TUFF STUFF'S™

BASEBALL MEMORABILIA

PRICE GUIDE

2ND EDITION

BY LARRY CANALE

AND THE TUFF STUFF™ STAFF

Published by
Tuff Stuff Books, A Division of

krause publications

700 East State Street • Iola, WI 54990-0001
715/445-2214 • FAX: 715/445-4087   www.krause.com

Please call or write for our free catalog of publications.
Our toll-free number to place an order or obtain a free catalog is 800-258-0929
or please use our regular business telephone: 715-445-2214.

Library of Congress Catalog Number: 2001088588
ISBN: 0-87349-267-6

Printed in the United States of America

ACKNOWLEDGEMENTS

Assembling a book about absolutely everything in the baseball memorabilia collectibles field can be daunting. And updating a book that went to press four long years ago is not much easier.

Fortunately, some of the sports collecting hobby's foremost authorities were available to help by writing chapter introductions, updating page after page of lists or checking the pricing of the ever-fluid marketplace.

Rocky Landsverk, editor of *Tuff Stuff*, got the project off to a great start in the planning stages. Dennis Thornton, *Tuff Stuff's* managing editor, took on the task of organizing mountains of material into a cohesive format.

And the hobby veterans who pitched in to help are a veritable Hall of Fame in the sports memorabilia field.

Larry Canale, who edited *Tuff Stuff* for 6 years, used all of his sports background and writing skills to produce the chapters on autographs and publications and to review the entire manuscript. One of the authors of the first edition of *Tuff Stuff's Baseball Memorabilia Price Guide*, Jerry Shaver, added introductions and pricing for the chapters on multi-signed items, collectible plates, and movies and videos. And *Tuff Stuff* columnist Phil Wood wrote about his specialty, baseball uniforms, in his unmistakable style.

Hobby specialists made other contributions. Lou Criscione shared his extensive knowledge as a longtime collector of sports figures, writing introductions and updating the database in several figurine areas. And Paul Ferrante wrote about his specialty, stadium seats and memorabilia, adding information about the historical importance of hallowed places such as Forbes Field and the Polo Grounds.

The editors of *Sports Collectors Digest* also made valuable contributions to this book. T.S. O'Connell wrote the whimsical foreword and combed through hundreds of auctions to compile the authoritative Top 100 Auction Items chapter. Scott Kelnhofer wrote about limited edition medallions, Tom Hultman added the chapter on cereal boxes and Bert Lehman updated lists and pricing of Starting Lineup figures. And longtime *SCD* editor Tom Mortenson laid important groundwork with hundreds of hours of research into every nook and cranny of sports memorabilia.

Others who provided valuable assistance in various ways, and who deserve a round of applause, include: Shelly Johnson, Mike Breeden, Jamie Martin, Kevin Ulrich, Cheryl Hayburn, and Gordie Ullom.

TABLE OF CONTENTS

Foreword **8**
By T.S. O'Connell

Chapter 1:   **Autographs** **12**
Hall of Fame Players................................. 18
Active Players...................................... 32
Retired Players..................................... 39
Managers and Announcers.......................... 52
Negro League Players............................... 54
MLB Authentication................................ 56

Chapter 2:   **Multi-Signed Items** **58**
World Series Team-Signed Balls..................... 58
Team-Signed Balls 63
All-Star Team-Signed Balls.......................... 88
Milestone Autographs 91

Chapter 3:   **Uniforms** **98**
Jerseys 98
Caps 105
Bats 108
Gloves 117

Chapter 4:   **Publications**.................................... **124**
Baseball Digest.................................... 125
Baseball Magazine 134
ESPN The Magazine................................ 138
Sport 139
Sports Illustrated.................................. 144
Sporting News 152
Street & Smith 155
Dell Sports Publishing 158
News Magazines................................... 161
Media Guides 165
Yearbooks.. 182
Books.. 195
Comic Books 206

Chapter 5:   **Programs, Press Pins, Tickets, Pennants** **211**
World Series Press Pins 211
Phantom Press Pins................................ 214
All-Star Press Pins 215
Hall of Fame Press Pins 216
Pennants.. 217
World Series Programs 222
LCS/Division Series Programs 225
Special Programs and Tickets 227
All-Star Programs.................................. 230
Ticket Stubs, Schedules, Baseball Tickets 232
Awards/Rings/Trophies............................. 237

Chapter 6:   **Figures** **238**
Banks 238
Bobbin' Heads 240

Gartlan 243
Hartland 245
Hall of Fame 247
Headliners 248
Romito 250
Starting Lineup 251
Miscellaneous Figures 269

Chapter 7: **Plates** **276**
Bradford Exchange 276
Gartlan USA 279
Hackett American Plates 280
Sports Impressions Plates 281

Chapter 8: **Limited Edition** **283**
Bleachers 283
Chicago Processing Enviromint Medallions 284
Highland Mint 292
Topps 298
Gulfstream Mint Sportstrikes 303
Hobby Editions 303
Premier Instand Replay 304
Pro Mint 304
Upper Deck 304

Chapter 9: **Stadium Memorabilia** **321**
Seats 322
Signs 324
Turnstiles 325
Usher/Vendor/Police Items 326
Other Fixtures 327
Miniature Stadiums 328

Chapter 10: **Cereal Boxes** **330**

Chapter 11: **Bottles & Cans** **338**
Beer Cans 338
Coca-Cola Products 339
1977-78 Royal Crown Cola Soda Cans 341
Bottle Caps 343
7-Eleven Cups 346

Chapter 12: **Baseball Games** **348**
Selected Baseball Board Games 348
Baseball Card Games 353
Miscellaneous Baseball Games 355

Chapter 13: **Movies, Videos** **357**
Movie Memorabilia 357
Videos 361
Music and Recordings 362
Sheet Music 367

Chapter 14: **Auctions** **368**
Chapter 15: **Miscellaneous Baseball Memorabilia** **381**
Glossary of terms **395**
Sports addresses and Web guide **396**

FOREWORD

By T.S. O'Connell

It's hard to imagine an area of the sports collecting hobby that has been more robust over the past decade than vintage memorabilia. No less of a hobby pioneer than Frank Nagy once said (actually, he said it more than once), "We'll never mature as a hobby until this stuff is worth something."

Well, the hobby may not be completely mature at this point, but it certainly is a lot more grown-up than it was 10 years ago. The "stuff" is worth quite a lot at the moment, and the price escalation shows no sign of easing up.

If Rip Van Winkle had begun one of his epic slumbers in the mid-1980s and then returned to the land of the conscious just as the millennium came to a close, he no doubt would have been startled to see a hobby awash in baseballs, bats, uniforms and equipment, along with a host of spectacular collectibles like display advertising pieces and pennants. Such was not the case as the hobby started to expand in the 1980s.

In those days, the emergence of "new" cards, mostly baseball, but more and more from the other three major sports as well, dominated the advertising space in the nearly dozen publications that catered to the collector. Dealers handled literally hundreds of cases of new cards every year, often selling "bricks" of 25, 50 and even 100 cards of various rookie or star cards of the same player. Cardboard was king.

Which is not surprising, since the baseball card remains at the epicenter of the hobby even today. "All of us started by collecting cards," said Bill Mastro, CEO of MastroNet Inc., the auction giant that annually handles sales of more than $30 million in cards and memorabilia, virtually all of it vintage, most of it expensive and a good deal of it awe-inspiring. "It's unusual to find a guy in the hobby who never collected cards or doesn't have a fondness for baseball. That's the connection."

That connection, according to Mastro, means that as collectors return to the hobby as adults, they might start out collecting cards at first, but they often move on fairly quickly to other things. There are a number of reasons for that, not the least of which is the relative rarity between a Christy Mathewson baseball card and, for example, a Tuxedo Tobacco advertising display of the same player.

While there may be dozens of high-grade specimens of T206 Mathewsons, the classy and attractive Tuxedo Tobacco display is much more rare, at least in relative numbers. Add to that the fact that more advanced col-

lectors have a desire to be able to show off their treasures, and the penchant for collectors to turn to any number of vintage alternatives is easily understood.

It's often said that the hobby reached a major turning point when price guides arrived on the scene to make the hobby accessible to more casual collectors. Such a nuance doesn't apply as easily to memorabilia, where the need to actually see the item is much greater and less simply encapsulated by a specific "grade."

Mastro figures that the memorabilia boom got its biggest assist with the growth of conventions in the 1980s, when many of the most experienced hobbyists started bringing some of their favorite items out for all the world to see. "The buying and selling of memorabilia requires a lot more expertise, and conventions changed the face of the hobby," Mastro said, as guys, who in many cases were the most-respected names in the hobby, finally got to meet one another in person.

Mastro explained that many of these memorabilia collectors were actually considered experts in their various fields, historians even, who often parlayed a lifelong hobby into a minor avocation. One of the things that helped fuel the expansion was the fact that much of the memorabilia wasn't terribly expensive … yet. And collectors didn't have to pick and choose as much as they would years later.

At the center of this world was a man named Barry Halper. Nobody in the history of the hobby personified what collecting is all about more than the man from New Jersey who diligently accumulated tens of thousands of pieces over almost 50 years.

Halper started out with cards just like almost everybody else, but the difference was that he quickly turned to more esoteric treasures. Even in the late 1940s as a teen-ager, he was acquiring uniforms at a time when these heirlooms-in-waiting were often unceremoniously discarded by the team or recycled and reused by affiliated clubs in the minor leagues.

The irony of such eventual treasures being relegated to the bushes notwithstanding, Halper embarked on a crusade to acquire items from virtually every significant figure in baseball history, and anyone who knows the noted collector is well aware that he is first and foremost a baseball fan and historian.

For Halper, every piece had a story attached to it, and not simply the story of how he acquired it, though of course he had plenty of those. For many years it was not uncommon for him to acquire pieces simply by writing to the player or family and requesting something; years later, when an awareness of the growing value of such items made that course less effective,

Halper would frequently trade pieces from his always expanding collection for those items he wanted. And ultimately he would pay for items, especially as his own fame grew and most experienced collectors and dealers understood whom they were dealing with.

Ultimately, Halper would stand alone atop the mountain with a collection he initially estimated at being worth around $40 million. That figure sounded outlandish when he first uttered it in the early 1990s, but few people were laughing by September of 1999 when the liquidation had begun.

Halper had hoped that his collection could be kept intact and, indeed, he labored for several years to find either a private buyer or even a corporation or municipality willing to purchase the entire inventory and preserve it in a museum setting. But that particular aspect of his dream was not to be.

Halper quietly sold a reported $5 million-plus of prized items to Major League Baseball, which in turn consigned the assortment to the Baseball Hall of Fame, where much of it is displayed in the "Halper Wing." Only months after that sale to MLB, the most important auction in the history of the collecting hobby got under way at Sotheby's in New York City, with several hundred bidders on hand for the week-long auction and thousands more taking part over the phone.

Such an historic event, not surprisingly, enticed a host of celebrities to take part in the bidding for Halper's treasures, a flashy aspect to the proceedings that was capped by film star Billy Crystal joyously announcing that he was the winning bidder for Mickey Mantle's glove, all $239,000 worth of it.

When the smoke cleared, nearly 2,500 lots of the most famous collection in the world had passed into private hands, at a price tag of more than $22 million. Ultimately, Halper would place several thousand more items up for auction via the Internet, leaving absolutely no one to chuckle at his original estimate of $40 million.

And as most experts had predicted at the time, the Halper sale in September 1999 gave the hobby another boost, because it didn't take long for the Halper pile to reappear in many of the most prominent auctions around the country.

Nobody would have suggested at the time of the Halper auction that much of the material would be available at wholesale prices, but even though there were few bargains, an enormous chunk of the auction was purchased by dealers and auction houses, to say nothing of nearly $1 million worth of stuff purchased by Upper Deck, the baseball card maker that quickly turned around and placed a dozen items into a sweepstakes that grabbed national attention.

Even without the presence of the Halper gold mine, the 1990s would have been an extraordinary decade for memorabilia collectors. Halper just heightened the experience. The next 10 years figure to be just as exciting, and probably just as rewarding for those who know where to look.

And if you are looking for a hint, here's the sage advice of none other than Mastro, whose company figures to be smack dab in the middle of all that activity. "The $1,000 and $2,000 items of today are tomorrow's $10,000 pieces," said Mastro, citing rare vintage photography as a particular area of potential expansion.

Uh, let's see. If a picture is worth a thousand words and $10,000, where does that leave us with the capital gains guy?

WANTED

For My Personal Collection
Cards From The Following Sets...

1) E107 Breisch-Williams
2) D381 Fleischmann, Ferguson Bread
3) Worch Cigars
4) Colgan's Chips
5) JuJu Drums
6) 1954-68 Seattle Popcorn
7) M101-6 Sporting News
8) 1908-09 Rose Postcards
9) 1936 Overland Candy
10) 1937-39 Orcajo, Val Decker, etal, Reds Postcards
11) 1949-51 Hage's Dairy
12) Green Bay Packer Programs Before 1970

NAME YOUR PRICE on my wants in these sets.
FOR - Larry Fritsch Cards
we are also buying cards 1965 and earlier from all sets - we pay the highest prices in the hobby - TRY US!

TOPPS BASEBALL SETS

These are cards that were purchased from Topps in the given year and have been in our warehouse since. These cards have been virtually untouched by human hands. We grade these sets in at least excellent mint to near mint condition.

2001 Factory (791 cards) $74.95	1986 (792 cards)...........................$35.00
2000 Factory (478 cards) $61.95	1985 (792 cards)..........................$275.00
1999 Factory (462 cards) $62.95	1984 (792 cards)...........................$55.00
1998 Factory (510 cards) $109.95	1983 (792 cards).........................$135.00
1997 Factory (504 cards) $249.95	1982 (726 cards).........................$140.00
1996 Factory (449 cards) $95.00	1981 (726 cards)...........................$85.00
1995 Factory (677 cards) $95.00	1980 (726 cards).........................$200.00
1994 Factory (808 cards) $75.00	1979 (726 cards).........................$225.00
1993 Factory (838 cards) $54.00	1978 (726 cards).........................$350.00
1992 Factory (802 cards) $39.00	1977 (660 cards).........................$360.00
1991 Factory (792 cards) $27.00	1976 (660 cards).........................$425.00
1990 Factory (792 cards) $30.00	1975 (660 cards).........................$775.00
1989 Factory (792 cards) $25.00	1974 (660 cards).........................$735.00
1988 (792 cards)............................$20.00	1973 (660 cards).........................$950.00
1987 (792 cards)............................$24.00	

We also stock Bowman, Donruss, Fleer, Leaf, Pinnacle, Score, Upper Deck Baseball Cards. Please write for our catalog.

REPRINT SETS

WHO BUYS REPRINT SETS!

THE TRUE COLLECTOR!

1880's Old Judge Type Set (80)........$35.95	1949 Bowman (240) $37.95
1909 T204 Ramly (121)....................$29.95	1950 Bowman (252) $44.95
1909-11 T206 (523)...........................$59.95	1950 Bowman Football (144)........$40.95
1910 Plow Boy (42)..............................$9.95	1951 Bowman (324).......................$74.95
1911 D304 General Baking (25)........$10.95	1952 Bowman (252).....................$174.95
1915 Cracker Jack (176) $29.95	1952 Redman (52).........................$19.95
1915 M101-5 The Sporting News (200)	1953 Bowman B&W Extension (16) ..$19.95
....$29.95	1953 Topps (330)...........................$89.95
1922 E120 American Camel (240) $32.95	1954 Johnston Cookies (34)..........$12.95
1933 Goudey (240) $44.95	1954 Wilson Franks (19)................$11.95
1933 Tattoo Orbit (60) $10.95	1955 Johnston Cookies (34)..........$12.95
1939 Play Ball (161) $24.95	1956 Topps Football (120) $43.95
1940 Play Ball (240) $44.95	1957 Spic & Span Braves (20).........$7.95
1941 Play Ball (72) $17.95	1957 Topps Football (154) $52.95
1941 Superman (72) $14.95	1959 Home Run Derby (19) $7.95
1947 Tip Top Bread (163)..................$29.95	1960 Lake To Lake Braves (28)........$8.95
1948 Bowman Football (108)............$21.95	

We have many other reprint sets in stock, write for our latest catalog.

FREE 272-PAGE SPORTS CARD & MEMORABILIA CATALOGS!!

"The World's #1 Sports Card Catalog!"
Specializing In Pre-1980 Cards

Shop our inventory of over 65 million cards at your convenience. We specialize in Vintage cards from the 1880's to the 1980's in all four major sports and some non-sports cards too. Newer items include singles, sets, wax boxes, reprints and supplies - WE HAVE IT ALL! Combine the Vintage One-of-a-Kind catalog just released along with our Regular issues and New Items, we offer over 270 pages of cards and collectibles in two different catalogs.

Up-to-$10.00-off coupon included in catalogs!
By far the largest selection in the hobby!

NEGRO LEAGUE BASEBALL STARS

For 48 Years The Negro Leagues Had Some Of The Best Players In The Nation. Now You Can Have Them Too!

Larry Fritsch Cards, Inc. has produced and now offers the only set of cards available using actual vintage photographs of some of the greatest baseball players of all time. These rare photos capture the excitement and rich tradition of an important part of baseball history, and the men who never got the recognition they deserved.

There is a rich history in this 119-card set, depicted in 19th and 20th century photographs of some of the greatest baseball players of all time. Rare photographs of Satchel Paige, Josh Gibson, Cool Papa Bell, Buck Leonard, Monte Irvin, Judy Johnson and Lou Dials, to name a few. Rare photographs of many historic Negro League uniforms are also included, among them are the Kansas City Monarchs, Homestead Grays and Pittsburgh Crawfords.

Complete Set (119 Cards) (Factory Sealed)	$14.95
2 Complete Sets (238 Cards) (Factory Sealed)	$26.50
5 Complete Sets (595 Cards) (Factory Sealed)	$56.25

1984 THE SPORTING NEWS CONLON COLLECTION

This 60 card set of mostly Hall of Famers, was produced in conjunction with the Smithsonian Institution's "Baseball Immortals" photo exhibition featuring the work of Charles Martin Conlon. Conlon's career in sports photography spanned over 4 decades and this collection represents some of the finest stills from who is universally agreed to be baseball's premier photographer. The cards are 4-1/2" x 6-1/8" and sepia toned photos on the front. Backs are printed in black and white and include extensive biographies of each player along with their major league totals.

Complete Set (60 cards) $49.95

Full-Time Since 1970

LARRY FRITSCH CARDS, INC.

MasterCard
VISA

LARRY FRITSCH CARDS
To order call (715) 344-8687
735 OLD WAUSAU ROAD, P.O. BOX 863 • DEPT. 960
STEVENS POINT, WI 54481
Serving Collectors Since 1948
Fax (715) 344-1778
Web site: www.fritschcards.com

Wisconsin residents please add 5.5% sales tax.
Postage & Handling:
Please add $5.95 per total order unless otherwise stated.

Krause Publications 15

Chapter 1

AUTOGRAPHS

By Larry Canale

Baseball memorabilia comes in all sizes, shapes and forms—from equipment, jersey, cans and coins to cards, programs, schedules and paper collectibles. But for legions of collectors, no type of memorabilia has as much allure and appeal as a player's signature. The hobby of collecting autographs—"philography," as it is formally known—is all at once exhilarating and challenging, frustrating and rewarding. The end result for baseball collectors—a signed item—is the fan's strongest, most tangible connection to our national pastime.

Those who don't collect autographs may not appreciate the sheer thrill of the hobby: "So you got somebody to scribble his name on a ball—what's the big deal?"

But anyone who got to watch, say, Joe DiMaggio sign his name in that fastidious and precise handwriting knows what it's all about. If you've seen the flair with which Reggie Jackson signs his John Hancock (those artistic "g"s in his first name, and that big-looped "J" in his last), you understand. If you've ever leaned way over the railing during batting practice at a big league stadium—or waited in the parking lot after a game—and asked player after player for an autograph, you understand. And if you've attended autograph shows and witnessed the rushed, frantic pace of a Pete Rose signing session, the relaxed and friendly pace of a Harmon Killebrew session, or the buttoned-up professionalism of a Sandy Koufax session, you get it. Collecting autographs can be as addictive a hobby as any. Once you score one signature, you want more. It doesn't matter whether you call them "sigs" or "autos" or "graphs," and it doesn't matter how you get them, and it may not even matter whether you're getting them from baseball's star sluggers or backup catchers. You just want more.

When we actually *watch* a player sign an item, we're looking at indisputable proof that our paths have crossed. The signature represents a brush with fame, whether it happened during pre-game warm-ups at the ballpark, during a brief meeting at an autograph show or celebrity event, or through a chance encounter at a random location (an airport, mall or a hotel). In cases where we buy an autograph, second-hand, of a player we admire, the "I was there" element is missing. But—assuming it's a legit autograph—the connection to a hero is no less real.

Speaking of legit vs. faked autographs, that topic is an entire book subject by itself. The guide you're holding assumes you have acquired authentic autographs either in person or through a source that's absolutely foolproof. Some would say that the latter is impossible—if you didn't see an item signed, you can't be 100 percent certain that it's real. But even the most cynical collectors know of a source or two that they trust unconditionally. That source might be a show promoter who sells pre-ordered (or excess) autographs through the mail. Or it might be an athlete's own marketing company. Or it might be a reputable memorabilia company. Your trusted source also might be any of the major trading card manufacturers that routinely—and randomly, of course—seed signed insert cards into packs. There have been occasional snafus involving signed insert cards. (Football collectors might remember the news in the mid-1990s that Errict Rhett—not realizing the stir it would cause—had his girlfriend help him sign insert cards for one now-defunct company.) But generally, if you pull an autographed card out of a Topps or Fleer or Upper Deck pack, you have a high degree of confidence that it's real.

But back to the project at hand: The point of this section isn't to dig into the subject of counterfeit autographs. Rather, we've set out to give you an estimated value of the autographs you own—or the ones you're intending to buy. This chapter in *Tuff Stuff's Baseball Memorabilia Guide* includes a wealth of new information added since the first edition: from the addition of popular players who have made a recent impact (what baseball fan wouldn't love to have an Ichiro Suzuki autograph?) to updated prices for autographs of the thousands of players whose names appeared in the first edition.

A HOBBY'S HUMBLE BEGINNINGS

The first professional baseball team, most history books agree, was the 1869 Cincinnati Redlegs. So you can bet your signed Ted Williams baseball that 1869 was also the year that the baseball autograph-collecting hobby began. Granted, the number of fans who turned out to watch the Redlegs play such teams as the Troy (N.Y.) Haymakers or the New York Mutuels back in '69 was far lower than what we see even at Montreal Expos games in April nowadays. Attendance at baseball's earliest games was anywhere from a few hundred people to a few thousand. But those first fans were there to watch real pros—men who were actu-

CREAM OF THE CROP

Ask the average person the question "Which baseball player's autograph is the most valuable?" and you're likely to hear "Babe Ruth" as the answer. That's not the case, however. The Babe's signature is one of the most desired in the hobby, but the most valuable belong to players who either pioneered the game in the late 1800s or who rarely signed autographs, making them almost impossible to come by today. At the top of the list is "Shoeless" Joe Jackson, the great White Sox hitter who was banned from baseball (unfairly, some admirers insist to this day) after the Black Sox scandal of 1919. Jackson, who batted .356 in his career (and .375 in the 1919 World Series), was unable to read and write, a problem that resulted in very few autographs from him.

Adrian C Anson

MOST VALUABLE BASEBALL AUTOGRAPHS

Player (b.-d.)	Signed Baseball Value	Player (b.-d.)	Signed Baseball Value
1. Joe Jackson (1888-1951)	$30,000	7. Pud Galvin (1856-1902)	$12,000
2. Cap Anson (1852-1922)	$17,000	8. Monte Ward (1860-1925)	$12,000
3. Rube Foster (1879-1930)	$13,000	9. Jim O'Rourke (1850-1919)	$10,000
4. Christy Mathewson (1880-1925)	$13,000	10. Sam Thompson (1860-1922)	$10,000
5. Rube Waddell (1876-1914)	$12,500	11. Jack Chesbro (1874-1931)	$10,000
6. Albert Spalding (1850-1915)	$12,000	12. Addie Joss (1880-1911)	$10,000

Source: Tuff Stuff *magazine*

The following lists were compiled in May 2001 by Quality Autographs & Memorabilia of Virginia (QAM), an Alexandria, Va.-based dealer of sports autographs. Owner Kevin Keating, who co-authored *The Negro Leagues Autograph Guide* (Tuff Stuff Books, 1999), based the selections on the demand for autographs he receives at QAM (www.qualityautographs.com).

The lists are in no particular order, he notes. "But I would say that Babe Ruth's autographs remains the most popular baseball signatures of all-time," Keating says. "To this day, it's the 'John Hancock' of sports autographs."

Also, Keating explains, he has seen forged autographs of each of the following 20 players. He has denoted the "problem areas" with these symbols:

#: often forged
##: widely forged

MOST POPULAR BASEBALL AUTOGRAPHS

Living Players
- Hank Aaron
- Yogi Berra
- Whitey Ford
- Willie Mays
- Mark McGwire ##
- Stan Musial
- Cal Ripken
- Nolan Ryan
- Sammy Sosa #
- Ted Williams ##

Deceased Players
- Ty Cobb ##
- Joe DiMaggio ##
- Lou Gehrig ##
- Walter Johnson #
- Mickey Mantle ##
- Christy Mathewson ##
- Jackie Robinson #
- Babe Ruth ##
- Jim Thorpe #
- Honus Wagner #

Note: Thorpe's autograph crosses several genres within the memorabilia market: baseball, football, track, Olympics, Americana and Native American.

ally getting paid money to play a kid's game. And because philography as a general hobby was already in existence, it stands to reason that at least a handful of autograph-seekers approached the stars of the day in search of a signature. (The stud of the 1869 Cincinnati Redlegs was shortstop George Wright, brother of the team's captain and center fielder, Harry Wright. George's autograph on a ball is so rare today that it's worth around $10,000.)

After those humble beginnings, it took years for baseball to catch on as our national pastime. But as the sport grew, so did the desirability of player autographs. By the time Babe Ruth captured the country's imagination in the 1910s and 1920s, more and more fans were coveting the signatures of the stars, from Honus Wagner and Ty Cobb to Walter Johnson and Christy Mathewson. Ruth, of course, set new standards for popularity. Fortunately, he was known to be fan-friendly and a willing signer (not to mention the player who popularized the practice of signing on a ball's "sweet spot"), so high-roller collectors will encounter legitimate samples coming up for auction from time to time. They can be expensive, too: A superb-condition Ruth ball brought more than $70,000 at a recent auction, while three others sold for upwards of $20,000 at auction. Other examples have sold for a few thousand dollars.

Each generation of baseball stars that followed Ruth's era featured its own marquee players who became fan favorites—and, naturally, the game's most desirable autograph subjects: from Joe DiMaggio, Ted Williams, Stan Musial and Jackie Robinson to Willie Mays, Mickey Mantle, Hank Aaron and Roberto Clemente, and from Pete Rose, Nolan Ryan and Johnny Bench to George Brett, Cal Ripken Jr. and Mark McGwire. Own an autograph from any of these Hall of Famers and HOFers-to-be and you've got something special—something that most certainly will hold long-term value.

COLLECTING STRATEGIES

Every autograph collector has his own preferences. Some of us score the bulk of our sigs inside or around ballparks in spring training or during the regular season. Players often sign before and after games, so have your items ready, hang around close to the dugout or bullpen, and, most of all, be polite. This "grass-roots" method is probably the most rewarding way to collect baseball autographs. Not only are you getting a one-on-one meeting—however brief it may be—with a player, but there's a certain amount of suspense leading up to the autograph (will he or won't he sign?) and great satisfaction when you succeed. Another thrill with this approach is the price you pay for the autograph—nothing. We've never heard of a player asking for money to sign an autograph during warm-ups—have you?

If you've never made the trek to spring training in search of autographs, consider heading to Florida or Arizona in mid- to late-February or March. Spring training is an ideal atmosphere for interacting with players and snagging multiple signatures. Players are usually more relaxed and more willing to take the time to sign for fans. Spring training is also a great opportunity to put together team-signed baseballs and secure autographs from former players who may be instructors or coaches during the spring. But don't wait until mid-February to book your trip. Start planning an itinerary in November or December. Because the teams train relatively close to each other, you can visit several camps over the course of a few days.

Other autograph collectors prefer the show circuit. By traveling to regional conventions or card shows that offer a lineup of autograph guests, you can build a collection fairly quickly. You'll pay a fee for autographs at most of these shows, of course, but at least you get the satisfaction—and security—of watching an athlete sign a handpicked item. And because you're a paying customer, a lot of athletes spend a few seconds to say hello and answer a quick question or two—and maybe to pose for a photograph.

Still other collectors focus mainly on collecting autographs through the mail, sending a short, polite letter, an item to be signed and a self-addressed, stamped envelope (SASE) to individual players. There are basic rules of etiquette you should follow when requesting an autograph by mail:

- Don't send a form letter—very tacky. Short, personal letters are most effective. Some say a handwritten note is better than a printed-out letter, but if your handwriting is atrocious, hit the word processor.
- Don't send big or bulky items, like bats or wall-sized posters that need to be rolled and unrolled. Stick with easy-to-handle items like trading cards, index cards or photos.
- Don't send valuable items. You might never see them again.
- Ask for a single autograph, not multiples. If a player opens your package and sees a stack of 30 cards and a note asking him to sign all of them, he'll likely be turned off right away.
- Don't assume that the autograph will be free. Some players charge a fee or ask for a donation to a charity or cause they're involved with in exchange for the autograph.
- And don't forget that SASE. Your chances of getting a reply without one are minimal.

And where should you send autograph requests? There are publications and newsletters that list players' home addresses, and some collectors have experienced success going that route. We recommend, however, that you mail your request to a player via the team most closely associated to him. In sending a request to a player's place of residence, you run the risk of him feeling as if you've imposed on his privacy—as opposed to having him receive your request along with other mail forwarded by his team or former team.

When requesting for autographs in the mail, be reasonable in your expectations. Sending an autograph request to Mark McGwire, Alex Rodriguez and Ken Griffey Jr. might not get you very quick replies (if any at all) because of the volume of mail these types of superstars receive. Sending requests to minor stars, future stars and average players will result in more successes. Even with lesser players, though, it helps if you don't expect anything to come back. Requests have been known to bounce back, unsigned, to the sender—or to never return at all.

One other point on the autographs-by-mail strategy: This approach doesn't give you the satisfaction—or security—of actually seeing a player sign his name. Rather, the big kick here is when you see your SASE land in your mailbox. Again, just understand that the wait can be long—several months, maybe, or more than a year—but the payoff can be worth it.

WHAT TO GET SIGNED

Today's autograph collectors seek signatures on an increasingly wide array of items. Some hobbyists are fairly consistent in building their collections: They'll stick with one type of item for each signature they pursue. Other collectors strive for variety—a signed napkin might be as thrilling to them as an autographed jersey. Autograph-collecting is, after all, a very personal hobby.

Every collector likely would agree, however, that one item is more popular than any other when it comes to autographs: a brand new, clean, official baseball. Whether it's signed by one player or by an entire team, an autographed ball makes for a smart, attractive, timeless collectible. It's big enough to absorb a decent-sized signature, but small enough to display without taking up a lot of space. Plus, the smooth writing surface of a baseball's horsehide is an ideal match for a simple ballpoint pen.

Keep in mind that if you're getting baseballs signed, it's best (from a value perspective) to use official baseballs.

Traditionally, official American League and National League baseballs included a signature stamp of the league president. But the era of AL- and NL-stamped baseballs ended in 1999. Today, all official Major League baseballs bear the signature stamp of Commissioner Bud Selig. (Actually, the stamp reads "Allan H. Selig.") That's because in September 1999, baseball's powers-that-be voted to abandon its system of autonomous AL and NL presidents—a system that had been in operation for nearly 100 years. The reorganization brought such responsibilities as scheduling and disciplinary decisions into Selig's office. The last NL president, Leonard Coleman, resigned shortly after the announcement, and AL President Gene Budig took on an advisory role in Selig's office through 2002. Essentially, the move means the AL and NL are no longer separate leagues—except on paper, and mainly for the purpose of retaining traditional divisional standings.

Even so, baseballs with pre-2000 signature stamps are important for authenticating older autographs. For example, it would be impossible for Babe Ruth to have signed an AL baseball with Joseph E. Cronin's signature stamped on it because Cronin didn't become league president until 1959, 11 years after Ruth died.

Here's the list of league presidents along with the years they served. Any baseballs not bearing their names are considered unofficial.

American League	National League
1901-1927: Byron B. "Ban" Johnson	1885-1902: Nicholas Young
1927-1931: Ernest S. Barnard	1903-1909: Harry Pulliam
1931-1959: William Harridge	1909-1910: John A. Heydler
1959-1973: Joseph E. Cronin	1910-1913: Thomas Lynch
1974-1983: Leland S. McPhail Jr.	1913-1918: John Tener
1984-1993: Robert W. Brown	1918-1934: John A. Heydler
1994-1999: Gene Budig	1934-1951: Ford C. Frick
	1951-1969: Warren C. Giles
	1970-1986: Charles S. Feeney
	1986-1989: A. Bartlett Giamatti
	1989-1993: William D. White
	1994-1999: Leonard Coleman

The autograph collector's favorite alternative to baseballs is the 8x10 photograph. Signed photos have less value than signed baseballs, but they offer the advantage of putting a face with a name, so to speak. They're also easier to display (matted and framed) or to store (in albums). Plus, they're readily available. Collectibles show promoters generally carry at least a couple of choices for each athlete appearing at every event, and the photos (unsigned) shouldn't cost you more than $3-$4. Outside of the show circuit, you often can find unsigned 8x10 glossies at sports collectibles and baseball card shops. One of the leading suppliers of licensed baseball photographs, Photo File Inc. (www.photofile.com), reports that more than 3,000 dealers nationally carry its photos.

The key for signed-photo collectors is picture quality. Survey any sports collectibles show and you'll be sure to find examples of sub-par photographs that have been signed or are available for signing. Common problems: poor focus, grainy or washed-out appearance and poor contrast. In picking out photos of players whose signatures you expect to get, be fussy about quality.

As for photography style, some collectors prefer portraits and posed shots, while others prefer action shots. But keep in mind that action photography earlier than, say, the 1970s is a far cry from today's sharp stop-action pictures. Even so, some collectors enjoy the aura and charm of a grainy black-and-white shot of Ted Williams or Stan Musial in mid-swing. Again, collecting is a very personal hobby.

When picking out a photograph that you expect to get signed, you sometimes have a choice in size. Some collectors like to mix a larger

photo or two into their collection. Popular choices are 11x14 and 16x20 photos—both of which offer greater impact when displayed than 8x10s.

Beyond baseballs and photographs, collectors are selecting from a wide range of items that will hold an autograph. Magazine covers (especially *Sports Illustrated*) can make attractive pieces when signed. The April 15, 1974, issue of *Sports Illustrated*—with its cover line of "715" in celebration of Henry Aaron's new all-time home run record—looks great with Hammerin' Hank's signature across the front. The same goes for hundreds and hundreds of other *SI* covers bearing images of baseball's best. And don't overlook old issues of *Sport*, baseball annuals from such publishers as Street & Smith and Athlon, and the pocket-sized *Baseball Digest*—all of which have published fitting items worthy of an autograph.

Autographed baseball books, schedules, programs, caps and posters, among other items, add a unique touch to a collection. Some collectors go outside the diamond to build a collection of baseball signatures, getting players to sign such items as golf balls, business cards or product packages bearing the athlete's image. (Wouldn't you love to have snagged Joe DiMaggio's autograph on a Mr. Coffee box?) One *Tuff Stuff* magazine reader once described his own envelope-pushing collection: He had athletes sign oddball items that connected to the player's skills or reputation. At one show, for example, he asked slick-fielding Hall-of-Fame third baseman Brooks Robinson to sign a small Hoover vacuum cleaner. Brooks, naturally, complied.

In the early days of baseball autographs, collectors weren't necessarily fussy about what they'd ask an athlete to sign. From the 1800s through the mid-1900s, collectors often had players sign such items as autograph books, scraps of paper, programs or notebooks.

Later, they (or other collectors) would extract the autograph, with the result being a "cut" signature. A cut is the most primitive form of autograph and is generally the easiest to find—and thus the least expensive. Oftentimes, cut signatures (some of which have come from letters, checks or legal documents), are matted and framed with a photo of the

player. Autographs of legendary players from the late 19th century and early 20th century are found on cuts more frequently than on any other type of item.

Plain old 3x5 index cards also became popular items among early baseball autograph collectors and remain so today. They've always been readily available; plus, they're inexpensive and they're more convenient to carry around than bats or boxes of baseballs. Like cuts, autographed index cards are ideal for matting and framing with player photographs or for compiling in an album. Older players' autographs are more prominent on index cards, which boast modestly higher values than cut signatures.

What else looks good with a signature on it? With the proliferation of autograph shows in the 1980s, baseball bats and jerseys became popular high-end items among autograph collectors. Bats can be attractively displayed, but they should be kept in clear plastic tubes to protect both the wood and the signature. Most athletes on the show circuit charge more to autograph a bat than they do for other items, so the values for signed bats run higher. In the case of, say, Frank Robinson, a signed ball is valued at $35, while a signed bat is around $165. Athletes also tend to charge more to sign a jersey, and, again, the value runs higher than other items—especially because collectors tend to want game-used jerseys (as opposed to replica jerseys).

Another frequently signed item in the world of baseball autographs is the postcard. Even within this niche, collectors have options:

- From 1946–64, the Hall of Fame issued commemorative black-and-white postcards of each of its members. Each postcard bears a picture of the player's Cooperstown plaque. Because these postcards were issued for such a limited time, they're tough to find with autographs and thus command a steep price. After 1964, the Hall of Fame replaced the black-and-white plaque cards with gold editions. These postcards are much more plentiful, but not necessarily cheaper. In the case of Jimmie Foxx, for example, a signed black-and-white HOF postcard is valued at $525 vs. $2,500 for a gold-plaque postcard. Foxx passed away in 1967, just three years after the gold-plaque series commenced, so there are few signed copies of the postcard.
- Signed Perez-Steele postcards—created by Dick Perez and Frank Steele—have long been hot items among collectors of limited-edition memorabilia. The first set appeared in 1980, and new cards are released every two years for the Hall-of-Fame's newest inductees. Only 10,000 postcards are produced of each player.
- Signed Perez-Steele Great Moments were introduced in 1985 with production runs of 5,000 sets, which are periodically updated. These cards are larger than regular Perez-Steele postcards and feature action photography. Eight series of cards are in circulation, with the last being produced in 1992.
- Signed Perez-Steele Celebration Cards were produced to commemorate the 50th anniversary of the Hall of Fame in 1989. A total of 10,000 44-card sets were produced. Players in the set include Hank Aaron, Mickey Mantle, and Ted Williams.

We would be remiss to ignore one other item that's popular with autograph collectors: the good old baseball card. And we're not talking about those autographed insert cards seeded into today's packs. We're talking about the practice of using unsigned cards in collecting autographs on your own. More and more collectors are taking this approach. Some may bring a stack of new Indians and Red Sox cards to a Cleveland/Boston game at Fenway Park, hoping to snag a host of signatures, while others may mail away 50-cent common cards to various players with a request for an autograph (a self-addressed, stamped envelope, of course, is a necessity when collecting through the mail).

Most serious collectors and dealers would advise against the idea of obtaining an autograph on an extremely valuable trading card—a Willie Mays or Nolan Ryan rookie, for example—insisting that a signature would lower the card's value. But there are thousands of players whose baseball cards actually gain in value with an autograph. A $1 Tony Gwynn card from the late 1980s or early 1990s, for example, suddenly becomes a $10 or $15 piece with the Padres star's signature. (Signed trading cards generally are worth slightly less than a signed 8x10 photograph. In Gwynn's case, an autographed 8x10 has a value of around $30.)

THE COA QUESTION

Today, practically every seller of autographs provides a Certificate of Authenticity, or COA (also called Letter of Authenticity, or LOA). What does a COA mean for the buyer? Opinions differ on the topic. Some collectors feel a sense of security when an autograph they buy is accompanied by a COA. Detractors point out that forgery artists can fake a COA as easily as an autograph.

Ultimately, collectors should consider that a COA is only as legitimate as the person or company providing it. This doesn't mean you should ignore certificates when they're offered; just make sure that the seller who's offering it is someone you trust. If it's a company with whom you haven't dealt, do some research. Ask other collectors about the seller's reputation. Learn what a certain player's autograph looks like, and compare it to the one you're considering. Forgeries are the most serious problem in the autograph hobby, and collectors must proceed with caution.

The bigger the star, the greater the temptation for an unscrupulous dealer to sell fakes. Such legends as Mickey Mantle and Ted Williams have had their names forged so often and with such accuracy that it's difficult even for experts to tell the difference between a fake and the real deal.

Forgeries are nothing new to the hobby. It's a poorly kept secret that years ago, bat boys and clubhouse attendants forged autographs for the stars. (Ted Williams is one player who admitted to having clubhouse boys sign in his stead.) More recently, autopens, rubber stamps and other instruments have contributed to the problem. If you're not getting your autographs in person, be selective and make sure you trust the person with whom you are dealing. If the dealer can't remember where the gem came from, or has a story that sounds too good to be true, hold on to your cash.

HOW TO DISPLAY AND STORE YOUR COLLECTION

What's the best way to display and/or store your autograph collection? Well, every collector would answer that question in a different way.

If you focus on collecting signed baseballs, the easy way to handle your prizes is to keep them in clear plastic ball cubes, which will keep dust from settling on the baseball and fingers from smudging the autograph. If you collect mainly 8x10s, you likely have taken the steps of matting, framing and hanging a selection of your favorites while storing the rest in clear plastic sleeves in a binder. Signed cards, magazines and other flat items also work well in binders, which allow for easy access and viewing.

If you buy mainly signed baseball bats, keep them in clear plastic tubes. You also can find racks designed to display bats; check the advertisements in hobby publications for information on where to find them. As for autographed jerseys, they look wonderful when framed, encased and hung, although they do take up a fair amount of space.

Regardless of what you collect, one storage principle applies: Keep your autographs out of direct sunlight and extreme heat, which can cause the signatures to fade over time. You also should make sure you don't keep your autographs in a damp room.

To provide the ultimate protection, more and more collectors are buying insurance for their collections. A standard homeowner's insurance policy generally doesn't cover collectibles. Find out what your policy says, and if you need to buy an insurance "rider" that would reimburse you in case the unthinkable ever happens, it's money well-spent.

AUTOGRAPH LEGEND

1. Cuts—Signatures have value even if they aren't on items considered collectible or suitable for display. They are often referred to as "cuts" because collectors cut them from original sources (documents, autograph books, and scrapbooks, for example), and matte and/or frame them along with a photo or other attractive item. Values in the section that follows are for clear, uninscribed signatures in ink.

2. Signed 3x5 cards—Before the explosive 1980s, collecting signatures on 3x5 cards was an extremely popular hobby. Index cards have been used for autographs since at least the early 1900s. (Note: Values decrease 15-25 percent for signatures on the lined side of the card.)

3. Signed Photos—8x10 color photos are the standard for modern players. For older players, the clarity and quality of the photograph and signature are more important than the size. The values here are for uninscribed photos with clear signatures in ink.

4. Signed Baseballs—Prices for modern players are based on single-signed official balls in Near Mint condition with the signatures in ballpoint pen on the sweet spot. Pre-1940s prices are based on single-signed (in ink) balls, Excellent or better. Most single-signed balls from the past, except for Babe Ruth, are signed on a side panel. Clarity and boldness of the signature and condition of the ball are factors for grading.

5. Signed Bats—This medium was not widely available to autograph collectors until players began signing at card shows. Values are for signed game-model bats; deduct 15-20 percent for a generic, no-name bat.

6. Signed Black & White "Plaques"—These postcards, issued by the Hall of Fame, depict the member's Cooperstown plaque. The B&Ws were released during the years 1946-1964. Values are for front-signed plaques.

7. Signed Gold Plaques—These gold (or yellow) postcards were issued by the Hall of Fame. They're similar to B&W postcards. In fact, they replaced the B&Ws in 1964, and the HOF has continued to print them to this date. Most collectors prefer the signature across the top of the front of the card; values are for cards signed in this manner.

8. Signed Perez-Steele Postcards—Only 10,000 of these attractive postcards were printed of each Hall of Famer. Of course, the number that have been autographed varies from player to player. Perez-Steele Galleries issues updates as new members are inducted into the Hall.

9. Signed Perez-Steele "Great Moments"—First offered in 1985 with 5,000 numbered sets, these cards are periodically updated. The cards are oversized and typically show the featured player in action.

10. Signed Perez-Steele "Celebration" Cards—These cards were offered in 1989 to celebrate the 50th anniversary of the Hall of Fame. There were 10,000 sets produced, with 44 boxed cards completing the set. An attractive book was included as part of the set.

11. Store model gloves—Values in this column are for player model gloves sold at retail outlets and made in the USA. Prices are based on Excellent condition. Expect a slightly decrease value for child sizes and a slight increase for models matching the hand of the player (left-handed glove for left-handed player).

12. Mini-helmets—In 1997, Riddell released replica mini-helmets for all 30 Major League teams. Prices are for helmets signed in either Sharpie or paint pen. By 1999, the minis were discontinued.

HALL OF FAME AUTOGRAPHS

Any baseball autograph collection worth its salt includes players who have reached the Hall of Fame. Why? Because those players represent the best of the best: the most successful and usually the most popular players to ever play the game.

When it comes to the signatures of Hall of Famers, some are naturally harder to find than others. The toughest ones are from those players who passed away in the late 19th or first part of the 20th century. That would include Cap Anson, Jake Beckley, Dan Brouthers and Alexander Cartwright—baseball figures whose autographs are virtually impossible to find on anything but a cut or a 3x5 card. Collectors pay a steep premium for these autographs, but their addition will enhance any collection.

At the other end of the spectrum is the group of living Hall of Famers who appear frequently on the autograph show circuit. In fact, some of these players earn far more money signing at shows than they did for swinging a bat or pitching a ball. Keep an eye on autograph show schedules published in hobby magazines and newspapers and you'll see such names as Ernie Banks, Bob Feller, Harmon Killebrew and Brooks Robinson turning up. It's worth your while to snag signatures of these stars, if you haven't already done so. Even Hall of Famers' autographs can be affordable—especially when you compare them to the prices current stars charge.

If a player—even a Hall of Famer—is especially active on the show circuit, his autograph value will tend to stay at moderate levels. To the uninitiated, it might seem odd that the value of a baseball signed by the game's all-time home run king, Hank Aaron, is in the $60-$75 range when you might have to pay more for Derek Jeter's autograph. Similarly, a ball autographed by one of baseball's all-time best catchers, Johnny Bench, is valued at $34-$40, the same as a Mike Piazza-signed baseball is in the $100 range. In those examples, The Big Apple is one factor; Jeter and Piazza play in the media mecca of New York. But the big reason for the difference in the values we've cited is that Aaron and Bench were fairly active throughout the 1990s as autograph show guests (and still make appearances), while Jeter and Piazza appearances are rare—and probably will be as long as they're active players.

Many collectors try the autograph-by-mail approach with Hall of Fame players. (The institution's address: National Baseball Hall of Fame and Museum, 25 Main St., P.O. Box 590, Cooperstown, N.Y. 13326.) The success rate for certain players is good, especially if you donate money to their charities. Other players simply don't sign through the mail, period. If you do choose to send something through the mail, A) make sure it's not a valuable item that you can't replace, and B) be patient. Some players will eventually respond, but may take months to do so.

Looking ahead, remember that it helps to anticipate which players are destined for the Hall of Fame in coming years. Around the time a player is inducted, the demand for his signature rises—and so does his autograph's value. Consider the example of George Brett from the class of '99: A baseball signed by Brett was worth $35-$40 before his election to the Hall was announced. After his induction, the price rose to $60.

Another factor that affects the value of Hall of Famer autographs, unfortunately, is a player's death. The great Willie Stargell, for example, passed away on April 9, 2001. Afterward, collectors understandably wanted mementos related to the longtime Pittsburgh Pirate slugger, but were faced with paying a higher price than they would have paid several years ago. Patience in such cases will benefit the collector: Eventually, values of a deceased player's autograph will peak and then often drop slightly in value before stabilizing.

The following section provides current Hall of Famers' autograph values. A total of 253 men had been inducted into the Hall through 2001; that figure includes not only players but managers, executives, and umpires as well.

Hall of Fame Autographs
(with year inducted into Hall of Fame appearing above pricing columns)

Hank Aaron (1934-)   1982

Cut signature	$15
Single-signature ball	$60-$75
3x5 index card	$30
Photograph/baseball card	$50
HOF plaque postcard	$40
Perez-Steele postcards	$30

Grover Cleveland Alexander (1887-1950)   1938

Cut signature	$500-$700
Single-signature baseball	$5,000
3x5 index card	$700-$800
Photograph/baseball card	$900
HOF plaque postcard	$1,000
Perez-Steele postcards	Impossible

Walter Alston (1911-1984)   1983

Cut signature	$35
Single-signature baseball	$700
3x5 index card	$40-$50
Photograph/baseball card	$300
HOF plaque postcard	$100-$150
Perez-Steele postcards	$750-$800

Sparky Anderson (1934-)   2000

Cut signature	$8-$10
Single-signature baseball	$35
3x5 index card	$10
Photograph/baseball card	$20-$25
HOF plaque postcard	$25
Perez-Steele postcards	$25

Cap Anson (1852-1922)   1939

Cut signature	$1,500
Single-signature baseball	$23,000
3x5 index card	$2,000
Photograph/baseball card	$8,000
HOF plaque postcard	Impossible
Perez-Steele postcards	Impossible

Luis Aparicio (1934-)   1984

Cut signature	$8
Single-signature baseball	$35
3x5 index card	$10
Photograph/baseball card	$20
HOF plaque postcard	$15
Perez-Steele postcards	$20

Luke Appling (1907-1991)   1964

Cut signature	$10
Single-signature baseball	$75-$100
3x5 index card	$15
Photograph/baseball card	$35
HOF plaque postcard	$20
Perez-Steele postcards	$40

Richie Ashburn (1927-1997)   1995

Cut signature	$8
Single-signature baseball	$50
3x5 index card	$10-$15
Photograph/baseball card	$25
HOF plaque postcard	$75
Perez-Steele postcards	$100

Earl Averill (1902-1983) — **1975**
Cut signature — $25
Single-signature baseball — $450-$500
3x5 index card — $40
Photograph/baseball card — $150
HOF plaque postcard — $35
Perez-Steele postcards — $450-$550

Frank "Home Run" Baker (1886-1963) — **1955**
Cut signature — $150
Single-signature baseball — $3,600
3x5 index card — $300-$350
Photograph/baseball card — $800
HOF plaque postcard — $700
Perez-Steele postcards — Impossible

Dave Bancroft (1891-1972) — **1971**
Cut signature — $50
Single-signature baseball — $2,800
3x5 index card — $100
Photograph/baseball card — $250
HOF plaque postcard — $800
Perez-Steele postcards — Impossible

Ernie Banks (1931-) — **1977**
Cut signature — $10
Single-signature baseball — $45
3x5 index card — $15
Photograph/baseball card — $35
HOF plaque postcard — $15-$25
Perez-Steele postcards — $30-$35

Al Barlick (1915-1995) — **1989**
Cut signature — $10
Single-signature baseball — $50
3x5 index card — $8-$10
Photograph/baseball card — $25
HOF plaque postcard — $15-$20
Perez-Steele postcards — $25

Edward Barrow (1868-1953) — **1953**
Cut signature — $75
Single-signature baseball — $3,300
3x5 index card — $150-$200
Photograph/baseball card — $400
HOF plaque postcard — Impossible
Perez-Steele postcards — Impossible

Jake Beckley (1867-1918) — **1971**
Cut signature — $1,200-$1,300
Single-signature baseball — $4,800-$5,500
3x5 index card — $1,700
Photograph/baseball card — $3,500
HOF plaque postcard — Impossible
Perez-Steele postcards — Impossible

Cool Papa Bell (1903-1991) — **1974**
Cut signature — $20
Single-signature baseball — $350
3x5 index card — $35
Photograph/baseball card — $150
HOF plaque postcard — $35
Perez-Steele postcards — $45-$70

Johnny Bench (1947-) — **1989**
Cut signature — $10
Single-signature baseball — $40-$45
3x5 index card — $15-$20
Photograph/baseball card — $30-$35
HOF plaque postcard — $25-$35
Perez-Steele postcards — $35-$40

Chief Bender (1883-1954) — **1953**
Cut signature — $100
Single-signature baseball — $2,000-$3,500
3x5 index card — $250
Photograph/baseball card — $450-$500
HOF plaque postcard — $1,200
Perez-Steele postcards — Impossible

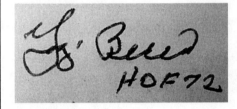

Yogi Berra (1925-) — **1972**
Cut signature — $8
Single-signature baseball — $40-$50
3x5 index card — $15
Photograph/baseball card — $20-$25
HOF plaque postcard — $20-$25
Perez-Steele postcards — $25-$30

Jim Bottomley (1900-1959) — **1974**
Cut signature — $150
Single-signature baseball — $3,000
3x5 index card — $300
Photograph/baseball card — $400
HOF plaque postcard — Impossible
Perez-Steele postcards — Impossible

Lou Boudreau (1917-2001) — **1970**
Cut signature — $8
Single-signature baseball — $40-$50
3x5 index card — $10
Photograph/baseball card — $12-$15
HOF plaque postcard — $10-$15
Perez-Steele postcards — $15-$25

Roger Bresnahan (1879-1944) — **1945**
Cut signature — $500
Single-signature baseball — $6,000
3x5 index card — $650-$700
Photograph/baseball card — $1,200
HOF plaque postcard — Impossible
Perez-Steele postcards — Impossible

George Brett (1953-) — **1999**
Cut signature — $10
Single-signature baseball — $60-$75
3x5 index card — $15
Photograph/baseball card — $40-$50
HOF plaque postcard — $60-$75
Perez-Steele postcards — $60-$75

Lou Brock (1939-) — **1985**
Cut signature — $5-$8
Single-signature baseball — $30-$35
3x5 index card — $10-$12
Photograph/baseball card — $20
HOF plaque postcard — $15
Perez-Steele postcards — $25

Dan Brouthers (1858-1932) — **1945**
Cut signature — $1,250
Single-signature baseball — $15,000-$20,000
3x5 index card — $1,700
Photograph/baseball card — $5,000
HOF plaque postcard — Impossible
Perez-Steele postcards — Impossible

Mordecai Brown (1876-1948) — **1949**
Cut signature — $250-$300
Single-signature baseball — $3,000-$5,500
3x5 index card — $350-$500
Photograph/baseball card — $900
HOF plaque postcard — Impossible
Perez-Steele postcards — Impossible

Morgan Bulkeley (1837-1922) — **1937**
Cut signature — $800-$1,450
Single-signature baseball — $6,000
3x5 index card — $1,200
Photograph/baseball card — $4,000
HOF plaque postcard — Impossible
Perez-Steele postcards — Impossible

Jim Bunning (1931-) — 1996
Cut signature	$5-$7
Single-signature baseball	$35
3x5 index card	$10-$15
Photograph/baseball card	$20-$25
HOF plaque postcard	$25
Perez-Steele postcards	$30

Jesse Burkett (1868-1953) — 1946
Cut signature	$450
Single-signature baseball	$5,500
3x5 index card	$800
Photograph/baseball card	$1,000
HOF plaque postcard	$1,500
Perez-Steele postcards	Impossible

Roy Campanella (1921-1993) — 1969
Cut signature	$350-$400
Single-signature baseball	$3,500-$4,500
3x5 index card	$500
Photograph/baseball card	$800
HOF plaque postcard	$325
Perez-Steele postcards	$200-$250

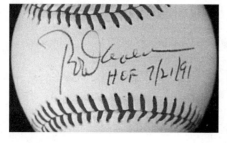

Rod Carew (1945-) — 1991
Cut signature	$8
Single-signature baseball	$35-$40
3x5 index card	$7-$9
Photograph/baseball card	$20
HOF plaque postcard	$25-$30
Perez-Steele postcards	$40-$50

Max Carey (1890-1976) — 1961
Cut signature	$30
Single-signature baseball	$750
3x5 index card	$40-$50
Photograph/baseball card	$125
HOF plaque postcard	$95
Perez-Steele postcards	Impossible

Steve Carlton (1944-) — 1994
Cut signature	$8
Single-signature baseball	$25-$30
3x5 index card	$10
Photograph/baseball card	$20-$25
HOF plaque postcard	$35
Perez-Steele postcards	$30

Alexander Cartwright (1820-1892) — 1938
Cut signature	$1,500
Single-signature baseball	Unknown
3x5 index card	$1,750
Photograph/baseball card	$3,500
HOF plaque postcard	Impossible
Perez-Steele postcards	Impossible

Orlando Cepeda (1937-) — 1999
Cut signature	$7
Single-signature baseball	$35
3x5 index card	$10
Photograph/baseball card	$25
HOF plaque postcard	$25
Perez-Steele postcards	$30

Henry Chadwick (1824-1908) — 1938
Cut signature	$1,000-$1,500
Single-signature baseball	Unknown
3x5 index card	$1,200
Photograph/baseball card	$3,200
HOF plaque postcard	Impossible
Perez-Steele postcards	Impossible

Frank Chance (1877-1924) — 1946
Cut signature	$750-$800
Single-signature baseball	$5,500-$7,000
3x5 index card	$1,700
Photograph/baseball card	$2,000
HOF plaque postcard	Impossible
Perez-Steele postcards	Impossible

Happy Chandler (1898-1991) — 1982
Cut signature	$20
Single-signature baseball	$100-$150
3x5 index card	$15-$25
Photograph/baseball card	$50
HOF plaque postcard	$25
Perez-Steele postcards	$40

Oscar Charleston (1896-1954) — 1976
Cut signature	$2,500
Single-signature baseball	$7,000
3x5 index card	$2,000-$3,000
Photograph/baseball card	$4,000
HOF plaque postcard	Impossible
Perez-Steele postcards	Impossible

Jack Chesbro (1874-1931) — 1946
Cut signature	$600-$1,150
Single-signature baseball	$10,000-$20,000
3x5 index card	$750
Photograph/baseball card	$2,000-$2,750
HOF plaque postcard	Impossible
Perez-Steele postcards	Impossible

Nestor Chylak (1922-1982) — 1999
Cut signature	$200-$250
Single-signature baseball	$800-$1,000
3x5 index card	$250-$300
Photograph/baseball card	$300-$350
HOF plaque postcard	Impossible
Perez-Steele postcards	Impossible

Fred Clarke (1872-1960) — 1945
Cut signature	$100
Single-signature baseball	$1,500-$3,000
3x5 index card	$200
Photograph/baseball card	$400
HOF plaque postcard	$400-$500
Perez-Steele postcards	Impossible

John Clarkson (1861-1909) — 1963
Cut signature	$1,200-$1,845
Single-signature baseball	Unknown
3x5 index card	$2,000
Photograph/baseball card	$2,500
HOF plaque postcard	Impossible
Perez-Steele postcards	Impossible

Roberto Clemente (1934-1972) — 1973
Cut signature	$300-$350
Single-signature baseball	$2,000-$4,000
3x5 index card	$400
Photograph/baseball card	$350-$600
HOF plaque postcard	Impossible
Perez-Steele postcards	Impossible

Ty Cobb (1886-1961) 1936
Cut signature	$500-$600
Single-signature baseball	$4,000-$5,000
3x5 index card	$700
Photograph/baseball card	$1,200
HOF plaque postcard	$1,000
Perez-Steele postcards	Impossible

Mickey Cochrane (1903-1962) 1947
Cut signature	$150
Single-signature baseball	$1,500-$2,000
3x5 index card	$200-$250
Photograph/baseball card	$350
HOF plaque postcard	$500
Perez-Steele postcards	Impossible

Eddie Collins (1887-1951) 1939
Cut signature	$100
Single-signature baseball	$2,250-$5,000
3x5 index card	$175-$225
Photograph/baseball card	$400
HOF plaque postcard	$550
Perez-Steele postcards	Impossible

Jimmy Collins (1870-1943) 1945
Cut signature	$500-$750
Single-signature baseball	$6,000
3x5 index card	$700-$950
Photograph/baseball card	$1,500
HOF plaque postcard	Impossible
Perez-Steele postcards	Impossible

Earle Combs (1899-1976) 1970
Cut signature	$15-$17
Single-signature baseball	$500-$2,000
3x5 index card	$40
Photograph/baseball card	$350
HOF plaque postcard	$100
Perez-Steele postcards	Impossible

Charles Comiskey (1859-1931) 1939
Cut signature	$350-$375
Single-signature baseball	$12,000-$15,000
3x5 index card	$500-$600
Photograph/baseball card	$2,000
HOF plaque postcard	Impossible
Perez-Steele postcards	Impossible

Jocko Conlan (1899-1989) 1974
Cut signature	$10
Single-signature baseball	$100-$125
3x5 index card	$15-$20
Photograph/baseball card	$35
HOF plaque postcard	$15-$20
Perez-Steele postcards	$60-$500

Thomas Connolly (1870-1963) 1953
Cut signature	$275
Single-signature baseball	$2,345-$7,000
3x5 index card	$350-$500
Photograph/baseball card	$900
HOF plaque postcard	$1,000-$1,200
Perez-Steele postcards	Impossible

Roger Connor (1857-1931) 1976
Cut signature	$1,000-$1,185
Single-signature baseball	$5,600-$8,000
3x5 index card	$2,700
Photograph/baseball card	$2,500
HOF plaque postcard	Impossible
Perez-Steele postcards	Impossible

Stan Coveleski (1889-1984) 1969
Cut signature	$20
Single-signature baseball	$450
3x5 index card	$35-$40
Photograph/baseball card	$150
HOF plaque postcard	$30
Perez-Steele postcards	$325-$400

Sam Crawford (1880-1968) 1957
Cut signature	$75-$100
Single-signature baseball	$1,900-$2,500
3x5 index card	$125
Photograph/baseball card	$250
HOF plaque postcard	$250-$400
Perez-Steele postcards	Impossible

Joe Cronin (1906-1984) 1956
Cut signature	$20
Single-signature baseball	$350-$500
3x5 index card	$25
Photograph/baseball card	$100
HOF plaque postcard	$35-$50
Perez-Steele postcards	$700-$750

Candy Cummings (1848-1924) 1939
Cut signature	$1,500-$1,750
Single-signature baseball	Unknown
3x5 index card	$1,700
Photograph/baseball card	$4,500
HOF plaque postcard	Impossible
Perez-Steele postcards	Impossible

Ki Ki Cuyler (1899-1950) 1968
Cut signature	$150
Single-signature baseball	$1,500-$3,500
3x5 index card	$175
Photograph/baseball card	$400-$425
HOF plaque postcard	Impossible
Perez-Steele postcards	Impossible

Ray Dandridge (1913-1994) 1987
Cut signature	$15-$20
Single-signature baseball	$40-$50
3x5 index card	$25
Photograph/baseball card	$25-$30
HOF plaque postcard	$15-$25
Perez-Steele postcards	$15-$25

George Davis (1870-1940) 1998
Cut signature	Unknown
Single-signature baseball	Unknown
3x5 index card	Unknown
Photograph/baseball card	Unknown
HOF plaque postcard	Impossible
Perez-Steele postcards	Impossible

Leon Day (1916-1995) 1995
Cut signature	$20
Single-signature baseball	$150-$200
3x5 index card	$25
Photograph/baseball card	$40-$50
HOF plaque postcard	Impossible
Perez-Steele postcards	Impossible

Dizzy Dean (1911-1974) — 1953
Cut signature	$75-$80
Single-signature baseball	$1,000
3x5 index card	$90-$100
Photograph/baseball card	$250-$350
HOF plaque postcard	$125-$150
Perez-Steele postcards	Impossible

Ed Delahanty (1867-1903) — 1945
Cut signature	$1,500
Single-signature baseball	Unknown
3x5 index card	$2,000
Photograph/baseball card	$4,000
HOF plaque postcard	Impossible
Perez-Steele postcards	Impossible

Bill Dickey (1907-1993) — 1954
Cut signature	$15
Single-signature baseball	$150-$200
3x5 index card	$30
Photograph/baseball card	$50
HOF plaque postcard	$35-$45
Perez-Steele postcards	$45-$80

Martin DiHigo (1905-1971) — 1977
Cut signature	$650-$675
Single-signature baseball	$4,000
3x5 index card	$800-$1,000
Photograph/baseball card	$1,500-$2,000
HOF plaque postcard	Impossible
Perez-Steele postcards	Impossible

Joe DiMaggio (1914-1999) — 1955
Cut signature	$40-$60
Single-signature baseball	$300-$350
3x5 index card	$150
Photograph/baseball card	$150-$200
HOF plaque postcard	$175-$200
Perez-Steele postcards	$300-$350

Larry Doby (1924-) — 1998
Cut signature	$7-$10
Single-signature baseball	$30-$35
3x5 Index card	$10-$12
Photograph/baseball card	$20
HOF plaque postcard	$15
Perez-Steele postcards	$15-$20

Bobby Doerr (1918-) — 1986
Cut signature	$5-$7
Single-signature baseball	$25
3x5 index card	$3-$7
Photograph/baseball card	$10-$13
HOF plaque postcard	$6-$10
Perez-Steele postcards	$15-$20

Don Drysdale (1936-1993) — 1984
Cut signature	$25-$30
Single-signature baseball	$125-$150
3x5 index card	$30-$35
Photograph/baseball card	$75-$90
HOF plaque postcard	$35
Perez-Steele postcards	$40

Hugh Duffy (1866-1954) — 1945
Cut signature	$300-$350
Single-signature baseball	$2,200-$3,500
3x5 index card	$350-$450
Photograph/baseball card	$600-$750
HOF plaque postcard	$900
Perez-Steele postcards	Impossible

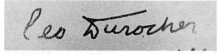

Leo Durocher (1905-1991) — 1994
Cut signature	$15-$20
Single-signature baseball	$150
3x5 index card	$25
Photograph/baseball card	$40-$50
HOF plaque postcard	Impossible
Perez-Steele postcards	Impossible

Billy Evans (1864-1956) — 1973
Cut signature	$225
Single-signature baseball	$10,000
3x5 index card	$300-$350
Photograph/baseball card	$500-$525
HOF plaque postcard	Impossible
Perez-Steele postcards	Impossible

Johnny Evers (1881-1947) — 1946
Cut signature	$300
Single-signature baseball	$3,500-$6,000
3x5 index card	$400
Photograph/baseball card	$1,000-$1,200
HOF plaque postcard	$1,100
Perez-Steele postcards	Impossible

Buck Ewing (1859-1906) — 1939
Cut signature	$1,000
Single-signature baseball	$3,000
3x5 index card	$2,400
Photograph/baseball card	$2,500-$4,000
HOF plaque postcard	Impossible
Perez-Steele postcards	Impossible

Red Faber (1888-1976) — 1964
Cut signature	$15
Single-signature baseball	$450-$1,800
3x5 index card	$35-$45
Photograph/baseball card	$75-$100
HOF plaque postcard	$85
Perez-Steele postcards	Impossible

Bob Feller (1918-) — 1962
Cut signature	$5
Single-signature baseball	$20-$25
3x5 index card	$7-$10
Photograph/baseball card	$10-$12
HOF plaque postcard	$20-$25
Perez-Steele postcards	$15-$35

Rick Ferrell (1905-1995) — 1984
Cut signature	$6-$8
Single-signature baseball	$70-$80
3x5 index card	$9
Photograph/baseball card	$25
HOF plaque postcard	$25
Perez-Steele postcards	$30-$35

Rollie Fingers (1946-) — 1992
Cut signature	$5-$7
Single-signature baseball	$25-$30
3x5 index card	$8-$12
Photograph/baseball card	$25
HOF plaque postcard	$10
Perez-Steele postcards	$25

Carlton Fisk (1947-) — 2000
Cut signature	$8-$12
Single-signature baseball	$35-$40
3x5 index card	$10
Photograph/baseball card	$25
HOF plaque postcard	$15-$20
Perez-Steele postcards	$25

Elmer Flick (1876-1971) — 1963
Cut signature	$45-$50
Single-signature baseball	$2,200-$2,500
3x5 index card	$50-$60
Photograph baseball card	$175-$250
HOF plaque postcard	$300-$450
Perez-Steele postcards	Impossible

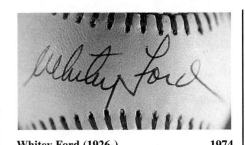

Whitey Ford (1926-) — 1974
Cut signature	$8-$10
Single-signature baseball	$30-$40
3x5 index card	$10-$12
Photograph/baseball card	$20-$30
HOF plaque postcard	$12-$20
Perez-Steele postcards	$20-$30

Bill Foster (1904-1978) — 1995
Cut signature	$2,000
Single-signature baseball	$5,000-$7500
3x5 index card	$3,000
Photograph/baseball card	Unknown
HOF plaque postcard	Impossible
Perez-Steele postcards	Impossible

Rube Foster (1878-1930) — 1981
Cut signature	$2,000
Single-signature baseball	$13,000
3x5 index card	$3,800
Photograph/baseball card	$3,150-$5,500
HOF plaque postcard	Impossible
Perez-Steele postcards	Impossible

Nellie Fox (1927-1975) — 1997
Cut signature	$150-$200
Single-signature baseball	$1,000-$1,500
3x5 index card	$250
Photograph/baseball card	$350-$400
HOF plaque postcard	Impossible
Perez-Steele postcard	Impossible

Jimmie Foxx (1907-1967) — 1951
Cut signature	$200-$250
Single-signature baseball	$3,000
3x5 index card	$300-$350
Photograph/baseball card	$500-$900
HOF plaque postcard	$550
Perez-Steele postcards	Impossible

Ford Frick (1894-1978) — 1970
Cut signature	$25-$30
Single-signature baseball	$500-$800
3x5 index card	$40-$50
Photograph/baseball card	$75-$100
HOF plaque postcard	$125
Perez-Steele postcards	Impossible

Frankie Frisch (1898-1973) — 1947
Cut signature	$50-$75
Single-signature baseball	$1,700-$1,800
3x5 index card	$75-$90
Photograph/baseball card	$100-$150
HOF plaque postcard	$100-$150
Perez-Steele postcards	Impossible

Pud Galvin (1855-1902) — 1965
Cut signature	$1,300
Single-signature baseball	$10,000-$12,000
3x5 index card	$2,500
Photograph/baseball card	$3,000
HOF plaque postcard	Impossible
Perez-Steele postcards	Impossible

Lou Gehrig (1903-1941) — 1939
Cut signature	$650
Single-signature baseball	$5,000-$7,000
3x5 index card	$800
Photograph/baseball card	$2,000-$4,000
HOF plaque postcard	Impossible
Perez-Steele postcards	Impossible

Charlie Gehringer (1903-1993) — 1949
Cut signature	$20-$25
Single-signature baseball	$150-$200
3x5 index card	$35
Photograph/baseball card	$85-$100
HOF plaque postcard	$35-$40
Perez-Steele postcards	$45-$65

Bob Gibson (1935-) — 1972
Cut signature	$8-$10
Single-signature baseball	$30-$35
3x5 index card	$12
Photograph/baseball card	$20-$25
HOF plaque postcard	$15-$20
Perez-Steele postcards	$20

Josh Gibson (1911-1947) — 1972
Cut signature	$700-$950
Single-signature baseball	$4,500-$6,500
3x5 index card	$800
Photograph/baseball card	$1,200-$1,700
HOF plaque postcard	Impossible
Perez-Steele postcards	Impossible

Warren Giles (1896-1979) — 1979
Cut signature	$20
Single-signature baseball	$250-$1,000
3x5 index card	$35-$45
Photograph/baseball card	$75-$125
HOF plaque postcard	Impossible
Perez-Steele postcards	Impossible

Lefty Gomez (1908-1989) — 1972
Cut signature	$15-$20
Single-signature baseball	$150-$200
3x5 index card	$20-$25
Photograph/baseball card	$35-$45
HOF plaque postcard	$20-$25
Perez-Steele postcards	$40-$65

Goose Goslin (1900-1971) — 1968
Cut signature	$70-$75
Single-signature baseball	$800-$2,700
3x5 index card	$75-$100
Photograph/baseball card	$300
HOF plaque postcard	$1,000-$3,000
Perez-Steele postcards	Impossible

Hank Greenberg (1911-1986) — 1956
Cut signature	$20-$30
Single-signature baseball	$500-$700
3x5 index card	$35-$75
Photograph/baseball card	$75-$100
HOF plaque postcard	$50-$75
Perez-Steele postcards	$300-$325

Clark Griffith (1869-1955) — 1946
Cut signature	$130-$135
Single-signature baseball	$1,000-$2,200
3x5 index card	$150-$175
Photograph/baseball card	$350
HOF plaque postcard	$600
Perez-Steele postcards	Impossible

Burleigh Grimes (1893-1985) — 1964
Cut signature	$20
Single-signature baseball	$90-$200
3x5 index card	$20-$25
Photograph/baseball card	$50-$60
HOF plaque postcard	$25-$30
Perez-Steele postcards	$150-$200

Lefty Grove (1900-1975) — 1947
Cut signature	$75
Single-signature baseball	$1,200-$1,300
3x5 index card	$100
Photograph/baseball card	$200
HOF plaque postcard	$150-$175
Perez-Steele postcards	Impossible

Chick Hafey (1903-1973) — 1971
Cut signature	$40-$45
Single-signature baseball	$425-$1,500
3x5 index card	$50
Photograph/baseball card	$75-$175
HOF plaque postcard	$600
Perez-Steele postcards	Impossible

Jesse Haines (1893-1978) — 1970
Cut signature	$30-$35
Single-signature baseball	$300-$950
3x5 index card	$20-$40
Photograph/baseball card	$75-$125
HOF plaque postcard	$75
Perez-Steele postcards	Impossible

Billy Hamilton (1866-1940) — 1961
Cut signature	$500-$1,500
Single-signature baseball	$4,250-$5,500
3x5 index card	$750
Photograph/baseball card	$2,150-$2,500
HOF plaque postcard	Impossible
Perez-Steele postcards	Impossible

Ned Hanlon (1857-1937) — 1996
Cut signature	Unknown
Single-signature baseball	Unknown
3x5 index card	Unknown
Photograph/baseball card	Unknown
HOF plaque postcard	Impossible
Perez-Steele postcards	Impossible

Will Harridge (1883-1971) — 1972
Cut signature	$85-$90
Single-signature baseball	$875-$2,500
3x5 index card	$125
Photograph/baseball card	$225-$300
HOF plaque postcard	Impossible
Perez-Steele postcards	Impossible

Bucky Harris (1896-1977) — 1975
Cut signature	$25-$30
Single-signature baseball	$450-$1,200
3x5 index card	$40
Photograph/baseball card	$200
HOF plaque postcard	$150-$200
Perez-Steele postcards	Impossible

Gabby Hartnett (1900-1972) — 1955
Cut signature	$40-$50
Single-signature baseball	$1,000-$2,000
3x5 index card	$60-$75
Photograph/baseball card	$200-$250
HOF plaque postcard	$200-$325
Perez-Steele postcards	Impossible

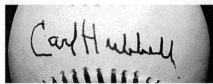

Harry Heilmann (1894-1951) — 1952
Cut signature	$175-$250
Single-signature baseball	$2,000-$2,500
3x5 index card	$300-$350
Photograph/baseball card	$475-$500
HOF plaque postcard	Impossible
Perez-Steele postcards	Impossible

Billy Herman (1909-1992) — 1975
Cut signature	$8
Single-signature baseball	$90-$100
3x5 index card	$12
Photograph/baseball card	$60
HOF plaque postcard	$20
Perez-Steele postcards	$25-$30

Harry Hooper (1887-1974) — 1971
Cut signature	$25-$30
Single-signature baseball	$450-$1,200
3x5 index card	$35
Photograph/baseball card	$80-$150
HOF plaque postcard	$100-$125
Perez-Steele postcards	Impossible

Rogers Hornsby (1896-1963) — 1942
Cut signature	$250-$300
Single-signature baseball	$2,500
3x5 index card	$300
Photograph/baseball card	$500-$700
HOF plaque postcard	$650
Perez-Steele postcards	Impossible

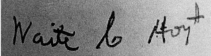

Waite Hoyt (1899-1984) — 1969
Cut signature	$30-$40
Single-signature baseball	$175-$450
3x5 index card	$45
Photograph/baseball card	$50-$80
HOF plaque postcard	$30-$35
Perez-Steele postcards	$450-$550

Cal Hubbard (1900-1977) — 1976
Cut signature	$30-$35
Single-signature baseball	$500-$1,000
3x5 index card	$40
Photograph/baseball card	$175-$250
HOF plaque postcard	$500
Perez-Steele postcards	Impossible

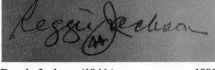

Carl Hubbell (1903-1988) — 1947
Cut signature	$15-$20
Single-signature baseball	$160-$175
3x5 index card	$25
Photograph/baseball card	$30-$35
HOF plaque postcard	$35-$40
Perez-Steele postcards	$60-$80

Miller Huggins (1879-1929) — 1964
Cut signature	$700-$750
Single-signature baseball	$4,500-$6,000
3x5 index card	$1,000
Photograph/baseball card	$1,500
HOF plaque postcard	Impossible
Perez-Steele postcards	Impossible

William Hulbert (1832-1882) — 1995
Cut signature - letter	$8000
Single-signature baseball	Unknown
3x5 index card	Unknown
Photograph/baseball card	Unknown
HOF plaque postcard	Impossible
Perez-Steele postcards	Impossible

Catfish Hunter (1946-1999) — 1987
Cut signature	$8
Single-signature baseball	$50-$60
3x5 index card	$10
Photograph/baseball card	$35
HOF plaque postcard	$20
Perez-Steele postcards	$25-$30

Monte Irvin (1911-) — 1973
Cut signature	$5-$8
Single-signature baseball	$20-$25
3x5 index card	$10
Photograph/baseball card	$15-$20
HOF plaque postcard	$10-$15
Perez-Steele postcards	$20-$25

Reggie Jackson (1946-) — 1993
Cut signature	$15
Single-signature baseball	$60-$65
3x5 index card	$20
Photograph/baseball card	$40-$50
HOF plaque postcard	$65
Perez-Steele postcards	$60

Travis Jackson (1903-1987) — 1982
Cut signature	$15
Single-signature baseball	$350
3x5 index card	$25
Photograph/baseball card	$80
HOF plaque postcard	$40
Perez-Steele postcards	$75-$80

Fergie Jenkins (1943-) — 1991
Cut signature	$3-$5
Single-signature baseball	$22-$28
3x5 index card	$7
Photograph/baseball card	$12-$15
HOF plaque postcard	$10-$15
Perez-Steele postcards	$10-$15

Hugh Jennings (1869-1928)   **1945**
Cut signature	$500-$825
Single-signature baseball	$4,750-$6,000
3x5 index card	$900
Photograph/baseball card	$1,000-$1,500
HOF plaque postcard	Impossible
Perez-Steele postcards	Impossible

Ban Johnson (1864-1931)   **1937**
Cut signature	$200
Single-signature baseball	$2,700-$3,500
3x5 index card	$250
Photograph/baseball card	$500-$550
HOF plaque postcard	Impossible
Perez-Steele postcards	Impossible

Judy Johnson (1900-1989)   **1975**
Cut signature	$10-$15
Single-signature baseball	$175-$200
3x5 index card	$15-$20
Photograph/baseball card	$30-$60
HOF plaque postcard	$25
Perez-Steele postcards	$80-$90

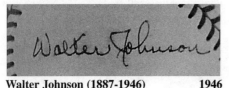

Walter Johnson (1887-1946)   **1946**
Cut signature	$600-$650
Single-signature baseball	$5,000
3x5 index card	$750
Photograph/baseball card	$1,200-$1,400
HOF plaque postcard	Unknown
Perez-Steele postcards	Impossible

Addie Joss (1880-1911)   **1978**
Cut signature	$1,500
Single-signature baseball	$7,500-$10,000
3x5 index card	$2,500
Photograph/baseball card	$3,900-$4,000
HOF plaque postcard	Impossible
Perez-Steele postcards	Impossible

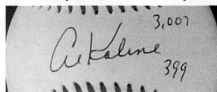

Al Kaline (1934-)   **1980**
Cut signature	$5-$7
Single-signature baseball	$30-$35
3x5 index card	$8-$10
Photograph/baseball card	$15-$25
HOF plaque postcard	$12-$15
Perez-Steele postcards	$20-$25

Tim Keefe (1857-1933)   **1964**
Cut signature	$600-$1,500
Single-signature baseball	$7,000
3x5 index card	$800
Photograph/baseball card	$2,000
HOF plaque postcard	Impossible
Perez-Steele postcards	Impossible

Wee Willie Keeler (1872-1923)   **1939**
Cut signature	$1,000-$1,400
Single-signature baseball	$8,000
3x5 index card	$2,000
Photograph/baseball card	$3,000-$3,250
HOF plaque postcard	Impossible
Perez-Steele postcards	Impossible

George Kell (1922-)   **1983**
Cut signature	$5-$7
Single-signature baseball	$25-$30
3x5 index card	$7
Photograph/baseball card	$10-$12
HOF plaque postcard	$6-$10
Perez-Steele postcards	$10-$15

Joe Kelley (1871-1943)   **1971**
Cut signature	$800-$1,100
Single-signature baseball	$7,300-$8,000
3x5 index card	$1,000
Photograph/baseball card	$1,500-$2,250
HOF plaque postcard	Impossible
Perez-Steele postcards	Impossible

George Kelly (1895-1984)   **1973**
Cut signature	$7-$8
Single-signature baseball	$350
3x5 index card	$15
Photograph/baseball card	$50-$75
HOF plaque postcard	$30
Perez-Steele postcards	$300-$325

Mike "King" Kelly (1857-1894)   **1945**
Cut signature	$2,000
Single-signature baseball	$7,000
3x5 index card	$3,500
Photograph/baseball card	$5,000
HOF plaque postcard	Impossible
Perez-Steele postcards	Impossible

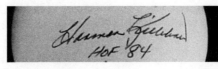

Harmon Killebrew (1936-)   **1984**
Cut signature	$8
Single-signature baseball	$30-$40
3x5 index card	$10
Photograph/baseball card	$20-$25
HOF plaque postcard	$25
Perez-Steele postcards	$20-$30

Ralph Kiner (1922-)   **1975**
Cut signature	$8
Single-signature baseball	$25-$30
3x5 index card	$10
Photograph/baseball card	$20
HOF plaque postcard	$15-$20
Perez-Steele postcards	$20-$25

Chuck Klein (1904-1958)   **1980**
Cut signature	$200
Single-signature baseball	$1,500-$3,000
3x5 index card	$300
Photograph/baseball card	$400-$500
HOF plaque postcard	Impossible
Perez-Steele postcards	Impossible

Bill Klem (1874-1951)   **1953**
Cut signature	$230-$400
Single-signature baseball	$2,750-$3,500
3x5 index card	$600
Photograph/baseball card	$900-$1,200
HOF plaque postcard	Impossible
Perez-Steele postcards	Impossible

Sandy Koufax (1935-)   **1971**
Cut signature	$10
Single-signature baseball	$75-$100
3x5 index card	$15
Photograph/baseball card	$50-$60
HOF plaque postcard	$40-$50
Perez-Steele postcards	$50-$75

Nap Lajoie (1875-1959)   **1937**
Cut signature	$250
Single-signature baseball	$4,500-$4,950
3x5 index card	$350
Photograph/baseball card	$900-$1,000
HOF plaque postcard	$750
Perez-Steele postcards	Impossible

Kenesaw Landis (1866-1944)   **1944**
Cut signature	$475-$500
Single-signature baseball	$3,500
3x5 index card	$600
Photograph/baseball card	$750-$900
HOF plaque postcard	Impossible
Perez-Steele postcards	Impossible

Tommy Lasorda (1927-)   **1997**
Cut signature	$8
Single-signature baseball	$35-$50
3x5 index card	$8-$10
Photograph/baseball card	$20-$30
HOF plaque postcard	$30-$40
Perez-Steele postcards	$40-$50

Tony Lazzeri (1903-1946)   **1991**
Cut signature	$275
Single-signature baseball	$2,500-$4,000
3x5 index card	$450
Photograph/baseball card	$500-$700
HOF plaque postcard	Impossible
Perez-Steele postcards	Impossible

Bob Lemon (1920-2000)   **1976**
Cut signature	$7-$9
Single-signature baseball	$40-$50
3x5 index card	$10
Photograph/baseball card	$25-$30
HOF plaque postcard	$10-$15
Perez-Steele postcards	$15-$20

Buck Leonard (1907-1997)   **1972**
Cut signature	$10
Single-signature baseball	$50-$75
3x5 index card	$12-$15
Photograph/baseball card	$25-$35
HOF plaque postcard	$15
Perez-Steele postcards	$25-$30

Freddie Lindstrom (1905-1981)   **1976**
Cut signature	$12-$15
Single-signature baseball	$400-$700
3x5 index card	$20
Photograph/baseball card	$75-$100
HOF plaque postcard	$75
Perez-Steele postcards	Impossible

John "Pop" Lloyd (1884-1964)   **1977**
Cut signature	$700
Single-signature baseball	$5,600-$7,000
3x5 index card	$750
Photograph/baseball card	$1,200-$2,500
HOF plaque postcard	Impossible
Perez-Steele postcards	Impossible

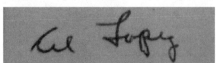

Ernie Lombardi (1908-1977)   **1986**
Cut signature	$35-$50
Single-signature baseball	$525-$1,200
3x5 index card	$50-$60
Photograph/baseball card	$225-$300
HOF plaque postcard	Impossible
Perez-Steele postcards	Impossible

Al Lopez (1908-)   **1977**
Cut signature	$15
Single-signature baseball	$75-$100
3x5 index card	$20
Photograph/baseball card	$50-$60
HOF plaque postcard	$45
Perez-Steele postcards	$50-$75

Ted Lyons (1900-1986)   **1955**
Cut signature	$8-$12
Single-signature baseball	$125-$225
3x5 index card	$15
Photograph/baseball card	$45-$75
HOF plaque postcard	$30-$35
Perez-Steele postcards	$200-$250

Connie Mack (1862-1956)   **1937**
Cut signature	$300
Single-signature baseball	$1,000
3x5 index card	$350
Photograph/baseball card	$400-$450
HOF plaque postcard	$600
Perez-Steele postcards	Impossible

Larry MacPhail (1890-1975)   **1978**
Cut signature	$60
Single-signature baseball	$785-$1,700
3x5 index card	$175
Photograph/baseball card	$300-$400
HOF plaque postcard	Impossible
Perez-Steele postcards	Impossible

Lee MacPhail (1917-)   **1998**
Cut signature	$10
Single-signature baseball	$75
3x5 index card	$15
Photograph	$35
HOF plaque postcard	$35
Perez-Steele postcard	$50

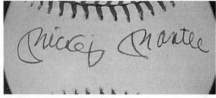

Mickey Mantle (1931-1995)   **1974**
Cut signature	$70
Single-signature baseball	$250-$350
3x5 index card	$75-$100
Photograph/baseball card	$125
HOF plaque postcard	$150-$200
Perez-Steele postcards	$200-$250

Heinie Manush (1901-1971)   **1964**
Cut signature	$25-$40
Single-signature baseball	$1,500-$2,200
3x5 index card	$60
Photograph/baseball card	$200-$300
HOF plaque postcard	$250-$300
Perez-Steele postcards	Impossible

Rabbit Maranville (1891-1954)   **1954**
Cut signature	$140-$150
Single-signature baseball	$1,600-$2,000
3x5 index card	$250
Photograph/baseball card	$350-$425
HOF plaque postcard	Impossible
Perez-Steele postcards	Impossible

Juan Marichal (1938-)   **1983**
Cut signature	$6-$8
Single-signature baseball	$25-$35
3x5 index card	$10
Photograph/baseball card	$15-$18
HOF plaque postcard	$12
Perez-Steele postcards	$10-$20

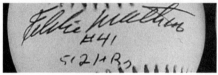

Rube Marquard (1889-1980)   **1971**
Cut signature	$10-$15
Single-signature baseball	$450-$700
3x5 index card	$20
Photograph/baseball card	$100-$150
HOF plaque postcard	$45
Perez-Steele postcards	Impossible

Eddie Mathews (1931-2001)   **1978**
Cut signature	$10
Single-signature baseball	$30-$40
3x5 index card	$10-$12
Photograph/baseball card	$15-$25
HOF plaque postcard	$15
Perez-Steele postcards	$20-$25

Christy Mathewson (1880-1925)   **1936**
Cut signature	$1,200
Single-signature baseball	$11,500-$13,000
3x5 index card	$1,400
Photograph/baseball card	$2,900-$3,000
HOF plaque postcard	Impossible
Perez-Steele postcards	Impossible

Willie Mays (1931-)   **1979**
Cut signature	$15
Single-signature baseball	$60-$80
3x5 index card	$20
Photograph/baseball card	$35-$50
HOF plaque postcard	$50
Perez-Steele postcards	$40-$35

Bill Mazeroski (1936-)   **2001**
Cut signature	$10
Single-signature baseball	$25-$35
3x5 index card	$10
Photograph/baseball card	$20-$25
HOF plaque postcard	$25-$30
Perez-Steele postcards	$25-$30

Joe McCarthy [signature]

Joe McCarthy (1887-1978)   **1957**
Cut signature	$25-$35
Single-signature baseball	$650-$1,000
3x5 index card	$40
Photograph/baseball card	$100-$150
HOF plaque postcard	$50-$80
Perez-Steele postcards	Impossible

Tom McCarthy (1864-1922)   **1946**
Cut signature	$1,500-$1,675
Single-signature baseball	$4,000-$4,250
3x5 index card	$2,000
Photograph/baseball card	$4,000-$4,250
HOF plaque postcard	Impossible
Perez-Steele postcards	Impossible

Willie McCovey (1938-)   **1986**
Cut signature	$4-$5
Single-signature baseball	$35-$50
3x5 index card	$8
Photograph/baseball card	$25-$35
HOF plaque postcard	$20
Perez-Steele postcards	$10-$25

Joe McGinnity (1871-1929)   **1946**
Cut signature	$800-$1,250
Single-signature baseball	$5,000-$9,000
3x5 index card	$1,500
Photograph/baseball card	$4,000-$5,000
HOF plaque postcard	Impossible
Perez-Steele postcards	Impossible

Bill McGowan (1871-1954)   **1992**
Cut signature	$300
Single-signature baseball	$5,000
3x5 index card	$400
Photograph/baseball card	$2,000
HOF plaque postcard	Impossible
Perez-Steele postcards	Impossible

John McGraw (1873-1934)   **1937**
Cut signature	$450-$500
Single-signature baseball	$3,500-$6,000
3x5 index card	$650
Photograph/baseball card	$1,250-$1,500
HOF plaque postcard	Impossible
Perez-Steele postcards	Impossible

Bill McKechnie (1886-1965)   **1962**
Cut signature	$60-$75
Single-signature baseball	$1,500-$2,000
3x5 index card	$150
Photograph/baseball card	$300-$350
HOF plaque postcard	$300
Perez-Steele postcards	Impossible

Bid McPhee (1859-1943)   **2000**
Cut signature	$250
Single-signature baseball	$2,000-$2,500
3x5 index card	$350
Photograph/baseball card	$350-$400
HOF plaque postcard	Impossible
Perez-Steele postcards	Impossible

Joe Medwick [signature]

Joe "Ducky" Medwick (1911-1975)   **1968**
Cut signature	$20-$25
Single-signature baseball	$500-$1,700
3x5 index card	$45
Photograph/baseball card	$150-$200
HOF plaque postcard	$125-$150
Perez-Steele postcards	Impossible

Johnny Mize (1913-1993)   **1981**
Cut signature	$10
Single-signature baseball	$75-$100
3x5 index card	$15
Photograph/baseball card	$30-$35
HOF plaque postcard	$25
Perez-Steele postcards	$40

Joe Morgan (1943-)   **1990**
Cut signature	$8-$10
Single-signature baseball	$25-$30
3x5 index card	$10-$12
Photograph/baseball card	$20-$30
HOF plaque postcard	$15-$20
Perez-Steele postcards	$20-$25

Stan Musial (1920-)   **1969**
Cut signature	$10-$12
Single-signature baseball	$50
3x5 index card	$15
Photograph/baseball card	$30-$35
HOF plaque postcard	$25
Perez-Steele postcards	$30-$80

Hal Newhouser (1921-1998)   **1992**
Cut signature	$3-$5
Single-signature baseball	$30-$50
3x5 index card	$7
Photograph/baseball card	$15-$20
HOF plaque postcard	$15
Perez-Steele postcards	$15-$20

Kid Nichols (1869-1953)   **1949**
Cut signature	$150-$200
Single-signature baseball	$3,200-$4,000
3x5 index card	$300
Photograph/baseball card	$475-$500
HOF plaque postcard	$1,000
Perez-Steele postcards	Impossible

Phil Niekro (1939-)   **1997**
Cut signature	$7
Single-signature baseball	$25-$35
3x5 index card	$10
Photograph/baseball card	$15-$20
HOF plaque postcard	$25
Perez-Steele postcards	$25

James O'Rourke (1852-1919)   **1945**
Cut signature	$1,500-$1,750
Single-signature baseball	$5,200-$10,000
3x5 index card	$2,500
Photograph/baseball card	$3,500-$3,700
HOF plaque postcard	Impossible
Perez-Steele postcards	Impossible

Mel Ott (1909-1958)   **1951**
Cut signature	$200-$300
Single-signature baseball	$2,500-$3,500
3x5 index card	$300
Photograph/baseball card	$500-$725
HOF plaque postcard	$650
Perez-Steele postcards	Impossible

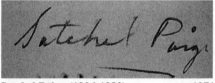

Satchel Paige (1906-1982)   **1971**
Cut signature	$75-$100
Single-signature baseball	$1,000
3x5 index card	$100-$10
Photograph/baseball card	$200-$235
HOF plaque postcard	$175
Perez-Steele postcards	$3,500

Jim Palmer (1945-)   **1990**
Cut signature	$7
Single-signature baseball	$25-$30
3x5 index card	$10
Photograph/baseball card	$15-$20
HOF plaque postcard	$12-$20
Perez-Steele postcards	$15-$25

Herb Pennock (1894-1948)   **1948**
Cut signature	$175
Single-signature baseball	$1,625-$2,500
3x5 index card	$200
Photograph/baseball card	$350
HOF plaque postcard	Impossible
Perez-Steele postcards	Impossible

Tony Perez (1943-)   **2000**
Cut signature	$7
Single-signature baseball	$25-$35
3x5 index card	$10
Photograph/baseball card	$15-$20
HOF plaque postcard	$20
Perez-Steele postcards	$20

Gaylord Perry (1938-)   **1991**
Cut signature	$5-$7
Single-signature baseball	$20-$25
3x5 index card	$10
Photograph/baseball card	$15-$20
HOF plaque postcard	$10
Perez-Steele postcards	$15

Ed Plank (1875-1926) — **1946**

Cut signature	$1,500-$1,775
Single-signature baseball	$8,000
3x5 index card	$2,200
Photograph/baseball card	$3,200-$3,500
HOF plaque postcard	Impossible
Perez-Steele postcards	Impossible

Kirby Puckett (1960-) — **2001**

Cut signature	$7
Single-signature baseball	$50-$75
3x5 index card	$10
Photograph/baseball card	$30-$50
HOF plaque postcard	$60
Perez-Steele postcards	$60

Charles Radbourne (1854-1897) — **1948**

Cut signature	$1,425-$2,000
Single-signature baseball	$7,500
3x5 index card	$2,500
Photograph/baseball card	$3,200-$3,500
HOF plaque postcard	Impossible
Perez-Steele postcards	Impossible

Pee Wee Reese (1918-1999) — **1984**

Cut signature	$10
Single-signature baseball	$75-$100
3x5 index card	$15
Photograph/baseball card	$45-$50
HOF plaque postcard	$40-$45
Perez-Steele postcards	$55-$60

Sam Rice (1890-1974) — **1963**

Cut signature	$25-$50
Single-signature baseball	$625-$1,500
3x5 index card	$60
Photograph/baseball card	$125-$150
HOF plaque postcard	$100-$135
Perez-Steele postcards	Impossible

Branch Rickey (1881-1965) — **1967**

Cut signature	$175-$225
Single-signature baseball	$1,100-$2,500
3x5 index card	$300
Photograph/baseball card	$525-$750
HOF plaque postcard	Impossible
Perez-Steele postcards	Impossible

Eppa Rixey (1891-1963) — **1963**

Cut signature	$70-$85
Single-signature baseball	$800-$3,500
3x5 index card	$100
Photograph/baseball card	$250-$350
HOF plaque postcard	Impossible
Perez-Steele postcards	Impossible

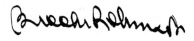

Phil Rizzuto (1918-) — **1994**

Cut signature	$5-$7
Single-signature baseball	$30-$40
3x5 index card	$10
Photograph/baseball card	$15-$25
HOF plaque postcard	$20
Perez-Steele postcards	$35

Robin Roberts (1926-) — **1976**

Cut signature	$5-$7
Single-signature baseball	$25
3x5 index card	$10
Photograph/baseball card	$15
HOF plaque postcard	$10
Perez-Steele postcards	$15-$20

Brooks Robinson (1937-) — **1983**

Cut signature	$5-$7
Single-signature baseball	$25-$30
3x5 index card	$10
Photograph/baseball card	$15-$20
HOF plaque postcard	$10
Perez-Steele postcards	$12-$20

Frank Robinson (1935-) — **1982**

Cut signature	$4-$5
Single-signature baseball	$35-$45
3x5 index card	$8
Photograph/baseball card	$20-$30
HOF plaque postcard	$25
Perez-Steele postcards	$25

Jackie Robinson (1919-1972) — **1962**

Cut signature	$400-$450
Single-signature baseball	$3,000
3x5 index card	$500
Photograph/baseball card	$750-$800
HOF plaque postcard	$750-$800
Perez-Steele postcards	Impossible

Wilbert Robinson (1863-1934) — **1945**

Cut signature	$700-$750
Single-signature baseball	$4,225-$6,000
3x5 index card	$750
Photograph/baseball card	$2,000
HOF plaque postcard	Impossible
Perez-Steele postcards	Impossible

Joe "Bullet" Rogan (1889-1967) — **1998**

Cut signature	$2,500
Single-signature baseball	$10,000
3x5 index card	$2,500
Photograph	$3,000
HOF plaque postcard	Impossible
Perez-Steele postcards	Impossible

Edd Roush (1893-1988) — **1962**

Cut signature	$9-$12
Single-signature baseball	$80-$160
3x5 index card	$10
Photograph/baseball card	$45-$75
HOF plaque postcard	$30-$80
Perez-Steele postcards	$65-$80

Red Ruffing (1904-1986) — **1967**

Cut signature	$20-$35
Single-signature baseball	$250-$500
3x5 index card	$40
Photograph/baseball card	$70-$125
HOF plaque postcard	$100
Perez-Steele postcards	$350-$400

Amos Rusie (1871-1942) — **1977**

Cut signature	$700-$1,100
Single-signature baseball	$5,000-$6,500
3x5 index card	$750
Photograph/baseball card	$2,000-$2,300
HOF plaque postcard	Impossible
Perez-Steele postcards	Impossible

Babe Ruth (1895-1948) — **1936**

Cut signature	$1,000
Single-signature baseball	$5,000-$10,000
3x5 index card	$1,500
Photograph/baseball card	$2,500-$5,000
HOF plaque postcard	$4,500
Perez-Steele postcards	Impossible

Nolan Ryan (1947-) — **1999**
Cut signature — $10-$12
Single-signature baseball — $60-$75
3x5 index card — $15
Photograph/baseball card — $40-$45
HOF plaque postcard — $60-$75
Perez-Steele postcards — $60-$75

Ray Schalk (1892-1970) — **1955**
Cut signature — $35-$45
Single-signature baseball — $600-$1,700
3x5 index card — $75-$85
Photograph/baseball card — $225-$350
HOF plaque postcard — $300-$450
Perez-Steele postcards — Impossible

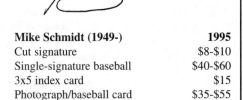

Mike Schmidt (1949-) — **1995**
Cut signature — $8-$10
Single-signature baseball — $40-$60
3x5 index card — $15
Photograph/baseball card — $35-$55
HOF plaque postcard — $40
Perez-Steele postcards — $40

Al "Red" Schoendienst (1923-) — **1989**
Cut signature — $5-$7
Single-signature baseball — $25-$30
3x5 index card — $10
Photograph/baseball card — $15-$20
HOF plaque postcard — $15
Perez-Steele postcards — $15-$20

Tom Seaver (1944-) — **1992**
Cut signature — $7-$10
Single-signature baseball — $40-$45
3x5 index card — $15
Photograph/baseball card — $35
HOF plaque postcard — $30
Perez-Steele postcards — $35-$40

Frank Selee (1859-1909) — **1999**
Cut signature — $550
Single-signature baseball — Unknown
3x5 index card — Unknown
Photograph/baseball card — Unknown
HOF plaque postcard — Impossible
Perez-Steele postcards — Impossible

Joe Sewell (1898-1990) — **1977**
Cut signature — $8-$10
Single-signature baseball — $80-$125
3x5 index card — $12
Photograph/baseball card — $30-$35
HOF plaque postcard — $20
Perez-Steele postcards — $35-$60

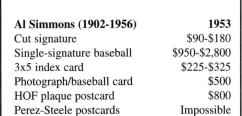

Al Simmons (1902-1956) — **1953**
Cut signature — $90-$180
Single-signature baseball — $950-$2,800
3x5 index card — $225-$325
Photograph/baseball card — $500
HOF plaque postcard — $800
Perez-Steele postcards — Impossible

George Sisler (1893-1973) — **1939**
Cut signature — $25-$40
Single-signature baseball — $550-$1,200
3x5 index card — $50-$60
Photograph/baseball card — $135-$175
HOF plaque postcard — $150
Perez-Steele postcards — Impossible

Enos Slaughter (1916-) — **1985**
Cut signature — $5
Single-signature baseball — $20-$25
3x5 index card — $7
Photograph/baseball card — $12-$15
HOF plaque postcard — $8-$10
Perez-Steele postcards — $12-$20

Hilton Smith (1907-1983) — **2001**
Cut signature — $550
Single-signature baseball — $850
3x5 index card — $600
Photograph/baseball card — $700-$800
HOF plaque postcard — Impossible
Perez-Steele postcards — Impossible

Duke Snider (1926-) — **1980**
Cut signature — $5-$8
Single-signature baseball — $30-$40
3x5 index card — $10
Photograph/baseball card — $20-$25
HOF plaque postcard — $15-$20
Perez-Steele postcards — $15-$25

Warren Spahn (1921-) — **1973**
Cut signature — $5-$8
Single-signature baseball — $20-$30
3x5 index card — $10
Photograph/baseball card — $15-$20
HOF plaque postcard — $10
Perez-Steele postcards — $20-$30

Al Spalding (1850-1915) — **1939**
Cut signature — $750-$1,250
Single-signature baseball — $12,000
3x5 index card — $1,750
Photograph/baseball card — $1,800-$2,200
HOF plaque postcard — Impossible
Perez-Steele postcards — Impossible

Tris Speaker (1888-1958) — **1937**
Cut signature — $125-$200
Single-signature baseball — $2,900-$3,000
3x5 index card — $225-$275
Photograph/baseball card — $500-$700
HOF plaque postcard — $600
Perez-Steele postcards — Impossible

Willie Stargell (1940-2001) — **1988**
Cut signature — $5-$8
Single-signature baseball — $30-$40
3x5 index card — $10
Photograph/baseball card — $15-$25
HOF plaque postcard — $15
Perez-Steele postcards — $15-$20

Turkey Stearnes (1901-1979) — **2000**
Cut signature — $250
Single-signature baseball — $800
3x5 index card — $300
Photograph/baseball card — $700
HOF plaque postcard — Impossible
Perez-Steele postcards — Impossible

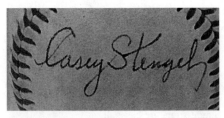

Casey Stengel (1890-1975)   **1966**
Cut signature	$50-$75
Single-signature baseball	$480-$1,000
3x5 index card	$90-$100
Photograph/baseball card	$150
HOF plaque postcard	$150
Perez-Steele postcards	Impossible

Don Sutton (1945-)   **1998**
Cut signature	$5-$8
Single-signature baseball	$25-$35
3x5 index card	$10
Photograph/baseball card	$15-$20
HOF plaque postcard	$12-$20
Perez-Steele postcards	$20-$25

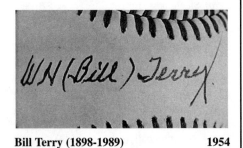

Bill Terry (1898-1989)   **1954**
Cut signature	$15
Single-signature baseball	$160-$175
3x5 index card	$20
Photograph/baseball card	$45-$50
HOF plaque postcard	$25-$30
Perez-Steele postcards	$65-$80

Sam Thompson (1860-1922)   **1974**
Cut signature	$1,200-$2,125
Single-signature baseball	$10,000
3x5 index card	$3,250
Photograph/baseball card	$6,000
HOF plaque postcard	Impossible
Perez-Steele postcards	Impossible

Joe Tinker (1880-1948)   **1946**
Cut signature	$300-$350
Single-signature baseball	$6,000
3x5 index card	$375-$400
Photograph/baseball card	$900-$1,200
HOF plaque postcard	$1,000
Perez-Steele postcards	Impossible

Pie Traynor (1899-1972)   **1948**
Cut signature	$50-$100
Single-signature baseball	$1,175-$1,200
3x5 index card	$125-$175
Photograph/baseball card	$300
HOF plaque postcard	$450
Perez-Steele postcards	Impossible

Dazzy Vance (1891-1961)   **1955**
Cut signature	$70-$200
Single-signature baseball	$1,500-$3,200
3x5 index card	$250-$300
Photograph/baseball card	$650-$750
HOF plaque postcard	$600
Perez-Steele postcards	Impossible

Arky Vaughan (1912-1952)   **1985**
Cut signature	$150-$175
Single-signature baseball	$1,525-$3,500
3x5 index card	$250
Photograph/baseball card	$500-$650
HOF plaque postcard	Impossible
Perez-Steele postcards	Impossible

Bill Veeck (1914-1986)   **1991**
Cut signature	$50-$75
Single-signature baseball	$1,500-$2,000
3x5 index card	$100
Photograph/baseball card	$250-$325
HOF plaque postcard	Impossible
Perez-Steele postcards	Impossible

Rube Waddell (1876-1914)   **1946**
Cut signature	$1,000-$1,400
Single-signature baseball	$12,500
3x5 index card	$1,500
Photograph/baseball card	$4,500
HOF plaque postcard	Impossible
Perez-Steele postcards	Impossible

Honus Wagner (1874-1955)   **1936**
Cut signature	$275-$300
Single-signature baseball	$4,000
3x5 index card	$350
Photograph/baseball card	$800-$850
HOF plaque postcard	$1,200
Perez-Steele postcards	Impossible

Bobby Wallace (1873-1960)   **1953**
Cut signature	$175-$225
Single-signature baseball	$3,000-$4,500
3x5 index card	$300
Photograph/baseball card	$625-$700
HOF plaque postcard	$800
Perez-Steele postcards	Impossible

Ed Walsh (1881-1959)   **1946**
Cut signature	$125-$150
Single-signature baseball	$2,725-$3,600
3x5 index card	$200
Photograph/baseball card	$350-$400
HOF plaque postcard	$350
Perez-Steele postcards	Impossible

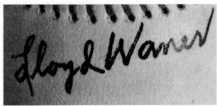

Lloyd Waner (1906-1982)   **1967**
Cut signature	$15-$20
Single-signature baseball	$500-$700
3x5 index card	$25
Photograph/baseball card	$150
HOF plaque postcard	$30
Perez-Steele postcards	$3,500

Paul Waner (1903-1965)   **1952**
Cut signature	$50-$100
Single-signature baseball	$2,300-$2,500
3x5 index card	$125
Photograph/baseball card	$200-$300
HOF plaque postcard	$350
Perez-Steele postcards	Impossible

Monte Ward (1860-1925)   **1964**
Cut signature	$1,000-$1,450
Single-signature baseball	$12,000
3x5 index card	$1,500
Photograph/baseball card	$3,000-$3,250
HOF plaque postcard	Impossible
Perez-Steele postcards	Impossible

Earl Weaver (1930-)   **1996**
Cut signature	$5-$7
Single-signature baseball	$25-$30
3x5 index card	$10
Photograph/baseball card	$15
HOF plaque/postcard	$10
Perez-Steele postcards	$15

George Weiss (1895-1972)   **1971**
Cut signature	$40-$45
Single-signature baseball	$675-$3,500
3x5 index card	$75-$100
Photograph/baseball card	$250-$300
HOF plaque postcard	Unknown
Perez-Steele postcards	Impossible

Mickey Welch (1859-1941)   **1973**
Cut signature	$1,700-$2,000
Single-signature baseball	$5,800-$8,500
3x5 index card	$2,750
Photograph/baseball card	$4,000
HOF plaque postcard	Impossible
Perez-Steele postcards	Impossible

Willie Wells (1905-1989)   **1997**
Cut signature	$200-$250
Single-signature baseball	$1,000-$1,500
3x5 index card	$300-$400
Photograph/baseball card	$500-$700
HOF plaque postcard	Impossible
Perez-Steele postcards	Impossible

Zack Wheat (1888-1972)   **1959**
Cut signature $20-$50
Single-signature baseball $975-$1,600
3x5 index card $80
Photograph/baseball card $175-$200
HOF plaque postcard $200-$350
Perez-Steele postcards   Impossible

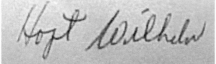

Hoyt Wilhelm (1923-)   **1985**
Cut signature $5
Single-signature baseball $25-$30
3x5 index card $8
Photograph/baseball card $12-$16
HOF plaque postcard $10-$15
Perez-Steele postcards $15

Billy Williams (1938-)   **1987**
Cut signature $5-$7
Single-signature baseball $25
3x5 index card $10
Photograph/baseball card $15-$20
HOF plaque postcard $10
Perez-Steele postcards $12-$20

Smokey Joe Williams (1885-1946) **1999**
Cut signature $400-$450
Single-signature baseball $800-$1,000
3x5 index card $450
Photograph/baseball card $500-$600
HOF plaque postcard   Impossible
Perez-Steele postcards   Impossible

Ted Williams (1918-)   **1966**
Cut signature $40
Single-signature baseball $275-$300
3x5 index card $60
Photograph/baseball card $150
HOF plaque postcard $200
Perez-Steele postcards $250-$300

Vic Willis (1876-1947)   **1995**
Cut signature $1,500
Single-signature baseball   Unknown
3x5 index card $425
Photograph/baseball card   Unknown
HOF plaque postcard   Impossible
Perez-Steele postcards   Impossible

Hack Wilson (1900-1948)   **1979**
Cut signature $235-$300
Single-signature baseball $2,400-$3,000
3x5 index card $450
Photograph/baseball card $675-$800
HOF plaque postcard   Impossible
Perez-Steele postcards   Impossible

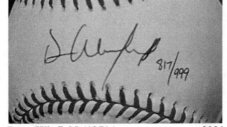

Dave Winfield (1951-)   **2001**
Cut signature $10
Single-signature baseball $40-$50
3x5 index card $15
Photograph/baseball card $25-$35
HOF plaque postcard $50
Perez-Steele postcards $50

George Wright (1847-1937)   **1937**
Cut signature $800-$900
Single-signature baseball $5,725-$8,500
3x5 index card $1,200
Photograph/baseball card $2,750
HOF plaque postcard   Impossible
Perez-Steele postcards   Impossible

Harry Wright (1835-1895)   **1953**
Cut signature $1,200-$1,600
Single-signature baseball $5,000
3x5 index card $2,000
Photograph/baseball card $3,500
HOF plaque postcard   Impossible
Perez-Steele postcards   Impossible

Early Wynn (1920-1999)   **1972**
Cut signature $7-$10
Single-signature baseball $40-$50
3x5 index card $10-$12
Photograph/baseball card $20-$30
HOF plaque postcard $15
Perez-Steele postcards $20-$25

Carl Yastrzemski (1939-)   **1989**
Cut signature $8-$10
Single-signature baseball $35-$45
3x5 index card $15
Photograph/baseball card $30
HOF plaque postcard $25
Perez-Steele postcards $20-$30

Tom Yawkey (1903-1976)   **1980**
Cut signature $100-$150
Single-signature baseball $1,000-$2,000
3x5 index card $125-$175
Photograph/baseball card $325-$400
HOF plaque postcard   Impossible
Perez-Steele postcards   Impossible

Cy Young (1867-1955)   **1937**
Cut signature $300
Single-signature baseball $3,400-$3,500
3x5 index card $350
Photograph/baseball card $700-$825
HOF plaque postcard $1,000
Perez-Steele postcards   Impossible

Ross Youngs (1897-1927)   **1972**
Cut signature $1,000-$1,150
Single-signature baseball $7,000
3x5 index card $1,500
Photograph/baseball card $2,500
HOF plaque postcard   Impossible
Perez-Steele postcards   Impossible

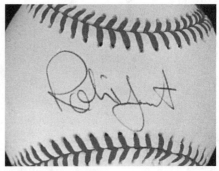

Robin Yount (1955-)   **1999**
Cut signature $8
Single-signature baseball $50-$60
3x5 index card $15
Photograph/baseball card $30-$40
HOF plaque postcard $50
Perez-Steele postcards $50

ACTIVE PLAYER AUTOGRAPHS

In the years following our national pastime's World Series-stopping strike of 1994 and early 1995, Major League Baseball embarked on a mission to win back its fans. One of the methods, in theory, was for players to be more accommodating to autograph requests. Not surprisingly, many players carried out the mission and continue to do so. (Cal Ripken Jr., for example, has always been a model for other players in the area of fan interaction; He built his reputation in large part by signing for as many fans as he possibly can before or after a game.) Other players, though, try to avoid autograph requests.

Ultimately, though, the demand for autographs outweighs the time a star player can devote to signing. Derek Jeter, Mike Piazza and Alex Rodriguez couldn't possibly fulfill every request for an autograph; if they sign for 50 people during batting practice before a game, there may be hundreds of others who get "shut out." Some players hesitate to sign even one autograph because it opens a veritable floodgate of other requests. Unlike Hall of Famers and retired players—who may go months at a time without mention in the media—today's stars are in the news practically every day during the season. Many of them are so recognizable that they get autograph requests whenever they're in a public place. Unfortunately for collectors, these heavy everyday demands on players make their autographs difficult to obtain.

But none of this means that autograph collectors should stop asking today's players to sign a ball or photo or card. Persistence is the key to this hobby. With some players, you may actually have to wait until they retire (*that's* persistence). Retired players, as we know, have the time to make several autograph show appearances a year—appearances that can supple-

ment their income. (On the other hand, today's stars may never need any extra income—average salaries recently surpassed the $2 million mark.)

So where can you get autographs from active players? The best time remains at spring training. Teams work out from mid-February through late March in either Florida or Arizona, and the atmosphere is much more relaxed than during the season, so players are generally more willing to sign.

Spring training is also the best time to snag autographs of up-and-coming players who may become less and less accessible as their stars rise. Albert Pujols of the St. Louis Cardinals, Dee Brown of the Kansas City Royals and, of course, former Japanese batting champion Ichiro Suzuki of the Seattle Mariners will get much more swamped with autograph requests in coming years than what they experienced in their first spring training camps.

If you can't make it to Florida or Arizona in February or March, the end of the winter is a good time to start mailing requests to players in care of their respective teams' spring training headquarters. (Such publications as *USA Today's Baseball Weekly* list spring training addresses during the off-season.) You'll find the response rate for mail-order requests is better during spring training than it is during the season.

The most obvious place to try for in-person autograph of current players is at the ballpark during the regular season. But the competition from other fans and collectors can be fierce, even if you take the steps outlined in "Collecting Strategy" (see p. 14). If you want a little less competition, keep an eye on events calendars in your local newspapers. An athlete's occasional speaking engagement, promotional appearance, seminar or charity dinner can provide autograph opportunities that don't necessarily draw a crowd.

Active Players' Autographs

Jeff Abbott
Ball	$22
Photo	$12
3x5 card	$5

Bobby Abreu
Ball	$25
Photo	$15
3x5 card	$6

Antonio Alfonseca
Ball	$20
Photo	$12
3x5 card	$5

Edgardo Alfonzo
Ball	$20
Photo	$12
3x5 card	$5

Luis Alicia
Ball	$20
Photo	$12
3x5 card	$5

Roberto Alomar
Ball	$30
Photo	$20
3x5 card	$6

Sandy Alomar Jr.
Ball	$23
Photo	$13
3x5 card	$5

Moises Alou
Ball	$30
Photo	$14
3x5 card	$7

Wilson Alvarez
Ball	$20
Photo	$10
3x5 card	$5

Brady Anderson
Ball	$30
Photo	$12
3x5 card	$5

Garret Anderson
Ball	$23
Photo	$14
3x5 card	$5

Rich Ankiel
Ball	$30
Photo	$17
3x5 card	$7

Kevin Appier
Ball	$22
Photo	$13
3x5 card	$6

Rich Aurilia
Ball	$20
Photo	$12
3x5 card	$5

Brad Ausmus
Ball	$21
Photo	$12
3x5 card	$5

Jeff Bagwell
Ball	$40
Photo	$25
3x5 card	$8

Harold Baines
Ball	$30
Photo	$20
3x5 index card	$5

Michael Barrett
Ball	$23
Photo	$13
3x5 card	$5

Rod Beck
Ball	$20
Photo	$11
3x5 card	$5

Josh Beckett
Ball	$19
Photo	$10
3x5 card	$5

Derek Bell
Ball	$23
Photo	$14
3x5 card	$6

Jay Bell
Ball	$23
Photo	$14
3x5 card	$6

Ronnie Belliard
Ball	$24
Photo	$13
3x5 card	$6

Carlos Beltran
Ball	$20
Photo	$12
3x5 card	$5

Adrian Beltre
Ball	$20
Photo	$9
3x5 card	$5

Alan Benes
Ball	$22
Photo	$13
3x5 card	$6-$7

Andy Benes
Ball	$23
Photo	$14
3x5 card	$6

Jason Bere
Ball	$21
Photo	$10
3x5 card	$5

Dante Bichette
Ball	$24
Photo	$13
3x5 card	$6

Craig Biggio
Ball	$25
Photo	$15
3x5 card	$6

Barry Bonds
Ball	$125
Photo	$50
3x5 card	$20

Bobby Bonilla
Ball	$25
Photo	$17
3x5 card	$7

Aaron Boone
Ball	$21
Photo	$10
3x5 card	$5

Bret Boone
Ball	$25
Photo	$12
3x5 card	$6

Mike Bordick
Ball	$22
Photo	$12
3x5 card	$6

Jeff Brantley
Ball	$23
Photo	$13
3x5 card	$6

Russ Branyan
Ball	$20
Photo	$12
3x5 card	$5

Scott Brosius
Ball	$30
Photo	$13
3x5 card	$6

Dee Brown
Ball	$20
Photo	$12
3x5 card	$5

Kevin Brown
Ball	$30
Photo	$15
3x5 card	$7

Jay Buhner
Ball	$28
Photo	$15
3x5 card	$7

A. J. Burnett
Ball	$20
Photo	$12
3x5 card	$5

Jeromy Burnitz
Ball	$25
Photo	$15
3x5 card	$7

John Burkett
Ball	$25
Photo	$15
3x5 card	$7

Ellis Burks
Ball	$25
Photo	$15
3x5 card	$5

Pat Burrell
Ball	$20
Photo	$12
3x5 card	$5

Paul Byrd
Ball	$24
Photo	$13
3x5 card	$6

Ken Caminiti
Ball	$26
Photo	$15
3x5 card	$6

Mike Caruso
Ball	$21
Photo	$12
3x5 card	$5

Sean Casey
Ball	$28
Photo	$15
3x5 card	$7

Vinny Castilla
Ball	$25
Photo	$15
3x5 card	$6

Eric Chavez
Ball	$20
Photo	$12
3x5 card	$5

Jeff Cirillo
Ball	$24
Photo	$15
3x5 card	$6

Tony Clark
Ball	$27
Photo	$15
3x5 card	$6

Royce Clayton
Ball	$24
Photo	$13
3x5 card	$6

Roger Clemens
Ball	$75
Photo	$40
3x5 card	$10

Bartolo Colon
Ball	$20
Photo	$12
3x5 card	$5

David Cone
Ball	$25
Photo	$15
3x5 card	$6

Jeff Conine
Ball	$23
Photo	$13
3x5 card	$6

Marty Cordova
Ball	$23
Photo	$13
3x5 card	$5

Craig Counsell
Ball	$21
Photo	$12
3x5 card	$5

Jose Cruz Jr.
Ball	$28
Photo	$17
3x5 card	$7

Chad Curtis
Ball	$20
Photo	$10
3x5 card	$5

Johnny Damon
Ball	$21
Photo	$12
3x5 card	$5

Eric Davis
Ball	$24
Photo	$15
3x5 card	$6

Russ Davis
Ball	$23
Photo	$11
3x5 card	$6

Carlos Delgado
Ball	$27
Photo	$18
3x5 card	$8

Delino DeShields
Ball	$25
Photo	$15
3x5 card	$6

Jason Dickson
Ball	$21
Photo	$12
3x5 card	$5

Gary DiSarcina
Ball	$21
Photo	$12
3x5 card	$5

J. D. Drew
Ball	$35
Photo	$20
3x5 card	$8

Shawon Dunston
Ball	$20
Photo	$10
3x5 card	$5

Ray Durham
Ball	$25
Photo	$17
3x5 card	$6

Jermaine Dye
Ball	$25
Photo	$12
3x5 card	$5

Damion Easley
Ball	$25
Photo	$15
3x5 card	$6

David Eckstein
Ball	$20
Photo	$12
3x5 card	$5

Jim Edmonds

Ball	$30
Photo	$15
3x5 card	$6

Cal Eldred

Ball	$18
Photo	$9
3x5 card	$5

Juan Encaracion

Ball	$20
Photo	$9
3x5 card	$5

Darin Erstad

Ball	$25
Photo	$16
3x5 card	$6

Carl Everett

Ball	$20
Photo	$12
3x5 card	$5

Tony Fernandez

Ball	$22
Photo	$15
3x5 card	$5

Darrin Fletcher

Ball	$20
Photo	$11
3x5 card	$5

Cliff Floyd

Ball	$26
Photo	$14
3x5 card	$6

Andy Fox

Ball	$23
Photo	$14
3x5 card	$5

John Franco

Ball	$24
Photo	$12
3x5 card	$6

Travis Fryman

Ball	$25
Photo	$16
3x5 card	$6

Brad Fullmer

Ball	$20
Photo	$12
3x5 card	$5

Andres Galarraga

Ball	$26
Photo	$16
3x5 card	$7

Ron Gant

Ball	$24
Photo	$14
3x5 card	$6

Freddy Garcia

Ball	$21
Photo	$11
3x5 card	$5

Nomar Garciaparra

Ball	$50
Photo	$30
3x5 card	$8

Jason Giambi

Ball	$23
Photo	$12
3x5 card	$6

Brian Giles

Ball	$24
Photo	$12
3x5 card	$5

Doug Glanville

Ball	$22
Photo	$11
3x5 card	$5

Troy Glaus

Ball	$22
Photo	$11
3x5 card	$6-$7

Tom Glavine

Ball	$35
Photo	$20
3x5 card	$6

Tom Goodwin

Ball	$22
Photo	$12
3x5 card	$5

Wayne Gomes

Ball	$20
Photo	$9
3x5 card	$5

Alex Gonzalez

Ball	$30
Photo	$20
3x5 card	$7

Juan Gonzalez

Ball	$35
Photo	$20
3x5 card	$7

Luis Gonzalez

Ball	$24
Photo	$12
3x5 card	$5

Tom Gordon

Ball	$18
Photo	$14
3x5 card	$5

Mark Grace

Ball	$25
Photo	$13
3x5 card	$6

Shawn Green

Ball	$24
Photo	$12
3x5 card	$6

Rusty Greer

Ball	$22
Photo	$12
3x5 card	$5

Ben Grieve

Ball	$30
Photo	$18
3x5 card	$7-$8

Ken Griffey Jr.

Ball	$60
Photo	$40
3x5 card	$20

Mark Grudzielanek

Ball	$20
Photo	$10
3x5 card	$5

Marquis Grissom

Ball	$25
Photo	$18
3x5 card	$7

Vladamir Guerrero

Ball	$35
Photo	$22
3x5 card	$9

Jose Guillen

Ball	$22
Photo	$12
3x5 card	$5

Ricky Gutierrez

Ball	$19
Photo	$11
3x5 card	$5

Cristian Guzman

Ball	$20
Photo	$12
3x5 card	$5

Darryl Hamilton

Ball	$20
Photo	$10
3x5 card	$5

Mike Hampton

Ball	$24
Photo	$13
3x5 card	$6

Pete Harnisch

Ball	$16
Photo	$10
3x5 card	$5

Charlie Hayes

Ball	$24
Photo	$12
3x5 card	$6

Todd Helton

Ball	$20
Photo	$10
3x5 card	$5

Rickey Henderson

Ball	$50
Photo	$25
3x5 card	$8

Livan Hernandez

Ball	$22
Photo	$12
3x5 card	$5

Orlando Hernandez

Ball	$40
Photo	$25
3x5 card	$7

Richard Hidalgo

Ball	$20
Photo	$12
3x5 card	$5

Bobby Higginson

Ball	$20
Photo	$13
3x5 card	$5

Ken Hill

Ball	$24
Photo	$13
3x5 card	$6

Sterling Hitchcock
Ball	$20
Photo	$10
3x5 card	$5

Trevor Hoffman
Ball	$25
Photo	$15
3x5 card	$6

Todd Hollandsworth
Ball	$25
Photo	$14
3x5 card	$6

Brian Hunter
Ball	$22
Photo	$12
3x5 card	$5

Hideki Irabu
Ball	$20
Photo	$10
3x5 card	$6

Mike Jackson
Ball	$22
Photo	$11
3x5 card	$5

Stan Javier
Ball	$21
Photo	$12
3x5 card	$5

Geoff Jenkins
Ball	$26
Photo	$14
3x5 card	$7

Derek Jeter
Ball	$75
Photo	$40
3x5 card	$12

Jose Jimenez
Ball	$24
Photo	$13
3x5 card	$6

Charles Johnson
Ball	$23
Photo	$12
3x5 card	$6

Randy Johnson
Ball	$50
Photo	$30
3x5 card	$8

Andruw Jones
Ball	$35
Photo	$22
3x5 card	$8

Chipper Jones
Ball	$40
Photo	$25
3x5 card	$9

David Justice
Ball	$35
Photo	$21
3x5 card	$7

Gabe Kapler
Ball	$27
Photo	$15
3x5 card	$6

Eric Karros
Ball	$26
Photo	$16
3x5 card	$6

Takashi Kashiwada
Ball	$24
Photo	$13
3x5 card	$6

Roberto Kelly
Ball	$22
Photo	$11
3x5 card	$5

Jason Kendall
Ball	$30
Photo	$20
3x5 card	$7

Adam Kennedy
Ball	$20
Photo	$12
3x5 card	$5

Darryl Kile
Ball	$23
Photo	$13
3x5 card	$5

Chuck Knoblauch
Ball	$26
Photo	$14
3x5 card	$6

Billy Koch
Ball	$20
Photo	$12
3x5 card	$5

Corey Koskie
Ball	$20
Photo	$12
3x5 card	$5

Paul Konerko
Ball	$19
Photo	$10
3x5 card	$5

Ray Lankford
Ball	$25
Photo	$15
3x5 card	$6

Mike Lansing
Ball	$22
Photo	$14
3x5 card	$5

Barry Larkin
Ball	$25
Photo	$14
3x5 card	$6

Matt Lawton
Ball	$22
Photo	$11
3x5 card	$5

Ricky Ledee
Ball	$20
Photo	$10
3x5 card	$5

Carlos Lee
Ball	$20
Photo	$12
3x5 card	$5

Derek Lee
Ball	$23
Photo	$13
3x5 card	$5

Travis Lee
Ball	$30
Photo	$18
3x5 card	$7

Al Leiter
Ball	$23
Photo	$13
3x5 card	$5

Mike Lieberthal
Ball	$24
Photo	$15
3x5 card	$6

Kerry Lightenberg
Ball	$22
Photo	$13
3x5 card	$5

Keith Lockhart
Ball	$19
Photo	$9
3x5 card	$5

Kenny Lofton
Ball	$30
Photo	$20
3x5 card	$7

Rich Loiselle
Ball	$21
Photo	$11
3x5 card	$5

Terrance Long
Ball	$20
Photo	$12
3x5 card	$5

Javier Lopez
Ball	$28
Photo	$16
3x5 card	$6

Mark Loretta
Ball	$20
Photo	$12
3x5 card	$5

Greg Maddux
Ball	$75
Photo	$35
3x5 card	$10

Eli Marrero
Ball	$22
Photo	$11
3x5 card	$5

Edgar Martinez
Ball	$25
Photo	$15
3x5 card	$6

Pedro Martinez
Ball	$75
Photo	$35
3x5 card	$11

Tino Martinez

Ball	$35
Photo	$20
3x5 card	$7

Ruben Mateo

Ball	$20
Photo	$12
3x5 card	$5

Brent Mayne

Ball	$21
Photo	$11
3x5 card	$5

Fred McGriff

Ball	$30
Photo	$15
3x5 card	$6

Mark McGwire

Ball	$500
Photo	$125
3x5 card	$40

Mark McLemore

Ball	$21
Photo	$11
3x5 card	$5

Pat Meares

Ball	$21
Photo	$11
3x5 card	$5

Orlando Merced

Ball	$22
Photo	$11
3x5 card	$5

Jose Mesa

Ball	$24
Photo	$14
3x5 card	$6

Doug Mientkiewicz

Ball	$20
Photo	$12
3x5 card	$5

Kevin Millwood

Ball	$25
Photo	$14
3x5 card	$6

Raul Mondesi

Ball	$30
Photo	$24
3x5 card	$7

Matt Morris

Ball	$23
Photo	$13
3x5 card	$5

Jamie Moyer

Ball	$20
Photo	$10
3x5 card	$5

Bill Mueller

Ball	$24
Photo	$14
3x5 card	$5

Mark Mulder

Ball	$20
Photo	$12
3x5 card	$5

Mike Mussina

Ball	$30
Photo	$18
3x5 card	$7

Charles Nagy

Ball	$24
Photo	$15
3x5 card	$6

Denny Neagle

Ball	$24
Photo	$14
3x5 card	$6

Robb Nen

Ball	$23
Photo	$14
3x5 card	$5

Phil Nevin

Ball	$23
Photo	$14
3x5 card	$5

Trot Nixon

Ball	$25
Photo	$12
3x5 card	$5

Hideo Nomo

Ball	$29
Photo	$18
3x5 card	$7

Jose Offerman

Ball	$26
Photo	$18
3x5 card	$6

Tomakazu Ohka

Ball	$20
Photo	$12
3x5 card	$5

Troy O'Leary

Ball	$23
Photo	$12
3x5 card	$5

John Olerud

Ball	$27
Photo	$17
3x5 card	$6

Paul O'Neill

Ball	$30
Photo	$15
3x5 card	$6

Magglio Ordonez

Ball	$25
Photo	$13
3x5 card	$6

David Ortiz

Ball	$22
Photo	$12
3x5 card	$10

Jose Ortiz

Ball	$20
Photo	$12
3x5 card	$5

Rafael Palmeiro

Ball	$30
Photo	$20
3x5 card	$7

Dean Palmer

Ball	$23
Photo	$12
3x5 card	$5

Chan Ho Park

Ball	$23
Photo	$13
3x5 card	$5

Troy Percival

Ball	$21
Photo	$12
3x5 card	$5

Andy Pettitte

Ball	$32
Photo	$19
3x5 card	$7

Mike Piazza

Ball	$60
Photo	$30
3x5 card	$7

Juan Pierre

Ball	$20
Photo	$12
3x5 card	$5

Jorge Posada

Ball	$23
Photo	$13
3x5 card	$5

Albert Pujols

Ball	$25
Photo	$12
3x5 card	$5

Mark Quinn

Ball	$20
Photo	$12
3x5 card	$5

Aramis Ramirez

Ball	$20
Photo	$12
3x5 card	$5

Manny Ramirez

Ball	$50
Photo	$25
3x5 card	$7

Joe Randa

Ball	$20
Photo	$10
3x5 card	$5

Pokey Reese

Ball	$20
Photo	$14
3x5 card	$6

Edgar Renteria

Ball	$22
Photo	$12
3x5 card	$5

Mariano Rivera

Ball	$35
Photo	$15
3x5 card	$6

John Rocker

Ball	$25
Photo	$15
3x5 card	$5

Alex Rodriguez

Ball	$75
Photo	$40
3x5 card	$12

Ivan Rodriguez
Ball	$35
Photo	$25
3x5 card	$7

Kenny Rogers
Ball	$20
Photo	$12
3x5 card	$5

Scott Rolen
Ball	$30
Photo	$18
3x5 card	$6

Jimmy Rollins
Ball	$25
Photo	$12
3x5 card	$5

Tim Salmon
Ball	$28
Photo	$20
3x5 card	$6

Rey Sanchez
Ball	$20
Photo	$12
3x5 card	$5

Reggie Sanders
Ball	$22
Photo	$13
3x5 card	$5

Benito Santiago
Ball	$24
Photo	$14
3x5 card	$5

Kazuhiro Sasaki
Ball	$20
Photo	$12
3x5 card	$5

Jason Schmidt
Ball	$20
Photo	$11
3x5 card	$5

Aaron Sele
Ball	$20
Photo	$12
3x5 card	$5

Richie Sexson
Ball	$25
Photo	$14
3x5 card	$6

Jeff Shaw
Ball	$22
Photo	$12
3x5 card	$5

Gary Sheffield
Ball	$28
Photo	$16
3x5 card	$6

Ruben Sierra
Ball	$22
Photo	$11-$15
3x5 card	$5

Heathcliff Slocumb
Ball	$22
Photo	$13
3x5 card	$5

John Smoltz
Ball	$35
Photo	$20
3x5 card	$7

J.T. Snow
Ball	$24
Photo	$14
3x5 card	$6

Alfonso Soriano
Ball	$20
Photo	$12
3x5 card	$5

Sammy Sosa
Ball	$125
Photo	$75
3x5 card	$15

Shane Spencer
Ball	$20
Photo	$12
3x5 card	$5

Ed Sprague
Ball	$21
Photo	$12
3x5 card	$5

Kevin Stocker
Ball	$20
Photo	$10
3x5 card	$5

Shannon Stewart
Ball	$20
Photo	$12
3x5 card	$5

B. J. Surhoff
Ball	$23
Photo	$13
3x5 card	$5

Ichiro Suzuki
Ball	$100
Photo	$50
3x5 card	$25

Mike Sweeney
Ball	$25
Photo	$12
3x5 card	$5

Bill Swift
Ball	$21
Photo	$12
3x5 card	$5

Greg Swindell
Ball	$18
Photo	$9
3x5 card	$5

Kevin Tapani
Ball	$22
Photo	$13
3x5 card	$5

Fernando Tatis
Ball	$25
Photo	$15
3x5 card	$6

Eddie Taubensee
Ball	$23
Photo	$12
3x5 card	$5

Miguel Tejada
Ball	$24
Photo	$14
3x5 card	$5

Frank E. Thomas
Ball	$40
Photo	$25
3x5 card	$8

Jim Thome
Ball	$25
Photo	$15
3x5 card	$6

Ugueth Urbina
Ball	$22
Photo	$11
3x5 card	$5

John Valentin
Ball	$18
Photo	$10
3x5 card	$6

Jose Valentin
Ball	$20
Photo	$12
3x5 card	$5

Greg Vaughn
Ball	$28
Photo	$17
3x5 card	$6

Mo Vaughn
Ball	$30
Photo	$20
3x5 card	$7

Robin Ventura
Ball	$30
Photo	$18
3x5 card	$6

Jose Vidro
Ball	$20
Photo	$12
3x5 card	$5

Fernando Vina
Ball	$24
Photo	$15
3x5 card	$6

Omar Vizquel
Ball	$24
Photo	$15
3x5 card	$6

Billy Wagner
Ball	$26
Photo	$15
3x5 card	$6

Tim Wakefield
Ball	$23
Photo	$13
3x5 card	$5

Matt Walbeck
Ball	$21
Photo	$10
3x5 card	$5

Larry Walker
Ball	$40
Photo	$20
3x5 card	$7

Todd Walker
Ball	$25
Photo	$18
3x5 card	$8

Jeff Weaver
Ball	$20
Photo	$12
3x5 card	$5

David Wells
Ball	$35
Photo	$17
3x5 card	$6

Rondell White
Ball	$25
Photo	$14
3x5 card	$5\

Bernie Williams
Ball	$50
Photo	$25
3x5 card	$8

Matt Williams
Ball	$35
Photo	$25
3x5 card	$7

Scott Williamson
Ball	$27
Photo	$18
3x5 card	$6

Dan Wilson
Ball	$21
Photo	$12
3x5 card	$5

Preston Wilson
Ball	$20
Photo	$12
3x5 card	$5

Kerry Wood
Ball	$40
Photo	$20
3x5 card	$8

Jaret Wright
Ball	$22
Photo	$13
3x5 card	$5

Dmitri Young
Ball	$21
Photo	$11
3x5 card	$5

Kevin Young
Ball	$23
Photo	$14
3x5 card	$5

Todd Zeile
Ball	$22
Photo	$14
3x5 card	$5

Barry Zito
Ball	$20
Photo	$12
3x5 card	$5

RETIRED PLAYERS

This section is devoted mainly—but not exclusively—to prominent former baseball players whose credentials were solid, but not quite enough to merit Hall of Fame induction. That means you'll find current autograph values for hundreds of players who put up impressive stats during their careers and became fan favorites in the process. There are:

- sluggers like Dave Kingman (442 career home runs), Graig Nettles (389 HRs), Frank "Hondo" Howard (382 HRs) and Dick Allen (351 HRs).
- popular, productive Yankees stars like Nettles, Roger Maris (275 HRs), Bobby Murcer (252 HRs), Thurman Munson (.292 career average) and Don Mattingly (.307, 222 HRs), who played for the Bronx Bombers for all or much of their careers.
- fathers of famous sons—baseball-playing dads who were pretty talented in their own right: Ken Griffey Jr.'s father Ken Sr. (.296 career average) and Barry Bonds' father Bobby (332 HRs, 461 steals).
- such personalities as Joe Garagiola and Bob Uecker, who followed unspectacular playing careers (Garagiola: .257 batting average; Uecker: .200) with long stints as popular announcers.

The section also includes would-be Hall of Famers like Tony Oliva and Tony Conigliaro, who suffered serious injuries that curtailed their playing days.

But the most prominent names in this section are two "should-be" Hall of Famers (at least in the minds of their supporters): Joe Jackson and Pete Rose. These two legends are connected in baseball lore, unfortunately, through their alleged ties to gambling and subsequent ban from the game. In terms of autographs, though, they reflect the extremes of the marketplace.

Rose, one of baseball's most active signers, has been extremely visible on the show circuit. In recent years, his autograph prices have been stable at around $50 for a signed baseball and $30 for a signed photo. On the surface, he's undervalued (considering that he was a popular player and manager, is baseball's all-time hits leader, and is always controversial). But the healthy supply of Rose signatures keeps the price affordable.

"Shoeless" Joe Jackson's autograph, on the other hand, is one of the scarcest in baseball history. Because he was unable to read and write, he didn't sign many autographs. Thus, serious collectors have to pay a small fortune to get one when it surfaces. How rare is Shoeless Joe's autograph? The Web site BlackBetsy.com wrote in December 2000, "We

are aware of about 30 verified and authenticated Joe Jackson autographs and we are aware of about 10 to 20 more that are Joe Jackson-signed items…but that have not been verified or authenticated." As a result, Jackson's signature on photos, balls or cuts can cost tens of thousands of dollars.

Finally, this section is home to a handful of retired players who might be destined for the Hall of Fame but who—at this writing—haven't yet been voted in.

In some cases (Eddie Murray, Paul Molitor and Wade Boggs), it's simply a matter of time. In other cases (Gary Carter, Jim Rice and Bruce Sutter), it's not so automatic.

Murray is considered a shoo-in for the Hall mainly because of his 504 career home runs. After playing 21 seasons for the Orioles, Dodgers, Mets, Indians, and Angels, Murray retired after the 1997 season and thus becomes eligible for induction in 2003. Likewise, Molitor—who retired after the 1998 campaign and is eligible for induction in 2004—is a lock for the Hall. In his 21 seasons for the Brewers, Blue Jays and Twins, Molitor had a .306 average, 3,319 hits and 504 stolen bases. And Boggs' 3,010 hits in 18 seasons for the Red Sox, Yankees and Devil Rays all but ensures his spot in the Hall of Fame. Boggs retired after the 1999 season and is eligible for induction in 2005. Murray's autograph is already somewhat pricey, compared to Boggs'—a reflection of the 500 Home Run Club's status. A Murray-signed ball goes for around $75 , vs. $40 for a Boggs-signed baseball.

Carter, Rice and Sutter, on the other hand, are on the bubble. Carter hit 324 homers while playing most of his 19 seasons at baseball's toughest position, catcher. Rice blasted 382 HRs and had a .298 average in 16 seasons. And Bruce Sutter posted 300 saves and a 2.83 ERA in 12 seasons. To earn HOF induction, a player needs to be named on at least 75 percent of the ballots cast by the Baseball Writers' Association of America (BBWAA). In 1999, 2000 and 2001, Carter garnered 33.8 percent, 49.70 percent and 64.85 percent of the ballots, respectively. Rice received 29.4 percent, 51.5 percent and 57.86 percent of the necessary votes. And Sutter pulled 24.3 percent, 38.48 percent and 47.57 of the votes in '99, '00 and '01. So all three have been getting closer to Hall of Fame status in recent years. Only time will tell whether these players will make it to Cooperstown—but that's part of the fun for those who might try to collect their autographs now.

Note: George Brett, Orlando Cepeda, Carlton Fisk, Tony Perez, Kirby Puckett, Nolan Ryan, Dave Winfield and Robin Yount are recent "graduates" of this section, with each having been voted into the Hall of Fame since our first edition was published.

Retired Players Autographs

* Indicates player is deceased

Cal Abrams *
Ball	$30-$40
Photo	$15
3x5 index card	$5

Joe Adcock *
Ball	$50-$75
Photo	$25
3x5 index card	$10-$12

Tommie Agee *
Ball	$20
Photo	$10
3x5 index card	$4

Harry Agganis *
Ball	$500
Photo	$200
3x5 index card	$90-$100

Willie Aikens
Ball	$17
Photo	$10
3x5 index card	$5

Danny Ainge
Ball	$40
Photo	$25
3x5 index card	$4-$6

Dick Allen
Ball	$30-$40
Photo	$20-$25
3x5 index card	$5

Sandy Alomar Sr.
Ball	$20
Photo	$15
3x5 index card	$5

Felipe Alou
Ball	$25
Photo	$15
3x5 index card	$5

Jesus Alou
Ball	$20
Photo	$10
3x5 index card	$4

Matty Alou
Ball	$23
Photo	$13
3x5 index card	$5-$6

Sandy Amoros *
Ball	$100
Photo	$30
3x5 index card	$12-$15

Joaquin Andujar
Ball	$18
Photo	$10
3x5 index card	$4-$5

Johnny Antonelli
Ball	$21
Photo	$13
3x5 index card	$5

Tony Armas
Ball	$20
Photo	$11
3x5 index card	$5

Alan Ashby
Ball	$17
Photo	$9
3x5 index card	$4

Bobby Avila
Ball	$25
Photo	$17
3x5 index card	$5

Ed Bailey
Ball	$20
Photo	$10
3x5 index card	$4-$5

Bob Bailor
Ball	$15
Photo	$8
3x5 index card	$4

Dusty Baker
Ball	$30
Photo	$15
3x5 index card	$5

Chris Bando
Ball	$14
Photo	$8
3x5 index card	$3-$4

Sal Bando
Ball	$20
Photo	$12
3x5 index card	$5

Floyd Bannister
Ball	$14
Photo	$8
3x5 index card	$4

George Bamberger
Ball	$23
Photo	$12
3x5 index card	$5

Steve Barber
Ball	$21
Photo	$12
3x5 index card	$5

Jesse Barfield
Ball	$19
Photo	$10
3x5 index card	$4-$5

Len Barker
Ball	$18
Photo	$9
3x5 index card	$4

Kevin Bass
Ball	$16
Photo	$9-$12
3x5 index card	$4

Earl Battey
Ball	$21
Photo	$12
3x5 index card	$4

Don Baylor
Ball	$30
Photo	$15
3x5 index card	$4

Glenn Beckert
Ball	$18
Photo	$10
3x5 index card	$4-$5

Mark Belanger *
Ball	$40-$50
Photo	$20-$25
3x5 index card	$5

Bo Belinsky
Ball	$25-$30
Photo	$15-$20
3x5 index card	$6

Albert Belle
Ball	$40
Photo	$24
3x5 index card	$9

Buddy Bell
Ball	$20
Photo	$10
3x5 index card	$4

George Bell
Ball	$20
Photo	$11
3x5 index card	$4

Gus Bell *
Ball	$50-$60
Photo	$20-$25
3x5 index card	$8-$10

Johnny Berardino *
Ball	$40-$50
Photo	$20-$25
3x5 index card	$8-$10

Moe Berg *
Ball	$500-$700
Photo	$150-$250
3x5 index card	$75-$100

Dale Berra
Ball	$20
Photo	$10
3x5 index card	$5

Joe Black
Ball	$25
Photo	$15
3x5 index card	$5

Ewell Blackwell *
Ball	$50-$75
Photo	$20-$30
3x5 index card	$10-$12

Paul Blair
Ball	$20
Photo	$12
3x5 index card	$5

Johnny Blanchard
Ball	$21
Photo	$11
3x5 index card	$4-$5

Steve Blass
Ball	$18
Photo	$9
3x5 index card	$4-$5

Ron Blomberg
Ball	$18
Photo	$9
3x5 index card	$4-$5

Vida Blue
Ball	$25-$30
Photo	$15-$20
3x5 index card	$6

Bert Blyleven
Ball	$25-$30
Photo	$15
3x5 index card	$5

Mike Boddicker
Ball	$22
Photo	$12
3x5 index card	$5

Wade Boggs
Ball	$40-$50
Photo	$25-$30
3x5 card	$10

Frank Bolling
Ball	$20
Photo	$12
3x5 index card	$5

Milt Bolling
Ball	$18
Photo	$10
3x5 index card	$4-$5

Bobby Bonds
Ball	$25
Photo	$12
3x5 index card	$6

Bob Boone
Ball	$23
Photo	$14
3x5 index card	$5

Ray Boone
Ball	$30
Photo	$20
3x5 index card	$4-$5

Frenchy Bordagaray *
Ball	$25-$35
Photo	$15-$20
3x5 index card	$5

Lyman Bostock Jr. *
Ball	$500-$600
Photo	$150-$200
3x5 index card	$40-$50

Jim Bouton
Ball	$21
Photo	$10
3x5 index card	$4-$5

Larry Bowa
Ball	$25
Photo	$12
3x5 index card	$4-$5

Clete Boyer
Ball	$23
Photo	$12
3x5 index card	$5

Kill Boyer (signature)

Ken Boyer *
Ball	$300-$500
Photo	$100-$200
3x5 index card	$50-$75

Ralph Branca
Ball	$22
Photo	$12-$15
3x5 index card	$5-$6

Ken Brett
Ball	$19
Photo	$11
3x5 index card	$4-$5

Rocky Bridges
Ball	$24
Photo	$10
3x5 index card	$5-$6

Nelson Briles
Ball	$19-$20
Photo	$10
3x5 index card	$4

Greg Brock
Ball	$17
Photo	$8
3x5 index card	$4

Hubie Brooks
Ball	$18
Photo	$10-$15
3x5 index card	$4

Tom Browning
Ball	$24
Photo	$15
3x5 index card	$5-$6

Tom Brunansky
Ball	$16
Photo	$8-$10
3x5 index card	$4

Billy Bruton *
Ball	$30-$40
Photo	$20-$25
3x5 index card	$10-$12

Bill Buckner
Ball	$25
Photo	$15
3x5 index card	$5-$6

Don Buford
Ball	$20
Photo	$15-$20
3x5 index card	$4-$5

Bob Buhl *
Ball	$25-$35
Photo	$10-$15
3x5 index card	$4-$5

Al Bumbry
Ball	$18
Photo	$10
3x5 index card	$4

Lew Burdette
Ball	$24-$28
Photo	$15-$20
3x5 index card	$5-$6

Smoky Burgess *
Ball	$40-$50
Photo	$20-$25
3x5 index card	$12-$15

Jeff Burroughs
Ball	$19
Photo	$10
3x5 index card	$4

Brett Butler
Ball	$25-$30
Photo	$12-$15
3x5 index card	$5

Enos Cabell
Ball	$22
Photo	$11
3x5 index card	$4-$5

Mike Caldwell
Ball	$18
Photo	$10
3x5 index card	$4

Johnny Callison
Ball	$19
Photo	$9
3x5 index card	$4

Bert Campaneris
Ball	$20
Photo	$11
3x5 index card	$4-$5

Bill Campbell
Ball	$19
Photo	$9
3x5 index card	$4-$5

Dave Campbell
Ball	$22
Photo	$11
3x5 index card	$4-$5

John Candelaria
Ball	$19
Photo	$10
3x5 index card	$4-$5

Bernie Carbo
Ball	$20
Photo	$10
3x5 index card	$4-$5

Chico Carrasquel
Ball	$22
Photo	$10
3x5 index card	$5

Jose Cardenal
Ball	$24
Photo	$15
3x5 index card	$5

Gary Carter (signature)

Gary Carter
Ball	$30-$35
Photo	$15-$20
3x5 index card	$8-$10

Joe Carter
Ball	$25
Photo	$15
3x5 index card	$7-$8

Rico Carty
Ball	$25
Photo	$15
3x5 index card	$7-$8

Dave Cash
Ball	$22
Photo	$11
3x5 index card	$4-$5

Norm Cash *
Ball	$300-$500
Photo	$75-$125
3x5 index card	$40-$50

Phil Cavarretta
Ball	$30
Photo	$15
3x5 index card	$6-$7

Cesar Cedeno
Ball	$28
Photo	$14
3x5 index card	$5-$6

Rick Cerone
Ball	$18-$20
Photo	$8
3x5 index card	$4

Bob Cerv
Ball	$25
Photo	$15
3x5 index card	$4

Ron Cey
Ball	$24
Photo	$13
3x5 index card	$5

Chris Chambliss
Ball	$24
Photo	$15
3x5 index card	$5-$6

Dean Chance
Ball	$25
Photo	$10-$15
3x5 index card	$4-$5

Spud Chandler *
Ball	$60-$75
Photo	$25-$30
3x5 index card	$12-$15

Joe Charboneau
Ball	$20
Photo	$10
3x5 index card	$5

Eddie V. Cicotte (signature)

Eddie Cicotte *
Ball	$1,000-$1,400
Photo	$500-$700
3x5 index card	$300-$500

Jack Clark
Ball	$23
Photo	$13
3x5 index card	$5

Will Clark
Ball	$35-$40
Photo	$20-$25
3x5 index card	$7

Donn Clendenon
Ball	$20-$24
Photo	$11-$15
3x5 index card	$5-$6

Harlond Clift *
Ball	$45
Photo	$23
3x5 index card	$12-$15

Rocky Colavito (signature)

Rocky Colavito
Ball	$40-$50
Photo	$25-$30
3x5 index card	$10-$12

Nate Colbert
Ball	$22
Photo	$13
3x5 index card	$4-$5

Jerry Coleman
Ball	$25
Photo	$15
3x5 index card	$5-$6

Joe Collins *
Ball	$30-$40
Photo	$20
3x5 index card	$9-$11

Dave Concepcion
Ball	$25
Photo	$15
3x5 index card	$5

Tony Conigliaro *
Ball	$250-$350
Photo	$100-$150
3x5 index card	$40-$60

Gene Conley
Ball	$18-$20
Photo	$12-$15
3x5 index card	$4-$5

Chuck Connors *
Ball	$125-$150
Photo	$40-$50
3x5 index card	$15-$20

Cecil Cooper
Ball	$20-$24
Photo	$13-$15
3x5 index card	$5

Wes Covington
Ball	$55-$60
Photo	$30-$40
3x5 index card	$15-$18

Roger Craig
Ball	$24
Photo	$13
3x5 index card	$4-$5

Roger Cramer *
Ball	$150-$200
Photo	$30-$40
3x5 index card	$10-$15

Del Crandall
Ball	$22
Photo	$12
3x5 index card	$5

Warren Cromartie
Ball	$17
Photo	$9
3x5 index card	$4

Jose Cruz
Ball	$23
Photo	$14
3x5 index card	$5

Frank Crosetti
Ball	$30
Photo	$20
3x5 index card	$6-$8

Mike Cuellar
Ball	$24
Photo	$12
3x5 index card	$5

Babe Dahlgren *
Ball	$50
Photo	$20-$25
3x5 index card	$12-$15

Kal Daniels
Ball	$18
Photo	$9
3x5 index card	$4

Alvin Dark
Ball	$23
Photo	$11
3x5 index card	$4-$5

Ron Darling
Ball	$20
Photo	$10-$12
3x5 index card	$4-$5

Darren Daulton
Ball	$23
Photo	$11
3x5 index card	$5

Alvin Davis
Ball	$20
Photo	$10
3x5 index card	$4

Chili Davis
Ball	$23
Photo	$11
3x5 index card	$5

Glenn Davis
Ball	$21
Photo	$12
3x5 index card	$4

Tommy Davis
Ball	$25
Photo	$15-$20
3x5 index card	$5-$6

Willie Davis
Ball	$20
Photo	$15
3x5 index card	$4-$5

Andre Dawson
Ball	$30
Photo	$18-$24
3x5 index card	$10-$12

Paul "Daffy" Dean *
Ball	$150-$250
Photo	$75-$100
3x5 index card	$20-$25

Doug DeCinces
Ball	$20
Photo	$10
3x5 index card	$4

Rick Dempsey
Ball	$22
Photo	$12
3x5 index card	$4

John Denny
Ball	$22
Photo	$12
3x5 index card	$4

Bucky Dent
Ball	$25-$30
Photo	$15-$20
3x5 index card	$6-$8

Bob Dernier
Ball	$15
Photo	$8-$10
3x5 index card	$4

Dom DiMaggio
Ball	$35-$50
Photo	$20-$30
3x5 index card	$7

Al Downing
Ball	$24
Photo	$14
3x5 index card	$5

Doug Drabek
Ball	$23
Photo	$13
3x5 index card	$5

Dave Dravecky
Ball	$23
Photo	$13
3x5 index card	$5

Charlie Dressen *
Ball	$40-$50
Photo	$20-$25
3x5 index card	$7

Walt Dropo
Ball	$20
Photo	$10
3x5 index card	$4

Ryne Duren
Ball	$25
Photo	$9-$12
3x5 index card	$4

Leon Durham
Ball	$20
Photo	$10
3x5 index card	$4

Duffy Dyer
Ball	$17
Photo	$8
3x5 index card	$4

Len Dykstra
Ball	$30-$35
Photo	$20
3x5 index card	$6

Dennis Eckersley
Ball	$35-$40
Photo	$20-$25
3x5 index card	$8-$10

Jim Eisenreich
Ball	$18-$20
Photo	$10
3x5 card	$4

Bob Elliot *
Ball	$50
Photo	$35
3x5 index card	$10-$12

Dock Ellis
Ball	$20
Photo	$11
3x5 index card	$4

Woody English *
Ball	$50
Photo	$30-$35
3x5 index card	$10-$12

Del Ennis *
Ball	$30-$40
Photo	$15
3x5 index card	$7-$9

Carl Erskine

Ball	$26
Photo	$12-$15
3x5 index card	$5

Nick Esasky

Ball	$17
Photo	$9
3x5 index card	$4

Darrell Evans

Ball	$22
Photo	$12
3x5 index card	$4-$5

Dwight Evans

Ball	$25
Photo	$12
3x5 index card	$5

Hoot Evers *

Ball	$30-$35
Photo	$20-$25
3x5 index card	$8-$10

Elroy Face

Ball	$22
Photo	$10
3x5 index card	$4-$5

Ferris Fain

Ball	$20
Photo	$12
3x5 index card	$5

Dick Farrell *

Ball	$75-$100
Photo	$30-$50
3x5 index card	$10-$12

Chico Fernandez

Ball	$24
Photo	$12
3x5 index card	$5

Wes Ferrell *

Ball	$45-$50
Photo	$25-$30
3x5 index card	$12-$14

Boo Ferriss

Ball	$15-$18
Photo	$8-$10
3x5 index card	$4

Cecil Fielder

Ball	$25
Photo	$15
3x5 index card	$6

Mark Fidrych

Ball	$24
Photo	$11
3x5 index card	$5

Ed Figueroa

Ball	$15
Photo	$8-$10
3x5 index card	$4

Mike Flanagan

Ball	$22
Photo	$12
3x5 index card	$5

Elbie Fletcher *

Ball	$30-$40
Photo	$25-$30
3x5 index card	$12-$15

Curt Flood *

Ball	$150-$250
Photo	$50-$75
3x5 index card	$30-$40

Dan Ford

Ball	$20
Photo	$13
3x5 index card	$4

George Foster

Ball	$24
Photo	$12
3x5 index card	$5

Julio Franco

Ball	$20
Photo	$10
3x5 index card	$5

Terry Francona

Ball	$21
Photo	$11
3x5 index card	$5

Tito Francona

Ball	$20-$24
Photo	$10-$15
3x5 index card	$5

Jim Fregosi

Ball	$23
Photo	$12
3x5 index card	$5

Bill Freehan

Ball	$21
Photo	$11
3x5 index card	$4-$5

Bob Friend

Ball	$20
Photo	$12-$15
3x5 index card	$4-$5

Carl Furillo *

Ball	$400
Photo	$90
3x5 index card	$50-$60

Gary Gaetti

Ball	$19
Photo	$12
3x5 card	$5

Chick Gandel *

Ball	$1,000-$1,500
Photo	$500
3x5 index card	$250

Oscar Gamble

Ball	$20
Photo	$12
3x5 index card	$5

Jim Gantner

Ball	$15-$18
Photo	$9-$12
3x5 index card	$4

Joe Garagiola

Ball	$30-$40
Photo	$20-$30
3x5 index card	$6-$7

Mike Garcia *

Ball	$200-$300
Photo	$50-$60
3x5 index card	$15-$20

Phil Garner

Ball	$23
Photo	$13
3x5 index card	$5

Ralph Garr

Ball	$20
Photo	$12
3x5 index card	$4

Ned Garver

Ball	$22
Photo	$12-$15
3x5 index card	$4-$5

Steve Garvey

Ball	$25
Photo	$14
3x5 index card	$5-$6

Cito Gaston

Ball	$25
Photo	$13
3x5 index card	$5

Jim Gentile

Ball	$21
Photo	$10
3x5 index card	$4-$5

Cesar Geronimo

Ball	$23
Photo	$12-$15
3x5 index card	$5

Kirk Gibson

Ball	$28-$30
Photo	$18
3x5 index card	$5-$6

Jim Gilliam *

Ball	$50-$60
Photo	$30-$40
3x5 index card	$12-$15

Al Gionfriddo

Ball	$15
Photo	$9
3x5 index card	$4

Dan Gladden

Ball	$18
Photo	$9
3x5 index card	$4

Dwight Gooden

Ball	$23
Photo	$13
3x5 index card	$5

Joe Gordon *

Ball	$400-$500
Photo	$75-$100
3x5 index card	$20-$30

Sid Gordon *

Ball	$60-$65
Photo	$35-$40
3x5 index card	$15-$18

Goose Gossage

Ball	$25
Photo	$14
3x5 index card	$5-$6

Mudcat Grant
Ball	$21
Photo	$11
3x5 index card	$

Pete Gray
Ball	$30
Photo	$18-$20
3x5 index card	$8-$9

Mike Greenwell
Ball	$19
Photo	$9
3x5 index card	$4-$5

Bobby Grich
Ball	$22
Photo	$10
3x5 index card	$4-$5

Ken Griffey Sr.
Ball	$28
Photo	$17
3x5 index card	$6-$7

Charlie Grimm *
Ball	$125-$150
Photo	$45-$50
3x5 index card	$25

Dick Groat
Ball	$25
Photo	$12
3x5 index card	$5

Jerry Grote
Ball	$22
Photo	$11
3x5 index card	$4

Kelly Gruber
Ball	$23
Photo	$13
3x5 index card	$5-$6

Pedro Guerrero
Ball	$22
Photo	$13
3x5 index card	$4-$5

Ron Guidry
Ball	$28
Photo	$15
3x5 index card	$6-$7

Don Gullett
Ball	$19
Photo	$9
3x5 index card	$4

Randy Gumpert
Ball	$18
Photo	$9
3x5 index card	$4

Tony Gwynn
Ball	$40
Photo	$25
3x5 card	$10

Harvey Haddix *
Ball	$50-$75
Photo	$20-$30
3x5 index card	$10

Fred Haney *
Ball	$150-$200
Photo	$40-$60
3x5 index card	$15-$20

Mel Harder
Ball	$28
Photo	$16-$18
3x5 index card	$5-$6

Tommy Harper
Ball	$21
Photo	$11
3x5 index card	$4

Bud Harrelson
Ball	$20
Photo	$10
3x5 index card	$4-$5

Bob Hazle *
Ball	$30-$35
Photo	$18-$20
3x5 index card	$9-$12

Richie Hebner
Ball	$22
Photo	$13
3x5 index card	$4

Jim Hegan *
Ball	$45-$50
Photo	$25
3x5 index card	$15-$18

Mike Hegan
Ball	$19
Photo	$9
3x5 index card	$4

Dave Henderson
Ball	$20
Photo	$10
3x5 index card	$4

George Hendrick
Ball	$21
Photo	$12
3x5 index card	$4

Ellie Hendricks
Ball	$17
Photo	$8
3x5 index card	$4

Tom Henke
Ball	$22
Photo	$11
3x5 index card	$4

Tommy Henrich
Ball	$25-$30
Photo	$15-$20
3x5 index card	$5

Keith Hernandez
Ball	$28
Photo	$18-$20
3x5 index card	$7-$10

Orel Hershiser
Ball	$25-$30
Photo	$15-$20
3x5 index card	$4-$5

Whitey Herzog
Ball	$28
Photo	$15
3x5 index card	$6

Ted Higuera
Ball	$23
Photo	$11
3x5 index card	$5

Larry Hisle
Ball	$21
Photo	$10
3x5 index card	$4-$5

Butch Hobson
Ball	$20
Photo	$10
3x5 index card	$4

Gil Hodges *
Ball	$1,450
Photo	$400-$500
3x5 index card	$200

Billy Hoeft
Ball	$20-$25
Photo	$15-$18
3x5 index card	$4-$5

Tommy Holmes
Ball	$24
Photo	$14
3x5 index card	$4-$5

Bob Horner
Ball	$22
Photo	$11
3x5 index card	$4-$5

Willie Horton
Ball	$21
Photo	$11
3x5 index card	$4-$5

Charlie Hough
Ball	$20
Photo	$10
3x5 index card	$4

Ralph Houk
Ball	$25-$30
Photo	$12-$15
3x5 index card	$5

Elston Howard *
Ball	$500
Photo	$100-$200
3x5 index card	$75-$100

Frank Howard
Ball	$25
Photo	$11
3x5 index card	$5

Steve Howe
Ball	$18
Photo	$9
3x5 index card	$4

Roy Howell
Ball	$18
Photo	$9
3x5 index card	$4

Al Hrabosky
Ball	$25
Photo	$14-$20
3x5 index card	$5

Kent Hrbek
Ball	$25
Photo	$13
3x5 index card	$5

Randy Hundley
Ball	$17
Photo	$9
3x5 index card	$4

Fred Hutchinson *
Ball	$150-$200
Photo	$50-$100
3x5 index card	$20-$25

Bo Jackson
Ball	$30-$40
Photo	$20-$30
3x5 index card	$7-$10

Joe Jackson *
Ball	$25,000-$30,000
Photo	$10,000-$15,000
3x5 index card	$8,000-$12,000

Joey Jay
Ball	$30-$35
Photo	$20-$25
3x5 index card	$7

Jackie Jensen *
Ball	$300-$500
Photo	$100-$200
3x5 index card	$40-$60

Sam Jethroe *
Ball	$30
Photo	$15
3x5 index card	$5

Tommy John
Ball	$25
Photo	$15
3x5 index card	$5

Davey Johnson
Ball	$25-$30
Photo	$12-$20
3x5 index card	$5-$6

Alex Johnson
Ball	$17
Photo	$8
3x5 index card	$4

Howard Johnson
Ball	$24
Photo	$13
3x5 index card	$4-$5

Jay Johnstone
Ball	$25
Photo	$14
3x5 index card	$5

Cleon Jones
Ball	$19-$24
Photo	$10-$15
3x5 index card	$4-$5

Doug Jones
Ball	$23
Photo	$13
3x5 index card	$5

Jim Kaat
Ball	$25
Photo	$14
3x5 index card	$5

Don Kessinger
Ball	$19
Photo	$10
3x5 index card	$4-$5

Jimmy Key
Ball	$25
Photo	$13
3x5 index card	$5

Jeff King
Ball	$23
Photo	$13
3x5 index card	$5

Dave Kingman
Ball	$25
Photo	$13
3x5 index card	$5

Ron Kittle
Ball	$20
Photo	$9
3x5 index card	$4

Ted Kluszewski *
Ball	$300
Photo	$75
3x5 index card	$35

Ray Knight
Ball	$25
Photo	$14
3x5 index card	$4-$5

Mark Koenig *
Ball	$35
Photo	$20-$25
3x5 index card	$6-$8

John Kruk
Ball	$25
Photo	$15-$18
3x5 index card	$5

Jerry Koosman
Ball	$22
Photo	$10
3x5 index card	$4

Tony Kubek
Ball	$75-$100
Photo	$50-$60
3x5 index card	$20

Whitey Kurowski *
Ball	$20-$24
Photo	$15-$20
3x5 index card	$5

Harvey Kuenn *
Ball	$200-$300
Photo	$50-$75
3x5 index card	$15-$20

Ed Kranepool
Ball	$20
Photo	$10
3x5 index card	$4-$5

Clem Labine
Ball	$24
Photo	$12-$15
3x5 index card	$5

Ken Landreaux
Ball	$17
Photo	$8
3x5 index card	$4

Mark Langston
Ball	$22
Photo	$11
3x5 index card	$5

Don Larsen
Ball	$25-$30
Photo	$15-$20
3x5 index card	$6-$8

Tony LaRussa
Ball	$24
Photo	$13
3x5 index card	$5

Vance Law
Ball	$18
Photo	$9
3x5 index card	$4

Vern Law
Ball	$24
Photo	$12-$15
3x5 index card	$5

Bill Lee
Ball	$26
Photo	$16-$20
3x5 index card	$6

Ron LeFlore
Ball	$23
Photo	$12
3x5 index card	$5

Mark Lemke
Ball	$18
Photo	$9
3x5 card	$4

Jeffrey Leonard
Ball	$19
Photo	$9
3x5 index card	$4-$5

Phil Linz
Ball	$20-$25
Photo	$12-$15
3x5 index card	$5

Johnny Logan
Ball	$19
Photo	$9
3x5 index card	$4

Mickey Lolich
Ball	$20
Photo	$10
3x5 index card	$4

Sherm Lollar *
Ball	$60
Photo	$28-$34
3x5 index card	$15-$20

Vic Lombardi
Ball	$20
Photo	$8
3x5 index card	$4

Jim Lonborg
Ball	$23
Photo	$11-$15
3x5 index card	$4

Dale Long *
Ball	$75-$100
Photo	$25-$30
3x5 index card	$8-$10

Ed Lopat *
Ball	$40
Photo	$20-$25
3x5 index card	$12

Stan Lopata
Ball	$18
Photo	$9
3x5 index card	$4

Davey Lopes
Ball	$22
Photo	$12
3x5 index card	$4-$5

Greg Luzinski
Ball	$20-$25
Photo	$12-$15
3x5 index card	$5

Sparky Lyle
Ball	$22
Photo	$12
3x5 index card	$5

Fred Lynn
Ball	$25
Photo	$14
3x5 index card	$5-$6

Garry Maddox
Ball	$24
Photo	$14
3x5 index card	$5

Bill Madlock
Ball	$23
Photo	$12
3x5 index card	$5

Sal Maglie *
Ball	$150-$250
Photo	$50-$100
3x5 index card	$10-$12

Frank Malzone
Ball	$22
Photo	$12
3x5 index card	$5

Rick Manning
Ball	$18
Photo	$9
3x5 index card	$4

Felix Mantilla
Ball	$20
Photo	$10
3x5 index card	$4-$5

Marty Marion
Ball	$25
Photo	$15-$18
3x5 index card	$5

Roger Maris *
Ball	$1,000-$2,000
Photo	$400-$600
3x5 index card	$200-$400

Mike A. Marshall
Ball	$200-$300
Photo	$100-$150
3x5 index card	$40-$50

Mike G. Marshall
Ball	$100-$125
Photo	$50-$60
3x5 index card	$15-$20

Billy Martin *
Ball	$200
Photo	$70-$100
3x5 index card	$35-$45

Dennis Martinez
Ball	$24
Photo	$13
3x5 index card	$5

Ramon Martinez
Ball	$23
Photo	$13
3x5 index card	$5

Don Mattingly
Ball	$45
Photo	$25-$30
3x5 index card	$9-$12

John Matlack
Ball	$17
Photo	$9
3x5 index card	$4

Gary Matthews
Ball	$22
Photo	$11
3x5 index card	$4-$5

Gene Mauch
Ball	$25
Photo	$10-$15
3x5 index card	$5

Carlos May
Ball	$17
Photo	$8
3x5 index card	$4

Lee May
Ball	$19
Photo	$10
3x5 index card	$4

Rudy May
Ball	$20
Photo	$10
3x5 index card	$4-$5

John Mayberry
Ball	$20
Photo	$10
3x5 index card	$4

Lee Maye
Ball	$18
Photo	$9-$12
3x5 index card	$4

Bill Mazeroski
Ball	$30
Photo	$18-$20
3x5 index card	$6-$8

Lee Mazzilli
Ball	$17
Photo	$9
3x5 index card	$4

Bake McBride
Ball	$22
Photo	$11
3x5 index card	$5

Al McBean
Ball	$28
Photo	$18
3x5 index card	$6-$7

Tim McCarver
Ball	$27-$30
Photo	$15-$20
3x5 index card	$6-$8

Willie McGee
Ball	$23
Photo	$14-$18
3x5 index card	$5-$6

Mickey McDermott
Ball	$17
Photo	$9
3x5 index card	$4

Jack McDowell
Ball	$23
Photo	$13
3x5 index card	$5

Oddibe McDowell
Ball	$17
Photo	$8
3x5 index card	$4

Gil McDougald
Ball	$25-$30
Photo	$10-$20
3x5 index card	$5

Sam McDowell
Ball	$18
Photo	$9
3x5 index card	$4

Tug McGraw
Ball	$25
Photo	$14-$18
3x5 index card	$5-$6

Denny McLain
Ball	$25-$30
Photo	$12-$15
3x5 index card	$5

Roy McMillan *
Ball	$30-$50
Photo	$20-$25
3x5 index card	$8

Dave McNally
Ball	$22
Photo	$10
3x5 index card	$4-$5

Brian McRae
Ball	$23
Photo	$13
3x5 index card	$5

Hal McRae
Ball	$23
Photo	$13
3x5 index card	$4-$5

Kevin McReynolds
Ball	$19
Photo	$10
3x5 index card	$4-$5

Bill Melton
Ball	$22-$24
Photo	$12-$15
3x5 index card	$5

Gene Michael
Ball	$17
Photo	$8
3x5 index card	$4

Felix Millan
Ball	$23
Photo	$12-$15
3x5 index card	$5-$6

Don Mincher
Ball	$21
Photo	$16-$18
3x5 index card	$4-$5

Minnie Minoso
Ball	$25-$30
Photo	$20
3x5 index card	$6-$7

Kevin Mitchell
Ball	$24
Photo	$13
3x5 index card	$4-$5

Wilmer Mizell *
Ball	$40-$60
Photo	$15-$20
3x5 index card	$7-$8

Paul Molitor
Ball	$40-$50
Photo	$25-$30
3x5 index card	$9-$10

Rick Monday
Ball	$23
Photo	$13
3x5 index card	$5

Don Money
Ball	$21
Photo	$12
3x5 index card	$4-$5

Wally Moon
Ball	$19
Photo	$10
3x5 index card	$4

Charlie Moore
Ball	$19
Photo	$10
3x5 index card	$4

Terry Moore *
Ball	$40-$60
Photo	$20-$30
3x5 index card	$12

Mickey Morandini
Ball	$21
Photo	$12
3x5 index card	$5

Keith Moreland
Ball	$18
Photo	$9
3x5 index card	$4

Jack Morris
Ball	$22
Photo	$11
3x5 index card	$4-$5

Omar Moreno
Ball	$25
Photo	$15
3x5 index card	$5

Manny Mota
Ball	$27
Photo	$15-$20
3x5 index card	$6

Van Lingle Mungo *
Ball	$90-$125
Photo	$45-$50
3x5 index card	$15-$20

Thurman Munson *
Ball	$1,000-$2,000
Photo	$300-$500
3x5 index card	$150-$250

Bobby Murcer
Ball	$25
Photo	$12
3x5 index card	$5

Dale Murphy
Ball	$35-$40
Photo	$25-$30
3x5 index card	$6-$7

Eddie Murray
Ball	$65-$75
Photo	$35-$50
3x5 index card	$12-$15

Danny Murtaugh *
Ball	$200-$300
Photo	$75-$100
3x5 index card	$25-$40

Graig Nettles
Ball	$25
Photo	$13
3x5 index card	$5

Don Newcombe
Ball	$25
Photo	$12
3x5 index card	$5

Bo Bo Newsom *
Ball	$90-$125
Photo	$45
3x5 index card	$15

Joe Niekro
Ball	$21
Photo	$11-$15
3x5 index card	$4-$5

Otis Nixon
Ball	$23
Photo	$13
3x5 index card	$5

Gary Nolan
Ball	$17
Photo	$8
3x5 index card	$4

Irv Noren
Ball	$20
Photo	$10-$15
3x5 index card	$4-$5

Joe Nuxhall
Ball	$17
Photo	$9
3x5 index card	$4

Lefty O'Doul *
Ball	$300-$500
Photo	$175-$250
3x5 index card	$50-$75

Blue Moon Odom
Ball	$20
Photo	$9
3x5 index card	$4-$5

Ben Oglivie
Ball	$19
Photo	$9
3x5 index card	$4

Tony Oliva
Ball	$23
Photo	$14
3x5 index card	$5

Al Oliver
Ball	$19
Photo	$13
3x5 index card	$4

Gene Oliver
Ball	$19
Photo	$12
3x5 index card	$4

Claude Osteen
Ball	$24
Photo	$12
3x5 index card	$4-$5

Amos Otis
Ball	$22
Photo	$12
3x5 index card	$4

Ed Ott
Ball	$19
Photo	$9
3x5 index card	$4

Mickey Owen
Ball	$21
Photo	$10
3x5 index card	$4-$5

Andy Pafko
Ball	$22-$25
Photo	$12-$15
3x5 index card	$5

Dave Parker
Ball	$25-$27
Photo	$13-$15
3x5 index card	$5-$6

Wes Parker
Ball	$22
Photo	$11
3x5 index card	$4

Mel Parnell
Ball	$24
Photo	$12
3x5 index card	$5

Camilo Pascual
Ball	$30-$35
Photo	$15-$20
3x5 index card	$5-$6

Alejandro Pena
Ball	$22
Photo	$11
3x5 index card	$4-$5

Tony Pena
Ball	$24
Photo	$13
3x5 index card	$5

Terry Pendleton
Ball	$20
Photo	$10
3x5 index card	$4-$5

Joe Pepitone
Ball	$25-$30
Photo	$15-$20
3x5 index card	$7-$8

Jim Perry
Ball	$20
Photo	$10-$15
3x5 index card	$4-$5

Johnny Pesky
Ball	$21
Photo	$11
3x5 index card	$4

Rico Petrocelli
Ball	$15-$17
Photo	$8
3x5 index card	$4

Billy Pierce
Ball	$21
Photo	$12
3x5 index card	$4-$5

Jimmy Piersall
Ball	$24
Photo	$14
3x5 index card	$5

Lou Piniella
Ball	$24
Photo	$14
3x5 index card	$4

Vada Pinson *
Ball	$75-$125
Photo	$50-$60
3x5 index card	$20-$25

Juan Pizzaro
Ball	$28-$30
Photo	$18-$20
3x5 index card	$7

Johnny Podres
Ball	$24
Photo	$13-$15
3x5 index card	$5

Darrell Porter
Ball	$23
Photo	$12
3x5 index card	$5

Boog Powell
Ball	$23-$25
Photo	$13-$15
3x5 index card	$6

Vic Power
Ball	$25
Photo	$15-$18
3x5 index card	$6-$7

Pedro Ramos
Ball	$23
Photo	$13
3x5 index card	$4-$5

Willie Randolph
Ball	$25
Photo	$13
3x5 index card	$5

Vic Raschi *
Ball	$150-$200
Photo	$50-$75
3x5 index card	$20-$30

Dick Radatz
Ball	$19
Photo	$9
3x5 index card	$4

Tim Raines
Ball	$25
Photo	$14
3x5 card	$5

Jeff Reardon
Ball	$22
Photo	$11
3x5 index card	$4-$5

Jimmie Reese *
Ball	$35-$50
Photo	$20-$30
3x5 index card	$9-$10

Pete Reiser *
Ball	$60-$75
Photo	$35-$40
3x5 index card	$12-$15

Allie Reynolds *
Ball	$100-$200
Photo	$35-$40
3x5 index card	$12-$15

Harold Reynolds
Ball	$20
Photo	$10
3x5 index card	$4

Dusty Rhodes
Ball	$24
Photo	$12-$15
3x5 index card	$5

Jim Rice
Ball	$30
Photo	$15-$20
3x5 index card	$7-$9

J.R. Richard
Ball	$23
Photo	$14
3x5 index card	$4-$5

Bobby Richardson
Ball	$20
Photo	$10
3x5 index card	$4

Bill Rigney
Ball	$25-$30
Photo	$18-$25
3x5 index card	$7

Dave Righetti
Ball	$20
Photo	$10
3x5 index card	$4

Billy Ripken
Ball	$18
Photo	$9
3x5 index card	$4

Cal Ripken Jr.
Ball	$100
Photo	$50
3x5 card	$25

Mickey Rivers
Ball	$21
Photo	$11
3x5 index card	$4

Eddie Robinson
Ball	$24
Photo	$15
3x5 index card	$5

Preacher Roe
Ball	$25
Photo	$14
3x5 index card	$5

Bob "Buck" Rodgers
Ball	$19
Photo	$10
3x5 index card	$4

Steve Rogers
Ball	$20
Photo	$10
3x5 index card	$4-$5

Cookie Rojas
Ball	$21
Photo	$12-$15
3x5 index card	$4-$5

Red Rolfe*
Ball	$50-$60
Photo	$35-$40
3x5 index card	$12-$14

Pete Rose
Ball	$40-$50
Photo	$25-$30
3x5 index card	$10-$14

Al Rosen
Ball	$30-$40
Photo	$20-$25
3x5 index card	$5

John Roseboro
Ball	$20
Photo	$10
3x5 index card	$4-$5

Joe Rudi
Ball	$24
Photo	$13
3x5 index card	$5

Bill Russell
Ball	$21
Photo	$11
3x5 index card	$4

Bret Saberhagen
Ball	$24
Photo	$14
3x5 card	$6

Chris Sabo
Ball	$24
Photo	$12
3x5 index card	$4-$5

Deion Sanders
Ball	$50-$75
Photo	$30-$50
3x5 index card	$7-$10

Johnny Sain
Ball	$25
Photo	$13
3x5 index card	$5

Ryne Sandberg
Ball	$35-$40
Photo	$25-$30
3x5 index card	$10-$12

Manny Sanguillen
Ball	$28
Photo	$17
3x5 index card	$6

Ron Santo
Ball	$25-$30
Photo	$15-$20
3x5 index card	$6

Hank Sauer*
Ball	$30-$35
Photo	$15-$20
3x5 index card	$5

Steve Sax
Ball	$20
Photo	$10
3x5 index card	$4-$5

Herb Score
Ball	$23
Photo	$14
3x5 index card	$5

George Scott
Ball	$23
Photo	$12
3x5 index card	$5

Mike Scott
Ball	$19-$25
Photo	$12-$15
3x5 index card	$4-$6

Bobby Shantz
Ball	$25-$30
Photo	$10-$15
3x5 index card	$4-$6

Kevin Seitzer
Ball	$20
Photo	$10
3x5 index card	$4-$5

Chris Short*
Ball	$100-$150
Photo	$40-$60
3x5 index card	$15-$25

Roy Sievers
Ball	$21
Photo	$11
3x5 index card	$4-$5

Ken Singleton
Ball	$20
Photo	$10
3x5 index card	$4

Ted Simmons
Ball	$25
Photo	$16
3x5 index card	$5

Sibby Sisti
Ball	$18-$20
Photo	$10-$12
3x5 index card	$4

Bill "Moose" Skowron
Ball	$24
Photo	$12
3x5 index card	$5

Don Slaught
Ball	$18
Photo	$9
3x5 index card	$4

Roy Smalley Jr.
Ball	$20
Photo	$11
3x5 index card	$4

Roy Smalley Sr.
Ball	$19
Photo	$9
3x5 index card	$4

Lee Smith
Ball	$24
Photo	$15
3x5 index card	$5

Lonnie Smith
Ball	$19
Photo	$9
3x5 index card	$4

Ozzie Smith
Ball	$25-$35
Photo	$18-$20
3x5 index card	$6-$7

Reggie Smith
Ball	$22
Photo	$12
3x5 index card	$4-$5

Cory Snyder
Ball	$18
Photo	$9
3x5 index card	$4

Billy Southworth*
Ball	$60-$75
Photo	$35-$40
3x5 index card	$15-$20

Eddie Stanky*
Ball	$50-$75
Photo	$25-$35
3x5 index card	$7-$8

Bob Stanley
Ball	$16-$18
Photo	$8-$9
3x5 index card	$4

Fred Stanley
Ball	$21
Photo	$10
3x5 index card	$4-$5

Rusty Staub
Ball	$23
Photo	$12
3x5 index card	$5

Darryl Strawberry
Ball	$23
Photo	$13
3x5 index card	$5

Terry Steinbach
Ball	$21
Photo	$12
3x5 index card	$4-$5

Vern Stephens*
Ball	$150-$175
Photo	$90-$100
3x5 index card	$25

Dave Stewart
Ball	$24
Photo	$12
3x5 index card	$5

Dave Stieb
Ball	$22
Photo	$11
3x5 index card	$4-$5

Steve Stone
Ball	$25
Photo	$13-$18
3x5 index card	$5

Mel Stottlemyre
Ball	$30-$35
Photo	$12-$15
3x5 index card	$5

Billy Sunday*
Ball	$400-$500
Photo	$300-$350
3x5 index card	$90-$100

Rick Sutcliffe
Ball	$22
Photo	$12
3x5 index card	$4-$5

Bruce Sutter
Ball	$23
Photo	$12
3x5 index card	$5

Ron Swoboda
Ball	$20
Photo	$10
3x5 index card	$4

Frank Tanana
Ball	$21
Photo	$12
3x5 index card	$4

Danny Tartabull
Ball	$20
Photo	$10
3x5 index card	$4

Birdie Tebbetts *
Ball	$40-$60
Photo	$20-$30
3x5 index card	$5-$6

Johnny Temple *
Ball	$30-$40
Photo	$15
3x5 index card	$6

Ralph Terry
Ball	$25-$35
Photo	$15-$20
3x5 index card	$4-$5

Chuck Tanner
Ball	$25
Photo	$18-$20
3x5 index card	$5

Kent Tekulve
Ball	$23
Photo	$12
3x5 index card	$5

Garry Templeton
Ball	$24
Photo	$12
3x5 index card	$5

Gene Tenace
Ball	$24
Photo	$12
3x5 index card	$5

Wayne Terwilliger
Ball	$18
Photo	$9
3x5 index card	$4

Mickey Tettleton
Ball	$24
Photo	$12
3x5 index card	$5

Bob Tewksbury
Ball	$17
Photo	$9
3x5 index card	$4

Frank J. Thomas
Ball	$20
Photo	$9
3x5 index card	$4

Gorman Thomas
Ball	$24
Photo	$12
3x5 index card	$5

Bobby Thomson
Ball	$25
Photo	$15
3x5 index card	$5-$6

Andre Thornton
Ball	$24
Photo	$17
3x5 index card	$5

Faye Throneberry *
Ball	$25
Photo	$17
3x5 index card	$6

Marv Throneberry *
Ball	$50
Photo	$25
3x5 index card	$8-$10

Luis Tiant
Ball	$25
Photo	$12
3x5 index card	$5

Frank Torre
Ball	$25
Photo	$10
3x5 index card	$4-$5

Joe Torre
Ball	$40-$50
Photo	$20-$30
3x5 index card	$10-$15

Alan Trammell
Ball	$30-$35
Photo	$16
3x5 index card	$5-$6

Tom Tresh
Ball	$21
Photo	$11
3x5 index card	$4-$5

Manny Trillo
Ball	$21
Photo	$12
3x5 index card	$4

Virgil Trucks
Ball	$24
Photo	$14
3x5 index card	$5

Bob Turley
Ball	$25-$30
Photo	$15-$20
3x5 index card	$4

Bob Uecker
Ball	$40-$50
Photo	$20-$25
3x5 index card	$8

Del Unser
Ball	$17
Photo	$8
3x5 index card	$4

Elmer Valo *
Ball	$30-$40
Photo	$$25-$35
3x5 index card	$5

Johnny VanderMeer *
Ball	$28-$30
Photo	$15-$20
3x5 index card	$6

Andy Van Slyke
Ball	$24
Photo	$14
3x5 index card	$5

Mickey Vernon
Ball	$25
Photo	$12-$15
3x5 index card	$4-$5

Frank Viola
Ball	$23
Photo	$12
3x5 index card	$5

Bill Virdon
Ball	$25
Photo	$9-$12
3x5 index card	$4-$5

Pete Vuckovich
Ball	$40-$50
Photo	$30-$40
3x5 index card	$10-$15

Dixie Walker *
Ball	$50-$75
Photo	$25-$30
3x5 index card	$10-$12

Harry Walker *
Ball	$50-$75
Photo	$20-$30
3x5 index card	$5-$6

Rube Walker *
Ball	$30-$35
Photo	$18-$20
3x5 index card	$7

Bucky Walters *
Ball	$40-$60
Photo	$25-$30
3x5 index card	$12-$15

Bill Wambsganss*
Ball	$150-$200
Photo	$75-$100
3x5 index card	$40-$50

Claudell Washington
Ball	$17
Photo	$8-$10
3x5 index card	$4

Bob Watson
Ball	$18
Photo	$9
3x5 index card	$4

Walt Weiss

Ball	$21
Photo	$11
3x5 index card	$5

Bob Welch

Ball	$21
Photo	$12
3x5 index card	$4

John Wetteland

Ball	$23
Photo	$13
3x5 index card	$5

Lou Whitaker

Ball	$25
Photo	$15
3x5 index card	$5

Bill White

Ball	$25
Photo	$13
3x5 index card	$5

Roy White

Ball	$21
Photo	$10
3x5 index card	$4

Dick Williams

Ball	$25-$30
Photo	$15-$20
3x5 index card	$5

Ken Williams *

Ball	$200
Photo	$100-$125
3x5 index card	$40

Mitch Williams

Ball	$20
Photo	$10
3x5 index card	$4

Maury Wills

Ball	$25-$30
Photo	$15-$20
3x5 index card	$5-$6

Mookie Wilson

Ball	$22
Photo	$10
3x5 index card	$4-$5

Smoky Joe Wood*

Ball	$125-$150
Photo	$75
3x5 index card	$35

Wilbur Wood

Ball	$20
Photo	$10-$15
3x5 index card	$4-$5

Gene Woodling *

Ball	$30-$40
Photo	$20-$30
3x5 index card	$4-$5

Jimmy Wynn

Ball	$21
Photo	$11
3x5 index card	$4-$5

Steve Yeager

Ball	$18
Photo	$9
3x5 index card	$4

Rudy York *

Ball	$150-$200
Photo	$100
3x5 index card	$50-$60

Gus Zernial

Ball	$22
Photo	$10
3x5 index card	$4-$5

Don Zimmer

Ball	$30-$35
Photo	$20-$25
3x5 index card	$5

MANAGERS, ANNOUNCERS & EXECUTIVES

Most collectors covet autographs of baseball's superstars—the Mantles, Aarons and McGwires of the world. But the men who call the shots in baseball—from managers and owners to commissioners and announcers—also make worthy subjects. This section is devoted to pricing on current and former managers' autographs as well as those from a variety of important figures who helped shape the game from outside the white lines.

Among current managers, Joe Torre of the New York Yankees is the most popular figure—not only because of the modern-day dynasty he helped build in New York, but because he also had a stellar career as a player. Torre batted .297 with 252 homers in his 18 years as a player, winning the National League Most Valuable Player Award in 1971, when he batted .363 for the St. Louis Cardinals. A host of other current managers also had distinguished careers as players; among them are former sluggers Don Baylor (331 home runs) and Dusty Baker (242 homers), accomplished hitter Lou Piniella (.291), and former 20-game winner Larry Dierker.

This section also offers autograph pricing on baseball's most popular announcers. Our listings focus on pure announcers (as opposed to play-er-turned-announcer types) from baseball's golden days. A collection of autographs from baseball's legendary voices might include Mel Allen, Red Barber, Jack Brickhouse, Harry Caray, and Ernie Harwell.

Among commissioners' autographs, one of the toughest to find is Bartlett Giamatti. A scholar for most of his professional career, Giamatti served as president of Yale University from 1978-86. After making a comment that he'd like to work in baseball, he got his wish, becoming president of the National League in 1986. In April 1989, the Boston-born Giamatti (a lifelong Red Sox fan, by the way), succeeded Peter Ueberroth as commissioner of baseball. Four months later, he handed down his most famous decision—a lifetime ban of Pete Rose. On September 1, 1989—just eight days after the Rose ruling—Giamatti died of a heart attack at age 51. As a result, Giamatti's autograph on a baseball is many times more valuable then Ueberroth's or Fay Vincent's.

Note: Prices in this section are for 8x10 photos and official league baseballs only. An ampersand (&) denotes that an autographed item isn't known to exist or is so rare that it's virtually impossible to price.
* Indicates manager, announcer or executive is deceased.

Managers–Current

Dusty Baker	Photo:	$15	Bob Brenly	Photo:	$10	Buck Martinez	Photo:	$10
	Ball:	$30		Ball:	$22		Ball:	$20
			Bobby Cox	Photo:	$20	Lloyd McClendon	Photo:	$10
				Ball:	$35		Ball:	$20
			Larry Dierker	Photo:	$10	Hal McRae	Photo:	$15
				Ball:	$15		Ball:	$30
			Phil Garner	Photo:	$12	Tony Muser	Photo:	$10
				Ball:	$22		Ball:	$20
			Mike Hargrove	Photo:	$10	Jerry Narron	Photo:	$10
				Ball:	$25		Ball:	$20
			Art Howe	Photo:	$12	Lou Piniella	Photo:	$20
				Ball:	$22		Ball:	$35
Don Baylor	Photo:	$15	Tom Kelly	Photo:	$15	Mike Scioscia	Photo:	$10
	Ball:	$30		Ball:	$25		Ball:	$20
Buddy Bell	Photo:	$10	Tony LaRussa	Photo:	$20	Joe Torre	Photo:	$30
	Ball:	$20		Ball:	$40		Ball:	$50
Bruce Bochy	Photo:	$10	Davey Lopes	Photo:	$15	Jim Tracy	Photo:	$10
	Ball:	$20		Ball:	$20		Ball:	$20
Bob Boone	Photo:	$12	Charlie Manuel	Photo:	$15	Bobby Valentine	Photo:	$15
	Ball:	$25		Ball:	$25		Ball:	$20
Larry Bowa	Photo:	$12	Jerry Manuel	Photo:	$10			
	Ball:	$25		Ball:	$20			

Managers–Retired

Sparky Anderson	Photo:	$15	Jim Leyland	Photo:	$15	John McNamara	Photo:	$10
	Ball:	$25		Ball:	$25		Ball:	$22
Cito Gaston	Photo:	$12	Billy Martin*	Photo:	$75	Chuck Tanner	Photo:	$15
	Ball:	$20		Ball:	$200		Ball:	$25
Whitey Herzog	Photo:	$15	Gene Mauch	Photo:	$15	Bill Virdon	Photo:	$15
	Ball:	$25		Ball:	$25		Ball:	$25
Davey Johnson	Photo:	$15	Jack McKeon	Photo:	$10	Dick Williams	Photo:	$15
	Ball:	$30		Ball:	$20		Ball:	$30
						Don Zimmer	Photo:	$25
							Ball:	$35

Announcers

Mel Allen*	Photo:	$40
	Ball:	$100
Red Barber*	Photo:	$40
	Ball:	$100
Rex Barney*	Photo:	$25
	Ball:	$75
Jack Brickhouse*	Photo:	$20
	Ball:	$50

Jack Buck	Photo:	$15
	Ball:	$22
Harry Caray*	Photo:	$75
	Ball:	$150
Ernie Harwell	Photo:	$25
	Ball:	$35
Vin Scully	Photo:	$15
	Ball:	$35

Commissioners

William Eckert*	Photo:	$100
	Ball:	$200
A. Bartlett Giamatti*	Photo:	$75
	Ball:	$300
Bowie Kuhn	Photo:	$20
	Ball:	$40

Bud Selig	Photo:	$25
	Ball:	$50
Peter Ueberroth	Photo:	$25
	Ball:	$35
Fay Vincent	Photo:	$25
	Ball:	$35

Owners/Executives

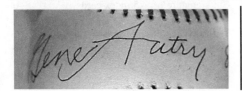

Gene Autry*	Photo:	$75
	Ball:	$200
Charles O. Finley*	Photo:	$50
	Ball:	$100
Ray Kroc*	Photo:	$75
	Ball:	$200

Walter O'Malley*	Photo:	$50
	Ball:	$100
George Steinbrenner	Photo:	$50
	Ball:	$75
Ted Turner	Photo:	$25
	Ball:	$75

NEGRO LEAGUES

* Deceased

Newt Allen *
Photo	$100
Ball	$250
Cut signature or 3x5 index card	$50-$75

Tom Alston *
Photo	$30-$35
Ball	$50
Cut signature or 3x5 index card	$10-$12

George Altman
Photo	$20-$25
Ball	$30
Cut signature or 3x5 index card	$6-$8

Russell Awkard
Photo	$20-$25
Ball	$30
Cut signature or 3x5 index card	$6

Gene Baker *
Photo	$25
Ball	$30
Cut signature or 3x5 index card	$7-$8

Dan Bankhead *
Photo	$50-$75
Ball	$150
Cut signature or 3x5 index card	$15-$20

Sam Bankhead (signature)

Sam Bankhead *
Photo	$75-$100
Ball	$200
Cut signature or 3x5 index card	$20-$25

David Barnhill *
Photo	$60-$75
Ball	$100
Cut signature or 3x5 index card	$20-$25

Frank Barnes
Photo	$20-$25
Ball	$25-$30
Cut signature or 3x5 index card	$6-$8

Gene Benson
Photo	$20-$25
Ball	$30
Cut signature or 3x5 index card	$5-$6

Bill "Fireball" Beverly *
Photo	$25-$30
Ball	$35
Cut signature or 3x5 index card	$8-$10

Dennis Biddle
Photo	$20
Ball	$25
Cut signature or 3x5 index card	$5

Charlie Biot*
Photo	$20-$25
Ball	$25-$30
Cut signature or 3x5 index card	$6-$8

Joe Black
Photo	$15
Ball	$25
Cut signature or 3x5 index card	$6-$8

Lyman Bostock Sr.
Photo	$20-$25
Ball	$30
Cut signature or 3x5 index card	$6

Chet Brewer *
Photo	$25-$40
Ball	$75-$100
Cut signature or 3x5 index card	$10

Bill Byrd *
Photo	$25-$30
Ball	$50-$75
Cut signature or 3x5 index card	$10-$12

Bill "Ready" Cash
Photo	$25-$30
Ball	$30-$35
Cut signature or 3x5 index card	$6-$8

Bus Clarkson *
Photo	$40-$50
Ball	$100-$150
Cut signature or 3x5 index card	$15

Sam Crawford *
Photo	$150-$250
Ball	$300-$400
Cut signature or 3x5 index card	$25

George Crowe
Photo	$20-$25
Ball	$25-$30
Cut signature or 3x5 index card	$6-$7

Jimmie Crutchfield *
Photo	$40
Ball	$50-$75
Cut signature or 3x5 index card	$12-$15

Piper Davis *
Photo	$35-$40
Ball	$40-$50
Cut signature or 3x5 index card	$9-$10

Lou Dials *
Photo	$20-$25
Ball	$40-$50
Cut signature or 3x5 index card	$7-$9

Mahlon Duckett
Photo	$10-$15
Ball	$30
Cut signature or 3x5 index card	$7-$9

Luke Easter *
Photo	$50-$75
Ball	$200-$300
Cut signature or 3x5 index card	$30-$40

Wilmer Fields
Photo	$10-$15
Ball	$25
Cut signature or 3x5 index card	$8

Josh Gibson Jr.
Photo	$10-$15
Ball	$25
Cut signature or 3x5 index card	$8

George Giles *
Photo	$30-$35
Ball	$50-$75
Cut signature or 3x5 index card	$10

Willie Grace
Photo	$25-$30
Ball	$30
Cut signature or 3x5 index card	$8-$10

Nap Gulley *
Photo	$25-$30
Ball	$50-$75
Cut signature or 3x5 index card	$5-$7

Sam Hairston *
Photo	$20
Ball	$25
Cut signature or 3x5 index card	$5-$7

Jehosie Heard
Photo	$25
Ball	$30
Cut signature or 3x5 index card	$6-$8

Bill Holland (signature)

Bill Holland *
Photo	$35-$40
Ball	$40-$50
Cut signature or 3x5 index card	$10-$12

Cowan "Bubba" Hyde
Photo	$20-$25
Ball	$25-$30
Cut signature or 3x5 index card	$5-$7

Connie Johnson
Photo	$20-$25
Ball	$30
Cut signature or 3x5 index card	$7-$8

Don Johnson
Photo	$25
Ball	$30
Cut signature or 3x5 index card	$6-$8

Josh Johnson
Photo	$25
Ball	$30
Cut signature or 3x5 index card	$6-$8

Clinton "Casey" Jones
Photo	$25-$30
Ball	$30-$35
Cut signature or 3x5 index card	$9-$12

Brooks Lawrence *
Photo	$25
Ball	$30
Cut signature or 3x5 index card	$7-$9

Rufus Lewis *
Photo	$20-$25
Ball	$30
Cut signature or 3x5 index card	$7

Lester Lockett
Photo	$20
Ball	$30
Cut signature or 3x5 index card	$7-$9

Biz Mackey *
Photo	$125-$150
Ball	$200-$250
Cut signature or 3x5 index card	$50-$75

Danid J. Malacchor

Dave Malarcher *
Photo	$150-$175
Ball	$200-$300
Cut signature or 3x5 index card	$75-$100

Max Manning
Photo	$20
Ball	$25
Cut signature or 3x5 index card	$5

Luis Marquez *
Photo	$50-$75
Ball	$75-$100
Cut signature or 3x5 index card	$15-$20

Verdell "Lefty" Mathis *
Photo	$20-$25
Ball	$30-$40
Cut signature or 3x5 index card	$7-$8

Charlie Neal *
Photo	$25-$30
Ball	$40
Cut signature or 3x5 index card	$8-$10

Ray Noble *
Photo	$25-$30
Ball	$35-$40
Cut signature or 3x5 index card	$8-$10

Buck O'Neil *
Photo	$25-$30
Ball	$35
Cut signature or 3x5 index card	$6-$8

William Warren Peace
Photo	$20-$25
Ball	$25-$30
Cut signature or 3x5 index card	$7-$8

Jim Pendleton *
Photo	$25-$30
Ball	$30-$35
Cut signature or 3x5 index card	$6-$8

Art "Superman" Pennington
Photo	$25
Ball	$30
Cut signature or 3x5 index card	$6-$8

Willie Pope
Photo	$20-$25
Ball	$25-$30
Cut signature or 3x5 index card	$5-$7

Dave Pope *
Photo	$25
Ball	$50
Cut signature or 3x5 index card	$15

Ted "Double Duty" Radcliffe
Photo	$20-$25
Ball	$30
Cut signature or 3x5 index card	$6-$8

Bobby Robinson
Photo	$20
Ball	$25
Cut signature or 3x5 index card	$5-$7

Hilton Smith

Hilton Smith *
Photo	$75-$100
Ball	$100-$150
Cut signature or 3x5 index card	$25-$30

Toni Stone *
Photo	$50-$75
Ball	$100
Cut signature or 3x5 index card	$20

Alfred "Slick" Surratt
Photo	$20
Ball	$25
Cut signature or 3x5 index card	$5-$7

Mule Suttles *
Photo	$150
Ball	$200
Cut signature or 3x5 index card	$50-$75

Hank Thompson *
Photo	$75-$90
Ball	$100
Cut signature or 3x5 index card	$15-$20

Bob Thurman *
Photo	$25
Ball	$30
Cut signature or 3x5 index card	$6-$8

Luis Tiant Sr. *
Photo	$30-$35
Ball	$40
Cut signature or 3x5 index card	$10-$12

Quincy Trouppe *
Photo	$40-$50
Ball	$75-$100
Cut signature or 3x5 index card	$8-$10

Armando Vasquez
Photo	$15-$20
Ball	$25-$30
Cut signature or 3x5 index card	$12

Artie Wilson
Photo	$25
Ball	$30
Cut signature or 3x5 index card	$6-$8

Earl Wilson Sr. *
Photo	$25
Ball	$30
Cut signature or 3x5 index card	$7-$8

Wild Bill Wright *
Photo	$25-$40
Ball	$50-$75
Cut signature or 3x5 index card	$8-$10

MAJOR LEAGUE BASEBALL AUTHENTICATION PROGRAM

Arthur Andersen is on board for the 2001 baseball season, giving baseball fans an added measure of assurance that their memorabilia and autographs are authentic.

The national accounting firm is overseeing the Major League Baseball Authentication Program.

MLB launched its authentication program early in 2001 to chase fakes out of the hobby and to assure collectors that their autographed items are real. Arthur Andersen's workers are marking autographed and game-used items with an official MLB hologram that will be entered in an online registry.

The effort started with a pilot program in 2000 that included 150 game-used sessions.

Five companies have become official licensees of the MLB Authentication Program, including Upper Deck Authenticated, Mounted Memories, Steiner Sports, Tri-Star Productions and Legends Collectibles.

Mounted Memories held official autograph sessions with Roger Clemens, Manny Ramirez and retired legends Nolan Ryan, Reggie Jackson and Willie Mays. Steiner Sports' list of signees included Nomar Garciaparra, Ramirez and the famous home run combination of Bobby Thomson and Ralph Branca.

Upper Deck Authenticated held an early signing with Alex Rodriguez, shortly after he joined the Texas Rangers. Randy Johnson and Rafael Furcal were among signees for Tri-Star Productions.

Most ballplayers have accepted the presence of the Arthur Andersen observers, said Joe Grippo, licensing manager for collectibles and memorabilia for Major League Baseball Properties. "We are confident that once the players are aware of the program they will be happy to participate," he said. "In fact, we have heard on a couple of occasions that the players thought this program will be a great tool in protecting the fans from purchasing fraudulent memorabilia."

Russell Halsted, president and CEO of Legends Collectibles, said his company has been careful to work around players' superstitions and emotions. Arthur Andersen representatives collect game-used jerseys at the locker room door, he said.

Grippo said he wanted to assure fans that the program wasn't set up to discourage fans from seeking autographs from ballplayers in person. "This could not be further from the truth," he said. "We encourage fans to create that magical bond that makes us all fans."

Major League Baseball also started auctioning game-used and autographed items on its MLB.com Web site in 2001. Some of the items auctioned on the site during the 2001 season included a bat signed by Hank Aaron, a glove autographed by Don Mattingly and a base signed by Willie McCovey.

This section offers pricing for items certified via an authentication system, including a sticker or hologram on the item, at the time of signing. While companies that utilize an authentication system will guarantee the authenticity of their items, that guarantee is only as good as the company itself. Pricing is for open editions; limited editions are worth more.

Player	Baseball	8x10	11x14+	Jersey	Helmet	Bat
Hank Aaron	$150	$120				
Roberto Alomar	$90					
Jeff Bagwell	$90	$70				
Johnny Bench	$65	$40				$230
Yogi Berra	$75	$45				
Craig Biggio	$80	$60				
Wade Boggs	$100					$160
Barry Bonds	$80	$170				
Branca/Thomson	$100	$70	$120			
Buckner/Wilson	$70	$60	$115			
Steve Carlton	$70	$40				
Gary Carter	$80					
Roger Clemens	$180		$180	$450	$250	
Carlos Delgado					$150	$150
Joe DiMaggio	$500	$1,200				
DiMaggio/Williams		$1,200				
J. D. Drew	$70	$60		$400	$150	$100
Carlton Fisk	$90			$600		$300
Whitey Ford	$90	$80	$130			
Bob Gibson	$100					
Tom Glavine	$150	$100	$150			
Ken Griffey Jr.	$200	$120		$500		$500

Player	Baseball	8x10	11x14+	Jersey	Helmet	Bat
Vladimir Guerrero	$210		$350	$620		$400
Tony Gwynn	$140	$100		$350		
Keith Hernandez	$70		$90	$450		
Orel Hershiser	$100	$80	$100			
Reggie Jackson	$130					
Derek Jeter	$350	$350	$525	$600	$1,000	$500-700
Andruw Jones	$90					
David Justice	$150	$130	$160	$600		$600
Al Kaline	$90					
Jeff Kent	$80					
Harmon Killebrew						$500
Ralph Kiner	$60	$40	$70			
Sandy Koufax	$350		$430	$1,100		
Don Mattingly				$600		
Willie Mays	$180	$250	$350			$700
Bill Mazeroski	$70					
Paul Molitor	$150			$600		$400
Raul Mondesi	$80					
Dale Murphy	$80					$80
Stan Musial	$80					
Manny Ramirez	$175					
Cal Ripken Jr.	$200	$125		$700		$450-700
Mariano Rivera	$175					
Phil Rizzuto	$70		$70	$350		$300
Brooks Robinson	$95			$550		$350
Frank Robinson	$80	$80		$600		$400
Alex Rodriguez	$150			$625		$300
Pete Rose	$90	$70	$115	$350-550		$170-350
Nolan Ryan	$150			$500		
Mike Schmidt	$100					
Tom Seaver	$100			$650		
Ozzie Smith	$100					
Duke Snider	$60	$80	$100	$500		$350
Sammy Sosa	$300			$500		
Darryl Strawberry	$60	$60	$80			$200
Joe Torre	$200	$180	$200	$500		
Bernie Williams	$150					
Ted Williams			$700			$2,500
Maury Wills	$50					
Dave Winfield	$120			$550		
Carl Yastrzemski	$160	$130				

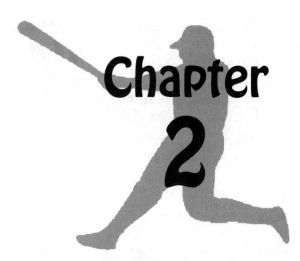

Chapter 2

MULTI-SIGNED ITEMS

By Jerry Shaver

In January 1998, Tony Gwynn appeared at Tuff Stuff's Winter Classic autograph show in Richmond, Va. At the time, Gwynn stood just 220 hits shy of the magical 3,000 mark and the atmosphere in the room was electric. Collector after collector asked Gwynn to sign treasured 3,000-Hit Club items—bats, balls and posters that featured the autographs of some of baseball's greatest players. Gwynn lived up to his reputation as an obliging and willing signer—and he autographed everything that was put in front of him—but time and again he shook his head and said, "Man, this is a nice piece. Are you sure you want me to ruin it?"

Of course, Gwynn did go on to join the 3,000 Hit Club in early 2000, but his comments point out the dangers of collecting multi-signed items. One mistake can turn a valuable piece of baseball history into an interesting, but virtually worthless, curiosity. If you've ever started a team-signed ball during spring training—only to have one of your signees get traded before the season started—you understand this dilemma. As this book was being put together, Sammy Sosa had just stroked his 400th home run. No doubt many collectors will be rushing to add Sammy to their 500-HR Club pieces in the coming months, but don't forget that guys like Albert Belle and Jose Canseco looked like shoo-ins for the club just a few years ago.

That said, collecting multi-signed memorabilia can be one of the more interesting and challenging aspects of the hobby. Obviously, you'll want to pick a theme for each item. (Items containing random signatures of unrelated ballplayers aren't very interesting, and they carry little value in the hobby.)

The major milestones—500 HRs, 3,000 hits, 3,000 strikeouts, 300 wins—seem to be the most popular. And since the inception of periodic milestone autograph shows in Atlantic City, N.J., collecting signatures of members of these clubs has never been easier.

Team-signed items also are popular, with premiums placed on balls or bats signed by all the members of a World Series champ. For collectors interested only in the very best, All-Star baseballs are a great way to collect autographs of the game's biggest superstars. Still another option is to collect great players who played the same position during the same era (Willie, Mickey and the Duke; or A-Rod, Jeter and Nomar). Regardless of your preference, be aware that obtaining sigs of all the members of a particular theme can be extremely difficult, but the rewards for success are definitely worth the effort

WORLD SERIES BASEBALLS

Prices are listed for both the winning and losing teams for each year the World Series has been played since 1920. (The scarcity of multi-signed items from before 1920 makes pricing highly speculative.) The price assumes that the ball contains the signatures of the majority of the players on the team, including all of the key players listed.

Year	W/L	Team	Key Signatures	NM Price
1920	Winner	Cleveland Indians	Bagby, Caldwell, Chapman, Coveleski, Gardner, Jamieson, O'Neill, J. Sewell, Smith, Speaker, Wambsganss	$2,000
	Loser	Brooklyn Dodgers	Grimes, Konetchy, Marquard, Myers, Pfeffer, W. Robinson, Wheat	$1,500
1921	Winner	New York Giants	Bancroft, Barnes, Burns, Frisch, Kelly, McGraw, Meusel, Nehf, Smith, Snyder, Toney, Youngs	$2,500
	Loser	New York Yankees	Baker, Hoyt, Huggins, Mays, Meusel, Pipp, Ruth, Shawkey, Ward	$3,500
1922	Winner	New York Giants	Bancroft, Barnes, Frisch, Kelly, McGraw, Meusel, Nehf, Stengel, Snyder, Youngs	$2,500
	Loser	New York Yankees	Baker, Bush, Hoyt, Huggins, Meusel, Pipp, Ruth, Schang, Shawkey	$2,800

1932 New York Yankees

1936 New York Yankees

Year	W/L	Team	Key Signatures	NM Price
1923	Winner	New York Yankees	Bush, Gehrig, Hoyt, Huggins, Jones, Meusel, Pennock, Pipp, Ruth, Ward, Witt	$3,000
	Loser	New York Giants	Bancroft, Frisch, Jackson, Kelly, McGraw, Meusel, Ryan, Stengel, Youngs	$2,500
1924	Winner	Washington Senators	Goslin, Harris, Johnson, Judge, Rice, Zachery	$1,800
	Loser	New York Giants	Barnes, Frisch, Gowdy, Jackson, Kelly, McGraw, Meusel, Snyder, Terry Wilson, Youngs	$2,200
1925	Winner	Pittsburgh Pirates	Barnhart, Carey, Cuyler, Grantham, McKechnie, Meadows, Smith, Traynor, Wright	$1,000
	Loser	Washington Senators	Coveleski, Goslin, Harris, Johnson, Judge, Rice	$1,500
1926	Winner	St. Louis Cardinals	Alexander, Bell, Blades, Bottomley, Douthit, Hafey, Haines, Hornsby, Rhem, Southworth	$1,800
	Loser	New York Yankees	Combs, Hoyt, Huggins, Gehrig, Lazzeri, Meusel, Pennock, Ruth	$4,000
1927	Winner	New York Yankees	Combs, Hoyt, Huggins, Gehrig, Lazzeri, Meusel, Moore, Pennock, Ruth	$20,000-$60,000
	Loser	Pittsburgh Pirates	Barnhart, Cronin, Cuyler, Grantham, Groh, Harris, Hill, Kremer, Traynor, L. Waner, P. Waner	$900
1928	Winner	New York Yankees	Combs, Durocher, Gehrig, Hoyt, Huggins, Lazzeri, Meusel, Pipgras, Pennock, Ruth	$10,000
	Loser	St. Louis Cardinals	Alexander, Bottomley, Frisch, Hafey, Haines, Maranville, McKechnie	$1,250-$2,000
1929	Winner	Philadelphia Athletics	Cochrane, Collins, Cronin, Earnshaw, Foxx, Grove, Haas, Mack, Miller, Simmons	$1,000
	Loser	Chicago Cubs	Cuyler, Hartnett, Hornsby, Malone, McCarthy, Root, Wilson	$1,000
1930	Winner	Philadelphia Athletics	Cochrane, Collins, Dykes, Foxx, Grove, Mack, Miller, Simmons	$800-$1,000
	Loser	St. Louis Cardinals	Adams, Bottomley, Douthit, Frisch, Gelbert, Grimes, Hafey, Haines, Street, Watkins, Wilson	$800-$1,000
1931	Winner	St. Louis Cardinals	Cochrane, Earnshaw, Foxx, Grove, Hoyt, Mack, Simmons	$900-$1,000
	Loser	Philadelphia Athletics	Mack, Foxx, Simmons, Cochrane, Grove, Earnshaw, Hoyt	$1,000-$1,500
1932	Winner	New York Yankees	Allen, Combs, Dickey, Gehrig, Gomez, Lazzeri, McCarthy, Ruffing, Ruth, Sewell	$4,000
	Loser	Chicago Cubs	Bush, Cuyler, Grimes, Grimm, Hartnett, Herman, Hornsby, Moore, Stephenson, Warneke	$900
1933	Winner	New York Giants	Hubbell, Jackson, Ott, Schumacher, Terry, Vergez	$800-$1,000
	Loser	Washington Senators	Cronin, Crowder, Goslin, Kuhel, Manush, Myer, Whitehill	$650-$800
1934	Winner	St. Louis Cardinals	Collins, D. Dean, P. Dean, Durocher, Frisch, Haines, Martin, Medwick	$800-$1,000
	Loser	Detroit Tigers	Bridges, Cochrane, Gehringer, Goslin, Greenberg, Rowe	$850
1935	Winner	Detroit Tigers	Bridges, Cochrane, Gehringer, Goslin, Greenberg, Rowe	$700
	Loser	Chicago Cubs	Cuyler, Demaree, Galan, Grimm, Hack, Hartnett, Herman, Klein, Lee, Lindstrom, Warneke	$700
1936	Winner	New York Yankees	Dickey, DiMaggio, Gehrig, Gomez, Lazzeri, McCarthy, Pearson, Ruffing	$1,700-$2,000
	Loser	New York Giants	Hubbell, Jackson, Leiber, Mancuso, Moore, Ott, Terry	$700-$1,900
1937	Winner	New York Yankees	Dickey, DiMaggio, Gehrig, Gomez, Lazzeri, McCarthy, Ruffing	$2,000-$7,000
	Loser	New York Giants	Bartell, Hubbell, Leiber, Melton, Moore, Ott, Ripple, Terry	$600-$700
1938	Winner	New York Yankees	Dickey, DiMaggio, Gehrig, Gomez, McCarthy, Ruffing	$1,200-$1,500
	Loser	Chicago Cubs	Bryant, Dean, Garbark, Grimm, Hack, Hartnett, Herman, Lazzeri, Lee, Reynolds	$750-$900
1939	Winner	New York Yankees	Dickey, DiMaggio, Gomez, Keller, McCarthy, Rolfe, Ruffing, Selkirk	$1,500
	Loser	Cincinnati Reds	Derringer, Goodman, Lombardi, McCormick, Walters	$400
1940	Winner	Cincinnati Reds	Derringer, Lombardi, McCormick, Ripple, Walters, Werber	$450
	Loser	Detroit Tigers	Averill, Gehringer, Greenberg, McCosky, Newsom, Rowe, York	$500-$600
1941	Winner	New York Yankees	Dickey, DiMaggio, Gomez, McCarthy, Rizzuto, Ruffing	$1,000
	Loser	Brooklyn Dodgers	Camilli, Durocher, Herman, Higbe, Medwick, Reese, Reiser, Wyatt	$600-$900
1942	Winner	St. Louis Cardinals	Slaughter, Musial, W. Cooper, M. Cooper, Beazley	$750-$900
	Loser	New York Yankees	Dickey, DiMaggio, Gomez, Gordon, McCarthy, Rizzuto, Ruffing	$800-$1,000

1955 Brooklyn Dodgers

1957 Milwaukee Braves

Year	W/L	Team	Key Signatures	NM Price
1943	Winner	New York Yankees	Chandler, Dickey, Johnson, Keller, McCarthy, Russo	$750-$1,200
	Loser	St. Louis Cardinals	M. Cooper, W. Cooper, Lanier, Musial	$450
1944	Winner	St. Louis Cardinals	M. Cooper, W. Cooper, Hopp, Marion, Musial	$450
	Loser	St. Louis Browns	Kreevich, Kramer, McQuinn, Potter, Stephens	$350-$600
1945	Winner	Detroit Tigers	Cramer, Greenberg, Newhouser, Trout, York	$350-$400
	Loser	Chicago Cubs	Cavarretta, Grimm, Hack, Johnson, Nicholson, Pafko, Wyse	$350-$400
1946	Winner	St. Louis Cardinals	Garagiola, Kurowski, Musial, Pollet, Schoendienst, Slaughter, Walker	$600-$700
	Loser	Boston Red Sox	Cronin, DiMaggio, Doerr, Ferriss, Hughson, Pesky, Williams	$450-$700
1947	Winner	New York Yankees	Berra, DiMaggio, Henrich, McQuinn, Reynolds, Rizzuto, Shea	$1,000-$1,200
	Loser	Brooklyn Dodgers	Branca, Furillo, Hatten, Hodges, Reese, Robinson, Snider, Stankey, Vaughan	$1,000
1948	Winner	Cleveland Indians	Bearden, Boudreau, Feller, Gordon, Keltner, Lemon, Mitchell, Paige	$500
	Loser	Boston Braves	Dark, B. Elliott, Heath, Holmes, Sain, Spahn, Stankey	$500
1949	Winner	New York Yankees	Bauer, Berra, DiMaggio, Henrich, Raschi, Rizzuto, Reynolds, Stengel	$1,200-$1,500
	Loser	Brooklyn Dodgers	Branca, Campanella, Connors, Furillo, Hodges, Newcombe, Reese, Robinson, Snider	$800-$1,000
1950	Winner	New York Yankees	Bauer, Berra, DiMaggio, Ford, Henrich, Mize, Raschi, Rizzuto, Stengel	$800-$1,000
	Loser	Philadelphia Phillies	Ashburn, Ennis, Hammer, Konstanty, Roberts, Simmons	$400
1951	Winner	New York Yankees	Bauer, Berra, DiMaggio, Jensen, Mantle, McDougald, Mize, Raschi, Rizzuto, Stengel	$4,000
	Loser	New York Giants	Dark, Durocher, Irvin, Jansen, Maglie, Mays, Thomson	$750-$1,000
1952	Winner	New York Yankees	Bauer, Berra, Mantle, Martin, Mize, Raschi, Reynolds, Rizzuto, Stengel	$800-$1,000
	Loser	Brooklyn Dodgers	Avila, Easter, Doby, Feller, Garcia, Lemon, Mitchell, Rosen, Wynn	$900-$1,200
1953	Winner	New York Yankees	Bauer, Berra, Ford, Mantle, Martin, Mize, Raschi, Rizzuto, Stengel	$1,000
	Loser	Brooklyn Dodgers	Doby, Feller, Garcia, Lopez, Lemon, Mitchell, Rosen, Westlake, Wynn	$900
1954	Winner	New York Giants	Antonelli, Dark, Durocher, Irvin, Mueller, Mays, Wilhelm	$1,000-$1,500
	Loser	Cleveland Indians	Avila, Doby, Feller, Garcia, Lemon, Lopez, Rosen, Wynn	$450
1955	Winner	Brooklyn Dodgers	Alston, Campanella, Erskine, Furillo, Gilliam, Hodges, Koufax, Newcombe, Podres, Reese, Snider, Robinson, Zimmer	$3,000
	Loser	New York Yankees	Bauer, Berra, Ford, Howard, Larsen, Mantle, Stengel	$900-$1,200
1956	Winner	New York Yankees	Bauer, Berra, Ford, Howard, Larsen, Mantle, Martin, Skowron, Stengel	$1,000-$1,200
	Loser	Brooklyn Dodgers	Alston, Campanella, Drysdale, Erskine, Furillo, Gilliam, Hodges, Koufax, Newcombe, Reese, Robinson, Snider	$900
1957	Winner	Milwaukee Braves	Aaron, Adcock, Burdette, Mathews, Schoendienst, Spahn	$1,200
	Loser	New York Yankees	Bauer, Berra, Ford, Howard, Larsen, Kubek, Mantle, Skowron, Stengel, Sturdivant	$1,000
1958	Winner	New York Yankees	Berra, Ford, Howard, Kubek, Larsen, Mantle, Stengel, Turley	$1,000-$1,200
	Loser	Milwaukee Braves	Aaron, Adcock, Burdette, Mathews, Schoendienst, Spahn	$700
1959	Winner	Los Angeles Dodgers	Alston, Drysdale, Gilliam, Hodges, Howard, Koufax, Snider, Wills, Zimmer	$700-$900
	Loser	Chicago White Sox	Aparicio, Cash, Fox, Kluszewski, Lopez, Shaw, Wynn	$500-$750
1960	Winner	Pittsburgh Pirates	Clemente, Friend, Groat, Law, Mazeroski, Stuart, Vernon	$1,200-$1,500
	Loser	New York Yankees	Berra, Ford, Howard, Kubek, Mantle, Maris, Skowron, Stengel	$700
1961	Winner	New York Yankees	Berra, Ford, Howard, Kubek, Mantle, Maris	$1,800-$2,000
	Loser	Cincinnati Reds	Coleman, Freese, Jay, O'Toole, Pinson, Robinson	$600-$1,200
1962	Winner	New York Yankees	Berra, Ford, Howard, Kubek, Mantle, Maris, Terry, Tresh	$750
	Loser	San Francisco Giants	Cepeda, Marichal, Mays, McCormick, McCovey	$500

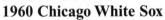

1960 Chicago White Sox

1969 New York Mets

Year	W/L	Team	Key Signatures	NM Price
1963	Winner	Los Angeles Dodgers	Alston, T. Davis, W. Davis, Drysdale, Gilliam, Koufax, Wills	$550
	Loser	New York Yankees	Berra, Ford, Howard, Kubek, Mantle, Maris, Terry, Tresh	$700
1964	Winner	St. Louis Cardinals	Boyer, Brock, Flood, Gibson, Groat, McCarver, White	$500
	Loser	New York Yankees	Berra, Ford, Howard, Kubek, Mantle, Maris, Stottlemyre, Tresh	$500-$700
1965	Winner	Los Angeles Dodgers	Alston, W. Davis, Drysdale, Gilliam, Lefebvre, Koufax, Wills	$400-$500
	Loser	Minnesota Twins	Grant, Kaat, Killebrew, Oliva, Versalles	$350
1966	Winner	Baltimore Orioles	Aparicio, Blair, Blefary, Johnson, McNally, Palmer, Powell, B. Robinson, F. Robinson	$350-$450
	Loser	Los Angeles Dodgers	Alston, T. Davis, W. Davis, Drysdale, Koufax, Sutton, Wills	$350
1967	Winner	St. Louis Cardinals	Brock, Carlton, Cepeda, Flood, Gibson, Maris, McCarver, Schoendienst	$400-$600
	Loser	Boston Red Sox	Conigliaro, Lonborg, Lyle, Petrocelli, Scott, Williams, Yastrzemski	$800
1968	Winner	Detroit Tigers	Cash, Freehan, Kaline, Lolich, McLain	$500
	Loser	St. Louis Cardinals	Brock, Carlton, Cepeda, Flood, Gibson, Maris, McCarver, Schoendienst	$350-$450
1969	Winner	New York Mets	Agee, Hodges, Koosman, Kranepool, Ryan, Seaver, Swoboda	$2,000-$2,500
	Loser	Baltimore Orioles	Blair, Cuellar, McNally, B. Robinson, F. Robinson, Palmer, Powell, Weaver	$300-$500
1970	Winner	Baltimore Orioles	Blair, Cueller, McNally, B. Robinson, F. Robinson, Palmer, Powell, Weaver	$325
	Loser	Cincinnati Reds	Anderson, Bench, Carbo, Concepcion, May, McRae, Perez, Rose	$300-$600
1971	Winner	Pittsburgh Pirates	Blass, Clemente, Mazeroski, Oliver, Sanguillen, Stargell	$550
	Loser	Baltimore Orioles	Cueller, Dobson, McNally, B. Robinson, F. Robinson, Palmer, Powell, Weaver	$300
1972	Winner	Oakland Athletics	Bando, Blue, Campaneris, Fingers, Hunter, Jackson, Williams	$200-$400
	Loser	Cincinnati Reds	Anderson, Bench, Concepcion, Foster, McRae, Morgan, Perez, Rose	$300
1973	Winner	Oakland Athletics	Bando, Blue, Campaneris, Fingers, Hunter, Jackson, Williams	$300-$450
	Loser	New York Mets	Berra, Koosman, Kranepool, Mays, Milner, Seaver, Staub	$300-$400
1974	Winner	Oakland Athletics	Bando, Blue, Campaneris, Fingers, Hunter, Jackson, Williams	$450-$1,000
	Loser	Los Angeles Dodgers	Alston, Buckner, Cey, Garvey, John, Lopes, Russell, Sutton, Wynn	$300
1975	Winner	Cincinnati Reds	Anderson, Bench, Concepcion, Foster, Griffey, Morgan, Perez, Rose	$500
	Loser	Boston Red Sox	Carbo, Cooper, Evans, Fisk, Lee, Lynn, Petrocelli, Rice, Tiant, Wise, Yastrzemski	$350-$500
1976	Winner	Cincinnati Reds	Anderson, Bench, Concepcion, Foster, Griffey, Morgan, Perez, Rose, Zachary	$500
	Loser	New York Yankees	Chambliss, Hunter, Lyle, Martin, Munson, Nettles, Randolph	$300-$800
1977	Winner	New York Yankees	Guidry, Hunter, Jackson, Lyle, Martin, Munson, Nettles, Piniella	$400-$750
	Loser	Los Angeles Dodgers	Baker, Cey, Garvey, John, Lasorda, Lopes, Russell, Smith, Sutton	$300
1978	Winner	New York Yankees	Gossage, Guidry, Hunter, Jackson, Lyle, Martin, Munson, Piniella	$400-$700
	Loser	Los Angeles Dodgers	Baker, Cey, Garvey, John, Lasorda, Lopes, Russell, Smith, Sutton	$250
1979	Winner	Pittsburgh Pirates	Blyleven, Candelaria, Madlock, Parker, Stargell, Tekulve	$300
	Loser	Baltimore Orioles	Flanagan, D. Martinez, Murray, Palmer, Singleton, Weaver	$200
1980	Winner	Philadelphia Phillies	Boone, Bowa, Carlton, Luzinski, Rose, Schmidt, Trillo	$300-$600
	Loser	Kansas City Royals	Brett, Leonard, McRae, Otis, Porter, Quisenberry, White, Wilson	$250-700
1981	Winner	Los Angeles Dodgers	Baker, Cey, Garvey, Guerrero, Lasorda, Lopes, Russell, Sax, Valenzuela	$325
	Loser	New York Yankees	Gossage, Guidry, Jackson, John, Murcer, Nettles, Piniella, Winfield	$400
1982	Winner	St. Louis Cardinals	Andujar, Hernandez, Kaat, McGee, O. Smith, Sutter	$350
	Loser	Milwaukee Brewers	Caldwell, Cooper, Fingers, Molitor, Oglivie, Thomas, Vuckovich, Yount	$350
1983	Winner	Baltimore Orioles	Altobelli, Boddicker, D. Martinez, Murray, Palmer, C. Ripken Jr.	$450
	Loser	Philadelphia Phillies	Carlton, Denny, Morgan, Perez, Rose, Schmidt	$250

1975 Cincinnati Reds

1993 Toronto Blue Jays

1996 New York Yankees

Year	W/L	Team	Key Signatures	NM Price
1984	Winner	Detroit Tigers	Anderson, Gibson, Evans, Hernandez, Johnson, Morris, Parrish, Trammell, Whitaker	$500
	Loser	San Diego Padres	Garvey, Gossage, Gwynn, Nettles	$250
1985	Winner	Kansas City Royals	Brett, Howser, McRae, Saberhagen, Quisenberry, White, Wilson	$400-$900
	Loser	St. Louis Cardinals	Clark, Coleman, McGee, O. Smith, Tudor	$250
1986	Winner	New York Mets	Carter, Dykstra, Gooden, Hernandez, D. Johnson, Mitchell, Strawberry, Wilson	$400-$900
	Loser	Boston Red Sox	Baylor, Boggs, Boyd, Buckner, Clemens, Evans, D. Henderson, Hurst, Rice, Seaver	$300
1987	Winner	Minnesota Twins	Blyleven, Brunansky, Gaetti, Hrbek, Kelly, J. Niekro, Puckett, Reardon, Viola	$400
	Loser	St. Louis Cardinals	Clark, Coleman, McGee, O. Smith, Tudor	$200
1988	Winner	Los Angeles Dodgers	Gibson, Guerrero, Hershiser, Lasorda, Sax, Valenzuela	$250
	Loser	Oakland Athletics	Canseco, Eckersley, LaRussa, McGwire, Steinbach, Stewart,Weiss	$225
1989	Winner	Oakland Athletics	Canseco, Eckersley, R. Henderson, LaRussa, McGwire, Steinbach, Stewart, Weiss	$300
	Loser	San Francisco Giants	Butler, Clark, Mitchell, Williams	$225
1990	Winner	Cincinnati Reds	Davis, Dibble, Larkin, Morris, Myers, O'Neill, Piniella, Rijo, Sabo	$300
	Loser	Oakland Athletics	Canseco, Eckersley, R. Henderson, LaRussa, McGwire, Stewart, Welch	$225
1991	Winner	Minnesota Twins	Aguilera, Davis, Erickson, Hrbek, Kelly, Knoblauch, Morris, Puckett, Tapani	$400
	Loser	Atlanta Braves	Avery, Blauser, Cox, Gant, Glavine, Justice, Pendleton, Smoltz, Wohlers	$250
1992	Winner	Toronto Blue Jays	Alomar, Borders Carter, Cone, Gaston, Key, Morris, Olerud, Stieb, Stottlemyre, Winfield, White	$400
	Loser	Atlanta Braves	Avery, Cox, Gant, Glavine, Justice, Pendleton, Reardon, Sanders, Smoltz	$300
1993	Winner	Toronto Blue Jays	Alomar, Carter, Gaston, Henderson, Hentgen, Key, Molitor, Morris, Olerud, Stottlemyre, Stewart, White	$400
	Loser	Philadelphia Phillies	Daulton, Dykstra, Green, Hollins, Kruk, Schilling, Williams	$250
1994			No World Series	
1995	Winner	Atlanta Braves	Avery, Cox, Glavine, Grissom, C. Jones, Justice, Klesko, Lopez, Maddux, McGriff, Smoltz, Wohlers	$400
	Loser	Cleveland Indians	Alomar, Baerga, Belle, Hershiser, Lofton, D. Martinez, Mesa, Murray, Nagy, Ramirez, Thome	$350
1996	Winner	New York Yankees	Boggs, Cone, Jeter, T. Martinez, Pettitte, Rivera, Torre, Wetteland, Williams	$600
	Loser	Atlanta Braves	Cox, Glavine, C. Jones, Justice, Klesko, Lopez, Maddux, McGriff, Smoltz, Wohlers	$300
1997	Winner	Florida Marlins	Bonilla, Brown, Fernandez, Hernandez, Johnson, Leyland, Nen, Renteria, Sheffield	$500
	Loser	Cleveland Indians	Alomar, Grissom, Hershiser, Ramirez, Thome, Vizquel	$300
1998	Winner	New York Yankees	Brosius, Jeter, Knoblauch, Wells, Williams	$500-$600
	Loser	San Diego Padres	Gwynn, Vaughn	$300
1999	Winner	New York Yankees	Jeter, Hernandez, Leyritz, T. Martinez, Rivera, Williams	$1,300-$1,500
	Loser	Atlanta Braves	Glavine, C. Jones, A. Jones, Maddux	$200
2000	Winner	New York Yankees	Brosius, Jeter, Justice, T. Martinez, Rivera, Williams	$2,100-$2,600
	Loser	New York Mets	Hampton, Payton, Piazza, Ventura	$300

AUTOGRAPHED TEAM BASEBALLS

Key signatures follow each team name

1920 Boston (AL) - Barrow, Hendryx, Hooper, Pennock,
Hoyt . . . .$800-$1,250

1920 Boston (NL) - Maranville, Powell, Mann . . . .$600-$900

1920 Brooklyn - Robinson, Konetchy, Myers, Wheat,
Grimes, Marquard . . . .$1,200-$1,750

1920 Chicago (AL) - Collins, Risberg, Weaver, Leibold,
Felsch, Jackson, Schalk, Faber, Williams, Kerr, Cicotte . .$ uncertain

1920 Chicago (NL) - Hollocher, Flack, Robertson, Alexander
. . . .$900-$1,400

1920 Cincinnati - Daubert, Roush . . . .$450-$700

1920 Cleveland - Wambsganss, Chapman, Gardner, Smith,
Speaker, Jamieson, O'Neill, Sewell, Coveleski . . . . .$1,300-$2,000

1920 Detroit - Jennings, Heilmann, Cobb, Veach . . . . . .$1,700-$2,500

1920 New York (AL) - Huggins, Pratt, Ruth, Mays,
Shawkey . . . .$2,200-$3,400

1920 New York (NL) - McGraw, Kelly, Bancroft, Frisch,
Youngs, Toney, Nehf, Barnes . . . .$1,700-$2,750

1920 Philadelphia (AL) - Mack . . . .$600-$850

1920 Philadelphia (NL) - Stengel, Williams, Meusel,
Wheat, Rixey . . . .$800-$1,300

1920 Pittsburgh - Carey, McKechnie, Traynor, Cooper . . .$675-$1,000

1920 St. Louis (AL) - Sisler, Tobin, Jacobson, Williams,
Shocker . . . .$425-$675

1920 St. Louis (NL) - Rickey, Fournier, Hornsby, Stock,
Doak, Haines . . . .$1,150-$1,750

1920 Washington - Griffith, Judge, Harris, Rice, Milan,
Johnson . . . .$1,300-$2,000

1921 Boston (AL) - Duffy, McInnis, Pratt, Leibold,
Menosky, Jones, Pennock . . . .$550-$875

1921 Boston (NL) - Barbare, Boeckel, Southworth, Powell,
Cruise, Oeschger . . . .$400-$600

1921 Brooklyn - Robinson, Schmandt, Johnston, Griffith,
Wheat, Grimes . . . .$800-$1,200

1921 Chicago (AL) - Sheely, Collins, Hooper, Strunk, Schalk,
Faber . . . .$725-$1,100

1921 Chicago (NL) - Evers, Grimes, Flack, Maisel, Barber,
Alexander . . . .$1,200-$1,800

1921 Cincinnati - Daubert, Groh, Bressler, Roush, Duncan,
Rixey, Marquard . . . .$550-$825

1921 Cleveland - Speaker, Sewell, Gardner, Jamieson,
O'Neill, Coveleski . . . .$725-$1,200

1921 Detroit - Cobb, Blue, Heilmann, Veach, Bassler,
Jones . . . .$800-$1,200

1921 New York (AL) - Huggins, Ward, Baker, Meusel,
Ruth, Mays, Hoyt . . . .$3,000-$6,000

1921 New York (NL) - McGraw, Kelly, Bancroft, Frisch,
Youngs, Meusel, Snyder, Stengel, Nehf . . . .$2,000-$3,000

1921 Philadelphia (AL) - Mack, Witt, T. Walker . . . .$500-$775

1921 Philadelphia (NL) - Konetchy, Williams, Meusel,
Bruggy, Stengel . . . .$400-$600

1921 Pittsburgh - Cuthsaw, Maranville, Carey, Bigbee,
Traynor, Cuyler, Cooper . . . .$800-$1,200

1921 St. Louis (AL) - Sisler, Tobin, Jacobson, Williams,
Severeid, Shocker . . . .$425-$625

1921 St. Louis (NL) - Rickey, Fournier, Hornsby, Stock,
Smith, Mann, McHenry, Clemons, Dillhoefer, Haines,
Doak . . . .$1,075-$1,600

1921 Washington - Judge, Harris, Shanks, Rice, Gharrity,
Goslin, Johnson . . . .$1,000-$1,500

1922 Boston (AL) - Duffy, Burns, Pratt, Harris, Pennock . . .$500-$750

1922 Boston (NL) - Marquard . . . .$400-$575

1922 Brooklyn - Johnston, Robinson, Myers, Wheat,
DeBerry, Ruether, Vance, Grimes, T. Griffith . . . . . .$1,000-$1,500

1922 Chicago (AL) - Sheely, Collins, Hooper, Mostil,
Schalk, Evers, Faber . . . .$1,200-$1,750

1922 Chicago (NL) - Grimes, Hollocher, Friberg, Miller,
O'Farrell, Hartnett, Alexander . . . .$800-$1,200

1922 Cincinnati - Daubert, Pinelli, Harper, Duncan,
Hargrave, Roush, Rixey . . . .$450-$700

1922 Cleveland - Speaker, McGinnis, Sewell, Uhle,
Jamieson, O'Neill, Coveleski . . . .$675-$1,000

1922 Detroit - Cobb, Blue, Rigney, Heilmann, Veach,
Bassler . . . .$800-$1,200

1922 New York (AL) - Pipp, Meusel, Ruth, Schang, Baker,
Bush, Shawkey, Hoyt, Huggins . . . .$2,000-$3,000

1922 New York (NL) - McGraw, Kelly, Frisch, Bancroft,
Youngs, Stengel, Meusel, Snyder, Jackson, Nehf . . . .$2,000-$3,000

1922 Philadelphia (AL) - Mack, Hauser, Galloway,
Rommel, Miller . . . .$500-$750

1922 Philadelphia (NL) - Walker, Williams, Lee, Henline . .$325-$500

1922 Pittsburgh - McKechnie, Tierney, Carey, Maranville,
Traynor, Russell, Bigbee, Gooch, Cuyler, Cooper . . .$1,100-$1,600

1922 St. Louis (AL) - Sisler, McManus, Tobin, Jacobson,
Williams, Severeid, Shocker . . . .$400-$650

1922 St. Louis (NL) - Rickey, Hornsby, Toporcer, Stock,
Smith, Schultz, Bottomley, Haines . . . .$1,350-$2,000

1922 Washington - Harris, Rice, Goslin, Johnson . . . . . .$900-$1,400

1923 Boston (AL) - Burns, Flagstead, Harris, Ehmke,
Chance . . . .$900-$1,400

1923 Boston (NL) - McInnis, Southworth, Powell,
Marquard . . . .$375-$550

1923 Brooklyn - Robinson, Fournier, Johnston, Wheat,
Grimes, Vance . . . .$1,100-$1,600

1923 Chicago (AL) - Collins, Hooper, Falk, Schalk, Faber,
Lyons . . . .$750-$1,200

1923 Chicago (NL) - Grimes, Friberg, Statz, Miller,
O'Farrell, Hartnett, Alexander, Aldridge . . . .$800-$1,000

1923 Cincinnati - Roush, Duncan, Hargrave, Luque,
Rixey . . . .$400-$600

1923 Cleveland - Speaker, Sewell, Summa, Jamieson,
Uhle, Coveleski . . . .$800-$1,200

1923 Detroit - Cobb, Rigney, Heilmann, Manush, Daus . .$900-$1,500

1923 New York (AL) - Huggins, Pipp, Ruth, Witt, Meusel,
Gehrig, Pennock, Hoyt . . . .$2500-$3,750

1931 Philadelphia Athletics

1926 St. Louis Cardinals

1941 Cleveland Indians

1923 New York (NL) - McGraw, Kelly, Frisch, Bancroft, Youngs, Jackson, Stengel, Terry, Wilson, Ryan . . . . .$2,100-$3,150

1923 Philadelphia (AL) - Mack, Hauser . . . .$475-$700

1923 Philadelphia (NL) - Holke, Tierney, Mokan, Henline . .$300-$450

1923 Pittsburgh - McKechnie, Grimm, Maranville, Traynor, Barnhart, Carey, Cuyler, Morrison . . . .$1,000-$1,500

1923 St. Louis (AL) - McManus, Tobin, Jacobson, Williams, Severeid, Shocker . . . .$350-$525

1923 St. Louis (NL) - Rickey, Bottomley, Hornsby, Myers, Smith, Haines . . . .$1,200-$1,800

1923 Washington - Judge, Harris, Rice, Leibold, Goslin, Ruel, Johnson . . . .$900-$1,400

1924 Boston (AL) - Harris, Boone, Flagstead, Ruffing . . . .$350-$525

1924 Boston (NL) - Stengel, Bancroft, Marquard . . . .$700-$900

1924 Brooklyn - Robinson, Fournier, High, Brown, Wheat, Grimes, Vance . . . .$1,000-$1,500

1924 Chicago (AL) - Evers, Sheely, Collins, Hooper, Mostil, Falk, Schalk, Thurston, Lyons, Faber . . . . . .$1,300-$1,800

1924 Chicago (NL) - Grantham, Heathcote, Hartnett, Alexander . . . .$725-$1,200

1924 Cincinnati - Critz, Pinelli, Walker, Roush, Mays, Rixey . . . .$400-$600

1924 Cleveland - Speaker, Burns, Sewell, Jamieson, Myatt, Shaute, Coveleski . . . .$800-$1,000

1924 Detroit - Cobb, Blue, Pratt, Heilmann, Manush, Bassler, Gehringer . . . .$1,000-$1,550

1924 New York (AL) - Huggins, Dugan, Ruth, Meusel, Combs, Gehrig, Pennock, Hoyt . . . .$3,000-$4,500

1924 New York (NL) - McGraw, Kelly, Frisch, Jackson, Youngs, Wilson, Snyder, Terry, Lindstrom, Bentley . .$1,900-$2,900

1924 Philadelphia (AL) - Miller, Simmons, Lamar . . . . . .$600-$1,000

1924 Philadelphia (NL) - Holke, Wrightstone, Williams . . . .$300-$450

1924 Pittsburgh - McKechnie, Maranville, Traynor, Carey, Cuyler, Cooper . . . .$800-$1,225

1924 St. Louis (AL) - Sisler, McManus, Robertson, Jacobson, Williams, Severeid . . . .$400-$600

1924 St. Louis (NL) - Rickey, Bottomley, Hornsby, Blades, Hafey . . . .$1,300-$1,800

1924 Washington - Harris, Judge, Rice, Goslin, Johnson . .$1,000-$1,500

1925 Boston (AL) - Prothro, Boone, Carlyle, Ruffing . . . .$300-$500

1925 Boston (NL) - Bancroft, Burrus, Welsh, Felix, Stengel, Marquard . . . .$600-$900

1925 Brooklyn - Robinson, Fournier, Stock, Cox, Brown, Wheat, Taylor, Vance, Grimes . . . .$900-$1,500

1925 Chicago (AL) - Collins, Sheely, Hooper, Falk, Schalk, Lyons, Faber, Bender . . . .$900-$1,500

1925 Chicago (NL) - Maranville, Grimm, Freigau, Jahn, Hartnett, Alexander . . . .$800-$1,200

1925 Cincinnati- Walker, Roush, Hargrave, Rixey . . . .$350-$575

1925 Cleveland - Speaker, Burns, Sewell, McNulty, Buckeye . . . .$550-$925

1925 Detroit - Cobb, Blue, Heilmann, Wingo, Manush, Gehringer . . . .$900-$1,300

1925 New York (AL) - Huggins, Gehrig, Ruth, Hoyt, Pennock, Durocher . . . .$2,750-$4,175

1925 New York (NL) - McGraw, Terry, Kelly, Jackson, Lindstrom, Youngs, Meusel, Frisch, Wilson . . . .$1,800-$2,700

1925 Philadelphia (AL) - Mack, Hale, Miller, Simmons, Lamar, Cochrane, Foxx, Rommel, Grove . . . .$1,400-$2,100

1925 Philadelphia (NL) - Hawks, Williams, Harper . . . .$300-$475

1925 Pittsburgh - McKechnie, Grantham, Wright, Traynor, Cuyler, Carey, Barnhart, Smith, Meadows . . . .$800-$1,200

1925 St. Louis (AL) - Sisler, Rice, Jacobson, Williams . . . .$375-$600

1925 St. Louis (NL) - Rickey, Bottomley, Hornsby, Hafey, Mueller, Blades, Haines . . . .$1,300-$2,000

1925 Washington - Harris, Judge, Rice, Goslin, Johnson, Coveleski . . . .$1,000-$1,500

1926 Boston (AL) - Jacobson, Ruffing . . . .$300-$475

1926 Boston (NL) - Bancroft, J. Smith, Brown . . . .$325-$525

1926 Brooklyn - Robinson, Herman, Wheat, Maranville, Carey, Grimes, Vance . . . .$1,200-$1,800

1926 Chicago - McCarthy, Adams, Wilson, Stephenson, Hartnett, Alexander . . . .$900-$1,400

1926 Chicago (AL) - Collins, Barrett, Mostil, Falk, Schalk, Lyons,Faber . . . .$600-$900

1926 Cincinnati- Walker, Roush, Donahue, Rixey . . . .$325-$575

1926 Cleveland - Speaker, Burns, J. Sewell, Summa, Uhle . .$600-$900

1926 Detroit - Cobb, Gehringer, Heilmann, Manush, Fothergill . . . .$800-$1,200

1926 New York (AL) - Huggins, Gehrig, Lazzeri, Ruth, Combs, Meusel, Pennock, Hoyt . . . .$3,500-$5,000

1926 New York (NL) - McGraw, Kelly, Frisch, Jackson, Lindstrom, Youngs, Terry, Ott . . . .$1,800-$2,750

1926 Philadelphia (AL) - Mack, French, Simmons, Cochrane, Foxx . . . .$1,300-$2,100

1926 Philadelphia (NL) - Williams, Leach, Mokan, Wilson . . . .$250-$400

1926 Pittsburgh- McKechnie, Grantham, Wright, Traynor, Waner, Carey, Cuyler, Smith, Cronin, Kremer, Meadows . . . .$800-$1,200

1926 St. Louis (AL) - Sisler, Miller, Rice, Shang . . . .$350-$500

1926 St. Louis (NL) - Hornsby, Bottomley, Bell, Southworth, Douthit, Blades, Hafey, Rhem, Haines, Alexander . . . .$1,600-$2,300

1926 Washington - Harris, Myer, Rice, McNeely, Goslin, Johnson, Coveleski . . . .$800-$1,200

1927 Boston (AL) - Tobin, Ruffing . . . .$300-$450

1927 Boston (NL) - Bancroft, High, Richbourg, Brown . . . .$300-$450

1927 Brooklyn - Robinson, Carey, Vance . . . .$800-$1,200

1927 Chicago (AL) - Schalk, Clancy, Metzler, Falk, Lyons, Faber . . . .$350-$550

1927 Chicago (NL) - McCarthy, Grimm, Webb, Wilson, Stephenson, Hartnett, Root . . . .$500-$800

1927 Cincinnati - Hargrave, Kelly, Rixey . . . .$300-$450

1927 Cleveland - Burns, Fonseca, J. Sewell, Jamieson, Miller . . . .$300-$450

1927 Detroit - Gehringer, Heilmann, Manush, Fothergill, Collins . . . .$375-$625

1927 New York (AL) - Gehrig, Lazzeri, Ruth, Combs, Meusel, Hoyt, Moore, Pennock . . . .$8,000-$16,000

1927 New York (NL) - McGraw, Terry, Hornsby, Jackson, Lindstrom, Harper, Roush, Grimes . . . .$1,800-$2,700

1927 Philadelphia (AL) - Mack, Dykes, Hale, Cobb, Simmons, French, Cochrane, Collins, Wheat, Foxx, Grove . . . .$2,200-$3,300

1927 Philadelphia (NL) - Wrightstone, Thompson, Leach . .$275-$400

1927 Pittsburgh - Harris, Grantham, Traynor, P. Waner, L. Waner, Barnhart, Cuyler, Groh, Cronin, Kremer . . . .$700-$1,000

1927 St. Louis (AL) - Sisler, Miller, Williams, Schang . . . .$400-$650

1927 St. Louis (NL) - Bottomley, Frisch, Maranville, Haines, Alexander . . . .$1,200-$1,750

1927 Washington - Harris, Judge, Rice, Speaker, Goslin, Ruel, Lisenbee, Hadley, Johnson, Coveleski . . . .$1,200-$1,800

1928 Boston (AL) - Myer, Williams, Ruffing . . . .$300-$475

1928 Boston (NL) - Hornsby, Sisler, Richbourg . . . .$800-$1,200

1928 Brooklyn - Robinson, Bissonette, Bancroft, Hendrick, Herman, Carey, Lopez, Vance . . . .$1,000-$1,400

1928 Chicago (AL) - Schalk, Kamm, Metzler, Lyons, Walsh, Faber . . . .$500-$775

1928 Chicago (NL) - McCarthy, Cuyler, Wilson, Stephenson, Hartnett . . . .$450-$725

1928 Cincinnati- Kelly, Allen, Rixey . . . .$300-$425

1928 Cleveland- Fonseca, Sewell, Hodapp, Jamieson . . . . . .$300-$425

1928 Detroit - Gehringer, Heilmann, Rice . . . .$325-$500

1928 New York (AL) - Huggins, Gehrig, Lazzeri, Koenig, Ruth, Combs, Dickey, Pipgras, Hoyt, Pennock, Coveleski . . . .$3,500-$5,000

1928 New York (NL) - McGraw, Terry, Jackson, Lindstrom, Ott, Welsh, O'Doul, Hogan, Roush, Benton, Fitzsimmons, Hubbell . . . .$1,300-$1,750

1928 Philadelphia (AL) - Mack, Bishop, Hale, Cobb, Miller, Simmons, Cochrane, Foxx, Speaker, Collins, Grove, Quinn . . . .$2,000-$3,000

1928 Philadelphia (NL) - Whitney, Klein, Leach . . . .$300-$500

1928 Pittsburgh - Grantham, Wright, Traynor, P. Waner, L. Waner, Brickell, Grimes . . . .$500-$750

1928 St. Louis (AL) - Manush, Crowder . . . .$300-$450

1928 St. Louis (NL) - McKechnie, Bottomley, Frisch, Maranville, Hafey, Haines, Alexander . . . .$1,200-$1,800

1928 Washington - Harris, Judge, Reeves, Rice, Barnes, Goslin, Cronin, Sisler, Jones . . . .$500-$750

1929 Boston (AL) - Rothrock, Ruffing . . . .$250-$350

1929 Boston (NL) - Sisler, Maranville, Richbourg, Clark, Evers . . . .$700-$1,200

1929 Brooklyn - Robinson, Bancroft, Gilbert, Herman, Frederick, Bressler, Carey, Vance . . . .$850-$1,300

1929 Chicago (AL) - Shires, Reynolds, Lyons, Faber . . . . .$275-$450

1929 Chicago (NL) - McCarthy, Hornsby, Cuyler, Wilson, Hartnett, Malone . . . .$800-$1,200

1929 Cincinnati - Kelly, Dressen, Swanson, Gooch, Rixey . .$275-$425

1929 Cleveland - Fonseca, Hodapp, Sewell, Falk, Averill, Sewell, Ferrell . . . .$300-$500

1929 Detroit - Harris, Alexander, Gehringer, Heilmann, Rice, Johnson . . . .$300-$500

1929 New York (AL) - Huggins, Gehrig, Lazzeri, Ruth, Combs, Dickey, Wells, Hoyt, Pennock . . . .$2,800-$4,250

1929 New York (NL) - McGraw, Terry, Jackson, Lindstrom, Ott, Roush, Hubbell . . . .$1,000-$1,600

1929 Philadelphia (AL) - Mack, Foxx, Miller, Haas, Simmons, Cochrane, Cronin, Collins, Earnshaw, Grove . . . .$800-$1,200

1929 Philadelphia (NL) - Hurst, Thompson, Thevenow, Whitney, Klein, Sothern, O'Doul . . . .$300-$450

1929 Pittsburgh - Grantham, Bartell, Traynor, P. Waner, L. Waner, Comorosky, Grimes . . . .$500-$800

1929 St. Louis (AL) - Kress, Schulte, Manush, Ferrell . . . . .$325-$550

1929 St. Louis (NL) - McKechnie, Bottomley, Frisch, Orsatti, Douthit, Hafey, Wilson, Johnson, Haines, Alexander . . . .$900-$1,400

1929 Washington - Johnson, Judge, Myer, Cronin, Rice, Goslin . . . .$1,300-$1,850

1930 Boston (AL) - Webb, Ruffing . . . .$225-$350

1930 Boston (NL) - McKechnie, Sisler, Maranville, Grimes . . . .$450-$750

1930 Brooklyn - Robinson, Bissonette, Wright, Herman, Frederick, Lopez, Vance . . . .$650-$1,200

1930 Chicago (AL) - Watwood, Jolley, Reynolds, Lyons, Appling, Faber . . . .$250-$400

1930 Chicago (NL) - McCarthy, Grimm, Cuyler, Wilson, Hartnett, Hornsby, Kelly . . . .$900-$1,450

1941 Brooklyn Dodgers

1943 St. Louis Browns

1947 Chicago Cubs

1930 Cincinnati - Durocher, Cuccinello, Heilmann, Walker, Kelly, Rixey . . . .$900-$1,450

1930 Cleveland - Morgan, Hodapp, J. Sewell, Porter, Averill, Jamieson, L. Sewell, Ferrell . . . .$300-$475

1930 Detroit - Harris, Alexander, Gehringer, McManus, Stone, Hoyt, Greenberg . . . .$300-$475

1930 New York (AL) - Gehrig, Lazzeri, Chapman, Ruth, Hoyt, Combs, Ruffing, Gomez, Pennock, Dickey . . . .$2,500-$3,750

1930 New York (NL) - McGraw, Terry, Jackson, Lindstrom, Ott, Leach, Hogan, Bancroft, Roush, Hubbell . . . . . .$1,200-$1,800

1930 Philadelphia (AL) - Mack, Foxx, Dykes, Miller, Simmons, Cochrane, Collins, Grove . . . .$700-$1,000

1930 Philadelphia (NL) - Hurst, Whitney, O'Doul, Davis, Alexander, Klein . . . .$500-$700

1930 Pittsburgh - Grantham, Bartell, Traynor, P. Waner, L. Waner, Comorosky . . . .$450-$700

1930 St. Louis (AL) - Kress, Goslin, Ferrell, Manush . . . . $375-$575

1930 St. Louis (NL) - Street, Bottomley, Frisch, Gelbert, Adams, Watkins, Douthit, Hafey, Wilson, Grimes, Haines, Dean . . . .$700-$1,000

1930 Washington - Johnson, Judge, Myer, Cronin, Rice, Manush, Goslin, Marberry . . . .$1,500-$2,250

1931 Boston (AL) - Webb . . . .$200-$300

1931 Boston (NL) - Maranville, Schulmerich, Berger, McKechnie . . . .$300-$500

1931 Brooklyn - O'Doul, Lopez, Lombardi, Vance, Robinson . . . .$800-$1,200

1931 Chicago (AL) - Blue, Appling, Faber, Lyons . . . .$250-$375

1931 Chicago (NL) - Grimm, Hornsby, English, Cuyler, Wilson, Taylor, Hartnett, Herman . . . .$750-$1,200

1931 Cincinnati - Hendrick, Cuccinello, Stripp, Roush, Heilmann, Rixey . . . .$325-$500

1931 Cleveland - Morgan, Porter, Averill . . . .$250-$375

1931 Detroit - Alexander, Gehringer, Rogell, Stone, Hoyt, Harris . . . .$300-$500

1931 New York (AL) - Gehrig, Lazzeri, Sewell, Ruth, Combs, Chapman, Dickey, Ruffing, Gomez, Pennock, McCarthy . . . .$3,000-$4,500

1931 New York (NL) - Terry, Jackson, Lindstrom, Ott, Leach, Hogan, Walker, Hubbell, McGraw . . . .$1,000-$1,500

1931 Philadelphia (AL) - Mack, Foxx, Simmons, Cochrane, Grove, Earnshaw, Hoyt . . . .$700-$1,000

1931 Philadelphia (NL) - Hurst, Mallon, Arlett, Klein, Davis . . . .$300-$450

1931 Pittsburgh - Grantham, Traynor, Waner, Waner . . . . .$425-$700

1931 St. Louis (AL) - Melillo, Kress, Schulte, Goslin, Ferrell . . . .$300-$450

1931 St. Louis (NL) - Bottomley, Frisch, Hafey, Hallahan, Grimes, Haines . . . .$550-$900

1931 Washington - Cronin, Rice, West, Manush, Crowder, Marberry, Johnson . . . .$1,200-$1,800

1932 Boston (AL) - Alexander, Jolley, Morris . . . .$225-$350

1932 Boston (NL) - Maranville, Berger, Worthington, McKechnie . . . .$300-$450

1932 Brooklyn - Kelly, Wright, Stripp, Wilson, Taylor, O'Doul, Lopez, Clark, Vance, Hoyt, Carey . . . .$600-$950

1932 Chicago (AL) - Appling, Lyons, Faber . . . .$325-$500

1932 Chicago (NL) - Grimm, Herman, Cuyler, Moore, Stephenson, Hartnett, Hornsby, Warneke, Grimes . . . .$700-$1,000

1932 Cincinnati - Hendrick, Durocher, Herman, Lombardi, Hafey, Heilmann, Frey . . . .$450-$750

1932 Cleveland - Cissell, Porter, Averill, Vosmik . . . .$250-$375

1932 Detroit - Gehringer, Walker, Harris . . . .$300-$500

1932 New York (AL) - Gehrig, Lazzeri, Sewell, Ruth, Combs, Dickey, Ruffing, Gomez, Allen, Pennock, McCarthy . . . .$1,750-$4,000

1932 New York (NL) - Terry, Ott, Lindstrom, McGraw, Hogan, Jackson, Jo-Jo Moore, Hoyt, Hubbell . . . .$900-$1,325

1932 Philadelphia (AL) - Cramer, Haas, Simmons, Cochrane, Grove, Mack . . . .$500-$750

1932 Philadelphia (NL) - Hurst, Bartell, Klein, Davis, Lee, Davis . . . .$300-$425

1932 Pittsburgh - Vaughn, Traynor, Waner, Waner . . . .$525-$750

1932 St. Louis (AL) - Burns, Scharien, Goslin, Ferrell . . . .$300-$450

1932 St. Louis (NL) - Watkins, Martin, Orsatti, Frisch, Bottomley, Medwick, Dean, Haines . . . .$500-$700

1932 Washington - Cronin, Reynolds, Manush, Rice, Crowder, Johnson . . . .$1,200-$1,800

1933 Boston (AL) - Hodapp, Johnson, Ferrell . . . .$250-$375

1933 Boston (NL) - Maranville, Moore, Cantwell, McKechnie ....$300-$450

1933 Brooklyn - Wright, Frederick, Wilson, Lopez, Mungo, Carey ....$700-$1,000

1933 Chicago (AL) - Appling, Swanson, Simmons, Lyons, Faber ....$375-$575

1933 Chicago (NL) - Grimm, Stephenson, Hartnett, Cuyler, Bush, Grimes, Billy Herman ....$400-$600

1933 Cincinnati - Bottomley, Hafey, Lombardi, Durocher, Rixey ....$400-$600

1933 Cleveland - Averill, Johnson ....$800-$1,200

1933 Detroit - Greenberg, Gehringer, Harris ....$375-$600

1933 New York (AL) - Gehrig, Lazzeri, Sewell, Ruth, Combs, Chapman, Dickey, Gomez, Allen, Ruffing, Pennock, McCarthy ....$2,800-$4,200

1933 New York (NL) - Terry, Ott, Jackson, Hubbell .....$750-$1,000

1933 Philadelphia (AL) - Foxx, Higgins, Cochrane, Grove, Mack ....$400-$600

1933 Philadelphia (NL) - Klein, Fullis, Schulmerich, Davis ..$300-$450

1933 Pittsburgh - Piet, Vaughan, Traynor, Waner, Lindstrom, Waner, Hoyt ....$575-$900

1933 St. Louis (AL) - West, Ferrell, Hornsby ....$450-$675

1933 St. Louis (NL) - Collins, Frisch, Durocher, Martin, Medwick, Hornsby, Haines, Dean, Vance, Grimes ....$900-$1,500

1933 Washington - Kuhel, Myer, Cronin, Goslin, Manush, Rice, Crowder, Whitehill ....$475-$725

1934 Boston (AL) - Harris, Reynolds, Johnson, R. Ferrell, W. Ferrell, Grove, Pennock ....$375-$525

1934 Boston (NL) - McKechnie, Jordan, Maranville, Frankhouse ....$325-$450

1934 Brooklyn - Stengel, Leslie, Stripp, Boyle, Koenecke, Lopez, Mungo ....$250-$500

1934 Chicago (AL) - Appling, Simmons, Conlan ....$400-$575

1934 Chicago (NL) - Grimm, Billy Herman, Hack, Cuyler, Klein, Hartnett ....$325-$600

1934 Cincinnati - Bottomley, Hafey, Lombardi ....$300-$525

1934 Cleveland - Johnson, Trosky, Hale, Knickerbocker, Averill, Vosmik, Harder ....$775-$1,250

1934 Detroit - Cochrane, Greenberg, Gehringer, Fox, Goslin, Rowe, Bridges ....$525-$800

1934 New York (AL) - McCarthy, Gomez, Lazzeri, Dickey, Gehrig, Ruffing, Grimes, Ruth, Combs ....$2,600-$3,900

1934 New York (NL) - Terry, Jackson, Ott, Hubbell ......$400-$575

1934 Philadelphia (AL) - Mack, Foxx, Higgins, Cramer, Johnson ....$300-$500

1934 Philadelphia (NL) - Chiozza, Bartell, J. Moore, Allen, Todd ....$200-$300

1934 Pittsburgh - Traynor, Vaughan, P. Waner, L. Waner, Lindstrom, Hoyt, Grimes ....$550-$875

1934 St. Louis (AL) - Hornsby, West, Hemsley ....$400-$675

1934 St. Louis (NL) - Frisch, Collins, Durocher, Martin, Orsatti, Medwick, Davis, Dean, Haines, Grimes, Vance ..$575-$900

1934 Washington - Cronin, Manush ....$275-$450

1935 Boston (AL) - Cronin, Cooke, R. Johnson, R. Ferrell, W. Ferrell, Grove ....$300-$500

1935 Boston (NL) - McKechnie, Lee, Ruth, Maranville ..$1,000-$1,500

1935 Brooklyn - Stengel, Leslie, Stripp, Lopez ....$300-$475

1935 Chicago (AL) - Appling, Simmons, Conlan, Lyons, Stratton ....$375-$575

1935 Chicago (NL) - Grimm, Herman, Lee, Klein, Demaree, Galan, Hartnett, Cuyler, Lindstrom, Hack ....$500-$750

1935 Cincinnati - Bottomley, Herman, Lombardi, Cuyler, Hafey, Derringer ....$350-$575

1935 Cleveland - Johnson, Averill ....$700-$1,200

1935 Detroit - Cochrane, Greenberg, Gehringer, Goslin ....$500-$750

1935 New York (AL) - McCarthy, Gehrig, Lazzeri, Dickey, Combs, Ruffing, Gomez ....$1,300-$2,000

1935 New York (NL) - Terry, Jackson, Ott, Leiber, Hubbell ....$475-$800

1935 Philadelphia (AL) - Mack, Foxx, Moses, Cramer ....$300-$450

1935 Philadelphia (NL) - Moore, Allen ....$500-$1,000

1935 Pittsburgh - Traynor, Vaughan, P. Waner, L. Waner, Hoyt ....$500-$700

1935 St. Louis (AL) - Hornsby, West, Solters, Andrews ....$450-$675

1935 St. Louis (NL) - Frisch, Collins, Durocher, Martin, Medwick, Haines, P. Dean, D. Dean ....$350-$575

1935 Washington - Harris, Myer, Travis, Powell, Manush, Bolton ....$250-$375

1936 Boston (AL) - Cronin, Foxx, R. Ferrell, Hanush, Grove ....$400-$600

1936 Boston (NL) - McKechnie, Jordan, Cuccinello, Lopez ....$250-$350

1936 Brooklyn - Stengel, Hassett, Stripp, Bordagaray, Lindstrom ....$275-$425

1936 Chicago (AL) - Appling, Lyons, Stratton ....$250-$400

1936 Chicago (NL) - Grimm, Herman, Demaree, Hartnett, Klein, French ....$300-$450

1936 Cincinnati - Scarsella, Cuyler, Lombardi, Hafey ....$275-$450

1936 Cleveland - Trosky, Hale, Weatherly, Averill, Sullivan, Allen ....$200-$325

1936 Detroit - Cochrane, Gehringer, Simmons, Goslin, Greenberg ....$400-$575

1936 New York (AL) - McCarthy, Gehrig, Lazzeri, DiMaggio, Dickey, Ruffing, Gomez ....$1,150-$1,750

1936 New York (NL) - Terry, Jackson, Ott, Moore, Mancuso, Hubbell ....$450-$700

1936 Philadelphia (AL) - Mack, Finney, Moses ....$250-$375

1936 Philadelphia (NL) - Camilli, Klein, Moore ....$200-$300

1936 Pittsburgh - Traynor, Suhr, Vaughan, P. Waner, L. Waner, Hoyt ....$425-$700

1936 St. Louis (AL) - Hornsby, Bottomley, Clift, Bell .....$450-$725

1936 St. Louis (NL) - Frisch, Mize, Durocher, Martin, Alston, Dean, Haines ....$425-$675

1936 Washington - Harris, Travis, Chapman, Stone ......$200-$350

1937 Boston (AL) - Foxx, Cronin, Higgins, Chapman, Cramer, Doerr, Ferrell, Grove ....$450-$550

1937 Boston (NL) - Lopez, McKechnie ....$200-$350

1937 Brooklyn - Hassett, Manush, Phelps, Hoyt, Grimes ..$350-$500

1937 Chicago (AL) - Appling, Stratton, Lyons ....$250-$425

1946 New York Giants

1946 New York Yankees

1943 Boston Red Sox

1937 Chicago (NL) - Herman, Demaree, Hartnett, Carleton, Grimm ....$275-$400

1937 Cincinnati - Wallace, Hafey, Cuyler, Lombardi ......$350-$500

1937 Cleveland - Campbell, Sotters, Pytlak, Feller, Averill ..$225-$375

1937 Detroit - Greenberg, Gehringer, Goslin, Cochrane ....$400-$700

1937 New York (AL) - Gehrig, Lazzeri, DiMaggio, Dickey, Gomez, Ruffing, McCarthy ....$1,450-$2,500

1937 New York (NL) - Bartell, Ott, Ripple, Moore, Hubbell, Melton, Terry ....$400-$600

1937 Philadelphia (AL) - Moses, Johnson, Mack ....$225-$375

1937 Philadelphia (NL) - Camilli, Whitney, Klein ....$200-$300

1937 Pittsburgh - Vaughan, Waner, Waner, Todd, Traynor, Hoyt ....$425-$650

1937 St. Louis (AL) - Clift, Bell, West, Vosmik, Hornsby, Bottomley ....$425-$650

1937 St. Louis (NL) - Mize, Durocher, Padgett, Medwick, Martin, Frisch, Dean, Haines ....$375-$600

1937 Washington (AL) - Travis, Lewis, Stone, Almada, Simmons, R. Ferrell, Harris ....$300-$425

1938 Boston (AL) - Foxx, Doerr, Cronin, Higgins, Chapman, Cramer, Vosmik, Grove ....$550-$900

1938 Boston (NL) - Stengel, Lopez, MacFayden ....$350-$575

1938 Brooklyn - Grimes, Durocher, Phelps, Cuyler, Manush, Hoyt ....$2,000-$2,750

1938 Chicago (AL) - Hayes, Appling, Steinbacher, Walker, Stratton ....$250-$450

1938 Chicago (NL) - Herman, Hack, Reynolds, Hartnett, Garbark, Lee, Grimm, Dean, Lazzeri ....$800-$1000

1938 Cincinnati - McKechnie, McCormick, Berger, Lombardi, Derringer, Vander Meer ....$250-$400

1938 Cleveland - Trosky, Averill, Heath, Pytlak, Boudreau, Feller ....$250-$400

1938 Detroit - Cochrane, Greenberg, Gehringer, Walker, Bridges ....$400-$700

1938 New York (AL) - McCarthy, Gehrig, DiMaggio, Dickey, Ruffing, Gomez ....$900-$1,200

1938 New York (NL) - Terry, Ott, Moore, Danning, Hubbell ....$350-$550

1938 Philadelphia (AL) - Mack, Moses, Johnson ....$400-$600

1938 Philadelphia (NL) - Weintraub ....$250-$325

1938 Pittsburgh - Traynor, Vaughan, Waner, Waner, Rizzo, Manush, Brown ....$700-$1,000

1938 St. Louis (AL) - McQuinn, Kress, Almada ....$200-$300

1938 St. Louis (NL) - Frisch, Mize, Slaughter, Medwick, Martin ....$400-$650

1938 Washington - Harris, Myer, Travis, Case, Simmons, Ferrell, Goslin, Ferrell ....$300-$475

1939 Boston (AL) - Cronin, Foxx, Doerr, Williams, Cramer, Grove ....$450-$650

1939 Boston (NL) - Stengel, Hassett, Cuccinello, Lopez, Simmons ....$300-$450

1939 Brooklyn - Durocher, Lazzeri ....$250-$450

1939 Chicago (AL) - Kuhel, Appling, McNair, Lyons ....$200-$350

1939 Chicago (NL) - Hartnett, Herman, Leiber, Galan, Hartnett, Dean ....$275-$400

1939 Cincinnati - McKechnie, McCormick, Goodman, Lombardi, Simmons, Walters, Derringer ....$325-$500

1939 Cleveland - Trosky, Hale, Keltner, Boudreau, Feller ..$225-$350

1939 Detroit - Greenberg, Gehringer, McCosky, Averill, Bridges ....$300-$500

1939 New York (AL) - McCarthy, Rolfe, Keller, DiMaggio, Selkirk, Dickey, Ruffing, Gehring, Gomez ....$750-$1,400

1939 New York (NL) - Terry, Bonura, Ott, Demaree, Danning, Lazzeri, Hubbell ....$325-$550

1939 Philadelphia (AL) - Mack, Moses, Johnson, Collins ..$300-$400

1939 Philadelphia (NL) - Suhr, Arnovich, Davis ....$175-$275

1939 Pittsburgh - Traynor, Fletcher, Vaughan, P. Waner, L. Waner, Manush ....$500-$1,000

1939 St. Louis (AL) - McQuinn, Laabs ....$200-$300

1939 St. Louis (NL) - Mize, Slaughter, Medwick, P. Martin ....$375-$550

1939 Washington - Harris, Vernon, Lewis, Case, Wright, Ferrell, Leonard ....$200-$300

1940 Boston (AL) - Cronin, Foxx, Doerr, Williams, Wilson, Grove ....$600-$1,000

1940 Boston (NL) - Stengel, Rowell, Cooney, Lopez ......$500-$750

1940 Brooklyn - Durocher, Reese, Medwick ....$450-$800

1940 Chicago (AL) - Appling, Wright, Solters, Lyons ....$200-$300

1940 Chicago (NL) - Hartnett, Herman, Dean ....$200-$300

1940 Cincinnati - McKechnie, F. McCormick, Lombardi . . .$350-$550

1940 Cleveland - Boudreau, Weatherly, Feller, Smith . . . . .$200-$300

1940 Detroit - York, Gehringer, McCosky, Greenberg, Averill, Newsom . . . .$500-$750

1940 New York (AL) - McCarthy, DiMaggio, Dickey, Ruffing, Gomez . . . .$450-$700

1940 New York (NL) - Terry, Ott, Demaree, Danning, Hubbell . . . .$400-$600

1940 Philadelphia (AL) - Mack, Moses, Hayes, Simmons . .$400-$750

1940 Philadelphia (NL) - . . . .$250-$400

1940 Pittsburgh - Frisch, Vaughan, P. Waner, L. Waner, Lopez . . . .$500-$1,000

1940 St. Louis (AL) - Judnich, Radcliff . . . .$175-$275

1940 St. Louis (NL) - Mize, Slaughter, P. Martin, Medwick . . . .$325-$475

1940 Washington - Harris, Lewis, Ferrell, Vernon . . . .$200-$325

1941 Boston (AL) - Cronin, Foxx, Doerr, DiMaggio, Williams, Grove . . . .$500-$675

1941 Boston (NL) - Cooney, Waner, Stengel . . . .$300-$400

1941 Brooklyn - Durocher, Camilli, Herman, Reese, Medwick, Waner . . . .$750-$1,250

1941 Chicago (AL) - Appling, Lyons . . . .$225-$350

1941 Chicago (NL) - Hack, Herman, Dean . . . .$175-$300

1941 Cincinnati - McKechnie, Lombardi, Waner . . . .$400-$600

1941 Cleveland - Boudreau, Heath, Lemon, Feller . . . .$200-$400

1941 Detroit - Gehringer, McCosky, Radcliff, Greenberg, Benton . . . .$450-$700

1941 New York (AL) - McCarthy, Rizzuto, DiMaggio, Dickey, Gomez, Ruffing . . . .$800-$1,200

1941 New York (NL) - Terry, Bartell, Ott, Hubbell . . . .$525-$600

1941 Philadelphia (AL) - Mack, Siebert, Moses, Chapman, Collins, Simmons . . . .$325-$500

1941 Philadelphia (NL) - Litwhiler, Etten . . . .$400-$500

1941 Pittsburgh - Frisch, Vaughan, Lopez, Waner . . . .$700-$800

1941 St. Louis (AL) - Ferrell . . . .$200-$325

1941 St. Louis (NL) - Mize, Brown, Slaughter, Hopp, Musial . . . .$300-$450

1941 Washington - Harris, Vernon, Travis, Ferrell, Wynn . .$225-$350

1942 Boston (AL) - Cronin, Doerr, Williams, Foxx . . . . . .$400-$575

1942 Boston (NL) - Stengel, Lombardi, Sain, Spahn . . . .$800-$1,000

1942 Brooklyn - Durocher, Herman, Reese, Vaughan, Reiser, Medwick, Wyatt, French . . . .$400-$600

1942 Chicago (AL) - Appling, Lyons . . . .$250-$350

1942 Chicago (NL) - Cavarretta, Hack, Novikoff, Foxx . . . .$250-$400

1942 Cincinnati - McKechnie, Vander Meer . . . .$200-$325

1942 Cleveland - Boudreau . . . .$200-$300

1942 Detroit - Gehringer, Trucks, Newhouser . . . .$300-$400

1942 New York (AL) - McCarthy, Gordon, Rizzuto, DiMaggio, Dickey, Ruffing, Gomez . . . .$600-$900

1942 New York (NL) - Ott, Mize, Hubbell . . . .$500-$800

1942 Philadelphia (AL) - Mack, Collins . . . .$300-$450

1942 Philadelphia (NL) - Waner . . . .$500-$750

1942 Pittsburgh - Frisch, Lopez . . . .$700-$900

1942 St. Louis (AL) - Ferrell . . . .$200-$375

1942 St. Louis (NL) - Slaughter, Musial, W. Cooper, M. Cooper, Beazley . . . .$750-$1,000

1942 Washington - Harris, Vernon, Wynn . . . .$200-$300

1943 Boston (AL) - Cronin, Doerr . . . .$300-$550

1943 Boston (NL) - Stengel, McCarthy . . . .$250-$325

1943 Brooklyn - Durocher, Herman, Vaughan, Bordagaray, Walker, Olmo, Waner, Hodges, Medwick, Wyatt . . . .$350-$700

1943 Chicago (AL) - Appling, Grove . . . .$200-$350

1943 Chicago (NL) - Cavarretta, Nicholson, Goodman . . . .$250-$400

1943 Cincinnati - McKechnie, McCormick, VanderMeer . . .$200-$350

1943 Cleveland - Boudreau, Smith . . . .$200-$275

1943 Detroit - Cramer, Wakefield, Trout, Trucks . . . .$200-$300

1943 New York (AL) - McCarthy, Dickey, Chandler . . . .$1,200-$1,500

1943 New York (NL) - Ott, Witek, Medwick, Lombardi, Adams . . . .$325-$500

1943 Philadelphia (AL) - Mack, Kell . . . .$200-$350

1943 Philadelphia (NL) - Rowe, Barrett . . . .$400-$600

1943 Pittsburgh - Frisch, Elliott, Lopez, Sewell . . . .$225-$350

1943 St. Louis (AL) - Ferrell, Dean . . . .$200-$350

1943 St. Louis (NL) - Musial, W. Cooper . . . .$350-$475

1943 Washington - Vernon, Wynn, Gomez . . . .$200-$300

1944 Boston (AL) - Cronin, Doerr, Fox, Johnson, Hughson . . . .$225-$350

1944 Boston (NL) - Holmes . . . .$200-$300

1944 Brooklyn - Durocher, Walker, Galan, P. Waner, L. Waner, Vaughan . . . .$250-$500

1944 Chicago (AL) - Schalk . . . .$200-$325

1944 Chicago (NL) - Grimm, Cavarretta, Dallessandro, Foxx . . . .$175-$325

1944 Cincinnati - McKechnie, McCormick, Tiptop, Walters .$200-$325

1944 Cleveland - Boudreau . . . .$275-$450

1944 Detroit - Wakefield, Newhouser . . . .$225-$375

1944 New York (AL) - McCarthy, Lindell, Martin, Waner . .$250-$425

1944 New York (NL) - Ott, Weintraub, Medwick, Lombardi, Voiselle . . . .$400-$600

1944 Philadelphia (AL) - Mack, Simmons . . . .$250-$400

1944 Philadelphia (NL) . . . .$300-$500

1944 Pittsburgh - Russell, Lopez, Sewell, Frisch . . . .,$300-$400

1944 St. Louis (AL) - Kreevich, Potter . . . .$300-$500

1944 St. Louis (NL) - Marion, Musial, Hopp, W. Cooper, Martin, M. Cooper . . . .$400-$500

1944 Washington - Spence, Ferrell, Wynn . . . .$200-$300

1945 Boston (AL) - Cronin . . . .$200-$300

1945 Boston (NL) - Holmes . . . .$175-$250

1945 Brooklyn - Durocher, Galan, Walker, Rosen, Olmo . . .$200-$350

1945 Chicago (AL) - Appling . . . .$175-$300

1945 Chicago (NL) - Grimm, Cavarretta, Johnson, Hack, Wyse . . . .$350-$500

1945 Cincinnati - McKechnie . . . .$225-$325

1945 Cleveland - Boudreau, Feller . . . .$275-$350

1945 Detroit (AL) - Greenberg, Newhouser . . . .$325-$450

1949 St. Luois Browns

1949 Chicago Cubs

1952 New York Yankees

1945 New York (AL) - McCarthy, Waner, Ruffing ....$200-$325

1945 New York (NL) - Ott, Lombardi, Mungo ....$300-$650

1945 Philadelphia (AL) - Mack, Kell ....$225-$350

1945 Philadelphia (NL) - Wasdell, Foxx ....$700-$900

1945 Pittsburgh - Frisch, Lopez, Waner ....$600-$800

1945 St. Louis (AL) - Muncrief ....$600-$800

1945 St. Louis (NL) - Kurowski, Schoendienst, Barrett, Burkhart, Brecheen ....$200-$350

1945 Washington - Lewis, Ferrell, Wolff ....$200-$300

1946 Boston (AL) - Cronin, Doerr, Pesky, DiMaggio, Williams, Ferriss ....$300-$450

1946 Boston (NL) - Holmes, Herman, Sain, Spahn ......$200-$350

1946 Brooklyn - Durocher, Reese, Medwick, Higbe ......$350-$500

1946 Chicago (AL) - Lyons, Appling, Caldwell ....$250-$350

1946 Chicago (NL) - Grimm, Waitkus ....$175-$275

1946 Cincinnati - McKechnie, Walters ....$200-$300

1946 Cleveland - Boudreau, Edwards, Lemon, Feller .....$250-$350

1946 Detroit - Kell, Newhouser ....$225-$350

1946 New York (AL) - McCarthy, Rizzuto, DiMaggio, Dickey, Berra, Ruffing, Chandler ....$550-$1,000

1946 New York (NL) - Ott, Mize, Lombardi ....$500-$650

1946 Philadelphia (AL) - Mack, Valo, McCosky, Kell ....$300-$400

1946 Philadelphia (NL) - Ennis, Rowe ....$200-$300

1946 Pittsburgh - Frisch, Kiner, Lopez ....$800-$950

1946 St. Louis (AL) - Stephens ....$200-$300

1946 St. Louis (NL) - Musial, Schoendienst, Kurowski, Slaughter, Walker, Garagiola, Pollet ....$400-$600

1946 Washington - Vernon, Grace, Leonard, Wynn ......$200-$300

1947 Boston (AL) - Cronin, Doerr, Pesky, Williams, Dobson ....$250-$400

1947 Boston (NL) - Elliott, Holmes, Spahn, Sain ....$200-$325

1947 Brooklyn - Robinson, Reese, Vaughan, Snider, Hodges, Branca, Hatten ....$900-$1,100

1947 Chicago (AL) - Lyons, Appling, Wright ....$200-$300

1947 Chicago (NL) - Grimm, Pafko, Cavarretta ....$200-$300

1947 Cincinnati - Galan, Kluszewski, Blackwell ....$200-$300

1947 Cleveland - Boudreau, Mitchell, Feller, Lemon .....$250-$350

1947 Detroit - Kell, Newhouser, Trucks ....$250-$350

1947 New York (AL) - McQuinn, Rizzuto, DiMaggio, Berra, Reynolds, Shea ....$1,000-$1,250

1947 New York (NL) - Ott, Mize, Cooper, Jansen ....$350-$600

1947 Philadelphia (AL) - Mack, Valo, Fox, Marchildon ....$225-$350

1947 Philadelphia (NL) - Walker, Leonard, Rowe ....$250-$400

1947 Pittsburgh - Herman, Greenberg, Kiner ....$200-$300

1947 St. Louis (AL) - Dean, V. Stephens ....$225-$350

1947 St. Louis (NL) - Musial, Schoendienst, Garagiola, Medwick, Munger ....$275-$400

1947 Washington - Vernon, Wynn ....$200-$300

1948 Boston (AL) - McCarthy, Doerr, Pesky, Williams ....$250-$375

1948 Boston (NL) - Dark, Sain, Spahn, Holmes, Southworth ....$500-$600

1948 Brooklyn - Durocher, Hodges, Robinson, Reese, Furillo, Campanella, Roe, Vaughan, Snider, Branca, Erskine ....$600-$900

1948 Chicago (AL) - Lyons, Appling ....$200-$300

1948 Chicago (NL) - Grimm ....$200-$300

1948 Cincinnati- Kluszewski ....$200-$300

1948 Cleveland - Boudreau, Mitchell, Bearden, Lemon, Feller, Paige ....$400-$575

1948 Detroit - Kell, Cramer, Newhouser, Trucks ....$250-$350

1948 New York (AL) - Rizzuto, DiMaggio, Berra, Raschi ..$400-$750

1948 New York (NL) - Ott, Durocher, Mize ....$400-$600

1948 Philadelphia (AL) - Mack, Fox ....$225-$350

1948 Philadelphia (NL) - Sisler, Ashburn, Leonard, Rowe, Roberts ....$300-$450

1948 Pittsburgh - Kiner, Murtaugh, Sewell ....$275-$375

1948 St. Louis (AL) - Zanilla, Sanford ....$200-$400

1948 St. Louis (NL) - Schoendienst, Slaughter, Musial, Garagiola, Medwick ....$275-$400

1948 Washington - Vernon, Wynn ....$225-$325

1949 Boston (AL) - McCarthy, Doerr, Williams, Parnell ..$200-$325

1949 Boston (NL) - Spahn, Sain ....$275-$350

1949 Brooklyn - Hodges, Robinson, Reese, Furillo, Roe, Newcombe, Campanella, Snider, Connors ....$700-$900

1949 Chicago (AL) - Appling ....$200-$300

1949 Chicago (NL) - Grimm, Frisch, Burgess ....$250-$350

1949 Cincinnati - Kluszewski ....$200-$275

1949 Cleveland - Boudreau, Vernon, Mitchell, Lemon,
Feller, Wynn ....$225-$300

1949 Detroit - Kell, Wertz, Evers, Trucks ....$200-$300

1949 New York (AL) - Stengel, Rizzuto, Berra, DiMaggio,
Mize, Raschi, Reynolds ....$1,200-$1,500

1949 New York (NL) - Durocher, Mize, Marshall, Thomson,
Irvin ....$275-$550

1949 Philadelphia (AL) - Mack, Fox ....$225-$325

1949 Philadelphia (NL) - Sisler, Meyer, Roberts ....$300-$500

1949 Pittsburgh - Hopp, Kiner ....$300-$500

1949 St. Louis (AL) - Dillinger, Sievers ....$200-$300

1949 St. Louis (NL) - Schoendienst, Musial, Slaughter,
Garagiola, Pollet ....$225-$350

1949 Washington - E. Robinson, Yost ....$200-$300

1950 Boston (AL) - McCarthy, Dropo, Doerr, Pesky, Williams
....$250-$350

1950 Boston (NL) - Jethroe, Spahn, Sain ....$200-$300

1950 Brooklyn - Hodges, Robinson, Reese, Furillo, Roe, Campanella,
Newcombe, Snider ....$600-$900

1950 Chicago (AL) - Fox, Appling ....$200-$300

1950 Chicago (NL) - Frisch, Pafko ....$200-$300

1950 Cincinnati - Kluszewski, Adcock ....$200-$300

1950 Cleveland - Boudreau, Rosen, Doby, Mitchell, Lemon,
Wynn, Feller ....$250-$350

1950 Detroit - Kell, Wertz, Groth, Evers ....$300-$400

1950 New York (AL) - Stengel, Martin, Rizzuto, Bauer,
DiMaggio, Woodling, Berra, Mize, Ford ....$675-$1,000

1950 New York (NL) - Dark, Irvin, Jansen, Maglie ......$300-$450

1950 Philadelphia (AL) - Mack, Dillinger, Lehner ....$300-$400

1950 Philadelphia (NL) - Ennis, Ashburn, Roberts, Simmons,
Konstanty ....$300-$450

1950 Pittsburgh - Hopp, Kiner ....$200-$300

1950 St. Louis (AL) - Garver, Siever ....$200-$275

1950 St. Louis (NL) - Musial, Schoendienst, Garagiola ....$225-$325

1950 Washington - Vernon ....$200-$275

1951 Boston (AL) - Doerr, Pesky, Boudreau ....$200-$300

1951 Boston (NL) - Spahn, Sain ....$200-$250

1951 Brooklyn - Hodges, Robinson, Reese, Snider,
Campanella, Roe, Newcombe ....$575-$675

1951 Chicago (AL) - Fox, Minoso ....$200-$300

1951 Chicago (NL) - Frisch, Connors, Burgess ....$225-$325

1951 Cincinnati - Kluszewski, Adcock ....$175-$275

1951 Cleveland - Lopez, Avila, Feller, Wynn, Lemon .....$225-$325

1951 Detroit - Kell, Trucks ....$250-$400

1951 New York (AL) - Stengel, Mize, Rizzuto, Brown,
DiMaggio, Mantle, McDougald, Berra, Martin .....$2,500-$4,500

1951 New York (NL) - Durocher, Dark, Mays, Irvin,
Maglie ....$1,000-$1,150

1951 Philadelphia (AL) - Fain, Shantz ....$200-$400

1951 Philadelphia (NL) - Ashburn, Roberts ....$175-$275

1951 Pittsburgh - Kiner, Garagiola ....$275-$375

1951 St. Louis (AL) - Paige, Gaedel ....$400-$600

1951 St. Louis (NL) - Schoendienst, Slaughter, Musial,
Garagiola ....$225-$325

1951 Washington - Vernon ....$100-$225

1952 Boston (AL) - Boudreau, Goodman, Kell, Williams ...$175-$275

1952 Boston (NL) - Grimm, Mathews, Spahn ....$250-$325

1952 Brooklyn - Hodges, Robinson, Reese, Furillo, Snider,
Campanella, Black, Erskine ....$500-$750

1952 Chicago (AL) - Fox, Minoso ....$200-$300

1952 Chicago (NL) - Fondy, Baumholtz, Sauer, Hacker ....$175-$275

1952 Cincinnati - Hornsby, Kluszewski, Adcock ....$275-$400

1952 Cleveland - Avila, Rosen, Mitchell, Wynn, Garcia,
Lemon, Feller ....$300-$500

1952 Detroit - Kell, Kuenn ....$200-$300

1952 New York (AL) - Stengel, Martin, Reynolds, Mantle,
Berra, Raschi, Woodling, Brown, Mize, Rizzuto ......$650-$800

1952 New York (NL) - Durocher, Dark, Irvin, Maglie,
Wilhelm ....$300-$425

1952 Philadelphia (AL) - Fain, Shantz ....$200-$300

1952 Philadelphia (NL) - Ashburn, Roberts ....$200-$300

1952 Pittsburgh - Groat, Kiner, Garagiola ....$200-$300

1952 St. Louis (AL) - Hornsby, Paige ....$350-$500

1952 St. Louis (NL) - Schoendienst, Slaughter, Musial ....$275-$400

1952 Washington - Vernon ....$175-$250

1953 Boston - Boudreau, Goodman, Kell, Williams, Parnell
....$400-$550

1953 Brooklyn - Hodges, Meyer, Reese, Furillo, Snider,
Robinson, Campanella, Erskine, Gilliam ....$700-$1,000

1953 Chicago (AL) - Fox, Minoso, Trucks ....$225-$350

1953 Chicago (NL) - Fondy, Baumholtz, Kiner, Garagiola,
Banks ....$200-$300

1953 Cincinnati - Hornsby, Kluszewski, Bell ....$275-$400

1953 Cleveland - Lopez, Rosen, Westlake, Mitchell, Lemon,
Wynn, Feller ....$225-$300

1953 Detroit - Kuenn, Boone, Kaline ....$200-$275

1953 Milwaukee - Grimm, Adcock, Mathews, Spahn,
Burdette ....$300-$375

1953 New York (AL) - Stengel, Martin, Rizzuto, Mantle,
Berra, Mize, Ford ....$750-$1,200

1953 New York (NL) - Durocher, Dark, Mueller, Thomson,
Irvin ....$275-$450

1953 Philadelphia (AL) - Philley ....$200-$300

1953 Philadelphia (NL) - Ashburn, Roberts ....$175-$275

1953 Pittsburgh - Kiner, Garagiola ....$200-$300

1953 St. Louis (AL) - Marion, Paige, Wertz ....$175-$250

1953 St. Louis (NL) - Schoendienst, Slaughter, Musial,
Haddix, Staley ....$225-$275

1953 Washington - Vernon, Busby, Porterfield ....$175-$250

1954 Baltimore - Larsen, Turley ....$150-$225

1954 Boston - Boudreau, Jensen, Williams ....$400-$500

1954 Brooklyn- Alston, Hodges, Gilliam, Reese, Furillo,
Lasorda, Robinson, Campanella, Erskine, Newcombe,
Snider ....$1,200-$1,400

1954 Chicago (AL) - Fox, Kell, Trucks, Minoso ....$200-$325

1958 Baltimore Orioles

1955 Boston Red Sox

1963 New York Yankees

1954 Chicago (NL) - Banks, Kiner, Garagiola . . . .$300-$500

1954 Cincinnati - Kluszewski, Temple . . . .$175-$275

1954 Cleveland - Lopez, Avila, Lemon, Wynn, Feller . . . . .$300-$450

1954 Detroit - Kuenn, Kaline . . . .$350-$425

1954 Milwaukee - Grimm, Adcock, Mathews, Aaron, Spahn,
Burdette . . . .$275-$400

1954 New York (AL) - Stengel, Rizzuto, Mantle, Berra,
Slaughter, Grim, Ford . . . .$500-$900

1954 New York (NL) - Durocher, Mays, Irvin, Antonelli,
Maglie, Wilhelm . . . .$1,200-$1,500

1954 Philadelphia (NL) - Ashburn, Burgess, Roberts . . . . .$250-$350

1954 Philadelphia (AL) - Finigan . . . .$175-$250

1954 Pittsburgh - Gordon . . . .$150-$250

1954 St. Louis - Schoendienst, Musial, Moon . . . .$200-$300

1954 Washington - Vernon, Killebrew . . . .$150-$225

1955 Baltimore - Robinson . . . .$225-$325

1955 Boston - Goodman, Jensen, Piersall, Williams . . . . . .$175-$300

1955 Brooklyn - Hodges, Gilliam, Reese, Labine, Furillo, Snider,
Campanella, Newcombe, Robinson, Erskine, Koufax
. . . .$2,500-$4,000

1955 Chicago (AL) - Fox, Kell, Donovan, Trucks . . . .$200-$300

1955 Chicago (NL) - Banks . . . .$175-$250

1955 Cincinnati - Kluszewski, Burgess . . . .$200-$300

1955 Cleveland - Lopez, Smith, Kiner, Colavito, Lemon,
Wynn, Score, Feller . . . .$375-$525

1955 Detroit - Kuenn, Kaline, Bunning . . . .$175-$275

1955 Kansas City - Boudreau, Slaughter . . . .$200-$275

1955 Milwaukee - Mathews, Aaron, Adcock, Spahn,
Burdette . . . .$250-$400

1955 New York (AL) - Stengel, Mantle, Slaughter, Howard,
Martin, Berra, Rizzuto, Ford, Larsen . . . .$500-$900

1955 New York (NL) - Durocher, Mays, Irvin, Antonelli . . .$275-$475

1955 Philadelphia - Ashburn, Roberts . . . .$175-$250

1955 Pittsburgh - Groat, Clemente, Friend . . . .$500-$800

1955 St. Louis - Musial, Schoendienst, Boyer, Virdon,
Haddix . . . .$200-$300

1955 Washington - Vernon, Killebrew . . . .$150-$225

1956 Baltimore - Kell, Gastall, Robinson . . . .$175-$250

1956 Boston - Vernon, Jensen, Williams . . . .$300-$400

1956 Brooklyn - Hodges, Gilliam, Reese, Furillo, Snider, Campanella,
Koufax, Newcombe, Erskine, Drysdale, Robinson . . . . . .$700-$900

1956 Chicago (AL) - Fox, Aparicio, Kell . . . .$200-$300

1956 Chicago (NL) - Banks, Irvin . . . .$200-$275

1956 Cincinnati - Kluszewski, Robinson . . . .$225-$325

1956 Cleveland - Lopez, Colavito, Lemon, Wynn, Score,
Feller . . . .$300-$400

1956 Detroit - Kuenn, Kaline, Bunning . . . .$200-$300

1956 Kansas City - Boudreau, Slaughter, Lasorda . . . .$200-$300

1956 Milwaukee - Grimm, Adcock, Mathews, Aaron, Spahn,
Burdette . . . .$275-$425

1956 New York (AL) - Stengel, Martin, Mantle, Howard,
Rizzuto, Slaughter, Berra, Bauer, Ford . . . .$650-$1,000

1956 New York (NL) - White, Schoendienst, Mays,
Antonelli . . . .$275-$475

1956 Philadelphia - Ashburn, Roberts . . . .$150-$225

1956 Pittsburgh - Mazeroski, Groat, Clemente, Virdon . . . .$600-$850

1956 St. Louis - Musial, Boyer, Schoendienst, Pettee . . . . .$175-$300

1956 Washington - Killebrew . . . .$150-$225

1957 Baltimore - Kell, Robinson . . . .$200-$300

1957 Boston - Jensen, Williams, Vernon . . . .$200-$275

1957 Brooklyn - Hodges, Gilliam, Reese, Furillo, Snider,
Campanella, Koufax, Drysdale . . . .$1,000-$1,300

1957 Chicago (AL) - Lopez, Fox, Aparicio . . . .$200-$300

1957 Chicago (NL) - Banks . . . .$175-$250

1957 Cincinnati - Robinson, Kluszewski . . . .$250-$375

1957 Cleveland - Colavito, Maris, Wynn, Wilhelm . . . .$450-$600

1957 Detroit - Kuenn, Kaline, Bunning . . . .$180-$270

1957 Kansas City - Martin . . . .$175-$275

1957 Milwaukee - Schoendienst, Mathews, Aaron, Adcock,
Spahn . . . .$1,000-$1,500

1957 New York (AL) - Stengel, Slaughter, Berra, Howard,
Sturdivant, Ford . . . .$700-$900

1957 New York (NL) - Mays, Schoendienst, McCormick,
White . . . .$250-$350

1957 Philadelphia - Ashburn, Sanford, Roberts . . . .$275-$375

1957 Pittsburgh - Mazeroski, Groat, Clemente, Friend . .$900-$1,000

1957 St. Louis - Musial, Boyer, Wilhelm . . . .$200-$300

1957 Washington - Killebrew . . . .$150-$225

1958 Baltimore - Robinson, Wilhelm . . . .$150-$225

1958 Boston - Runnels, Williams . . . .$275-$500

1958 Chicago (AL) - Fox, Aparicio, Cash, Wynn . . . .$200-$300

1958 Chicago (NL) - Banks . . . .$175-$250

1958 Cincinnati - Robinson, Pinson . . . .$150-$300

1958 Cleveland - Vernon, Colavito, Maris, Wilhelm, Lemon
. . . .$200-$300

1958 Detroit - Martin, Kaline, Kuenn, Bunning . . . .$200-$300

1958 Kansas City - Maris . . . .$400-$550

1958 Los Angeles - Alston, Hodges, Furillo, Snider, Reese,
Drysdale, Koufax, Howard . . . .$350-$600

1958 Milwaukee - Schoendienst, Mathews, Aaron, Spahn,
Burdette . . . .$525-$800

1958 New York - Kubek, Mantle, Berra, Howard, Slaughter,
Turley, Ford, Larsen . . . .$1,100-$1,350

1958 Philadelphia - Ashburn, Roberts . . . .$200-$350

1958 Pittsburgh - Kluszewski, Mazeroski, Groat, Clemente,
Friend . . . .$575-$850

1958 San Francisco - Cepeda, Mays, White, McCormick . . .$450-$600

1958 St. Louis - Musial, Boyer . . . .$175-$250

1958 Washington - Pearson, Killebrew . . . .$150-$225

1959 Baltimore - Robinson, Wilhelm . . . .$175-$250

1959 Boston - Runnels, Williams . . . .$150-$250

1959 Chicago (AL) - Lopez, Fox, Aparicio, Cash, Kluszewski,
Wynn . . . .$350-$525

1959 Chicago (NL) - Banks, Williams . . . .$175-$250

1959 Cincinnati - Robinson, Pinson . . . .$300-$500

1959 Cleveland - Martin, Colavito, Perry, Score . . . .$175-$250

1959 Detroit - Kaline, Bunning $250

1959 Kansas City - Maris . . . .$200-$400

1959 Los Angeles - Alston, Hodges, Gilliam, Snider,
Koufax, Furillo, Drysdale, Howard, Wills . . . . . .$800-$1,000

1959 Milwaukee - Adcock, Mathews, Aaron, Vernon,
Slaughter, Schoendienst, Spahn . . . .$350-$500

1959 New York - Stengel, Kubek, Mantle, Berra, Howard,
Slaughter, Ford, Larsen . . . .$450-$600

1959 Philadelphia - Sparky Anderson, Ashburn, Roberts . .$300-$400

1959 Pittsburgh - Stuart, Mazeroski, Groat, Clemente,
Kluszewski, Friend . . . .$600-$800

1959 San Francisco - Cepeda, Mays, McCovey,
McCormick . . . .$250-$375

1959 St. Louis - Musial, Boyer, White, McDaniel, Gibson . .$175-$250

1959 Washington - Killebrew, Allison, Kaat . . . .$150-$225

1960 Baltimore - Hansen, Robinson, Wilhelm . . . .$175-$250

1960 Boston - Runnels, Williams . . . .$375-$500

1960 Chicago (AL) - Lopez, Fox, Aparicio, Kluszewski,
Wynn, Score . . . .$300-$500

1960 Chicago (NL) - Grimm, Boudreau, Banks, Santo,
Ashburn, Williams . . . .$175-$250

1960 Cincinnati - Robinson, Martin, Pinson . . . .$250-$350

1960 Cleveland - Aspromonte, Kuenn, Piersall, Perry . . . .$150-$250

1960 Detroit - Cash, Colavito, Kaline, Bunning . . . .$250-$350

1960 Kansas City - Bauer, Herzog, Throneberry . . . .$150-$225

1960 Los Angeles - Alston, Wills, Howard, Davis, Snider,
Hodges, Davis, Koufax, Drysdale, Gilliam . . . .$425-$500

1960 Milwaukee - Adcock, Mathews, Aaron, Schoendienst,
Spahn, Burdette, Torre . . . .$300-$400

1960 New York - Stengel, Kubek, Maris, Mantle, Howard,
Berra, Ford . . . .$500-$750

1960 Philadelphia - Callison, Roberts . . . .$100-$150

1960 Pittsburgh - Stuart, Mazeroski, Clemente, Law, Vernon
. . . .$800-$1,200

1960 San Francisco - McCovey, Mays, Cepeda, McCormick,
Marichal . . . .$250-$375

1960 St. Louis - White, Boyer, Musial, McCarver, Gibson . .$250-$350

1960 Washington - Killebrew, Versalles, Kaat . . . .$175-$275

1961 Baltimore - Robinson, Powell, Wilhelm . . . .$150-$225

1961 Boston - Jensen, Yastrzemski . . . .$175-$250

1961 Chicago (AL) - Lopez, Fox, Aparicio, Pierce, Wynn . .$175-$250

1961 Chicago (NL) - Banks, Santo, Ashburn, Hubbs, Brock,
Williams . . . .$175-$275

1961 Cincinnati - Robinson, Pinson, Jay . . . .$325-$500

1961 Cleveland - Piersall, McDowell . . . .$125-$175

1961 Detroit - Cash, Kaline, Colavito, Bunning, Freehan . . .$250-$350

1961 Kansas City - Howser, Throneberry . . . .$75-$250

1961 Los Angeles (AL) - Kluszewsky, Wagner . . . .$200-$300

1961 Los Angeles (NL) - Alston, Wills, T. Davis, W. Davis,
Howard, Snider, Drysdale, Koufax . . . .$275-$400

1961 Milwaukee - Adcock, Mathews, Aaron, Torre, Spahn,
Martin . . . .$175-$275

1961 Minnesota - Lavagetto, Killebrew, Martin, Versalles,
Kaat . . . .$200-$300

1961 New York - Kubek, Maris, Mantle, Berra, Howard,
Tresh, Ford . . . .$1,400-$1,800

1961 Philadelphia - Callisom, Roberts . . . .$100-$150

1961 Pittsburgh - Stuart, Mazeroski, Clemente, Clendenon,
Friend . . . .$550-$850

1961 San Francisco - McCovey, Mays, Cepeda, Marichal,
McCormick . . . .$250-$350

1961 St. Louis - White, Boyer, Musial, Schoendienst,
McCarver, Gibson . . . .$275-$350

1961 Washington - Vernon . . . .$150-$225

1962 Baltimore - Robinson, Powell, Roberts, Wilhelm . . . . .$175-$250

1962 Boston - Yastrzemski . . . .$175-$250

1962 Chicago (AL) - Lopez, Fox, Wynn, Peters, DeBusschere
. . . .$200-$400

1962 Chicago (NL) - Banks, Hubbs, Santo, Brock, Williams
. . . .$172-$275

1962 Cincinnati - Robinson, Pinson . . . .$250-$450

1962 Cleveland - McDowell . . . .$125-$200

1962 Detroit - Cash, Kaline, Colavito, Bunning . . . .$125-$200

1962 Houston - Aspromonte . . . .$300-$425

1962 Kansas City - Howser, Segui . . . .$100-$175

1962 Los Angeles (AL) - Lee Thomas, Fregosi . . . .$150-$225

1961 Detroit Tigers

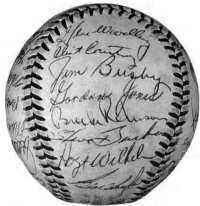

1961 Baltimore Orioles

1958 Milwaukee Braves

1962 Los Angeles (NL) - Alston, Gilliam, Wills, Howard, W. Davis, T. Davis, Snider, Drysdale, Koufax ....$400-$800

1962 Milwaukee - Adcock, Mathews, Aaron, Uecker, Spahn . .$300-$400

1962 Minnesota - Versalles, Killebrew, Oliva, Kaat ......$175-$275

1962 New York (AL) - Tresh, Maris, Mantle, Howard, Berra, Kubek, Terry, Ford ....$550-$800

1962 New York (NL) - Stengel, Hodges, Kranepool ......$300-$450

1962 Philadelphia - Callison, Maheffey ....$100-$150

1962 Pittsburgh - Mazeroski, Groat, Clemente, Clendenon, Stargell ....$500-$750

1962 San Francisco - Cepeda, Mays, McCovey, Marichal, McCormick, Perry ....$400-$600

1962 St. Louis - White, Boyer, Musial, Schoendienst, Gibson ....$275-$350

1962 Washington - Vernon ....$150-$275

1963 Baltimore - Aparicio, Robinson, Powell, Roberts ....$200-$250

1963 Boston - Yastrzemski ....$150-$250

1963 Chicago (AL) - Lopez, Fox, Peters, Wilhelm, DeBusschere ....$175-$250

1963 Chicago (NL) - Banks, Hubbs, Santo, Brock, Williams . . .$175-$250

1963 Cincinnati - Rose, Harper, Pinson, Robinson ....$200-$275

1963 Cleveland - Adcock, McDowell, John ....$100-$150

1963 Detroit - Cash, Kaline, Colavito, Lolich, McLain ....$125-$200

1963 Houston - Staub, Aspromonte, Morgan, Umbricht ....$175-$250

1963 Kansas City - Harrelson, Segui ....$150-$225

1963 Los Angeles (AL) - Fregosi, Chance ....$100-$150

1963 Los Angeles (NL) - Alston, Gilliam, Wills, Howard, W. Davis, T. Davis, Koufax, Drysdale ....$450-$650

1963 Milwaukee - Mathews, Aaron, Torre, Uecker, Spahn . .$150-$225

1963 Minnesota - Versalles, Killebrew, Oliva, Kaat ......$175-$275

1963 New York (AL) - Maris, Howard, Mantle, Berra, Ford . .$450-$650

1963 New York (NL) - Stengel, Snider, Kranepool, Hodges . .$275-$400

1963 Philadelphia - Allen ....$100-$150

1963 Pittsburgh - Clendenon, Mazeroski, Clemente, Stargell, Mota ....$450-$800

1963 San Francisco - Cepeda, Mays, McCovey, Marichal, Larsen, Perry ....$225-$450

1963 St. Louis - Groat, Boyer, McCarver, Musial, Gibson . .$300-$550

1963 Washington - Vernon, Hodges ....$100-$150

1964 Baltimore - Aparicio, Robinson, Powell, Piniella, Roberts ....$200-$275

1964 Boston - Herman, Yastrzemski ....$200-$300

1964 Chicago (AL) - Lopez, Wilhelm ....$100-$150

1964 Chicago (NL) - Banks, Santo, Williams, Brock, Kessinger ....$150-$225

1964 Cincinnati - Rose, Robinson, Pinson, Perez ....$175-$250

1964 Cleveland - McDowell, Tiant, John ....$100-$150

1964 Detroit - Cash, Kaline, Freehan, Lolich, McLain .....$150-$200

1964 Houston - Fox, Aspromonte, Staub, Morgan ....$200-$300

1964 Kansas City - Colavito, Campaneris, Odom ....$150-$250

1964 Los Angeles (AL) - Adcock, Fregosi, Chance ....$75-$100

1964 Los Angeles (NL) - Alston, Wills, Howard, W. Davis, T. Davis, Koufax, Drysdale ....$250-$400

1964 Milwaukee - Mathews, Aaron, Carty, Torre, Spahn, Niekro ....$175-$250

1964 Minnesota - Versalles, Oliva, Killebrew, Kaat ....$200-$250

1964 New York (AL) - Berra, Maris, Mantle, Howard, Ford, Stottlemyre ....$350-$500

1964 New York (NL) - Stengel, Kranepool ....$350-$500

1964 Philadelphia - Allen, Bunning ....$100-$135

1964 Pittsburgh - Clendenon, Mazeroski, Clemente, Mota . .$450-$650

1964 San Francisco - Cepeda, Mays, McCovey, Snider, Marichal, Perry, Larsen ....$200-$300

1964 St. Louis - White, Boyer, Brock, McCarver, Uecker, Gibson ....$375-$550

1964 Washington - Hodges ....$225-$350

1965 Baltimore - Powell, Aparicio, Robinson, Blefary, Palmer, Roberts ....$200-$300

1965 Boston - Herman, Yastrzemski ....$200-$275

1965 California - Fregosi ....$115-$200

1965 Chicago (AL) - Lopez, John, Wilhelm ....$125-$175

1965 Chicago (NL) - Banks, Santo, Williams ....$100-$150

1965 Cincinnati - Rose, Robinson, Pinson, Perez ....$200-$400

1965 Cleveland - Colavito, McDowell, Tiant ....$125-$325

1965 Detroit - Cash, Kaline, Freehan, McLain, Lolich .....$150-$200

1965 Houston - Morgan, Staub, Fox, Roberts . . . .$150-$225

1965 Kansas City - Campaneris, Hunter, Paige, Odom . . . . .$200-$400

1965 Los Angeles - Alston, Lefebvre, Wills, W. Davis,
Koufax, Drysdale . . . .$350-$550

1965 Milwaukee - Mathews, Aaron, Torre, Niekro . . . .$250-$350

1965 Minnesota - Versalles, Oliva, Killebrew, Kaat . . . . . .$325-$575

1965 New York (AL) - Mantle, Howard, Maris, Murcer,
Stottlemyre, Ford . . . .$400-$575

1965 New York (NL) - Stengel, Kranepool, Swoboda, Berra,
Spahn . . . .$300-$375

1965 Philadelphia - Allen, Bunning, Jenkins . . . .$150-$250

1965 Pittsburgh - Mazeroski, Clemente, Stargell . . . . . .$1,300-$1,400

1965 San Francisco - McCovey, Mays, Cepeda, Marichal,
Perry, Spahn . . . .$200-$350

1965 St. Louis - Schoendienst, White, Boyer, Brock, McCarver,
Uecker, Gibson, Carlton . . . .$300-$350

1965 Washington - Hodges, Howard, McCormick . . . .$150-$225

1966 Atlanta - Mathews, Aaron, Torre, Niekro . . . .$325-$400

1966 Baltimore - Aparicio, B. Robinson, F. Robinson, Palmer
. . . .$250-$450

1966 Boston - Herman, Yastrzemski, Lonborg . . . .$200-$300

1966 California - Fregosi . . . .$80-$120

1966 Chicago (AL) - Agee, John, Wilhelm . . . .$150-$250

1966 Chicago (NL) - Banks, Santo, Jenkins, Roberts . . . . .$125-$200

1966 Cincinnati - Perez, Rose, Helms, Harper, Pinson . . . .$125-$175

1966 Cleveland - Colavito, Tiant, McDowell . . . .$100-$175

1966 Detroit - Cash, Kaline, Freehan, McLain, Lolich . . . .$125-$200

1966 Houston - Morgan, Staub, Roberts . . . .$100-$150

1966 Kansas City - Campaneris, Hunter, Odom . . . .$100-$150

1966 Los Angeles - Wills, W. Davis, T. Davis, Koufax,
Drysdale, Sutton . . . .$175-$400

1966 Minnesota - Killebrew, Oliva, Kaat . . . .$150-$225

1966 New York (AL) - Maris, Mantle, Howard, Stottlemyre,
Ford . . . .$400-$600

1966 New York (NL) - Kranepool, Boyer, Swoboda, Ryan . .$175-$250

1966 Philadelphia - White, Allen, Uecker, Bunning, Jenkins . .$100-$150

1966 Pittsburgh - Clendenon, Mazeroski, Clemente, Stargell,
Mota . . . .$800-$1,200

1966 San Francisco - McCovey, Mays, Cepeda, Marichal,
Perry . . . .$175-$250

1966 St. Louis - Schoendienst, Cepeda, Brock, McCarver,
Gibson, Carlton . . . .$250-$400

1966 Washington - Hodges, Howard . . . .$125-$200

1967 Atlanta - Aaron, Carty, Uecker, Niekro . . . .
. . . .$150-$225

1967 Baltimore (AL) - Powell, Aparicio, B. Robinson,
F. Robinson, Palmer . . . .$200-$300

1967 Boston (AL) - Yastrzemski, Howard, Lonborg, Lyle . .$600-$1,200

1967 California (AL) - Fregosi . . . .$75-$125

1967 Chicago (AL) - Colavito, Boyer, John, Wilhelm . . . .$100-$175

1967 Chicago (NL) - Durocher, Banks, Santo, Williams,
Jenkins . . . .$125-$175

1967 Cincinnati - Pinson, Rose, Bench . . . .$150-$225

1967 Cleveland (AL) - Adcock, McDowell, Tiant . . . .$100-$150

1967 Detroit (AL) - Cash, Kaline, Freehan, Mathews,
McLain, Lolich . . . .$150-$225

1967 Houston - Mathews, Morgan, Staub . . . .$100-$150

1967 Kansas City (AL) - Appling, Jackson, Hunter, Odom . . .$150-$225

1967 Los Angeles - Alston, Davis, Drysdale, Sutton . . . . .$200-$275

1967 Minnesota (AL) - Killebrew, Carew, Oliva, Kaat . . . .$275-$375

1967 New York (AL) - Mantle, Howard, Stottlemyre, Ford . . .$350-$450

1967 New York (NL) - Kranepool, Harrelson, Swoboda,
Seaver, Koosman . . . .$325-$475

1967 Philadelphia - White, Allen, Uecker, Groat, Bunning . .$100-$150

1967 Pittsburgh - Mazeroski, Wills, Clemente, Stargell . . . .$400-$600

1967 San Francisco (NL) - McCovey, Mays, McCormick,
Perry, Marichal . . . .$175-$250

1967 St. Louis - Schoendienst, Cepeda, Maris, Brock, McCarver,
Carlton, Gibson . . . .$550-$750

1967 Washington (AL) - Hodges, Howard . . . .$175-$250

1968 Atlanta - Aaron, Torre, Niekro . . . .$200-$300

1968 Baltimore - Weaver, Powell, B. Robinson, F. Robinson . . .$150-$250

1968 Boston - Yastrzemski, Howard, Lyle . . . .$150-$200

1968 California - Fregosi . . . .$100-$125

1968 Chicago (AL) - Lopez, Aparicio, John . . . .$100-$150

1968 Chicago (NL) - Durocher, Banks, Santo, Williams,
Jenkins . . . .$125-$200

1968 Cincinnati - Perez, Rose, Pinson, Bench . . . .$175-$250

1968 Cleveland - Tiant, McDowell . . . .$100-$150

1968 Detroit - Cash, Freehan, Kaline, McLain, Lolich,
Mathews . . . .$375-$600

1968 Houston - Staub, Morgan . . . .$100-$150

1968 Los Angeles - Alston, Davis, Drysdale, Sutton . . . . .$125-$200

1968 Minnesota - Carew, Oliva, Killebrew, Kaat . . . .$175-$250

1968 New York (AL) - Mantle, Bahnsen . . . .$200-$300

1968 New York (NL) - Hodges, Kranepool, Harrelson,
Swoboda, Koosman, Seaver, Ryan . . . .$500-$800

1968 Oakland - Bando, Jackson, Odom, Hunter, Fingers . . .$200-$300

1968 Philadelphia - White, Allen . . . .$75-$125

1968 Pittsburgh - Mazeroski, Wills, Clemente, Stargell,
Oliver, Bunning . . . .$450-$650

1968 San Francisco - McCovey, Bonds, Mays, Marichal,
Perry, McCormick . . . .$175-$250

1968 St. Louis - Schoendienst, Cepeda, Maris, Brock,
Simmons, Gibson, Carlton, McCarver . . . .$450-$600

1968 Washington - Howard . . . .$100-$150

1969 Atlanta - Cepeda, Aaron, Evans, Niekro, Wilhelm . . . .$200-$300

1969 Baltimore - Weaver, Powell, B. Robinson, F. Robinson,
Cueller, Palmer . . . .$150-$275

1969 Boston - Yastrzemski, Lyle . . . .$300-$400

1969 California - Fregosi, Wilhelm . . . .$75-$125

1969 Chicago (AL) - Lopez, Aparicio, John . . . .$150-$200

1969 Chicago (NL) - Durocher, Banks, Santo, Williams,
Jenkins . . . .$125-$200

1969 Cincinnati - Perez, Rose, Bench . . . .$175-$250

1958 New York Yankees

1966 California Angels

1965 San Francisco Giants

1969 Cleveland - McDowell, Tiant . . . .$75-$125

1969 Detroit - Cash, Kaline, Freehan, McLain, Lolich . . . . .$125-$175

1969 Houston - Morgan . . . .$75-$125

1969 Kansas City - Piniella . . . .$250-$375

1969 Los Angeles - Alston, Sizemore, Wills, Davis, Drysdale,
   Bunning, Buckner, Garvey . . . .$175-$250

1969 Minnesota - Carew, Killebrew, Oliva, Nettles, Kaat . . .$275-$375

1969 Montreal - Staub . . . .$275-$450

1969 New York (AL) - Murcer, Munson, Stottlemyre . . . . .$200-$275

1969 New York (NL) - Harrelson, Swoboda, Seaver,
   Koosman, Ryan . . . .$750-$2,000

1969 Oakland - Bando, Jackson, Odom, Hunter, Fingers,
   Blue . . . .$250-$325

1969 Philadelphia - Allen . . . .$100-$150

1969 Pittsburgh - Oliver, Mazeroski, Clemente, Stargell,
   Bunning . . . .$325-$575

1969 San Diego - Colbert, Gaston, J. Niekro . . . .$200-$300

1969 San Francisco - McCovey, Bonds, Mays, Marichal,
   Perry . . . .$125-$250

1969 Seattle - T. Davis, Harper, Segui . . . .$400-$600

1969 St. Louis - Pinson, Torre, Simmons, Gibson, Carlton,
   Schoendienst, Brock, McCarver . . . .$125-$225

1969 Washington - Williams, Howard . . . .$150-$200

1970 Atlanta - Cepeda, Aaron, Evans, Niekro, Wilhelm . . . .$125-$200

1970 Baltimore - Weaver, Powell, B. Robinson, F. Robinson,
   Palmer . . . .$325-$400

1970 Boston - Yastrzemski, Lyle . . . .$125-$175

1970 California - Fregosi . . . .$75-$125

1970 Chicago (AL) - Aparicio, John . . . .$150-$200

1970 Chicago (NL) - Durocher, Banks, Santo, Williams,
   Jenkins, Wilhelm . . . .$150-$225

1970 Cincinnati - Anderson, Concepcion, Perez, Rose,
   Bench . . . .$225-$300

1970 Cleveland - Nettles, Pinson, McDowell . . . .$75-$125

1970 Detroit - Cash, Kaline, Freehan, Lolich . . . .$100-$150

1970 Houston - Morgan . . . .$75-$125

1970 Kansas City - Lemon, Piniella . . . .$125-$175

1970 Los Angeles - Alston, Wills, Garvey, Buckner, Sutton . . .$175-$250

1970 Milwaukee - Harper . . . .$100-$175

1970 Minnesota - Killebrew, Oliva, Carew, Perry, Kaat,
   Tiant . . . .$200-$400

1970 Montreal - Staub, Morton . . . .$100-$150

1970 New York (AL) - Murcer, Munson, Stottlemyre . . . . .$275-$375

1970 New York (NL) - Hodges, Koosman, Harrelson, Swoboda,
   Kranepool, Seaver, Ryan, Clendenon . . . .$275-$400

1970 Oakland - Bando, Jackson, Hunter, Fingers . . . .$150-$250

1970 Philadelphia - Bowa, McCarver, Bunning, Luzinski . . .$100-$150

1970 Pittsburgh - Mazeroski, Clemente, Stargell, Oliver . . .$600-$800

1970 San Diego - Colbert, Gaston . . . .$100-$150

1970 San Francisco - McCovey, Bonds, Mays, Foster, Perry,
   Marichal . . . .$175-$275

1970 St. Louis - Allen, Torre, Brock, Simmons, Gibson,
   Carlton . . . .$150-$200

1970 Washington - Williams, Howard . . . .$150-$200

1971 Atlanta - Aaron, Evans, Williams, Cepeda, Niekro,
   Wilhelm . . . .$125-$200

1971 Baltimore - Weaver, Powell, B. Robinson, F. Robinson,
   Palmer . . . .$250-$300

1971 Boston - Aparicio, Fisk, Lyle, Tiant . . . .$125-$175

1971 California - Fregosi . . . .$100-$125

1971 Chicago (AL) - John . . . .$100-$125

1971 Chicago (NL) - Santo, Williams, Banks, Jenkins . . . . .$100-$150

1971 Cincinnati - Concepcion, Perez, Rose, Foster, Bench . .$175-$250

1971 Cleveland - Chambliss, Nettles, Pinson, McDowell . . .$100-$125

1971 Detroit - Martin, Cash, Kaline, Freehan, Lolich . . . . . .$150-$200

1971 Houston - Morgan . . . .$75-$125

1971 Kansas City - Lemon, Piniella . . . .$75-$125

1971 Los Angeles - Alston, Wills, Garvey, Buckner, Sutton,
   Wilhelm . . . .$175-$250

1971 Milwaukee - Harper . . . .$75-$100

1971 Minnesota - Killebrew, Carew, Oliva, Blyleven, Kaat
   . . . .$100-$150

1971 Montreal - Staub . . . .$75-$100

1971 New York (AL) - Murcer, Munson, Stottlemyre . . . . .$250-$450

1971 New York (NL) - Hodges, Kranepool, Harrelson,
   Seaver, Ryan, Koosman . . . .$250-$375

1971 Oakland - Bando, Jackson, Hunter, Blue, Fingers . . .$200-$275

1971 Philadelphia - Bowa, McCarver, Luzinski, Bunning . . .$100-$150

1971 Pittsburgh - Clemente, Oliver, Stargell, Mazeroski . . . .$500-$700

1971 San Diego - Colbert, Gaston . . . .$100-$150

1971 San Francisco - McCovey, Bonds, Mays, Kingman,
Foster, Marichal, Perry . . . .$175-$300

1971 St. Louis - Schoendienst, Torre, Brock, Simmons,
Carlton, Gibson . . . .$150-$250

1971 Washington - Williams, Harrah, Howard, McLain . . . .$200-$250

1972 Atlanta - Mathews, Aaron, Evans, Cepeda, Niekro . . . .$125-$200

1972 Baltimore - Weaver, Powell, Robinson . . . .$150-$175

1972 Boston - Aparicio, Yastrzemski, Fisk, Tiant . . . .$150-$200

1972 California - Pinson, Ryan . . . .$100-$150

1972 Chicago (AL) - Allen, Gossage . . . .$50-$125

1972 Chicago (NL) - Durocher, Santo, Williams, Jenkins . . .$100-$150

1972 Cincinnati - Anderson, Perez, Morgan, Concepcion,
Rose, Bench, Foster . . . .$275-$375

1972 Cleveland - Nettles, Bell, Perry . . . .$100-$125

1972 Detroit - Cash, Northrup, Freehan, Kaline, Lolich . . . .$150-$225

1972 Houston - Durocher . . . .$65-$85

1972 Kansas City - Piniella . . . .$85-$110

1972 Los Angeles - Alston, Garvey, Robinson, Davis, Sutton,
John, Wilhelm . . . .$175-$250

1972 Milwaukee - Scott . . . .$75-$110

1972 Minnesota - Killebrew, Carew, Oliva, Blyleven, Kaat . . .$125-$175

1972 Montreal - Singleton, McCarver . . . .$100-$150

1972 New York (AL) - Murcer, Munson, Stottlemyre . . . . .$200-$275

1972 New York (NL) - Hodges, Berra, Staub, Kranepool,
Harrelson, Mays, Seaver, Matlack, Koosman . . . .$200-$300

1972 Oakland - Bando, Jackson, Cepeda, Hunter, Fingers,
Blue . . . .$350-$400

1972 Philadelphia - Bowa, Luzinski, McCarver, Boone,
Schmidt, Carlton . . . .$125-$175

1972 Pittsburgh - Stargell, Clemente, Oliver, Mazeroski . . . .$500-$725

1972 San Diego - Colbert, Gaston . . . .$75-$100

1972 San Francisco - McCovey, Bonds, Mays, Marichal . .$200-$300

1972 St. Louis - Schoendienst, Torre, Brock, Simmons,
Gibson . . . .$150-$200

1972 Texas - Williams, Howard, Harrah . . . .$150-$210

1973 Atlanta - Mathews, Aaron, P. Niekro, J. Niekro . . . . .$125-$200

1973 Baltimore - Weaver, Powell, Robinson, Bumbry,
Palmer . . . .$175-$250

1973 Boston - Yastrzemski, Aparicio, Fisk, Cepeda, Evans,
Tiant . . . .$100-$175

1973 California - Pinson, Robinson, Ryan . . . .$75-$150

1973 Chicago (AL) - Kaat, Gossage . . . .$75-$125

1973 Chicago (NL) - Kessinger, Williams, Jenkins . . . .$75-$100

1973 Cincinnati - Anderson, Perez, Concepcion, Rose, Bench,
Foster . . . .$225-$350

1973 Cleveland - Perry . . . .$85-$125

1973 Detroit - Martin, Cash, Northrup, Freehan, Kaline, Lolich,
Perry . . . .$150-$180

1973 Houston - Richard . . . .$75-$100

1973 Kansas City - Piniella, Brett . . . .$175-$300

1973 Los Angeles - Alston, Buckner, Cey, Davis, Garvey,
Sutton, John . . . .$125-$200

1973 Milwaukee - Thomas . . . .$80-$120

1973 Minnesota - Carew, Oliva, Killebrew, Kaat, Blyleven . . .$100-$150

1973 Montreal - Singleton . . . .$80-$100

1973 New York (AL) - Nettles, Murcer, Munson, Stottlemyre,
McDowell, Lyle . . . .$200-$235

1973 New York (NL) - Berra, Harrelson, Staub, Jones,
Kranepool, Seaver, Koosman . . . .$275-$425

1973 Oakland - Bando, Jackson, Hunter, Blue, Fingers . . .$275-$425

1973 Philadelphia - Bowa, Schmidt, Luzinski, Boone,
Carlton . . . .$125-$175

1973 Pittsburgh - Oliver, Stargell, Parker . . . .$125-$175

1973 San Diego - Winfield . . . .$100-$125

1973 San Francisco - McCovey, Bonds, Matthews,
Marichal . . . .$100-$150

1973 St. Louis - Schoendienst, Torre, Brock, Simmons,
McCarver, Gibson . . . .$100-$150

1973 Texas - Martin, Harrah, Burroughs, Madlock . . . .$65-$125

1974 Atlanta - Mathews, Evans, Aaron, P. Niekro . . . .$150-$200

1974 Baltimore - Weaver, Powell, Robinson, Palmer . . . . .$200-$300

1974 Boston - Yastrzemski, Evans, Fisk, Cooper, Rice, Lynn,
McCarver, Marichal . . . .$150-$225

1974 California - Robinson, Ryan . . . .$100-$150

1974 Chicago (AL) - Allen, Kaat, Gossage . . . .$75-$125

1974 Chicago (NL) - Kessinger, Madlock . . . .$75-$100

1974 Cincinnati - Anderson, Perez, Morgan, Concepcion,
Foster, Rose, Bench . . . .$225-$350

1974 Cleveland - G. Perry, J. Perry . . . .$100-$150

1974 Detroit - Freehan, Horton, Kaline, Lolich . . . .$150-$200

1974 Houston - Wilson, Richard . . . .$75-$100

1974 Kansas City - Brett, Pinson . . . .$100-$150

1974 Los Angeles - Alston, Garvey, Cey, Buckner, Sutton,
Marshall, John . . . .$150-$225

1974 Milwaukee - Yount . . . .$150-$200

1974 Minnesota - Carew, Oliva, Killebrew, Blyleven . . . . . .$125-$150

1974 Montreal - Singleton, Davis, Carter . . . .$75-$100

1974 New York (AL) - Nettles, Murcer, Munson, Lyle,
McDowell . . . .$175-$250

1974 New York (NL) - Harrelson, Staub, Jones, Kranepool,
Koosman, Seaver . . . .$135-$200

1974 Oakland - Bando, Jackson, Hunter, Blue, Fingers . . .$250-$375

1974 Philadelphia - Bowa, Schmidt, Luzinski, Boone . . . . .$100-$150

1974 Pittsburgh - Oliver, Stargell, Parker, Tekulve . . . .$150-$200

1974 San Diego - McCovey, Winfield . . . .$75-$125

1974 San Francisco - Kingman, Bonds . . . .$50-$100

1974 St. Louis - Torre, McBride, Brock, Simmons, McCarver,
Gibson . . . .$125-$175

1974 Texas - Martin, Hargrove, Harrah, Burroughs, Jenkins . . .$100-$145

1975 Atlanta - Evans, Niekro . . . .$100-$150

1965 Houston Astros

1964 Philadelphia Phillies

1963 New York Mets

1975 Baltimore - Weaver, Robinson, Palmer ....$150-$250

1975 Boston - Yastrzemski, Evans, Lynn, Rice, Fisk, Cooper,
Conigliaro, Tiant ....$375-$550

1975 California - Ryan ....$200-$275

1975 Chicago (AL) - Kaat, Gossage ....$75-$100

1975 Chicago (NL) - Madlock ....$75-$125

1975 Cincinnati - Anderson, Perez, Morgan, Concepcion,
Rose, Foster, Bench ....$350-$400

1975 Cleveland - Robinson ....$150-$225

1975 Detroit - Freehan, Horton, Lolich ....$75-$115

1975 Houston - Richard ....$65-$95

1975 Kansas City - Brett, Killebrew ....$150-$200

1975 Los Angeles - Alston, Garvey, Cey, Buckner, Sutton,
John ....$125-$175

1975 Milwaukee - Yount, Aaron ....$200-$275

1975 Minnesota - Carew, Bostock, Oliva, Blyleven ......$200-$300

1975 Montreal - Carter ....$75-$125

1975 New York (AL) - Martin, Nettles, Bonds, Munson,
Piniella, Hunter, Lyle, Guidry ....$250-$450

1975 New York (NL) - Kranepool, Staub, Kingman, Grote,
Seaver, Koosman ....$115-$125

1975 Oakland - Bando, Jackson, Williams, Blue, Fingers,
Odom ....$250-$350

1975 Philadelphia - Allen, Schmidt, Luzinski, Boone,
McCarver, Carlton ....$100-$150

1975 Pittsburgh - Stargell, Parker, Oliver, Candelaria,
Tekulve ....$175-$225

1975 San Diego - McCovey, Winfield ....$85-$125

1975 San Francisco - Murcer, Clark ....$45-$100

1975 St. Louis - Schoendienst, Brock, Simmons, Hernandez,
Gibson ....$100-$150

1975 Texas - Martin, Harrah, Jenkins, Perry ....$100-$200

1976 Atlanta - Murphy, Niekro ....$75-$100

1976 Baltimore - Weaver, Jackson, Robinson, Palmer .....$150-$200

1976 Boston - Yastrzemski, Evans, Lynn, Rice, Fisk, Cooper,
Tiant, Jenkins ....$175-$300

1976 California - Ryan ....$125-$175

1976 Chicago (AL) - Gossage ....$60-$90

1976 Chicago (NL) - Madlock ....$60-$90

1976 Cincinnati - Anderson, Perez, Morgan, Concepcion, Rose,
Griffey, Foster, Bench, Zachry ....$400-$600

1976 Cleveland - Robinson, Powell, Bell ....$75-$125

1976 Detroit - Staub, Freehan, Horton, Fidrych ....$100-$125

1976 Houston - Richard ....$60-$90

1976 Kansas City - Brett ....$125-$200

1976 Los Angeles - Alston, Garvey, Cey, Buckner, Sutton,
John ....$100-$150

1976 Milwaukee - Yount, Aaron, Frisella ....$100-$150

1976 Minnesota - Carew, Bostock, Oliva, Blyleven ....$75-$125

1976 Montreal - Carter, Dawson ....$75-$125

1976 New York (AL) - Martin, Nettles, Munson, Hunter, Lyle
....$150-$300

1976 New York (NL) - Kranepool, Harrelson, Kingman, Torre,
Koosman, Seaver, Lolich ....$150-$200

1976 Oakland - Williams, Blue, Fingers ....$100-$125

1976 Philadelphia - Allen, Bowa, Schmidt, Luzinski, Boone,
McCarver, Carlton, Kaat ....$125-$200

1976 Pittsburgh - Stargell, Parker, Oliver, Candelaria,
Tekulve ....$150-$175

1976 San Diego - Winfield, McCovey, Jones, Metzger .....$100-$125

1976 San Francisco - Evans, Murcer, Clark ....$75-$100

1976 St. Louis - Schoendienst, Hernandez, Brock,
Simmons ....$125-$200

1976 Texas - Harrah, Thompson, Perry, Blyleven ....$75-$100

1977 Atlanta - Niekro ....$60-$90

1977 Baltimore - Weaver, Murray, Robinson, Palmer .....$100-$150

1977 Boston - Evans, Lynn, Yastrzemski, Fisk, Rice, Tiant,
Jenkins ....$125-$175

1977 California - Grich, Bonds, Ryan ....$100-$150

1977 Chicago (AL) - B. Lemon ....$60-$90

1977 Chicago (NL) - Buckner, Trillo, Murcer, R. Reuschel ...$60-$75

1977 Cincinnati - Anderson, Morgan, Concepcion, Rose,
Griffey, Foster, Bench, Seaver ....$125-$175

1977 Cleveland - Robinson, Bell, Eckersley ....$125-$175

1977 Detroit - Staub, Trammell, Whitaker, Morris ....$100-$150

1977 Houston - Richard ....$60-$90

1977 Kansas City - Brett . . . .$150-$200

1977 Los Angeles - Lasorda, Garvey, Cey, Mota, John, Sutton
. . . .$175-$250

1977 Milwaukee - Cooper, Yount . . . .$75-$125

1977 Minnesota - Carew, Bostock . . . .$85-$100

1977 Montreal - Perez, Dawson, Carter . . . .$80-$120

1977 New York (AL) - Martin, Nettles, Jackson, Munson,
Piniella, Guidry, Lyle, Hunter . . . .$350-$450

1977 New York (NL) - Harrelson, Kranepool, Kingman,
Grote, Koosman, Seaver . . . .$100-$150

1977 Oakland - Allen, Armas, Blue . . . .$60-$90

1977 Philadelphia - Bowa, Schmidt, Luzinski, Boone,
McCarver, Carlton, Kaat . . . .$125-$175

1977 Pittsburgh - Stargell, Parker, Oliver, Gossage, Tekulve . . .$125-$200

1977 San Diego - Winfield, Kingman, Fingers . . . .$100-$150

1977 San Francisco - McCovey, Madlock, Clark . . . .$100-$150

1977 Seattle - R. Jones, Segui . . . .$125-$175

1977 St. Louis - Hernandez, Brock, Simmons . . . .$80-$120

1977 Texas - Perry, Blyleven . . . .$50-$100

1977 Toronto - Rader, Fairly . . . .$150-$200

1978 Atlanta - Murphy, Horner, Neikro . . . .$75-$100

1978 Baltimore - Weaver, Murray, Palmer . . . .$125-$175

1978 Boston - Evans, Lynn, Yastrzemski, Fisk, Rice,
Eckersley . . . .$100-$150

1978 California - Bostock, Ryan . . . .$80-$120

1978 Chicago (AL) - Bob Lemon . . . .$60-$90

1978 Chicago (NL) - Murcer, Kingman . . . .$60-$90

1978 Cincinnati - Anderson, Morgan, Concepcion, Rose, Foster,
Bench, Seaver . . . .$150-$200

1978 Cleveland - Bell . . . .$85-$100

1978 Detroit - Whitaker, Trammell, Staub, Morris . . . .$100-$150

1978 Houston - Richard . . . .$60-$90

1978 Kansas City - Brett . . . .$120-$180

1978 Los Angeles - Lasorda, Garvey, Cey, Guerrero, John,
Sutton . . . .$150-$225

1978 Milwaukee - Molitor, Yount . . . .$80-$120

1978 Minnesota - Carew . . . .$70-$125

1978 Montreal - Perez, Dawson, Carter . . . .$80-$120

1978 New York (AL) - Martin, Jackson, Lyle, Munson, Guidry,
Hunter, Gossage, Lemon, Piniella . . . .$275-$400

1978 New York (NL) - Kranepool, Koosman . . . .$75-$100

1978 Oakland - Armas, Carty . . . .$60-$90

1978 Philadephia - Schmidt, Luzinski, Boone, Carlton,
Kaat . . . .$125-$175

1978 Pittsburgh - Stargell, Parker, Blyleven, Candelaria,
Tekulve . . . .$125-$175

1978 San Diego - Smith, Winfield, Perry, Fingers . . . .$125-$175

1978 San Francisco - McCovey, Clark, Blue . . . .$100-$150

1978 Seattle - R. Jones, B. Robertson . . . .$60-$90

1978 St. Louis - Boyer, Hernandez, Brock, Simmons . . . . .$130-$160

1978 Texas - Harrah, Oliver, Jenkins . . . .$75-$100

1978 Toronto - Carty, Mayberry . . . .$65-$150

1979 Atlanta - Murphy, Horner, Niekro . . . .$75-$125

1979 Baltimore - Weaver, Murray, Flanagan, Palmer . . . . .$175-$250

1979 Boston - Lynn, Rice, Fisk, Yastrzemski, Eckersley . . .$125-$175

1979 California - Carew, Lansford, Baylor, Ryan . . . .$125-$175

1979 Chicago (AL) - Ortz . . . .$75-$100

1979 Chicago (NL) - Buckner, Kingman, Sutter . . . .$60-$90

1979 Cincinnati - Morgan, Concepcion, Griffey, Foster,
Bench, Seaver . . . .$125-$175

1979 Cleveland - Harrah . . . .$60-$90

1979 Detroit - Anderson, Whitaker, Trammell, Staub, Morris
. . . .$100-$150

1979 Houston - Richard . . . .$75-$100

1979 Kansas City - Brett, Quisenberry . . . .$100-$150

1979 Los Angeles - Lasorda, Garvey, Cey, Guerrero, Sutcliffe,
Sutton . . . .$100-$150

1979 Milwaukee - Molitor, Yount . . . .$150-$200

1979 Minnesota - Castino, Koosman . . . .$75-$90

1979 Montreal - Perez, Dawson, Carter, Staub, Raines . . . .$100-$150

1979 New York (AL) - Martin, Nettles, Jackson, Munson,
Murcer, John, Guidry, Tiant, Gossage, Kaat, Hunter . . . .$175-$250

1979 New York (NL) - Kranepool . . . .$85-$100

1979 Oakland - Armas, Henderson . . . .$75-$90

1979 Philadelphia - Rose, Trillo, Bowa, Schmidt, Luzinski,
Boone, Carlton, Kaat . . . .$150-$200

1979 Pittsburgh - Stargell, Madlock, Parker, Candelaria,
Blyleven, Tekulve . . . .$275-$375

1979 San Diego - Smith, Winfield, Perry, Fingers, Lolich . .$125-$175

1979 San Francisco - McCovey, Clark, Madlock, Blue . . . . .$125-$150

1979 Seattle - Bochte, W. Horton . . . .$60-$90

1979 St. Louis - Boyer, Hernandez, Brock, Simmons . . . . .$125-$175

1979 Texas - Bell, Oliver, Jenkins, Lyle . . . .$65-$95

1979 Toronto - Griffin, Stieb . . . .$60-$90

1980 Atlanta - Horner, Murphy, Niekro . . . .$90-$125

1980 Baltimore - Weaver, Murray, Stone, Palmer . . . .$150-$225

1980 Boston - Perez, Evans, Lynn, Rice, Fisk, Yastrzemski,
Eckersley . . . .$125-$200

1980 California - Carew, Lansford . . . .$75-$100

1980 Chicago (AL) - Baines . . . .$60-$90

1980 Chicago (NL) - Buckner, Kingman . . . .$60-$90

1980 Cincinnati - Concepcion, Griffey, Foster, Bench, Seaver
. . . .$75-$100

1980 Cleveland - Harrah, Charboneau . . . .$45-$75

1980 Detroit - Anderson, Whitaker, Trammell, Gibson, Morris
. . . .$100-$150

1980 Houston - Morgan, Ryan . . . .$125-$175

1980 Kansas City - Brett, Quisenberry . . . .$175-$250

1980 Los Angeles - Lasorda, Garvey, Guerrero, Welch,
Sutton, Howe, Valenzuela . . . .$100-$150

1980 Milwaukee - Molitor, Yount . . . .$80-$120

1980 Minnesota - Koosman . . . .$60-$85

1980 Montreal - Dawson, Carter, Raines . . . .$100-$150

1968 St. Louis Cardinals

1969 Atlanta Braves

1972 Houston Astros

1980 New York (AL) - Nettles, Jackson, Piniella, Murcer, Guidry, Tiant, Gossage, John, Perry, Kaat . . . .$200-$250

1980 New York (NL) - Wilson . . . .$75-$100

1980 Oakland - Martin, Henderson . . . .$140-$210

1980 Philadelphia - Rose, Bowa, Schmidt, Luzinski, Boone, Carlton, Lyle . . . .$275-$350

1980 Pittsburgh - Stargell, Madlock, Parker, Candelaria, Tekulve, Blyleven . . . .$150-$175

1980 San Diego - Smith, Winfield, Fingers . . . .$80-$120

1980 San Francisco - Clark, McCovey, Blue . . . .$75-$120

1980 Seattle - Bachte, W. Horton . . . .$60-$90

1980 St. Louis - Schoendienst, Hernandez, Simmons, Kaat . .$80-$120

1980 Texas - Bell, Oliver, Staub, Jenkins, Perry, Lyle . . . . . .$75-$100

1980 Toronto - Stieb . . . .$60-$90

1981 Atlanta - Murphy, Butler, Perry, Niekro . . . .$100-$150

1981 Baltimore - Weaver, Murray, C. Ripken Jr., Palmer . . .$100-$150

1981 Boston - Lansford, Rice, Yastrzemski, Eckersley . . . . .$100-$150

1981 California - Carew, Lynn . . . .$60-$90

1981 Chicago (AL) - Baines, Fisk, Luzinski, Hoyt . . . .$75-$100

1981 Chicago (NL) - Buckner . . . .$60-$90

1981 Cincinnati - Concepcion, Griffey, Foster, Bench, Seaver . . . .$80-$120

1981 Cleveland - Harrah, Blyleven . . . .$60-$90

1981 Detroit - Anderson, Whitaker, Trammell, Gibson, Morris . . . .$100-$125

1981 Houston - Ryan, Sutton . . . .$100-$125

1981 Kansas City - Brett, Quisenberry . . . .$75-$100

1981 Los Angeles - Garvey, Cey, Guerrero, Sax, Valenzuela, Stewart . . . .$275-$350

1981 Milwaukee - Yount, Molitor, Fingers . . . .$100-$150

1981 Minnesota - Koosman, Ward . . . .$60-$90

1981 Montreal - Dawson, Raines, Carter . . . .$150-$175

1981 New York - Kingman, Staub . . . .$100-$125

1981 New York (AL) - Nettles, Jackson, Winfield, Murcer, Piniella, Guidry, John, Gossage . . . .$200-$250

1981 Oakland - Martin, Henderson . . . .$125-$200

1981 Philadelphia - Rose, Bowa, Schmidt, Boone, Sandberg, Carlton, Lyle . . . .$100-$150

1981 Pittsburgh - Parker, Stargell, Madlock . . . .$75-$125

1981 San Diego - Smith, Kennedy . . . .$60-$95

1981 San Francisco - Morgan, Clark, Blue . . . .$65-$95

1981 Seattle - Henderson . . . .$50-$85

1981 St. Louis- Hernandez, Kaat . . . .$100-$135

1981 Texas - Bell, Oliver, Jenkins . . . .$65-$95

1981 Toronto - Bell, Barfield, Stieb . . . .$60-$100

1982 Atlanta - Murphy, Butler, Niekro . . . .$90-$150

1982 Baltimore - Weaver, Murray, Ripken, Palmer . . . .$100-$150

1982 Boston - Lansford, Rice, Yastrzemski, Boggs, Perez, Eckersley . . . .$150-$250

1982 California - Carew, Jackson, Lynn, Boone, John, Tiant . . .$125-$200

1982 Chicago (AL) - Baines, Fisk, Luzinski, Hoyt, Lyle . . . .$75-$125

1982 Chicago (NL) - Buckner, Sandberg, Jenkins, Hernandez . . .$80-$120

1982 Cincinnati - Concepcion, Bench, Seaver . . . .$75-$125

1982 Cleveland - Harrah, Blyleven . . . .$60-$90

1982 Detroit - Anderson, Whitaker, Trammell, Gibson, Johnson, Morris . . . .$100-$150

1982 Houston - Ryan, Sutton . . . .$75-$125

1982 Kansas City - Brett, Quisenberry . . . .$75-$100

1982 Los Angeles - Garvey, Sax, Guerrero, Valenzuela, Stewart . . . .$100-$150

1982 Milwaukee - Yount, Molitor, Vuckovich, Fingers, Sutton . . . .$250-$350

1982 Minnesota- Hrbek, Brunansky, Viola . . . .$60-$90

1982 Montreal - Oliver, Dawson, Raines, Carter, Reardon . . .$75-$125

1982 New York(AL) - Lemon, Nettles, Winfield, Piniella, Murcer, Mattingly, John, Guidry, Gossage . . . .$125-$175

1982 New York (NL) - Kingman, Foster . . . .$80-$120

1982 Oakland - Martin, Henderson . . . .$150-$180

1982 Philadelphia - Rose, Schmidt, Carlton, Lyle . . . .$150-$175

1982 Pittsburgh - Madlock, Parker, Stargell, Candelaria, Tekulve . . . .$90-$135

1982 San Diego - Kennedy, Gwynn . . . .$80-$120

1982 San Francisco - Robinson, Morgan, Clark, Leonard . . . .$60-$90

1982 Seattle - Perry . . . .$60-$90

1982 St. Louis - Hernandez, Smith, McGee . . . .$275-$350

1982 Texas - Bell ....$60-$90

1982 Toronto - Barfield, Stieb ....$60-$90

1983 Atlanta - Murphy, Butler, Niekro ....$60-$90

1983 Baltimore - Murray, Ripken, Palmer ....$300-$450

1983 Boston - Boggs, Rice, Yastrzemski, Eckersley ....$150-$200

1983 California - Carew, Lynn, Boone, Jackson, John .....$80-$120

1983 Chicago (AL) - Baines, Kittle, Fisk, Hoyt ....$150-$180

1983 Chicago (NL) - Buckner, Sandberg, Jenkins, Hernandez ....$100-$150

1983 Cincinnati - Concepcion, Bench ....$75-$100

1983 Cleveland - Franco, Harrah, Blyleven ....$60-$90

1983 Detroit - Anderson, Whitaker, Trammell, Johnson, Morris ....$125-$150

1983 Houston - Ryan ....$100-$150

1983 Kansas City - Brett, Quisenberry, Perry ....$80-$120

1983 Los Angeles - Sax, Guerrero, Valenzuela, Welch, Stewart, Hershiser ....$125-$175

1983 Milwaukee - Yount, Molitor, Simmons, Fingers, Kuenn ....$100-$200

1983 Minnesota - Hrbek, Brunansky, Viola ....$60-$90

1983 Montreal - Oliver, Dawson, Raines, Carter ....$75-$100

1983 New York (AL) - Martin, Nettles, Winfield, Piniella, Murcer, Guidry, Gossage ....$200-$300

1983 New York (NL) - Strawberry, Foster, Staub, Kingman, Seaver ....$100-$150

1983 Oakland - Lansford, Henderson ....$75-$85

1983 Philadelphia - Rose, Morgan, Schmidt, Perez, Denny, Hernandez ....$175-$250

1983 Pittsburgh - Madlock, Parker, Candelaria, Tekulve .....$60-$90

1983 San Diego - Garvey, Gwynn ....$100-$150

1983 San Francisco - Robinson ....$60-$90

1983 Seattle - Perry ....$60-$90

1983 St. Louis - Smith, McGee, Hernandez ....$100-$125.

1983 Texas - Bell, Stewart ....$60-$90

1983 Toronto - Bell, Fernandez, Stieb ....$60-$90.

1984 Atlanta - Murphy ....$60-$90.

1984 Baltimore - Murray, Ripken, Palmer ....$175-$225.

1984 Boston - Buckner, Boggs, Rice, Clemens ....$85-$110

1984 California - Carew, Lynn, Boone, Jackson, John .....$80-$120

1984 Chicago (AL) - Baines, Fisk, Seaver ....$75-$90.

1984 Chicago (NL) - Sandberg, Sutcliffe, Eckersley .....$175-$275

1984 Cincinnati - Rose, Concepcion, Parker, Perez, Davis ...$75-$125

1984 Cleveland - Franco, Blyleven. ....$75-$90

1984 Detroit - Anderson, Whitaker, Trammell, Johnson, Gibson, Morris, Hemandez ....$350-$500

1984 Houston - Davis, Ryan ....$65-$100

1984 Kansas City - Brett, Saberhagen ....$100-$150

1984 Los Angeles - Sax, Guerrero, Valenzuela, Hershiser ..$125-$150

1984 Milwaukee - Yount, Sutton ....$100-$125

1984 Minnesota - Hrbek, Puckett, Viola ....$85-$150

1984 Montreal - Dawson, Raines, Carter, Rose ....$100-$150

1984 New York (AL) - Berra, Mattingly, Winfield, Piniella, Niekro, Guidry. ....$125-$175

1984 New York (NL) - Hernandez, Strawberry, Foster, Gooden ....$125-$150

1984 Oakland - Morgan, Lansford, Henderson ....$85-$100

1984 Philadelphia - Schmidt, Carlton ....$100-$150

1984 Pittsburgh - Madlock, Candelaria, Tekulve ....$65-$90

1984 San Diego - Garvey, Nettles, Gwynn, Gossage .....$175-$250

1984 San Francisco - Oliver, Leonard, Clark ....$75-$90

1984 Seattle - Davis, Tartabull, Langston ....$60-$90

1984 St. Louis - O. Smith, McGee ....$125-$150

1984 Texas - Stewart ....$60-$90

1984 Toronto - Bell, Fernandez, Stieb ....$100-$125

1985 Atlanta - Murphy ....$60-$90

1985 Baltimore - Weaver, Murray, Ripken, Lynn ....$50-$85

1985 Boston - Boggs, Rice, Clemens ....$60-$90

1985 California - Carew, Jackson, Boone, Sutton, John .....$80-$120

1985 Chicago (AL) - Guillen, Baines, Fisk, Seaver ....$75-$100

1985 Chicago (NL) - Sandberg, Eckersley ....$60-$90

1985 Cincinnati - Rose, Concepcion, Parker, Perez, Davis ...$75-$125

1985 Cleveland - Franco, Carter, Blyleven ....$50-$85

1985 Detroit - Anderson, Whitaker, Trammell, Gibson, Morris ....$75-$125

1985 Houston - Davis, Ryan ....$75-$100

1985 Kansas City - Brett, Saberhagen ....$300-$400

1985 Los Angeles - Sax, Oliver, Hershiser, Valenzuela. .....$60-$150

1985 Milwaukee - Yount, Fingers ....$60-$90

1985 Minnesota - Hrbek, Puckett, Viola, Blyleven ....$75-$100

1985 Montreal - Dawson, Raines ....$45-$75

1985 New York (AL) - Berra, Martin, Mattingly, Winfield, Henderson, Guidry, Niekro ....$125-$175

1985 New York (NL) - Hernandez, Johnson, Strawberry, Foster, Carter, Gooden ....$200-$300

1985 Oakland - Lansford, Kingman, Sutton ....$60-$90

1985 Philadelphia - Schmidt, Carlton ....$75-$100

1985 Pittsburgh - Madlock ....$60-$90

1985 San Diego - Garvey, Nettles, Gwynn, Gossage ....$75-$100

1985 San Francisco - Leonard ....$60-$90

1985 Seattle - Tartabull, Langston ....$60-$90

1985 St. Louis - Clark, McGee, Coleman ....$175-$250

1985 Texas - Harrah ....$70-$95

1985 Toronto - Fernandez, Bell, Fielder, Stieb ....$100-$150

1986 Atlanta - Murphy ....$50-$80

1986 Baltimore - Weaver, Murray, Ripken, Lynn ....$75-$100

1986 Boston - Boggs, Rice, Clemens, Seaver ....$200-$400

1986 California - Joyner, Boone, Jackson, Sutton ....$60-$90

1986 Chicago (AL) - Baines, Fisk, Carlton, Seaver ....$75-$100

1986 Chicago (NL) - Sandberg, Palmeiro, Eckersley ....$75-$100

1986 Cincinnati - Parker, Davis, Concepcion, Perez, Rose ....$60-$90

1986 Cleveland - Franco, Carter, Niekro ....$60-$75

1972 Oakland A's

1982 New York Yankees

1983 Milwaukee Brewers

1986 Detroit - Anderson, Whitaker, Trammell, Gibson, Morris
. . . .$100-$125

1986 Houston - Davis, Scott, Ryan . . . .$75-$100

1986 Kansas City - Howser, Brett, Jackson, Saberhagen . . . .$60-$90

1986 Los Angeles - Guerrero, Valenzuela, Hershiser . . . . . .$75-$100

1986 Milwaukee - Yount, Molitor . . . .$50-$75

1986 Minnesota - Hrbek, Puckett, Blyleven, Viola . . . .$80-$120

1986 Montreal - Dawson, Raines . . . .$50-$75

1986 New York (AL) - Mattingly, Winfield, Henderson,
Guidry, John . . . .$125-$200

1986 New York (NL) - Hernandez, Strawberry, Carter,
Mitchell, Foster, Gooden . . . .$350-$525

1986 Oakland - Canseco, McGwire, Stewart . . . .$100-$125

1986 Philadelphia - Schmidt, Carlton . . . .$75-$100

1986 Pittsburgh - Bonds, Bonilla . . . .$50-$75

1986 San Diego - Garvey, Gwynn, Gossage . . . .$60-$75

1986 San Francisco - Clark, Carlton . . . .$50-$75

1986 Seattle - Tartabull, Langston . . . .$60-$75

1986 St. Louis - Smith, McGee . . . .$75-$100

1986 Texas - Sierra . . . .$60-$75

1986 Toronto - Fernandez, Bell, Stieb . . . .$60-$75

1987 Atlanta - Murphy, Niekro . . . .$50-$75

1987 Baltimore - Murray, Ripken, Lynn . . . .$60-$85

1987 Boston - Boggs, Rice, Clemens . . . .$75-$100

1987 California - Joyner, Boone, Buckner, Sutton . . . .$65-$80

1987 Chicago (AL) - Fisk, Baines . . . .$75-$115

1987 Chicago (NL) - Sandberg, Dawson, Palmeiro . . . .$50-$75

1987 Cincinnati - Rose, Parker, Davis, Concepcion . . . .$75-$100

1987 Cleveland - Carter, Franco, Niekro, Carlton . . . .$75-$100

1987 Detroit - Anderson, Whitaker, Trammell, Gibson, Morris
. . . .$175-$200

1987 Houston - Davis, Ryan . . . .$100-$165

1987 Kansas City - Brett, Tartabull, Jackson, Saberhagen . . .$85-$100

1987 Los Angeles - Lasorda, Sax, Guerrero, Hershiser,
Valenzuela . . . .$80-$120

1987 Milwaukee - Molitor, Yount . . . .$45-$90

1987 Minnesota - Hrbek, Puckett, Viola, Blyleven, Carlton . . .$300-$400

1987 Montreal - Raines . . . .$75-$100

1987 New York (AL) - Mattingly, Henderson, Winfield, John,
Guidry . . . .$100-$150

1987 New York (NL) - Hernandez, Johnson, Strawberry,
Carter, Gooden . . . .$150-$175

1987 Oakland - McGwire, Canseco, Jackson, Stewart,
Eckersley . . . .$100-$150

1987 Philadelphia - Schmidt . . . .$50-$75

1987 Pittsburgh - Bonilla, Van Slyke, Bonds . . . .$75-$100

1987 San Diego - Gwynn, Garvey, Gossage . . . .$50-$75

1987 San Francisco - Clark, Mitchell, Williams . . . .$100-$150

1987 Seattle - Langston . . . .$50-$75

1987 St. Louis - Smith, McGee . . . .$175-$225

1987 Texas - Sierra . . . .$60-$90

1987 Toronto - Fernandez, Bell, McGriff, Stieb, Niekro . . . . .$75-$100

1988 Atlanta - Murphy . . . .$50-$80

1988 Baltimore - Robinson, Murray, Ripken, Lynn . . . .$75-$100

1988 Boston - Boggs, Rice, Clemens . . . .$75-$125

1988 California - Joyner, Boone, Buckner . . . .$60-$75

1988 Chicago (AL) - Fisk, Baines . . . .$65-$75

1988 Chicago (NL) - Grace, Sandberg, Dawson, Palmeiro,
Gossage . . . .$50-$80

1988 Cincinnati - Sabo . . . .$75-$100

1988 Cleveland - Franco, Carter . . . .$50-$75

1988 Detroit - Whitaker, Trammell, Lynn, Morris . . . .$85-$100

1988 Houston - Davis, Ryan . . . .$75-$125

1988 Kansas City - Brett, Tartabull, Jackson, Buckner,
Saberhagen . . . .$100-$125

1988 Los Angeles - Sax, Gibson, Hershiser, Valenzuela . . . .$200-$300

1988 Milwaukee - Yount, Molitor . . . .$50-$75

1988 Minnesota - Hrbek, Puckett, Viola, Blyleven, Carlton . . .$60-$85

1988 Montreal - Raines . . . .$50-$75

1988 New York (AL) - Martin, Mattingly, Winfield, Henderson,
John, Guidry . . . .$150-$200

1988 New York (NL) - Hernandez, Johnson, Strawberry, Carter,
Gooden . . . .$75-$150

1988 Oakland - McGwire, Lansford, Canseco, Parker,
Stewart, Welch, Eckersley . . . .$200-$250

1988 Philadelphia - Schmidt . . . .$75-$100

1988 Pittsburgh - Bonilla, Van Slyke, Bonds, Drabek . . . .$50-$75

1988 San Diego - Gwynn . . . .$60-$80

1988 San Francisco - Clark, Mitchell, Williams . . . .$60-$85

1988 Seattle - Langston . . . .$50-$75

1988 St. Louis - Smith, McGee, Guerrero . . . .$45-$70

1988 Texas - Sierra . . . .$50-$75

1988 Toronto - McGriff, Fernandez, Bell, Stieb . . . .$60-$85

1989 Atlanta - Murphy . . . .$100-$150

1989 Baltimore - Robinson, Ripken . . . .$75-$125

1989 Boston - Boggs, Clemens . . . .$75-$100

1989 California - Joyner, Blyleven . . . .$50-$75

1989 Chicago (AL) - Fisk, Baines . . . .$50-$75

1989 Chicago (NL) - Grace, Sandberg, Dawson . . . .$150-$225

1989 Cincinnati - Davis . . . .$50-$85

1989 Cleveland - Carter . . . .$50-$75

1989 Detroit - Anderson, Trammell, Lynn, Morris . . . .$50-$75

1989 Houston - Davis . . . .$40-$60

1989 Kansas City - Brett, Jackson, Boone, Tartabull,
Saberhagen . . . .$100-$150

1989 Los Angeles - Lasorda, Murray, Randolph, Gibson,
Hershiser, Valenzuela . . . .$125-$175

1989 Milwaukee - Yount, Molitor . . . .$90-$125

1989 Minnesota - Hrbek, Puckett, Viola . . . .$50-$85

1989 Montreal - Raines . . . .$75-$100

1989 New York (AL) - Mattingly, Sax, Winfield, Gossage . .$125-$150

1989 New York (NL) - Johnson, Strawberry, Hernandez, Carter,
Gooden . . . .$75-$145

1989 Oakland - LaRussa, McGwire, Canseco, D. Henderson,
R. Henderson, Parker, Stewart, Eckersley . . . .$225-$300

1989 Philadelphia - Dykstra, Schmidt . . . .$60-$100

1989 Pittsburgh - Bonilla, Van Slyke, Bonds . . . .$75-$100

1989 San Diego - Clark, Gwynn . . . .$50-$85

1989 San Francisco - Clark, Williams, Mitchell, Gossage . .$150-$200

1989 Seattle - Griffey Jr. . . . .$175-$250

1989 St. Louis - Guerrero, Smith, McGee . . . .$85-$125

1989 Texas - Palmeiro, Franco, Sierra, Baines, Ryan . . . . . .$75-$100

1989 Toronto - McGriff, Fernandez, Stieb . . . .$100-$150

1990 Atlanta - Justice, Murphy . . . .$100-$175

1990 Baltimore - F. Robinson, C. Ripken Jr. . . . .$75-$100

1990 Boston - Boggs, Clemens . . . .$100-$150

1990 California - Joyner, Winfield, Blyleven . . . .$75-$100

1990 Chicago (AL) - Fisk . . . .$50-$85

1990 Chicago (NL) - Dawson, Grace, Sandberg . . . .$100-$135

1990 Cincinnati - Larkin, Davis, Piniella . . . .$225-$300

1990 Cleveland - Hernandez . . . .$40-$60

1990 Detroit - Anderson, Fielder, Morris, Trammell,
Whitaker . . . .$75-$100

1990 Houston - Davis . . . .$40-$60

1990 Kansas City - Brett, Tartabull, Jackson, Saberhagen . . .$75-$125

1990 Los Angeles - Lasorda, Murray, Gibson, Valenzuela . . .$85-$125

1990 Milwaukee - Yount, Molitor, Parker . . . .$50-$75

1990 Minnesota - Hrbek, Puckett . . . .$50-$85

1990 Montreal - Raines . . . .$50-$85

1990 New York (AL) - Mattingly . . . .$125-$175

1990 New York (NL) - Strawberry, Johnson, Viola, Gooden . .$100-$125

1990 Oakland - McGwire, Randolph, Canseco, R. Henderson,
D. Henderson, Baines, McGee, Welch, Stewart,
Eckersley . . . .$150-$200

1990 Philadelphia - Dykstra, Murphy . . . .$40-$60

1990 Pittsburgh - Bonds, Bonilla, Van Slyke, Drabek . . . . .$100-$135

1990 San Diego - Gwynn, Carter, Clark . . . .$50-$75

1990 San Francisco - Clark, Mitchell, Williams . . . .$75-$100

1990 Seattle - Ken Griffey Jr., Ken Griffey Sr. . . . .$75-$100

1990 St. Louis - Guerrero, Smith, McGee . . . .$50-$85

1990 Texas - Palmeiro, Franco, Sierra, Ryan . . . .$85-$100

1990 Toronto - McGriff, Stieb, Fernandez . . . .$60-$85

1991 Atlanta - Glavine, Pendleton . . . .$150-$200

1991 Baltimore - F. Robinson, Ripken . . . .$65-$100

1991 Boston - Boggs, Clemens . . . .$80-$100

1991 California - Joyner, Winfield . . . .$45-$65

1991 Chicago (AL) - Fisk, Thomas . . . .$85-$150

1991 Chicago (NL) - Sandberg, Dawson . . . .$75-$100

1991 Cincinnati - Larkin, Davis, Piniella . . . .$65-$85

1991 Cleveland - Swindell . . . .$45-$75

1991 Detroit - Anderson, Whitaker, Trammell, Fielder . . . . .$75-$100

1991 Houston - Bagwell, Harnisch . . . .$50-$75

1991 Kansas City - Brett, Saberhagen, Tartabull . . . .$85-$100

1991 Los Angeles - Lasorda, Murray, Strawberry . . . .$65-$90

1991 Milwaukee - Yount, Molitor . . . .$85-$100

1991 Minnesota - Knoblauch, Morris, Puckett, Hrbek . . . . .$150-$225

1991 Montreal - Calderon . . . .$30-$50

1991 New York (AL) - Mattingly . . . .$75-$125

1991 New York (NL) - Johnson, Gooden, Viola . . . .$60-$90

1991 Oakland - R. Henderson, Stewart, Eckersley, Canseco . .$80-$120

1991 Philadelphia - Dykstra, Murphy . . . .$50-$85

1991 Pittsburgh - Bonds, Bonilla . . . .$100-$150

1991 San Diego - Gwynn, McGriff, Fernandez . . . .$50-$80

1991 San Francisco - Mitchell, Clark . . . .$40-$60

1991 Seattle - Griffey Jr., Griffey Sr. . . . .$75-$100

1991 St. Louis - O. Smith, L. Smith . . . .$45-$60

1991 Texas - Franco, Ryan, Sierra, Palmeiro . . . .$60-$85

1991 Toronto - Carter, Alomar, Stieb . . . .$80-$125

1992 Atlanta - Pendleton, Justice, Glavine $325

1992 Baltimore - Devereaux, Ripken, Mussina $115

1992 Boston - Boggs, Clemens $100

1992 California - Langston $75

1992 Chicago (AL) - Thomas, McDowell $85

1992 Chicago (NL) - Maddux, Grace, Dawson, Sandberg $125

1992 Cincinnati - Larkin, Rijo $85

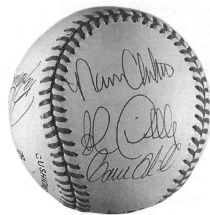

1981 New York Yankees   **1986 New York Mets**   **1991 Cincinnati Reds**

1992 Cleveland - Baerga, Belle, Nagy $100

1992 Detroit - Fryman, Whitaker, Trammell, Fielder $85

1992 Houston - Biggio, Bagwell $40

1992 Kansas City - Brett, Jefferies, Joyner $85

1992 Los Angeles - Karros, Butler $80

1992 Milwaukee - Listach, Yount, Eldred, Molitor $60

1992 Minnesota - Puckett, Knoblauch $85

1992 Montreal - Grissom, Walker, Martinez $50

1992 New York (AL) - Mattingly $90

1992 New York (NL) - Murray, Bonilla, Cone $85

1992 Oakland - Eckersley, McGwire, Henderson, Canseco $150

1992 Philadelphia - Hollins, Dykstra, Kruk, Schilling, Daulton . . .$100

1992 Pittsburgh - Bonds, Van Slyke, Drabek $125

1992 San Diego - Gwynn, Sheffield, McGriff $85

1992 San Francisco - Clark, Williams $110

1992 Seattle - Griffey Jr., Martinez $115

1992 St. Louis - O. Smith, L. Smith, Lankford $60

1992 Texas - Sierra, Gonzalez $125

1992 Toronto - Alomar, Carter, Winfield, Morris $200

1993 Atlanta - Maddux, McGriff $250

1993 Baltimore - Ripken, Mussina $115

1993 Boston - Dawson, Clemens, Vaughn $80

1993 California - Salmon, Langston $75

1993 Chicago (AL) - Thomas, McDowell $175

1993 Chicago (NL) - Sandberg, Grace $85

1993 Cincinnati - Larkin, Rijo $45

1993 Cleveland - Baerga, Belle, Nagy $125

1993 Colorado - Galarraga, Hayes $150

1993 Detroit - Whitaker, Trammell, Fielder $90

1993 Florida - Harvey, Weiss, Destrade $150

1993 Houston - Swindell, Drabek, Bagwell $40

1993 Kansas City - Brett, Cone $125

1993 Los Angeles - Piazza, Karros $150

1993 Milwaukee - Listach, Hamilton, Vaughn, Yount $50

1993 Minnesota - Puckett, Winfield $100

1993 Montreal - D. Martinez, Grissom, Walker $50

1993 New York (AL) - Boggs, Mattingly $115

1993 New York (NL) - Bonilla, Murray, Gooden $75

1993 Oakland - Sierra, McGwire, Eckersley $75

1993 Philadelphia - Schilling, Dykstra, Kruk, Daulton $300

1993 Pittsburgh - Van Slyke, Bell $95

1993 San Diego - Gwynn, Sheffield $80

1993 San Francisco - Bonds, Clark $150

1993 Seattle - Griffey Jr., R Johnson $85

1993 St. Louis - O. Smith, Lankford $50

1993 Texas - Ryan, Gonzalez, Canseco $125

1993 Toronto - Alomar, Molitor, Carter, Olerud, Stewart $200

1994 Atlanta - Maddux, McGriff $275

1994 Baltimore - Ripken, Mussina $125

1994 Boston - Greenwell, Clemens, Vaughn $125

1994 California - Salmon, Langston, Edmonds $95

1994 Chicago (AL) - Thomas, McDowell, Ventura $125

1994 Chicago (NL) - Sandberg, Grace $95

1994 Cincinnati - Larkin $65

1994 Cleveland - Baerga, Belle, Lofton, Martinez, Nagy $175

1994 Colorado - Galarraga, Hayes $150

1994 Detroit - Whitaker, Trammell, Fielder, Anderson $95

1994 Florida - Sheffield, Harvey $75

1994 Houston - Drabek, Bagwell $50

1994 Kansas City - Appier, Cone $95

1994 Los Angeles - Piazza, Karros $150

1994 Milwaukee - Eldred, Vaughn $85

1994 Minnesota - Puckett, Winfield, Knoblauch $110

1994 Montreal - D. Martinez, Grissom, Walker $60

1994 New York (AL) - Boggs, Mattingly, Key, Abbott $125

1994 New York (NL) - Bonilla $75

1994 Oakland - Sierra, McGwire, Eckersley $110

1994 Philadelphia - Dykstra, Kruk, Daulton $250

1994 Pittsburgh - Van Slyke, Bell $85

1994 San Diego - Gwynn $80

1994 San Francisco - Bonds, Clark $150

1994 Seattle - Griffey Jr., R. Johnson, Piniella $85

1994 St. Louis - O. Smith, Lankford $65

1994 Texas - Ryan, Gonzalez, Canseco $125

1994 Toronto - Alomar, Molitor, Carter, Olerud, Stewart $125

1995 Atlanta - Smoltz, Glavine $250

1995 Baltimore - Ripken, Mussina $125

1995 Boston - Canseco $110

1995 California - D. Easley, C. Davis $125

1995 Chicago (AL) - Thomas, Ventura, Guillen $110

1995 Chicago (NL) - Sosa, Sandberg $145

1995 Cincinnati - Larkin $150

1995 Cleveland - Thome, A. Belle $250

1995 Colorado - Bichette, Castilla, Galarraga, Walker, Burks $135

1995 Detroit - Fielder, Fryman, Trammell $100

1995 Florida - Sheffield, W. Fraser $175

1995 Houston- Bagwell, D. Bell $125

1995 Kansas City- Hamelin, Gaetti, Cone, Gagne $90

1995 Los Angeles - Piazza, Nomo $125

1995 Milwaukee - Garner, Seitzer, Cirillo $75

1995 Minnesota - Knoblauch, Puckett $90

1995 Montreal - P. Martinez, M. Alou, Grissom $110

1995 New York (AL) O'Neill, Boggs $125

1995 New York (NL) Saberhagen $95

1995 Oakland - McGwire $75

1995 Philadelphia - Dykstra, Daulton, Morandini, Schilling $95

1995 Pittsburgh - King $100

1995 San Diego - Gwynn, Caminiti, Finley $90

1995 San Francisco - Bonds $140

1995 Seattle - Griffey, Buhner $150

1995 St. Louis - O. Smith, Gilkey $125

1995 Texas - Gonzalez, Rodriguez $125

1995 Toronto - R. Alomar, Molitor, J. Carter $100

1996 Atlanta - Maddux, Glavine, Justice, Grissom $175

1996 Baltimore - Ripken, R. Alomar, Mussina $100

1996 Boston - Vaughn, Clemens $110

1996 California - Salmon $90

1996 Chicago (AL) - Thomas, Ventura, Guillen $100

1996 Chicago (NL) - Sosa, Grace $110

1996 Cincinnati - Larkin, Boone $90

1996 Cleveland - Thome, Lofton, Nagy $175

1996 Colorado - Bichette, Castilla, Walker, Galarraga, Burks $145

1996 Detroit - Clark $80

1996 Florida - Sheffield, K. Brown, C. Johnson, A. Leiter $100

1996 Houston - Bagwell, Biggio $100

1996 Kansas City - $80

1996 Los Angeles - Piazza, Mondesi, Nomo, Karros $110

1996 Milwaukee - G. Vaughn $90

1996 Minnesota - Molitor, Knoblauch $90

1996 Montreal - P. Martinez, M. Alou, Grudzielanek $75

1996 New York (AL) - Jeter, T. Martinez, Torre, Williams, O'Neill $325

1996 New York (NL) - Hundley, Gilkey, J. Kent $175

1996 Oakland - McGwire $120

1996 Philadelphia - Dykstra, Schilling $90

1996 Pittsburgh - Kendall $80

1996 San Diego - Gwynn, R. Henderson $100

1996 San Francisco - Bonds, Baker $90

1996 Seattle - Griffey, Buhner, Rodriguez $120

1996 St. Louis - O. Smith, Gaetti $100

1996 Texas - Gonzalez, Clark $90

1996 Toronto - J. Guzman, Olerud, Hentgen $80

1997 Anaheim - Edmonds, Salmon $100

1997 Atlanta - C. Jones, Maddux, Glavine, Lofton, Smoltz $150

1997 Baltimore - C. Ripken, Mussina $110

1997 Boston - Vaughn, Garciaparra $100

1997 Chicago (AL) - Thomas, Belle $110

1997 Chicago (NL) - Sosa, Grace $120

1997 Cincinnati- Larkin, Tomko, Stynes $100

1997 Cleveland - Thome, Justice, M. Williams $175

1997 Colorado - Bichette, Castilla, Galarraga, Walker $140

1997 Detroit - Easley, Clark, Higginson $75

1997 Florida - M. Alou, K. Brown, Sheffield, Bonilla, Leyland . . .$155

1997 Houston - Bagwell, Biggio, Kile $145

1997 Kansas City - Damon, Bell $125

1997 Los Angeles - Piazza, Mondesi, Nomo $110

1997 Milwaukee - Garner, Cirillo $90

1997 Minnesota - Molitor, Knoblauch $90

1997 Montreal - Guerrero, P. Martinez, F. Alou $80

1997 New York (AL) - Jeter, Williams, Torre, O'Neill $395

1997 New York (NL) - Hundley, Franco $150

1997 Oakland - Canseco $100

1997 Philadelphia - Rolen, Jefferies $135

1997 Pittsburgh - Kendall $125

1997 San Diego - Gwynn, Caminiti $175

1997 San Francisco - Bonds, Baker $100

1997 Seattle - A. Rodriguez, Griffey $125

1997 St. Louis - McGwire, Gant $150

1997 Texas - Gonzalez, Rodriguez $100

1997 Toronto - Clemens, Delgado $100

1998 Anaheim - Edmonds, Salmon $110

1998 Arizona - Lee, Bell, M. Williams, Showalter $245

1998 Atlanta - Glavine, Maddux, C. Jones, Galarraga $295

1998 Baltimore - Ripken, Mussina $120

1998 Boston - Vaughn, Garciaparra, P. Martinez $110

1998 Chicago (AL) - Thomas, Belle $100

1998 Chicago (NL) - Sosa, Wood $200

1998 Cincinnati - Larkin, Tomko, Greene $125

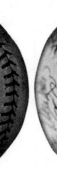

1995 Cleveland Indians **1956 Brooklyn Dodgers** **1987 Los Angeles Dodgers** **1974 Los Angeles Dodgers**

1998 Cleveland - Thome, Justice, Lofton $210

1998 Colorado - Bichette, Castilla, Walker $190

1998 Detroit - Clark, Higginson, Easley, Cruz $130

1998 Florida - Renteria, Hernandez, Leyland $80

1998 Houston - Bagwell, Biggio, R. Johnson, M. Alou $180

1998 Kansas City - Palmer $90

1998 Los Angeles - Sheffield, Mondesi $110

1998 Milwaukee - Cirillo, Vina, Jenkins $90

1998 Minnesota - Molitor $100

1998 Montreal - Guerrero, F. Alou $90

1998 New York (AL) - Jeter, Wells, Williams, Brosius, Torre $320

1998 New York (NL) - Piazza, Nomo, Franco $225

1998 Oakland - Grieve, Henderson $120

1998 Philadelphia - Rolen, Schilling $110

1998 Pittsburgh - Kendall, Guillen $125

1998 San Diego - K. Brown, Gwynn, Caminiti, Hoffman, Vaughn . . .$225

1998 San Francisco - Bonds, Baker $100

1998 Seattle - Griffey, A. Rodriguez $160

1998 St. Louis - McGwire, Drew, LaRussa $250

1998 Tampa Bay - McGriff, Boggs $275

1998 Texas - Gonzalez, Rodriguez $100

1998 Toronto - Clemens, Canseco $140

1999 Anaheim - Edmonds, Salmon, Vaughn $110

1999 Arizona - M. Williams, Showalter, R. Johnson $245

1999 Atlanta - Glavine, Maddux, C. Jones, Smoltz $295

1999 Baltimore - C. Ripken, Mussina, Belle $120

1999 Boston - Garciaparra, P. Martinez $110

1999 Chicago (AL) - Thomas, Durham $100

1999 Chicago (NL) - Sosa, Grace $200

1999 Cincinnati - Larkin, Tomko, Greene, Vaughn $125

1999 Cleveland - Thome, Justice, Lofton $190

1999 Colorado - Bichette, Castilla, Walker $180

1999 Detroit - Clark, Higginson, Easley, Cruz $135

1999 Florida - Hernandez, Floyd $80

1999 Houston - Bagwell, Biggio, M. Alou $180

1999 Kansas City - Beltran, Dye $90

1999 Los Angeles - K. Brown, Sheffield, Mondesi $110

1999 Milwaukee - Cirillo, Vina, Nomo, Jenkins $90

1999 Minnesota - Radke, Walker $100

1999 Montreal - Guerrero, F. Alou $90

1999 New York (AL) - Jeter, Clemens, Williams, Brosius, Torre . .$320

1999 New York (NL) - Piazza, Franco $140

1999 Oakland - Grieve, Giambi $110

1999 Philadelphia - Rolen, Schilling $110

1999 Pittsburgh - Kendall, Guillen $125

1999 San Diego - Gwynn, Caminiti, Hoffman, ...$225

1999 San Francisco - Bonds, Baker, Kent $120

1999 Seattle - Griffey, A. Rodriguez, Buhner $130

1999 St. Louis - McGwire, Drew, Tatis, Renteria, ...$240

1999 Tampa Bay - McGriff, Boggs, Canseco $275

1999 Texas - Gonzalez, Rodriguez $110

1999 Toronto - Wells, Delgado $90

2000 Anaheim - Salmon, Vaughn $110

2000 Arizona - M. Williams, R. Johnson $245

2000 Atlanta - Glavine, Maddux, C. Jones, Smoltz $295

2000 Baltimore - Ripken, Mussina, Belle $120

2000 Boston - Garciaparra, P. Martinez $110

2000 Chicago (AL) - Thomas, Durham $100

2000 Chicago (NL) - Sosa, Grace $200

2000 Cincinnati - Griffey, Casey $125

2000 Cleveland - Thome, Lofton $190

2000 Colorado - Cirillo, Walker $180

2000 Detroit - Clark, Higginson, Easley, Cruz $135

2000 Florida - Floyd, Lee $80

2000 Houston - Bagwell, Biggio, M. Alou $180

2000 Kansas City - Beltran, Dye $90

2000 Los Angeles - K. Brown, Sheffield $110

2000 Milwaukee - Burnitz, Jenkins $90

2000 Minnesota - Lawton, Radke $100

2000 Montreal - Guerrero, F. Alou $90

2000 New York (AL) - Jeter, Clemens, Williams, Brosius, Torre . . .$320

2000 New York (NL) - Piazza, Franco $140

2000 Oakland - Grieve, Giambi $110

2000 Philadelphia - Rolen, Lieberthal $110

2000 Pittsburgh - Kendall, Giles $125

2000 San Diego - Gwynn, Hoffman $225

2000 San Francisco - Bonds, Baker, Kent $120

2000 Seattle - A. Rodriguez, Buhner $130

2000 St. Louis - McGwire, Drew, Tatis, Renteria, ...$240

2000 Tampa Bay - McGriff, Williams $275

2000 Texas - Martinez, Rodriguez $110

2000 Toronto - Wells, Delgado $90

2001 Anaheim - Anderson, Salmon $110

2001 Arizona - M. Williams, R. Johnson $245

2001 Atlanta - Glavine, Maddux, C. Jones, Smoltz $295

2001 Baltimore - Ripken, Hairston $120

2001 Boston - Garciaparra, P. Martinez $110

2001 Chicago (AL) - Thomas, Durham $100

2001 Chicago (NL) - Sosa, Wood $200

2001 Cincinnati - Griffey, Casey $125

2001 Cleveland - Thome, Lofton $190

2001 Colorado - Helton, Walker $180

2001 Detroit - Clark, Higginson, Easley, Cruz $135

2001 Florida - Floyd, Johnson $80

2001 Houston - Bagwell, Biggio, M. Alou $180

2001 Kansas City - Beltran, Dye $90

2001 Los Angeles - K. Brown, Sheffield $110

2001 Milwaukee - Burnitz, Jenkins, Sexson $90

2001 Minnesota - Radke, Lawton $100

2001 Montreal - Guerrero, F. Alou $90

2001 New York (AL) - Jeter, Clemens, Williams, Brosius, Torre ..$320

2001 New York (NL) - Piazza, Franco $140

2001 Oakland - Giambi, Hudson $110

2001 Philadelphia - Rolen, Lee $110

2001 Pittsburgh - Kendall, Giles $125

2001 San Diego - Gwynn, Hoffman, ...$225

2001 San Francisco - Bonds, Baker, Kent $120

2001 Seattle - Martinez, Cameron, Suzuki $130

2001 St. Louis - McGwire, Drew, Renteria, ...$240

2001 Tampa Bay - McGriff, Grieve $275

2001 Texas - A. Rodriguez, I. Rodriguez $110

2001 Toronto - Fullmer, Delgado $90

AUTOGRAPHED ALL-STAR BASEBALLS

Prices are listed for American and National League teams for each year that the All-Star game has been played. Like other team-signed balls, All-Star balls aren't considered complete unless they contain signatures of all the key members of the team.

Key signatures follow each team name

1933 American League All-Star Team - Mack, Collins,
  Gehrig, Ruth . . . .$6500-$9750
1933 National League All-Star Team - McGraw, Traynor,
  Waner, Frisch . . . .$2500-$3500
1934 American League All-Star Team - Gehrig, Ruth,
  Foxx . . . .$7000-$8500
1934 National League All-Star Team - Ott, Traynor,
  Vaughan, Waner . . . .$2000-$3000
1935 American League All-Star Team - Foxx, Gehrig,
  Hornsby . . . .$4000-$6000
1935 National League All-Star Team - Frisch, Ott,
  Vaughan . . . .$1400-$2100
1936 American League All-Star Team - Foxx, Gehrig,
  DiMaggio . . . .$5000-$7500
1936 National League All-Star Team - Ott, Vaughan,
  Traynor . . . .$1200-$1800
1937 American League All-Star Team - Foxx, DiMaggio,
  Gehrig . . . .$4500-$6750
1937 National League All-Star Team - Frisch, Ott,
  Vaughan . . . .$1500-$2350
1938 American League All-Star Team - Foxx, DiMaggio,
  Gehrig . . . .$4500-$6800
1938 National League All-Star Team - Ott, Vaughan,
  Frisch . . . .$1200-$1800
1939 American League All-Star Team - Foxx, DiMaggio,
  Gehrig . . . .$4000-$6000
1939 National League All-Star Team - Ott, Vaughan . . . .$1000-$1200
1940 American League All-Star Team - Foxx, Williams,
  DiMaggio . . . .$600-$850
1940 National League All-Star Team - Ott, Vaughan . . . .$1000-$1200
1941 American League All-Star Team - Foxx, Williams,
  DiMaggio . . . .$600-$900
1941 National League All-Star Team - Ott, Vaughan . . . . .$650-$1000
1942 American League All-Star Team - Williams,
  Joe DiMaggio . . . .$500-$750
1942 National League All-Star Team - McKechnie, Frisch,
  Ott, Vaughan . . . .$700-$1200

1943 A.L. All-Star Team

1943 American League All-Star Team - McCarthy . . . .$400-$600
1943 National League All-Star Team - Frisch, Ott, Musial . .$500-$750
1944 American League All-Star Team - McCarthy, Cronin . .$400-$600
1944 National League All-Star Team - Wagner, Ott, Musial . .$500-$750
1945 (There was no All-Star Game)
1946 American League All-Star Team - Williams,
  DiMaggio . . . .$450-$675
1946 National League All-Star Team - Musial . . . .$500-$750
1947 American League All-Star Team - Williams,
  DiMaggio . . . .$500-$725
1947 National League All-Star Team - Ott, Musial . . . .$525-$800
1948 American League All-Star Team - Williams,
  DiMaggio . . . .$475-$750
1948 National League All-Star Team - Ott, Musial . . . .$525-$800
1949 American League All-Star Team - Williams,
  DiMaggio . . . .$475-$750
1949 National League All-Star Team - Campanella,
  Robinson, Musial . . . .$550-$850
1950 American League All-Star Team - Williams,
  DiMaggio . . . .$500-$750
1950 National League All-Star Team - Campanella,
  Robinson, Musial . . . .$550-$850
1951 American League All-Star Team - Williams,
  J. DiMaggio . . . .$500-$725
1951 National League All-Star Team - Campanella,
  Robinson, Musial . . . .$575-$875
1952 American League All-Star Team - Mantle, Paige . . . .$800-$1300
1952 National League All-Star Team - Campanella,
  Robinson, Musial . . . .$575-$825
1953 American League All-Star Team - Mantle, Williams,
  Paige . . . .$600-$800
1953 National League All-Star Team - Campanella,
  Robinson, Musial . . . .$650-$1500
1954 American League All-Star Team - Williams, Mantle . .$450-$675
1954 National League All-Star Team - Campanella,
  Robinson, Musial . . . .$550-$825
1955 American League All-Star Team - Williams, Mantle . .$600-$700
1955 National League All-Star Team - Aaron, Banks,
  Musial . . . .$600-$800
1956 American League All-Star Team Williams, Mantle,
  Berra, Martin, Ford . . . .$450-$675
1956 National League All-Star Team - Campanella, Musial .$500-$750
1957 American League All-Star Team - Williams, Mantle . .$600-$700
1957 National League All-Star Team - Mathews, Mays,
  Musial . . . . $400-$600
1958 American League All-Star Team - Williams, Mantle,
  Martin, Berra, Ford . . . .$600-$800
1958 National League All-Star Team - Aaron, Banks,
  Musial, Spahn . . . .$700-$900
1959 American League All-Star Team - Williams, Mantle . .$400-$600
1959 American League 2nd Game All-Stars - Mantle,
  Maris, Williams . . . .$475-$725
1959 National League All-Star Team - Musial, Drysdale . . .$450-$600
1959 National League 2nd Game All-Stars - Musial,
  Drysdale . . . .$450-$600
1960 American League All-Star Team, both teams - Mantle,
  Maris . . . .$475-$700
1960 National League All-Star Team, both teams - Clemente
  . . . .$425-$650
1961 American League All-Star Team - Mantle, Maris . . . . .$500-$750
1961 American League 2nd Game All-Stars - Mantle, Maris . . .$500-$725
1961 National League All-Star Team - Clemente, Koufax . .$450-$650

1961 National League 2nd Game All-Stars - Clemente,
Koufax . . . .$450-$650
1962 American League All-Star Team - Mantle, Maris . . . . .$400-$600
1962 American League 2nd Game All-Stars - Mantle, Maris . . .$400-$600
1962 National League All-Star Team - Clemente . . . .$420-$630
1962 National League 2nd Game All-Stars - Clemente . . . . .$425-$625
1963 American League All-Star Team - Fox, Yastrzemski . .$325-$425
1963 National League All-Star Team - Musial, Clemente . . .$375-$550
1964 American League All-Star Team - Mantle, E. Howard . .$325-$500
1964 National League All-Star Team - Clemente . . . .$400-$800
1965 American League All-Star Team - Kaline, Killebrew . .$325-$450
1965 National League All-Star Team - Clemente . . . .$450-$675
1966 American League All-Star Team - Killebrew, Kaline,
B. Robinson, F. Robinson . . . .$375-$550
1966 National League All-Star Team - Clemente . . . .$400-$600
1967 American League All-Star Team - Mantle . . . .$375-$550
1967 National League All-Star Team - Clemente . . . .$400-$600
1968 American League All-Star Team - Mantle . . . .$350-$525
1968 National League All-Star Team Aaron, Drysdale,
Mays, Seaver . . . .$350-$525
1969 American League All-Star Team - Carew, Jackson,
Williams . . . .$400-$525
1969 National League All-Star Team - Aaron, Clemente . . .$400-$600
1970 American League All-Star Team - Aparicio, Killebrew,
B. Robinson, F. Robinson, Yastrzemski . . . .$325-$500
1970 National League All-Star Team - Hodges, Clemente,
Aaron, Bench, Mays, Rose, Seaver . . . .$400-$600
1971 American League All-Star Team - Munson, Martin,
Killebrew, B. Robinson, F. Robinson, Yastrzemski . . . . .$375-$550
1971 National League All-Star Team - Clemente, Aaron,
Mays, Rose, Seaver, McCovey . . . .$400-$600
1972 American League All-Star Team - R. Jackson,
B. Robinson, Yastrzemski . . . .$300-$450
1972 National League All-Star Team - Clemente, Aaron,
Bench, Carlton, Stargell . . . .$400-$600
1973 American League All-Star Team - Munson, R. Jackson,
B. Robinson, Ryan . . . .$325-$500
1973 National League All-Star Team - Aaron, Bench, Mays,
Rose, Seaver, Stargell . . . .$300-$450

1974 American League All-Star Team - R. Jackson,
B. Robinson, F. Robinson, Kaline, Yastrzemski . . . .$325-$500
1974 National League All-Star Team - Aaron, Rose,
Schmidt . . . .$325-$500
1975 American League All-Star Team - Munson, Martin,
Aaron, Yastrzemski . . . .$325-$500
1975 National League All-Star Team - Bench, Brock, Rose,
Seaver . . . .$300-$425
1976 American League All-Star Team - Munson, Brett,
Carew, Yastrzemski . . . .$325-$500
1976 National League All-Star Team - Bench, Rose,
Schmidt, Seaver . . . .$300-$425
1977 American League All-Star Team - Munson, Martin,
Brett, Carew, R. Jackson, Yastrzemski . . . .$350-$550
1977 National League All-Star Team - Bench, Rose,
Schmidt, Seaver . . . .$275-$425
1978 American League All-Star Team - Martin, Brett,
Carew, Palmer . . . .$300-$450
1978 National League All-Star Team - Rose, Seaver,
Stargell, Winfield . . . .$275-$425
1979 American League All-Star Team - Brett, Carew,
R. Jackson, Ryan, Yastrzemski . . . .$300-$450
1979 National League All-Star Team - Brock, Carlton,
Rose, Schmidt . . . .$300-$450
1980 American League All-Star Team - Carew, Yount . . . . .$300-$425
1980 National League All-Star Team - Bench, Rose,
Schmidt, Winfield . . . .$250-$375
1981 American League All-Star Team - Brett, Carew,
R. Jackson, Winfield . . . .$300-$425
1981 National League All-Star Team - Rose, Ryan, Schmidt.
Seaver . . . .$300-$425
1982 American League All-Star Team - Brett, Carew,
R. Jackson, Winfield, Yastrzemski, Yount . . . .$300-$450
1982 National League All-Star Team - Carlton, Rose,
Schmidt . . . .$275-$400
1983 American League All-Star Team - Brett, Carew,
R. Jackson, Ripken, Winfield, Yastrzemski, Yount . . . . . .$250-$375
1983 National League All-Star Team - Bench, Schmidt . . . .$250-$375
1984 American League All-Star Team - Brett, Carew,
R. Jackson, Ripken, Winfield . . . .$250-$375
1984 National League All-Star Team - Sandberg, Schmidt . .$250-$375
1985 American League All-Star Team - Brett, Mattingly . . .$250-$375

1983 A.L. All-Star Team

1980 A.L. All-Star Team

1984 N.L. All-Star Team

1985 National League All-Star Team - Rose, Ryan ......$275-$425
1986 American League All-Star Team - Clemens, Mattingly,
  Ripken ....$250-$375
1986 National League All-Star Team - Sandberg, Schmidt ..$250-$375
1987 American League All-Star Team - Mattingly, McGwire,
  Ripken ....$250-$375
1987 National League All-Star Team - Gwynn, Sandberg,
  Schmidt ....$250-$375
1988 American League All-Star Team - Mattingly, McGwire,
  Ripken ....$225-$350
1988 National League All-Star Team - Sandberg ....$225-$350
1989 American League All-Star Team - Mattingly, Ripken,
  Ryan ....$225-$350

1989 National League All-Star Team - Gwynn, Sandberg ...$225-$350
1990 American League All-Star Team - Clemens, Griffey Jr.,
  Ripken ....$225-$350
1990 National League All-Star Team - Bonds, Gwynn .....$225-$350
1991 American League All-Star Team - Clemens, Griffey Jr.,
  Ripken ....$150-$200
1991 National League All-Star Team - E. Murray, Sandberg $150-$200
1992 American League All-Star Team - Griffey Jr., McGwire,
  Ripken ....$150-$225
1992 National League All-Star Team - Bonds, Maddux,
  Sandberg ....$125-$200
1993 American League All-Star Team - Griffey Jr., Puckett,
  F. Thomas, Ripken, R. Johnson, J. Gonzalez ....$100-$150
1993 National League All-Star Team - Bonds, Gwynn, Piazza,
  Sandberg ....$100-$150
1994 American League All-Star Team - Griffey Jr., Puckett,
  C. Ripken ....$250-$300
1994 National League All-Star Team - Bonds, Maddux,
  Piazza ....$250-$300
1995 American League All-Star Team - F. Thomas,
  Griffey Jr. $300
1995 National League All-Star Team - Sosa $275
1996 American League All-Star Team - McGwire,
  F. Thomas ....$250-$375
1996 National League All-Star Team - Bonds ....$250-$375
1997 American League All-Star Team - Griffey Jr.,
  F. Thomas ....$250-$375
1997 National League All-Star Team - Piazza, Sosa ......$250-$375
1998 American League All-Star Team - Griffey Jr. ....$225-$350
1998 National League All-Star Team - McGwire, Bonds,
  Sosa ....$225-$350
1999 American League All-Star Team - Griffey Jr., Ripken,
  Garciaparra ....$225-$350
1999 National League All-Star Team - McGwire, Piazza,
  Sosa ....$225-$350
2000 American League All-Star Team - Jeter, Griffey Jr. ..$225-$350
2000 National League All-Star Team - Sosa, Bonds ......$225-$350

MULTIPLE-SIGNED MILESTONE BASEBALL ITEMS

500 Home Run Club

Collecting items signed by all the members of the 500 Home Run Club has never been more difficult. Because the autographs of Babe Ruth, Mel Ott, and Jimmie Foxx are extremely pricey and difficult to come by, collectors have long been content to focus on the sigs of the club's more attainable members.

The recent addition of Mark McGwire and Barry Bonds to the ranks of 500-HR hitters, however, has caused some difficulty for the hobby. Bonds is fairly accessible, and there's little doubt his signature will begin appearing on a multitude of 500-HR-Club items in the near future.

McGwire, however, has all but refused to sign any 500-HR items since joining the club. If this trend continues, collectors may have to add another name to the club's "unattainable" list.

(Unless otherwise noted, prices listed are for items containing the signatures of 12 Club members—Hank Aaron, Willie Mays, Mickey Mantle, Ted Williams, Frank Robinson, Harmon Killebrew, Reggie Jackson, Mike Schmidt, Willie McCovey, Ernie Banks, Eddie Matthews, and Eddie Murray.)

COURTESY OF PETE ROSE HIT KING MARKETING INC. / CAPITAL CARDS

Official Baseball

Signed (w/o Ruth, Foxx, Ott)	$750-$2,000
Signed (w/o Mantle)	$500-$700
Signed (w/o McGwire)	$700

Baseball Bat

Signed (w/o Ruth, Foxx, Ott)	$3,500-$4,000
Signed (w/o Mantle)	$1,500-$2,500
Signed (w/o Williams)	$1,800

8x10 Photo

Signed (w/o Ruth, Foxx, Ott, Murray, McGwire)	$750

Limited Edition 1989

Ron Lewis Litho of 100

Signed (w/o Ruth, Foxx, Ott)	$3,200-$3,800

*Murray and McGwire are not featured on artwork

500 Home Run Club

The 500 Home Run Club Book
by Bob Allen and Bill Gilbert

Limited Edition 1989 Ron Lewis Litho of 5,000
Signed (w/o Ruth, Foxx, Ott) $2,000-$3,000
Unsigned $75

1996 Doo S. Oh Poster
Limited Edition of 5,000
Signed (w/o Ruth, Foxx, Ott) $1,500-$2,000

Craig Pursley Painting 40x28
Signed (w/o Ruth, Foxx, Ott) $3,000

1999 Bob Allen/Bill Gilbert Book
The 500 Home Run Club
Signed by Hank Aaron $75

Mitchell & Ness Replica Hank Aaron 1957 Braves Tomahawk Jersey
Signed (w/o Ruth, Foxx, Ott) $3,500

500 Home Run Club painting by Craig Pursley

**500 Home Run Club
poster by Doo S. Oh**

**500 Home Run Club signed
baseball**

**500 Home Run Club poster by
Ron Lewis**

500 Home Run Club bat

3,000 Hit Club

Currently, there are 23 members of the 3,000 Hit Club, and like the 500 HR Club, collectors are content to chase the autographs of only the most attainable members. Keep in mind that 3,000 Hit Club items are generally considered complete without the signatures of Ty Cobb, Tris Speaker, Honus Wagner, Eddie Collins, Nap Lajoie, Paul Waner and Roberto Clemente.

Since no less than three new members—Wade Boggs, Cal Ripken Jr. and Tony Gwynn—have entered the club recently, many of the items on the market do not yet bear their signatures. All three men are fairly generous signers, however, so their autographs should begin appearing on more and more 3,000 Hit Club items in the near future—bringing with them, of course, a significant increase in price.

Unless otherwise noted, prices are for items that do not contain the signatures of Gwynn, Ripken or Boggs.

Official Baseball
Signed (w/o Cobb, Wagner, Speaker, Collins, Lajoie, Waner or Clemente) $500-$1,500

Bat
Signed (w/o Cobb, Wagner, Speaker, Collins, Lajoie, Waner or Clemente) $1,250

1995 Ron Lewis Limited Edition Poster
Signed (w/o Cobb, Wagner, Speaker, Collins, Lajoie, Waner or Clemente) $800-$1,500
Unsigned $25
*Murray, Molitor, Ripken, Gwynn and Boggs are not featured on poster

1997 Doo S. Oh Limited Edition (4,000) Poster
Signed (w/o Cobb, Wagner, Speaker, Collins, Lajoie, Waner or Clemente) $900-$2,500
Unsigned $25
*Ripken, Gwynn, Boggs are not featured on poster

3,000 Hit Club poster by Ron Lewis

3,000 Hit Club signed baseball

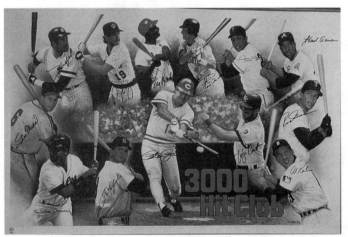

**3,000 Hit Club poster
by Doo S. Oh**

500 Home Runs and 3,000 Hits

To date, only three players in baseball history have amassed both 500 Home Runs and 3,000 Hits—Hank Aaron, Willie Mays and Eddie Murray. Since all three are still living, and make appearances on the autograph circuit, obtaining items signed by the members of this club is a relatively easy and inexpensive challenge.

300 Wins

Pitchers have never been as popular in the hobby as hitters, but many collectors still enjoy chasing down members of this exclusive club. Of the 20 men who have recorded 300 wins, only eight—Warren Spahn,

Steve Carlton, Nolan Ryan, Don Sutton, Phil Niekro, Gaylord Perry, Tom Seaver and Early Wynn—are easily attainable. Prices listed are for items containing only their signatures.

Official baseball	$300-$500
Baseball bat	$300-$750
Pitching rubber	$200-$600
1994 Brunelli Lithograph	
signed	$1,000
unsigned	$50

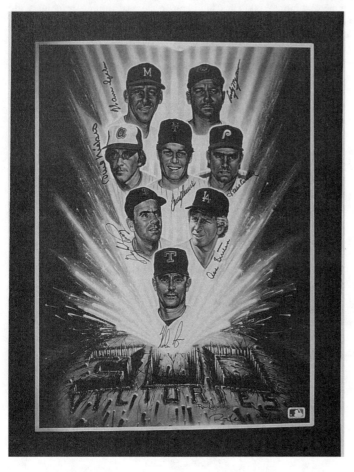

300 Game Winners Litho by Anthony Brunelli

300 Game Winners poster by Ron Lewis

3,000 Strikeouts

While not as popular as the 300 Win Club, memorabilia bearing the autographs of members of the 3,000 Strikeout Club has been gaining momentum in the hobby. The recent addition of Roger Clemens has brought the number of attainable members of this club to 10–Clemens,

Phil Niekro, Don Sutton, Bob Gibson, Fergie Jenkins, Steve Carlton, Gaylord Perry, Tom Seaver, Bert Blyleven and Nolan Ryan. The following prices are for items signed by all 10.

Official American or National League Baseball Signed $500
Baseball Bat Signed $700

Pitching Rubber Signed $600
Limited-Edition Poster Signed $1,000

300 Wins & 3,000 Strikeouts

Six of the attainable members of the 300 Win Club also have more than 3,000 Strikeouts. Items featuring the signatures of Tom Seaver, Steve Carlton, Gaylord Perry, Nolan Ryan, Phil Niekro and Don Sutton

are fairly prized among collectors of pitching memorabilia, especially since all six men are now members of the Hall of Fame.

Official American or National League Baseball Signed $400
Baseball Bat Signed $500

Pitching Rubber Signed $500
Limited-Edition Poster Signed $1,000

Stat Leaders

In 1998, artist Ron Lewis created artwork for limited edition (5,000) posters of major league baseball career leaders in four major statistical categories: Pete Rose (hits), Hank Aaron (home runs), Nolan Ryan (strikeouts) and Rickey Henderson (stolen bases).

1998 Baseball Kings
Limited Edition of 150
   Signed $575
   Unsigned $25
Official Baseball
   Signed . . . .$200-$250
Bat
   Signed $325

Baseball Kings by Ron Lewis

Chapter 3

UNIFORMS

JERSEYS

By Phil Wood

On an episode of the classic TV sitcom "The Honeymooners," blustery bus driver Ralph Kramden, during one of his weekly battles with wife Alice, looks her in the eye and says "You don't love me. You've never loved me. You were in love with my uniform." Mrs. Kramden's response notwithstanding, it's the love of the uniform that drives what has become an extremely popular, yet occasionally scary, avenue of collecting.

The future uniform collectors of America were easy to spot in the 1950s and '60s; they were the ones who were doodling redesigns of the home team's logo, instead of race cars or airplanes, on their school notebooks. Today, a fan can go to his local shopping mall and buy, off-the-rack, replicas of his favorite team's jersey, frequently complete with the name and number of a star player already applied to the back.

Baseball marketing was in its infancy 40-50 years ago, consisting largely of a sign that read "GAME TODAY." The idea that fans would be willing to pony up serious money for a major league quality uniform or warm-up jacket was simply unthinkable. Sports collecting in those days was pretty much limited to paper items: cards, programs, yearbooks and ticket stubs. If there was any fabric in your collection, chances are it was a pennant, or ribbon attached to a button or pin of some kind.

When the sports collecting boom got under way in the mid '70s, a baseball card show was usually just that: dealer after dealer with tables full of cards. If anyone had a jersey or two on his table, it always brought out a lot of tire kickers. Everyone wanted to look at it, or try it on, but with cards selling for pennies (this was before price guides, grading services and the creation of the designation "rookie card"), the price usually meant the dealer would take his shirt(s) home at the show's conclusion. Case in point: When the EPSCC Show (now at Ft. Washington, Pa.) was in its infancy at Spring Garden College in Philadelphia, one dealer set up with vintage Phillies' road flannels he had acquired from an old minor league affiliate. He charged $25 each and sold very few, but at the same show, a decent green background T-206 Ty Cobb portrait could be found for $5. A 1952 Topps Mickey Mantle in EX condition went for $35. Heck, a complete set of 1954 Bowman—albeit without the Ted Williams card—was $75. A single uniform of an everyday player for $25 didn't seem like much of a bargain, all things considered.

Part of the apparent lack of appeal for uniform collecting then stemmed from the fact that every major league team had, by 1973,

switched from flannel to polyester. The new doubleknit material had a sleek look, far more modern than flannel, more often than not, with a shirt that pulled over instead of buttoning up, and pants that had a waistband and drawstring rather than beltloops. If a dealer had a knit uniform available—usually priced at least 50 percent higher than what he'd charge for a flannel—he might actually find a buyer. A quarter century ago, polyester was what you'd find on the backs of the crowd at the local disco, and it clearly drove the early popularity of uniform collecting.

By the early '80s, someone figured out that while disco was dead, polyester uniforms were here to stay, and that there wouldn't be any more flannel uniforms. Perhaps the pricing of these garments was a little skewed. Almost overnight, pricing schemes flip-flopped. Suddenly polyester was the bargain, and flannels were treated more like the antiques they were becoming. It was also during this decade that fakery and misrepresentation became a bigger problem along this avenue of the hobby than any other.

Anyone who ever attended baseball's winter meetings knows that a big part of the weeklong festivities is an exhibit hall full of vendors whose products are related to the national pastime. Everything from snack manufacturers to advertising specialties is arranged under one roof for the purpose of drumming up business with baseball. Also on hand are the companies that manufacture uniforms. On display in their booths are samples of the uniforms they've manufactured for big league clubs, usually featuring the name and number on the back of properly sized shirts of that club's star players. Additional samples would be distributed for use by regional company representatives to show the quality of their manufacturer's work. It doesn't require much of a stretch of the imagination to figure out that many of these shirts eventually made their way to a dealer's inventory represented as "game worn."

Also in the '80s, Scoreboard, a now-defunct enterprise that advertised extensively in various hobby publications, entered into agreements with several name players to sell autographed replicas of their game jerseys. These shirts, like the aforementioned salesman samples, were sized and tagged exactly like the shirts the players wore on the field, and Scoreboard sold dozens of them, along with a letter of authenticity that applied more to the signature than to the shirt. Unfortunately, because the shirts were called "Game Jerseys," many consumers who received them secondhand confused "game" with "game worn." In the ensuing years, the line between these shirts and the genuine articles has become even more blurred.

There have been numerous instances of downright fraud over the years, with several unscrupulous types manufacturing their own superstar uniforms. One famous case involved a former major league batboy in the greater Cincinnati area who would doctor examples of a common player's uniform into a Hall of Famer. He even came up with a way to create documentation using vintage paper and ink. Eventually, he was caught and prosecuted, but he told investigators that a number of his pieces had made their way into the collections of some of the hobby's high rollers—even passing muster from paid authenticators. (More on them later.)

That's the bad news. The good news is that many teams over the past 10-15 years have opted to sell their game-used shirts in bulk to dealers, or make them available in their own retail outlets. Buying a real shirt worn in a major league game has never been easier, as long as you're willing to pay the price and accept less than an all-star caliber player. In 2001, Major League Baseball announced a program by which they would take over the marketing effort of their game-used equipment, and offer an ironclad guarantee of authenticity. It's a decision that will have a positive impact on collectors, though most likely a negative impact on their wallets. The decision's impact on dealers may simply be that they'll be limited to a 20th century vintage inventory.

If you're considering collecting game worn uniforms—and really, nothing spruces up a display of baseball memorabilia more than the shirt off someone's back—there are several points to consider:

> What's your game plan? Do you want to collect a shirt from every team, or just the various styles of your favorite team, or favorite players? Pick a theme and try to stick to it.

> Do you know any other uniform collectors? Networking with others of the same bent as yourself can only increase your knowledge, and being able to go through other collections can keep you from making some serious errors.

> Do you regularly receive catalogs from the major auction houses? Whether you're going to bid or not, these catalogs usually contain good quality color photos of shirts, showing tagging and manufacturer variations.

Are you assertive enough to ask difficult questions of dealers? Skepticism is a very healthy thing. It's your money. Don't buy an item because someone offers a good story. Get the facts.

Are you collecting shirts because you love baseball or because you think it's a good investment? If you don't love the game, you're setting yourself up to be fleeced, since you're probably not willing to do the homework required to build a solid collection. Start by buying the books *Baseball Uniforms of the 20th Century/The Official Major League Baseball Guide*, by Marc Okkonen (Sterling Publishing Co., Inc., New York, 1993, softcover) and *Baseball By the Numbers, a Guide to the Uniform Numbers of Major League Teams*, by Mark Stang & Linda Harkness (Scarecrow Press, Lanham, MD, 1997). You'll use them frequently.

Authentication is a tricky, and often expensive, process when done by a third party. Some authenticators charge a fee based upon what they judge to be the retail value of the item. Something is either good or it's not, but much like card-grading services, these authenticators believe that their letter is the seal of approval required for you to sell your shirt, and they want a piece of the action upfront. They will toss around the buzzwords "shows good game use," when in fact, they've never played the game or had daily access to a major league clubhouse.

Even if the letter comes from the team itself, it's frequently meaningless. For example, the Colorado Rockies sold uniforms in 1993, their inaugural season, as "game worn," with team letters of authenticity. Yet, close inspection by anyone with even the slightest bit of sophistication in uniform collecting revealed that the shirts were tagged for retail sale rather than field use, and had never seen the inside of a washing machine, the appliqué work still stiff as cardboard.

If you've ever been to the Hall of Fame in Cooperstown, N.Y., you've no doubt noticed that the displays around which people linger the longest feature uniforms. Balls and bats all look fairly similar, but the texture of the fabric, the design of the logo and the colors of the trim make uniforms baseball's most compelling collectible.

Game-Used

"NIC" - Name in collar.   "NOB" - Name on back.

Hank Aaron: 1967 Atlanta Braves home.....................................$16,995
Jim Abbott: 1999 Milwaukee Brewers home....................................$395
Rick Aguilera: 1988 Minnesota Twins road $495
Sparky Anderson: 1974 Cincinnati Reds home, NOB, signed $1,000
Sparky Anderson: 1994 Detroit Tigers road $850
Cap Anson: 1898 New York Giants road, NIT $100,000
Luis Aparicio: 1968 Chicago White Sox home, with pants, NOB, signed $5,500
Luke Appling: 1971 Chicago White Sox road, NIC, coaching jersey $3,750
Ernie Banks: 1968 Cubs home jersey, game-used........................$2,500
Harold Baines: 1992 Oakland A's home $275
Sal Bando: 1968 Oakland A's away $700
Don Baylor: 1979 California Angels home $995
Don Baylor: 1994 Colorado Rockies road.......................................$450
Derek Bell: 1997 Houston Astros road $400
George Bell: 1985 Toronto Blue Jays road $495
Albert Belle: 1997 Chicago White Sox jersey, home, NOB........$1,595
Johnny Bench: 1976 Cincinnati Reds road.................................$2,495
Johnny Bench: 1981 Cincinnati Reds jersey, signed $2,500
Andy Benes: San Diego Padres road, 1993 All-Star Game.............$950
Dante Bichette: 1998 Colorado Rockies home $850
Bert Blyleven: 1987 Minnesota Twins home..................................$545
Vida Blue: 1986 San Francisco Giants road, game worn, NOB restored $275

Wade Boggs: 1991 Boston Red Sox away, game worn $1,795
Wade Boggs: 1994 New York Yankees home, game worn $1,450
Barry Bonds: 1989 Pittsburgh Pirates road, game worn, NOB $3,000
Barry Bonds: 1998 San Francisco Giants home, game worn $2,195
Bobby Bonds: 1981 Chicago Cubs home, game worn $400
Bobby Bonilla: 1989 Pittsburgh Pirates road, game worn, NOB $375
Larry Bowa: 1977 Philadelphia Phillies home, game worn $275

**1968 Ernie Banks game-used
Chicago Cubs home jersey**

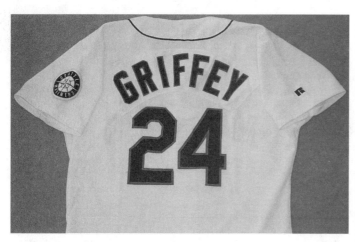

Ken Griffey Jr. Seattle Mariners home jersey

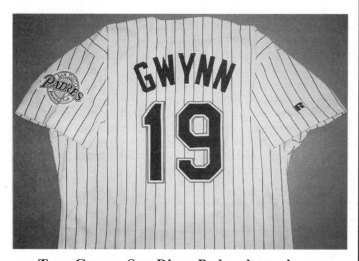

Tony Gwynn San Diego Padres home jersey

1997 Andruw Jones Atlanta Braves home jersey

Dennis "Oil Can" Boyd: 1987 Boston Red Sox, game worn $195
George Brett: 1984 Kansas City Royals road, game worn, NOB $3,000
George Brett: 1991 Kansas City Royals road, game worn $2,500
George Brett: Kansas City Royals blue warm-up jersey $200
Brett Butler: 1986 Cleveland Indians road, game worn, NOB $275
Roy Campanella: 1950 Brooklyn Dodgers home, game worn, NIT $16,000
Jose Canseco: 1991 Oakland A's road, game worn, with pants, NOB $900
Jose Canseco: 1998 Toronto Blue Jays road, game worn.............$695
Rod Carew: 1980 California Angels home, game worn $1,095
Steve Carlton: 1969 St. Louis Cardinals road, signed $1,495
Joe Carter: 1994 Toronto Blue Jays home, signed.....................$995
Rico Carty: 1968 Atlanta Braves home.............................$1,375
Dave Cash: 1978 Montreal Expos home, NOB $175
Ron Cey: 1987 Oakland A's road, signed $395
Will Clark: 1987 San Francisco Giants home, game worn..........$1,050
Roger Clemens: 1987 Boston Red Sox road, with pants..............$1,800
Roberto Clemente: 1957 Pittsburgh Pirates road, restored..........$15,000
Ty Cobb: 1925 Detroit Tigers home, NIC $110,000
Cecil Cooper: 1975 Boston Red Sox home $350
Eric Davis: 1985 Cincinnati Reds home, NOB, signed $575
Willie Davis: 1963 Los Angeles Dodgers home, NIT $1,395
Andre Dawson: 1988 Chicago Cubs hom.........................$695
Rick Dempsey: 1974 New York Yankees road.....................$425
Paul Derringer: 1944 Chicago Cubs home flannel $2,795
Delino DeShields: 1994 Los Angeles Dodgers road $450
Joe DiMaggio: 1947 New York Yankees road......................$34,100
Al Downing: 1974 Los Angeles Dodgers home $800
Don Drysdale: 1959 Los Angeles Dodgers home, signed $14,500
Shawon Dunston: 1988 Chicago Cubs home, game worn, signed ...$195
Darrell Evans: 1971 Atlanta Braves home, game worn, NOB $900
Chico Fernandez: 1962 Detroit Tigers home $2,000
Tony Fernandez: 1989 Toronto Blue Jays blue, game worn.............$350
Tony Fernandez: 1991 San Diego Padres road, game worn $225
Cecil Fielder: 1994 Detroit Tigers road, game worn $895
Carlton Fisk: 1990 Chicago White Sox road, game worn $895
Andres Galarraga: 1994 Colorado Rockies home, game worn $1,150
Ron Gant: 1989 Atlanta Braves home, game worn, signed $895
Steve Garvey: 1981 Los Angeles Dodgers home, game worn, NOB, signed $1,195
Jim Gentile: 1965 Houston Astros home, game worn $1,500
Dan Gladden: 1989 Minnesota Twins home, game worn................$295
Fred Gladding: 1965 Detroit Tigers home, game worn................$1,250
Tom Glavine: 1994 Atlanta Braves road, game worn $695
Juan Gonzalez: 1993 Texas Rangers home, game worn, NOB $1,200
Juan Gonzalez: 1997 Texas Rangers road, game worn, NOB $950
Rich Gossage: 1988 Chicago Cubs road, game worn................$350
Mark Grace: 1988 Chicago Cubs home, game worn.....................$550
Mike Greenwell: 1989 Boston Red Sox road, game worn $475
Ken Griffey Jr.: 1989 Seattle Mariners road $2,495
Ken Griffey Sr.: 1981 Cincinnati Reds road, game worn................$425
Marquis Grissom: 1993 Montreal Expos home $395
Ron Guidry: 1988 New York Yankees road, game worn $995
Tony Gwynn: 1989 San Diego Padres road................$1,050
Mike Hampton: 1996 Houston Astros home $600
Tommy Harper: Seattle Pilots road jersey, restored.....................$1,200
Charlie Hayes: 1994 Colorado Rockies home $395
Rickey Henderson: 1991 Oakland A's home, NOB, signed $1,495
Orel Hershiser: 1987 Los Angeles Dodgers road $595
Keith Hernandez: 1988 New York Mets road, NOB, signed $600
Teddy Higuera: 1992 Milwaukee Brewers road $240
Al Hollingsworth: 1939 Philadelphia Phillies road $8,470
Bob Horner: 1982 Atlanta Braves road.............................$350
Kent Hrbek: 1992 Minnesota Twins home $695
Catfish Hunter: 1971 Oakland A's road NOB.........................$2,250
Bo Jackson: 1987 Kansas City Royals home.............................$650

Reggie Jackson: 1968 Oakland A's road vest $12,995
Reggie Jackson: 1983 California Angels home, NOB, with pants $2,795
Gregg Jefferies: 1990 New York Mets home, NOB.........................$450
Davey Johnson: 1967 Baltimore Orioles home, NIT....................$1,250
Randy Johnson: 1994 Seattle Mariners home, game worn.............$795
Andruw Jones: 1998 Atlanta Braves home $1,250
Chipper Jones: 1997 Atlanta Braves home $1,695
Wally Joyner: 1987 California Angels road, NOB, signed.............$295
David Justice: 1992 Atlanta Braves home, NOB, signed $1,150
Al Kaline: 1974 Detroit Tigers road, game worn $1,695
Eric Karros: 1994 Los Angeles Dodgers road $850
Harmon Killebrew: 1961 Minnesota Twins home, NIC $7,000
Dave Kingman: 1986 Oakland A's gold, game worn, NOB $325
Ryan Klesko: 1998 Atlanta Braves home, ...$695
Ted Kluszewski: 1964 Cincinnati Reds home $1,800
Chuck Knoblauch: 1993 Minnesota Twins home $495
Sandy Koufax: 1961 Los Angeles Dodgers home, NIT $19,950
Barry Larkin: 1993 Cincinnati Reds home, NOB, signed $695
Tony LaRussa: 1992 Oakland A's home $375
Ron LeFlore: 1980 Montreal Expos away, NOB...........................$250
Chet Lemon: 1982 Detroit Tigers home $325
Kenny Lofton: 1994 Cleveland Indians road $795
Earle Mack: 1950 Philadelphia Phillies road................................$8,470
Mickey Mantle: 1981 New York Yankees home (spring training coach) $7,700
Greg Maddux: 1994 Atlanta Braves road......................................$1,795
Juan Marichal: 1966 San Francisco Giants home, NIC, signed $5,500
Roger Maris: 1960 New York Yankees home, NIC $25,000
Dennis Martinez: 1988 Montreal Expos road, game worn..............$250
Eddie Mathews: 1966 Atlanta Braves road, signed $12,500
Don Mattingly: 1993 New York Yankees home $1,495
Willie McCovey: 1972 San Francisco Giants road, game worn, with pants, NIC $11,500
Jack McDowell: 1995 New York Yankees road, Mantle armband....$795
Mark McGwire: 1987 Oakland A's home $2,950
Hal McRae: 1986 Kansas City Royals away, NOB $275
Andy Messersmith: 1970 California Angels $550
Kevin Mitchell: 1988 San Francisco Giants, signed $250
Paul Molitor: 1988 Milwaukee Brewers road $1,095
Bill Monbouquette: 1961 Boston Red Sox road............................$750
Raul Mondesi: 1994 Los Angeles Dodgers home, game worn $1,250
Joe Morgan: 1968 Houston Astros road $5,500
Jack Morris: 1983 Detroit Tigers road, NOB $850
Rance Mulliniks: 1982 Kansas City Royals road $190
Dale Murphy: 1981 Atlanta Braves road, signed...........................$650
Eddie Murray: 1994 Cleveland Indians road $795
Eddie Murray: 1995 Cleveland Indians World Series jersey $2,495
Stan Musial: 1960 St. Louis Cardinals road $13,500
Phil Niekro: 1979 Atlanta Braves road $895

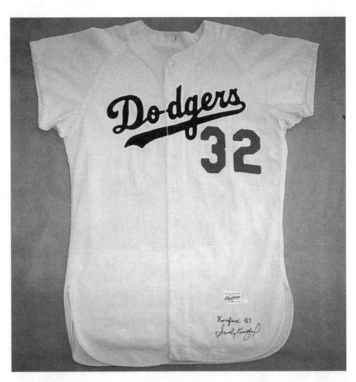

1961 Sandy Koufax Los Angeles Dodgers home jersey

Greg Maddux Atlanta Braves road jersey

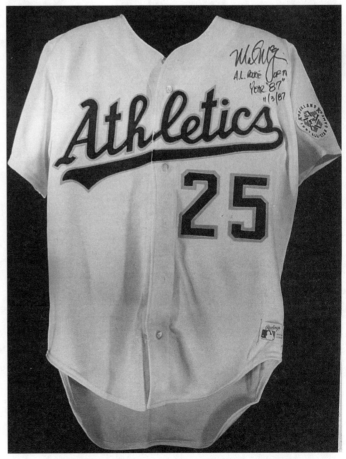

1987 Mark McGwire Oakland A's jersey

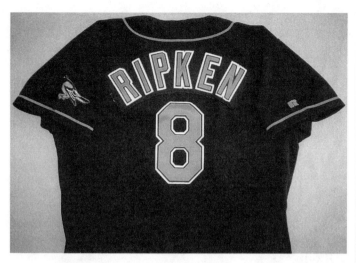

Cal Ripken Jr. Baltimore Orioles jersey

1994 Ryne Sandberg Chicago Cubs home jersey

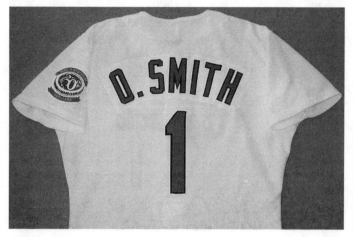

1996 Ozzie Smith St. Louis Cardinals home jersey

Hideo Nomo: 1998 New York Mets road..$650
Blue Moon Odom: 1968 Oakland A's green vest, game worn $450
Mel Ott: 1947 New York Giants road, game worn, NIC $45,000
Jim Palmer: 1970 Baltimore Orioles road, game worn, signed.....$3,500
Jim Palmer: 1981 Baltimore Orioles road $4,730
Rafael Palmeiro: 1990 Texas Rangers road, NOB, signed $650
Chan Ho Park: 1997 Los Angeles Dodgers home $795
Dave Parker: 1984 Cincinnati Reds home $395
Terry Pendleton: 1988 St. Louis Cardinals, NOB $575
Mike Piazza: 1994 Los Angeles Dodgers road............................$1,495
Boog Powell: 1972 Baltimore Orioles home $2,750
Kirby Puckett: 1985 Minnesota Twins road, NOB $2,195
Kirby Puckett: 1993 Minnesota Twins home $995
Tim Raines: 1987 Montreal Expos road, NOB, signed $595
Manny Ramirez: 1994 Cleveland Indians road..............................$495
Allie Raynolds: 1951 New York Yankees home $5,000
Jim Rice: 1975 Boston Red Sox road $1,495
Cal Ripken Jr.: 1994 Baltimore Orioles road...............................$2,995
Bip Roberts: 1991 San Diego Padres road....................................$350
Robin Roberts: 1964 Baltimore Orioles home, signed..................$4,495
Brooks Robinson: 1957 Baltimore Orioles road, signed $5,000
Frank Robinson: 1973 California Angels home.............................$1,695
Ivan Rodriguez: 1995 Texas Rangers home, All-Star patch $595
Pete Rose: 1974 Cincinnati Reds home, game worn, NOB $2,500
Pete Rose: Cincinnati Reds red warm-up jersey, #14......................$250
Pete Rose: Philadelphia Phillies #14 pre-game jersey, signed..........$895
Pete Rose: 1980 Philadelphia Phillies, game worn.......................$1,400
Babe Ruth: 1938 Brooklyn Dodgers road, game worn, with pants, NIC
....$110,000
Nolan Ryan: 1987 Houston Astros home, NOB $4,000
Nolan Ryan: 1990 Texas Rangers road, with pants $2,750
Bret Saberhagen: 1993 New York Mets road, signed $600
Tim Salmon: 1992 California Angels road, NOB.........................$1,395
Ryne Sandberg: 1988 Chicago Cubs home $1,350
Deion Sanders: 1992 Atlanta Braves road $695
Mike Schmidt: 1989 Philadelphia Phillies home..........................$2,495
Mike Scott: 1980 New York Mets road, game worn, NOB $250
Tom Seaver: 1983 New York Mets road, game worn $3,295
Gary Sheffield: 1998 Los Angeles Dodgers home..........................$950
Al Simmons: 1943 Boston Red Sox road, NIC $12,500
John Smiley: 1990 Pittsburgh Pirates home..................................$175
Ozzie Smith: 1996 St. Louis Cardinals home..............................$1,350
Duke Snider: 1962 Los Angeles Dodgers road, NIT, signed.......$11,000
Willie Stargell: 1970 Pittsburgh Pirates home, signed..................$4,495
Willie Stargell: 1982 Pittsburgh Pirates black $4,150
Terry Steinbach: 1992 Oakland A's road, NOB $350
Casey Stengel: 1962 New York Mets road, with pants.................$14,750
Rennie Stennett: 1978 Pittsburgh Pirates home $350
Dave Stewart: 1983 Los Angeles Dodgers home, NOB $495
Darryl Strawberry: 1988 New York Mets road, signed...................$350
Rick Sutcliffe: 1994 St. Louis Cardinals road, NOB $395
Bruce Sutter: 1985 Atlanta Braves road $350
Don Sutton: 1974 Los Angeles Dodgers home, NOB, signed.......$1,495
Don Sutton: 1986 California Angels road, NOB $1,025
Danny Tartabull: 1993 New York Yankees home...........................$695
Frank Thomas: 1995 Chicago White Sox home $2,500
Alan Trammell: 1994 Detroit Tigers home....................................$895
Mo Vaughn: 1997 Boston Red Sox home......................................$895
Robin Ventura: 1994 Chicago White Sox road $695
Frank Viola: 1988 Minnesota Twins road, signed $495
Devon White: 1989 California Angeles home, signed.....................$600
Frank White: 1988 Kansas City Royals road, NOB $350
Hoyt Wilhelm: 1970 Atlanta Braves home, signed.......................$3,350
Matt Williams: 1988 San Francisco Giants road $950
Ted Williams: 1960 Boston Red Sox home $60,000
Dave Winfield: 1993 Minnesota Twins home..............................$1,200
Carl Yastrzemski: 1978 Boston Red Sox home, signed.................$1,795
Robin Yount: 1993 Milwaukee Brewers home $1,195

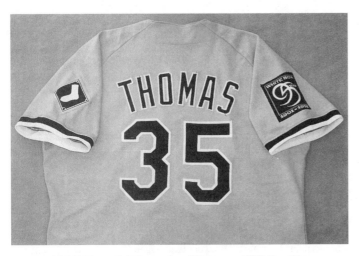

**1995 Frank Thomas Chicago White Sox
road jersey**

**Ted Williams game-used
Boston Red Sox home jersey**

Replica Jerseys

Hank Aaron: Late 1950s Milwaukee Braves tomahawk, signed $425
Hank Aaron: Late 1960s Atlanta Braves flannel, signed $350
Sparky Anderson: Detroit Tigers home #11, signed $295
Luis Aparicio: Chicago White Sox flannel, signed............................$275
Ernie Banks: 1969 Chicago Cubs flannel, signed.............................$275
Johnny Bench: 1969 Cincinnati Reds home, signed.........................$250
Yogi Berra: 1952 New York Yankees home flannel, signed $275
Vida Blue: San Francisco Giants home, signed................................$175
Wade Boggs: New York Yankees home, signed................................$275
Lou Boudreau: Cleveland Indians flannel, signed $275
George Brett: Kansas City Royals home, signed..............................$325
Lou Brock: St. Louis Cardinals flannel, signed................................$575
Bill Buckner: Chicago Cubs home, signed $185
Roy Campanella: Brooklyn Dodgers, signed....................................$895
Jose Canseco: Oakland A's with elephant patch, signed.................$275
Jose Canseco: Texas Rangers, signed $225
Rod Carew: California Angels home, signed.....................................$395
Steve Carlton: St. Louis Cardinals flannel, signed $325
Steve Carlton: Philadelphia Phillies home, signed $225
Will Clark: San Francisco Giants home, signed $275
Roger Clemens: Boston Red Sox home, signed $295
Roberto Clemente: Pittsburgh Pirates home, flannel $195
Ty Cobb: 1920s Detroit Tigers grey flannel $195
Rocky Colavito: 1959 Cleveland Indians road flannel $250
Eric Davis: Cincinnati Reds home, signed.......................................$185
Joe DiMaggio: 1939 New York Yankees pinstripe, signed $2,450
Don Drysdale: Los Angeles Dodgers grey flannel, signed...............$850
Rollie Fingers: Oakland A's road flannel, signed $275
Rollie Fingers: Milwaukee Brewers home, signed $255
Carlton Fisk: Chicago White Sox road, signed................................$275
Lou Gehrig: 1930s New York Yankees pinstripe flannel $195
Charlie Gehringer: Detroit Tigers home, signed..............................$575
Bob Gibson: St. Louis Cardinals home, signed...............................$275
Juan Gonzalez: Texas Rangers home, signed $275
Dwight Gooden: New York Mets pinstripe, signed $160
Ken Griffey Jr.: Seattle Mariners home, signed...............................$375
Tony Gwynn: San Diego Padres home, signed................................$250
Rickey Henderson: New York Yankees pinstripe, signed $250
Keith Hernandez: New York Mets road, signed...............................$150
Orel Hershiser: Los Angeles Dodgers home, signed.......................$295

1997 Juan Gonzalez Texas Rangers road jersey

Rogers Hornsby: 1920s St. Louis Cardinals grey flannel................$225
Reggie Jackson: 1969 Oakland As road, flannel, signed.................$350
Reggie Jackson: New York Yankees grey, signed $295
Fergie Jenkins: Chicago Cubs home, signed $250
Al Kaline: Detroit Tigers grey flannel, signed...................................$275
Harmon Killebrew: Minnesota Twins road, signed..........................$250
Harmon Killebrew: Washington Senators home, signed $250
Barry Larkin: Cincinnati Reds home, signed....................................$225
Kenny Lofton: Cleveland Indians home, signed...............................$275
Mickey Lolich: 1968 Detroit Tigers grey, signed.............................$275
Greg Maddux: Atlanat Braves home, signed $375
Mickey Mantle: 1951 New York Yankees pinstripe, signed $675
Mickey Mantle: 1952 New York Yankees home, signed...................$675
Mickey Mantle: 1952 New York Yankees away, signed $600
Juan Marichal: San Francisco Giants road, signed.........................$250
Roger Maris: New York Yankees home..$185
Eddie Mathews: 1957 Milwaukee Braves tomahawk, signed..........$295
Don Mattingly: New York Yankees road, signed $275
Willie Mays: San Francisco Giants flannel, signed $325
Willie McCovey: San Francisco Giants road, signed $250

Mark McGwire: Oakland A's, signed..........................$450
Joe Morgan: 1969 Houston Astros flannel, signed $250
Eddie Murray: Baltimore Orioles or Cleveland Indians, signed.......$300
Stan Musial: 1942 St. Louis Cardinals flannel, signed....................$325
Phil Niekro: 1969 Atlanta Braves flannel, signed............................$275
Jim Palmer: Baltimore Orioles home, signed $275
Tony Perez: Cincinnati Reds home, signed $275
Gaylord Perry: 1962 San Francisco Giants flannel, signed..............$250
Mike Piazza: Los Angeles Dodgers home, signed..........................$350
Kirby Puckett: Minnesota Twins home, signed $300
Pee Wee Reese: Brooklyn Dodgers away flannel, signed $250
Cal Ripken Jr.: Baltimore Orioles home, signed $325
Brooks Robinson: Baltimore Orioles grey flannel, signed..............$225
Frank Robinson: Cincinnati Reds flannel, signed...........................$250
Pete Rose: 1963 Cincinnati Reds flannel vest, signed....................$275
Babe Ruth: 1920s N. Y. Yankees road flannel................................$200
Nolan Ryan: N. Y. Mets flannel, signed..$375
Nolan Ryan: California Angels, signed..$375

Nolan Ryan: Houston Astros, signed $350
Nolan Ryan: Texas Rangers, signed..$350
Ryne Sandberg: Chicago Cubs road, signed...................................$325
Mike Schmidt: Philadelphia Phillies grey flannel, signed $325
Tom Seaver: 1969 New York Mets home, signed $325
Ozzie Smith: St. Louis Cardinals home, signed $275
Duke Snider: Los Angeles Dodgers flannel, signed $250
Warren Spahn: 1957 Milwaukee Braves home, signed $325
Darryl Strawberry: New York Mets road, signed...........................$150
Don Sutton: Los Angeles Dodgers home, signed...........................$250
Frank Thomas: Chicago White Sox road, signed $295
Mo Vaughn: Boston Red Sox home, signed $300
Ted Williams: 1939 Boston Red Sox home flannel, signed $795
Dave Winfield: New York Yankees road, signed............................$250
Early Wynn: Cleveland Indians flannel, signed $275
Carl Yastrzemski: Boston Red Sox home flannel, signed..............$595
Robin Yount: Milwaukee Brewers road, signed..............................$350

**Harmon Killebrew Mitchell &
Ness replica jerseys**

CAPS

By Phil Wood

The most universally worn piece of apparel in this country is the baseball cap. No matter where you travel in North America (and many other parts of the world as well), you'll see men, women and children wearing a cap with a bill. Descriptions of armed robbers frequently include "…and wearing a baseball cap." Not all of these lids feature baseball logos, but whatever the color or appliqué, the basic description stays the same. A baseball cap.

If you collect uniforms, invariably you'll want to match up the correct cap with the jersey. It makes for a terrific display, and these days, acquiring the exact cap style of contemporary big league uniforms is usually no more difficult than driving to your local mall. Over the past 20 years or so, the availability of real major league caps has turned into a real marketing bonanza for Major League Baseball. Collecting game-worn caps, however, presents a different challenge.

The availability of authentic pre-1980 game-worn caps is pretty limited, and logically, becomes even more so going backwards. By the time you reach World War II and before, they become exceedingly scarce. In fact, you're may be more likely to find uniforms of that vintage than the caps that go with them.

Why? The answer's pretty easy. As caps were worn—and in the early days players were issued caps one-at-a-time—they would get soiled, torn or simply just wear out. When that happened, the player (or the equipment manager) would simply throw it away. Caps weren't seen as having great value, certainly weren't considered "collectible" and were disposed of with no remorse. The thing to remember is that on some teams a player had to turn in an old hat to get a new one. Clubs weren't about to give their players new caps every time they turned around. In fact, the cap was considered part of the uniform, and up until just before the beginning of free agency, players were required to leave a cash deposit on their uniforms. Before six-figure salaries were the norm, most players wanted that money back.

Many early caps can be found with the player's name stitched into the leather sweatband. Others can be found with the player's uniform numbers stitched in. These caps are highly prized, but there is a caveat: Clubs also had caps with no names (or numbers) stitched inside for players who joined the team during the season. There have been instances where these caps have been embroidered with the names of famous players and sold as the real thing. Some early caps will have the cap size stitched in as well.

New Era Cap Company is currently the official milliner to Major League Baseball, but in years past, big league caps were manufactured by a plethora of companies, including Wilson, Spalding, Rawlings, MacGregor, Goldsmith, Leslie, Devon, AJD, Roman Pro, and many others. Many caps can be found with a Tim McAuliffe label, though McAuliffe wasn't a manufacturer, per se. He was a salesman who, after getting an order from a club, would contract with a manufacturer to make the caps and sew in his label. In later years the "KM Pro" label would occasionally accompany a McAuliffe tag, designating the part-

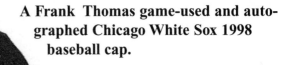

A Frank Thomas game-used and autographed Chicago White Sox 1998 baseball cap.

nership he formed with Kauffman Sporting Goods. And, while you rarely see New Era labels in caps prior to the 1950s, they actually made caps for other sporting goods companies at times going back into the 1920s.

Only one cap manufacturer has ever stamped a date code into its caps. Wilson Sporting Goods designed a letter code that can be found in most of its caps from the early 1950s through the end of their dominance in the major league cap field, the early 1970s. Inside the sweatband you'll see a rubber-stamped three-letter code. The first letter signifies the year, the second letter the month of manufacture and the third letter is always "C" for cap. Here's how the code works:

First Letter
A – last digit of the year is 8
B - 9
C – 0
D – 1
E – 2
F – 3
G – 4
H – 5   (NOTE: There's no "I" in this code)
J – 6
K - 7

Second Letter
Z – January
Y – February
X – March
W – April
V – May
U – June
And so on…

So, a Wilson cap with a date code of AZC would have been manufactured in January 1968 (or 1958). The style of the cap usually makes it easy to pin down the precise year. The date code makes authenticating a specific player's cap somewhat easier. Obviously, if a cap was manufactured after a player had already been sent elsewhere, he couldn't have worn that cap.

Collecting vintage game-worn caps is a challenging sidebar to collecting uniforms. The search for certain team's caps may take years, but the hunt is half the fun.

Hank Aaron: 1970s Milwaukee Brewers, blue/gold with M $1,250

Johnny Bench: 1970s Cincinnati Reds, game used, New Era $450

Wade Boggs: 1995 New York Yankees, used in the All-Star game, signed $350

Barry Bonds: 1994 San Francisco Giants, game used, New Era......$225

Bobby Bonilla: 1992-93 New York Mets, game used, New Era, signed $95

George Brett: Kansas City Royals, game used $550

Lou Brock: 1970s St. Louis Cardinals, game used, New Era $350

Ellis Burks: 1994 Colorado Rockies, game used, New Era $75

Joe Carter: 1990s Toronto Blue Jays, game used, New Era, signed......... ....$250

Ron Cey: 1970s Los Angeles Dodgers, game used, New Era..........$125

Will Clark: 1990s San Francisco Giants, game used, New Era........$195

Will Clark: 1997 Texas Rangers, game used, New Era, signed........$165

Royce Clayton: 1993 San Francisco Giants, game used, New Era, signed $85

Dave Concepcion: 1970s Cincinnati Reds, game used St. Patrick's Day, New Era..$150

Andre Dawson: 1993 Boston Red Sox, game used, New Era, signed $140

Andre Dawson: 1994 Florida Marlins, game used, signed...............$125

Bucky Dent: 1970s New York Yankees cap, game used, Wilson........$95

Steve Finley: 1990s Houston Astros, game used, New Era, signed ...$50

Andres Galarraga: 1994 Colorado Rockies, game used, New Era, 125 year pin...$150

Juan Gonzalez: 1990s Texas Rangers, game used, New Era, signed $145

Mike Greenwell: 1992 Boston Red Sox, game used, New Era, signed $90

Ozzie Guillen: 1990s Chicago White Sox, game used, New Era, signed $80

Rickey Henderson: New York Yankees, game used, New Era, signed $325

Bo Jackson: 1994 California Angles, game used, New Era $80

Reggie Jackson: New York Yankees, game used..............................$550

Tommy John: Chicago White Sox, game used $175

Howard Johnson: Detroit Tigers, game used $60

Barry Larkin: 1990s Cincinnati Reds, game used, New Era, signed $125

Dennis Martinez: 1995 Cleveland Indians, game used, New Era.....$175

Jack McDowell: 1992 Chicago White Sox cap, game used, New Era, signed $110

Fred McGriff: 1990s San Diego Padres, game used, Sports Specialties $125

Joe Morgan: 1978 Cincinnati Reds, green, game used on St. Patrick's Day, signed...$350

Dale Murphy: Atlanta Braves, game used $125

Jim Palmer: 1970s Baltimore Orioles, game used, AJD, signed $350

Vada Pinson: 1968 Cincinnati Reds, game used, Wilson $150

Kirby Puckett: 1993 Minnesota Twins, game used, New Era $250

Tim Raines: 1980s Montreal Expos, game used, New Era, signed....$95

Jim Rice: 1980s Boston Red Sox, game used, Devon, signed $115

Cal Ripken Jr.: Baltimore Orioles, game used, signed $450

Brooks Robinson: Baltimore Orioles, game used, Tim McAuliffe, 1964 ....$495

Bret Saberhagen: 1993-94 New York Mets, game used, New Era $80

Ryne Sandberg: Chicago Cubs, game used $175

Gary Sheffield: 1989 Milwaukee Brewers, game used, Sports Specialties, signed...$125

Ruben Sierra: Texas Rangers cap, #21 under bill, game used, signed $250

Darryl Strawberry: Los Angeles Dodgers cap, #44 under bill, game used, signed $250

Greg Swindell: 1980s Cleveland Indians cap, game used, New Era..$75

Frank Thomas: 1998 Chicago White Sox, game used, signed $225

Larry Walker: 1995 Colorado Rockies cap, game used, New Era, signed $160

Walt Weiss: 1990s Oakland As cap, game used, New Era, signed.....$65

Lou Whitaker: Detroit Tigers cap, #1 under bill, game used............$135

Matt Williams: San Francisco Giants cap, game used, 1994...........$175

Dave Winfield: 1993 Minnesota Twins cap, game used, New Era...$150

Major League Baseball Caps

Major League Baseball Caps

Game-Used Batting Helmets

Hank Aaron: Milwaukee Brewers, mid-1970s...............................$1,500
Roberto Alomar: San Diego Padres $695
Roberto Alomar: Toronto Blue Jays $795
Carlos Baerga: Cleveland Indians $550
Wade Boggs: Boston Red Sox $795
Bobby Bonilla: 1992 New York Mets $195
George Brett: Kansas City Royals, signed........................$1,300
Jeff Burroughs: 1988 Toronto Blue Jays $125
Jose Canseco: 1980s Oakland A's batting helmet, signed $750
Jose Canseco: Texas Rangers batting helmet, #33, signed $750
Rod Carew: Minnesota Twins, signed...............................$795
Gary Carter: Montreal Expos, signed $795
Will Clark: Texas Rangers, 1994, signed.........................$450
Roberto Clemente: Pittsburgh Pirates, 1960s....................$3,000
Andre Dawson: Boston Red Sox, 1994, signed $550
Darrell Evans: Detroit Tigers, 1980s.............................$225
Julio Franco: 1980s Cleveland Indians $175
Andres Galarraga: late-1980s Montreal Expos $150

Juan Gonzalez: Texas Rangers, 1993, signed $300
Rickey Henderson: Oakland A's, signed $900
Reggie Jackson: California Angels, 1984, signed...........................$900
Javy Lopez: Atlanta Braves catchers helmet, signed $250
Hal McRae: 1980s Kansas City Royals $175
Paul Molitor: Milwaukee Brewers, #4, signed....................$700
Dale Murphy: Atlanta Braves, #3, signed $575
Kirby Puckett: Minnesota Twins, #34, signed $1,000
Willie Randolph: 1980s New York Yankees $250
Ryne Sandberg: 1991 Chicago Cubs $1,195
Gary Sheffield: 1990 Milwaukee Brewers......................$175
Ruben Sierra: Texas Rangers $395
Dave Winfield: San Diego Padres, mid-1970s.....................$950
Dave Winfield: 1991 California Angels, game used......................$800
Dave Winfield: New York Yankees, game used $1,295
Robin Yount: 1970s Milwaukee Brewers $900
Robin Yount: Milwaukee Brewers, game used $895

BASEBALL BATS

There are basically four categories of baseball bats that collectors pursue. They are:

1) Authentic cracked or uncracked game-used bat. The player has actually used the bat in a game; it shows wear and tear from use, including scuffs, dents, tape, filing of the handle, uniform numbers on the handles, use of pine tar, hollowed ends and cracks. The value of a bat decreases according to the size of the crack.

This bat is made to a player's specifications, with his name and signature on it, or it could be a bat ordered by the team, with the team name branded into it. Pitchers and coaches generally use these bats. Coaches' bats may carry the player's name, but are not necessarily made according to the specifics he used as an active player.

2) Authentic bats, made to the players' specifications, but which have not been used in a game. It's possible the player didn't even own the bat, which could have been ordered by the team for promotions or giveaways, or made for other businesses for resale. These bats are often used for autographing.

3) Retail or store model bats, which are purchased in sporting goods stores. They are not made according to the player's specifications, but often carry his name as an endorsement. Vintage model bats of stars before the 1950s generally sell well. Naive collectors can end up purchasing these bats for $100 to $200, thinking they are game-used bats when they aren't.

Store models can be distinguished from game-used bats because the knobs carry inch markings, a single-digit number or both initials of the player whose name is on the barrel. Also, if the bat number in the brand oval is followed by any letters, probably player initials, it's likely the bat is a store model.

4) Commemoratives: These bats are made to recognize a particular person, place or event in baseball history, such as a World Series or Hall of Fame induction. These customized bats, generally more desirable than store models, are often created for display purposes and are suitable for autographing, which makes them more valuable. Black Sharpie pens work best.

Many collectors have their commemorative bats signed by the players involved.

Here are some general guidelines for bat collectors:

Baseball's rules limit the length of bats to 42 inches long. Generally, bats weigh between 30-50 ounces.

These are the most common bat brands used by major leaguers:

1) Hillerich & Bradsby: This company has undergone several name modifications from 1884 until 1979, when its bats became more commonly known as Louisville Sluggers, H&B's most popular style. Since 1945, H&B has labeled bats with player initials and a model number on the knob, which is an identifying number for each individual style. In 1976, those numbers were moved to the barrel of the bat. If the player is contracted by the manufacturer, his name is burned into the bat barrel in autograph form. If he isn't, his name is in block letters.

Hillerich & Bradsby adopted the slogan "Powerized" in 1932 and began putting model numbers—which have one letter and at least one number—on the knob in 1944. Those numbers were removed beginning in 1976 and then placed on the barrel. The H&B logo was dropped in 1979, with Louisville Slugger becoming the brand label.

2) A.G. Spalding & Bros. bats, used primarily before the turn of the century.

3) A.J. Reach bats, which were prominent at the beginning of the century.

4) Rawlings, which labels its bats as Adirondacks. They feature a single-colored ring around the neck and a diamond-shaped trademark.

5) Worth, which entered the market in the 1970s and offers its Tennessee Thumper bats.

6) Cooper bats, produced in Canada since 1986.

7) Mizuno bats, made in Japan.

It is very difficult to verify a bat actually used by a player in a major league game. (Was it scuffed at a softball game last week? Did the player himself use it, or did one of his teammates? Was it used only in batting practice? Often, players themselves cannot remember which stick they used.)

If you invest in one of these bats, deal only with a dealer who is an expert in the area and insist on written documentation. Reliable dealers usually get these items from unimpeachable sources—the player's attorney or agent, a family member, the clubhouse attendant or a batboy.

Game-Used Bats

A game-used Hank Aaron Adirondack Big Stick personal model bat from the 1969 season.

Hank Aaron: Hillerich & Bradsby, late 1950s	$2,595
Hank Aaron: Adirondack, uncracked, early 1970s	$2,295
Joe Adcock: Hillerich & Bradsby, 1965-71	$295
Dick Allen: Hillerich & Bradsby, 1973-75	$495
Bob Allison: Hillerich & Bradsby, 1960s	$395
Roberto Alomar: Louisville Slugger, 1990	$425
Roberto Alomar: Adirondack, 1999	$250
Sandy Alomar Jr.: Rose, 1994-95	$95
Matty Alou: Hillerich & Bradsby, 1965-72	$295
Moises Alou: Adirondack, 1992	$140
Brady Anderson: Louisville Slugger	$85
Luis Aparicio: Hillerich & Bradsby, 1960s	$795
Tony Armas: Louisville Slugger, cracked, 1984-85	$40
Carlos Baerga: Adirondack, 1995, signed	$275
Harold Baines: Adirondack, uncracked, 1991-94, signed	$80

Dusty Baker: Louisville Slugger, 1975-79.................................$100
Steve Balboni: Louisville Slugger, cracked, 1984-85......................$40
Sal Bando: Hillerich & Bradsby, 1965-72.................................$175
Don Baylor: Louisville Slugger, 1977-79.................................$150
Albert Belle: Louisville Slugger, 1995 ....$600
Johnny Bench: Adirondack, 1960s, signed $750
Dante Bichette: Louisville Slugger, 1988 ....$195
Dante Bichette: Adirondack, cracked, 1999...............................$125
Craig Biggio: Louisville Slugger, 1993-94, signed $195
Jeff Blauser: Louisville Slugger, cracked, 1995 ....$50
Wade Boggs: Hillerich & Bradsby, 1977-79 (minor leagues)...$1,795
Wade Boggs: Louisville Slugger, 1982................................$1,295
Wade Boggs: Louisville Slugger, uncracked, 1994 ....$450
Barry Bonds: Louisville Slugger, 1993-95, signed.......................$595
Bobby Bonilla: Louisville Slugger, 1986-89 ....$130
Bob Boone: Louisville Slugger, 1984-85, signed $265
Bret Boone: Louisville Slugger, 1992-93, signed $75
Lyman Bostock: Louisville Slugger, 1977-79 ....$125
Clete Boyer: Hillerich & Bradsby, 1965-72..............................$295
Ken Boyer: Adirondack, 1959 All-Star Game $1,495
George Brett: Louisvillle Slugger, uncracked, early 1980s...........$1,150
Lou Brock: Hillerich & Bradsby, 1967 All-Star Game, signed.....$1,595
Lou Brock: Hillerich & Bradsby, 1973-75 ....$495
Gates Brown: Hillerich & Bradsby, 1965-72..............................$295
Bill Buckner: Louisville Slugger, 1973-75 ....$150
Jay Buhner: Adirondack, 1994...$150
Ellis Burks: Louisville Slugger, uncracked, 1995........................$45
Jeromy Burnitz: Louisville Slugger, 1997 ....$195
Jeff Burroughs: Worth, 1987...$70
Brett Butler: Louisville Slugger, 1986-89...............................$90
Ken Caminiti: Adirondack, 1995 ....$80
Jose Canseco: Adirondack, uncracked, 1991, signed $450
Jose Canseco: Cooper, 1995...$295
Leo Cardenas: Hillerich & Bradsby, 1973-75, signed......................$75
Rod Carew: Hillerich & Bradsby, cracked, 1965-72, signed...........$995
Rod Carew: Louisville Slugger, uncracked, 1979, signed.............$290
Rod Carew: Adirondack, 1980, signed $350
Steve Carlton: Louisville Slugger, mid-1980s $750
Gary Carter: Hillerich & Bradsby, 1972-75..............................$695
Gary Carter: Adirondack, uncracked, mid-1980s $275
Joe Carter: Louisville Slugger, 1982-83 ....$395
Joe Carter: Louisville, 1995...$195
Rico Carty: Hillerich & Bradsby, 1965-72, signed $225
Vinny Castilla: Adirondack, 1999.......................................$150
Cesar Cedeno: Hillerich & Bradsby, 1970-71, signed.....................$140
Ron Cey: Louisville Slugger, 1975-79...................................$150

Jack Clark: Louisville Slugger, 1984-85.................................$80
Will Clark: Adirondack, uncracked, 1991, signed $450
Will Clark: Louisville Slugger, uncracked..............................$375
Roberto Clemente: Hillerich & Bradsby, cracked, late 1960s.......$3,295
Rocky Colavito: Hillerich & Bradsby, 1965-68...........................$895
Dave Concepcion: Louisville Slugger, 1984-85, signed...................$140
Cecil Cooper: Louisville Slugger, 1980..................................$75
Al Cowens: Hillerich & Bradsby, 1977-79.................................$40
Vic Davalillo: Louisville Slugger, 1977-79.............................$150
Alvin Davis: Louisville Slugger,1986-89.................................$25
Chili Davis: Adirondack, 1996..$100
Eric Davis: Louisville Slugger, 1999...................................$125
Tommy Davis: Hillerich & Bradsby, game used, uncracked, 1961-64
....$350
Willie Davis: Hillerich & Bradsby, 1973-75.............................$125
Andre Dawson: Louisville Slugger, cracked, early 1980s.............$275
Doug DeCinces: Adirondack, 1987...$70
Joe DiMaggio: Hillerich & Bradsby, uncracked, 1930s $16,500
Joe DiMaggio: Hillerich & Bradsby, 1945-51 ....$9,995
Bobby Doerr: Hillerich & Bradsby, cracked, repaired, 1949-59 ...$1,200
Shawon Dunston: Worth, cracked, 1988-89.................................$70
Len Dykstra: Louisville Slugger, 1986-89...............................$200
Damion Easley: Louisville Slugger, 1998, cracked........................$95
Jim Eisenrich: Louisville Slugger, 1995.................................$45
Mike Epstein: Hillerich & Bradsby, 1973-75.............................$125
Darrell Evans: Worth, 1988...$125
Dwight Evans: Hillerich & Bradsby, 1977-79, signed $395
Dwight Evans: Louisville Slugger, 1984-85...............................$80
Hoot Evers: Adirondack, 1952-57..$295
Tony Fernandez: Adirondack, 1991 ....$50
Cecil Fielder: Cooper, cracked, 1994...................................$250
Steve Finley: Cooper, cracked, 1993.....................................$40
Carlton Fisk: Worth, cracked, 1970s, signed $550
Carlton Fisk: Hillerich & Bradsby, 1977-79..........................$1,295
George Foster: Louisville Slugger, 1977-79.............................$125
Nellie Fox: Louisville Slugger...$400
Bill Freehan: Hillerich & Bradsby, 1973-75.............................$495
Jim Fregosi: Hillerich & Bradsby, 1965-71, signed $175
Andres Galarraga: Louisville Slugger, cracked, 1995 ....$175
Ron Gant: Adirondack, 1992 NLCS..$350
Jim Gantner: Louisville Slugger, 1991-94................................$50
Nomar Garciaparra: Louisville Slugger, 1999, autographed $995
Steve Garvey: Adirondack, cracked, late 1970s..........................$325
Steve Garvey: Louisville Slugger, 1985 All-Star Game $595
Cito Gaston: Adirondack, 1970s...$110
Lou Gehrig: Hillerich & Bradsby, 1925 ....$13,500

A game-used Barry Bonds personal Louisville Slugger model bat.

A Nellie Fox game-used Hillerich and Bradsby Lousville Slugger model bat.

A game-used Gil Hodges personal model Louisville Slugger bat from the 1953 World Series.

A game-used Eddie Mathews personal Louisville Slugger model bat.

A Game-used Willie Mays personal model Adirondack bat from the 1959 All-Star Game.

Cesar Geronimo: Hillerich & Bradsby, 1977-79	$295
Bob Gibson: Hillerich & Bradsby, 1965-72	$995
Dan Gladden: Worth, cracked, 1988	$50
Juan Gonzalez: Adirondack, 1995	$285
Dwight Gooden: Adirondack, 1984, signed	$195
Mark Grace: Adirondack, 1993	$295
Mark Grace: Adirondack, cracked, 1995	$150
Mike Greenwell: Louisville Slugger, 1995	$100
Bobby Grich: Adirondack, cracked, 1981	$80
Tom Grieve: Hillerich & Bradsby, 1965-72	$110
Ken Griffey Jr.: Louisville Slugger, 1991-95, signed	$795
Ken Griffey Sr.: Louisville Slugger, 1973-75	$125
Ken Griffey Sr.: Louisville Slugger, 1990	$90
Marquis Grissom: Adirondack, 1993	$70
Dick Groat: Hillerich & Bradsby, 1965-72	$595
Pedro Guerrero: Louisville Slugger, 1983-85	$85
Ozzie Guillen: Worth, game used, 1995	$90
Tony Gwynn: Louisville Slugger, uncracked, 1998	$895
Tony Gwynn: Adirondack, 1992 All-Star Game	$800
Von Hayes: Louisville Slugger, 1986-89	$40
Rickey Henderson: Louisville Slugger, 1993 World Series	$995
Rickey Henderson: Louisville Slugger, 1995	$290
George Hendrick: Louisville Slugger, 1984-85	$55
Tommy Henrich: Hillerich & Bradsby, 1940s	$1,395
Keith Hernandez: Louisville Slugger, cracked, 1980s	$150
Babe Herman: Hillerich & Bradsby, uncracked, 1930s	$375
Orel Hershiser: Louisville Slugger, 1984-85	$200
Butch Hobson: Hillerich & Bradsby, 1977-79	$70
Gil Hodges: Louisville Slugger, 1953 World Series	$1,500
Chris Hoiles: Adirondack, cracked, 1994	$70
Elston Howard: Hillerich & Bradsby, pre-1964	$1,395
Frank Howard: Hillerich & Bradsby, 1965-72, signed	$595
Todd Hundley: Lousiville Slugger, cracked, 1995	$50
Bo Jackson: Louisville Slugger, 1991-93	$295
Joe Jackson: Hillerich & Bradsby, 1921-30	$11,000
Reggie Jackson: Louisville Slugger, 1968-72	$2,400
Reggie Jackson: Hillerich & Bradsby, 1968-71, signed	$1,795
Reggie Jackson: Adirondack, cracked, 1971-79	$695
Reggie Jackson: Adirondack, 1985	$695
Alex Johnson: Hillerich & Bradsby, 1973-75, signed	$295
Cliff Johnson: Louisville Slugger, cracked, early 1980s	$40
Davey Johnson: Hillerich & Bradsby, cracked 1970s, signed	$185
Howard Johnson: Adirondack, 1988	$95
Felix Jose: Louisville Slugger, 1986-89	$50

Von Joshua: Hillerich & Bradsby, 1977-79	$40
Wally Joyner: Louisville Slugger, 1991-94	$90
Dave Justice: Louisville Slugger, 1995	$275
Al Kaline: Hillerich & Bradsby, 1965-72, signed	$795
Al Kaline: Hillerich & Bradsby, chipped, late 1970s	$450
Ron Karkovice: Louisville Slugger, cracked	$40
Eric Karros: Louisville Slugger, 1992	$175
Don Kessinger: Louisville Slugger, 1973-75	$90
Harmon Killebrew: Louisville Slugger, 1965-71, signed	$1,595
Harmon Killebrew: Louisville Slugger, 1971	$2,000
Dave Kingman: Louisville Slugger, cracked, signed, 1984-85	$190
Ted Kluszewski: Hillerich & Bradsby, 1958	$995
Ray Knight: Hillerich & Bradsby, 1977-79	$95
Chuck Knoblauch: Louisville Slugger, 1991-93	$175
John Kruk: Louisville Slugger, cracked, 1993	$85
Tony Kubek: Hillerich & Bradsby, 1965-72	$895
Harvey Kuenn: Hillerich & Bradsby, 1965-72	$695
Lee Lacy: Adirondack, cracked, 1971-79	$60
Carney Lansford: Hillerich & Bradsby, 1977-79	$65
Barry Larkin: Louisville Slugger, 1986-89	$180
Ron LeFlore: Louisville Slugger, 1977-79	$95
Chet Lemon: Louisville Slugger, 1990	$45
Davey Lopes: Adirondack, 1981	$150
John Lowenstein: Hillerich & Bradsby, 1980s	$85
Greg Luzinski: Adirondack, 1971-79	$125
Fred Lynn: Adirondack, 1990	$140
Bill Madlock: Louisville Slugger, 1984-85	$195
Greg Maddux: Louisville Slugger, 1995, signed	$1,295
Mickey Mantle: Louisville Slugger, 1965-68, signed	$10,995
Marty Marion: Hillerich & Bradsby, 1940s, signed	$850
Roger Maris: Hillerich & Bradsby, cracked, 1960s	$2,775
Roger Maris: Hillerich & Bradsby, 1961	$4,995
Tino Martinez: Rose, 1995	$110
Eddie Mathews: Hillerich & Bradsby, uncracked, 1968, signed	$2,500
Don Mattingly: Worth, 1980s	$495
Don Mattingly: Worth, 1995	$350
Willie Mays: Hillerich & Bradsby, 1965-72	$2,250
Willie Mays: Hillerich & Bradsby, early 1970s	$1,895
Bill Mazeroski: Adirondack, 1960 All-Star Game	$2,000
Tim McCarver: Hillerich & Bradsby, cracked, 1976	$285
Willie McCovey: Louisville Slugger, cracked, 1965-71, signed	$1,495
Willie McCovey: Louisville Slugger, 1974-75	$1,195
Fred McGriff: Louisville Slugger, 1986-89	$195
Mark McGwire: Adirondack, uncracked, 1992	$1,095

A game-used 1951 Jackie Robinson model Louisville Slugger All-Star Game bat.

A game-used Babe Ruth personal model bat

Mark McGwire: Adirondack, 1991 All-Star Game, signed $1,295
Hal McRae: Hillerich & Bradsby, 1973-75 ....$60
Hal McRae: Louisville Slugger, 1977-79 ....$95
Kevin McReynolds: Adirondack, game used, 1988 ....$75
Minnie Minoso: Hillerich & Bradsby, 1960 All-Star Game $1,495
Kevin Mitchell: Mizuno, cracked, 1994 ....$50
Johnny Mize: Hillerich & Bradsby, 1944-49 ....$995
Paul Molitor: Hillerich & Bradsby, 1977-79 ....$795
Paul Molitor: Cooper, cracked, signed, 1995 ....$250
Rick Monday: Hillerich & Bradsby, uncracked, 1965-71, signed....$175
Joe Morgan: Louisville Slugger, 1977-79 ....$400
Manny Mota: Hillerich & Bradsby, 1965-72 ....$295
Thurman Munson: Hillerich & Bradsby, 1977-79 ....$1,495
Bobby Murcer: Hillerich & Bradsby, 1973-75 ....$175
Eddie Murray: Hillerich & Bradsby, 1977-79, signed $1,295
Eddie Murray: Lousville Slugger, cracked, 1988, signed $595
Stan Musial: Hillerich & Bradsby, pre-1964 ....$4,199
Tim Naehring: Louisville Slugger, 1995 ....$90
Graig Nettles: Louisville Slugger, 1984-85 ....$195
Otis Nixon: Cooper, 1995 ....$60
Matt Nokes: Louisville Slugger, 1984-85 ....$80
Ben Oglivie: Louisville Slugger, cracked, 1980-83 ....$60
John Olerud: Adirondack, 1994 ....$125
Tony Oliva: Hillerich & Bradsby, missing knob, early 1970s.........$175
Al Oliver: Louisville Slugger, 1965-72 ....$100
Jorge Orta: Louisville Slugger, 1977-79 ....$50
Paul O'Neill: Louisville Slugger, uncracked $180
Rafael Palmeiro: Louisville Slugger, 1986 ....$195
Rafael Palmeiro: Cooper, cracked, 1995 ....$85
Dave Parker: Louisville Slugger, cracked, 1980-83 ....$125
Lance Parrish: Worth, 1980s $95
Dan Pasqua: Louisville Slugger, cracked, 1994 ....$30
Tony Pena: Louisville Slugger, 1986-89 ....$50
Terry Pendleton: Louisville Slugger, 1985 World Series, signed $595
Tony Perez: Adirondack, slight crack, late 1960s $550
Tony Perez: Louisville Slugger, 1986-89, signed $150
Mike Piazza: Louisville Slugger, 1993 ....$595
Jim Piersall: Hillerich & Bradsby, 1950s $995
Vada Pinson: Hillerich & Bradsby, 1973-75 ....$250
Kirby Puckett: 1991 Adirondack, ALCS $595
Kirby Puckett; 1994 Louisville Slugger, ...$300
Tim Raines: Louisville Slugger, early 1980s, signed $175
Tim Raines: Louisville Slugger, 1982 All-Star Game, signed.........$495
Manny Ramirez: Louisville Slugger, 1999 ....$495
Willie Randolph: Louisville Slugger, cracked, 1980s $95
Jody Reed: Louisville Slugger, 1995 ....$50
Pee Wee Reese: Hillerich & Bradsby, 1949-59 ....$1,595
Rich Reese: Hillerich & Bradsby, 1965-72 ....$85
Harold Reynolds: Louisville Slugger, 1984-85 ....$30
Jim Rice: Louisville Slugger, 1984-85 ....$175

Jose Rijo: Louisville Slugger, 1994 ....$125
Cal Ripken Jr.: Louisville Slugger, 1981 ....$2,250
Brooks Robinson: Hillerich & Bradsby, 1972-75, signed $750
Frank Robinson: Hillerich & Bradsby, 1965-71 ....$695
Jackie Robinson: Adirondack, 1952-56 ....$6,995
Pete Rose: Hillerich & Bradsby, 1965-72, signed $1,795
Pete Rose: Hillerich & Bradsby, 1972-75, signed $1,595
Pete Rose: Mizuno, cracked, 1980-83, signed $1,250
Joe Rudi: Hillerich & Bradsby, 1973-75 ....$150
Babe Ruth: Hillerich & Bradsby, uncracked, 1922 ....$8,955
Babe Ruth: Hillerich & Bradsby, 1920s $18,995
Nolan Ryan: Louisville Slugger, 1983-85, signed $2,495
Tim Salmon: Mizuno, 1995 ....$150
Ryne Sandberg: Adirondack, cracked, 1988 ....$475
Manny Sanguillen: Hillerich & Bradsby, 1965-72, signed..............$195
Benito Santiago: Worth, cracked, 1995 ....$40
Mike Schmidt: Louisville Slugger, 1974-75 ....$1,700
Mike Schmidt: Adirondack, uncracked, 1980s $750
Red Schoendienst: Adirondack, cracked, 1950s $895
George Scott: Louisville Slugger, 1973-75 ....$50
Tom Seaver: Hillerich & Bradsby, 1972-75, signed $1,495
Tom Seaver: Hillerich & Bradsby, uncracked, 1977-79 ....$1,625
Kevin Seitzer: Louisville Slugger, 1986-89 ....$50
Richie Sexson: Louisville Slugger, uncracked, 1999 ....$195
Ruben Sierra: Louisville Slugger, 1991-92, signed $125
Ruben Sierra: Adirondack, 1991 All-Star Game $245
Ted Simmons: Louisville Slugger, 1984-85 ....$150
Moose Skowron: Hillerich & Bradsby, 1950s $995
Roy Smalley: Louisville Slugger, 1965-72 ....$50
Ozzie Smith: Hillerich & Bradsby, 1977-79, signed $695
Cory Snyder: Louisville Slugger, uncracked, signed $95
Sammy Sosa: Adirondack, 1995 ....$185
Mario Soto: Louisville Slugger, 1984-85 ....$60
Willie Stargell: Hillerich & Bradsby, 1964 All-Star Game, signed
....$2,495
Willie Stargell: Hillerich & Bradsby, late 1970s $475
Terry Steinbach: Adirondack, cracked, 1994 ....$70
Rennie Stennett: Louisville Slugger, 1975-79 ....$50
B.J. Surhoff: Adirondack, 1995 ....$80
Danny Tartabull: Worth, cracked, 1992 ....$80
Frank Thomas: Worth, two-toned, 1994, cracked $350
Gorman Thomas: Adirondack, 1981, cracked $80
Luis Tiant: Hillerich & Bradsby, 1965-72, signed $695
Alan Trammell: Worth, early 1980s, signed $175
Alan Trammell: Louisville Slugger, 1980-83, signed $395
Andy Van Slyke: Louisville Slugger, 1995 ....$275
Greg Vaughn: Adirondack, 1991 ....$70
Mo Vaughn: Louisville Slugger, 1995 ....$495
Otto Velez: Hillerich & Bradsby, 1976, cracked $90
Robin Ventura: Louisville Slugger, 1993 ....$175

Bob Watson: Adirondack, 1971-79 ....$95
Walt Weiss: Louisville Slugger, cracked, 1995 ....$45
Walt Weiss: Worth, 1989 ALCS $235
Bill White: Hillerich & Bradsby, 1950s $895
Devon White: Louisville Slugger, 1990 ....$100
Frank White: Adirondack, cracked, 1971-79 ....$60
Roy White: Hillerich & Bradsby, 1979 ....$175
Ernie Whitt: Louisville Slugger, 1990 ....$20
Dick Willams: Hillerich & Bradsby, 1950s $450
Matt Williams: Cooper, slight crack, 1994 ....$295

Dave Winfield: Hillerich & Bradsby, 1973-75, signed $1,295
Dave Winfield: Cooper, uncracked, 1994 ....$225
Dave Winfield: Adirondack, 1979 All-Star Game, uncracked ..$1,850
Jimmy Wynn: Hillerich & Bradsby, cracked, 1976 ....$180
Carl Yastrzemski: Hillerich & Bradsby, 1960-64 ....$1,695
Carl Yastrzemski: Hillerich & Bradsby, 1965-72 ....$995
Carl Yastrzemski: Louisville Slugger, early 1980s $575
Robin Yount: Hillerich & Bradsby, 1973-75 ....$1,995
Robin Yount: Louisville Slugger,1984-85 ....$295
Richie Zisk: Adirondack, cracked, 1981 ....$60

Unused Game Bats

**An unused Louisville Slugger R161 model bat autographed
by several members of the Hall of Fame.**

Roberto Alomar: Cooper, 1992, C243 ....$150
Carlos Baerga: Louisville Slugger, 1994 ....$250
Carlos Baerga: Adirondack, 1995 World Series $595
Albert Belle: Cooper, B343 ....$150
Barry Bonds: Louisville Slugger H238, 1994 ....$295
Bobby Bonilla: Cooper, S318 ....$75
George Brett: Louisville Slugger, P89, 1983-84, signed $395
Jose Canseco: Cooper, R161 ....$150
Gary Carter: Louisville Slugger, P89, 1984-85 ....$135
Gary Carter: Louisville Slugger, 1982 All-Star Game, signed ..$450
Joe Carter: Cooper, B343, 1993 World Series $695
Will Clark: Cooper, C271 ....$150
Andre Dawson: Louisville Slugger, 1980-83, C271, signed ...$195
Tony Fernandez: Cooper, F322, 1993 World Series $175
Cecil Fielder: Cooper, C271 ....$95
Travis Fryman: Adirondack, 1992 All-Star Game $495
Andres Galarraga: Cooper, C243 ....$75
Juan Gonzalez: Cooper, P72 ....$150

Ken Griffey Jr.: Louisville Slugger, C271, 1994, signed ...$350
Bo Jackson: Louisville Slugger, J93, 1990 ....$125
Reggie Jackson: Louisville Slugger, H174, 1980-83, #44 ....$295
Chipper Jones: Adirondack, 1995 World Series $595
Michael Jordan: Worth, black, signed $275
Eddie Murray: Louisville Slugger, R161, 1983-84, signed ...$350
Eddie Murray: Adirondack, 1995 World Series, signed $695
John Olerud: Cooper, T141, 1993 World Series $695
Rafael Palmeiro: Cooper, S329 ....$85
Jim Rice: Cooper, R206 ....$85
Jim Rice: Hillerich & Bradsby, M159 ....$295
Ryne Sandberg: Louisville Slugger, B267, 1983-84 ....$295
Mike Schmidt: Adirondack, 1986, 154A $495
Ruben Sierra: Louisville Slugger, 1991-92, T141 ....$125
Ruben Sierra: Louisville Slugger, 1992 All-Star, 484A $350
Matt Williams: Cooper, M110 ....$150
Dave Winfield: Cooper, DW20 ....$150
Robin Yount: Louisville Slugger, 1984-84, P72, signed $350

Team-Signed Bats

1971 Baltimore Orioles: 1968-72 Reggie Jackson Adirondack model, with 17 signatures, includes Dave McNally, Jim Palmer, Boog Powell, Brooks Robinson and Frank Robinson $1,350
1990 Boston Red Sox: Boston Red Sox bat, with 41 signatures, includes Wade Boggs, Ellis Burks, Roger Clemens, Dwight Evans, Mike Greenwell and Jeff Reardon..............................$325
1995 Boston Red Sox: game-used team bat, with 25 signatures, includes Rick Aguilcra, Josc Cansceco, Roger Clemens, Mike Greenwell, Mo Vaughn and Tim Wakefield......................................$195

1992 California Angels: Louisville Slugger, game used in spring training, with 25 signatures, includes Jim Abbott, Chuck Finley, Gary Gaetti and Mark Langston $200
1995 California Angels: Damon Easley's game-used Louisville Slugger, with 25 signatures, includes Jim Abbott, Chili Davis, Chuck Finley, Mark Langston, Tim Salmon, Lee Smith and J.T. Snow.............$125
1994 Chicago Cubs: generic Cooper model bat, with 25 signatures, includes Mark Grace, Ryne Sandberg and Sammy Sosa.............$150
1959 Chicago White Sox: Billy Martin game used, with 24 signatures,

**A Louisville Slugger bat signed by members of the 1959 A.L. champion
Chicago White Sox.**

includes Luis Aparicio, Norm Cash, Nellie Fox, Al Lopez and Early Wynn $1,150

1992 Chicago White Sox: Dan Pasqua model bat, with 17 signatures, includes Carlton Fisk, Bo Jackson, Tim Raines, Frank Thomas and Robin Ventura..$225

1978 Cincinnati Reds: 1977-79 Pete Rose Hillerich & Bradsby model, with 20 signatures, includes Dave Concepcion, George Foster, Ken Griffey, Pete Rose and Tom Seaver $1,150

1995 Colorado Rockies: store model Adirondack, black, with 28 signatures, includes Dante Bichette, Andres Galarraga and Larry Walker $350

1987 Detroit Tigers: Kirk Gibson model bat, with 29 signatures, includes Sparky Anderson, Darrell Evans, Kirk Gibson, Jack Morris, Alan Trammell and Lou Whitaker..$315

1993 Florida Marlins: Jim Corsi game-used bat, with 19 signatures, includes Jeff Conine, Gary Sheffield and Walt Weiss $400

1995 Houston Astros: generic black Adirondack, with 31 signatures, includes Jeff Bagwell, Craig Biggio and Doug Drabek $295

1982 Kansas City Royals: on a George Brett game-used Louisville Slugger, signed by the entire team..$795

1991 Milwaukee Brewers: on a Paul Molitor Milwaukee Brewers bat, with 24 signatures, includes Paul Molitor, Greg Vaughn and Robin Yount $150

1995 Montreal Expos: store model Adirondack, with 30 signatures, includes Moises Alou, Will Cordero and Rondell White $175

1969 New York Mets: Gil Hodges pro model Adirondack, with 25 signatures, includes Nolan Ryan and Tom Seaver $450

1956 New York Yankees: Moose Skowron game-used bat, with 22 signatures, includes Mickey Mantle and Casey Stengel $3,250

1990 Oakland A's: generic Adirondack model, with 27 signatures, includes Jose Canseco, Rickey Henderson, Mark McGwire and Dave Stewart..$250

1992 Oakland A's: Oakland A's team bat, with 17 signatures, includes Harold Baines, Jose Canseco, Dennis Eckersley, Rickey Henderson and Mark McGwire..$240

1982 St. Louis Cardinals: Steve Braun World Series bat, with 27 signatures, includes Keith Hernandez, Jim Kaat, Willie McGee, Ozzie Smith and Bruce Sutter..$495

1991 American League All-Stars: Danny Tartabull bat, with 29 signatures, includes Roberto Alomar, Wade Boggs, Roger Clemens, Cecil Fielder, Carlton Fisk, Ken Griffey Jr., Rickey Henderson, Jack McDowell, Cal Ripken Jr., Ruben Sierra and Danny Tartabull $495

Store Model Bats

Hank Aaron: Adirondack	$45
Hank Aaron: Wilson	$80
Dick Allen: Adirondack	$35
Ernie Banks: Louisville Slugger	$45
Hank Bauer: Adirondack	$45
Johnny Bench: Louisville Slugger	$50
Yogi Berra: Hillerich & Bradsby	$65
Bobby Bonds: Louisville Slugger	$45
Johnny Callison: Hillerich & Bradsby	$45
Fred Clarke: Gold Medal Spalding, 1908-10	$450
Roberto Clemente: Sears	$85
Roberto Clemente: Hillerich & Bradsby	$75
Mickey Cochrane: Hanna Batrite	$60
Rocky Colavito: Spalding	$75
Eddie Collins: Louisville Slugger	$95
Joe DiMaggio: J. C. Higgins	$125
Joe DiMaggio: Revelation	$175
Joe DiMaggio: Louisville Slugger	$200
Carlton Fisk: Adirondack	$50
Jimmie Foxx: J.C. Higgins	$85
Jimmie Foxx: Hanna Batrite	$150
Jimmie Foxx: Louisville Slugger	$125
Charlie Gehringer: Louisville Slugger	$165
Joe Gordon: Louisville Slugger	$100
Goose Goslin: Diamond Ace	$195
Ken Harrelson: Louisville Slugger	$55
Babe Herman: Hillerich & Bradsby	$155
Rogers Hornsby: Louisville Slugger	$275
Cleon Jones: Adirondack	$25
George Kell: Spalding	$135
George Kelly: Louisville Slugger	$100
Mickey Mantle: Adirondack Big Stick	$75
Mickey Mantle: Hillerich & Bradsby 1960s	$195
Mickey Mantle: Louisville Slugger	$100
Roger Maris: Hillerich & Bradsby	$75
Eddie Mathews: Hillerich & Bradsby	$45
Willie Mays: Adirondack	$60
Willie McCovey: Adirondack	$40
Joe Medwick: Hanna Batrite	$35
Felix Milan: Adirondack	$25
Joe Morgan: Hillerich & Bradsby	$35
Mel Ott: MacGregor Gold Smith	$150
Vada Pinson: Adirondack	$50
Kirby Puckett: Louisville Slugger	$75
Brooks Robinson: Louisville Slugger	$65
Frank Robinson: Hillerich & Bradsby	$65
Jackie Robinson: Hillerich & Bradsby	$75
Jackie Robinson: store model, signed	$1,995
Pete Rose: Hillerich & Bradsby	$60
Babe Ruth: Revelation Bat Co.	$95
Babe Ruth: Louisville Slugger	$95
Ron Santo: Adirondack	$35
Al Simmons: J.C. Higgins	$125
Tris Speaker: Hanna Batrite	$95
Tris Speaker: Hillerich & Bradsby	$295
Willie Stargell: Louisville Slugger	$65
Vern Stephens: MacGregor Gold Smith	$100
Joe Torre: Adirondack	$30
Paul Waner: Louisville Slugger	$125
Billy Williams: Louisville Slugger	$85
Ted Williams: Hillerich & Bradsby	$125
Ted Williams: Hanna Batrite	$75
Carl Yastrzemski: Louisville Slugger	$65
Heinie Zimmerman: Spalding, 1916-20	$495

Cooperstown Bat Co. Commemorative Bats

Cooperstown Bat Co., Cooperstown, N.Y., has produced several limited-edition bats to commemorate several players, stadiums and teams.

Cooperstown Bat Co.'s 10 Stadium Series bats include: 1) Fenway Park, 1986; 2) Wrigley Field, 1986; 3) Ebbets Field, 1987; 4) Polo Grounds, 1987; 5) Yankee Stadium, 1987; 6) Forbes Field, 1988; 7) Shibe Park, 1988; 8) Briggs/Tiger Stadium, 1989; 9) Sportsman's Park, 1989; and 10) Comiskey Park, 1990.

Cooperstown Bat Co's. Famous Players Series includes these players: Pee Wee Reese, 1988; Ted Williams, 1989; Yogi Berra, 1990; Ernie Banks, 1991; Carl Yastrzemski, 1992; Stan Musial, 1993; Duke Snider, 1994; Frank Robinson, 1995; and Mike Schmidt, 1996.

Cooperstown Bat Co. was commissioned by the National Baseball Hall of Fame to produce a limited edition of 500 sets of five bats and a display rack for the inaugural Class of 1936—Ty Cobb, Walter Johnson, Christy Mathewson, Babe Ruth and Honus Wagner.

The company also makes bats for autographing. A Cooperstown Bat Co. 1989 Cooperstown Hall of Fame autograph model bat, signed by 18 greats (including Stan Musial, Tom Seaver, Bob Gibson, Steve Carlton, Luis Aparicio, Willie Stargell and Enos Slaughter), was offered in an auction for a minimum bid of $350.

Another Cooperstown Bat Co. Hall of Fame autograph model bat, signed by 24 Hall of Famers (including Stan Musial, Ted Williams, Mike Schmidt, Willie Mays, Hank Aaron, Pete Rose, Johnny Bench, Lefty Gomez, Jocko Conlan, Happy Chandler, Duke Snider, Willie McCovey, Ernie Banks and Lou Brock), was offered in an auction for a minimum bid of $900.

Cooperstown Bat Co.'s Vintage Club Series includes bats for the Brooklyn Dodgers, 1990; Boston Braves, 1991; and Milwaukee Braves, 1992. A Brooklyn Dodgers bat, signed by 34 Dodger greats (including Sandy Koufax, Andy Pafko, Duke Snider, Carl Abrams, Ralph Branca, Don Drysdale, Billy Herman, Mickey Owen and Chuck Connor) was offered in an auction for a minimum bid of $250.

Cooperstown Bat Co. also creates bats for team autograph collectors. The 1992 Major League Team Series had bats for seven teams—California Angels, Chicago White Sox, Cincinnati Reds, Detroit Tigers, Pittsburgh Pirates, San Francisco Giants and Toronto Blue Jays.

The 1991 Major League Team Series featured six teams—Chicago Cubs, Kansas City Royals, Los Angeles Dodgers, Oakland Athletics, Philadelphia Phillies and St. Louis Cardinals.

The 1990 Major League Team Series included four teams—Baltimore Orioles, Boston Red Sox, New York Mets and New York Yankees.

Cooperstown Bat Co. has also created three Doubleday Field Bats—in 1983, 1985 and 1989. The 1983 bat is red and brown. Twenty have a plain red band at the throat of the bat; the remaining 124 had a red ring with a brown center stripe. The 1985 version was also red and brown and featured an enlarged drawing of the stadium compared to the first bat. The company has not limited production on these bats, and estimates about 1,900 have been made. About 900 of these were made before 1988 and have the red and brown stripe. Those made after 1988 have a red and brown band art reading "Stadium Series."

A limited edition of 1,000 bats were issued 1989 in red and blue to commemorate the 150th anniversary of baseball in America. The text was changed to reflect the history of the stadium, beginning with the Phinney Lot in 1839 and ending with the 1939 All-Star Game for the dedication of the Hall of Fame. The company did not number the bats in this series, so there is not an edition number stamped into the knob of the bat.

Bats have also been created to commemorate the Negro League teams; the 1993 and 1994 All-Star Games; the opening of Camden Yards in Baltimore; Cal Ripken's consecutive games played streak; baseball Immortals Shoeless Joe Jackson and Ty Cobb; Roberto Clemente; Rusty Staub; Ralph Kiner; Ted Williams Museum; and the Cincinnati Reds' Big Red Machine.

A Cooperstown Bat Co. model honoring "Boston's best." It's signed by Ted Williams and Carl Yastrzemski

Autographed individual Cooperstown Bat Co. bats honoring Hall of Famers Pee Wee Reese, Ted Williams, Yogi Berra and Ernie Banks.

Louisville Slugger Hall of Fame Induction Bats

Since 1983, Louisville Slugger, in conjunction with the Baseball Hall of Fame, has issued limited-edition bats commemorating the inductions of players, executives, managers and umpires into the Hall of Fame. Their names are engraved into the bat barrels with gold lettering.

Five hundred bats, each numbered, were made per induction ceremony from 1936-87. From 1988 on there have been 1,000 bats made per ceremony. The first 500 are sold through subscription. The Hall of Fame sells the others during the induction ceremonies.

1936 - Ty Cobb, Walter Johnson, Christy Mathewson, Babe Ruth, Honus Wagner ....$495-$575
1937 - Morgan Bulkeley, Ban Johnson, Nap Lajoie, Connie Mack, John McGraw, Tris Speaker, George Wright, Cy Young ....$250-$275
1938 - Grover Alexander, Alexander Cartwright, Henry Chadwick $195
1939 - Cap Anson, Eddie Collins, Charles Comiskey, Candy Cummings, Buck Ewing, Lou Gehrig, Willie Keeler, Charles Radbourn, George Sisler, Al Spalding ....$275-$295
1942 - Rogers Hornsby $195
1944 - Kenesaw Landis $195
1945 - Roger Bresnahan, Dan Brouthers, Fred Clarke, Jimmy Collins, Ed Delahanty, Hugh Duffy, Hugh Jennings, Mike Kelly, James O'Rourke, Wilbert Robinson ....$185-$195
1971 - Dave Bancroft, Chick Hafey, Harry Hooper, Rube Marquard, Satchel Paige, George Weiss $185
1972 - Yogi Berra, Josh Gibson, Lefty Gomez, Will Harridge, Sandy Koufax, Buck Leonard, Ross Youngs, Early Wynn ....$425-$500
1973 - Roberto Clemente, Billy Evans, Monte Irvin, George Kelly,

Warren Spahn, Mickey Welch $375
1974 - Cool Papa Bell, Jim Bottomley, Jocko Conlan, Whitey Ford, Mickey Mantle, Sam Thompson ....$350-$500
1975 - Earl Averill, Bucky Harris, Billy Herman, Judy Johnson, Ralph Kiner $225
1976 - Oscar Charleston, Roger Connor, Cal Hubbard, Bob Lemon, Freddie Lindstrom, Robin Roberts $185
1977 - Ernie Banks, Martin DiHigo, John Lloyd, Al Lopez, Amos Rusie, Joe Sewell ....$150-$175
1978 - Addie Joss, Larry MacPhail, Eddie Mathews $185
1979 - Warren Giles, Willie Mays, Hack Wilson $325
1980 - Al Kaline, Chuck Klein, Duke Snider, Tom Yawkey ...$150-$200
1981 - Rube Foster, Bob Gibson, Johnny Mize ....$150-$175
1982 - Hank Aaron, Happy Chandler, Travis Jackson, Frank Robinson $375
1983 - Walter Alston, George Kell, Juan Marichal, Brooks Robinson ....$375-$450
1984 - Luis Aparicio, Don Drysdale, Wes Ferrell, Harmon Killebrew, Pee Wee Reese ....$175-$395
1985 - Lou Brock, Enos Slaughter, Arky Vaughan, Hoyt Wilhelm ....$275-$295
1986 - Bobby Doerr, Willie McCovey, Ernie Lombardi $285
1987 - Ray Dandridge, Jim Hunter, Billy Williams $185
1988 - Willie Stargell $185
1989 - Al Barlick, Johnny Bench, Red Schoendienst, Carl Yastrzemski $195
1990 - Joe Morgan, Jim Palmer $250
1991 - Rod Carew, Fergie Jenkins, Tony Lazzeri, Gaylord Perry, Bill Veeck $225

World Series Black Bats

World Series Black Bats, created by Hillerich and Bradsby, are given to participating players and dignitaries from teams in the Series. They have facsimile signatures of the entire team in gold on a dark black ebony bat.

1934 Detroit Tigers ....$2,500-$3,000
1935 Detroit Tigers ....$1,500-$2,000
1936 New York Yankees ....$2,000-$2,750
1936 New York Giants ....$1,200-$1,500
1937 New York Yankees ....$1,500-$2,500
1937 New York Giants ....$1,000-$1,200
1938 New York Yankees ....$1,200-$1,500
1938 Chicago Cubs ....$1,200-$1,500
1939 New York Yankees ....$800-$1,250
1939 Cincinnati Reds ....$800-$1,000
1940 Cincinnati Reds ....$800-$1,250
1940 Detroit Tigers ....$800-$1,250
1941 New York Yankees ....$800-$1,200
1941 Brooklyn Dodgers ....$1,200-$1,500
1942 New York Yankees ....$700-$900
1942 St. Louis Cardinals ....$600-$800
1943 St. Louis Cardinals ....$500-$700
1943 New York Yankees ....$500-$700
1944 St. Louis Cardinals ....$1,000-$1,200
1944 St. Louis Browns ....$1,000-$1,200
1945 Detroit Tigers ....$600-$800
1945 Chicago Cubs ....$600-$800
1946 St. Louis Cardinals ....$500-$700
1946 Boston Red Sox ....$1,000-$1,200
1947 New York Yankees ....$500-$600
1947 Brooklyn Dodgers ....$500-$700

1948 Cleveland Indians ....$800-$1,200
1948 Boston Braves ....$600-$800
1949 New York Yankees ....$450-$650
1949 Brooklyn Dodgers ....$500-$700
1950 New York Yankees ....$500-$700
1950 Philadelphia Phillies ....$600-$800
1951 New York Yankees ....$800-$1,200
1951 New York Giants ....$700-$900
1952 New York Yankees ....$450-$650
1952 Brooklyn Dodgers ....$500-$700
1953 New York Yankees ....$425-$500
1953 Brooklyn Dodgers ....$500-$700
1954 New York Giants ....$500-$700
1954 Cleveland Indians ....$500-$700
1955 Brooklyn Dodgers ....$1,500-$1,900
1955 New York Yankees ....$400-$500
1956 New York Yankees ....$600-$800
1956 Brooklyn Dodgers ....$500-$700
1957 Milwaukee Braves ....$500-$700
1957 New York Yankees ....$400-$500
1958 Milwaukee Braves ....$350-$550
1958 New York Yankees ....$300-$400

A Hillerich & Bradsby New York Yankees 1953 World Championship black bat

A Hillerich & Bradsby Los Angeles Dodgers 1959 World Championship black bat

1959 Los Angeles Dodgers	$500-$700
1959 Chicago White Sox	$800-$1,000
1960 New York Yankees	$300-$400
1960 Pittsburgh Pirates	$500-$700
1961 New York Yankees	$800-$1,000
1961 Cincinnati Reds	$300-$400
1962 New York Yankees	$300-$400
1962 San Francisco Giants	$400-$600
1963 Los Angeles Dodgers	$300-$400
1963 New York Yankees	$300-$400
1964 St. Louis Cardinals	$300-$400
1964 New York Yankees	$300-$400
1965 Los Angeles Dodgers	$350-$450
1965 Minnesota Twins	$350-$500
1966 Baltimore Orioles	$300-$450
1966 Los Angeles Dodgers	$300-$400
1967 Boston Red Sox	$500-$700
1967 St. Louis Cardinals	$350-$450
1968 Detroit Tigers	$500-$700
1968 St. Louis Cardinals	$300-$400
1969 Baltimore Orioles	$250-$350
1969 New York Mets	$800-$1,000
1970 Baltimore Orioles	$200-$300
1970 Cincinnati Reds	$200-$300
1971 Pittsburgh Pirates	$200-$300
1971 Baltimore Orioles	$200-$300
1972 Oakland A's World	$200-$300
1972 Cincinnati Reds	$200-$300
1973 Oakland A's	$200-$300
1973 New York Mets	$300-$400
1974 Oakland A's	$200-$300
1974 Los Angeles Dodgers	$200-$300
1975 Cincinnati Reds	$300-$400
1975 Boston Red Sox	$300-$400
1976 Cincinnati Reds	$225-$325

A Hillerich & Bradsby Minnesota Twins 1991 World Championship black bat

1976 New York Yankees	$200-$300
1977 Los Angeles Dodgers	$225-$325
1977 New York Yankees	$200-$300
1978 Los Angeles Dodgers	$225-$325
1978 New York Yankees	$200-$300
1979 Baltimore Orioles	$200-$300
1979 Pittsburgh Pirates	$250-$350
1980 Kansas City Royals	$200-$300
1980 Philadelphia Phillies	$200-$300
1981 Los Angeles Dodgers	$225-$325
1981 New York Yankees	$200-$300
1982 St. Louis Cardinals	$200-$300
1982 Milwaukee Brewers	$150-$250
1983 Baltimore Orioles	$100-$200
1983 Philadelphia Phillies	$250-$350
1984 Detroit Tigers	$350-$450
1984 San Diego Padres	$225-$325
1985 St. Louis Cardinals	$225-$325
1985 Kansas City Royals	$225-$325
1986 New York Mets	$450-$600
1986 Boston Red Sox	$250-$300
1987 Minnesota Twins	$250-$350
1987 St. Louis Cardinals	$200-$300
1988 Los Angeles Dodgers	$150-$250
1988 Oakland A's	$100-$200
1989 San Francisco Giants	$100-$200
1989 Oakland A's	$100-$200
1990 Oakland A's	$100-$200
1990 Cincinnati Reds	$100-$200
1991 Minnesota Twins	$800-$1,000
1991 Atlanta Braves	$500-$700
1992 Toronto Blue Jays	$400-$500
1992 Atlanta Braves	$400-$500
1993 Toronto Blue Jays	$400-$500
1993 Philadelphia Phillies	$400-$500

Pro Insignia Inc.

Pro Insignia Inc. is a Hudson, Wis.-based company that produces regulation and miniature laser-engraved baseball bats. The bats, which are Rawlings/Adirondack or Worth professional model bats, are produced in limited editions and generally have an issue price of about $50. They are suitable for autographing. Among others, the company has produced commemorative bats for the World Series champions in 1989 (A's, 1,989 bats), 1990 (Reds, 1,990 bats), 1991 (Twins, 1,991 bats) and 1995 (Braves, 1,995 bats) the All-Star games in 1990, 1991 (two bats, 500 each), 1993 (1,993 bats), 1994 (1,994 bats) and 1995 (1,995 bats); the 100th anniversary of the Dodgers (500 bats); the centennial of the St. Louis Cardinals (1,992 bats); the closings of Comiskey Park in Chicago (500 bats), Cleveland Stadium (1,000 bats) and Arlington Stadium (1,000 bats); the 1955 World Champion Brooklyn Dodgers (1,955 bats), 1961 New York Yankees (1,961 bats) and 1966 Baltimore Orioles (1,966 bats); the 1957 World Series between the Milwaukee Braves and New York Yankees (1,957 bats); the 25th anniversaries of the Kansas City Royals, San Diego Padres, Milwaukee Brewers, Philadelphia Phillies and Montreal Expos (500 each); the 40th anniversary of the Baltimore Orioles (1,000 bats); the inaugural seasons for the Colorado Rockies and

Florida Marlins (1,000 each); the openings of Jacobs Field in Cleveland (1,994 bats) and Coors Field in Colorado (1,995 bats); and six bats capturing the final standings for each division in the strike-shortened 1994 season (94 each). The company has also created Louisville Sluggers that can be laser-engraved with a collector's name alongside the logo of his favorite team, plus team logo bats for the 1995 and 1996 seasons.

Pro Insignia Adirondack bats honoring the 1955 Brooklyn Dodgers and 1957 Milwaukee Braves

BASEBALL GLOVES

Store-Bought Gloves

Some of the hottest collectibles on the market today are baseball gloves. What makes a glove collectible? Is it the maker or the style of glove? Is it the player's name that appears embossed on it or is it the condition? The answer is all of these factors.

A store-bought glove is just that: an over-the-counter purchase. Those that bear a facsimile autograph of a player are called autograph models.

The most important factor in determining the value of a glove is the player's name that appears somewhere on the face of the glove. The bigger the name, the higher the price it brings, if all other variants are the same.

The second most important consideration when determining glove value is the condition. Even a relatively common player may be worth hundreds of dollars if in Near Mint to Mint condition. This is especially true with older gloves, because it is much harder to find a Near Mint to Mint common player from the 1920s or 1930s than it is to find a similar condition glove from the 1960s or 1970s.

Two very important factors in determining value: supply and demand, or the relative scarcity of some gloves versus the seemingly endless supply of others.

Rarely, if ever, is a post period glove of any player worth the same amount as one manufactured while the player was still on the diamond. So, too, are earlier model gloves of certain players.

It is generally accepted that fielder's gloves with unlaced fingers are prewar models or styles, while gloves with the fingers laced are considered postwar models or styles. Various companies produced both laced and unlaced gloves prior to and after World War II, but the terms "prewar" and "postwar" are used to determine the relative era of a fielder's glove using the criteria of whether or not the glove is laced.

Another important value factor has to do with which hand the glove fits on. This is the area that seems to cause the most confusion, even among advanced collectors. The factories, and hence the sporting good stores, used to designate a glove either right hand or left hand by determining which hand the glove actually fit, indicating right hand for a left-handed thrower. As a result, one might find the letters RH somewhere on the box label.

The reason for this is that most collectors are right-handed and they want to put the glove on and feel comfortable, so they will buy a nice right-handed model of a left-handed player for nearly the same price, yet they refuse to pay anywhere near the same price for a left-handed glove of a right-handed player.

Often, gloves were sold in individual boxes and with hang tags that were used to price and/or describe the features of the glove. Having them with the glove adds to the overall value of the glove. Prewar hang tags add $30 with a player photo and can add $50-$150, depending on the player. Postwar tags add $15, and can add $25-$75, depending on the player.

Plain boxes, those without pictures on them, in Good condition (intact, some corners may be split, light scuffing, small surface tears, slight soiling) can add 20-50 percent in value. Postwar plain boxes add 20 percent, 1930-45 add 30 percent, 1920-30 add 40 percent and pre-1920 boxes add 50 percent.

Picture boxes (those with a photo or illustration of the player either posed or in action) in Good condition can add two to six times to the price of the glove. Prewar boxes of Hall of Famers add four to six times the price, postwar boxes Hall of Famers add two to four times the value, while postwar boxes of non-Hall of Famers adds no more than twice the value.

Other factors involved in value include player popularity and condition of the glove.

Fair/Poor: Gloves in this condition are generally not collectible and often are good only for parts. They have irreparable tears, holes, severe magic marker, dry rot, water damage and any other major problem.

Good: A glove that has been used considerably. Most of the stamping will be gone or barely visible. Leather very chaffed, thinned in spots, no form left, may still be serviceable, but collectible only if an extremely rare model, usually used as a filler until a better similar type is available.

Very Good: Well used, but most stamping visible, no form but intact, cloth label gone or worn out, piping frayed and worn.

Excellent: Well used, but cared for. Stamping visible. Dark with age but nice patina. Cloth label intact, minor piping wear. Some form left.

Excellent/Mint: The most confusing grade. Much stronger than an Excellent glove but not Near Mint. It is an Excellent glove with certain strong characteristics of a higher grade glove; i.e. super strong, bright signature, perfect cloth label, no oil stains, perfect insides, etc.

Near Mint: A glove that has seen almost no use. Still stiff in form, all stamping strong, most original silver or black ink still within stamping. Perfect insides, perfect cloth patch, has caught but a few balls. Some otherwise Mint gloves may not have been used, but have significant enough blemishes such as staining, cracking from dryness, scratches from some handling, to drop them into this category.

Mint: Brand spanking new, never played with. This is regardless of age. A Mint glove may show some shelf wear due to years for example, minute piping wear, oxidation around brass grommets, stiff due to no use, slight fading of original color, all of which must be minute and from storage, not from use.

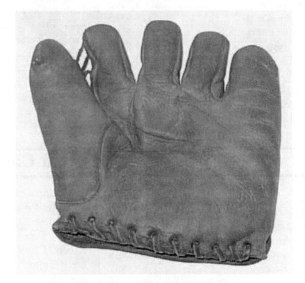

Luke Appling glove

Prewar Gloves (Hall of Famers)

Prices are for USA-made gloves, full size.

Player	Value
Grover Alexander	$250-$500
Luke Appling	$50-$150
Earl Averill	$75-$200
Frank Baker	$500-$1,200
Dave Bancroft	$400-$850
Chief Bender	$500-$1,200
Jim Bottomley	$250-$500
Roger Breshnahan	$500-$1,200
Mordecai Brown	$500-$1,200
Max Carey	$250-$500
Frank Chance	$500-$1,200
Jack Chesbro	$500-$1,200
Fred Clarke	$500-$1,200
Ty Cobb	$750-$1,500
Mickey Cochrane	$250-$500
Eddie Collins	$250-$500
Jimmy Collins	$400-$850
Earle Combs	$250-$500
Stan Coveleski	$400-$850
Sam Crawford	$500-$1,200
Joe Cronin	$50-$150
Kiki Cuyler	$125-$375
Dizzy Dean	$500-$1,200
Bill Dickey	$50-$150
Joe DiMaggio	$250-$500
Bobby Doerr	$50-$150
Johnny Evers	$500-$1,200
Red Faber	$400-$850
Bob Feller	$50-$150
Rick Ferrell	$250-$500
Elmer Flick	$400-$850
Jimmie Foxx	$250-$500
Frankie Frisch	$125-$375
Lou Gehrig	$850-$1,500
Charlie Gehringer	$125-$375
Lefty Gomez	$125-$375
Goose Goslin	$75-$200
Hank Greenberg	$125-$375
Burleigh Grimes	$400-$850
Lefty Grove	$125-$375
Chick Hafey	$250-$500
Jesse Haines	$250-$500
Bucky Harris	$750-$200
Gabby Hartnett	$125-$375
Harry Heilmann	$250-$500

A Wasco store model Charlie Keller fielder's glove.

Billy Herman	$50-$150
Harry Hooper	$500-$1,200
Rogers Hornsby	$125-$375
Waite Hoyt	$400-$850
Carl Hubbell	$250-$500
Travis Jackson	$125-$375
Walter Johnson	$250-$500
Charlie Keller	$250-$500
George Kelly	$250-$500
Chuck Klein	$125-$375
Nap Lajoie	$850-$1,500
Tony Lazzeri	$250-$500
Freddie Lindstrom	$250-$500
Ernie Lombardi	$75-$200
Al Lopez	$50-$150
Ted Lyons	$75-$200
Heinie Manush	$75-$200
Rube Marquard	$500-$1,200
Rabbit Maranville	$250-$500
Christy Mathewson	$750-$1,500
Joe McGinnity	$500-$1,200
Ducky Medwick	$50-$150
Johnny Mize	$50-$150
Mel Ott	$75-$200
Herb Pennock	$250-$500
Eddie Plank	$500-$1,200
Pee Wee Reese	$50-$150
Sam Rice	$250-$500
Eppa Rixey	$250-$500
Edd Roush	$250-$500
Red Ruffing	$125-$375
Babe Ruth	$500-$1,200
Ray Schalk	$125-$375

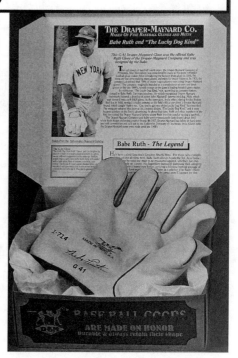

A Draper-Maynard Babe Ruth store model glove with original box

Joe Sewell	$250-$500
Al Simmons	$125-$375
George Sisler	$125-$375
Tris Speaker	$750-$1,500
Bill Terry	$250-$500
Joe Tinkers	$500-$1,200
Pie Traynor	$125-$375
Dazzy Vance	$125-$375
Arky Vaughn	$250-$500
Rube Waddell	$500-$1,200
Honus Wagner	$750-$1,500
Bobby Wallace	$500-$1,200
Ed Walsh	$500-$1,200
Lloyd Waner	$125-$375
Paul Waner	$250-$500
Zack Wheat	$500-$1,200
Ted Williams	$125-$375
Hack Wilson	$250-$500
Cy Young	$250-$500
Ross Youngs	$400-$850

Postwar Gloves (Hall of Famers)

Player	Price				
Hank Aaron	$100-$300	Roy Campanella	$50-$125	Bob Feller	$40-$95
Luis Aparicio	$30-$85	Steve Carlton	$35-$75	Rollie Fingers	$40-$95
Richie Ashburn	$30-$60	Rod Carew	$40-$95	Whitey Ford	$40-$95
Ernie Banks	$50-$125	Orlando Cepeda	$35-$75	Nelson Fox	$40-$85
Johnny Bench	$30-$85	Roberto Clemente	$30-$85	Bob Gibson	$40-$95
Yogi Berra	$50-$125	Steve Carlton	$50-$125	Lefty Gomez	$40-$95
Lou Boudreau	$30-$85	Joe DiMaggio	$150-$375	Catfish Hunter	$40-$95
Lou Brock	$65-$175	Larry Doby	$75-$200	Monte Irvin	$65-$175
		Don Drysdale	$40-$95	Joe Jackson	$150-$375

Reggie Jackson ....$30-$85
Fergie Jenkins ....$40-$95
Al Kaline ....$30-$50
George Kell ....$30-$85
Harmon Killebrew ....$40-$95
Ralph Kiner.......................................$30-$85
Sandy Koufax ....$85-$200
Bob Lemon ....$30-$85
Mickey Mantle ....$225-$500
Juan Marichal ....$40-$95
Eddie Mathews ....$50-$125
Willie Mays ....$125-$350
Willie McCovey ....$65-$175
Joe Morgan ....$40-$95
Stan Musial ....$100-$300
Hal Newhouser ....$50-$125
Jim Palmer ....$40-$95
Gaylord Perry....................................$40-$95
Pee Wee Reese ....$30-$85
Phil Rizzuto.......................................$25-$50
Robin Roberts ....$30-$85
Brooks Robinson................................$30-$85
Frank Robinson ....$40-$95
Red Schoendienst...............................$30-$85
Tom Seaver ....$40-$95
Enos Slaughter ....$30-$85

A store model Spalding Phil Rizzuto fielder's glove and a Sonnett Gil Hodges first baseman's mitt with original boxes

Duke Snider ....$50-$150
Warren Spahn ....$50-$150
Willie Stargell ....$40-$95
Hoyt Wilhelm...................................$85-$200

Billy Williams ....$40-$95
Ted Williams ....$100-$300
Early Wynn ....$30-$85
Carl Yastrzemski ....$30-$85

Prewar Gloves

Player	Price
Babe Adams	$100-$250
Jimmy Archer	$150-$375
Jimmy Austin	$150-$375
Jim Bagby	$75-$200
Dick Bartell	$50-$175
Moe Berg	$500-$1,200
Wally Berger	$50-$175
Zeke Bonura	$75-$200
Rube Bressler	$225-$500
Tommy Bridges	$100-$250
Mace Brown	$50-$175
Guy Bush	$75-$200
Joe Bush	$150-$375
Dolf Camilli	$50-$175
Tex Carleton	$75-$200
George Case	$150-$375
Ray Chapman	$400-$850
Hal Chase	$400-$850
Eddie Cicotte	$500-$1,200
Harlond Clift	$100-$250
Rip Collins	$35-$125
Mort Cooper	$75-$200
Walker Cooper	$75-$200
Harry Craft	$50-$175
Doc Cramer	$75-$200
Frank Crosetti	$75-$200
General Crowder	$150-$375
Harry Danning	$50-$175
Jake Daubert	$225-$500
Harry Davis	$225-$500
Paul (Daffy) Dean	$75-$200
Paul Derringer	$75-$200

Vince DiMaggio	$35-$125
Bill Doak	$75-$200
Larry Doyle	$225-$500
Joe Dugan	$225-$500
Leo Durocher	$50-$175
Jimmy Dykes	$150-$375
George Earnshaw	$100-$250
Bibb Falk	$150-$375
Hap Felsch	$500-$1,200
Wes Ferrell	$150-$375
Fred Fitzsimmons	$150-$375
Ira Flagstead	$150-$375
Jack Fournier	$150-$375
Larry French	$35-$125
Denny Galehouse	$100-$250
Chick Gandil	$500-$1,200
Wally Gerber	$150-$375
George Gibson	$100-$250
Ival Goodman	$35-$125
Hank Gowdy	$35-$125
Pete Gray	$225-$500
Heinie Groh	$225-$500
Haas, Mule	$50-$175
Stan Hack	$35-$125
Bump Hadley	$100-$250
Sammy Hale	$150-$375
Mel Harder	$150-$375
Bubbles Hargrave	$100-$250
Rollie Hemsley	$35-$125
Tommy Henrich	$50-$175
Herman, Babe	$100-$250
Pinky Higgins	$35-$125
Sam Jones	$150-$375

Joe Judge	$150-$375
Willie Kamm	$150-$375
Charlie Keller	$35-$125
Ken Keltner	$100-$250
Dickie Kerr	$225-$500
Mark Koenig	$225-$500
Joe Kuehl	$100-$250
Whitey Kurowski	$50-$175
Tommy Leach	$225-$500
Dutch Leonard	$225-$500
Duffy Lewis	$225-$500
Hans Lobert	$100-$250
Gus Mancuso	$50-$175
Firpo Marberry	$225-$500
Pepper Martin	$150-$375
Carl Mays	$225-$500
Snuffy J. McInnis	$225-$500
Chief Meyers	$400-$850
Bing Miller	$150-$375
Terry Moore	$35-$125
Wally Moses	$50-$175
Johnny Mostil	$50-$175
Bob Muesel	$225-$500
Irish Muesel	$150-$375
Van Lingle Mungo	$100-$250
Buddy Myer	$75-$200
Swish Nickelson	$50-$175
Lefty O'Doul	$75-$200
Bob O'Farrell	$75-$200
Mickey Owen	$35-$125
Monte Pearson	$35-$125
Roger Peckinpaugh	$225-$500
Wally Pipp	$100-$250
Swede Risberg	$500-$1,200

BASEBALL GLOVES

Player	Price		Player	Price		Player	Price
Red Rolfe	$100-$250		Billy Southworth	$150-$375		Bill Wambsganss	$400-$850
Eddie Rommel	$100-$250		Jake Stahl	$225-$500		Lon Warneke	$50-$175
Charlie Root	$75-$200		Riggs Stephenson	$150-$375		Buck Weaver	$500-$1,200
Schoolboy Rowe	$50-$175		Jake Tobin	$150-$375		Earl Whitehill	$150-$375
Muddy Ruel	$225-$500		Specs Toporcer	$150-$375		Claude Williams	$500-$1,200
Dutch Ruether	$225-$500		Hal Trosky	$75-$200		Cy Williams	$150-$375
Wally Schang	$225-$500		Dizzy Trout	$75-$200		Ken Williams	$75-$200
Urban Schocker	$400-$850		George Uhle	$150-$375		Vic Willis	$150-$375
Wildfire Schulte	$225-$500		Johnny VanderMeer	$75-$200		Jimmie Wilson	$100-$250
Hal Schumacher	$150-$375		Jim (Hippo)Vaughn	$400-$850		Joe Wood	$400-$850
George Selkirk	$50-$175		Bobby Veach	$150-$375		Rudy York	$35-$125
Luke Sewell	$100-$250		Dixie Walker	$35-$125		Heinie Zimmerman	$225-$500
Elmer Smith	$150-$375		Harry Walker	$50-$175			
Fred Snodgrass	$225-$500		Bucky Walters	$50-$175			

Postwar Gloves

Player	Price		Player	Price		Player	Price
Cal Abrams	$45-$95		Bob Buhl	$30-$60		John Edwards	$25-$50
Bobby Adams	$30-$60		Jim Bunning	$35-$75		Bob Elliott	$35-$75
Joe Adcock	$45-$95		Lew Burdette	$35-$75		Dick Ellsworth	$30-$60
Tommy Agee	$35-$75		Smoky Burgess	$35-$75		Del Ennis	$30-$60
Harry Agganis	$55-$100		Jim Busby	$30-$60		Mike Epstein	$30-$60
Richie Allen	$35-$75		Tommy Byrne	$25-$50		Carl Erskine	$55-$100
Gene Alley	$35-$75		John Callison	$30-$60		Hoot Evers	$30-$60
Bob Allison	$25-$50		Bert Campaneris	$30-$60		Elroy Face	$35-$75
Felipe Alou	$25-$50		Andy Carey	$30-$60		Ferris Fain	$30-$60
Matty Alou	$25-$50		Chico Carrasquel	$30-$60		Curt Flood	$40-$85
Sandy Amoros	$45-$95		Hugh Casey	$35-$75		Dee Fondy	$25-$50
Sparky Anderson	$45-$95		Norm Cash	$30-$60		Ray Fosse	$35-$75
Johnny Antonelli	$30-$60		Phil Cavaretta	$35-$75		Tito Francona	$25-$50
Bobby Avila	$35-$75		Bob Cerv	$25-$50		Bill Freehan	$40-$85
Ed Bailey	$35-$75		Gino Cimoli	$35-$75		Gene Freese	$35-$75
Steve Barber	$35-$75		Rocky Colavito	$50-$95		Jim Fregosi	$30-$60
Rex Barney	$35-$75		Jerry Coleman	$35-$75		Bob Friend	$35-$75
Earl Battey	$30-$60		Joe Collins	$30-$60		Carl Furillo	$40-$85
Hank Bauer	$45-$95		Tony Conigliaro	$35-$75		Joe Garagiola	$55-$100
Frank Baumholtz	$35-$75		Gene Conley	$55-$100		Mike Garcia	$45-$95
Glenn Beckert	$25-$50		Chuck Connors	$100-$300		Ned Garver	$30-$60
Gus Bell	$25-$50		Billy Consolo	$35-$75		Jim Gentile	$30-$60
Floyd Bevins	$35-$75		Walker Cooper	$75-$200		Jim Gilliam	$75-$200
Vern Bickford	$35-$75		Chuck Cottier	$35-$75		Billy Goodman	$30-$60
Joe Black	$75-$200		Clint Courtney	$30-$60		Joe Gordon	$25-$50
Ewell Blackwell	$45-$95		Wes Covington	$35-$75		Sid Gordon	$35-$75
Paul Blair	$30-$60		Billy Cox	$35-$75		Bob Grim	$45-$60
Don Blasingame	$30-$60		Roger Craig	$30-$60		Dick Groat	$35-$75
Curt Blefary	$30-$60		Del Crandall	$35-$75		Johnny Groth	$30-$60
Frank Bolling	$30-$60		George Crowe	$35-$75		Frankie Gustine	$25-$50
Milt Bolling	$35-$75		Mike Cuellar	$35-$75		Harvey Haddix	$45-$95
Ray Boone	$35-$75		Ray Culp	$35-$75		Ron Hansen	$25-$50
Steve Boros	$30-$60		Joe Cunningham	$30-$60		Ken Harrelson	$35-$75
Jim Bouton	$40-$85		Al Dark	$30-$60		Jim Ray Hart	$35-$75
Clete Boyer	$35-$75		Vic Davalillo	$35-$75		Clint Hartung	$35-$75
Ken Boyer	$45-$95		Jim Davenport	$25-$50		Jim Hegan	$30-$60
Bobby Bragan	$35-$75		Tommy Davis	$30-$60		Solly Hemus	$30-$60
Ralph Branca	$45-$95		Willie Davis	$30-$60		Tommy Henrich	$40-$85
Jackie Brandt	$30-$60		Murry Dickson	$35-$75		Whitey Herzog	$75-$200
Al Brazle	$35-$75		Larry Dierker	$35-$75		Don Hoak	$35-$75
Harry Brecheen	$35-$75		Bob Dillinger	$55-$100		Gil Hodges	$40-$85
Ernie Broglio	$25-$50		Dom DiMaggio	$55-$100		Billy Hoeft	$35-$75
Jim Brosnan	$30-$60		Dick Donovan	$30-$160		Tommy Holmes	$40-$85
Bobby Brown	$35-$75		Walt Dropo	$30-$60		Johnny Hopp	$35-$75
Bill Bruton	$35-$75		Ryne Duren	$25-$50		Ralph Houk	$35-$75
			Luke Easter	$55-$100		Elston Howard	$40-$85

Frank Howard	$40-$85	
Dixie Howell	$45-$95	
Ken Hubbs	$35-$75	
Fred Hutchinson	$45-$95	
Larry Jackson	$25-$50	
Vic Janowicz	$35-$75	
Larry Jansen	$35-$75	
Joey Jay	$25-$50	
Jackie Jenson	$30-$60	
Sam Jethroe	$40-$85	
Dave Johnson	$35-$75	
Sam Jones	$35-$75	
Willie Jones	$40-$85	
Jim Kaat	$40-$85	
Buddy Kerr	$25-$50	
Don Kessinger	$30-$60	
Ellis Kinder	$35-$75	
Ron Kline	$35-$75	
Johnny Klippstein	$35-$75	
Ted Kluszewski	$40-$85	
Bobby Knoop	$35-$75	
Jim Konstanty	$35-$75	
Dave Koslo	$35-$75	
Tony Kubek	$45-$95	
Johnny Kucks	$25-$50	
Harvey Kuenn	$30-$60	
Whitey Kurowski	$35-$75	
Clem Labine	$45-$95	
Jim Landis	$30-$60	
Max Lanier	$45-$95	
Don Larsen	$40-$85	
Frank Lary	$30-$60	
Tommy Lasorda	$75-$200	
Vern Law	$35-$75	
Brooks Lawrence	$30-$60	
Frank Leja	$25-$50	
Jim Lemon	$25-$50	
Dutch Leonard	$75-$200	
Buddy Lewis	$30-$60	
Whitey Lockman	$35-$75	
Billy Loes	$45-$95	
Johnny Logan	$35-$75	
Mickey Lolich	$35-$75	
Sherm Lollar	$35-$75	
Dale Long	$35-$75	
Eddie Lopat	$35-$75	
Stan Lopata	$30-$60	
Hector Lopez	$35-$75	
Peanuts Lowrey	$30-$60	
Jerry Lynch	$25-$50	
Sal Maglie	$35-$75	
Jim Maloney	$35-$75	
Frank Malzone	$35-$75	
Felix Mantilla	$35-$75	
Marty Marion	$35-$75	
Roger Maris	$55-$100	
Willard Marshall	$25-$50	
Billy Martin	$35-$75	
Gene Mauch	$35-$75	
Dal Maxvill	$30-$60	
Charlie Maxwell	$25-$50	
Bill Mazeroski	$45-$95	
Tim McCarver	$40-$85	
Mike F. McCormick	$35-$75	
Mike McCormick	$40-$85	
Barney McCosky	$40-$85	
Clyde McCullough	$25-$50	
Lindy McDaniel	$45-$95	
Mickey McDermott	$45-$95	
Gil McDougald	$30-$60	
Sam McDowell	$35-$75	
Denny McLain	$45-$95	
Roy McMillan	$30-$60	
George McQuinn	$55-$100	
Meyer Russ	$25-$50	
Felix Millan	$35-$75	
Eddie Miller	$30-$60	
Stu Miller	$40-$85	
Bob Milliken	$45-$95	
Minnie Minoso	$65-$125	
Dale Mitchell	$45-$95	
Wilmer Mizell	$45-$95	
Wally Moon	$35-$75	
Terry Moore	$40-$85	
Walt Moryn	$30-$60	
Don Mossi	$30-$60	
Don Mueller	$30-$60	
Danny Murtaugh	$35-$75	
Ray Narleski	$35-$75	
Charlie Neal	$35-$75	
Don Newcombe	$65-$125	
Bobo Newsom	$45-$95	
Bill Nicholson	$40-$85	
Phil Niekro	$45-$95	
Bob Nieman	$35-$75	
Irv Noren	$30-$60	
Joe Nuxall	$35-$75	
Tony Oliva	$35-$75	
Claude Osteen	$35-$75	
Amos Otis	$30-$60	
Jim O'Toole	$30-$60	
Andy Pafko	$30-$60	
Joe Page	$45-$95	
Milt Pappas	$35-$75	
Wes Parker	$30-$60	
Mel Parnell	$45-$95	
Camilo Pascual	$35-$75	
Albie Pearson	$30-$60	
Joe Pepitone	$35-$75	
Ron Perranoski	$25-$50	
Tony Perez	$30-$60	
John Pesky	$30-$60	
Gary Peters	$35-$75	
Dave Philley	$30-$60	
Billy Pierce	$30-$60	
Jimmy Piersall	$35-$75	
Vada Pinson	$30-$60	
Johnny Podres	$30-$60	
Howie Pollet	$40-$85	
Wally Post	$300-$600	
Boog Powell	$30-$60	
Vic Power	$30-$60	
Jerry Priddy	$30-$60	
Bob Purkey	$30-$60	
Ken Raffensberger	$40-$85	
Pete Reiser	$30-$60	
Rip Repulski	$30-$60	
Allie Reynolds	$75-$200	
Dusty Rhodes	$40-$85	
Del Rice	$30-$60	
Bobby Richardson	$40-$85	
Jim Rivera	$35-$75	
Eddie Robinson	$40-$85	
Preacher Roe	$40-$85	
Ed Roebuck	$35-$75	
John Romano	$35-$75	
Buddy Rosar	$30-$75	
Pete Rose	$40-$85	
John Roseboro	$35-$75	
Al Rosen	$40-$85	
Schoolboy Rowe	$40-$85	
Pete Runnels	$25-$50	
Bob Rush	$30-$60	
John Rutherford	$25-$50	
Johnny Sain	$40-$85	
Jack Sanford	$35-$75	
Ron Santo	$30-$60	
Hank Sauer	$25-$50	
Johnny Schmitz	$25-$50	
Dick Schofield	$30-$60	
Herb Score	$45-$95	
George Scott	$25-$50	
Andy Seminick	$25-$50	
Mike Shannon	$25-$50	
Bobby Shantz	$25-$50	
Frank Shea	$40-$85	
Larry Sherry	$25-$50	
Norm Sherry	$30-$60	
George Shuba	$45-$95	
Norm Siebern	$30-$60	
Roy Sievers	$25-$50	
Curt Simmons	$30-$60	
Dick Sisler	$30-$60	
Bob Skinner	$30-$60	
Moose Skowron	$30-$60	
Roy Smalley	$30-$60	
Al Smith	$30-$60	
Karl Spooner	$45-$95	
Gerry Staley	$40-$85	
Eddie Stanky	$35-$75	
Mickey Stanley	$30-$60	
Rusty Staub	$25-$50	
Vern Stephens	$30-$60	
Snuffy Stirnweiss	$30-$60	
Dick Stuart	$40-$85	
George Susce	$30-$60	
Haywood Sullivan	$25-$50	
Chuck Tanner	$35-$75	
Birdie Tebbetts	$40-$85	
Johnny Temple	$25-$50	
Ralph Terry	$30-$60	
Wayne Terwilliger	$35-$75	
Frank Thomas	$25-$50	
Hank Thompson	$25-$50	
Bobby Thomson	$30-$60	
Luis Tiant	$35-$75	
Earl Torgeson	$30-$60	
Frank Torre	$30-$60	
Joe Torre	$30-$60	
Tom Tresh	$35-$75	
Gus Triandos	$35-$75	
Virgil Trucks	$35-$75	

BASEBALL GLOVES

Bob Turley ....$40-$85	Eddie Waitkus ....$30-$60	Maury Wills ....$35-$75
Bill Tuttle ....$25-$50	Dick Wakefield ....$30-$60	Earl Wilson ....$25-$50
Bob Uecker ....$75-$200	Rube Walker ....$40-$85	Gene Woodling ....$40-$85
Elmer Valo ....$30-$60	Vic Wertz ....$75-$200	Eddie Yost ....$35-$75
Emil Verban ....$35-$75	Wes Westrum ....$40-$85	Babe Young ....$35-$75
Mickey Vernon ....$35-$75	Bill White ....$35-$75	Al Zarilla ....$30-$60
Zoilo Versalles ....$35-$75	Dave Williams ....$35-$75	Gus Zernial ....$35-$75
Bill Virdon................$30-$60	Dick Williams ....$35-$75	Don Zimmer ....$30-$60

Additional Player Model Gloves

Richie Allen: Spalding model $65	Reggie Jackson: Rawlings model.....................$45
Bobby Allison: 1960s Sonnett model..............$125	Tommy John: Wilson model, signed..................$65
Luke Appling: Wilson model $85	Harmon Killebrew: 1960s Wilson model............$65
Richie Ashburn: MacGregor model $45	Sandy Koufax: 1950s Denkert model $350
Sal Bando: Spalding model $65	Harvey Kuenn: 1950s Wilson model $125
Hank Bauer: 1950s Hurricane model, signed $85	Ron LeFlore: Wilson model...........................$45
Gus Bell: 1950s MacGregor model, signed $75	Bob Lemon: 1950s Hurricane model $50
Buddy Bell: Wilson model $45	Johnny Logan: TruPlay model $35
Johnny Bench: 1970s Rawlings catcher's mitt, signed..........$150	Ernie Lombardi: Goldsmith catcher's mitt............$125
Yogi Berra: 1950s Reach catcher's mitt, signed ...$50	Greg Luzinski: MacGregor model $45
Paul Blair: Montgomery Ward model $65	Fred Lynn: Wilson model.............................$75
Wade Boggs: Rawlings model $55	Billy Martin: 1950s Wilson model...................$100
Bobby Bonilla: Rawlings model $35	Don Mattingly: Franklin first baseman's mitt.........$95
Ken Boyer: Rawlings, three-finger $55	John Mayberry: 1970s MacGregor first baseman's mitt....$35
George Brett: 1970s Wilson model, signed $175	Willie Mays: MacGregor model.......................$75
Lou Brock: Franklin model $75	Bill Mazeroski: 1950s MacGregor model.............$50
Roy Campanella: 1950s Wilson catcher's mitt $135	Willie McGee: MacGregor model $45
Rod Carew: MacGregor model $65	Johnny Mize: Wilson first baseman's mitt............$95
Steve Carlton: 1970s Rawlings model, right-handed, signed............$85	Rick Monday: Spalding model.........................$55
Joe Carter: Wilson model $45	Joe Morgan: 1970s MacGregor model, signed $60
Norm Cash: Wilson first baseman's model $95	Don Mossi: Nokona model............................$45
Cesar Cedeno: Rawlings model $45	Stan Musial: 1960s Hawthorne model, signed $140
Ron Cey: MacGregor model $45	Stan Musial: Rawlings model..........................$85
Jack Clark: Spalding model $65	Graig Nettles: Louisville Slugger model $40
Roger Clemens: Wilson model.....................$65	Amos Otis: Rawlings model...........................$55
Roberto Clemente: 1950s Franklin model $150	Andy Pafko: J.C. Higgins model.......................$60
Roberto Clemente: J.C. Higgins model $145	Dave Parker: Rawlings model.........................$55
Tony Conigliaro: 1970s Hurricane model..........$110	Wes Parker: MacGregor model........................$30
Alvin Dark: 1950s Spalding model.................$60	Joe Pepitone: Trio-Hollander model $165
Bill Dickey: 1940s MacGregor Goldsmith catcher's mitt $125	Gaylord Perry: 1960s Wilson model, signed $90
Joe DiMaggio: 1950s Spalding model, signed $895	Rico Petrocelli: Spalding model.......................$55
Don Drysdale: 1960s Spalding model, signed $450	Jimmy Piersall: 1950s Wilson model..................$60
Dwight Evans: 1980s Wilson black model, signed ...$85	Lou Piniella: Spalding model..........................$75
Hoot Evers: Hutch model $95	Vic Power: Franklin model $50
Bob Feller: J.C. Higgins model....................$50	Willie Randolph: MacGregor model $45
Ron Fairly: Spalding six-finger model.............$85	Del Rice: 1960s black Denkert catcher's mitt, 1960s.....$100
Carlton Fisk: 1970s Wilson catcher's mitt $85	Jim Rice: 1970s Wilson model.........................$40
Whitey Ford: Spalding model $70	Cal Ripken Jr.: Rawlings model.......................$65
George Foster: 1970s MacGregor model, signed ...$40	Phil Rizzuto: Reach model............................$145
Nellie Fox: Wilson model fielder's glove..........$140	Brooks Robinson: Rawlings model....................$45
Steve Garvey: Rawlings first baseman's model $65	Frank Robinson: MacGregor model...................$45
Bob Gibson: 1970s Rawlings model, signed $100	Red Ruffing: 1930s J.C. Higgins model $275
Kirk Gibson: Wilson model $65	Babe Ruth: 1930s Spalding catcher's mitt.............$800
Pedro Guerrero: Wilson model.....................$35	Ryne Sandberg: Rawlings model......................$65
Bucky Harris: 1920s Spalding model $150	Ron Santo: 1960s Wilson model, signed $75
Hurricane Hazle: 1950s Rawlings model...........$80	Ray Schalk: 1920s Wilson model......................$195
Mike Hegan: Spalding first baseman's model $65	Mike Schmidt: Franklin model........................$45
Larry Hisle: Wilson model $45	Tom Seaver: 1970s MacGregor model, signed $100
Willie Horton: Wilson model $45	Luke Sewell: 1930s Wilson catcher's mitt.............$125
Gil Hodges: Denkert first baseman's mitt..........$75	Moose Skowron: 1950s Denkert model...............$45
Ken Hunt: Spalding model.........................$45	Enos Slaughter: 1950s J.C. Higgins model, signed ...$125
Catfish Hunter: 1970s Wilson model $40	Ozzie Smith: 1970s Rawlings model, signed $125

Roy Smalley Sr.: Rawlings model $50
Duke Snider: Rawlings model, unused $250
Snuffy Sternweiss: Spalding split-finger model $350
Mel Stottlemyre: Spalding model $30
Bruce Sutter: Wilson model $55
Bill Terry: Ken-Wel fielder's glove $350
Manny Trillo: Wilson model $55
Johnny VanderMeer: Goldsmith fielder's glove $295
Bill Virdon: 1950s Denkert model $65

Frank White: Rawlings model...$45
Ted Williams: Sears model..$65
Ted Williams: Hutch model...$200
Dave Winfield: Rawlings model $45
Carl Yastrzemski: 1970s Spalding, signed twice $125
Pep Young: 1940s Hutch model $75
Robin Yount: 1970s Rawlings model $150
Richie Zisk: Wilson model..$55
Wade Boggs: Franklin, signed $125

Batting Gloves

Barry Bonds: Franklin, signed $125
Ellis Burks: Franklin $65
Jose Canseco: Mizuno, blue and white, signed $90
Gary Carter: Mizuno, blue, signed...................................$75
Joe Carter: Franklin, one ripped, signed $110
Will Clark: Easton , signed $65
Eric Davis: Mizuno , scarlet, signed $50
Andre Dawson: Mizuno, black, signed ....$60 each
Lenny Dykstra: Franklin, red, signed ....$60 each
Cecil Fielder: Franklin, black ....$85 each
Julio Franco: Franklin $30
Ken Griffey Jr.: Franklin, blue...................................$90 each
Ken Griffey Sr.: Franklin, #30, signed $30
Ozzie Guillen: Saranac $65
Tony Gwynn: Franklin, signed..$125
Rickey Henderson: Mizuno, fluorescent, signed ......$90 each
Chuck Knoblauch: Franklin , unsigned.............................$35

John Kruk: Easton, red, signed $60
Barry Larkin: Franklin ....$25 each
Don Mattingly: Franklin $95
Paul Molitor: Franklin $75
Raul Mondesi: Worth, plus wristband, signed $165
Kirby Puckett: Franklin, red.....................................$75 each
Tim Raines: Franklin, blue, signed...........................$45 each
Manny Ramirez: Nike, signed..$125
Ivan Rodriguez: Wilson $35
Tim Salmon: Franklin $50
Mike Schmidt: Franklin, signed $225
Ozzie Smith: Franklin, signed..$75
Darryl Strawberry: Easton, signed............................$50 each
Mickey Tettleton: Franklin $45
Frank Thomas: Worth, signed $195
Alan Trammell: Franklin, signed $85
Robin Ventura: Louisville Slugger $65

Chapter 4

PUBLICATIONS

By Larry Canale

Let's be honest: Publications aren't the first items that come to mind when you think of baseball memorabilia. And they may never rank with trading cards and autographs in terms of sheer collector popularity. Not only do they create storage (and moving) challenges, but their secondary market values are far lower, generally speaking, than those of cards and autographs.

Even so, the collecting of baseball-related publications is an extremely rewarding pursuit—so much so that this niche has become an increasingly popular segment in the baseball memorabilia market. The reasons? First, publications often are inexpensive to buy. As the following pages illustrate, you can build—at a reasonable price—a healthy collection of magazines featuring, say, players from your favorite team. (Yankees collectors, of course, should expect to pay more.) Second, publications make ideal items for autographs, especially those publications with high-quality photography and a strong design. Third—and maybe most important—publications just might be the richest type of baseball collectible out there in terms of historical value. They feature pages and pages of words, stats, photos and advertisements that collectively capture an era or a great moment, define the state of the game at a given point in time and profile the more popular stars.

Publications are not only informative and historical, but they can be wonderfully entertaining, as longtime collectors will attest. What baseball fan doesn't enjoy reading old sports magazines, with their monthly selection of in-depth stories, top photography and, of course, "The Sport Interview"? Who can resist the chance to thumb through an old *Baseball Digest*, absorbing the simply presented stats, short features and analysis? And what baseball collector doesn't have at least a few issues of *Sports Illustrated*—with its high-impact action photography, news of the week and smart sports-writing—in his stash? Or how about a classic Street & Smith baseball annual, with its team-by-team rosters, stats, previews, and predictions? And years from now, you'll be glad if you had the foresight to put away copies of *ESPN/The Magazine*, which offers a consistently strong editorial package and high-impact, often dramatic cover photography. ESPN magazines aren't big-dollar items now, but give 'em a chance to age.

There are other baseball-related magazines worth collecting, too—from the classic periodical simply known as *Baseball* (published between 1908 and 1965) to general news magazines (like *Time* and *Newsweek*) that have given baseball fans a thrill with occasional cover stories devoted to the likes of Willie Mays, Mickey Mantle and Mark McGwire. The reports you'll see in the latter type of magazine are usually sweeping in their coverage, giving the subject a thorough going-over that extends beyond his baseball life.

Taking the "info-packed collectible" approach even further is the baseball media guide. For decades, teams have been publishing thick, exhaustive research guides for members of the press—softcover books that offer every type of stat imaginable along with biographical information, team histories and schedules for upcoming seasons. A complete set of one team's media guides is a collector's dream. Building such a set would be an eminently enjoyable pursuit, but financially, it could be surprisingly affordable—or it could be extremely expensive, depending on how far back a team's history extends. (A Yankees collection, obviously, would be a much more challenging chase than an Expos collection.)

Then there are team yearbooks, which, over the years, have become thick, slick presentations with up-close portrait photography of a team's players mixed with quality action shots. Yearbooks may not contain the globs of numbers you'll find in media guides, but there are stats nonetheless. And there's usually a lot more photography in yearbooks than in media guides. Plus, yearbooks (which generally have the same dimensions as standard magazines) simply look better than media guides (which often look, not surprisingly, like reference guides).

And let's not forget books. This is an area that requires focus on the part of the collector. Just like it would be impossible to collect one of every baseball card (and insert card) ever produced, it would be impossible to amass a collection of every baseball book ever printed. Thousands upon thousands of baseball-related tomes hit the bookshelves during the past century, and they're still coming. The good news is that collectors have no shortage of selection. You want vintage books? You'll pay more, of course, because first editions of such classics as *Ring Lardner's You Know Me Al* or *W.P. Kinsella's Shoeless Joe Jackson Comes to Iowa* cost $750-$800—and those examples aren't even the priciest. If you go after contemporary books, your collection might never be worth a fortune, but it'll provide as much enjoyment as any niche of the baseball memorabilia market.

BASEBALL DIGEST

Baseball Digest is the nation's oldest active and continuously published magazine devoted to baseball. The magazine was founded in 1942 by Herbert F. Simmons, a member of the Baseball Writers Association of America, as a collection of baseball articles from around the country. The original cover price was 15 cents. In the early years, *Baseball Digest* printed only 10 issues a year—typically not issuing a November or December issue. Starting in 1969, its frequency changed to 12 issues per year.

Today, the magazine is published by Century Sports Network, carries a $2.99 cover price, and measures 5-1/2x7-1/2 inches. It continues in the direction that its loyal readers demand: entertaining features, easily digestible anecdotes, and loads of stats and stats analysis.

Baseball Digest has a relatively small following (compared to *Sports Illustrated*) among publications collectors, so the secondary values of most issues are lower than those for other sports magazines. But as this area of the baseball memorabilia hobby continues its steady growth in popularity, the values of *Baseball Digest* back issues should grow as well. In fact, issues with Hall of Famer covers usually attract healthy amounts of attention in Internet auctions. Certain issues that normally book for around $10—a June 1952 (Pee Wee Reese) or an April 1954 (Whitey Ford), for example—can sell for $15-$20 at such sites as eBay.

The following prices are for magazines in Excellent/Near-Mint condition.

August 1942

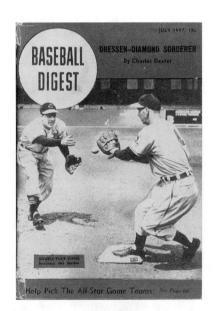

July 1947

Year	Month	Cover	Price
1942	August	Hit and run	$250
1942	October	Pete Reiser	$100
1942	November	Double play	$75
1942	December	Joe DiMaggio/Billy Southworth	$125
1943	February	At bat in Iceland	$25
1943	March	Back to school	$10
1943	April	Get two	$10
1943	May	Catching a popup	$20
1943	July	Play at second base	$10
1943	August	Safe at the plate	$10
1943	September	Stan Musial	$40
1943	October	Spud Chandler	$10

Year	Month	Cover	Price
1943	November	Johnny Lindell	$10
1944	February	Bill Johnson	$15
1944	March	Bill Nicholson/Rip Sewell	$15
1944	April	Dixie Ward	$15
1944	May	Lou Boudreau	$20
1944	July	Vern Stephens	$10
1944	August	Bucky Walters	$15
1944	September	Charlie Grimm	$10
1944	October	Walker Cooper	$10
1944	November	Marty Marion	$10
1945	February	Hal Newhouser	$15
1945	March	George McQuinn	$15
1945	April	Dixie Walker	$15

Year	Month	Cover	Price	Year	Month	Cover	Price
1945	May	Bill Voiselle	$15	1948	September	Stan Musial	$25
1945	July	Hank Borowy	$15	1948	October	Hank Sauer	$10
1945	August	Tommy Holmes	$15	1948	November	Paul Fagen	$10
1945	September	Stan Hack	$15	1949	January	Jim Hegan	$10
1945	October	Hank Greenberg	$15	1949	February	Red Rolfe	$10
1945	November	Al Lopez	$15	1949	March	Ted Williams	$25
1946	February	Charlie Keller	$15	1949	April	Joe DiMaggio	$25
1946	March	Play at the Plate	$10	1949	May	Play at the plate	$10
1946	April	Bobby Doerr	$15	1949	June	Robin Roberts	$15
1946	May	Bob Feller	$15	1949	July	Johnny Groth	$10
1946	July	Joe DiMaggio/Ted Williams	$50	1949	August	Frankie Frisch	$10
1946	August	Joe Cronin	$15	1949	September	Vic Raschi	$10
1946	September	Hank Wyse	$15	1949	October	Mel Parnell/Birdie Tebbets	$10
1946	October	Dave Ferriss	$15	1949	November	Tommy Henrich/Allie Reynolds	$10
1946	November	Johnny Pesky/Red Schoendienst	$15	1950	January	Richie Ashburn/Roy Smalley	$15
1947	February	Bucky Harris	$10	1950	February	Dave Koslo	$10
1947	March	Johnny Rigney	$10	1950	March	50 Baseball Rules	$10
1947	April	Johnny Van Cuyk	$10	1950	April	Bob Feller	$15
1947	May	Hank Greenberg/Billy Herman	$10	1950	May	Dark/Kramer/Stankey	$10
1947	July	Lou Boudreau/Joe Gordon	$15	1950	June	Joe DiMaggio	$25
1947	August	Buddy Kerr	$10	1950	July	Phil Rizzuto	$10
1947	September	Ewell Blackwell	$10	1950	August	Dick Sisler	$10
1947	October	Joe DiMaggio	$50	1950	September	Art Houtteman/Larry Jansen	$10
1947	November	Ralph Lapointe	$10	1950	October	Hoot Evans	$10
1948	January	Joe Page	$10	1950	November	Jim Konstanty	$10
1948	February	Leo Durocher/Branch Rickey	$10	1951	January	Yogi Berra/Whitey Ford	$15
1948	March	Ennis/Hubbard/Meyer	$10	1951	February	Gil Hodges	$10
1948	April	Joe McCarthy	$10	1951	March	Eddie Yost	$10
1948	May	Art Houtteman	$10	1951	April	Joe DiMaggio	$25
1948	June	Willard Marshall	$10	1951	May	George Earnshaw	$10
1948	July	Ralph Kiner	$10	1951	June	Ted Williams	$25
1948	August	Lou Boudreau	$10	1951	July	Irv Noren	$10

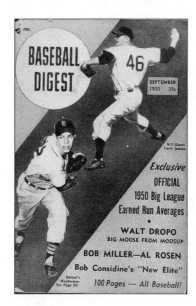

September 1950

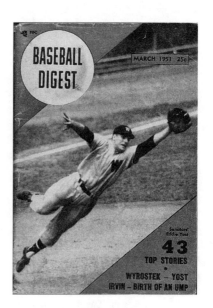

March 1951

Year	Month	Cover	Price
1951	August	Nellie Fox/Paul Richards	$15
1951	September	Stan Musial	$15
1951	October	Gil McDougald	$10
1951	November	Charlie Dressen	$10
1952	January	Eddie Lopat/Phil Rizzuto	$10
1952	February	Eddie Stanky	$10
1952	March	Sid Gordon	$10
1952	April	Mike Garcia	$10
1952	May	George Staley	$10
1952	June	Pee Wee Reese	$10
1952	July	Ted Kluszewski	$10
1952	August	Bobby Shantz	$10
1952	September	Sal Maglie	$10
1952	October	Carl Erskine	$10
1952	November	Duke Snider	$10
1953	January	Robin Roberts	$10
1953	February	Eddie Mathews	$15
1953	March	Billy Martin	$15
1953	April	Hornsby/Mantle/Musial	$25
1953	May	Carl Furillo	$10
1953	June	Bob Lemon	$10
1953	July	Dorish/Kellner/Logan	$10
1953	August	Robin Roberts	$10
1953	September	O'Connell/Strickland/Trucks	$10
1953	October	Casey Stengel	$10
1954	January	Billy Martin	$10
1954	March	Jimmy Piersall	$10
1954	April	Whitey Ford	$10
1954	May	Harvey Kuenn	$10
1954	June	Eddie Mathews/Bobby Morgan	$10
1954	July	Bob Turley	$10
1954	August	Bob Keegan	$10
1954	September	Willie Mays	$10
1954	October	World Series	$10
1954	November	Dusty Rhodes	$10
1955	January	Ralph Kiner	$10
1955	March	Rookies of '55	$10
1955	April	Alvin Dark	$10
1955	May	Bob Lemon/Don Mueller	$10
1955	June	Bobby Avila	$10
1955	July	Bill Skowron	$10
1955	August	Roy McMillian/Al Smith	$10
1955	September	Don Newcombe	$10
1955	October	Walt Alston/Tommy Byrne	$10
1955	November	Johnny Podres	$10
1956	February	Al Kaline	$10
1956	March	Rookie Report	$15
1956	April	Luis Aparicio	$10
1956	May	Mike Higgins	$10
1956	June	Clem Labine	$10
1956	July	Mickey Mantle	$25
1956	August	Dale Long	$10
1956	September	Yogi Berra	$15
1956	October	World Series	$10
1956	November	Don Larson	$15
1957	January	Robin Roberts	$10
1957	March	Scouting Reports	$10
1957	April	Farrell/Scheffing/Tighe	$10
1957	May	Don Blasingame	$10
1957	June	Breaking up double play	$10
1957	July	Don Hosak	$10
1957	August	Stan Musial	$15
1957	September	Bobby Shantz	$10

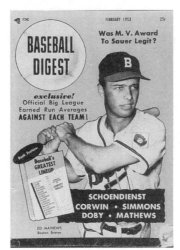
February 1953

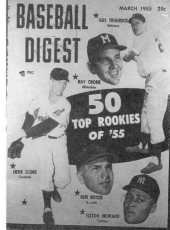
March 1955

August 1955

March 1957

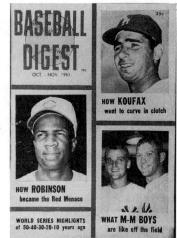

Oct.-Nov. 1961

February 1966

Year	Month	Cover	Price
1960	August	Dick Gary/Dick Stuart	$8
1960	September	Ron Hansen	$8
1960	October	Dick Groat	$8
1961	January	Bill Virdon	$8
1961	February	Ralph Houk	$8
1961	March	Scouting Reports	$8
1961	April	Tony Kubek/Al Sprangler	$8
1961	May	Glenn Hobbie	$8
1961	June	Earl Battey	$8
1961	July	Wally Moon	$8
1961	August	Norm Cash	$8
1961	September	Whitey Ford	$8
1961	October	Koufax/Mantle/Maris/F. Robinson	$25
1962	January	Elston Howard/Ralph Terry	$8
1962	February	Joey Jay	$8
1962	March	Scouting Reports	$8
1962	April	Orlando Cepeda	$8
1962	May	Jim Landis	$8
1962	June	Mickey Mantle	$25
1962	July	Dick Donavan	$8
1962	August	$20 home runs	$8
1962	September	Rich Rollins	$8
1962	October	Tom Tresh/Frank Howard	$8
1963	January	Ralph Terry	$8
1963	February	Ty Cobb/Maury Wills	$8
1963	March	Scouting Reports	$10
1963	April	Rosters	$8
1963	May	Drysdale/Dean/Grove	$8
1963	June	Al Kaline	$8
1963	July	Jim O'Toole	$8
1963	August	Jim Bouton	$8
1963	September	Denny Lemaster	$8
1963	October	Al Downing	$8
1964	January	Dodgers' Aces	$8
1964	February	Roger Maris	$10
1964	March	Scouting Reports	$8
1964	April	Sandy Koufax	$10
1964	May	Harmon Killebrew	$8
1964	June	Tommy Davis/Carl Yastrzemski	$8
1964	July	Jim Maloney	$8
1964	August	Dave Nicholson	$8
1964	September	Dennis Bennett/Willie Smith	$8
1964	October	Miracle Braves	$8
1965	January	Dick Groat	$8
1965	February	Winter Rrades	$8
1965	March	Scouting Reports	$8
1965	April	Which tag is phoney?	$8
1965	May	Bill Freehan	$8
1965	June	Tony Conigliaro	$8
1965	July	Yankees' Six Mistakes	$10
1965	August	Don Drysdale	$8
1965	September	Pete Ward/Joe Morgan	$8
1965	October	Biggest World Series mysteries	$8
1966	January	Sandy Koufax	$10
1966	February	Willie Mays	$8
1966	March	Scouting Reports	$8
1966	April	Rosters	$8
1966	May	Sam McDowell	$8
1966	June	Should the rules be changed?	$8
1966	July	Juan Marichal	$8
1966	August	Gene Alley/Bill Mazeroski	$8
1966	September	George Scott	$8
1966	October	World Series	$8

Year	Month	Cover	Price
1957	October	Babe Ruth	$10
1958	January	Lew Burdette	$10
1958	February	Lindy McDaniel	$10
1958	March	Scouting Reports	$10
1958	April	Willie Mays/Duke Snider	$10
1958	May	Ted Williams	$20
1958	June	Stan Musial	$25
1958	July	Warren Spahn	$10
1958	August	Bob Turley	$10
1958	September	Pete Runnels	$10
1958	October	World Series	$10
1959	January	Jensen/Roberts/Truly	$10
1959	February	Baseball's Darling Daughters	$10
1959	March	Scouting Reports	$10
1959	April	Ernie Banks	$10
1959	May	Juan Pizarro	$10
1959	June	Antonelli/Landis/Pascual	$10
1959	July	Vada Pinson	$10
1959	August	Hoyt Wilhem	$10
1959	September	Rocky Colavito/Roy Face	$10
1959	October	World Series	$10
1960	January	John Roseboro/Larry Sherry	$8
1960	February	Harvey Kuenn	$8
1960	March	Scouting Reports	$8
1960	April	Jim Landis/Charlie Neal	$8
1960	May	Early Wynn	$8
1960	June	Bunning/Francona/McDaniel	$8
1960	July	Vern Law	$8

Year	Month	Cover	Price
1967	January	Bunker/Drabowsky/Palmer	$8
1967	February	Allison/Drysdale/Mathews	$10
1967	March	Scouting Reports	$8
1967	April	Rosters	$8
1967	May	Roger Maris	$10
1967	June	Gaylord Perry/Juan Marichal	$8
1967	July	Denny McLain	$8
1967	August	Joe Horlen	$8
1967	September	Tim McCarver	$8
1967	October	World Series	$8
1968	January	Bob Gibson	$8
1968	February	Billy Williams	$8
1968	March	Scouting Reports	$8
1968	April	Rosters	$8
1968	May	Rod Carew/Jay Johnstone	$8
1968	June	Cookie Rojas/Nellie Briles	$8
1968	July	Jerry Koosman	$8
1968	August	Andy Kosco	$8
1968	September	Matty Alou/Ken Harrelson	$8
1968	October	World Series	$8
1969	January	Lou Brock/Bill Freehan	$8
1969	February	Mickey Mantle	$25
1969	March	Rookie/Scouting Reports	$8
1969	April	Rosters	$8
1969	May	Al Lopez	$8
1969	June	Ernie Banks	$8
1969	July	Tony Conigliaro	$8
1969	August	Frank Robinson	$8
1969	September	Brushback Tragedy	$8
1969	October	World Series	$8
1969	November	Future Superstars	$8
1969	December	Tom Seaver	$10
1970	January	Harmon Killebrew	$5
1970	February	Joe Pepitone	$5
1970	March	Gene Alley	$5
1970	April	Tony Perez	$5
1970	May	Roberto Clemente	$10
1970	June	Mel Stottlemyre	$5
1970	July	Ken Holtzman	$5
1970	August	Sal Bando	$5
1970	September	Tony Perez	$5
1970	October	Jim Palmer	$5
1970	November	Johnny Bench	$5
1970	December	Billy Williams	$5
1971	January	Brooks Robinson	$5
1971	February	Sal Bando/Juan Marichal	$5
1971	March	Carl Yastrzemski	$5
1971	April	Bob Gibson	$5
1971	May	Willie Mays	$5
1971	June	Tony Oliva	$5
1971	July	Hank Aaron	$5
1971	August	Vida Blue	$5
1971	September	Joe Pepitone	$5
1971	October	World Series	$5
1971	November	Bobby Murcer	$5
1971	December	Joe Torre	$5
1972	January	Steve Blass	$5
1972	February	Earl Williams	$5
1972	March	Frank Robinson	$5
1972	April	Bill Melton	$5
1972	May	Rosters	$5
1972	June	Reggie Jackson	$8
1972	July	Richie Allen	$5

January 1968

August 1968

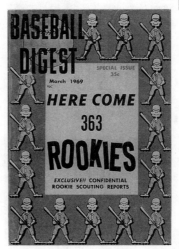

March 1969

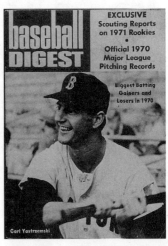

March 1971 Annual

Year	Month	Cover	Price
1972	August	Bud Harrelson	$5
1972	September	Roberto Clemente	$10
1972	October	World Series	$5
1972	November	Carlton Fisk	$5
1972	December	Richie Allen	$5
1973	January	Pete Rose	$5
1973	February	Cesar Cedeño	$5
1973	March	Harmon Killebrew	$5
1973	April	Don Kessinger	$5
1973	May	Nolan Ryan	$15
1973	June	Tom Seaver	$10
1973	July	Pete Rose	$5
1973	August	Allen/May/Melton	$5
1973	September	Ken Holtzman	$5
1973	October	Bill Russell	$5
1973	November	Jose Cardenal	$5
1973	December	Willie Stargell	$5
1974	January	World Series	$5
1974	February	Bobby Bonds	$5
1974	March	Bobby Grich	$5
1974	April	Hank Aaron	$5
1974	May	Ted Sizemore	$5
1974	June	Felix Millan	$5
1974	July	Brooks Robinson	$5
1974	August	Gaylord Perry	$5
1974	September	Tommy John	$5
1974	October	Richie Allen	$5
1974	November	Bando/Campaneris/Jackson	$8
1974	December	Lou Brock	$5
1975	January	Rollie Fingers	$5
1975	February	Steve Garvey	$5
1975	March	Jeff Burroughs	$5

Year	Month	Cover	Price
1975	April	Jim "Catfish" Hunter	$5
1975	May	Mike Schmidt	$8
1975	June	Rod Carew	$5
1975	July	Nolan Ryan	$15
1975	August	Rick Monday	$5
1975	September	Johnny Bench	$5
1975	October	Vida Blue	$5
1975	November	Fred Lynn	$5
1975	December	Joe Morgan	$5
1976	January	Pete Rose	$5
1976	February	Jim Palmer	$5
1976	March	George Brett	$5
1976	April	Carlton Fisk	$5
1976	May	Frank Tanana	$5
1976	June	Rick Manning	$5
1976	July	Bill Madlock	$5
1976	August	Randy Jones	$5
1976	September	Larry Bowa	$5
1976	October	Mickey Rivers	$5
1976	November	Mark Fidrych	$5
1976	December	Joe Morgan	$5
1977	January	World Series	$5
1977	February	Thurman Munson	$5
1977	March	Amos Otis	$5
1977	April	Mark Fidrych	$5
1977	May	John Montefusco	$5
1977	June	Steve Carlton	$5
1977	July	Dave Parker	$5
1977	August	Ivan DeJesus/Manny Trillo	$5
1977	September	Carl Yastrzemski	$5
1977	October	Steve Garvey	$5
1977	November	Bump Wills	$5
1977	December	George Foster	$5
1978	January	Reggie Jackson	$5
1978	February	Willie McCovey	$5
1978	March	Rod Carew	$5
1978	April	Tom Seaver	$10
1978	May	Cesar Cedeño	$5
1978	June	Garry Templeton	$5
1978	July	Dave Kingman	$5
1978	August	Jim Rice	$5
1978	September	Ron Guidry	$5
1978	October	Rich Gale/Clint Hurdle	$5
1978	November	Reggie Smith	$5
1978	December	Dave Parker	$5
1979	January	World Series	$5
1979	February	Dave Winfield	$5
1979	March	Greg Luzinski	$5
1979	April	Rich Gossage	$5
1979	May	Jack Clark	$5
1979	June	Steve Garvey	$5
1979	July	Al Oliver	$5
1979	August	Bill Buckner	$5
1979	September	Tommy John	$5
1979	October	Mike Schmidt	$5
1979	November	Omar Moreno	$5
1979	December	George Brett	$5
1980	January	World Series	$5
1980	February	Paul Molitor	$5
1980	March	Gary Carter	$5
1980	April	Willie Stargell	$5
1980	May	Don Baylor	$5
1980	June	J.R. Richard/Nolan Ryan	$5

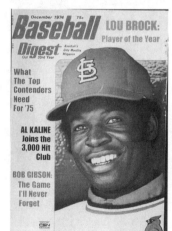

December 1974

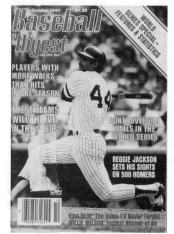

October 1980

Year	Month	Cover	Price	Year	Month	Cover	Price
1980	July	Baumgarten/Burns/Trout	$5	1985	October	Ron Guidry	$5
1980	August	Ken Landreaux	$5	1985	November	Pedro Guerrero	$5
1980	September	Steve Carlton	$5	1985	December	Dwight Gooden	$5
1980	October	Reggie Jackson	$5	1986	January	Willie McGee	$5
1980	November	Joe Charboneau	$5	1986	February	Bret Saberhagen	$5
1980	December	George Brett	$5	1986	March	Tom Browning	$5
1981	January	Tug McGraw	$5	1986	April	Harold Baines	$5
1981	February	Eddie Murray	$5	1986	May	Darryl Strawberry	$5
1981	March	Rickey Henderson	$5	1986	June	Eddie Murray	$5
1981	April	Mike Schmidt	$5	1986	July	Bert Blyleven	$5
1981	May	Gary Carter	$5	1986	August	Roger Clemens	$10
1981	June	Cecil Cooper	$5	1986	September	Gary Carter	$5
1981	July	Carlton Fisk	$5	1986	October	Jose Canseco/Wally Joyner	$5
1981	August	Fernando Valenzuela	$5	1986	November	Bill Doran	$5
1981	September	Danny Darwin	$5	1986	December	Roger Clemens/Teddy Higuera	$5
1981	October	Ron Davis	$5	1987	January	Wade Boggs/Don Mattingly	$5
1981	November	Pete Rose	$5	1987	February	Sid Fernandez	$5
1981	December	Tim Raines	$5	1987	March	Mike Scott	$5
1982	January	Steve Garvey	$5	1987	April	Chris Brown	$5
1982	February	Carney Lansford	$5	1987	May	Pete O'Brien	$5
1982	March	Rollie Fingers	$5	1987	June	Eric Davis/Jody Davis	$5
1982	April	Dave Winfield	$5	1987	July	Mike Witt	$5
1982	May	Nolan Ryan	$15	1987	August	Rickey Henderson	$5
1982	June	Jerry Reuss	$5	1987	September	Jack Clark/Ozzie Smith	$5
1982	July	Salome Barojas	$5	1987	October	Mark McGwire	$5
1982	August	Dale Murphy	$5	1987	November	George Bell	$5
1982	September	Rickey Henderson	$5	1987	December	Kevin Seitzer	$5
1982	October	Robin Yount	$5	1988	January	Andre Dawson	$5
1982	November	Kent Hrbek	$5	1988	February	Frank Viola	$5
1982	December	Lonnie Smith/Ozzie Smith	$5	1988	March	Jimmy Key	$5
1983	January	Darrell Porter	$5	1988	April	Kevin McReynolds/Mike Pagliarulo	$5
1983	February	Mario Soto	$5	1988	May	Eric Davis	$5
1983	March	Doug DeCinces	$5	1988	June	Royals Pitchers	$5
1983	April	Willie McGee	$5	1988	July	Andy Van Slyke	$5
1983	May	Pete Vuckovich	$5	1988	August	Dave Winfield	$5
1983	June	Cal Ripken Jr.	$5	1988	September	Greg Maddux	$5
1983	July	Tony Peña	$5	1988	October	Kirby Puckett	$5
1983	August	Dave Stieb	$5	1988	November	Jose Canseco	$5
1983	September	Chris Chambliss	$5	1988	December	Tony Gwynn	$5
1983	October	Ron Kittle	$5	1989	January	Jose Canseco	$5
1983	November	Steve Carlton	$5	1989	February	Orel Hershiser	$5
1983	December	Carlton Fisk	$5	1989	March	Greg Jefferies	$5
1984	January	Rick Dempsey	$5	1989	April	Kirk Gibson	$5
1984	February	Wade Boggs	$5	1989	May	Cory Snider	$5
1984	March	Dale Murphy	$5	1989	June	Fred McGriff	$5
1984	April	Mike Boddicker	$5	1989	July	Will Clark	$5
1984	May	Andre Dawson	$5	1989	August	Nolan Ryan	$12
1984	June	Lance Parrish	$5	1989	September	Bo Jackson	$5
1984	July	Bill Madlock	$5	1989	October	Dave Stewart	$5
1984	August	Leon Durham	$5	1989	November	Howard Johnson	$5
1984	September	Gwynn/Martinez/McReynolds	$5	1989	December	Jerome Walton/Dwight Smith	$5
1984	October	Ryne Sandberg	$5	1990	January	Abbott/Clark/Ryan	$8
1984	November	Keith Hernandez	$5	1990	February	Ruben Sierra	$5
1984	December	Mark Langston	$5	1990	March	Ken Griffey Jr.	$12
1985	January	Alan Trammell	$5	1990	April	Canseco/McGwire/Steinbach	$5
1985	February	Don Mattingly	$5	1990	May	Gibson/Strawberry/Winfield	$5
1985	March	Frank Viola	$5	1990	June	Mark Grace	$5
1985	April	Jack Morris	$5	1990	July	Bill Geren/Lou Whitaker	$5
1985	May	Tony Gwynn	$5	1990	August	Bobby Bonilla/Frank Viola	$5
1985	June	Dwight Gooden	$5	1990	September	Rickey Henderson	$5
1985	July	Bruce Sutter	$5	1990	October	Ozzie Guillen	$5
1985	August	Pete Rose	$5	1990	November	Cecil Fielder	$5
1985	September	Lee Smith	$5				

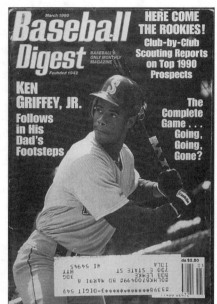

March 1990

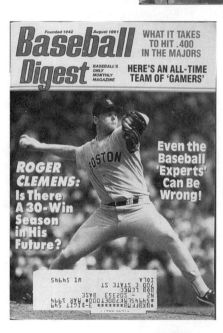

August 19991

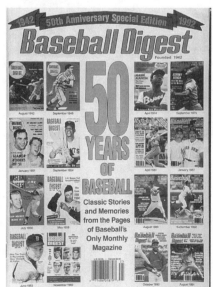

1992 Annual

Year	Month	Cover	Price
1990	December	Sandy Alomar/Dave Justice	$5
1991	January	Bob Welch	$3
1991	February	Chris Sabo	$3
1991	March	Ray Lankford	$3
1991	April	Charlton/Dibble/Myers	$3
1991	May	Darryl Strawberry	$3
1991	June	Tim Raines	$3
1991	July	Kevin Mitchell	$3
1991	August	Roger Clemens	$3
1991	September	Robin Yount	$3
1991	October	Cal Ripken Jr.	$8
1991	November	Rafael Palmeiro	$3
1991	December	Chuck Knoblauch	$3
1992	January	Steve Avery	$3
1992	February	Kirby Puckett	$3
1992	March	'92 Rookies	$3
1992	April	Frank Thomas	$3
1992	May	Wade Boggs	$3
1992	June	Dan Gladden/Greg Olson	$3
1992	July	Howard Johnson	$3
1992	August	Mark McGwire	$3
1992	September	Juan Guzman	$3
1992	October	Kirby Puckett	$3
1992	November	Dennis Eckersley/Tom Glavine	$3
1992	December	Pat Listach	$3
1993	January	Roberto Alomar	$3
1993	February	Gary Sheffield	$3
1993	March	Tim Wakefield	$3
1993	April	Jose Canseco	$3
1993	May	Curt Schilling	$3
1993	June	Robin Ventura	$3
1993	July	Juan Gonzalez	$3
1993	August	Barry Bonds	$3
1993	September	Joe Carter	$3
1993	October	John Kruk	$3
1993	November	Frank Thomas	$6
1993	December	Mike Piazza	$6
1994	January	Paul Molitor	$3
1994	February	Randy Johnson	$3
1994	March	Greg Maddux	$3
1994	April	Carlos Baerga	$3
1994	May	Lenny Dykstra	$3
1994	June	Rafael Palmeiro	$3
1994	July	Lance Johnson	$3
1994	August	Matt Williams	$3
1994	September	Kirby Puckett	$3
1994	October	Ozzie Smith	$3
1994	November	Jimmy Key	$3
1994	December	Bob Hamelin	$3
1995	January	Jeff Bagwell	$3
1995	February	Tony Gwynn	$3
1995	March	Raul Mondesi	$3
1995	April	Kenny Lofton	$3
1995	May	Don Mattingly	$3
1995	June	Fred McGriff	$3
1995	July	Cal Ripken Jr.	$8
1995	August	Eddie Mathews	$3
1995	September	John Valentin	$3
1995	October	Barry Larkin	$3
1995	November	Mickey Mantle	$15
1995	December	Hideo Nomo	$3
1996	January	Albert Belle	$3
1996	February	Tom Glavine	$3

Year	Month	Cover	Price	Year	Month	Cover	Price
1996	March	Tim Salmon	$3	1998	December	Sammy Sosa	$3
1996	April	Dante Bichette	$3	1999	January	Wells/Clemens/Brown	3
1996	May	Edgar Martinez	$3	1999	February	Omar Vizquel	$3
1996	June	Roberto Alomar	$3	1999	March	Juan Gonzalez	3
1996	July	Mike Piazza	$3	1999	April	Mark McGwire	$5
1996	August	Jason Giambi	$3	1999	May	Vladimir Guerrero	$3
1996	September	Harold Baines	$3	1999	June	Roger Clemens	$3
1996	October	John Smoltz	$3	1999	July	Thomas/Ripken Jr./Gwynn	$4
1996	November	Mark McGwire	$3	1999	August	Jose Canseco	$3
1996	December	Derek Jeter	$3	1999	September	Pedro Martinez	3
1997	January	Alex Rodriguez	$3	1999	October	Manny Ramirez	$3
1997	February	Ken Caminiti	$3	1999	November	Ventura/Piazza	$3
1997	March	Andruw Jones	$3	1999	December	Williams/Ruth/Mays	5
1997	April	Ken Griffey Jr.	$3	2000	January	Ivan Rodriguez	3
1997	May	Albert Belle/Frank Thomas	$3	2000	February	Mariano Rivera	$3
1997	June	Brown/Fernandez/A. Leiter	$3	2000	March	Randy Johnson	$3
1997	July	Ivan Rodriguez	$3	2000	April	Chipper Jones	3
1997	August	Larry Walker	$3	2000	May	McGwire/Griffey Jr./Sosa	$5
1997	September	Roger Clemens	$3	2000	June	Nomar Garciaparra	$3
1997	October	Tino Martinez	$3	2000	July	Jim Edmonds	3
1997	November	Chipper Jones	$3	2000	August	Greg Maddux	$3
1997	December	Nomar Garciaparra	$3	2000	September	Todd Helton	3
1998	January	Tony Gwynn	$3	2000	October	Magglio Ordonez	$3
1998	February	Charles Johnson	3	2000	November	Edgar Martinez	$3
1998	March	Curt Schilling	$3	2000	December	Bonds/Piazza/Delgado	$3
1998	April	Jay Bell/Matt Williams	$3	2001	January	Pedro Martinez	3
1998	May	Paul O'Neill	$3	2001	February	Derek Jeter	$4
1998	June	Mike Mussina	3	2001	March	Edgardo Alfonzo	3
1998	July	Jeromy Burnitz	3	2001	April	Mark McGwire/Jason Giambi	$4
1998	August	Kerry Wood	$3	2001	May	Andruw Jones	$3
1998	September	Mark McGwire	$5	2001	June	Jeff Kent	3
1998	October	Derek Jeter	$4	2001	July	Mike Mussina	$3
1998	November	Greg Vaughn	3	2001	August	Kevin Brown	3

BASEBALL MAGAZINE

Baseball Magazine, launched in 1908, was our nation's premier baseball publication for its first few decades of life. By the middle of the 20th century, such competitors as *The Sporting News*, *Sport* and *Sports Illustrated* started grabbing market share. Ultimately, 1953 was the beginning of the end for *Baseball Magazine*. Only eight issues appeared that year, followed by four each in '54 and '55, five in '56, and two final issues in 1957. An attempt to revive the magazine in 1964 and '65 was short-lived, and a lack of interest forced *Baseball Magazine* to vanish for good after its April 1965 issue.

Today, vintage copies of *Baseball Magazine* are the most valuable of all baseball publications in the hobby. Finding a Near Mint issue is almost impossible because the magazine has been out of print so long. Plus, relatively few fans saved their issues.

In our *Baseball Magazine* pricing section, we don't list cover subjects because most of the publication's covers were illustrations of baseball scenes, fans or action. The publisher rarely used photography of baseball stars on the cover.

The prices below reflect magazines in Excellent condition.

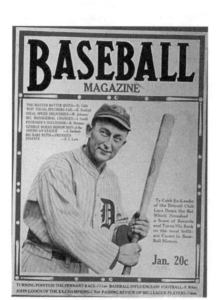

January 1919

September 1927

April 1912 Player	$90
May 1912 Opening Day	$90
December 1912 Football player	$90
March 1913 Frank Chase	$90
April 1915 Walter Johnson	$150
May 1916 Joe Jackson	$150
September 1916 Brown paper (no cover)	$20
October 1916 Brown paper (no cover)	$40
November 1916 Brown paper (no cover)	$40
January 1917 John McGraw	$35
February 1917 St. Louis players	$50
March 1917 Tris Speaker	$95
November 1917 Baseball fans	$65
January 1919 Ty Cobb	$200
March 1920 Pat Moran	$75
September 1920 Cleveland player	$90
October 1922 Play at third	$35
March 1923 Batter and catcher	$45
November 1924 Batter	$45
May 1925 Pitcher	$35
November 1925 Pitcher, World Series	$50
February 1926 Fielder	$35
April 1926 Play at the plate	$45
May 1926 Pitcher	$35
August 1926 Eddie Collins, George Sisler	$35
September 1926 Catcher	$45
February 1927 Batter	$40
April 1927 Play at first	$35

July 1927 Robert O'Farrell	$35
August 1927 Catcher	$35
September 1927 Lou Gehrig	$50
October 1927 Joe McCarthy	$30
May 1928 Pitcher	$35
June 1928 First baseman	$45
July 1928 Batter and catcher	$35
August 1928 Batter	$45
September 1928 Play at third	$35
January 1929 Play at plate	$40
February 1929 Sliding into base	$40
March 1929 Catcher	$40
April 1929 Base runner	$40
May 1929 Pitcher	$40
June 1929 Batter	$35
July 1929 Play at second	$40
August 1929 Mickey Cochrane	$40
September 1929 Batter	$40
January 1930 Pitcher illustration	$30
February 1930 Pitcher illustration	$30
March 1930 Lefty Grove	$30
April 1930 Batter illustration	$40
May 1930 Al Simmons	$40
June 1930 Batter illustration	$40
July 1930 Grover Alexander	$35
August 1930 Pitcher illustration	$25
September 1930 Play at the plate	$40
October 1930 Pitcher illustration	$40

November 1930 World Series crowd	$25
January 1931 Pitcher illustration	$35
March 1931 Fielder illustration	$30
April 1931 Play at second	$35
May 1931 1930-31 Champions banner	$35
June 1931 Batter illustration	$35
July 1931 Catcher and batter	$25
August 1931 Rabbit Maranville	$30
September 1931 Play at second	$30
October 1931 Wes Ferrell	$35
November 1931 World Series number	$25
December 1931 Fielder	$30
January 1932 Unknown	$35
February 1932 Chuck Klein	$45
March 1932 Play at the plate	$75
April 1932 Pepper Martin	$35
May 1932 Play ball	$35
June 1932 Max Carey	$35
July 1932 Fielder illustration	$30
August 1932 Catcher illustration	$35
September 1932 George Earnshaw	$35
October 1932 Earl Averill	$50
November 1932 World Series number	$35
December 1932 J. McCarthy, President Roosevelt	$75
February 1933 Jimmie Foxx	$45
March 1933 John Heydler	$35
April 1933 Dale Alexander	$35
May 1933 25th Anniversary issue	$45
June 1933 Bill Terry	$45
July 1933 Red Faber	$35
August 1933 Play at second	$35
February 1934 William Harridge	$40
May 1934 Play at the plate	$35
June 1934 Bob O'Farrell	$35
July 1934 Jimmy Dykes	$35
September 1934 Mel Harder	$30
January 1935 Ford Frick	$35
July 1935 Charles Dressen	$30
September 1935 Mel Ott	$45

October 1935 Hank Greenberg	$45
January 1936 Buddy Myers	$30
February 1936 Gabby Hartnett	$40
March 1936 Steve O'Neill	$35
May 1936 Play Ball	$35
June 1936 Roger Cramer	$35
July 1936 Joe Medwick	$75
August 1936 Bill Dickey	$35
September 1936 Lon Warneke	$35
October 1936 World Series bleacher fans	$35
November 1936 Joe McCarthy, Bill Terry	$30
December 1936 Luke Appling	$35
January 1937 Play at first	$40
February 1937 Hal Trotsky	$35
March 1937 Leo Durocher	$40
April 1937 Johnny Allen	$35
May 1937 Play Ball	$35
June 1937 Burleigh Grimes	$35
July 1937 Wally Moses	$35
August 1937 Dick Bartell	$35
October 1937 Play at the plate	$35
December 1937 Charlie Gehringer	$40
January 1938 Joe Medwick	$35
February 1938 Gee Walker	$30
March 1938 Play at the plate	$30
April 1938 Catchers mask	$30
June 1938 Gus Mancuso	$30
July 1938 Frank Crosetti	$30
August 1938 Gabby Hartnett, umpire	$75
September 1938 Red Rolfe	$30
October 1938 World Series issue	$75
November 1938 Gabby Hartnett, Joe McCarthy	$30
December 1938 Dizzy Dean	$30
January 1939 Ernie Lombardi	$35
February 1939 Bob Feller	$35
March 1939 Play at the plate	$35
April 1939 Bobby Doerr	$35
May 1939 D. Bartell, H. Leiber, G. Mancuso	$30
June 1939 Abner Doubleday	$75
July 1939 Baseball action photos	$75
September 1939 Dodgers on the mound	$35
October 1939 Red Rolfe	$50
November 1939 Bucky Walters, Joe DiMaggio	$50
December 1939 Ted Williams	$50
January 1940 Terry Moore	$25
February 1940 Baseball close-up	$25
March 1940 P. Coscarart, C. Dressen, L. Durocher	$25
April 1940 Joe Gordon	$25
May 1940 Umpire Bill Klem	$25
June 1940 B. Feller, R. Hemsley, O. Vitt	$35
July 1940 Ernie Lombardi, Johnny Mize	$35
August 1940 Flash Gordon	$25
September 1940 Harry Danning	$25
October 1940 Joe DiMaggio	$50
November 1940 Reds team photo	$30
December 1940 Tigers/Reds World Series	$30
January 1941 Jimmy Wilson	$25
February 1941 Connie Mack	$25
March 1941 Babe Young	$25
April 1941 Joe McCarthy	$25
May 1941 Bucky Walters	$25
June 1941 Jake Early, Ban Johnson	$25
July 1941 Johnny Hopp, Babe Young	$25
August 1941 Ted Williams	$45

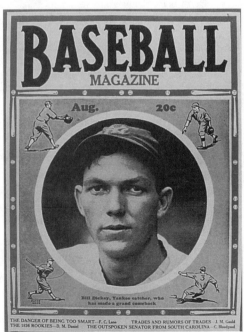

August 1936

February 1941

September 1941 Dolph Camilli, Enos Slaughter $25
October 1941 Umpire Bill Summers $30
November 1941 Yankees team $30
December 1941 Billy Herman $30
January 1942 Lou Boudreau $50
February 1942 Mel Ott, team executives $40
March 1942 Play at the plate $35
April 1942 Ebbets Field $35
May 1942 Hank Greenberg $45
June 1942 Enos Slaughter $35
July 1942 Play at the plate $35
August 1942 Paul Waner $35
September 1942 Joe Gordon, Elmer Valo $35
October 1942 Play at the plate $35
November 1942 J. McCarthy, B. Southworth $35
December 1942 Cal Griffith $35
January 1943 Pee Wee Reese $35
February 1943 Johnny Pesky, Phil Rizzuto $35
March 1943 Jimmy Brown $30
April 1943 Play at the plate $30
May 1943 Play at the plate $25
June 1943 Play at the plate $30
July 1943 Arguing with an umpire $30
August 1943 Play at first $30
September 1943 Arky Vaughn $30
October 1943 Bill Johnson $50
November 1943 J. McCarthy, B. Southworth $30
December 1943 Frank Crosetti $25
January 1944 Play at the plate $25
February 1944 Play at third $20
March 1944 Yankees bat boy $20
April 1944 Pirates player $25
May 1944 Senators pitchers $25
June 1944 Buy Bonds $25
July 1944 Jimmie Foxx $35
August 1944 Play at third $20
September 1944 Play at the plate $25
October 1944 The Cooper brothers $25
November 1944 Detroit Tigers players $25

December 1944 Cardinals team photo $25
January 1945 Play at the plate $25
February 1945 Ford Frick, William Harriot $25
March 1945 Play at the plate $25
April 1945 Play Ball $25
May 1945 Joe Cronin, Tom Yawkey $15
June 1945 Buy Bonds $25
July 1945 Happy Chandler $25
August 1945 Rundown play $25
September 1945 Boston Braves players $25
October 1945 Chicago Cubs players $25
November 1945 Chief Bender, Connie Mack $25
December 1945 Charlie Grimm, Steve O'Neill $25
January 1946 Play at the plate $25
February 1946 Play at the plate $25
March 1946 Play at the plate $25
April 1946 L. Durocher, J. McCarthy, M. Ott $35
May 1946 Lou Boudreau, Bob Feller $35
June 1946 President Truman $25
July 1946 Pee Wee Reese, Pete Reiser $35
August 1946 Rudy York $25
September 1946 Play at third $25
October 1946 Bobby Doerr, Ted Williams $45
November 1946 Bob Feller, Hal Newhouser $40
December 1946 Cardinals team photo $25
January 1947 Johnny Pesky $25
February 1947 George Case $25
March 1947 Happy Chandler $25
April 1947 Play at the plate $25
May 1947 Eddie Stanky $45
June 1947 Ted Williams $45
July 1947 Pete Reiser, Andy Seminick $35
August 1947 Luke Appling $25
September 1947 Ewell Blackwell $25
October 1947 Cincinnati Reds $25
November 1947 Ralph Kiner, Johnny Mize $30
December 1947 Jackie Robinson $45
January 1948 Play at third $25
February 1948 Joe Cronin, Joe McCarthy $35
March 1948 Yogi Berra, Jack Conway $30
April 1948 Play at the plate $25
May 1948 T. Holmes, D. Litwhiler, C. Ryan $25
June 1948 President Truman $20
July 1948 Clyde Kluttz, Johnny Mize $25
August 1948 Steve O'Neill, Dizzy Trout $25
September 1948 Stan Musial $35
October 1948 Lou Boudreau, Mike Guerra $50
November 1948 Connie Mack $20
December 1948 Lou Boudreau $25
January 1949 Joe DiMaggio, Bobby Doerr, Ted Williams $60
February 1949 Gil Coan, Joe Dobson $25
March 1949 Pat Mullin $25
April 1949 Bob Swift, Birdie Tebbetts $25
June 1949 Griffith Stadium $25
July 1949 Ralph Branca $25
August 1949 Del Rice $25
September 1949 Casey Stengel $25
October 1949 Richie Ashburn, Clyde McCullough, Andy Seminick .$35
November 1949 Connie Mack $30
December 1949 Ford Frick, William Harridge, Casey Stengel $20
January 1950 Red Sox pitchers $20
February 1950 Roy Sievers $20
March 1950 T. Henrich, J. Mize, C. Stengel $20
April 1950 Sherm Lollar, Birdie Tebbetts $20

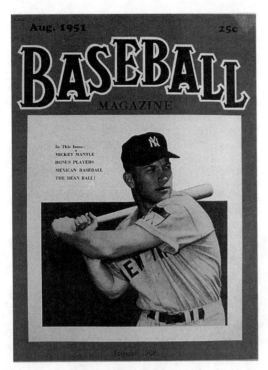

August 1951

May 1950 Stan Musial $25
June 1950 Earl Torgeson $20
July 1950 Connie Mack $25
August 1950 Eddie Sawyer...$20
September 1950 Johnny Lipon..$20
October 1950 Richie Ashburn $35
December 1950 Yankee Stadium...$35
January 1951 Play at second $20
February 1951 Billy Goodman..$20
March 1951 Braves vs. Cubs $20
April 1951 Joe Garagiola $15
May 1951 Vern Bickford, Johnny Sain, Warren Spahn $20
June 1951 Casey Stengel...$20
July 1951 Eddie Sawyer, Casey Stengel $15

August 1951 Mickey Mantle..$45
September 1951 Gil Hodges $35
October 1951 World Series issue $25
November 1951 Bob Feller..$25
December 1951 Cy Young..$25
January 1952 Out at the plate...$20
March 1952 Ned Garver...$20
April 1952 Rogers Hornsby, Eddie Stanky $40
May 1952 R. Ashburn, D. Ennis, T. Brown $35
June 1952 Willie Mays..$35
July/August 1952 All-Star Game issue $20
September 1952 Babe Ruth anniversary issue......................$35
October 1952 Pennant issue $45
November/December 1952 World Series issue....................$20
April 1953 Pee Wee Reese, Hank Sauer, Bobby Shantz $35
May 1953 Solly Hemus, Johnny Mize................................$20
June 1953 Joe DiMaggio, Hoot Evers, Allie Reynolds $40
July 1953 Billy Bruton, Mickey Mantle $45
August 1953 L. Appling, R. Boone, D. Gernert $15
September 1953 Karl Drews, Mickey Vernon, Del Wilber................$20
October 1953 Gus Bell, Gil Hodges $35
November 1953 Reese, Rizzuto, Roberts, fSchoendienst...................$35
August 1954 Mickey Mantle..$20
September 1954 Casey Stengel..$10
October 1954 World Series issue $10
March 1955 Connie Mack..$15
May 1955 Illustration..$10
June 1955 Illustration...$10
July 1955 All-Star Game issue...$15
May 1956 Play Ball...$25
June 1956 Ted Williams $30
July 1956 Mickey Mantle..$40
August 1956 Bob Friend $20
October 1956 Casey Stengel $20
May 1957 Don Larsen..$20
September 1957 Bob Feller..$20
November 1964 Johnny Callison..$30
December 1964 Brooks Robinson $30
January 1965 Cardinals team photo $20
February 1965 Cleveland's Municipal Stadium...................$20
March 1965 Frank Howard $30
April 1965 Wally Bunker $20

ESPN THE MAGAZINE

It may not have the history and tradition of *Sports Illustrated* magazine, but *ESPN The Magazine* does have the power of America's favorite sports television channel behind it. Launched in early 1998, *ESPN The Magazine* (which publishes every two weeks) takes a more trendy approach to sports than what you expect from *S.I.* The design is hip and flashy, the photography is bold and personal, and the writing mirrors the quick, often witty repartee of ESPN's best Sportscenter personalities.

Thus far, collectors have shown interest only in certain issues of *ESPN The Magazine* (especially those with the likes of basketball great Michael Jordan or golfer Tiger Woods on the cover). Plus, the publication boasts mass distribution, so it's not hard to find. Consequently, values aren't very high—yet. But 25 years from now, you may wish you had held on to these early issues of the magazine. Besides, *ESPN The Magazine*'s large format (10x12 inches) makes it an attractive object for autograph collectors.

Surprisingly, *ESPN The Magazine* has devoted relatively few of its covers to baseball players. Only 18 out of its first 85 issues (through June 2001) featured a baseball star—and one of those was a cover shared by athletes from three other sports. Mark McGwire has made the most appearances thus far: Five of those 18 baseball covers were devoted to Big Mac.

April 3, 2000

March 5, 2001

May 14, 2001

June 11, 2001

1998 (Volume 1; 20 issues)
03/23—Alex Rodriguez (w/Kobe Bryant, Kordell Stewart,
  Eric Lindros) $6
04/18—Mark McGwire...$5
05/18—Mark McGwire...$5
08/24—Ken Griffey Jr. $4
09/21—Mark McGwire and Sammy Sosa $5

1999 (Volume 2; 26 issues)
04/05—Roger Clemens $3
05/17—Mark McGwire...$5
07/12—Derek Jeter $5
08/23—Sammy Sosa and Mark McGwire...........................$5

2000 (Volume 3; 26 issues)
04/03—Alex Rodriguez $3
05/15—Barry Bonds $3
06/12—Randy Johnson, Pedro Martinez $3
06/26—Nomar Garciaparra...$3
08/07—John Rocker...$3

2001 (Volume 4; 26 issues)
03/05—Manny Ramirez $3
04/02—Jason Giambi $3
05/14—Gary Sheffield $3
06/11—Barry Bonds $3

SPORT MAGAZINE

Among memorabilia collectors, *Sport* magazine is second only to *Sports Illustrated* in popularity. In fact, during its heyday (the 1950s and '60s), *Sport* was the leader in its field.

Unfortunately, the magazine folded in September 2000, but *Sport's* classic issues live on in the collections of loyalists who remember its in-depth features covering all sports, its enthusiasm, and its quality writing and photography. *Sport* featured the work of a host of big-name sports journalists—from Roger Kahn, Ira Berkow and George Vecsey to Dick Young, Joe Garagiola and even Howard Cosell—who brought insider information to its pages. Another major factor behind the magazine's early success was the inimitable photography of Ozzie Sweet. A former *Newsweek* cover photographer, Sweet hooked up with *Sport* in 1949 and made an instant impact with his up-close, intimate portraits and his unique "simulated action" scenes—styles that put baseball's stars in heroic settings. Sweet's work appeared as covers as well as full-page interior photographs that *Sport's* readers frequently cut out of magazines and pinned up on walls.

Sweet photographed the majority of *Sport's* covers in the 1950s and early '60s. Ironically, the magazine began losing ground to *Sports Illustrated* after that time—a result due partly to (or largely because of) *S.I.*'s weekly publication schedule (vs. monthly for *Sport*). Between the 1970s and '80s, the magazine continued serving its loyal following, but the writing seemed less groundbreaking and the photography less special as more and more sports-related publications filled newsstand shelves.

The prices below are for baseball-related issues of *Sport*. The column of autograph pricing represents a magazine signed by the athlete on the cover. For covers featuring multiple personalities, the autographed price is for an issue signed by all pictured players. Keep in mind that some issues don't show an autographed price—either the player pictured had already passed away, making it impossible for him to have signed, or the cover featured an artist's rendition of the game as opposed to a single player or players.

September 1946

August 1947

September 1948

July 1950

1946 Month	Cover Subject	VG	EX	NM	Signed
September	J. DiMaggio	$300	$450	$750	$900
1947					
Apr	Leo Durocher	20	35	60	75
June	Bob Feller	25	40	70	90
July	E. Dyer/J. Cronin	20	35	60	200
August	Ted Williams	40	60	100	250
September	Joe/Dom DiMaggio	45	75	120	350
1948					
April	Ted Williams	30	50	70	250
May	Babe Ruth	20	30	60	—
August	Stan Musial	30	50	70	85
September	J. DiMaggio/T. Williams	40	60	100	500
October	Lou Gehrig	30	50	70	—
1949					
February	Lou Boudreau	10	20	30	50
April	Bob Feller	20	30	60	80
May	Enos Slaughter	15	25	40	50
June	Hal Newhouser	15	25	40	50
July	L. Boudreau/J. Gordon	15	25	40	75
August	Jackie Robinson	30	50	70	750
September	Joe DiMaggio	60	90	150	300
October	Christy Mathewson	15	25	40	—

1950 Month	Cover Subject	VG	EX	NM	Signed
April	Casey Stengel	15	25	40	275
May	Ralph Kiner	15	25	40	60
June	Bob Lemon	15	25	40	60
July	Stan Musial	20	30	60	80
September	Don Newcombe	15	25	40	60
October	World Series	12	24	35	—
1951					
April	Baseball Painting	12	24	35	—
May	Baseball Jubilee	12	24	35	—
August	Yogi Berra	15	25	40	50
September	Ted Williams	25	40	70	250
October	Jackie Robinson	25	40	70	750
1952					
March	Gil McDougald	10	20	30	50
April	Chico Carrasquel	10	20	30	50
May	Alvin Dark	10	20	30	50
June	Ralph Kiner	15	25	40	50
July	Stan Musial	20	30	60	75
August	A. Reynolds/Y. Berra	15	25	40	60
October	J. Robinson/Reese	25	40	70	800
November	J. Robinson/A. Reynolds	20	35	60	700

September 1951

October 1951

August 1953

July 1954

1953

Month	Cover Subject	VG	EX	NM	Signed
February	Bobby Shantz	10	20	30	50
April	Mickey Mantle	75	100	125	300
May	Bob Lemon	5	10	15	30
June	Hank Bauer	5	10	15	30
August	Warren Spahn	6	12	20	40
September	Robin Roberts	6	12	20	35
October	Roy Campanella	8	15	25	325
November	Phil Rizzuto	8	15	25	60

1954

Month	Cover Subject	VG	EX	NM	Signed
February	Eddie Mathews	15	25	35	60
March	Casey Stengel	6	12	20	250
April	Don Newcombe	6	12	20	50
May	Ted Kluszewski	8	15	25	90
July	Stan Musial	12	20	40	60
August	Minnie Minoso	6	12	20	35
September	Duke Snider	15	25	35	50
October	Al Rosen	5	10	20	40

1955

Month	Cover Subject	VG	EX	NM	Signed
February	Alvin Dark	4	6	10	25
April	Bob Turley	5	10	15	25
May	Bobby Thomson	5	10	15	25
August	Paul Richards	4	6	10	25
September	Duke Snider	8	15	25	50
October	Yogi Berra	6	12	20	50

1956

Month	Cover Subject	VG	EX	NM	Signed
March	Walter Alston	4	7	12	175
April	Larry Doby	5	10	15	30
May	Bob Lemon	6	12	20	25
June	Willie Mays	8	15	25	75
July	Ted Williams	15	25	40	250
October	Mickey Mantle	20	35	60	250

1957

Month	Cover Subject	VG	EX	NM	Signed
March	Mickey Mantle	15	25	50	250
April	Eddie Mathews	6	12	20	50
May	Campanella/Spahn/Roberts	6	12	20	450
Annual	Kluszewski	6	12	20	50
June	Early Wynn	12	22	40	60
July	Al Kaline	15	25	35	50
August	Joe Adcock	6	12	20	35
September	Duke Snider	15	25	35	50

1958

Month	Cover Subject	VG	EX	NM	Signed
January	Baseball Stars: Mays/Snider/Others	6	12	20	700
March	Lew Burdette	5	10	15	30
April	Nellie Fox	6	12	20	250
May	Yogi Berra	6	12	20	40
June	Willie Mays	8	15	25	60
July	Herb Score	5	10	15	40
August	Billy Martin	5	10	15	90
September	Eddie Mathews	6	12	20	50
October	B. Turley/H. Aaron/Snead	4	7	12	50

1959

Month	Cover Subject	VG	EX	NM	Signed
March	A. Kaline/O. Robertson/ F. Patterson	10	20	30	50
May	Hank Bauer/Gil Hodges	4	7	12	325
June	Mantle/T. Williams	15	25	50	500
July	Don Newcombe/ Jimmy Piersall	4	6	10	50
August	Mantle/Others	10	20	30	325
September	T. Williams/S. Musial	12	22	40	275
October	Warren Spahn	6	12	20	50

1960

Month	Cover Subject	VG	EX	NM	Signed
March	Willie Mays/Others	5	10	15	425
April	Duke Snider	5	10	15	50
May	Harmon Killebrew/ Willie McCovey	8	15	25	65
June	Don Drysdale	8	15	25	75
July	L. Aparicio/F. Howard	6	12	20	50
August	Mickey Mantle	12	22	40	240
September	R. Colavito/Mays/Fox	8	15	25	600
October	B. Ruth/L. Sherry	4	6	10	35
November	Roger Maris	10	20	30	500

1961

Month	Cover Subject	VG	EX	NM	Signed
April	Frank Howard	4	6	10	25
May	D. Groat/Mantle Insert	5	10	15	240
June	Willie Mays	5	10	15	60
August	Spahn/Boyer	5	10	15	40
September	J. DiMaggio/Mantle	12	22	40	450
October	Wally Moon	4	6	10	25

1962

Month	Cover Subject	VG	EX	NM	Signed
February	Roger Maris	8	15	25	500
April	N. Cash/V. Pinson	4	6	10	35
May	Baseball Sluggers	4	7	12	—

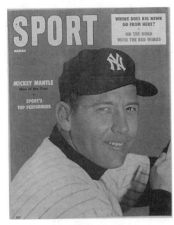

March 1957

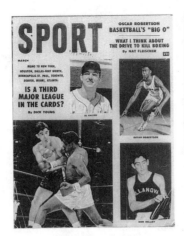

March 1959

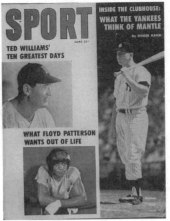

June 1959

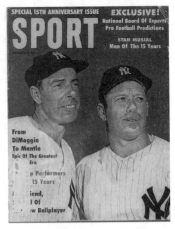

September 1961

Month	Cover Subject	VG	EX	NM	Signed
June	Hank Aaron	6	12	20	50
July	Mickey Mantle	15	30	50	225
August	Colavito/ Kuenn	6	12	20	35
September	Boyer/Musial	6	12	20	140
October	Willie Mays	5	10	15	50
1963					
February	Maury Wills	3	5	8	25
April	S. Musial/ W. Chamberlain	4	6	10	140
May	Berra/Mantle	12	22	40	250
June	Maury Wills	3	5	8	25
July	Kaline/Colavito	10	20	30	60
August	Willie Mays	5	10	15	50
September	Sandy Koufax	6	12	20	70
October	Mickey Mantle	10	20	30	225
November	Whitey Ford	5	10	15	40
1964					
February	Sandy Koufax	5	10	15	60
May	Warren Spahn	4	7	12	30
July	Yastrzemski/Davis/Tresh	3	5	8	60
August	J. DiMaggio/W. Mays	6	12	20	275
September	Mickey Mantle	10	20	30	225
October	Willie Mays	5	10	15	60
November	Harmon Killebrew	5	10	15	30
1965					
April	Dean Chance	3	5	8	30
May	Sandy Koufax	5	10	15	60
June	Willie Mays	4	7	12	50
August	Mickey Mantle	10	20	30	225
September	Gehrig/DiMaggio	6	12	20	240
October	S. Koufax/Wills	4	7	12	75
1966					
February	Sandy Koufax	4	7	12	30
April	W. Mays/P. Hornung	4	6	10	30
May	Maury Wills	3	5	8	30
July	Mickey Mantle	8	15	25	225
August	Frank Robinson	3	5	8	30
September	Willie Mays	4	7	12	50
October	Sandy Koufax	4	7	12	60
1967					
February	Frank Robinson	3	5	8	30
May	Mickey Mantle	8	15	25	225
June	Willie Mays	4	6	10	50

Month	Cover Subject	VG	EX	NM	Signed
July	Richie Allen/J. Ryan	1	3	6	30
August	Roberto Clemente	10	20	30	325
September	Pete Rose	6	12	20	40
1968					
February	Carl Yastrzemski	4	6	10	30
May	Willie Mays	3	5	8	50
June	Carl Yastrzemski	4	6	10	30
July	Hank Aaron	4	6	10	35
August	Pete Rose	4	7	12	30
September	Don Drysdale	3	5	8	60
1969					
April	Mickey Mantle	10	20	30	225
May	Koufax/DiMaggio/ Ruth/Mays	1	3	6	325
June	Ted Williams	4	7	12	225
July	Tony Conigliaro	4	6	10	150
September	Durocher/Banks/Santo	6	12	20	50
1970					
February	Lew Alcindor/Gil Hodges	3	5	8	400
May	Tom Seaver	4	6	10	35
June	Harmon Killebrew	4	6	10	30
August	Hank Aaron	4	6	10	50
September	Johnny Bench	4	7	12	40
1971					
May	T. Williams/McLain/Flood	5	10	15	250
June	Boog Powell	3	5	8	25
July	Carl Yastrzemski	4	6	10	30
September	Willie Mays	4	6	10	50
October	Vida Blue	1	3	6	25
1972					
June	Brooks Robinson	4	6	10	30
August	Tom Seaver	4	7	12	35
September	Frank Robinson	3	5	8	30
October	Johnny Bench	5	10	15	40
1973					
August	Bobby Murcer	3	5	8	20
September	Gaylord Perry	3	5	8	20
October	Pete Rose/Others	3	5	8	—
1974					
May	Hank Aaron #715	5	10	15	50
June	Pete Rose	4	6	10	30
October	Reggie Jackson	4	7	12	50

July 1963

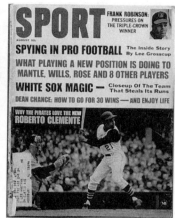

August 1967

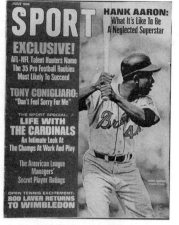

July 1968

September 1971

1975

Month	Cover Subject	VG	EX	NM	Signed
May	Frank Robinson	3	5	8	30
July	Bobby Bonds	3	5	8	25
August	Billy Martin	4	6	10	90
1976					
April	Steve Garvey	4	6	10	25
August	Rose/Morgan	5	10	15	50
1977					
July	Mark Fidrych	3	5	8	20
October	Rod Carew	1	3	6	30
1978					
April	S. Lyle/Gossage	3	5	8	50
May	Graig Nettles	3	5	8	20
July	Jim Rice	3	5	8	20
August	Tom Seaver	4	6	10	35
October	Carl Yastrzemski	3	5	8	25
1979					
April	Pete Rose	4	6	10	30
May	Ron Guidry	1	3	6	20
June	Dave Parker	1	3	6	20
July	Graig Nettles	1	3	6	20
August	Rod Carew	3	5	8	20
October	Reggie Jackson	4	6	10	50
1980					
April	Willie Stargell	3	5	8	50
April	Nolan Ryan	6	12	20	50

Month	Cover Subject	VG	EX	NM	Signed
May	George Brett	5	10	15	40
May	Lou Piniella	5	8	10	25
July	Gorman Thomas	1	3	6	15
1981					
April	George Brett	3	5	8	20
April	Tug McGraw	3	5	8	20
May	Billy Martin	1	3	6	80
May	Mike Schmidt	1	3	6	20
June	Dave Parker	1	3	6	20
June	Don Sutton	1	3	6	20
July	Bruce Sutter	—	2	5	20
July	Dave Parker	1	3	6	20
1982					
April	Fernando Valenzuela	1	3	6	20
May	Reggie Jackson	3	5	8	40
June	Tom Seaver	3	5	8	30
July	Billy Martin	1	3	6	80
1983					
April	Steve Garvey	1	3	6	20
May	Steve Carlton	3	5	8	25
June	Schmidt/Dawson/Yount	3	5	8	65
July	Reggie Jackson	3	5	8	40
1984					
April	Cal Ripken	3	5	8	60
June	Dale Murphy	1	3	6	20
July	Tommy Lasorda/Others	—	2	5	—

August 1972

October 1977

October 1979

May 1982

July 1982

July 1983

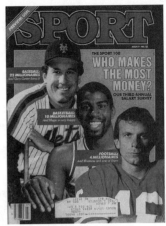

March 1985

May 1986

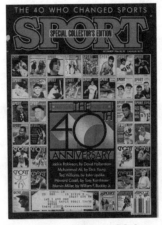

December 1986

1985 Month	Cover Subject	VG	EX	NM	Signed
February	D. Gooden/others	1	3	6	20
March	Gary Carter	1	3	6	20
April	Doc Gooden	1	3	6	20
May	Keith Hernandez/G. Matthews	2	5	8	20
June	George Brett	3	5	8	35
July	Kirk Gibson	1	3	6	25
August	Joe Montana	3	5	8	—
1986					
April	Bret Saberhagen	1	3	6	20
April	Dwight Gooden	1	3	6	20
May	George Brett	3	5	8	35
July	R. Jackson/P. Rose	3	5	8	35
1987					
March	R. Clemens/Schmidt	1	3	6	300
April	Darryl Strawberry	1	3	6	20
July	Dave Parker/Mike Schmidt	1	3	6	65
1988					
March	G. Jefferies/J. McDowell	—	2	5	30
April	Don Zimmer	1	2	5	15
1989					
April	K. Gibson/Mattingly	3	5	8	35
May	Orel Hershiser	1	3	6	20
June	Dan Marino/R. Clemens	1	3	6	20
July	Jose Canseco	1	3	6	25
October	Marino/Gooden	1	3	6	115
1990					
March	Bo Jackson	1	3	6	25
April	J. Canseco/others	1	3	6	60

Month	Cover Subject	VG	EX	NM	Signed
May	Baseball Preview	1	3	6	—
June	Salaries	—	2	5	—
July	Will Clark	1	3	6	20
September	Bo Jackson/Others	—	2	5	25
1991					
March	Ken Griffey Jr.	3	5	8	55
April	Jose Canseco	1	3	6	20
May	H. Johnson/J. Reardon	—	2	5	40
June	Darryl Strawberry	1	3	6	20
1992					
April	Bo Jackson/F. Thomas	1	3	6	40
May	Cal Ripken	3	5	8	50
1993					
March	Baseball '93	1	3	6	—
April	Bonds/Bonilla/Clemens	1	3	6	35
1994					
April	Barry Bonds	—	2	5	35
May	Mike Piazza	1	3	6	40
June	Scottie Pippen	1	3	6	—
1995					
January	Frank Thomas	1	3	6	40
April	Michael Jordan (White Sox)	4	6	10	200
1998					
May	Baseball's Best/Worst Values	—	2	5	—
July	Chipper Jones	1	3	6	20

SPORTS ILLUSTRATED

Its 3 million readers every week attest to the strength, tradition and quality of *Sports Illustrated*. The magazine has had to maintain those characteristics in recent years because of the launch in 1998 of *ESPN The Magazine*. From the collector's point of view, though, *S.I.* is the favorite because of its 44-year head start on *ESPN*.

Since that first issue of *Sports Illustrated*—featuring "Night Baseball in Milwaukee" and a photograph of the Braves' Eddie Mathews—rolled off the presses on August 16, 1954, the magazine has issued thousands of baseball covers. Virtually all of the game's biggest stars have appeared on an *S.I.* cover.

Early on, *SI* differentiated itself from its first major competitor, *Sport*, by using more action photography. In the 1950s and '60s, *Sport*—a monthly that offered top-notch feature stories—usually used finely detailed portraits on its covers, reflecting the depth of the material inside. *Sports Illustrated*—a weekly magazine—is known more for its exciting action shots, reflecting the magazine's sports news focus. That said, there are countless examples of high-quality portrait covers in *S.I.*'s past. But again, with four or five issues to put out every month, *S.I.* has always had the luxury of running a variety of styles.

Like *Sport*, *Sports Illustrated* became a popular piece of memorabilia among autograph collectors. And with so many more issues pub-lished per year, *Sports Illustrated* has always offered more choices for autograph collectors who prefer the signatures on magazine covers. Copies of *Sports Illustrated* are fairly widespread (although increasingly hard to find—if you're looking for early issues—in Near-Mint condition). They're also fairly inexpensive to collect, generally speaking (certain copies command a premium, usually because of the cover subject), so collectors can amass full-year sets or team collections at reasonable prices.

The prices here are for Near-Mint copies of the magazine, which often means that the mailing label is intact. (Because the vast majority of *Sports Illustrated* copies have subscriber mailing labels attached, and because the labels are tough to remove cleanly, the presence of the labels doesn't take much away from the magazines' value.)

Our pricing, of course, includes a value for an autographed *S.I.* On covers with multiple stars, the autograph price is for an issue signed by everyone pictured—adjust the price accordingly if there are "missing" signatures. In cases where we don't offer an autographed price, it's either because the subject was deceased at the time of publication or because the cover art was an illustration that didn't picture a specific or recognizable athlete.

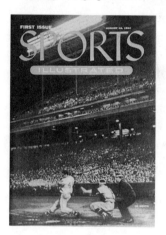

August 16, 1954

April 11, 1955

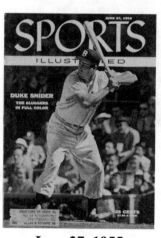

June 27, 1955

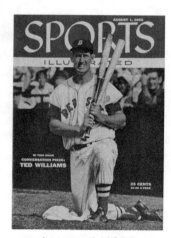

August 1, 1955

Date	Cover Subject	VG	EX	NM	Signed
1954					
08/16	Eddie Mathews	$125	$190	$300	$400
1955					
04/11	Durocher/Mays	75	100	125	300
04/18	Al Rosen	50	75	100	150
05/30	Herb Score	6	12	20	40
06/27	Duke Snider	30	50	75	90
07/11	Yogi Berra	15	25	50	60
08/01	Ted Williams	50	75	100	350
08/22	Don Newcombe	6	12	20	30
09/26	Walter Alston	8	15	25	225
1956					
01/02	Johnny Podres	15	25	35	60
03/05	Stan Musial	20	30	50	75
04/09	Special Baseball Issue	5	10	15	—
04/23	Billy Martin	15	25	35	125
05/14	A. Kaline/H. Kuenn	12	22	40	150
06/18	Mickey Mantle	90	140	200	350

Date	Cover Subject	VG	EX	NM	Signed
06/25	Warren Spahn	15	25	35	65
07/09	All-Star Game	10	20	30	—
07/16	Reds' Musclemen	25	35	60	130
07/30	Joe Adcock	5	10	15	25
08/20	Eddie Mathews	10	20	35	50
09/10	Whitey Ford	20	30	50	60
10/01	M. Mantle: World Series	50	75	100	250
1957					
03/04	Mantle: Spring Training	50	75	100	275
04/15	Spring Baseball	10	20	30	—
04/22	Wally Moon	5	10	15	35
05/13	Billy Pierce	5	10	15	20
06/03	Clem Labine	5	10	15	40
07/08	T. Williams/S. Musial	50	75	100	300
07/22	Hank Bauer	5	10	15	40
09/09	Roy McMillan	5	10	15	20
09/30	World Series Issue	8	15	25	—
11/04	Bobby Cox	4	6	10	20
12/23	Stan Musial	12	22	40	50

May 14, 1956

June 18, 1956

July 16, 1956

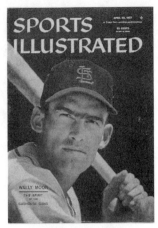

April 22, 1957

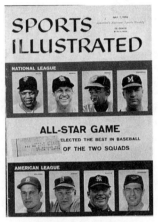

July 7, 1958

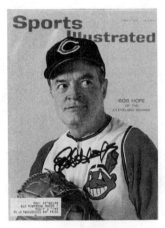

June 3, 1963

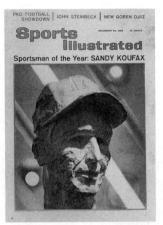

December 20, 1965

Date	Cover Subject	VG	EX	NM	Signed
1958					
03/03	Yankees Spring Training	6	12	20	—
03/17	Sal Maglie	5	10	15	75
03/31	Roy Sievers	5	10	15	40
04/14	Baseball Special	5	10	15	—
04/21	Del Crandall	5	10	15	50
05/05	Gil McDougald	5	10	15	40
05/19	Richie Ashburn	5	10	15	60
06/02	Eddie Mathews	9	20	35	50
06/23	Jackie Jensen	5	10	15	125
07/07	All-Stars Mays/Mantle	12	22	40	600
07/28	Frank Thomas	5	10	15	35
09/29	World Series	5	10	15	—
1959					
03/02	Casey Stengel	10	20	30	375
04/13	Willie Mays	20	30	50	75
05/04	Bob Turley	5	10	15	25
08/10	L. Aparicio/N. Fox	20	30	50	200
09/28	Chicago White Sox	5	10	15	—
1960					
03/07	Spring Training	5	10	15	—
04/11	Baseball Annual	5	10	15	—
06/06	Red Schoendienst	6	12	20	40
07/04	Comiskey Park Fireworks	5	10	15	—
07/18	Candlestick Park	4	6	10	—

Date	Cover Subject	VG	EX	NM	Signed
08/08	Dick Groat	6	12	20	35
10/10	Vernon Law	4	6	10	30
1961					
03/06	Spring Training/Reds	5	10	15	—
04/10	Baseball Issue	5	10	15	—
05/15	Cookie Lavagetto	4	7	12	65
06/26	W. Mays/E. Broglio	6	12	20	75
07/31	Split-Second Baseball	4	7	12	—
08/14	Murray/Rose/Mays	5	10	20	75
10/02	Roger Maris	12	22	40	650
10/09	Joey Jay	4	7	12	40
1962					
03/05	Casey Stengel	10	20	30	225
04/09	Frank Lary	4	7	12	45
04/30	Luis Aparicio	8	15	25	45
06/04	Willie Mays	11	21	35	80
07/02	Mickey Mantle	55	80	125	300
07/30	Ken Boyer	6	12	20	125
08/20	Don Drysdale	10	20	30	125
10/01	World Series	6	12	20	—
1963					
03/04	Sandy Koufax	14	23	45	80
04/08	Harmon Killebrew	10	20	30	50
04/29	Art Mahaffey	4	7	12	30
06/24	Roy Face	4	7	12	30

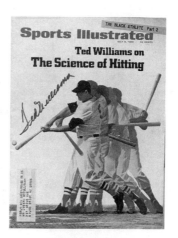

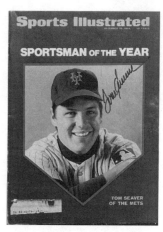

| October 16, 1967 | May 27, 1968 | July 8, 1968 | December 22, 1969 |

Date	Cover Subject	VG	EX	NM	Signed
07/22	Dick Groat	5	10	15	35
09/30	Whitey Ford	8	15	25	50
1964					
03/02	Y. Berra/C. Stengel	10	20	30	250
04/13	Sandy Koufax	10	20	30	85
05/11	Al Kaline	6	12	20	50
05/25	Frank Howard	4	7	12	25
07/06	Alvin Dark	4	7	12	25
08/10	Johnny Callison	4	6	10	35
08/31	Brooks Robinson	6	12	20	45
1965					
03/01	J. Bunning/B. Belinsky	5	10	15	40
04/19	Baseball 1965	5	10	15	—
05/17	Bill Veeck	4	7	12	110
06/21	Mickey Mantle	12	22	40	275
07/05	Bill Talbert	3	5	8	25
07/12	Maury Wills	5	10	15	30
08/09	Juan Marichal	6	12	20	50
08/23	Tony Oliva	5	10	15	25
10/04	Zoilo Versalles	4	7	12	20
12/20	Sandy Koufax	8	15	25	85
1966					
02/28	L. Durocher/E. Stanky	5	10	15	140
04/18	Dick Groat	5	10	15	35
05/23	Sam McDowell	4	7	12	20
07/11	Andy Etchebarren	4	6	10	60
09/26	Gaylord Perry	5	10	15	40
10/10	Brooks/F. Robinson	8	15	25	85
1967					
04/17	Maury Wills	5	10	15	25
05/08	Mickey Mantle	9	22	35	250
05/15	Koufax/Drysdale/Wills	10	20	30	275
06/05	Al Kaline	5	10	15	40
07/03	Roberto Clemente	10	20	30	650
07/31	The Spitball	4	6	10	—
08/21	Carl Yastrzemski	6	12	20	65
09/04	Tim McCarver	4	7	12	35
10/16	Lou Brock	6	12	20	35
12/25	Carl Yastrzemski	6	12	20	60
1968					
03/11	Johnny Bench	8	12	25	90
04/15	Lou Brock	5	10	15	30

Date	Cover Subject	VG	EX	NM	Signed
05/06	Ron Swoboda	4	6	10	20
05/27	Pete Rose	8	12	25	50
06/17	Don Drysdale	6	12	20	125
07/08	Ted Williams	10	20	30	225
07/29	Denny McLain	5	10	15	20
08/19	Curt Flood	5	10	15	25
09/02	Ken Harrelson	3	5	8	25
09/23	D. McLain/A. Kaline	5	10	15	50
10/07	St. Louis Cardinals	5	10	15	300
1969					
03/17	Ted Williams	8	15	25	225
05/19	Walter Alston	6	12	20	250
06/30	Ron Santo	5	10	15	30
07/07	Reggie Jackson	8	12	25	75
07/21	Billy Martin	5	10	15	100
08/18	Hank Aaron	8	12	25	60
09/08	P. Rose/E. Banks	6	12	20	75
10/06	Frank Robinson	5	10	15	40
10/20	Brooks Robinson	5	10	15	40
12/22	Tom Seaver	10	20	30	60
1970					
02/23	Denny McLain	4	6	10	20
03/23	Dick Allen	4	6	10	20
04/13	Jerry Koosman	4	7	12	25
05/25	Hank Aaron	4	7	12	50
06/22	Tony Conigliaro	4	7	12	200
07/13	Johnny Bench	4	7	12	45
07/27	Willie Mays	4	7	12	60
09/07	Bud Harrelson	3	5	8	15
09/28	L. Durocher/D. Murtaugh	3	5	8	100
10/19	Brooks Robinson	4	6	10	75
1971					
03/22	Wes Parker	2	4	7	25
04/12	Boog Powell	3	5	8	15
05/03	D. Duncan/J. Fregosi	3	5	8	35
05/31	Vida Blue	3	5	8	25
06/21	Jerry Grote	3	5	8	25
07/05	Alex Johnson	2	4	7	20
08/02	Willie Stargell	3	5	8	35
08/30	Ferguson Jenkins	3	5	8	35
09/27	Maury Wills	3	5	8	15
10/18	Frank Robinson	3	5	8	40

July 13, 1970

August 30, 1971

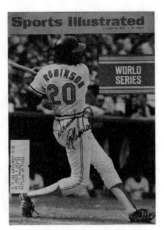

October 18, 1971

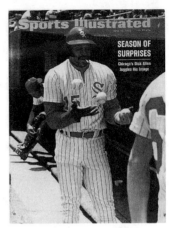

June 12, 1972

April 15, 1974

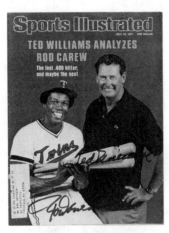

July 18, 1977

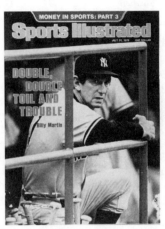

July 13, 1978

Date	Cover Subject	VG	EX	NM	Signed
1972					
03/13	Johnny Bench	3	5	8	40
03/27	Vida Blue	2	4	7	25
04/10	Joe Torre	4	6	10	25
05/01	Willie Davis	2	4	7	20
05/22	Willie Mays	4	6	10	55
06/12	Dick Allen	3	5	8	25
07/03	Steve Blass	2	4	7	20
08/21	Sparky Lyle	3	5	8	20
09/25	Carlton Fisk	3	5	8	40
10/23	Catfish Hunter	3	5	8	30
1973					
03/12	Bill Melton	3	5	8	20
04/09	Steve Carlton	3	6	10	30
04/30	Chris Speier	3	5	8	20
06/04	Wilbur Wood	3	5	8	20
07/30	Carlton Fisk	4	6	10	35
08/20	Dodgers/Russell/Osteen	4	6	10	45
09/24	Danny Murtaugh	3	5	8	100
10/22	Bert Campaneris	3	5	8	35
1974					
03/18	Babe Ruth	4	6	10	—
04/08	Pete Rose	4	6	10	40
04/15	Hank Aaron	6	12	20	55
05/27	Jim Wynn	2	4	7	20

Date	Cover Subject	VG	EX	NM	Signed
06/17	Reggie Jackson	4	6	10	45
07/01	Rod Carew	3	5	8	20
07/22	Lou Brock	3	5	8	30
08/12	Mike Marshall	2	4	7	35
10/07	Catfish Hunter	3	5	8	25
10/21	A's/Dodgers	3	5	8	100
1975					
03/03	Reds Spring Training	4	6	10	75
04/07	Steve Garvey	3	5	8	35
05/26	Jimmy Wynn	2	4	7	25
06/02	Billy Martin	3	5	8	80
06/16	Nolan Ryan	4	7	12	60
07/07	Fred Lynn	3	5	8	30
07/21	T. Seaver/J.Palmer	4	6	10	60
08/11	Baseball Boom	3	5	8	—
10/06	Reggie Jackson	4	6	10	45
10/20	J. Bench/L. Tiant	4	6	10	40
11/03	J. Bench/W. McEnaney	3	5	8	40
12/22	Pete Rose	4	6	10	50
1976					
03/15	Bill Veeck	2	4	7	100
04/12	Joe Morgan	3	5	8	40
05/03	Mike Schmidt	3	5	8	45
05/31	C. Fisk/L. Piniella	3	5	8	25
06/21	George Brett	4	6	10	45
07/12	Randy Jones	2	4	7	20

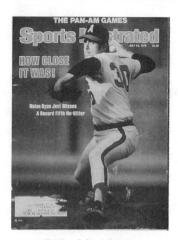

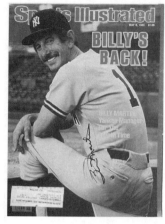

| July 23, 1979 | April 16, 1984 | March 25, 1985 | May 6, 1985 |

Date	Cover Subject	VG	EX	NM	Signed
08/30	Reggie Jackson	4	6	10	50
11/01	Johnny Bench	4	6	10	40
1977					
03/14	Tommy Lasorda	3	5	8	30
03/28	Bump Wills	2	4	7	20
04/11	Joe Rudi	3	5	8	20
05/02	Reggie Jackson	4	6	10	40
05/30	Dave Parker	3	5	8	50
06/06	Mark Fidrych	3	5	8	25
06/27	Tom Seaver	4	6	10	30
07/04	Ted Turner	2	4	7	25
07/18	R. Carew/T. Williams	4	6	10	225
08/15	Sadaharu Oh	3	5	8	65
08/29	Greg Luzinski	2	4	7	15
10/24	World Series	3	4	7	—
1978					
03/20	Clint Hurdle	2	4	7	15
04/10	R. Carew/G. Foster	3	5	8	50
04/24	Mark Fidrych	3	5	8	20
07/31	Billy Martin	3	5	8	80
08/07	Pete Rose's Streak	4	6	10	40
10/23	Lee Lacy/Brian Doyle	2	4	7	20
1979					
03/05	Spring Training	3	5	8	—
04/09	J. Rice/D. Parker	3	5	8	40
04/30	George Bamberger	2	4	7	20
05/28	Pete Rose: Phillies	3	5	8	30
06/18	Earl Weaver	3	5	8	20
07/23	Nolan Ryan	4	7	12	50
08/13	Silver Anniversary	4	6	10	—
08/27	BB's Golden Oldies	4	6	10	130
10/22	D. DeCinces/P. Garner	2	4	7	40
12/24	Stargell/Bradshaw	3	5	8	25
1980					
03/24	Kirk Gibson	3	5	8	25
04/07	Keith Hernandez	3	5	8	20
06/09	Darryl Porter	2	4	7	20
07/21	Steve Carlton	3	5	8	35
08/04	Reggie Jackson	4	6	10	45
08/18	J.R. Richard	2	4	7	35
08/25	Baltimore Orioles	3	5	8	40
10/06	Gary Carter	2	4	7	30
10/27	Schmidt/Porter	3	5	8	35

Date	Cover Subject	VG	EX	NM	Signed
1981					
01/05	Dave Winfield	3	5	8	35
03/02	J.R. Richard	2	4	7	35
03/16	Rollie Fingers	3	5	8	25
04/13	G. Brett/M. Schmidt	4	6	10	65
04/27	Oakland's 5 Aces	2	4	7	60
05/18	Fernando Valenzuela	3	5	8	25
06/08	Greg Luzinski	2	4	7	20
06/22	Strike	1	3	6	—
07/27	Tom Seaver	3	5	8	25
08/10	Brett/Schmidt	3	5	8	60
08/17	Gary Carter	2	4	7	25
10/26	Graig Nettles	2	4	7	20
11/02	World Series	2	4	7	25
1982					
03/15	Reggie Jackson	3	5	8	45
04/12	Steve Garvey	3	5	8	30
05/17	Gaylord Perry	2	4	7	25
07/05	Kent Hrbek	2	4	7	20
07/19	Rose/Yaz	3	5	8	60
08/09	Dale Murphy	3	5	8	25
09/06	Rickey Henderson	3	5	8	35
10/11	Robin Yount	4	6	10	25
10/25	Yount/Smith	3	5	8	50
1983					
03/14	Rose/Morgan/Perez	4	6	10	75
04/04	Gary Carter	2	4	7	25
04/18	Tom Seaver	3	5	8	25
04/25	Steve Garvey	3	5	8	25
06/13	Rod Carew	3	5	8	25
07/04	Dale Murphy	3	5	8	20
07/18	A. Dawson/D. Stieb	3	5	8	35
10/03	Steve Carlton	3	5	8	30
10/24	Rick Dempsey	2	4	7	20
1984					
03/12	George Brett	3	5	8	40
04/02	Yogi Berra	3	5	8	30
04/16	Gossage/Nettles	3	5	8	35
04/23	Darryl Strawberry	3	5	8	25
05/28	Alan Trammell	3	5	8	30
06/11	Leon Durham	2	4	7	20
08/27	Pete Rose	3	5	8	25
09/24	Gooden/Sutcliffe	3	5	8	35
10/22	Alan Trammell	2	4	7	30

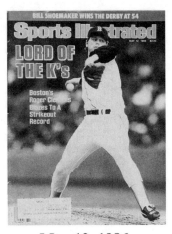

| September 23, 1985 | May 12, 1986 | November 2, 1987 | October 17, 1988 |

Date	Cover Subject	VG	EX	NM	Signed
1985					
03/04	Schmidt/Millionaires	3	5	8	40
03/18	Fred Lynn	2	4	7	20
03/25	Mantle/Mays/Ueberroth	5	10	15	325
04/15	Dwight Gooden	3	5	8	20
05/06	Billy Martin	3	5	8	80
07/08	Fernando Valenzuela	3	5	8	20
08/05	Pedro Guerrero	2	4	7	15
08/19	Pete Rose	3	5	8	30
09/02	Dwight Gooden	3	5	8	20
09/23	Ozzie Smith	3	5	8	30
10/28	Ozzie Smith	3	5	8	40
11/04	K.C. Royals	2	4	7	—
12/09	Kirk Gibson	2	4	7	20
1986					
04/14	Wade Boggs	3	5	8	25
05/12	Roger Clemens	4	6	10	30
07/14	Bo Jackson	3	5	8	30
07/28	Rickey Henderson	3	5	8	25
08/04	Oil Can Boyd	2	4	7	15
08/25	Ron Darling	2	4	7	15
10/06	Darryl Strawberry	3	5	8	20
10/20	DeCinces/Grich	2	4	7	25
10/27	Rice/Carter	2	4	7	20
11/03	Ray Knight	2	4	7	20
1987					
03/09	Ripken Family	3	5	8	125
03/16	Gary McLain	1	3	6	20
04/06	Carter/Snyder: BB Issue	3	5	8	30
04/27	Rob Deer	2	4	7	15
05/11	Reggie Jackson	4	6	10	40
07/06	One Day in Baseball	2	4	7	—
07/13	Strawberry/Mattingly	4	6	10	50
07/20	Andre Dawson	3	5	8	15
08/17	Alan Trammell	2	4	7	20
09/28	Ozzie Smith	3	5	8	25
10/05	Lloyd Moseby	2	4	7	15
10/19	Twins/World Series	3	5	8	—
10/26	Dan Gladden	2	4	7	15
11/02	Minnesota Twins	3	5	8	—
1988					
03/07	Kirk Gibson	2	4	7	15
03/14	Pam Postema	1	3	6	20

Date	Cover Subject	VG	EX	NM	Signed
04/04	M. McGwire/W. Clark	4	6	10	60
05/02	Billy Ripken	2	4	7	20
05/09	Pete Rose: Super Red	3	5	8	25
07/11	Darryl Strawberry	3	5	8	20
07/18	Casey at the Bat	2	4	7	—
09/26	Dwight Evans	2	4	7	20
10/17	Jose Canseco	3	5	8	25
10/31	Orel Hershiser	2	4	7	20
12/19	Orel Hershiser	2	4	7	20
1989					
03/06	Wade Boggs	3	5	8	25
04/03	Pete Rose: BB Issue	4	6	10	25
05/01	Nolan Ryan: Texas Heat	5	10	15	20
06/12	Bo Jackson	3	5	8	40
07/03	Pete Rose	3	5	8	25
07/10	Rick Rueschel	2	4	7	15
07/24	Gregg Jefferies	2	4	7	20
10/16	Rickey Henderson	3	5	8	30
10/30	Earthquake	1	3	6	—
1990					
03/12	Tony LaRussa	—	2	5	15
04/16	Ted Williams	2	4	7	225
05/07	Ken Griffey Jr.	5	8	15	50
05/28	Will Clark	—	2	5	25
06/04	Len Dykstra	—	2	5	20
07/09	Darryl Strawberry	—	2	5	25
07/23	Minor League Baseball	1	3	6	—
08/13	Autographs	1	3	6	—
08/20	Jose Canseco	1	3	6	20
10/01	Bobby Bonilla	1	3	6	20
10/22	Dennis Eckersley	1	3	6	20
10/29	Chris Sabo	2	4	7	20
1991					
03/04	Darryl Strawberry	—	2	5	20
04/15	N. Ryan: Baseball '91	3	5	8	45
05/13	Roger Clemens	4	7	7	20
05/27	M. Mantle/R. Maris	4	6	10	200
07/01	Orel Hershiser	—	2	5	20
07/29	Cal Ripken Jr.	5	10	15	50
09/30	Ramon Martinez	1	3	6	20
10/21	Kirby Puckett	3	5	8	25
10/28	Twins/Braves Series	2	4	7	20
11/04	Twins Win Series	3	5	8	—

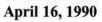

April 16, 1990

March 14, 1994

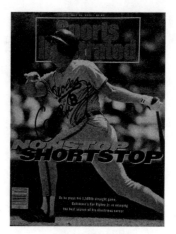

August 7, 1995

August 24, 1998

Date	Cover Subject	VG	EX	NM	Signed
1992					
03/16	Ryne Sandberg	4	7	12	20
04/06	K. Puckett: Baseball '92	2	4	7	25
04/27	Deion Sanders	1	3	6	25
05/04	Barry Bonds	3	5	8	25
05/18	Baseball '92	—	—	5	—
06/01	Mark McGwire	3	5	8	25
10/05	George Brett	1	3	6	15
10/19	Dave Winfield	1	3	6	30
10/26	R. Alomar/J. Smoltz	2	4	7	20
Fall Sp.	Willie Mays	2	4	7	50
11/02	Toronto Blue Jays	2	4	7	—
1993					
03/01	George Steinbrenner	—	2	5	25
03/22	Dwight Gooden	1	3	6	20
04/05	David Cone	1	3	6	20
05/03	Joe DiMaggio	4	6	10	225
05/24	Barry Bonds	1	3	6	25
07/19	B. Gibson/D. McLain	1	3	6	25
1994					
03/14	Michael Jordan (White Sox)	1	5	10	150
04/04	K. Griffey/M. Piazza	3	5	8	60
04/18	Mickey Mantle	4	6	10	200
05/23	Braves vs. Mets	1	3	6	—
06/06	Ken Griffey Jr.	—	6	10	60
07/18	Mussina/McDonald	1	3	6	20
08/08	Frank Thomas	2	4	7	45
08/15	Ed Mathews: 40th Anniv.	3	5	8	20
08/22	Baseball Strike	—	2	5	—
1995					
02/27	Gooden/Strawberry	1	3	6	20
03/20	Michael Jordan	4	7	12	50
03/27	Michael Jordan	4	7	12	50
05/01	Cal Ripken Jr.	3	5	8	60
07/10	Hideo Nomo	1	3	6	30
08/07	Cal Ripken Jr.	3	5	8	60
08/14	Greg Maddux	2	4	7	45
08/21	Mickey Mantle	4	6	10	—
09/11	Cal Ripken Jr.	3	5	8	60
10/02	Mo Vaughn	1	3	6	20
10/16	Ken Griffey Jr.	3	5	8	20
10/30	Bo Jackson	1	3	6	20

Date	Cover Subject	VG	EX	NM	Signed
11/07	Greg Maddux	1	3	6	15
12/18	Cal Ripken Jr.	3	5	8	50
1996					
03/18	Jay Buhner	1	3	6	20
04/01	Manny Ramirez	2	4	7	20
05/06	Albert Belle	—	2	5	20
05/20	Marge Schott	—	2	5	15
07/08	Alex Rodriguez	4	6	10	30
08/19	Al Simmons	1	3	6	—
10/14	Roberto Alomar	1	3	6	25
10/21	Derek Jeter	3	5	8	30
11/04	Joe Girardi	—	2	5	30
11/25	Ted Williams	2	4	7	200
	Special: Champion Yanks	4	6	10	—
1997					
03/31	Randy Johnson	—	2	5	30
05/05	Jackie Robinson	1	3	5	—
08/11	Pudge Rodriguez	1	3	6	30
11/03	Edgar Renteria	1	3	6	20
1998					
04/20	Pedro Martinez	1	3	6	20
05/25	Mike Piazza	1	3	6	20
06/20	Sammy Sosa	4	6	10	25
07/06	Alex Rodriguez	3	5	8	25
08/03	Mark McGwire	4	7	12	25
08/24	Babe Ruth	2	4	7	—
09/07	McGwire & Son	4	7	12	25
09/14	McGwire: "The Record"	4	7	12	50
09/14	*S.I.* Extra Edition.....				
	Mark McGwire "62!"	4	7	12	50
09/21	Sammy Sosa	4	6	10	30
10/05	Mark McGwire	4	7	12	50
10/07	Special Comm. Ed				
	McGwire/Sosa	5	10	15	75
10/12	Greg Vaughn	1	3	6	15
10/19	"Kill the Umps"	—	2	5	—
11/02	Yankees Celebration	2	4	7	—
1999					
03/01	Roger Clemens	2	4	6	15
03/29	Kevin Brown	2	4	6	15
05/17	Ken Griffey Jr.	2	4	6	20
06/21	Derek Jeter	2	4	6	20

September 14, 1998

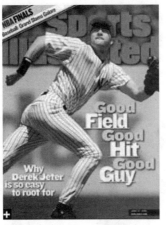
June 21, 1999

September 6, 1999

October 25, 1999

March 6, 2000

May 8, 2000

July 17, 2000

March 5, 2001

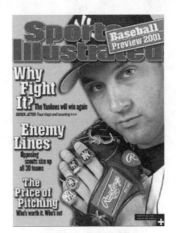
March 26, 2001

Date	Cover Subject	VG	EX	NM	Signed
07/12	Sandy Koufax	2	4	7	25
09/06	New York Mets Infield	2	4	7	40
10/25	Scott Brosius	2	4	6	15
2000					
02/21	Ken Griffey Jr.	2	4	6	20
03/06	McGwire/Sosa/Griffey	2	4	7	50
03/13	Frank Thomas	2	3	5	15
03/27	Baseball Preview	2	3	5	—
05/01	Vladimir Guerrero	2	3	5	15

Date	Cover Subject	VG	EX	NM	Signed
05/08	Randy Johnson	2	3	6	20
05/15	Ticket Prices	2	3	5	—
07/10	David Wells	2	4	6	15
07/17	Jason Giambi	2	4	6	20
08/21	Mike Piazza	2	3	5	20
10/16	Jim Edmonds	2	3	5	15
2001					
03/05	Nomar Garciaparra	2	3	5	15
03/26	Baseball Preview 2001	2	3	5	—

SPORTING NEWS

Baseball Guides

1962

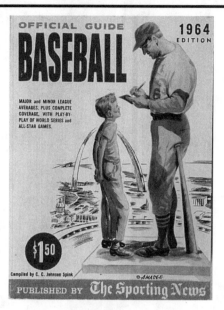

1964

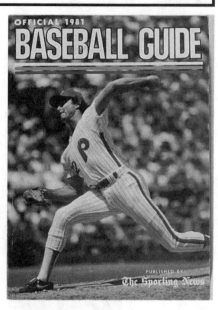

1981

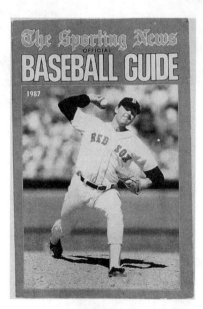

1987

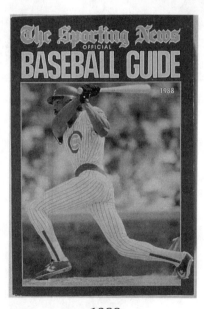

1988

These guides offer complete team recaps for the previous Major League season, plus statistics and lists of the award winners. From 1943-62 the guide was known as *The Sporting News Baseball Guide & Record Book*. It's been called *The Sporting News Official Baseball Guide* from 1963 to present.

1942 Baseball art	$165-$175
1943 Patriotic art	$60-$95
1944 B. Newsom/B. Dahlgren	$35-$40
1945 Marty Marion	$35-$45
1946 Hal Newhouser	$35-$45
1947 Harry Brecheen	$35-$45
1948 Ewell Blackwell	$50-$60

1949 Lou Boudreau	$50-$60
1950 P. Rizzuto/P.W. Reese	$40-$60
1951 Red Schoendienst	$40-$60
1952 Stan Musial	$35-$60
1953 Robin Roberts	$40-$60
1954 Casey Stengel	$40-$60
1955 Baseball action	$40-$60
1956 J. Coleman/B. Martin	$35-$60
1957 Mickey Mantle	$40-$60
1958 Ted Williams	$40-$60
1959 Baseballs	$40-$60
1960 Mullin Bum cartoon	$35-$60
1961 Trophy	$25-$35

1962 R. Maris/B. Ruth	$35-$50
1963 Mullin cartoon	$25-$50
1964 Stan Musial	$35-$50
1965 B. Robinson/K. Boyer	$35-$50
1966 W. Mays/S. Koufax	$40-$50
1967 F. Robinson/Koufax/Clemente	$40-$50
1968 Yastrzemski/Cepeda/Lonborg	$20-$35
1969 Rose/Gibson/McLain	$20-$35
1970 McCovey/Killebrew	$25-$35
1971 Bench/Gibson/Killebrew	$15-$25
1972 Jenkins/Blue/Torre	$10-$20
1973 Carlton/Bench/G. Perry	$10-$15
1974 Palmer/Jackson/Bonds	$12-$17
1975 Brock/Hunter	$15-$20
1976 Morgan/Seaver/Palmer	$15-$20
1977 Munson/Palmer	$10-$12
1978 Carew/Ryan/Carlton	$14-$15
1979 Guidry/Rice/Parker	$10-$15
1980 K. Hernandez/D. Baylor	$6-$10
1981 Steve Carlton	$8-$12
1982 Tom Seaver	$10-$15
1983 Robin Yount	$8-$12
1984 Cal Ripken Jr.	$10-$15
1985 Ryne Sandberg	$10-$15
1986 Willie McGee	$5-$7
1987 Roger Clemens	$10-$15
1988 Andre Dawson	$8-$10
1989 Jose Canseco	$8-$10
1990 Bret Saberhagen	$7-$10
1991 Bob Welch	$7-$10
1992 Will Clark	$7-$10
1993 Kirby Puckett	$5-$7
1994 Jack McDowell	$5-$7
1995 Ken Griffey Jr.	$7-$8
1996 Hideo Nomo	$5-$7
1997 John Smoltz	$5-$7
1998 Roger Clemens	$6-$7
1999 World Series Action	$5-$7
2000 Yankees Team Celebration	$5-$7
2001 Mike Piazza	$5-$7

Baseball Register

Lists statistics for active Major League players from the year before, for every player who appeared in at least one game. Minor League statistics and career accomplishments are also included.

1940 Ty Cobb	$75-$100
1941 Paul Derringer	$35-$45
1942 Joe DiMaggio	$40-$45
1943 Uncle Sam art	$30-$45
1944 Rube Waddell art	$30-$45
1945 Billy Southworth	$25-$45
1946 Baseball art	$35-$40
1947 Walter Johnson	$40-$45
1948 Baseball art	$35-$45
1949 Baseball art	$35-$45
1950 Joe DiMaggio	$35-$40
1951 Baseball art	$40-$75
1952 Baseball art	$25-$40
1953 Baseball art	$25-$40
1954 Baseball art	$22-$40
1955 Baseball art	$18-$40
1956 Baseball art	$18-$40
1957 Baseball art	$25-$40
1958 Baseball art	$15-$50
1959 Baseball art	$27-$40
1960 Baseball art	$20-$35
1961 Baseball art	$25-$35
1962 Baseball art	$25-$35
1963 Baseball art	$25-$35
1964 Yankee Stadium	$25-$35
1965 Ken Boyer	$25-$35
1966 Sandy Koufax	$25-$35
1967 Frank & Brooks Robinson	$25-$35
1968 Boston Red Sox	$20-$30
1969 Willie Horton	$20-$30

1944

1970

1976

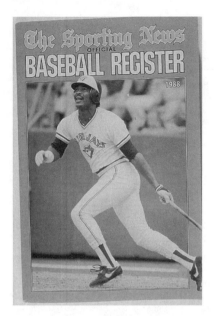

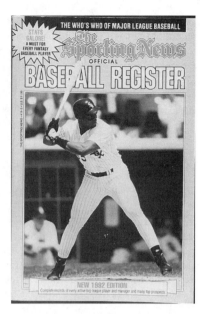

| 1988 | 1992 | 1997 |

1970 Tom Seaver..$20-$25	1986 Don Mattingly $10
1971 Willie Mays..$20-$25	1987 Mike Schmidt $10
1972 Joe Torre...$17-$25	1988 George Bell $10
1973 Wilbur Wood ....$15-$25	1989 Frank Viola $10
1974 Pete Rose...$20-$25	1990 Kevin Mitchell..$10
1975 Catfish Hunter ....$15-$20	1991 Barry Bonds $10
1976 Jim Palmer ....$15-$20	1992 Frank Thomas..$10
1977 Joe Morgan...$15-$20	1993 Gary Sheffield ....$5-$8
1978 Rod Carew ....$15-$20	1994 Lenny Dykstra...$5-$7
1979 Ron Guidry ....$15-$20	1995 Bret Saberhagen ....$5-$7
1980 Carl Yastrzemski ....$12-$15	1996 Greg Maddux ....$5-$7
1981 George Brett..$12-$15	1997 Ken Griffey Jr..$6-$8
1982 Fernando Valenzuela ....$12-$15	1998 Frank Thomas..$6-$8
1983 Bruce Sutter ....$10-$15	1999 Sammy Sosa..$6-$8
1984 John Denny ....$10-$15	2000 Pedro Martinez...$6-$8
1985 Willie Hernandez ....$10-$15	2001 Jason Giambi...$5-$7

STREET & SMITH

For years, *Street & Smith's Official Yearbook* was considered the most comprehensive baseball annual on the market. In today's market, a host of competitors in the annuals business have challenged *Street & Smith*, but the publication remains a leader. And among collectors, it's a familiar sight: It premiered in 1941, and in the decades that followed, it has produced a healthy supply of collectible magazines featuring as cover subjects baseball's brightest stars—from Bob Feller (on that first issue), Joe DiMaggio, Stan Musial, and Mickey Mantle to Hank Aaron, Tom Seaver, Nolan Ryan, and Mike Piazza, among other legends of the game.

Street & Smith was one of the first sports annual publishers to produce several different regional covers. Traditionally, its covers have featured a single player image, which makes the magazine perfect for autograph hounds. Although *Street & Smith* isn't as popular as *Sports Illustrated*, many baseball fans enjoy collecting the magazine because it serves as a superb "snapshot" of any given year in baseball since that '41 season. Of course, only the most devoted collector chases all the regional covers issued today.

The prices we list here are for magazines in Excellent condition through 1980 and in Near-Mint condition from 1980 to the present. The column of autograph prices below offers the price for an issue that has been signed by the "cover boy." For issues with multiple players on the cover, the autographed price reflects a signature from all players pictured. Adjust the price accordingly if you're missing some sigs. Issues don't have autograph prices if the player pictured has already passed away or if the cover featured an artist's rendition of the game but no particular player.

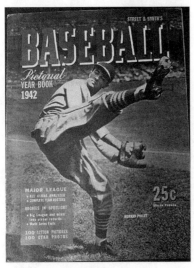

1942

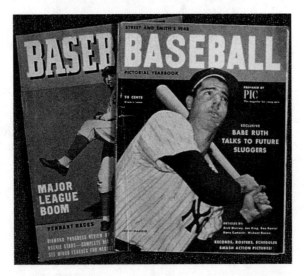

1948

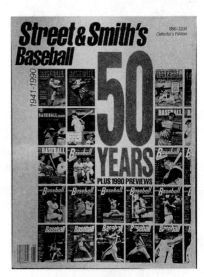

1990

Year	Player	Price range
1941	Bob Feller	$100-$250
1942	Howie Pollet	$75-$125
1943	New York Giants	$85-$120
1944	Joe McCarthy	$85-$100
1945	N.Y. Giants Spring Training	$95-$110
1946	Dick Fowler	$85-$100
1947	Leo Durocher	$75-$85
1948	Joe DiMaggio	$100-$150
1949	Lou Boudreau	$85-$100
1950	J. DiMaggio/T. Williams	$100-$125
1951	J. DiMaggio/R.Kiner	$100-$125
1952	Stan Musial	$85-$110
1953	Mickey Mantle	$100-$125
1954	Eddie Mathews	$85-$110
1955	Yogi Berra	$85-$100
1956	M. Mantle/D.Snider	$75-$125
1957	Mantle, D. Larsen, Y. Berra	$75-$125
1958	B. Buhl/L. Burdette	$50-$75
1959	Mantle/Spahn/Burdette	$50-$65
1960	L. Aparicio/N. Fox	$50-$60
1961	Dick Groat	$45-$55
1962	Roger Maris	$60-$70
1963	Tom Tresh	$35-$40
	Stan Musial	$40-$50
	Don Drysdale	$40-$50

Year	Player	Price range
1964	Mickey Mantle	$50-$60
	Warren Spahn	$40-$50
	Sandy Koufax	$45-$50
1965	Brooks Robinson	$40-$45
	Ken Boyer	$35-$40
	Dean Chance	$30-$40
1966	Ron Swoboda	$30-$35
	Rocky Colavito	$30-$45
	Sandy Koufax	$35-$40
1967	Andy Etchebarren	$25-$35
	Harmon Killebrew	$30-$35
	Juan Marichal	$25-$35
1968	Jim Lonborg	$25-$35
	Orlando Cepeda	$30-$35
	Jim McGlothlin	$25-$35
1969	B. Gibson/D. McLain	$30-$35
1970	Tom Seaver	$35-$45
	Harmon Killebrew	$25-$30
	Bill Singer	$20-$30
1971	Boog Powell	$20-$25
	Johnny Bench	$30-$35
	Gaylord Perry	$25-$30
1972	Roberto Clemente	$40-$45
	Joe Torre	$20-$25
	Vida Blue	$20-$25

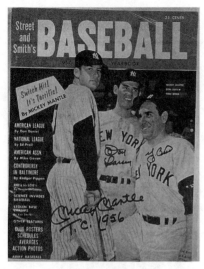

1957

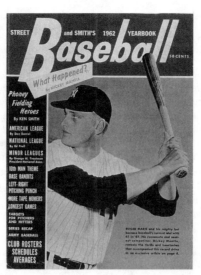

1962

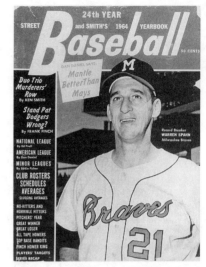

1964

Year	Player	Price range
1973	Steve Carlton	$20-$25
	Johnny Bench	$20-$25
	Reggie Jackson	$25-$35
1974	Hank Aaron	$20-$25
	Pete Rose	$20-$25
	Nolan Ryan	$35-$45
1975	Lou Brock	$15-$18
	Catfish Hunter	$15-$18
	Mike Marshall	$15
1976	Fred Lynn	$15
	Joe Morgan	$17-$20
	Davey Lopes	$15
1977	Thurman Munson	$17-$20
	Mark Fidrych	$15
	Randy Jones	$15
1978	Reggie Jackson	$20-$25
	Rod Carew	$17-$18
	Steve Garvey	$15-$18
1979	Ron Guidry	$15
	J.R. Richard	$15
	Burt Hooten	$15
1980	Mike Flanagan	$12
	Joe Niekro	$10
	Brian Downing	$10
1981	Mike Schmidt	$15-$20
	George Brett	$15-$20
	all other covers	$12-$15
1982	Nolan Ryan	$30-$45
	R. Gossage/P. Rose	$15-$20
	R. Fingers/T. Seaver	$17-$20
	Valenzuela/Martin	$15
	all other covers	$12.50-$15
1983	Steve Carlton	$12-$15
	Doug DeCinces	$10
	Robin Yount	$15-$17
	Dale Murphy	$12-$15
	all other covers	$12-$15
1984	Carlton Fisk	$12-$15
	Pedro Guerrero	$10
	McGregor/Dempsey	$10
	all other covers	$10
1985	Dwight Gooden	$12
	Detroit Tigers	$10

Year	Player	Price range
	Steve Garvey	$12
	all other covers	$10
1986	Nolan Ryan	$20-$25
	D. Gooden/D. Mattingly	$12
	Kansas City Royals	$10
	Orel Hershiser	$14
	all other covers	$10
1987	G. Carter/J. Orosco	$10-$12
	Jesse Barfield	$8
	Mike Scott	$8
	Joe Carter	$8
	Wally Joyner	$8
	Roger Clemens	$10-$12
	all other covers	$8-$12
1988	Don Mattingly	$12-$15
	Dale Murphy	$12
	Ozzie Smith	$12
	George Bell	$8
	Jeff Reardon	$8
	McGwire/Santiago	$10
	all other covers	$8-$12
1989	Jose Canseco	$10
	Mike Greenwell	$8
	Orel Hershiser	$10
	M. Grace/C. Sabo	$9
	Kevin McReynolds	$8
	Galarraga/McGriff	$9-$10
	all other covers	$7.50-$10
1990	Anniversary Issue	$7-$8
1991	Lou Piniella	$6
	Doug Drabek	$6
	Ryne Sandberg	$7
	Dave Justice	$6
	Nolan Ryan	$10
	Ramon Martinez	$6
	Kelly Gruber	$6
	Ken Griffey Jr.	$10
1992	Roberto Alomar	$7
	Roger Clemens	$8
	Bobby Bonilla	$7
	Terry Pendelton	$6
	L. Smith, J. Bagwell, R. Sierra, K. Puckett	$7

1978

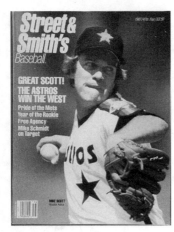

1987

1991

1999

Year	Player	Price range
	F. Thomas/C. Fielder/	
	B. Larkin/R. Sandberg	$8
	J. Abbott/W. Clark/	
	B. Butler/J. Canseco	$7
1993	Roger Clemens	$7
	Jim Abbott	$5
	Tom Glavine	$7
	Barry Larkin	$7
	Ryne Sandberg	$7
	Dennis Eckersley	$7
	Darryl Strawberry	$5
	Roberto Alomar	$7
1994	Aaron Sele	$5
	Lenny Dykstra	$5
	Carlos Baerga	$6
	Paul Molitor	$7
	Dave Justice	$7
	Barry Bonds	$8
	Mike Piazza	$10
	Frank Thomas	$8
1995	J. Key/B. Saberhagen	$5
	M. Alou/J. Carter	$5
	Greg Maddux	$5
	B. Larkin/K. Lofton	$5
	Frank Thomas	$6
	Matt Williams	$5
	Tony Gwynn	$5
	Gary Sheffield	$5
	Andres Galarraga	$5
	Jeff Bagwell	$5
	Cal Ripken Jr.	$6
	Len Dykstra	$5
	Mike Piazza	$6
	Cecil Fielder	$5
1996	Mo Vaughn	$5
	Paul O'Neill	$5
	Cal Ripken Jr.	$6
	Sammy Sosa	$6
	Kenny Lofton	$5
	Greg Maddux	$5

Year	Player	Price range
	Ken Griffey Jr.	$6
	Dante Bichette	$5
	Hideo Nomo	$5
1997	B. Gilkey/D. Jeter	$5
	Brady Anderson	$5
	B. Larkin/J. Thome	$5
	Chipper Jones	$5
	Gary Sheffield	$5
	J. Gonzalez/B. Jordan	$5
	A. Belle/S. Sosa	$5
	Ellis Burks	$5
	Alex Rodriguez	$5
	K. Caminiti/T. Hollandsworth	$5
	Roger Clemens/	
	Henry Rodriguez	$5
1998	Mark McGwire	$6
	Barry Bonds	$5
	S. Sosa/M. McGwire	$5
1999	Raul Mondesi	$5
	Scott Rolen	$5
	Mike Piazza	$5
	Pete Harnisch	$5
2000	Nomar Garciaparra/	
	Pedro Martinez	$5
	E. Alfonzo/D. Jeter	$5
	A. Jones/C. Jones	$5
	S. Sosa/K. Griffey Jr.	$5
	Mark McGwire	$5
	M. Tejada/J.f Kent/G. Sheffield $5	
2001	Nomar Garciaparra	$5
	Andruw Jones	$5
	Miguel Tejada	$5
	Sammy Sosa	$5
	Edgar Martinez	$5
	Chipper Jones	$5
	Jim Edmonds	$5
	Edgardo Alfonzo	$5
	Jeff Kent	$5
	Ken Griffey Jr.	$5
	Derek Jeter	$5

DELL SPORTS PUBLISHING

Baseball Annual

This magazine was issued from 1952-1968, skipping 1969, and then again from 1970-1978. It had several title modifications—*Dell Baseball Annual* (1953-1957); *Dell Sports Baseball* (1958-1959 and 1970-1978); *Dell Sports Magazine Baseball* (1960-1963); and *Dell Sports* March issue (1964-1968).

1952 Allie Reynolds...$30-$40
1953 Mickey Mantle...$45-$50
1954 Billy Martin..$35-$40
1955 Willie Mays ....$30-$40
1956 Pee Wee Reese ....$30-$35
1957 Mickey Mantle...$25-$35
1958 Lew Burdette...$25-$30
1959 Bob Turley ....$20-$30
1960 Gil Hodges/Nellie Fox ....$20-$25
1961 Richardson/Mazeroski/Ford $20
1962 Roger Maris $25
1963 Tom Tresh ....$15-$25
1964 Sandy Koufax...$20-$25
1965 Ken Boyer/Brooks Robinson ....$20-$25
1966 Sandy Koufax...$20-$25
1967 Frank Robinson...$15-$25
1968 Carl Yastrzemski ....$15-$25
1970 Tom Seaver/Jerry Koosman ....$15-$20
1971 Brooks Robinson...$10-$15
1972 Roberto Clemente/Vida Blue...........................$10-$15

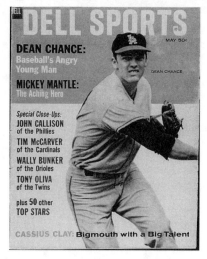

1965 Dell Sports Annual

1973 Richie Allen ....$10-$15
1974 Hank Aaron ....$10-$15
1975 Lou Brock ....$8-$12
1976 Fred Lynn ....$8-$10
1977 ....$10
1978 Reggie Jackson..$10-$15

Baseball Stars

This magazine was issued from 1949-1968, known as *Dell Sports Baseball Stars*. In 1958-1963 and from 1964-1968, it was the May issue of *Dell Sports*.

1949 Stan Musial ....$45-$50
1950 Ted Williams/Joe DiMaggio ....$45-$50
1951 Phil Rizzuto..$30-$35
1952 Bobby Thomson $30
1953 Robin Roberts ....$20-$30
1954 Ted Williams ....$30-$40
1955 Stan Musial ....$30-$35
1956 Mickey Mantle $35

1957 Don Larsen...$25-$30
1958 Ted Williams ....$30-$35
1959 Warren Spahn ....$15-$25
1960 Kuenn/Aaron/Wynn ....$15-$25
1961 Vern Law $20
1962 Cepeda/Gentile/Colavito ....$20-$25
1963 Maury Wills $20
1964 Sandy Koufax/Mickey Mantle $25
1965 Dean Chance $20
1966 Sandy Koufax..$25
1967 Sandy Koufax..$25
1968 Lou Brock ....$15-$20

Who's Who in the Big Leagues

This magazine was issued in 1953 and from 1955-1968. From 1964-1968 it was issued in the June or July issues of *Dell Sports*.

1953 Stan Musial ....$35-$45
1955 Yogi Berra..$40
1956 Roy Campanella...$25-$30
1957 Herb Score ....$20-$25
1958 Willie Mays $45
1959 Mickey Mantle..$45-$50

1960 Rocky Colavito ....$20-$25
1961 Chuck Estrada ....$20-$25
1962 Whitey Ford ....$20-$25
1963 Harmon Killebrew ....$20-$25
1964 Dick Stuart ....$15-$20
1965 Willie Mays ....$20-$25
1966 Tony Oliva ....$15-$20
1967 Boog Powell ....$15-$20
1968 Harmon Killebrew ....$15-$20

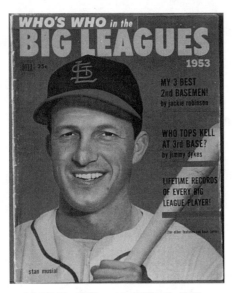

1953 Dell Sports Who's Who

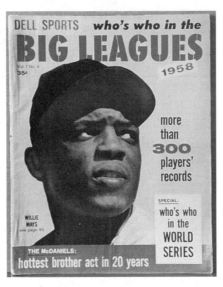

1958 Dell Sports Who's Who

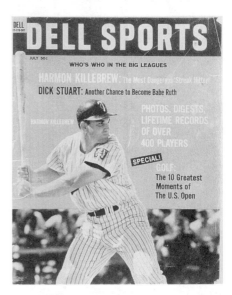

1968 Dell Sports Who's Who

Who's Who in the Baseball by Baseball Magazine

1912 Generic cover ....$1,000-$1,250	1930 Burleigh Grimes.................................$50-$125
1913-15 .... not issued	1931 Lefty Grove ....$50-$125
1916 Ty Cobb...$500-$1,000	1932 Al Simmons ....$50-$100
1917 Tris Speaker ....$400-$800	1933 Chuck Klein ....$50-$100
1918 George Sisler ....$300-$700	1934 Bill Terry ....$50-$100
1919 Grover Alexander......................................$400-$800	1935 Dizzy Dean ....$50-$100
1920 Babe Ruth ....$350-$700	1936 Hank Greenberg ....$50-$100
1921 Babe Ruth $700	1937 Lou Gehrig ....$75-$150
1922 Rogers Hornsby ....$250-$500	1938 Joe Medwick ....$40-$75
1923 George Sisler $300	1939 Jimmie Foxx ....$40-$75
1924 Walter Johnson...$150-$400	1940 Bucky Walters ....$30-$55
1925 Dizzy Vance $250	1941 Bob Feller ....$30-$60
1926 Max Carey...$100-$200	1942 Joe DiMaggio.....................................$35-$80
1927 Frankie Frisch ....$150-$300	1943 Ted Williams ....$50-$80
1928 Hack Wilson...$125-$250	1944 Stan Musial ....$25-$45
1929 Bob O'Farrell..$100-$175	1945 Hal Newhouser/Dizzy Trout ....$25-$30

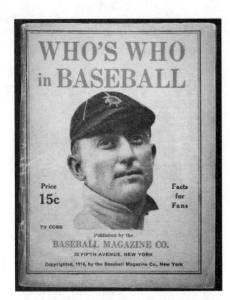

1916 Who's Who in Baseball

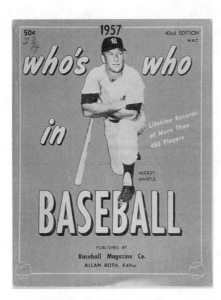

1957 Who's Who in Baseball

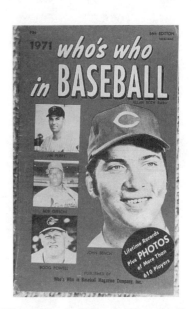

1971 Who's Who in Baseball

DELL SPORTS PUBLISHING

1946 Hal Newhouser	$25-$40	1969 Rose/Gibson/Yaz/McLain	$14-$18
1947 Eddie Dyer	$25-$40	1970 Seaver/Killebrew/McCovey	$12-$16
1948 Ralph Kiner/Johnny Mize	$25-$40	1971 Johnny Bench/Bob Gibson	$10-$15
1949 Lou Boudreau	$25-$40	1972 Vida Blue/Joe Torre	$10-$12
1950 Mel Parnell	$20-$30	1973 Steve Carlton/Dick Allen	$10-$15
1951 Jim Konstanty	$20-$30	1974 Ryan/Rose/Jackson	$12-$18
1952 Stan Musial	$20-$30	1975 Lou Brock/Steve Garvey	$10-$15
1953 Hank Sauer/Bobby Shantz	$20-$30	1976 Joe Morgan/Fred Lynn	$9-$12
1954 Al Rosen	$20-$25	1977 Joe Morgan/Thurman Munson	$10
1955 Al Dark	$20-$25	1978 Rod Carew/George Foster	$10
1956 Duke Snider	$20-$25	1979 Guidry/Parker/Rice	$9
1957 Mickey Mantle	$60-$80	1980 Willie Stargell/Keith Hernandez	$8
1958 Warren Spahn	$25-$35	1981 Mike Schmidt/George Brett	$8
1959 Bob Turley	$20-$30	1982 Fernando Valenzuela/Rollie Fingers	$8
1960 Don Drysdale	$25-$30	1983 Dale Murphy/Robin Yount	$8-$10
1961 Roger Maris	$20-$25	1984 Darryl Strawberry/Cal Ripken	$10
1962 Whitey Ford	$20-$25	1985 Ryne Sandberg	$8
1963 Don Drysdale	$25-$30	1986 Gooden/Mattingly/McGee	$8
1964 Sandy Koufax	$20-$25	1987 Mike Schmidt/Roger Clemens	$8
1965 Juan Marichal/Ken Boyer	$15-$20	1989 Kirk Gibson/Jose Canseco	$6-$8
1966 Willie Mays/Sandy Koufax	$18-$25	1990 Kevin Mitchell/Robin Yount	$8
1967 F. Robinson/Koufax/Clemente	$20-$25	1991 R. Sandberg/N. Ryan/C. Fielder	$6-$8
1968 Carl Yastrzemski	$18-$25	1992 to present	$5-$7 each

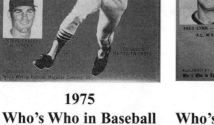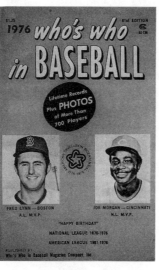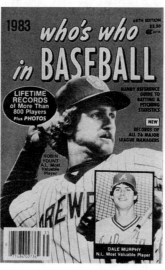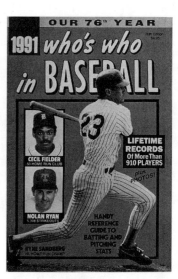

1975 Who's Who in Baseball **1976** Who's Who in Baseball **1983** Who's Who in Baseball **1991** Who's Who in Baseball

NEWS MAGAZINES

Life

May 1, 1939

September 1, 1941

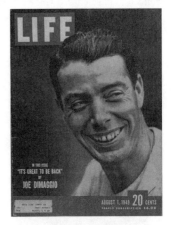

August 1, 1949

Is there a more American publication than *Life* magazine? For a long time (1936-72) *Life* was a weekly magazine that told the story—mainly through stunning photography—of life in the U.S.A. It changed its schedule (to monthly) through May 2000, when its parent company, Time Inc., announced that *Life* would publish only special issues, commemorative publications, and books. At the same time, *Life* has added an Internet presence (www.lifemag.com/Life) offering more of what it built its reputation on: vivid, lively photography.

So why is *Life* featured in *Tuff Stuff's Baseball Memorabilia Guide*? Because in its history, *Life* has occasionally featured baseball stars as cover subjects. Some of the best players in the game, in fact, have graced the cover of this magazine. The Joe DiMaggio issue from 1939 and the Mickey Mantle cover from 1956 were tremendously popular among autograph collectors. Ted Williams, Jackie Robinson, Roy Campanella, and Sandy Koufax are among the other legends that made *Life*'s cover. Because of *Life*'s large distribution numbers, issues of the magazine are more common than sports-only publications, so the values of *Life* on the secondary market are fairly low.

It's worth noting that there's one non-baseball Life cover among those we price: an April 1962 issue with Richard Burton on the cover. That issue featured baseball cards of Mantle and Roger Maris bound into the middle of the magazine. With those cards intact, it's a valuable piece.

May 8, 1950

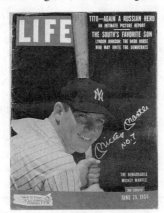

June 25, 1956

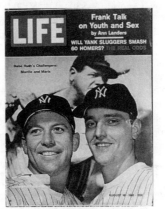

August 18, 1961

September 26, 1969

Year	Month	Cover	Price	Signed
1938	April	John Winsett	$20.00	$60.00
1939	May	Joe DiMaggio	$100.00	$300.00
1940	April	John Rucker	$15.00	$50.00
1941	September	Ted Williams	$100.00	$300.00
1946	April	Charles Barrett	$15.00	$60.00
1948	April	Dodger Rookies	$10.00	—
1949	August	Joe DiMaggio	$60.00	$250.00
1950	May	Jackie Robinson	$40.00	$350.00
1953	June	Roy Campanella	$40.00	$350.00
1953	September	Casey Stengel	$25.00	$350.00
1956	June	Mickey Mantle	$60.00	$250.00

Year	Month	Cover	Price	Signed
1957	October	Braves Motorcade	$20.00	—
1958	April	Willie Mays	$25.00	$75.00
1958	July	Roy Campanella	$40.00	$350.00
1961	August	Mickey Mantle/ Roger Maris	$50.00	$800.00
1962	April	Richard Burton (w/Mantle cards)	$125.00	—
1962	September	Don Drysdale	$20.00	$125.00
1963	August	Sandy Koufax	$25.00	$75.00
1965	July	Mickey Mantle	$40.00	$240.00
1967	September	Carl Yastrzemski	$25.00	$50.00
1969	September	Jerry Koosman	$15.00	$25.00

Newsweek

Newsweek has a rich history of baseball covers. Connie Mack, Babe Ruth, and Ted Williams are among the more popular cover subjects that collectors have chased since the magazine's first baseball cover in 1933. Despite a large circulation, issues of *Newsweek* can be tough to find because so many readers traditionally discarded the previous week's issue when the new one arrived.

Incidentally, the 1934 cover of Babe Ruth could have been signed by "The Bambino" (he died in 1948), making for a truly unique collectible.

| October 11, 1965 | June 16, 1975 | September 14, 1998 | March 22, 1999 |

Year	Month	Cover	Price	Signed
1933	April	Carl Hubbell	$60.00	$100.00
1933	September	Connie Mack	$40.00	$400.00
1933	September	Clark Griffith	$40.00	$400.00
1933	December	Judge Kenesaw Landis	$40.00	$700.00
1934	February	Babe Ruth	$75.00	$2,500.00
1934	March	Mel Ott	$40.00	$550.00
1934	October	Mickey Cochrane	$60.00	$400.00
1935	April	Judge Kenesaw Landis	$50.00	$700.00
1936	October	Carl Hubbell	$50.00	$100.00
1937	October	Carl Hubbell	$30.00	$80.00
1938	April	Rudy York	$20.00	—
1938	October	Gabby Hartnett/ Joe McCarthy	$30.00	$450.00
1939	June	Abner Doubleday	$50.00	—
1946	September	Ted Willliams	$50.00	$250.00
1947	June	Bob Feller	$40.00	$60.00
1947	October	Brooklyn World Series	$30.00	—

Year	Month	Cover	Price	Signed
1948	April	Joe McCarthy/ Bill Southworth	$30.00	$200.00
1949	August	Branch Rickey	$25.00	$750.00
1950	April	Mel Parnell	$15.00	$20.00
1952	March	Dodgers Spring Training	$12.00	—
1954	October	Bob Feller/Bob Lemon	$30.00	$70.00
1955	October	World Series	$20.00	—
1956	June	Mickey Mantle	$60.00	$260.00
1957	July	Stan Musial	$40.00	$70.00
1959	August	Casey Stengel	$25.00	$225.00
1961	August	Mickey Mantle/ Roger Maris	$20.00	$750.00
1965	April	The Astrodome	$10.00	—
1965	October	Sandy Koufax	$20.00	$60.00
1973	August	Hank Aaron/Babe Ruth	$20.00	$50.00
1975	June	Nolan Ryan	$20.00	$50.00

Time

More than a dozen issues of *Time* with baseball-related covers boast values of $100 or more. A George Sisler cover from 1925 (*Time*'s first nod to our national pastime) is tops among collectors, with a 1936 Joe DiMaggio right behind it.

With that recognizable red border, stately nameplate, and routinely striking cover images, *Time* has always been an attractive magazine. And, because readers have routinely tossed out old issues of *Time* as new ones arrived (just as *Newsweek* readers do), vintage issues are fairly scarce, hence the higher values.

Year	Month	Cover	Price	Signed
1925	March	George Sisler	$500.00	$800.00
1927	March	Connie Mack	$250.00	$650.00
1928	July	Rogers Hornsby	$200.00	$600.00
1929	July	Jimmie Foxx	$150.00	$450.00
1929	October	W. Wrigley Jr.	$100.00	$400.00
1930	August	W. Robinson	$125.00	$350.00
1932	March	Gabby Street	$100.00	$300.00
1932	September	Colonel Jacob Ruppert	$75.00	$350.00

Year	Month	Cover	Price	Signed
1934	July	Lefty Gomez	$75.00	$225.00
1935	April	Dizzy Dean	$75.00	$300.00
1935	October	Mickey Cochrane	$75.00	$400.00
1936	July	Joe DiMaggio	$450.00	$700.00
1936	October	Lou Gehrig/Carl Hubbell	$250.00	$1,500.00
1937	April	Bob Feller	$100.00	$125.00
1938	August	Happy Chandler	$65.00	$200.00
1945	July	Mel Ott	$50.00	$300.00

April 19, 1937

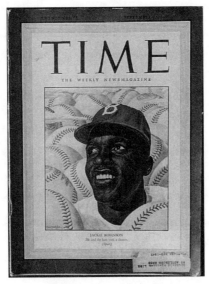

September 22, 1947

April 28, 1952

July 26, 1954

July 18, 1977

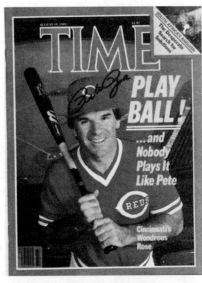

August 19, 1985

Year	Month	Cover	Price	Signed	Year	Month	Cover	Price	Signed
1947	April	Leo Durocher	$40.00	$250.00	1964	September	Hank Bauer	$30.00	$50.00
1947	September	Jackie Robinson	$85.00	$400.00	1966	June	Juan Marichal	$40.00	$60.00
1948	October	Joe DiMaggio	$200.00	$400.00	1967	October	Carl Yastrzemski	$25.00	$50.00
1949	September	Stan Musial	$150.00	$200.00	1968	September	Denny McLain	$30.00	$50.00
1950	April	Ted Williams	$200.00	$400.00	1969	September	New York Mets	$30.00	—
1951	October	Bert Lahr	$30.00	$75.00	1971	August	Vida Blue	$25.00	$40.00
1952	April	Eddie Stanky	$35.00	$75.00	1972	July	Johnny Bench	$25.00	$50.00
1953	July	Mickey Mantle	$125.00	$375.00	1974	June	Reggie Jackson	$30.00	$75.00
1954	July	Willie Mays	$200.00	$250.00	1975	August	Charles Finley	$15.00	$125.00
1955	June	Gwen Verdon	$25.00	$75.00	1976	April	Babe Ruth	$10.00	—
1955	July	Augusta Bush	$25.00	$75.00	1977	July	Rod Carew	$15.00	$40.00
1955	August	Roy Campanella	$65.00	$325.00	1981	May	Billy Martin	$15.00	$100.00
1955	October	Casey Stengel	$40.00	$250.00	1985	August	Pete Rose	$15.00	$30.00
1956	May	Robin Roberts	$40.00	$75.00	1986	April	Dwight Gooden	$5.00	$20.00
1957	July	Berdie Tebbetts	$25.00	$75.00	1989	July	Pete Rose	$5.00	$25.00
1958	April	Walter O'Malley	$25.00	$175.00	1992	January	Ted Turner	$5.00	$25.00
1959	August	Rocky Colavito	$30.00	$75.00	1994	August	Strike	$5.00	—
					1995	September	Cal Ripken Jr. (corner)	$5.00	$60.00

Collier's

Date	Cover	Price
11/14/42	Referee on cover, inside has Jim Thorpe story	$15
07/27/46	Joe DiMaggio	$60
07/19/47	Hal Newhouser	$30
06/21/52	Jackie Jensen family	$15

Look

Date	Cover	Price
10/10/39	Joe DiMaggio	$95
04/30/46	Hank Greenberg	$40
10/15/46	Ted Williams	$80
04/26/49	Joe DiMaggio Sr. & Jr.	$80
04/24/51	Phil Rizzuto	$45
05/22/51	J. DiMaggio/Others	$50
07/31/51	S. Musial/Others	$35
09/25/51	R. Campanella/Others	$25
10/09/51	T. Williams/Others	$45
03/11/52	Bob Feller	$25
04/22/52	Casey Stengel	$20
06/17/52	R. Hornsby/Others	$20
07/15/52	Al Rosen/Others	$20
08/12/52	M. Mantle/Others	$90
05/03/55	Willie Mays/Others	$30

Saturday Evening Post

Date	Cover	Price
05/11/63	Leo Durocher	$15

May 11, 1963

MEDIA GUIDES

In the 1920s, baseball journalists began using roster sheets and/or booklets—"publications" that were, essentially, the first media guides. Teams issued them to writers to provide player information for use in newspaper reports or radio broadcasts. These original guides provided little more than a complete roster and some player biographies and statistics, and were available only to ballpark insiders. It wasn't until much later that the guides were sold to the public.

Over the years, the original booklets evolved into 4x9-inch books with several hundred pages full of stats, including information about team executives, players, Minor League affiliates, prospects, team history, and spring training and post-season results. There's so much infor-mation that the guides have become popular with collectors and the general public.

Today, media guides are readily available to the public and give fans a chance to get to know their favorite team. Guides from the past 10 years can usually be found for the cover price or slightly more. Guides from the first half of the century—before the advent of mass production and distribution—are of course harder to find and more expensive. Collectors should also look out for media guides from a team's first season, from the first year in a new city or new ballpark, or with star players on the cover.

The list below includes original roster sheets, roster booklets, and media guides in Excellent condition.

Los Angeles Angels

1961 Player emerging from baseball	$75
1962 Baby with Angels logo	$75
1963 Angels logo, Rigney/Haney	$75
1964 Angels in action	$75
1965 Dean Chance/Cy Young Award	$40

California Angels

1966 Anaheim Stadium	$75
1967 League logos and Anaheim	$40
1968 Anaheim Stadium and logo	$30
1969 New-look A.L. West	$30
1970 Press box and player	$12-$15
1971 Four Angels in California	$12-$15
1972 Del Rice	$10-$12
1973 Nolan Ryan	$20
1974 Anaheim Stadium	$10
1975 Dick Williams	$10
1976 Angels baseball cards	$10
1977 Frank Tanana	$12
1978 Tanana/Ryan/Rudi	$15
1979 Anaheim Stadium	$10-$12
1980 Don Baylor	$7
1981 Angels equipment	$6
1982 Angels logo	$7
1983 Angels in action, R. Jackson	$8
1984 Angels celebrating, R. Jackson	$7
1985 25th Anniversary logo	$6
1986 DeCinces/Schofield/Downing	$6
1987 Donnie Moore	$6
1988 Wally Joyner/Brian Downing	$10
1989 All-Star Game logo	$10
1990 Angels stars, Joyner/Finley	$10
1991 Pitcher in action	$10
1992 Bryan Harvey	$10

1993 Old Angels uniforms	$10
1994 Tim Salmon	$7
1995 Anaheim Stadium	$5
1996 Anderson, Edmonds, Salmon	$5

Anaheim Angels

1997 New Anaheim Angels logo	$5
1998 Edison Int'l. Field of Anaheim	$5
1999 Gene Autry	$5
2000 Players in celebration of 40th season	$5
2001 Darin Erstad/Troy Glaus	$5

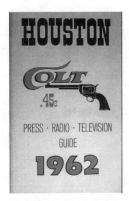

Houston Colt .45s

1962 .45s logo	$150
1963 .45s logo	$100
1964 Player art	$100

Houston Astros

1965 New logo	$75
1966 Catcher's mask	$75

1967 Astroturf $50
1968 Astrodome art...$40
1969 Baseball anniversary..$30
1970 Team roster...$20
1971 Locker room scene...$20
1972 Ball, bat as pool cue..$20
1973 Zodiac signs..$15
1974 Big orange..$10
1975 Equipment...$8-$10
1976 Bicentennial logo..$8-$10
1977 Player art..$6-$7
1978 Art..$6-$7
1979 Art..$6-$7
1980 Baseball scene..$6
1981 Team logo..$6
1982 20th Anniversary in Houston ....$5-$6
1983 Nolan Ryan...$5-$6
1984 Equipment..$5-$6
1985 Jersey..$4-$6
1986 Memorabilia...$10
1987 Mike Scott/Hal Lanier...$10
1988 Bill Doran...$10
1989 Glenn Davis...$10
1990 Team logo...$10
1991 Helmet, bat, ball...$10
1992 Craig Biggio/Pete Harnisch...$10
1993 Luis Gonzalez/Jeff Bagwell..$10
1994 Cap...$9
1995 Jeff Bagwell..$9
1996 Craig Biggio..$9
1997 Bell, Biggio, Bagwell...$9
1998 Biggio, Bagwell, Hampton celebrating...........................$10
1999 35 Great Years patch..$10
2000 Bagwell/Biggio at Enron Field $6
2001 Bagwell/Hidalgo...$6

Philadelphia Athletics

1928 Roster sheet $125
1929 Roster sheet $125
1930 Roster sheet (elephant)......................................$75-$100
1931 Roster sheet (elephant)......................................$75-$100
1932 Roster booklet (elephant)..$125
1933 Roster booklet (elephant)..$100
1934 Roster booklet (elephant)..$100
1935 Roster booklet (elephant)..$100
1936 Team mascot (elephant)......................................$55-$75
1937 Team mascot (elephant)......................................$50-$75
1938 Team mascot (elephant) ....$50-$75
1939 A's and elephant ....$50-$75
1940 Pennant and elephant ....$45-$75
1941 A's and baseball..$45-$75
1942...$40-$45
1943 Team mascot with flag..$40-$60
1944 Team mascot with flag..$40-$60
1945...$40-$60
1946 Connie Mack...$45-$60
1947...$35-$60
1948 Baseball and elephant ....$35-$60
1949..$60-$100
1950 Connie Mack..$60-$100
1951..$60-$100
1952 Team mascot (elephant) ....$60-$100
1953..$60-$100
1954 Eddie Joost..$60-$100

Kansas City Athletics

1955 K.C. Municipal Stadium $75
1956 Elephant logo $75

1957 Elephant logo $75
1958 Elephant logo $75
1959 A's baseball...$75
1960 Baseball and A's hat..$75
1961 K.C. Municipal Stadium $75
1962...$75
1963 Player sliding, baseball...$75
1964 1964 and A's logo...$75
1965 1965 and A's logo...$30
1966 1966 and A's logo...$30
1967 1967 and A's logo...$30

Oakland Athletics

1968 Oakland Stadium, ball, logo......................................$25
1969 Bando/Campaneris/Hunter.......................................$20
1970 Player at bat...$20
1971 A's logo and 1971 ....$15
1972 A's logo and 1972..$15
1973 A's logo and 1973..$15

1974 A's logo and 1974...$15
1975 A's logo and 1975...$15
1976 A's logo and 1976..$8-$10
1977 A's logo and 1977..$7-$10
1978 A's logo and 1978..$7-$10
1979 A's logo and 1979..$6-$10
1980 A's logo and 1980..$6
1981 Billy Ball baseball...$6-$7
1982 Running spikes..$6
1983 A's jukebox..$6
1984 Oakland sportswriters..$6
1985 Athletics memorabilia $6
1986 Dwayne Murphy...$10
1987 All-time Athletics team $10
1988 Batter hitting...$10
1989 Canseco/Eckersley/Weiss...$10

1990 World Series trophy..$10
1991 Team memorabilia...$10
1992 25th anniversary, A's greats.................................$10
1993 Dennis Eckersley..$10
1994 Players..$7
1995 A's logo..$7
1996 Baseballs spelling out "A's"..................................$7
1997 Mark McGwire swinging..$9
1998 Action at second base..$7
1999 Ben Grieve artwork..$7
2000 Century of A's Baseball logo................................$7
2001 Ja. Giambi, Chavez, Tejada.................................$7

Toronto Blue Jays

1977 Toronto Exhibition Stadium.................................$45
1978 Blue Jays pitcher...$15
1979 Blue Jays in action..$15
1980 Alfredo Griffin...$10
1981 Blue Jays equipment...$10
1982 Blue Jays in action, Bobby Cox...........................$10
1983 Blue Jays equipment and hat..............................$10
1984 Blue Jays in action..$10
1985 Blue Jays logo...$10
1986 Blue Jays 10th anniversary.................................$10
1987 Bell/Barfield/Fernandez......................................$10
1988 George Bell...$10
1989 Blue Jays stars, McGriff......................................$12
1990 Blue Jays, McGriff/Gruber...................................$12
1991 Dave Stieb..$10
1992 Roberto Alomar...$12
1993 World Series trophy...$10
1994 World Championship rings.....................................$7
1995 Blue Jays logo..$7
1996 Joe Carter/Blue Jays logo....................................$7
1997 Pat Henten holding Cy Young Award.....................$7

1998 Roger Clemens..$7
1999 Carlos Delgado..$7
2000 Shannon Stewart...$7
2001 25th Anniversary logo..$7

Boston Braves

1927 Roster sheet..$125
1928 Roster sheet..$100
1929 Roster sheet..$100
1930 Roster sheet..$100
1931 Roster booklet, Indian head................................$100
1932 Roster booklet, Indian head................................$100
1933 Roster booklet, Indian head................................$100
1934 Roster booklet, Indian head................................$100
1935 Roster booklet, Indian head................................$100
1936 Roster booklet...$75
1937 Roster booklet...$75
1938 Roster booklet, Bees Baseball.............................$75
1939 Roster booklet...$75
1940 Roster booklet, Casey Stengel............................$75
1941 Roster booklet, Casey Stengel............................$60
1942 Roster booklet, Indian head...........................$45-$60
1943 Roster booklet, Indian head...........................$40-$60
1944 Booklet/Bat, flag, airplane.............................$40-$60
1945 Roster booklet, Indian Head...........................$40-$60
1946 Booklet/Billy Southworth................................$40-$60
1947 Booklet/Billy Southworth..............................$60-$100
1948 Roster booklet/Bob Elliott.............................$60-$100
1949 Booklet/Billy Southworth..............................$50-$100
1950 Roster booklet/Braves Logo..........................$50-$100
1951 Roster booklet...$50-$100
1952 Booklet/Baseball/Indian head........................$50-$100

Milwaukee Braves

1953 State of Florida...$125
1954 Plaque honoring "the people of Wisconsin".........$125
1955..$125
1956..$125
1957..$100
1958..$100
1959..$100
1960 Pennant and Indian head....................................$75
1961 Pennant and Indian head....................................$75
1962 Pennant and Indian head....................................$75
1963 Pennant and Indian head....................................$75
1964 Aaron, Alou, Mathews, Spahn............................$75
1965 Felipe Alou, Bobby Bragan.................................$75

Atlanta Braves

1966 Player hitting..$40
1967 Felipe Alou...$40
1968 Hands gripping bat..$30
1969 Players in action...$30
1970 Hank Aaron..$20
1971 Foot sliding into base..$20
1972 Players in action..$12-$15
1973 Players in action..$12-$15
1974 Players in action...$10
1975 Knit baseballs...$10
1976 Dave Bristol..$8-$10
1977 Braves hat..$8-$10
1978 Atlanta-Fulton Co. Stadium................................$10
1979 Phil Niekro, All-Stars......................................$10-$12
1980 Baseball and stadium...$8
1981 Bob Horner/Dale Murphy..................................$6-$8

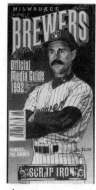

1982 Joe Torre $6
1983 Bedrosian/Murphy/Niekro/Torre......................$6-$7
1984 Braves logo..$6
1985 Dale Murphy/Bruce Sutter...........................$6-$7
1986 Bobby Cox/Chuck Tanner..............................$6
1987 Braves uniform..$5-$6
1988 Dale Murphy $8
1989 Gant/Glavine/Perry/Smith/Thomas $10
1990 25th anniversary logo....................................$10
1991 Ron Gant/Dave Justice...................................$10
1992 Greg Olson/John Smoltz.................................$10
1993 N.L. Champions...$10
1994 Maddux, McGriff, Glavine, Justice....................$7
1995 30th Season in Atlanta.....................................$7
1996 World Series Trophy...$7
1997 Maddux/Smoltz/Glavine jerseys $6
1998 Bobby Cox $5
1999 Hank Aaron, Home Run #715...........................$6
2000 ....$6
2001 World Series logos, Fulton County Stadium, Turner Field..........$6

1986 Brewers pitcher in action $6
1987 Ted Higuera $6
1988 Player running $6
1989 20th anniversary logo....................................$10
1990 Player running $10
1991 Team logo $10
1992 Phil Garner $10
1993 Pat Listach $10
1994 New uniforms/25th anniv. logo.........................$7
1995 Bob Uecker with huge bat.................................$8
1996 Outline of new Miller Park $6
1997 Jose Valentin $6
1998 Brewers logo $6
1999 County Stadium..$10
2000 Baseballs & Glove...$10
2001 Miller Park Roof $10

Seattle Pilots
1969 Pilots logo ....$100-$125
1970 Pilots logo...$100

Milwaukee Brewers
1971 Newspaper clipping ....$30-$40
1972 State of Wisconsin....................................$10
1973 Del Crandall/George Scott $12
1974 Team mascot..$10
1975 Team mascot ....$8-$10
1976 Baseball glove ....$8-$10
1977 Robin Yount..$15
1978 Larry Hisle $10
1979 George Bamberger $10
1980 Cooper/Lezcano/Thomas $6
1981 Cooper/Oglivie/Yount ....$6-$8
1982 Rollie Fingers.......................................$7-$8
1983 Kuenn/Vuckovich/Yount ....$6-$8
1984 County Stadium.......................................$6
1985 Brewers uniform #85................................$6

St. Louis Cardinals
1926 Roster sheet $200
1927 Roster sheet $125
1928 Roster sheet $125
1929 Roster sheet $100
1930 Logo and 1930, sheet $115
1931 Roster sheet $115
1932 Logo and 1932, booklet $125
1933 Logo and 1933, booklet $125
1934 Logo and 1934, booklet $115
1935 Logo and 1935, booklet $100
1936 Logo and 1936, booklet $75
1937 Logo and 1937, booklet ....$50-$75
1938 Roster booklet ....$50-$75
1939 Name and year, booklet ....$50-$75
1940 Logo and 1940, booklet ....$45-$75
1941 Logo and 1941, booklet ....$45-$60
1942 Logo, Statue of Liberty.......................$45-$65
1943 Flag and logo, booklet ....$40-$70
1944 Victory V and logo, booklet................$40-$70

1945 Logo and 1945, booklet	$40-$60
1946 Roster booklet	$35-$70
1947 Team logo, booklet	$35-$60
1948 Logo and baseball, booklet	$35-$60
1949 Logo and baseball, booklet	$30-$60
1950 Baseball and players	$150
1951 25th anniv. of World Champs	$125
1952 Team logo	$125
1953 It's the Cardinals	$125
1954 Team logo	$125
1955 Team logo	$125
1956 Team logo	$100
1957 Team logo	$100
1958 Team mascot	$75
1959 Stan Musial	$100
1960 Team mascot	$75
1961 Broglio/McDaniel/Sadecki/Simmons	$75
1962 Stan Musial	$75
1963 Player in action	$60
1964 Boyer/Groat/Javier/White	$60
1965 Team logo	$60
1966 Busch Stadium, team logo	$60
1967 Busch Stadium	$60
1968 World Series trophy	$45
1969 Bob Gibson	$45
1970 Joe Torre	$20
1971 Bob Gibson/Joe Torre	$25
1972 Red Schoendienst/Joe Torre	$20
1973 Brock, Gibson, Simmons, Torre	$20
1974 Cardinals uniform and hat	$10-$15
1975 Lou Brock and team logo	$10-$15
1976 Busch Stadium	$10-$15
1977 Lou Brock/Vern Rapp	$6-$7
1978 Cardinals equipment	$6-$7
1979 St. Louis Arch	$6
1980 Keith Hernandez	$6-$8
1981 Whitey Herzog	$6-$8
1982 Whitey Herzog	$7
1983 World Series celebration	$7
1984 Player running	$5-$6
1985 Busch Stadium, St. Louis Arch	$10
1986 Coleman/Herzog/McGee	$10
1987 Whitey Herzog, former managers	$10
1988 N.L. Champions celebrate	$10
1989 Action photos, Whitey Herzog	$10
1990 Team logo	$8
1991 Joe Torre	$10
1992 Todd Zeile	$10
1993 Team logo	$10
1994 Bats/home plate	$7
1995 Cardinals Mascot	$6
1996 Tony La Russa	$6
1997 Busch Stadium	$6
1998 Mark McGwire	$10
1999 Photo of McGwire hitting 62nd HR	$10
2000 Backs of Jerseys Stars, Hintten/Tatis/Lankford/Venis/Vina/ McGwire/Kyle/Veres	$10
2001 Edmonds/Kyle/Ankiel/Matheny/Renteria/Vina	$10

Chicago Cubs

1927 The year, booklet	$175
1928 The year, booklet	$150
1929 The year, booklet	$150
1930 The year, booklet	$100
1931 Rogers Hornsby, booklet	$100
1932 Rogers Hornsby, booklet	$125
1933 Team mascot, booklet	$100

1934 Team mascot, booklet	$100
1935 Team mascot, booklet	$115
1936 Team mascot, booklet	$75
1937 Team mascot throwing, booklet	$75
1938 Team mascot hitting, booklet	$85

1939 Mascot with pennant, booklet	$65
1940 Roster booklet	$65
1941 Jimmy Wilson, booklet	$65
1942 Roster booklet	$65
1943 Roster booklet	$65
1944 Roster booklet	$65
1945 Roster booklet	$75
1946 Charlie Grimm, booklet	$65
1947 Team mascot, booklet	$65
1948 Roster booklet	$100
1949 Roster booklet	$100
1950 Roster booklet	$100
1951 Roster booklet	$100
1952	$100
1953	$100
1954	$75
1955	$75
1956	$75
1957	$75
1958 Team logo	$75
1959 Team logo	$75
1960 Team logo	$50
1961 Team logo	$50
1962 Team logo	$50
1963 Team logo	$50
1964 Team logo	$50
1965 Team logo	$50
1966 Team logo	$30
1967 Team logo	$30
1968 Team logo	$30
1969 Team logo	$30
1970 Team logo	$15-$20
1971 Team logo	$15-$20
1972 Team logo	$15
1973 Team logo	$10-$15
1974 Team logo	$10
1975 Team logo	$8-$10
1976 Team logo	$8-$10
1977 Team logo	$7-$10
1978 Team logo	$7-$10
1979 Team logo	$6-$10
1980 Team logo	$6-$7
1981 Team logo	$6-$7
1982 Team logo	$5-$7
1983 Wrigley Field, celebration	$5-$7

1984 Autographed baseballs $6
1985 Frey/Green/Sandberg/Sutcliffe $10
1986 Cubs second baseman (Sandberg)......................$12
1987 Billy Williams $10
1988 Andre Dawson $10
1989 Wrigley Field $10
1990 Wrigley Field $10
1991 Ryne Sandberg $12
1992 Wrigley Field $10
1993 Wrigley Field $10
1994 Grace/Sandberg/Sosa...$7
1995 Collage $5
1996 Brian McRae $5
1997 Sammy Sosa $6
1998 Ball exploding through stat sheet........................$6
1999 Sammy Sosa, Kerry Wood $6
2000 Sosa/Banks/Grace/Wilson $6
2001 Nine Topps baseball cards used in promotion $6

Tampa Bay Devil Rays
1997 Montage of eight photos, including countdown billboard, construction of stadium................$10
1998 Inaugural season artwork, Ray chasing an AL ball $8
1999 Original art including Musial, Arrojo, Raymond.....................$8
2000 "Hitshow" with Canseco, Vaughn, McGriff, Castilla $7
2001 New uniforms, hats on the field........................$7

Arizona Diamondbacks
1998 Mountain background, jersey No. 98......................$8
1999 Interior of Bank One Ballpark $7
1999 Picture of Ballpark Opening night of new franchise $10
2000 Collage of 8 uniform personnel $10
2001 Randy Johnson $10

Brooklyn Dodgers
1927 Roster sheet $125
1928 Name and 1928, booklet $150
1929 Name and 1929, booklet $100
1930 Name and 1930, booklet $100
1931 Name and 1931, booklet $100
1932 Name and 1932, booklet $100
1933 Logo and 1933, booklet $100
1934 Logo and 1934, booklet $100
1935 Logo and 1935, booklet $100
1936 Logo and 1936, booklet ....$55-$75
1937 Logo and 1937, booklet ....$55-$75
1938 Logo and 1938, booklet ....$50-$75
1939 100th anniversary logo..............................$50-$75
1940 50th anniversary in Brooklyn ....$45-$75
1941 Team airplane $85
1942 V logo..$45-$65

1943 Roster booklet ....$40-$65
1944 Roster booklet ....$40-$65
1945 Roster booklet ....$40-$65
1946 Roster booklet ....$35-$65
1947 Roster booklet ....$35-$70
1948 Roster booklet ....$35-$65
1949 Roster booklet $150
1950 The Bum $125
1951 The Bum $125
1952 ....$125
1953 The Bum $125
1954 ....$125
1955 Walter Alston $125
1956 Walter Alston $100
1957 Walter Alston $100

Los Angeles Dodgers
1958 Walter Alston..$75
1959 L.A. Coliseum $75
1960 Dodger Stadium drawing $30
1961 Dodger Stadium $30
1962 Cartoon and airplane $50
1963 T. Davis/Drysdale/Koufax/Wills $50
1964 Players celebrating $40
1965 Championship pennants $40
1966 Mascot climbing mountains $40
1967 Mascot juggling crowns $40
1968 Walter Alston $30
1969 100th anniversary $30
1970 W. Davis/Osteen/Singer/Sizemore $30
1971 Dodgers in action $20
1972 Dodgers in action $20
1973 Dodgers in action $10
1974 Dodgers in action $10
1975 Steve Garvey $12
1976 Buckner/Cey/Garvey/Lopes/Sutton....................$14
1977 Tom Lasorda ....$9-$12
1978 Baker/Cey/Garvey/Smith ....$9-$14
1979 Dodger Stadium $6
1980 Team logo $6
1981 1980 highlights..$7
1982 World Series trophy, Howe/Yeager $8
1983 Sax/Guerrero/Valenzuela....................................$8
1984 Fireworks over Dodger Stadium......................$5-$6
1985 Bill Russell..$6-$7
1986 Player swinging bat ....$4-$6
1987 Dodger Stadium $10
1988 Baseballs $10
1989 World Series trophy..$10
1990 100th anniversary caps and pins $10
1991 Name and 1991 ....$10
1992 Team stadium $10

1993 Eric Karros $10
1994 Mike Piazza/Enz Karros $7
1995 Dodger Stadium $6
1996 Karros/Piazza/Mondesi/Nomo $6
1997 Rookies of the Year $6
1998 40th year anniversary logo $6
1999 Manager Davey Johnson, GM Kevin Malone $6
2000 Collection of Dodgers baseball memorabilia $6
2001 Baseball with ghosted small pictures $5

 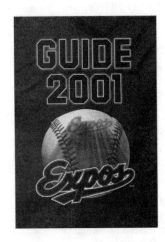

Montreal Expos

1969 Team logo $75
1970 Jarry Park..$40
1971 Baseball $20
1972 Action photos, Jarry Park $20
1973 Montreal photos ....$10-$12
1974 Gene Mauch $10
1975 Players in action.......................................$8-$10
1976 Players in action.......................................$8-$10
1977 Cash/McEnaney/Perez/D. Williams $6
1978 Gary Carter/Andre Dawson.............................$10
1979 Team logo $6
1980 Locker with uniform $6
1981 Pennant $6
1982 Players in action...$6
1983 Hands holding a bat...$6
1984 Team hats $6
1985 Olympic Stadium with dome $6
1986 Baseball and team logo $6
1987 Olympic Stadium with dome $10
1988 20th anniversary bat $10
1989 Hands giving hi-five $10
1990 Team logo $10
1991 Team logo $10
1992 Dennis Martinez $10
1993 25th anniversary $10
1994 New Expos logo $7
1995 Felipe Alou $5
1996 Autographed ball $5
1997 Baseball scene $5
1998 30 years anniversary logo...............................$6
1999 Vladimir Guerrero $6
2000 Vladimir Guerrero $6
2001 Expos logo $6

New York Giants

1927 Name and 1927, booklet $150
1928 Name and 1928, booklet $100
1929 Name and 1929, booklet $100

1930 Name and 1930, booklet $100
1931 Name and 1931, booklet $100
1932 Name and 1932, booklet $100
1933 Name and 1933, booklet $125
1934 Name and 1934, booklet ....$60-$100
1935 Name and 1935, booklet ....$60-$100
1936 Name and 1936......................................$55-$85
1937 Name and 1937......................................$55-$85
1938 Name and 1938......................................$50-$75
1939 New York World's Fair............................$50-$75
1940 Name and 1940......................................$45-$75
1941 Name and 1941......................................$45-$60
1942 Name and 1942......................................$45-$60
1943 Name and 1943......................................$40-$60
1944 Name and 1944......................................$40-$60
1945 Name and 1945......................................$40-$60
1946 Name and 1946...$150
1947 Baseball with 1947....................................$150
1948 Baseball with 1948....................................$150
1949 Baseball with 1949....................................$150
1950 Polo Grounds..$125
1951 Team logo...$125
1952 Leo Durocher, a Giant................................$125
1953 Polo Grounds..$125
1954 Team logo...$125
1955 The Giant...$125
1956 Team hat..$125
1957 Team hat..$125

San Francisco Giants

1958 Candlestick Park drawing............................$150
1959 Players in action $100
1960 Team logo..$80
1961 Giants in action $80
1962 Players in action $70
1963 Candlestick Park...$70
1964 Candlestick Park...$70
1965 Candlestick Park...$70
1966 Baseball and team logo $65
1967 Team logo..$45
1968 Team logo..$45
1969 Team logo..$45
1970 Willie Mays/Willie McCovey........................$25
1971 Year of the Fox $20
1972 Best in the West...$20
1973 Candlestick Park...$15
1974 Matthews/Bryant/Bonds..............................$15
1975 Team logo..$15
1976 Team logo...$8-$10

1977 Joe Altobelli/ John Montefusco ....$7-$10
1978 Players in action $6
1979 Blue/ Clark/ Giants management $6
1980 On deck circle with team logo $6
1981 Golden Gate Bridge...$6
1982 25th anniversary in city $6
1983 Team logo $6
1984 Team logo $6
1985 Team logo $6
1986 Team logo $6
1987 Team logo $6
1988 Team logo $10
1989 Team logo $10
1990 Team logo $10
1991 Team logo $10
1992 Team uniform $10
1993 Team logo $10
1994 Dusty Baker $7
1995 B. Bonds/M. Williams $6
1996 B. Bonds/M. Williams $6
1997 40 years in San Francisco $6
1998 J. T. Snow/B. Mueller/B. Johnson.........................$6
1999 "Tell it Goodbye (Candlestick)" $6
2001 Pacific Bell Park...
2001 ....

Cleveland Indians

1927 Roster sheet $125
1928 Roster sheet $100
1929 Roster sheet $100
1930 Roster sheet $100
1931 Roster sheet $100
1932 Roster booklet $100
1933 Roster booklet $100
1934 Roster booklet $100
1935 Roster booklet $100
1936 Chief and 1936, booklet.....................................$55-$75
1937 Chief and 1937, booklet.....................................$50-$75
1938 Chief and 1938, booklet.....................................$50-$75
1939 Chief and 1939, booklet.....................................$50-$75
1940 Chief and 1940, booklet.....................................$50-$75
1941 Chief and 1941, booklet.....................................$50-$60
1942 Lou Boudreau, booklet ....$55-$60
1943 Lou Boudreau, booklet ....$50-$60
1944 Mascot and year, booklet ....$40-$60
1945 Mascot and year, booklet ....$40-$60
1946 Lou Boudreau, booklet ....$45-$60
1947 Team mascot, booklet ....$35-$60
1948 Team mascot with media ....$100-$150
1949 Team mascot..$100

1950 Team mascot at bat $100
1951 Team mascot $100
1952 Garcia/Wynn/Lemon/Feller $100
1953 Press box and media...$100
1954 Al Rosen $100
1955 Mascot $100
1956 Mascot $100
1957 Kirby Farrell $75
1958 Bobby Bragan/Frank Lane $75
1959 Rocky Colavito $75
1960 Tito Francona $75
1961 Jim Perry $75
1962 Team mascot $75
1963 Team uniform #20 ....$75
1964 Team mascot $75
1965 Team mascot $35
1966 Baseball with feather...$35
1967 Cleveland Stadium $30
1968 Autographed baseball $30
1969 100th anniversary, mascot $30
1970 Team mascot $20
1971 Team hat, feather $20
1972 Players in action $20
1973 Team logo $10
1974 Team logo $10
1975 Frank Robinson ....$8-$10
1976 Baseball with feather...$8-$10
1977 Player hitting ....$6-$7
1978 Baseball, logo, glove ....$6-$7
1979 Team logo ....$6-$7
1980 Fireworks over stadium ....$6-$7
1981 Team logo ....$6-$7
1982 Cleveland Stadium ....$5-$7
1983 Team logo ....$5-$7
1984 Team memorabilia...$5-$6
1985 Bert Blyleven/Andre Thornton...............................$7
1986 Past team uniforms..$4-$6
1987 Joe Carter $7
1988 Indians uniform #88 ....$6
1989 Candiotti/Farrell/Jones/Swindell $10
1990 90 Years of Cleveland baseball $10
1991 Jacoby/Jones/Alomar $10
1992 60 years at Cleveland Stadium...............................$10
1993 Memorabilia collage $10
1994 A. Belle/C. Baerga/K. Lofton $7
1995 Jacobs Field at night..$7
1996 Player celebration $7
1997 Cleveland city outline $7
1998 Player celebration collage $7
1999 M. Hargrove/Thome/others $6
2000 ....
2001 Player collage, 100th anniversary logo ....

Seattle Mariners

1977 Kingdome $30
1978 Baseball with team logo..$10
1979 Kingdome $10
1980 Mariners equipment $6
1981 Maury Wills $7
1982 Team logo $6
1983 Gaylord Perry, team equipment $8
1984 Team logo $6
1985 Beattie/Davis/Henderson/Langston.........................$7
1986 Team memorabilia...$6
1987 Team logo $6
1988 Team bat $10
1989 Kingdome, baseball, logo $10
1990 A.L. baseballs, team logo $10
1991 Highlights..$10

1992 Team logo $10
1993 Team logo/Kingdome $10
1994 Mariners cap...$7
1995 Mariners logo $5
1996 A.L. West Championship $6
1997 Griffey Jr./A. Rodriguiz $7
1998 Griffey Jr. holding trophy......................................$7
1999 Logo, grass background $7
2000 Game at Safeco Field $6
2001 ALCS game, plus 2001 All-Star logo $5

Florida Marlins

1993 Logo, player $20
1994 Mascot $10
1995 Team logo $15
1996 Mascot $10
1997 Logo $10
1998 Players celebrating, trophy $5
1999 Alex Fernandez/others...$5
2000 Preston Wilson..$5
2001 Team picture $5

New York Mets

1962 First year..$500
1963 Mr. Met/Stadium $150
1964 Shea Stadium..$100
1965 Mr. Met $100
1966 Mass media...$100
1967 Donald Grant/George Weiss...................................$100
1968 Gil Hodges, crowd shot..$100
1969 Gil Hodges $100
1970 World Series ticket, action photos........................$75
1971 Scoreboard...$50

1972 Tom Seaver..$50
1973 Yogi Berra and pennant $50
1974 N.L. Champs flag $50
1975 Mets general managers..$20
1976 Joe Frazier $20
1977 Mets uniform #77 ....$20
1978 Team logo, hat, glove $20
1979 Willie Mays $15
1980 Team logo $15
1981 New York City, baseball $15
1982 George Bamberger locker $15
1983 Tom Seaver, others $15
1984 Davey Johnson $15
1985 Tom Seaver, Mets stars..$15
1986 R. Craig/Gooden/Shea Stadium $15
1987 World Series ring..$15
1988 Shea 25th anniversary $15
1989 Frank Cashen/Howard Johnson.................................$15
1990 Howard Johnson $15
1991 Bud Harrelson $15
1992 Bonilla/Murray/Saberhagen/Torborg $15
1993 Team uniform No. 93 ....$15
1994 Dwight Gooden $7
1995 Shea Stadium..$7
1996 Organization of the Year Trophy $6
1997 Hundley/Franco/Gilkey $6
1998 Valentine/Ordonez/others $6
1999 Piazza/Henderson/Ventura/others...............................$6
2000 Celebratory photo of 1999 Playoffs $5
2001 National League Championship Trophy, four pennants $5

St. Louis Browns

1927 Name and 1927, booklet $150
1928 Name and 1928, booklet $125

1929 Roster booklet $125
1930 Roster booklet $125
1931 Sportsmans Park, booklet..$125
1932 Sportsmans Park, booklet..$70-$100
1933 Sportsmans Park, booklet..$70-$100
1934 Roster booklet ....$65-$100
1935 Roster booklet ....$65-$100
1936 Rogers Hornsby, booklet..$75-$80
1937 Team logo, booklet ....$60-$75
1938 Roster booklet ....$60-$75
1939 Roster booklet ....$60-$75
1940 Fred Haney, booklet, ...$55-$75
1941 Statue and 1941, booklet..$55-$60
1942 Roster booklet ....$55-$60
1943 Team logo, booklet..$50-$60
1944 Roster booklet ....$70-$150
1945 ....$150
1946 Team logo, booklet..$150
1947 Baseball, logo $150
1948 Meet the Brownies $150
1949 ....$150
1950 Team logo $150
1951 Team logo $150
1952 Team mascot $150
1953 Team mascot $150

1980 Players celebrating $6
1981 Orioles locker room..$6
1982 Team logo and mascot..$6
1983 Frank and Brooks Robinson..$8
1984 World Series celebration $6
1985 Bumbry/Palmer/Singleton $7
1986 Eddie Murray/Cal Ripken $8
1987 Cal Ripken Sr. $6
1988 Team logo $10
1989 New team uniforms $10
1990 1989 highlights $10
1991 Team stadium drawing $10
1992 Team stadium $10
1993 Team stadium $10
1994 150 Years of Baseball $7
1995 Cal Ripken Jr. $20
1996 Davey Johnson $5
1997 Cartoon $5
1998 R. Miller/E. Weaver/others $5
1999 Camden Yards $10
2000 Collage of Players $10
2001 A Trophy..$10

Baltimore Orioles

1954 Team mascot..$125
1955 Team mascot..$100
1956 Team mascot..$100
1957 Team mascot..$100
1958 Team mascot..$100
1959 Team mascot..$100
1960 Team mascot..$75
1961 Team mascot..$75
1962 Team mascot..$75
1963 Team mascot..$75
1964 Team mascot..$75
1965 Hank Bauer..$40
1966 Team mascot..$40
1967 Dave McNally/Brooks Robinson $50
1968 Memorial Stadium...$40
1969 View from press box...$30
1970 Orioles dugout..$25
1971 World Series celebration $20
1972 Team mascot with pennants $15
1973 Player face drawing..$10
1974 Orioles award winners..$10
1975 Players in action...$10
1976 Team logo $10
1977 Palmer/L. May/Belanger $15
1978 Earl Weaver ....$10-$12
1979 25th anniversary hats..$10

San Diego Padres

1969 Preston Gomez, stadium..$75
1970 Jack Murphy Stadium $15
1971 Jack Murphy Stadium $15
1972 Padres vs. Dodgers, July 3, 1971 ....$15
1973 Nate Colbert...$15
1974 Player hitting...$10
1975 Players in action..$8
1976 Randy Jones $8
1977 Randy Jones/Butch Metzger $7
1978 Batter, pitcher in action..$6
1979 Roger Craig/Padres stars..$6
1980 Jerry Coleman/Dave Winfield $8
1981 Frank Howard, stadium..$7
1982 Dick Williams..$6
1983 Padres memorabilia..$6
1984 Team logo, Ray Kroc memorabilia.......................................$10
1985 N.L. Champions trophy $10
1986 Team logo $10
1987 Larry Bowa...$10
1988 Tony Gwynn/Benito Santiago $10
1989 Team logo, stadium $10
1990 Players in action...$10
1991 Padres uniform, ball, glove $10
1992 All-Star Game...$10
1993 Gary Sheffield/Fred McGriff...$10

1994 San Diego $7
1995 Gwynn/Caminiti/Finley $7
1996 Tony Gwynn $7
1997 Pitchers $7
1998 Padre players in the community............$10

Philadelphia Phillies

1927 Roster sheet $125
1928 Roster sheet $100
1929 Roster sheet $100
1930 Team logo, sheet ....$75-$100
1931 Roster sheet ....$70-$100
1932 Team logo, booklet.....................$65-$125
1933 Phillies golden anniversary ....$60-$100
1934 Team logo, booklet......................$60-$100
1935 Team logo, booklet......................$55-$100
1936 Team logo, booklet........................$55-$75
1937 Team logo, booklet........................$50-$75
1938 Roster booklet ....$50-$75
1939 Roster booklet ....$50-$75
1940 Roster booklet ....$45-$75
1941 Player hitting, booklet....................$45-$60
1942 Soldier with crossed bats ....$45-$60
1943 Roster booklet ....$40-$60
1944 Roster booklet ....$40-$60
1945 Roster booklet ....$40-$60
1946 Logo, Shibe Park, booklet ....$35-$60
1947 Logo, Shibe Park, booklet ....$35-$60
1948 Logo, Shibe Park, booklet ....$30-$70
1949 Roster booklet ....$30-$70
1950 ....$150
1951 ....$30-$50
1952 Shibe Park ....$25-$50
1953 Player hitting ....$25-$50
1954 Robin Roberts ....$35-$50
1955 Get Set To Go In '55....................$20-$50
1956 Crowd photo...............................$20-$40
1957 Crowd photo...............................$20-$40
1958 Crowd photo...............................$20-$40
1959 Team logo..................................$20-$40
1960 Team logo..................................$20-$40
1961 Team logo..................................$15-$40
1962...$15-$20
1963...$15-$20
1964 Team hat $150
1965 Team hat $100
1966 Team hat $100
1967 Team hat $75
1968 Team hat $75
1969 Team hat $50
1970 Phillies P...$50

1971 Frank Luchessi $35
1972 Team logo.......................................$35
1973 Steve Carlton/Cy Young Award $25
1974 Players in action.............................$20
1975 Players in action.............................$20
1976 Players in action.............................$15
1977 Division champs pennant $15
1978 Fireworks over stadium $15
1979 Team logo.......................................$15
1980 Team logo, baseball........................$10
1981 World Series trophy $10
1982 Basket of baseballs $10
1983 100th anniversary logo $10
1984 N.L. Championship trophy...............$10
1985 Hands holding bat $10
1986 Home plate with team logo $10
1987 Mike Schmidt, trophies $15
1988 Steve Bedrosian/Mike Schmidt $15
1989 Nick Leyva/Lee Thomas $15
1990 Ashburn/Carlton/Roberts/Schmidt ...$15
1991 Catchers mask, baseball $15
1992 Memorabilia collage........................$15
1993 Phillies league leaders $15
1994 Jim Fregosi $7
1995 Silver anniversary of stadium logo ...$6
1996 All-Star Game logo $6
1997 Terry Francona $5
1998 Scott Rolen/Curt Schilling $5
1999 Curt Schilling/Scott Rolen—"Leather and Ace" ...$5
2000 Lieberthal/Glanville/Abreu $5
2001 Larry Bowa.......................................$5

Pittsburgh Pirates

1927 Roster sheet $175
1928 Roster sheet $100
1929 Roster sheet $125
1930 Pirate and 1930, sheet $100
1931 Pirate and 1931, sheet $100
1932 Pirate and 1932, booklet..................$125
1933 Pirate and 1933, booklet ....$60-$100
1934 Pirate and 1934, booklet ....$60-$100
1935 Pirate and 1935, booklet ....$55-$100
1936 Pirate and 1936 ....$55-$75
1937 Pirate and 1937 ....$50-$75
1938 Pirate and 1938 ....$50-$75
1939 100th anniversary, Pirate.............$50-$75
1940 Pirate and 1940 ....$45-$75
1941 Pirate and 1941 ....$45-$60
1942 Pirate, Remember Pearl Harbor....$45-$60
1943 Pirate, Buy War Bonds, Stamps....$40-$60
1944 Pirate and 1944 ....$40-$60

1945 Pirate and 1945 ....$40-$60
1946 Pirate, Buy Victory Bonds ....$35-$60
1947 Billy Herman..$40-$60
1948 William Meyer ....$40-$60
1949 40th anniversary ....$30-$60
1950 Baseballs ....$30-$50
1951 Logo and 1951..$125
1952 Baseball and 1952 ....$125
1953 Fred Haney $125
1954 Honus Wagner statue...$125
1955 Baseball diamond and 1955 ....$125
1956 Pirate cartoon $125
1957 Pirate cartoon $100
1958 Danny Murtaugh $100
1959 Pirate cartoon $100
1960 Pirate cartoon $75
1961 Pirate cartoon $75
1962 Pitcher..$75
1963 Baseballs...$75
1964 Logo and 1964...$60
1965 Harry Walker $60
1966 Pirate cartoon $60
1967 Pirate cartoon $45
1968 Larry Shepard and coaches $45
1969 100th anniversary, Forbes..................................$30
1970 Three River Stadium model $30
1971 Danny Murtaugh $25
1972 World Series celebration $25
1973 Clemente memorial $35
1974 Three Rivers Stadium $10
1975 Championship Stars, logo $10
1976 Rennie Stennett $10
1977 Players in action $6
1978 Three Pirates..$6
1979 Team uniform $10
1980 Willie Stargell...$9
1981 Team logo $6
1982 Team hat $6
1983 Team logo $6
1984 Bill Madlock..$6
1985 Tony Pena $6
1986 Three Rivers Stadium $10
1987 100th anniversary logo $10
1988 Pirates memorabilia...$10
1989 Bonilla/LaValliere/Van Slyke $10
1990 Bonds/Bonilla/Drabek/Van Slyke $10
1991 N.L. Champions, logo $10
1992 Doug Drabek/Don Slaught..................................$10
1993 Jim Leyland $10
1994 Three Rivers Stadium $7
1995 Artwork of pirates $5
1996 Cap $5
1997 Uniforms/caps/logos... $5
1998 Previous Pirates media guides........................... $5
1999 Three bats $10
2000 30 Years of Three Rivers Stadium.....................$10
2001 PNC Park & Lloyd McClendon $10

Texas Rangers

1972 Team logo...$30
1973 Burke/Herzog/Short...$20
1974 Billy Martin $15
1975 Hargrove/Jenkins/Martin $15
1976 Toby Harrah, old-timers $6
1977 Team equipment, hat $6
1978 Billy Hunter..$6
1979 Baseball and 1979 ....$6
1980 Rangers catcher $6
1981 Fireworks over scoreboard $6
1982 Baseball with logo..$6

1983 Baseball glove $6
1984 Buddy Bell, others..$6
1985 Team hat $6
1986 Arlington Stadium $6
1987 Bobby Valentine $10
1988 Team logo and baseball $10
1989 Rangers uniforms $10
1990 Home plate with team logo $10
1991 Nolan Ryan...$15
1992 Julio Franco $10
1993 Arlington Stadium $10
1994 Jersey $7
1995 Ballpark at Arlington $5
1996 Ballpark at Arlington $5
1997 Juan Gonzalez $6
1998 Ivan Rodriguez $6
1999 Ivan Rodriguez $10
2000 Ivan Rodriguez $10
2001 I. Rodriguez, A. Rodriguez, R. Palmeiro..............$10

Cincinnati Reds

1927 Roster sheet $125
1928 Roster sheet $100
1929 Roster sheet $100
1930 Team logo, sheet ....$65-$100
1931 Team logo, sheet ....$60-$100
1932 Team logo, booklet...$60-$100
1933 Roster booklet...$60-$100
1934 Cincinnati Reds, booklet....................................$55-$100
1935 Team logo, booklet...$55-$100
1936 Team logo, booklet...$55-$75
1937 Team logo, booklet...$50-$75
1938 Bill McKechnie, booklet......................................$50-$75
1939 1869 Reds ....$50-$85
1940 Team logo...$45-$85
1941 Baseball, champions pennant $125

1942 Team logo, eagle $125
1943 Team logo, eagle $125
1944 Team logo, hitter $125
1945 Baseball, eagle $125
1946 Catcher and batter $125
1947 Baseball and eagle $125
1948 Team logo, batter $125
1949 City, team logo $125
1950 Cartoon sportswriter $100
1951 75th anniversary logo $100
1952 Team logo, eagle $100
1953 ....$100
1954 ....$100
1955 Team mascot $100
1956 Birdie Tebbetts $100
1957 Schedule $100
1958 Team mascot batting $100
1959 Mayo Smith $100
1960 Fred Hutchinson $75
1961 Fred Hutchinson, Bill DeWitt $75
1962 Team mascot $75
1963 Team mascot $75
1964 Team mascot $75
1965 Team mascot $75
1966 Team mascot $75
1967 ....$75
1968 ....$40
1969 100th anniversary logo $40
1970 N.L. hats $30
1971 ....$30
1972 Baseball field $20
1973 Sparky Anderson $20
1974 Jack Billingham/Don Gullett...........................$15
1975 Johnny Bench $15
1976 Joe Morgan, MVP Trophy...............................$20
1977 Johnny Bench $20
1978 George Foster $15
1979 John McNamara $15
1980 Riverfront Stadium $8
1981 Players in action $8
1982 Team uniform $8
1983 Russ Nixon $8
1984 Team logo $8
1985 Riverfront Stadium $8
1986 Pete Rose $10
1987 N.L. logos $8
1988 All-Star Game logo $8
1989 Autographed bats $8
1990 Lou Piniella $10
1991 World Series trophy $10
1992 Equipment $10
1993 Reds locker $10
1994 Team logo $7
1995 Riverfront Stadium $5
1996 Knight/Morris/Boone $5
1997 Larkin/Sanders/Boone $5
1998 Reds logo on uniform, cap $5
1999 "Cincinnati" on uniform.................................$10
2000 Player Collage $10
2001 Jerseys $10

Boston Red Sox

1927 Roster sheet $125
1928 Roster sheet $100
1929 Roster sheet $100

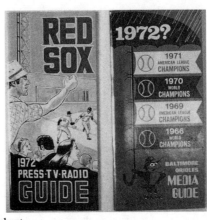

1930 Roster sheet $100
1931 Roster sheet $100
1932 Roster sheet $100
1933 Roster sheet $100
1934 Roster booklet $150
1935 Roster booklet $100
1936 Roster booklet $75
1937 Roster booklet $75
1938 Roster booklet $75
1939 Jimmie Foxx/ booklet ....$65-$70
1940 Team logo, booklet....................................$45-$65
1941 Fenway Park, booklet ....$45-$60
1942 Baseball bats &1942/booklet ....$45-$60
1943 Tufts College batting cage ....$40-$60
1944 Roster booklet ....$40-$60
1945 Name and 1945/booklet ....$40-$60
1946 Player in action ....$35-$70
1947 World Series pennant/booklet ....$35-$60
1948 Joe McCarthy, booklet.................................$45-$60
1949 Roster booklet ....$30-$60
1950 Team mascot ....$30-$50
1951 Old-timer, current player $125
1952 Fenway Park $125
1953 Team logo $125
1954 Team logo $125
1955 Team logo $125
1956 Name and 1956 ....$125
1957 Player in action...$125
1958 Red Sox media $100
1959 Player in mirror $100
1960 Player on horse $100
1961 Baseball glove, ball $100
1962 Carl Yastrzemski, others $125
1963 Johnny Pesky $75
1964 Team logo $75
1965 Team logo $75
1966 Showerhead, team logo $40
1967 Team logo $40
1968 A.L. Championship pennant $40
1969 100th anniversary $40
1970 Fenway Park $20
1971 Red Sox stars $20
1972 Cheering fan $10
1973 Player in action $10
1974 Darrell Johnson $10
1975 Fenway Park $10
1976 A.L. Championship pennant $10
1977 Don Zimmer $10
1978 Carl Yastrzemski/Jim Rice $15
1979 Jim Rice $12
1980 Carl Yastrzemski..$12
1981 Ralph Houk $6

1982 Ralph Houk and players.............................$6
1983 Dwight Evans/Bob Stanley $6
1984 Wade Boggs/Jim Rice $8
1985 Tony Armas $6
1986 Boggs/Boyd/Buckner/Gedman...................$8
1987 Roger Clemens/John McNamara $6
1988 Dwight Evans/Roger Clemens $8
1989 Joe Morgan $10
1990 Fenway Park $10
1991 Ellis Burks/Tony Pena $10
1992 Roger Clemens/Butch Hobson $10
1993 Red Sox baseball $10
1994 Mo Vaughn $7
1995 Team logos $5
1996 Mo Vaughn $5
1997 Mo Vaughn $5
1998 Nomar Garciaparra $6
1999 Garciaparra/Martinez, Gordon $6
2000 Pedro Martinez, Jimy Williams.....................

Colorado Rockies

1993 Silhouette..$20
1994 Coors Field $10
1995 Coors Field $15
1996 Coors Field $6
1997 Baseball scenes..$6
1998 All-Star Game logo, stars $6
1999 Coors Field, baseballs $6
2000 Coors Field photo......................................$6
2001 Bat, glove, baseball $6

Kansas City Royals

1969 Team logo...$60
1970 Player hitting $20

1971 Team bat rack $20
1972 Royals Stadium $15
1973 Players in action $15
1974 Royals Stadium $15
1975 Player hitting $15
1976 Whitey Herzog $10
1977 Players in action $6
1978 Players hitting, pitching $6
1979 1976-1978 A.L. West Champions $6
1980 Team logo, scoreboard $6
1981 Players in action, logo $6
1982 Team logo, pitcher.....................................$6
1983 Statue of hitter $6
1984 George Brett and fans $8
1985 Scoreboard (A.L. West Champions) $6
1986 World Series trophy $6
1987 Players in action $6
1988 Fireworks over scoreboard $10
1989 Team equipment $10
1990 Players in action $10
1991 George Brett $12
1992 Equipment $10
1993 25th anniversary $10
1994 Appier/Montgomery/Gagne $7
1995 Magazine covers $7
1996 Player photo collage $6
1997 25th Anniv. of Kaufman Stadium $6
1998 Royals logo on wood background................$6
1999 George Brett, Baseball HOF $7
2000 Art: player collage $6
2001 ....$6

Washington Senators

1928 Roster sheet...$125
1929 Roster sheet...$100
1930 Roster sheet...$100
1931 Roster sheet...$100
1932 Roster booklet $100
1933 Roster booklet $100
1933 Capitol and 1933, booklet....................$80-$115
1934 Capitol and 1934, booklet.....................$80-$100
1935 Capitol and 1935, booklet.....................$75-$100
1936 Capitol and 1936 ....$75
1937 Capitol and 1937 ....$75
1938 Capitol and 1938 ....$70-$75
1939 Capitol and 1939 ....$70-$75
1940 Capitol and 1940 ....$70-$75
1941 Capitol and 1941 ....$60-$65
1942 Capitol and 1942 ....$60-$65
1943 Capitol and 1943 ....$60-$65
1944 Capitol and 1944 ....$60
1945 Capitol and 1945 ....$60
1946 Capitol and 1946 ....$60
1947 Capitol and 1947 ....$55-$60
1948 Capitol and 1948 ....$55-$60
1949 Capitol and 1949 ....$55-$60
1950 Capitol and 1950 ....$50
1951 Capitol and 1951 ....$50
1952 Capitol and 1952 ....$50
1953 Capitol, bat, baseball...........................$45-$50
1954 Capitol, bat, baseball...........................$45-$50
1955 Capitol, bat, baseball...........................$45-$50
1956 Sportswriter $40
1957 Team mascot pitching...............................$40
1958 Golden anniversary of BBWAA.................$40
1959 Mascot blowing out candles ....$35-$40
1960 Home run celebration $75
Becomes Minnesota Twins
1961 Doherty, Quesada, Vernon.......................$75

1962 Stadium and team logo...$75
1963 Stadium and team logo...$75
1964 Stadium and team logo...$60
1965 Stadium and team logo...$35
1966 Stadium and team logo...$25
1967 Pitcher and baseball...$25
1968 Batter and baseball..$25
1969 Frank Howard..$25
1970 Bob Short/Ted Williams...$25
1971 Stadium and team logo...$25

Detroit Tigers

1927 Roster sheet...$125
1928 Roster sheet...$100
1929 Roster sheet...$100
1930 Roster sheet...$100
1931 Roster booklet...$100
1932 Roster booklet...$100
1933 Tiger head and 1933, booklet ....$60-$100
1934 Tiger head and 1934, booklet ....$55-$110
1935 Tiger head and 1935, booklet ....$55-$115
1936 Tiger head and 1936...$55-$75
1937..$50-$75
1938 Tiger head and 1938...$50-$75
1939 Tiger head and 1939...$50-$75
1940..$45-$85
1941 Briggs Stadium ....$45-$60
1942 Flag over Briggs Stadium ....$45-$60
1943 Tiger head and 1943...$40-$60
1944 Tiger head and 1944...$40-$60
1945 Tiger head and 1945...$40-$70
1946 Tiger head and 1946...$35-$60
1947 Tiger head and 1947...$35-$60
1948 Tiger head and 1948..$150
1949 Tiger head and 1949..$150
1950 Tiger head and 1950..$150
1951 Tiger head and 1951..$150
1952 Tiger head and 1952..$150
1953 Tiger head and 1953..$150
1954 Tiger head and 1954..$100
1955 Tiger head and 1955..$100
1956 Ray Boone/Al Kaline $100
1957 Frank Lary $100
1958 Jim Bunning $100
1959 Tiger head and 1959..$100
1960 Tiger head and 1960..$75
1961 Tiger Stadium $75
1962 Players and team logo..$75
1963 Team logo..$75
1964 Team logo..$50
1965 Team logo..$40

1966 Team mascot and 1966...$40
1967 Team mascot and 1967...$40
1968 Team mascot and 1968...$40
1969 Team mascot..$30
1970 Team mascot fielding...$20
1971 Team mascot throwing..$15
1972 Team mascot fielding...$10
1973 Team mascot fielding...$10
1974 Team mascot sliding..$10
1975 Team mascot in field..$10
1976 Team mascot pitching...$10
1977 Team mascot catching..$10
1978 Team mascot hitting...$10
1979 Team logo and 1979...$10
1980 Team mascot in action...$6
1981 Tiger jumping $6
1982 Team logo $6
1983 Greenberg and Gehringer uniforms $6
1984 Team mascot boxing..$6
1985 World Series trophy, logo...$6
1986 Team mascot in stadium..$6
1987 Baseball and Tiger..$6
1988 ....$6
1989 The Press Guide and logo $10
1990 Uniform D...$10
1991 And Once Again $10
1992 Alan Trammell/Lou Whitaker $10
1993 Tiger greats..$10
1994 Team logo $9
1995 Baseballs..$8
1996 Buddy Bell $8
1997 Stripes...$8
1998 J. Thompson/B. Higginson/T. Clark $8
1999 Tiger Stadium at night...$10
2000 Comerica Park inaugural celebration $10
2001 Comerica Park at night...$10

Minnesota Twins

1961 Metropolitan Stadium drawing $150
1962 Metropolitan Stadium...$75
1963 Player hitting $75
1964 Baseball and 1964..$75
1965 All-Star Game hosts $40
1966 Player fielding $40
1967 Twins uniform $30
1968 Pitcher throwing $30
1969 Metropolitan Stadium..$25
1970 Rod Carew, Twins stars..$25
1971 Jim Perry $25
1972 Minnesota media $25
1973 Rod Carew...$25

1974 Baseballs..$10
1975 Rod Carew/Ty Cobb..$15
1976 R. Carew/H. Killebrew/others $15
1977 Old press guide covers $10
1978 Rod Carew $10
1979 Metropolitan Stadium......................................$6
1980 Twins baseball cards...$6
1981 Twins bats, hats, uniforms..............................$6
1982 Metrodome $6
1983 Kent Hrbek...$7
1984 Twins uniforms...$6
1985 All-Star Game logo $6
1986 25th anniversary logo $6
1987 Gary Gaetti/Kirby Puckett................................$8
1988 World Series trophy..$10
1989 Kirby Puckett/Frank Viola.............................$10
1990 Carew/Oliva/Puckett.......................................$10
1991 Drawings of Carew/Killebrew........................$10
1992 Celebration, World Series trophy $10
1993 Kirby Puckett..$10
1994 Autographs...$7
1995 Bat/glove/uniform...$6
1996 Rookies of the Year...$5
1997 Team logo...$5
1998 Paul Molitor..$5
1999 Collage of Tom Kelly/Matt Lawton/Ron Coomer/Todd Walker$10
2000 Photos of All-time Twins/40th Anniversary...$10
2001 Carew, Killebrew, Puckett...............................$10

Chicago White Sox

1927 Roster sheet $125
1928 Roster sheet $100
1929 Roster sheet $100
1930 Roster sheet $100
1931 Roster sheet $100
1932 Roster sheet $100
1933 Name and 1933, sheet.........................$60-$100
1934 Name and 1934, booklet.....................$55-$100
1935 Name and 1935, booklet.....................$55-$100
1936 Name and 1936, booklet.......................$55-$75
1937 Name and 1937, booklet.......................$50-$75
1938 Name and 1938, booklet.......................$50-$75
1939 Name and 1939, booklet.......................$50-$75
1940 Name and 1940, booklet.......................$45-$75
1941 Ted Lyons, booklet...............................$50-$60
1942 Jimmy Dykes, booklet ....$45-$60
1943 Buy More War Bonds, booklet ....$40-$60
1944 Back the attack, booklet........................$40-$60
1945 Roster booklet ....$40-$60

1946 Name and 1946, booklet.......................$35-$60
1947 Ted Lyons, booklet...$100
1948 Team mascot and 1948, booklet....................$100
1949 Team logo and 1949, booklet.........................$100
1950 Luke Appling $100
1951 Paul Richards...$100
1952 Carrasquel, Fox, Minoso, Rogovin $100
1953 Player in action...$100
1954 Team mascot..$100
1955 Team mascot..$100
1956 Team mascot..$100
1957 Team mascot..$90
1958 Team mascot..$90
1959 Team mascot..$90
1960 Team mascot..$75
1961 Name and 1961...$75
1962 Player in action..$75
1963 Player in action..$75
1964 Player in action..$75
1965 Pitcher throwing $40
1966 Batter hitting..$30
1967 Player in action..$25
1968 Hitter up to bat $25
1969 Batter hitting..$25
1970 Fielder in action...$10
1971 Chuck Tanner $10
1972 Player in action..$10
1973 Allen/Tanner/Wood..$10
1974 Team logo...$10
1975 A.L. 75th anniversary $6
1976 Team logo...$6
1977 Team logo...$6
1978 Team logo, hitter..$6
1979 Don Kessinger..$6
1980 Fans in crowd...$6
1981 Pitcher in action...$6
1982 Team logo...$6
1983 Sportswriter equipment $6
1984 Scoreboard, A.L. West Champs $6
1985 Comiskey Park...$6
1986 Aparicio/Appling/Guillen......................................$7
1987 New White Sox uniform #87..................................$6
1988 Player in action...$6
1989 Former White Sox stars $6
1990 Comiskey Park 80 years..$10
1991 Catchers mask, uniform, bat.................................$10
1992 Team logo...$10
1993 Team logo...$10
1994 Lamont/Thomas/McDowell $7
1995 Comiskey Park...$6
1996 Thomas/Guillen/Fernandez $6
1997 Frank Thomas hitting $6
1998 Jerry Manuel...$6
1999 Players including Frank Thomas.............................$6
2000 Players including Ray Durham...............................$6
2001 Players including Magglio Ordonez $6

New York Yankees

1927 Roster sheet...$150-$175
1928 Roster sheet...$150
1929 Roster sheet...$150
1930 Roster sheet...$150
1931 Roster sheet...$150
1932 Roster booklet $200
1933 Roster booklet $100
1934 Roster booklet $100

1935 Roster booklet $100
1936 Joe McCarthy, booklet ....$70-$100
1937 Joe McCarthy, booklet ....$65-$100
1938 Joe McCarthy, booklet ....$65-$100
1939 Joe McCarthy, booklet ....$65-$100
1940 Joe McCarthy, booklet ....$60-$75
1941 Joe McCarthy, booklet ....$60-$65
1942 Joe McCarthy ....$60-$65
1943 ....$45-$65
1944 ....$45-$60
1945 Victory V and 1945 ....$40-$60
1946 Team logo and 1946 ....$40-$60
1947 Team logo and 1947..................................$35-$65
1948 Team logo and 1948 ....$35-$60
1949 Team logo and 1949 ....$30-$65
1950 Team logo and 1950 ....$150
1951 Team logo and 1950 ....$150
1952 Team logo and 1952 ....$150
1953 Team logo and 1953 ....$150
1954 Team logo and 1954 ....$150
1955 Team logo and 1955 ....$150
1956 Team logo and 1956 ....$150
1957 Team logo and 1957 ....$150
1958 Team logo and 1958 ....$150
1959 Team logo and 1959 ....$150
1960 Yankee Stadium $100

1961 Team logo and 1961 ....$100
1962 Team logo and 1962 ....$100
1963 Team logo and 1963 ....$100
1964 Yogi Berra and logo..$75
1965 Team logo $40
1966 Yankee Stadium and logo $40
1967 Team logo and hitter..$40
1968 Yankee Stadium $40
1969 Yankee glove and hat $40
1970 Mel Stottlemyre..$25
1971 Logo and players in action $20
1972 Bobby Murcer, Roy White $20
1973 Yankee Stadium $20
1974 Whitey Ford/Mickey Mantle $25
1975 Bobby Bonds/Catfish Hunter $20
1976 Yankee Stadium $20
1977 Chris Chambliss/Thurman Munson $25
1978 Reggie Jackson/Babe Ruth..............................$25
1979 Goose Gossage/Thurman Munson $20
1980 Dick Howser/Gene Michael.............................$15
1981 Team logo..$20
1982 Team logo..$5
1983 Billy Martin with umpire $8
1984 Righetti, Yankee no-hitters $6
1985 Don Mattingly $7
1986 Guidry/Henderson/Mattingly/Niekro $7
1987 Lou Piniella and team $15
1988 Team logo..$15
1989 Dallas Green..$15
1990 Baseball bat and ball $15
1991 Maas/Mattingly/Meulens/Sax $15
1992 A tradition of great moments $15
1993 Collage $10
1994 Players $10
1995 Babe Ruth's 100th birthday.............................$12
1996 Memorabilia $10
1997 Players $10
1998 Yankee Stadium at 75 years $13
1999 3 Players raising their hands after winning the championship ..$10
2000 Collage: Yankees Legends...............................$10
2001 World Series celebration $10

YEARBOOKS

With more pictures and general content than media guides, yearbooks appeal to the casual baseball fan. In addition to player biographies similar to those found in media guides, yearbooks often include lengthy team histories.

Yearbooks haven't proven as popular as media guides with fans or collectors, which may be why several teams didn't produce them in the 1980s and 1990s. The prices below are for specimens in excellent condition. Yearbooks from 1994 to the present typically sell for their cover price—around $5.

Los Angeles Angels

1961	None issued
1962 Angels baby with cake	$85-$100
1963 Rocket, Chavez Ravine	$35-$50
1964 Angels in action	$25-$35
1965 Angels in action	$25-$35

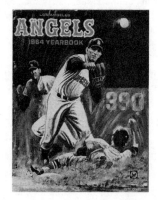 

California Angels

1966 Anaheim Stadium	$50-$65
1967 All About the Angels, with logo	$12-$15
1968-1982	None issued
1983 Lynn/Carew/Jackson, others	$8-$12
1984 Anaheim Stadium	$5-$10
1985 25th Anniversary, Angel greats	$7-$10
1986-1991	None issued
1992 Abbott, Langston/Harvey/Finley	$12
1993 Nolan Ryan	$12
1994 Tim Salmon	$8
1995-1997	None issued

Anaheim Angels

1988-1999	None issued
2000 Collage of current, former players	$8
2001 Troy Percival, Adam Kennedy	$6

Houston Colt .45s

1962 Baseball/ pistol/ Texas map	$150
1963	None issued
1964 Colt .45s logo	$125

Houston Astros

1965 Inside the Astrodome	$100
1966 Astrodome	$75
1967	None issued
1968	$45
1969-1971	None issued
1972	$25
1973-1976	None issued
1977 Photo album	$20
1978 Photo album	$20
1979 Photo album	$20
1980-1981	None issued
1982 Nolan Ryan	$12-$15
1983-1991	None issued
1992 Luis Gonzalez	$12
1993 Photo album	$12
1994 New logo, Bagwell, others	$10
1995-2001	None issued

Philadelphia Athletics

1949 Connie Mack	$60-$125
1950 Connie Mack Golden Jubiliee	$60-$125
1951 Team mascot (elephant)	$60-$125
1952 Team mascot (elephant)	$60-$125
1953 Elephant pitching baseball	$20
1954 Play at first base	$75

Kansas City Athletics

1955 A's batter ripping through map	$100-$150
1956 Elephant mascot	$100-$150
1957 Kansas City Municipal Stadium	$100-$150

1958 Play at first	$125
1959 Kansas City Municipal Stadium	$125
1960 Baseball wearing Athletics hat	$125
1961 Pitcher and baseball	$125
1962 A's players in action	$125
1963 Play at home plate	$25-$40
1964 Player making a catch	$25-$40
1965 A's donkey/ Finley flag	$25-$45
1966	$65
1967 Athletics pitcher	$40

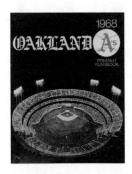

Oakland Athletics

1968 Oakland Coliseum	$45-$75
1969 Connie Mack	$25-$35
1970 Monday/Odom/Jackson/others	$25
1971 Sal Bando/Bert Campaneris	$15-$25
1972 Dick Williams/Vida Blue	$15-$22
1973 Rudi/Fingers/Williams/Hunter	$20
1974 One More in '74/ two trophies	$15-$20
1975 Keep it Alive in '75	$20
1976 Bicentennial celebration	$15
1977 A's logo/arch of baseballs	$7-$9
1978	None issued
1979 The Swingin A's, with logo	$20
1980-1981	None issued
1982 Billy Ball baseball	$5-$10
1983 A's baseball card collage	$15
1984-1999	None issued
2000 100th Anniversary of Athletcis baseball	$10
2001 Jason Giambi	$10

Toronto Blue Jays

1977 The First Year, fans	$15-$20
1978	None issued
1979 Rico Carty	$9
1980 Rico Carty/Roy Howell	$15
1981 Ernie Whitt/Jim Clancy	$15
1982 Martinez/Moseby/Whitt	$15
1983 Blue Jays baseball	$15
1984 Exhibition Stadium	$15

1985 Logo and year	$15
1986 American League baseball, bat	$15
1987 Barfield/Clancy/Whitt	$15
1988 Blue Jay player batting	$15
1989 Fred McGriff	$15
1990 George Bell	$15
1991 Player drawing	$15
1992 Roberto Alomar	$15
1993 Trophy	$15
1994 Carter/Molitor/White/others	$12
1995 Logo and baseball	$10
1996 20th Anniv. All-Time greats	$10
1997 Roger Clemens	$10
1998 Roger Clemens/Carlos Delgado	$10
1999 Shawn Green	$10
2000	$10
2001	$10

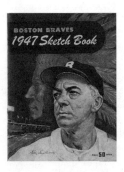

Boston Braves

1946 Billy Southworth	$300
1947 Billy Southworth	$150-$165
1948-1949	None issued
1950 Smiling Brave	$150
1951 Baseball diamond and ball	$125
1952 Braves players talking	$125

Milwaukee Braves

1953 Runner sliding into home	$150-$175
1954 To the People of Milwaukee	$75-$100
1955 Fans and stadium	$50-$60
1956 Cartoon of Braves fans	$100-$125
1957 Braves logo in crystal ball	$100-$125
1958 Brave raising World Series pennant	$100-$125
1959 Brave in hot-air balloon	$65-$70
1960 Brave with two baseball bats	$60
1961 Braves player, other N.L. players	$40-$65
1962 Braves logo	$45-$60
1963 Braves player/other N.L. players	$40
1964 Aaron/Mathews/Torre/Spahn	$40-$60
1965 Bobby Bragan/Felipe Alou	$40

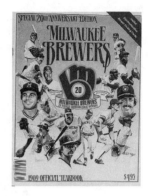

Atlanta Braves

1966 Aaron/Mathews/others ....$25-$50
1967 Play at home plate...$10-$30
1968 Play at second base ....$10-$25
1969 Braves infielder ....$15-$25
1970 Braves in action...$20
1971 Hank Aaron/Babe Ruth...$7-$9
1972 Five Braves...$5-$9
1973 Braves pitcher...$20
1974 Hank Aaron/Babe Ruth...$20
1975 Four Braves $15
1976 Niekro/Cepeda/Aaron/others $15
1977 Former Braves/Hank Aaron $10
1978 Spahn/Niekro/Burdette...$10
1979 Garber stops Roses streak...$12-$15
1980 Bob Horner/Bobby Cox $15
1981 D. Murphy/B. Horner/others $15
1982 Spahn/Horner/Aaron/others...$12-$15
1983 Phil Niekro in an Uncle Sam outfit..$10
1984 Horner/Murphy/Aaron..$10
1985 Aaron/Murphy/20th Anniversary $10
1986 Dale Murphy/Chuck Tanner..$12
1987 Dale Murphy $12
1988 Braves Illustrated...$10
1989 ....None issued
1990 25 years in Atlanta..$12
1991 ....None issued
1992 N.L. Champions $12
1993 .... None issued
1994 B. Cox/G. Maddux/others $7
1995-1997...None Issued
1998 Collage of players $10
1999 ....$7
2000 Art...$7
2001 Braves logo...$7

Seattle Pilots

1969 Pilot logos, 10 pictures..$150

Milwaukee Brewers

1970 Brewers hitter...$50-$75
1971-1978... None issued
1979 Larry Hisle ....$5-$9
1980 Gorman Thomas..$5-$9
1981 Molitor/Fingers/Yount/others...$5-$9
1982 Crowd celebrating $12
1983 Robin Yount and fans $10
1984 County Stadium ....$5-$9
1985 George Bamberger and fans ....$5-$9
1986 Brewers locker room ....$5-$9
1987 Brewers baseball cards...$5-$9
1988 Paul Molitor hologram $10
1989 Brewer greats/Hank Aaron $12
1990 Brewers logo/Milwaukee skyline $10
1991 Paul Molitor..$12
1992 Molitor/Yount/Gantner $12
1993 ....None issued
1994 New Brewer uniforms $7
1995 ....None issued
1996 John Jaha...$8
1997-1999 ....None issued

St. Louis Cardinals

1951 Cardinal in bottom right...$250
1952 Cardinal and soldier $125
1953 Stan Musial ....$125-$175
1954 Red Schoendienst $100
1955 Cardinal pitcher gets the sign...$75
1956 Cardinal pitcher gets the sign...$75
1957 Cardinal circles the bases...$40-$50
1958 Cardinal circles the bases..$50
1959 Stan Musial..$55
1960 Cardinal catches a ball $40
1961 Curt Simmons/Ray Sadecki, others $40
1962 Stan Musial and his milestones ....$40-$60
1963 Musial slides into second...$35-$50

1964 Groat/Boyer/Javier/White ....$35-$50
1965 Bob Gibson..$35
1966 New Busch Stadium photo..$65
1967 World Champs..$50-$75
1968 Busch Stadium $45
1969 Brock/Flood/Gibson/others $30
1970 Five Cardinal drawings ....$12-$15
1971 Brock/Torre/Gibson/others ....$12-$15
1972 Cardinals fielder $25
1973 Cardinals batter ....$15-$20
1974 Simmons/Torre $15
1975 Brock/Gibson/others..$20
1976 Centennial yearbook...$20
1977 Lou Brock/Ty Cobb ....$12-$15
1978 .... None issued
1979 St. Louis city skyline..$12
1980 Simmons/Hernandez $10
1981-1987... None issued
1988 Wraparound team photo...$12
1989 Coleman/Worrell...$7-$12
1990 Herzog, Busch Stadium..$10
1991 Lee Smith $12
1992 Moore/Slaughter/Musial/Guerrero/Lankford/Jose $10
1993 Ozzie Smith $12
1995 K. Hill/S. Cooper/D. Jackson/T. Henke................................$10
1996-98..None issued
1999 Mark McGwire...$10
2000 10 Greatest Moments $10
2001 Baseball card collage...$7

Chicago Cubs

1934 Wraparound batting scene..$200-$275
1939 Players records $200
1941 Players history/record book ....$175-$250
1942 Roster/record book..$150-$200
1948 Logo and blue 1948 ....$100-$150
1949 Logo and blue 1949 ....$35-$50
1950 Hat and red 1950...$35-$50
1951 Ball in center of red glove..$60
1952 Logo/year in red and blue ....$50-$70
1953 Cubs logo $50
1954 Name and year...$50
1955 Name and year...$50
1956 Name and year...$75-$100
1957 Head with Cubs hat $125
1958-1984... None issued
1985 Wrigley photo ....$5-$8
1986 70th Anniversary/Ryne Sandberg ....$5-$7
1987 Billy Williams/Ryne Sandberg ....$7-$8
1988 Andre Dawson...$7-$9
1989 Wrigley Field Diamond Anniv. $12
1990 Photo of six bats...$12

1991 Ryne Sandberg $12
1992 Scoreboard, celebration...$12
1993 Mark Grace..$12
1994 Moments from 1984 season $10
1995 Wrigley Field...$10
1996-98...None issued
1999 Cubs Quarterly covers: Sammy Sosa, others; Mark Grace; Sosa;
    Sosa $5
2000 Cubs Quarterly covers: Don Baylor; Mark Grace; Kerry Wood;
    Sammy Sosa $5
2001: Kerry Wood, Sammy Sosa, others $5

Tampa Bay Devil Rays

1998 ....None issued
1999 Celebration at home plate $10
2000 Fred McGriff $10
2001 Player collage $5

Arizona Diamondbacks

1998 Two hardbound books $10

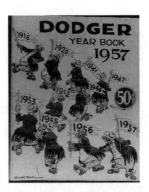

Brooklyn Dodgers

1947 League Champs..$100
1948 .... None issued
1949 League Champs..$250
1950 Artwork of a fielder...$175-$200
1951 Bum picking daisy petals $125
1952 The Bum holding a sign..$125
1953 The Bum holding a bat..$125
1954 The Bum with saw, hammer $125
1955 The Bum reaching for a star...$300
1956 The Bum holding #6 ....$50-$125
1957 The Bum holding pennants..$125-$150

Los Angeles Dodgers

1958 Autographed team baseball...$150-$175
1959 Play at second base ....$75-$135

1960 Dodger stadium drawing $50
1961 Artwork of Dodger Stadium.................................$50
1962 Map of area around Stadium ....$15-$20
1963 Maury Wills...$50
1964 World Champions banner.....................................$30
1965 Dodger Stadium $35
1966 Walter Alston...$20-$25
1967 Dodger juggling crowns.................................$10-$20
1968 Drysdale/Koufax/others ....$10-$20
1969 Baseball's centennial logo ....$10-$20
1970 Dodgers and Mets mascots ....$10-$20
1971 10th Anniversary of stadium ....$10-$20
1972 Dodger Stadium ....$10-$20
1973 Maury Wills/Walter Alston ....$15-$25
1974 Jimmy Wynn ....$10-$20
1975 Steve Garvey/N.L. Champions ....$12-$18
1976 Davey Lopes ....$12-$18
1977 20th Anniversary, players $10
1978 Lasorda/Garvey/Cey/others ....$12-$15
1979 Tommy Lasorda ....$10-$12
1980 Dodger baseball cards $10
1981 Dusty Baker/Steve Garvey ....$10-$12
1982 World Series trophy ....$8-$12
1983 25th Anniversary in Los Angeles $10
1984 A Winning Tradition/Lasorda ....$7-$10
1985 Russell/Valenzuela/Garvey ....$9-$10
1986 Guerrero/Hershiser/Marshall ....$7-$10
1987 24 previous Los Angeles yearbooks ....$7-$10
1988 Blueprint for Success..$8-$9
1989 World Series trophy ....$6-$10
1990 Dodger greats painting....................................$6-$10
1991 Dodgers Field of Dreams..................................$5-$7
1992 Dodger greats ....$5-$7
1993 Hershiser/Lasorda collage $8
1994 Team photo, uniform background.........................$8
1995 Dodger rookies of the year................................$8
1996 Nomo/Piazza/Mondesi/Karros $8
1997 Jackie Robinson patch, photo............................$10
1998 Art collage of 40 year anniversary $10
1999 Drysdale, Campanella Dodger "Hero" patches $10
2000 Stadium scenes with 2000 spelled out $10
2001 Reprinted covers of yearbooks from 1941-2000 ......$10

Montreal Expos

1969 Larry Jaster...$35-50
1970 Expos equipment and fan.............................$25-$35
1971 Fan with Expos pennant...............................$25-$35
1972 Four different covers, each ....$25-$35
1973-81 .... None issued
1982 Expos celebration, All-Star logo $10
1983 Dawson/Carter/Oliver/others ....$7-$12

1984 Raines/Rose/Dawson/others...........................$8-$12
1985 Wallach/Raines/Dawson/others $10
1986 Baseball in hand..$8
1987-91 .... None issued
1992 Gary Carter $10
1993-1998 ....None issued
1999 Vladimir Guerrero $6
2000 Vladimir Guerrero $6
2001 Vladimir Guerrero/Fernando Tatis/others $6

New York Giants

1947 First Year ....$150-$165
1948-1950 .... None issued
1951 Logo, art of leaping player..................................$125
1952 Durocher and Giant..$85
1953 Polo Grounds photo $85
1954 Giant cutting a 1951 book....................................$85
1955 Giant holding other mascots $125
1956 Giants cap ....$75-$85
1957 Photo of play at second...............................$85-$100

San Francisco Giants

1958 Giant with a load of books..................................$250
1959 Photo of a play at third ....$75-$100
1960 Al Dark/play at first...$50
1961 Giants hat $50
1962 N.L. Champs $50

1963 Trolley car w/Giants pennant ....$30-$40
1964 Child looking at Candlestick $30
1965 Painting of a play at second $30
1966 W. Mays with S.F. baseball ....$30-$50
1967 Willie Mays/Juan Marichal $40
1968 Willie Mays $25
1969 Mays/Bonds/McCovey $30
1970 Photos of Mays/McCovey ....$20-$25
1971 Willie McCovey ....$15-$20
1972 Willie Mays sliding into third ....$10-$15
1973 Marichal/Bonds/Speier ....$10-$15
1974 Young Giants '74 ....$10
1975 Gary Matthews/Mike Caldwell $12
1976 Giants memorabilia $15
1977-1979 .... None issued
1980 Giant batter $9
1981 Frank Robinson $10
1982 Silver Anniversary yearbook ....$8-$10
1983 Frank Robinson ....$7-$9
1984 Giants All-Star memorabilia ....$7-$9
1985 Horizontal A History of... ....$5-$7
1986-1991 .... None issued
1992 Will Clark $12
1993 .... None issued
1994 Willie Mays $10
1995 Matt Williams/Barry Bonds $10
1996 Mays/Bonds/McCovey/Marichal/Perry/Beck $10
1997 .... None issued
1998 Brian Johnson $9
2000 Pacific Bell Park $5

Cleveland Indians

1948 World Champs...$100-$125
1949 Logo wearing crown ....$40-$85
1950 Fans entering stadium ....$40-$75
1951 50th Anniversary with logo...............................$60-$75
1952 Chain with Indians logo...$60
1953 Umpire yelling Play ball ....$65-$95
1954 Lemon/Wynn/Doby/Rosen $100
1955 Indian wearing crown ....$75-$100
1956 Indian mascot $75
1957 Indian mascot ....$75-$125
1958 Herb Score..$250
1959 Indians logo...$125-$175
1960 Jim Perry, Indians pitcher....................................$100
1961 Sketch book $100
1962 Team photo $75
1963 Sketch book $100
1964 Indian sliding into home $75

1965 Past and present uniforms $65
1966 Sam McDowell...$50-$65
1967 Picture set..$50-$65
1968 Baseball and year ....$25-$40
1969 Runner sliding into base...$20
1970 Sam McDowell...$25
1971 Indians in action..$15
1972 Indians in action..$7-$9
1973 Jim Perry/others $15
1974-1983 .... None issued
1984 Franco/Sutcliffe/others.......................................$5-$6
1985-1988 .... None issued
1989 Autographed team ball $10
1990 90th Anniversary in Cleveland $10
1991 Score/Alomar/Chambliss $10
1992 Alomar/Hargrove $12
1993 .... None issued
1994 Hardcover, Jacobs Field $15
1995 Jacobs Field, Belle/Baerga/others $10
1996 A. L. Championship artwork...................................$10
1997 All-Star logo, Cleveland skyline $10
1998 Championship celebration......................................$10
1999 Manny Ramirez/Mike Hargrove/others......................$9
2000 ....$7
2001 100th Anniversary logo $7

Seattle Mariners

1978-1984... None issued
1985 Davis/Beattie/Langston $10
1986-1993 .... None issued
1994 Griffey/Martinez/others...$5
1995-1998 .... None issued
1999 K. Griffey Jr./A. Rodriguez......................................$9
2000 Alex Rodriguez at Safeco Field $9

Florida Marlins

1993 Marlins hitter/pitcher/catcher $10
1994 B. Harvey/R. Lachemann/others $8

YEARBOOKS

1995-1996 ....None issued
1997 Gary Sheffield/Jeff Conine/others.......................$7
1998 World Series ring..$7
1999 Alex Fernandez, Old-Time players $6
2000 Team photo collage $6
2001 Team photo collage $6

New York Mets

1962 First year ....$300-$350
1963 Mr. Met leaning on bat ....$125-$150
1964 Cartoon..$75-$100
1965 Cartoon, Shea Stadium ....$50-$60
1966 "Go-Go-Go" Mets banner $50
1967 Cartoon..$50-$75
1968 Gil Hodges $45
1969 Koosman/Grote/Seaver ....$100-$125
1970 Film strips, World Series celebration $35
1971 Play at the plate...................................$35-$50
1972 Harrelson/McGraw/Seaver $15
1973 All-Star gallery w/Mays/Seaver/others ...$15-$35
1974 N.L. Champions pennant.............................$15
1975 Tom Seaver...$15-$25
1976 Mr. Met ....$15-$20
1977 Jerry Koosman ....$10-$15
1978 Play at home plate..................................$6-$10
1979 Mets logo ....$10-$15
1980 Mazzilli with fan/others $30
1981 Joe Torre/All-Time Mets $15
1982 George Foster/George Bamberger ....$12-$15
1983 Foster/M. Wilson/Seaver $20
1984 Orosco/Hernandez/Strawberry.............$15-$20
1985 Hernandez/Gooden/D. Johnson...................$15
1986 25th Anniversary logo $20
1987 World Champions logo ....$10-$15
1988 Strawberry/Gooden/Johnson/others $15
1989 Strawberry/Gooden/Carter/others $15
1990 Mets starting pitchers.................................$15
1991 Shea Stadium..$10
1992 Bonilla/Saberhagen/Murray/Torborg $15
1993 30 years at Shea..$15
1994 25th Anniv. of 1969 Championship $10
1995 Logo on bats..$10
1996 Todd Hundley/Everett/others.......................$10
1997 Motion card of Hundley swing $10
1998 Player celebration photo..............................$10
1999 Al Leiter/Mike Piazza/Rey Ordonez/Rickey Henderson $10
2000 Edgardo Alfonzo/ Al Leiter/Mike Piazza/others.......................$10
2001 Mike Piazza/Armando Benitez/Edgardo Alfonzo/Al Leiter photo collage $10

St. Louis Browns

1944 ....$275
1945 ....$250
1946 ....$250
1947 ....$225
1948 ....$200
1949 ....$200
1950 Browns sketchbook $200
1951 Browns logo $200
1952 Logo on Browns sketchbook.......................$300
1953 ....$150

Baltimore Orioles

1954 Orioles mascot in spotlight $250
1955 Oriole mascot batting $150
1956 Oriole mascot on deck................................$125
1957 Oriole mascot pitching $125
1958 Oriole mascot riding a rocket.....................$125
1959 Oriole mascot with report ....$100-$125
1960 Oriole mascot sitting on eggs.....................$100
1961 Oriole mascot hitting opponent....................$75
1962 Jim Gentile $75
1963 Brooks Robinson $75
1964 Orioles catcher $75
1965 B. Robinson/Bauer/Bunker $75
1966 Robinsons/Blefary/Powell...........................$50
1967 Frank Robinson and fans.............................$50
1968 Brooks and Frank Robinson $25
1969 Dave McNally..$25
1970 Boog Powell...$20-$35
1971 B. Robinson/Palmer/others ....$15-$25
1972 Palmer/McNally/Cuellar $15
1973 Orioles player...$12-$15
1974 Orioles jukebox......................................$10-$12
1975-1979 ....None issued
1980 Orioles mascot ....$10-$12
1981 Orioles players ....$8-$10
1982 Frank Robinson/Earl Weaver $15
1983 Brooks Robinson.......................................$9-$10
1984 30th Anniversary in Baltimore................$10-$12
1985 ....None issued
1986 Robinsons/Ripken Jr./Murray......................$10
1987-1992 ....None issued
1993 Camden Yards..$10
1994 40th Anniversary Issue $10
1995-1997 ....None issued
1998 Cal Ripken Jr./Brady Anderson.....................$8

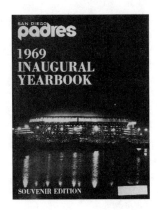

San Diego Padres

1969 Jack Murphy Stadium $75
1970-1978 .... None issued
1979 Dave Winfield ....$5-$6
1980 Dave Winfield ....$6-$7
1981 .... None issued
1982 Dick Williams ....$7-$12
1983 Dick Williams/Steve Garvey ....$7-$12
1984 Templeton/Williams/Garvey $12
1985 Padres hat, N.L. Championship ring $12
1986 Padres memorabilia $10
1987-1991 .... None issued
1992 Fernandez/Gwynn/Santiago $10
1993 25th Anniversary $10
1994-1998 ....None issued
1999 Yearbook/Media guide $10

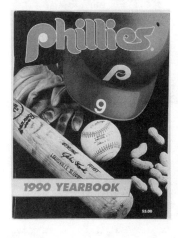

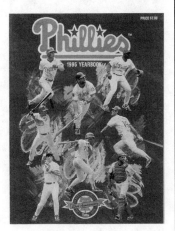

Philadelphia Phillies

1949 Batting scene ....$175-$250
1950 Phillie and sheet music $150
1951 Six player drawings $400
1952 Color stadium photo ....$100-$125
1953 Phillie batter ....$35-$75
1954 Smiling Phillie (head only) $100
1955 Phillie pitcher ....$75-$100
1956 Robin Roberts/Richie Ashburn $150
1957 Ball wearing a Phillies hat ....$50-$100
1958 Hat on pinstriped background ....$75-$80
1959 Five balls, one with a logo ....$50-$75
1960 New faces of 1960/11 photos $75
1961 First edition $150
1961 Second edition $150
1962 Four balls and logo ....$60-$75

1963 Bat, ball and logo $75
1964 First or second edition $75
1964 Third edition, Bunning/others $75
1965 Richie Allen/Jim Bunning $45
1966 Stadium photo $45
1967 Child eating a hot dog $45
1968 Phillie ballplayers ....$35-$45
1969 Connie Mack Stadium ....$35-$45
1970 Veterans Stadium in tree bark ....$20-$40
1971 Veterans Stadium drawing $45
1972 Stadium/fans and players $30
1973 12 drawings, with Carlton $45
1974 12 drawings, with Carlton/Bowa $20
1975 Schmidt/Carlton ....$20-$30
1976 Drawings with Schmidt/Carlton ....$12-$15
1977 Larry Bowa ....$12-$15
1978 Schmidt/Carlton, photos ....$7-$9
1979 Schmidt/Rose/Carlton ....$7-$9
1980 Schmidt/Rose/Carlton $30
1981 World Series ring photo $30
1982 Schmidt/Rose/Carlton $10
1983 Centennial celebration ....$9-$12
1984 Schmidt/Carlton/20 others ....$6-$7
1985 Schmidt/Carlton/Samuel/Hayes ....$7-$10
1986 Mike Schmidt at bat ....$10-$12
1987 Schmidt/Samuel, others $10
1988 Veterans Stadium photo $10
1989 Jordan/V. Hayes/Schmidt $10
1990 Photo of John Kruk's equipment $10
1991 Veterans Stadium $10
1992 Kruk/Dykstra/Daulton/others $10
1993 Kruk/Dykstra/Daulton/others $10
1994 1993 N.L. Championship ring $8
1995 L. Dykstra/D. Hollins/others $8
1996 Montage of action photos $8
1997 Curt Schilling $8
1998 S. Rolen/C. Jefferies/others $7
1999 C. Schilling/S. Rolen/others $7
2000 Phillies 2000 logo $7
2001 Robert Person/Larry Bowa/Doug Glanville/others $7

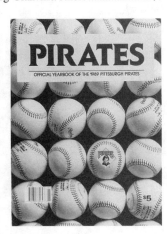

Pittsburgh Pirates

1951 Forbes Field photo $250
1952 Pirate with sword and pistol $125
1953 Buc youngster in sailboat $100
1954 Honus Wagner statue ....$100-$175
1955 Pirate batter—It's a hit! $100

1956 Pirate swinging at 1956 ball.................................$100
1957 Pirate winding up ....$85-$100
1958 Pirate head between two bats.............................$65
1959 Pirate with Pa Pitt...$50
1960 Pirate in sailboat...$50
1961 Pirate on a treasure chest...................................$35
1962 Ball wearing bandana and cap ....$35-$50
1963 Pirate batter ....$35-$50
1964 Pirate sliding into third......................................$15
1965 Mgr. Harry Walker and coaches........................$25
1966 Wraparound Forbes Field photo........................$25
1967 Clemente/Mazeroski/others...............................$25
1968 Clemente/Stargell/others $25
1969 Wraparound Forbes Field photo........................$25
1970 Three Rivers Stadium...$75
1971 Three Rivers Stadium...$75
1972 Clemente/Stargell/others....................................$20
1973 Clemente/Stargell/others....................................$20
1974 Stargell/Parker/others..$12
1975 Historical photos...$5-$6
1976 Yosemite Sam cartoon.......................................$5-$6
1977 Pirate baseball cards..$6-$7
1978 Tanner/Candelaria/others...................................$5-$6
1979 Dave Parker $20
1980 The Family of Stars...$5-$6
1981 Lacy/Rhoden/Madlock/others............................$10
1982 Stargell/Madlock/others.....................................$10
1983 Chuck Tanner ....$6-$7
1984 Madlock/Pena/Ray/others..................................$5-$6
1985 Painting of Mazs '60 homer ....$5-$9
1986 Leland/Pena/Ray/M. Brown..............................$7-$12
1987 Centennial yearbook..$7-$12
1988 Bonds/Bonilla/Van Slyke/others........................$7-$12
1989 Photo of official N.L. balls ....$7-$12
1990 Van Slyke bat/Leyland uniform.........................$10
1991 Pirates greats..$10
1992 Locker room/uniforms.......................................$10
1993 Jay Bell..$10
1994 Jim Leyland/Orlando Merced/others....................$9
1995 25th anniversary of stadium................................$9
1996-99 ....None issued

Texas Rangers

1972-1975.. None issued
1976 Rangers cowgirl on horse ....$15-$25
1977 Autographed Rangers ball..................................$7-$15
1978 Squared photo collage $12
1979 Jenkins/Oliver/others...$5-$9

1980 Arlington Stadium $15
1981 Rangers hitter ....$5-$9
1982 Rangers baseball ....$10-$12
1983 ....None issued
1984 George Wright...$10-$12
1985 Pete O'Brien equipment $10
1986-1987 ....None issued
1988 Ruben Sierra...$10
1989 ....None issued
1990 Rangers helmet rack...$6-$8
1991 20 Years in Texas...$10
1992 Nolan Ryan...$12
1993 Arlington Stadium tribute $10
1994 Ballpark at Arlington...$8
1995 Will Clark artwork...$8
1996 Nolan Ryan...$10
1997 25th Anniv. logo, Gonzalez/others $8
1998 J. Gonzalez/I Rodriguez.....................................$8

Washington Nationals/Senators

1947 "Photo Book", W. Johnson ....$250-$400
1948 ....None issued
1949...$150-$350
1950...$125-$300
1951 ....None issued
1952 Nationals batter $100
1953 Capitol building and baseball.............................$25
1954 Bob Porterfield, Mickey Vernon $75
1955 National with four bats.......................................$75
1956 Clark C. Griffith memorial..................................$100
1957 Senators pitcher...$75-$100
1958 Roy Sievers..$100
1959 100 Years of Baseball art...................................$50
1960 Harmon Killebrew..$65
Becomes Minnesota Twins
1961 A Team is Born ....$100-$150
1962 Washington Stadium $75
1963 Red cover with dedication ....$30-$45
1964 Off the Floor in '64 ....$15
1965 Frank Howard signing autograph........................$25
1966 Senators in action..$20
1967 Capitol and Washington Monument ....$25-$30
1968 Pitcher delivering ....$15-$20
1969 Ted Williams ....$20-$30
1970-1971 ....None issued
Becomes Texas Rangers

Cincinnati Reds

1948 Ewell Blackwell/Ray Lamanno...$150
1949 Bucky Walters/Harry Gumbert...$200
1950 .... None issued
1951 75th Anniversary of N.L. ....$100-$125
1952 Crosley Field...$100-$125
1953 Reds mascot leaning on bat...$75
1954 Reds mascot swinging bat...$75
1955 Reds mascot rising on bat...$75
1956 Reds mascot swinging bat...$75
1957 Reds mascot in space ship ....$60-$75
1958 Reds mascot in orbit ....$40-$50
1959 VanderMeer/Lombardi/others...$50
1960 Reds mascot, Goodman/Rixey $30
1961 Reds mascot running after ball $40
1962 Reds mascot raising pennant $40
1963 Reds mascot yelling Charge...$65
1964 Reds mascot in action ....$30-$40
1965 Reds mascot making catch...$30-$40
1966 Reds mascot reaching for ball $30
1967 Reds mascot/Crosley Field..$30
1968 Autographed team baseball...$15-$25
1969 Perez/Rose/Bench/others ....$15-$25
1970 Johnny Bench..$25
1971 Rose/Bench/Anderson, others $15
1972 Bench/Perez/other film strips $15
1973 Morgan/Bench/others $10
1974 Pete Rose sliding into home...$20
1975 Joe Morgan...$30
1976 Morgan/Rose/Perez $10
1977 Morgan/Bench/Foster/others $12
1978 Pete Rose..$10
1979 Bench/Perez/Griffey/Foster $10
1980 Reds equipment $8
1981 Riverfront Stadium and baseball.......................................$8
1982 Binoculars on stadium seat $8
1983 Red player signing autographs $8
1984 Bats and baseball equipment $8
1985 Pete Rose/Ty Cobb..$8-$10
1986 .... None issued
1987 Rose/Parker/E. Davis/others $12
1988 All-Star Game logo $10
1989 Baseball with Reds logo...$10
1990 Red player with fans $10
1991 World Series trophy...$10
1992 Equipment collage...$10
1993 Barry Larkin's jersey $10
1994 Reds pinstriped cap $8
1995 Big Red Machine commemorative..$8

1996 Marge Schott and Schottzie $7
1997 Jeff Brantley/Barry Larkin $8
1998 ....None issued
1999 Reds logo...$8

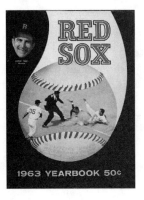
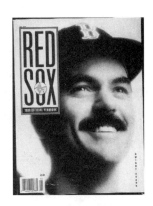

Boston Red Sox

1951 Fenway Park...$250
1952 Red Sox sliding into home...$150
1953-1954 ....None issued
1955 Red Sox fielder ....$115-$125
1956 Red Sox owners..$75
1957 Fenway Park...$75-$125
1958 Red Sox signing autograph $65
1959 Red Sox pitcher $65
1960 Gary Geiger $65
1961 Red Sox batter $65
1962 Carl Yastrzemski..$65
1963 Johnny Pesky/Play at third base.......................................$50
1964 Fenway Park at night...$50
1965 Dick Radatz...$40-$45
1966 Fenway Park...$35-$45
1967 Scott/T. Conigliaro/Yastrzemski ....$50-$75
1968 Yastrzemski/Lonborg/D. Williams $40
1969 Fenway Park...$40
1970 Lyle/Petrocelli/Yastrzemski...$40
1971 Scott/Yastrzemski/Petrocelli ....$12-$15
1972 Carl Yastrzemski and fans ....$7-$12
1973 Carlton Fisk and fans $25
1974 C. Fisk with T. Munson..$10
1975 Foxx/Williams/Yastrzemski/Fisk $10
1976 Fred Lynn $10
1977 Carl Yastrzemski..$10-$15
1978 Jim Rice/Carl Yastrzemski ....$12-$15
1979 Jim Rice...$10
1980 Fred Lynn $8
1981 Rice/Yastrzemski/Eckersley $10
1982 Yastrzemski/Evans/Rice/Lansford $10
1983 Carl Yastrzemski..$10
1984 Jim Rice...$7
1985 Tony Armas $6
1986 Wade Boggs...$8
1987 R. Clemens and Fenway Park...$7-$9
1988 Wade Boggs/Roger Clemens ....$7-$9
1989 Dwight Evans $10
1990 Mike Greenwell/Ellis Burks..$10
1991 Pena/Clemens/Burks...$10
1992 Clemens/Reardon/Viola..$12
1993 Roger Clemens...$10
1994-1998...cover
1999 Nomar Garciaparra/Pedro Martinez/others $9

Colorado Rockies

1993 Hologram of Rockies emblem $10
1994-1999 ....None issued

Kansas City Royals

1969 Pitcher inside large R $25
1970 Piniella/Otis/others $10
1971 Piniella/Otis/others $10
1972 Catcher's mitt with face $10
1973 Mayberry/Splittorff/others $10
1974 Otis, Mayberry, Splittorff $10
1975 Killebrew/McRae/Mayberry $15
1976-77 .... None issued
1978 Fans, Royals pitcher $12
1979 American League players $12
1981 Photo of A.L. Champions $12
1982 Royals action photos $12
1983 Bronze Royals statue $7-10
1984 Royals jacket and equipment $7-10
1985 Division championship celebration.......................................$10-12
1986 Hand wearing World Series ring...$5-10
1987 Royals championship pennants...$5-8
1988 Fireworks over Royals Stadium $10
1989 Royals' player locker $10
1990 Royals in action...$10
1991 Scoreboard replay...$10
1992 Newspaper format $10
1993 Memorabilia collage..$10
1994 Caricatures of players...$9
1995 Organization of year trophy $7
1996 Players celebrating $7
1997 25th anniv. of Kauffman Stadium $7
1998 Autographed baseballs $6
1999 George Brett in tuxedo...$7

Detroit Tigers

1934 Batter and Mascot head...$1,000
1935-1938 ....None issued

1939 "100 Years of Detroit baseball"...$750
1940-1954..None issued
1955 Catcher Drawing $300
1956 .... None issued
1957 Tiger sliding into home...$150-$175
1958 Tiger Hall of Famers, with Cobb $150
1959 Tiger batting and logo $150
1960 Tiger Stadium $100
1961 Tiger head and five baseballs...$50-$100
1962 Tiger head and nine players ....$75-$100
1963 Tiger head...$100
1964 Tiger head..$65
1965 Bill Freehan..$65
1966 Willie Horton..$65
1967 Denny McLain...$45
1968 Al Kaline...$40-$60
1969 World Series trophy $45
1970 Tiger hat, bats, baseballs $10
1971 Martin/Kaline/Horton...$20
1972 Mickey Lolich $10
1973 Tiger infielder in action...$10
1974 Tiger sliding into home...$10
1975 Ron LeFlore ....$12-$15
1976 75th Anniversary $15
1977 Fidrych/Staub/LeFlore ....$10-$12
1978..$8-$12
1979 A. Trammell/L. Whitaker..$8-$12
1980 Trammell/Whitaker/Morris/others ....$8-$15
1981 Trammell/Whitaker/Morris/others .... $7-$15
1982 Clubhouse photo with Gibson...$12
1983 H. Greenberg/C. Gehringer..$8
1984 Morris/Whitaker/Trammell/others ....$10-$12
1985 World Championship trophy $8
1986 Sparky Anderson $10
1987 Tiger on top of baseball...$8
1988 Tiger face, Eye of the Tiger $8
1989 Intend-a-Pennant $10
1990 Roaring into the '90s Tiger $8
1991 Whitaker/Trammell/Fielder/others $12
1992 Anderson/Stengel $10
1993-1999.. None issued

Minnesota Twins

1961 Twins batters ....$125-$175
1962 Metropolitan Stadium..$100
1963 Harmon Killebrew ....$75-$100
1964 Gloved hand and baseball $50
1965 Autographed Twins ball ....$40-$60
1966 Tony Oliva, A.L. Champions...$45

1967 Killebrew/Kaat/Oliva ....$25-$35
1968 Jim Kaat/Harmon Killebrew ....$15-$25
1969 Killebrew/Carew/Oliva/others $20
1970 Rod Carew $20
1971 Carew/Killebrew/Oliva/others $20
1972 Tony Oliva/Harmon Killebrew $15
1973 Frank Quilici $15
1974 Rod Carew ....$20-$25
1975 Rod Carew $15
1976 Rod Carew $25
1977 Past Twins yearbooks $10
1978 Rod Carew $12
1979 Twins batting helmet $10
1980 Twins baseball cards $10
1981 20th Anniversary, Rod Carew ....$8-$12
1982 Metrodome $8
1983-1984 .... None issued
1985 Yearbook/scorecard ....$6-$10
1986 25th Anniversary celebration ....$7-$10
1987 Twins uniforms $10
1988 World Champions celebration ....$8-$10
1989 Viola/Puckett/Gaetti/Reardon $10
1990 Carew/Puckett/Oliva $10
1991 Uniform collage ....$5-$7
1992 World Series trophy $10
1993 .... None issued
1994 Twins greats, Killebrew/others $9
1996 Puckett/Molitor/others $7
1997 .... None issued
1998 Molitor/Steinbach/others $9
1999 Matt Lawton/Ron Coomer/others $8

1953 Comiskey Park $125
1954 White Sox batter $100
1955 White Sox batter $75
1956 White Sox sliding into home $75
1957 White Sox fielder ....$70-$75
1958 White Sox batter ....$60-$65
1959 White Sox mascot with hat $125
1960 White Sox fielding ....$50-$65
1961 White Sox pitching $50
1962 White Sox batting $35
1963 White Sox fielding ....$15-$25
1964 Fireworks at Comiskey Park ....$30-$40
1965 White Sox uniform #80 ....$25-$35
1966 White Sox batter swinging $35
1967 White Sox in action $20
1968 White Sox batter at plate $20
1969 Tommy John $20
1970 White Sox in action $40
1971-1981 .... None issued
1982 LaRussa/Luzinski/Fisk $10
1983 All-Star Game with Fisk/others $10
1984 Hoyt/LaRussa/Kittle/Luzinski $10
1985 .... None issued
1986 Walker/Guillen/J. Davis/Baines $12
1987 .... None issued
1988 White Sox memorabilia $10
1989 .... None issued
1990 Comiskey Park ....$5-$6
1991 Comiskey Park $5
1992 Good Guys Wear Black $7
1993 Cooperstown Collection $7
1994 Frank Thomas $8
1995 1917 Championship team $8
1996 F. Thomas/R. Ventura/others $8
1997 F. Thomas/A. Belle $8
1998 Belle/Thomas/Manuel/others $7
1999 Five Players $7

Chicago White Sox

1951 ....$250
1952 White Sox and year $150

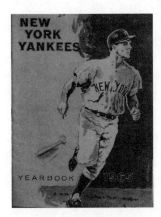

New York Yankees

1950 Yankees emblem, pennants...................................$300
1951 Balls on shelf ....$175-$250
1952 Yankee Stadium, action ....$150-$200
1953 Yankees infielder $150
1954 Yankee with World Series bats $150
1955 Yankees player drawing......................................$250
1956 Yankee sliding into home $250
1957 Bobby Richardson $250
1958 Yankee Stadium $150
1959 Yankee Stadium...$125-$150

1960 Yankee Stadium, players ....$100-$125
1961 Yankee Stadium sketch...$150
1962 Yankee Stadium sketch...$75
1963 Yankee holding three bats...$65
1964 Yogi Berra, Ralph Houk $65
1965 Photo inside Yankee Stadium $65
1966 Two autographed balls $50
1967 Mickey Mantle drawing $50
1968 Mantle/Stottlemyre/others..$25
1969 Mantle/Stottlemyre/others..$50
1970 Murcer/Stottlemyre/others $75
1971 Murcer/White/others $10
1972 Murcer/White/Stottlemyre $20
1973 Ruth/DiMaggio/Mantle/Gehrig..$20

1974 B. Murcer/T. Munson..$20
1975 25th Annual w/past yearbooks $15
1976 Yankees Stadium..$25
1977 Chris Chambliss $12
1978 World Series trophy...$15
1979 World Series celebration ....$10-$15
1980 Yankee Stadium $8
1981 Yankees Big Apple $15
1982 Winfield/Guidry/Gossage/others $8
1983 Billy Martin..$7
1984 Yankee greats $15
1985 Maris/Mantle/Ruth/Gehrig $8
1986 Yankees MVPs...$6
1987 Gehrig/Mattingly/Mantle $10
1988 Mattingly/Clark/Randolph ....$10-$15
1989 Yankees memorabilia...$10
1990 Don Mattingly $12
1991 Pitcher vs. batter $10
1992 Don Mattingly $12
1993 Team photo $10
1994 125th Anniv. logo, Yankee greats $12
1995 Babe Ruth $12
1996 Mickey Mantle $12
1997 Championship ring $12
1998 Yankee Stadium at 75 years $12
1999 Players celebrating $10
2000 Derek Jeter, the "Century's team"...$8
2001 World Series trophy...$8

BASEBALL BOOKS

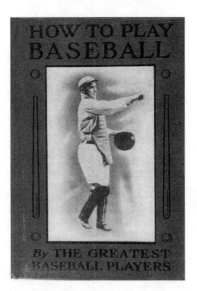

Once among the least expensive collectibles, baseball books have risen in both popularity and value in recent years. And why not? They make great items for autographing—either by the author or the subject—and they give collectors some insight into many aspects of the game and its best players.

Certain books should be part of every baseball fan's library, just for their writing: *Babe, The Legend Comes to Life*, by Robert Creamer, Roger Kahn's *The Boys of Summer*, and *The Summer Game*, by Roger Angell, to name just three And there are a dizzying number of biographies that make great additions to the libraries of single-player collectors or team-collectors.

Several factors—besides simple supply and demand—go into the task of determining the value of a book. First editions, of course, are far more valuable than subsequent printings. Condition is also important. And consider the condition of both the book and its dust jacket when trying to determine a value.

The following list is by no means comprehensive, but should offer collectors a snapshot of some of the more popular titles among book collectors. The price given is for a first-edition printing, with the book and original dust jacket in Excellent condition. Subtract about 50 percent if the book is missing its dust jacket and 25 percent for a second edition. (Not every book listed was issued with a dust jacket.)

Best of the Baseball Books

Here are some of the best baseball books ever published, books that would form the foundation of any worthy collection. While not truly rare, first editions of many of these titles are becoming quite scarce.

Babe, The Legend Comes to Life, Robert Creamer, 1974 .... $50
Considered by many as the best sports biography ever written, *Babe* increases our affection and respect for baseball's foremost hero.

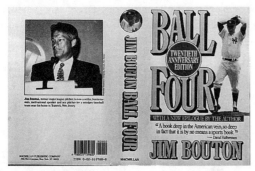

Ball Four, Jim Bouton, 1970 .... $50
Although rather tame by today's standards, Bouton's tell-all shocker of 1970 is still the funniest baseball book in captivity.

The Ballparks, Bill Shannon, 1965 .... more than $75
This photo-history, the first book on its subject, is tough to find and high on many collectors' want-lists.

Baseball: The Early Years (1960) & Baseball: The Golden Age (1971), Harold Seymour .... $50-$75
This as-yet-uncompleted triology ranks as baseball literature's most highly regarded general history.

The Baseball Encyclopedia, first edition $50
Now in its eighth edition, the original edition of the most famous baseball record book comes in a neat boxed slip cover.

Baseball I Gave You All the Best Years of My Life, edited by Richard Grossinger and Kevin Kerrane $50
A mind-bending anthology of eclectic poetry and prose, *Baseball I Gave You* is hard to find but worth the trouble.

The Boys of Summer, Roger Kahn, 1971 .... $50
The book that immortalized that Brooklyn Dodgers of the early 1950s, *The Boys of Summer* is the quintessential classic baseball book.

Bush League, Robert Obojski .... $50-$75
Conceived as a companion to *The Baseball Encyclopedia*, *Bush League* was published in 1975, but it is still the best reference book on the minors.

The Celebrant, Eric Rolfe Greenberg, 1993 .... more than $75
A novel about Christy Mathewson and his biggest fan, *The Celebrant* is a scarce book with a big following.

The Cincinnati Game, Lonnie Wheeler, 1988 .... $50
This is the most innovative team history ever, but only 3,000 copies of the hardback were published.

The Chrysanthemum and the Bat, Robert Whiting, 1977 .... $50-$75
The first major treatment of Japanese baseball, this is also a book about the clash of two cultures.

Eight Men Out, Eliot Asinof .... $50-$75
This is the best book about baseball's most infamous scandal, the fixed 1919 World Series.

False Spring, Pat Jordan $50
This beautifully written coming-of-age autobiography about failure in the minor leagues reads like a novel.

The Fireside Book of Baseball, Vol. I, II & III, edited by Charles Einstein ....$50, $50 and more than $75
These are the first great (and still unsurpassed) anthologies of baseball literature. *Vol. III* is especially tough to locate.

The Glory of Their Times, Lawrence Ritter, 1966 ....$85
This collection of first-person accounts by players from the '20s is a favorite with collectors.

The Great American Baseball Card Flipping, Trading and Bubble Gum Book, Brendan C. Boyd and Fred C. Harris. This most nostalgic of all baseball books was the first to demonstrate the enormous appeal of baseball cards.

The Long Season, 1960, and Pennant Race, Jim Brosnan ....$50-$75 each
Great inside looks at Major League Baseball, Brosnan's diaries remain the only books to be entirely written by an active Major League player.

Only the Ball Was White, Robert Peterson.........................more than $75
This pioneering history of Negro League baseball is a must for anyone interested in its popular topic.

Putnam Sports Series, various authors ....more than $75
Written by the leading sportswriters of the '50s, these team histories have stood the test of time and fetch increasingly higher prices.

Shoeless Joe, W. P. Kinsella...more than $75
The novel that *Field of Dreams* was based on, *Shoeless Joe* is highly sought-after by collectors of American fiction as well as collectors of great baseball books.

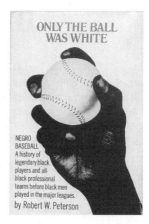

Ty Cobb, Charles C. Alexander ....A
This great biography of baseball's fiercest immortal was underestimated and underprinted by its original publisher.

The Ultimate Baseball Book, edited by Dan Okrent and Harry Levine.....$50
Great photos and superb writing by an all-star lineup highlight this coffee-table spectacular.

Veeck as in Wreck, Bill Veeck and Ed Linn ....$50-$75
Baseball's maverick promoter tells how it's done in a consistently entertaining and seldom-offered-for-sale book.

HC means hardcover. Books are all first editions.

Classics

How Life Imitates the World Series, by Tom Boswell, Doubleday (1982), HC $25

I Had a Hammer, by Hank Aaron with Lonnie Wheeler, Harper/Collins (1991), HC, signed, $40-$60, unsigned $15

Late Innings, by Roger Angell, Simon & Schuster (1982), HC ....$15-$50

Once More Around the Park, by Roger Angell, Ballantine (1991), HC $20

Season Ticket, by Roger Angell, Houghton-Mifflin, (1988), HC $20

The Heart of the Order, by Tom Boswell, Doubleday (1989), HC ...$15

The Image of Their Greatness, by Lawrence Ritter and Donald Honig, HC $35

The Summer Game, by Roger Angell, Viking (1972), HC ....$25-$50

Why Time Begins on Opening Day, by Tom Boswell, Doubleday (1984), HC ....$20-$35

Biographies/Autobiographies
(arranged by subject's name)

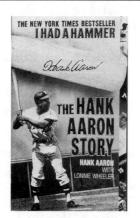

The Hank Aaron Story, by Milton Shapiro, Messner (1961), HC $15

Aaron R.F., by Henry Aaron and Furman Bisher, World (1968), HC $65

Hank Aaron—Quiet Superstar, by Al Hirshberg, Putnam (1974), HC $30

Hank Aaron 715, by Pat Reshen, Arco (1974), HC $30

The Man Who Made Milwaukee Famous, by Don Money (Hank Aaron), Agape (1976), HC $45

Crash, by Tom Whitaker and Dick Allen, Ticknor & Fields (1989), HC ....$15-$25

You Can't Beat the Hours, by Mel Allen and Ed Fitzgerald, Harper (1964), HC $75

The Bob Allison Story, by Hal Butler, Messner (1967), HC $50

My Life in Baseball, by Felipe Alou with Herm Weiskopf, Word (1967), HC, signed $45

Alston and the Dodgers, Walter Alston with Si Burick, Doubleday (1966), HC ....$22.50.

A Year at a Time, by Walt Alston and Jack Tobin, Word (1976), HC $17.50

Bless You Boys, Sparky Anderson with Dan Ewald (1984 season recap), Contemporary (1984), HC...................... $15

Sparky!, by Sparky Anderson with Dan Ewald, Prentice Hall (1990), HC, signed $40

Mr. Cub, by Ernie Banks and Jim Enright, Follet (1971), HC $40

Don Baylor, by Don Baylor and Claire Smith, St. Martins (1989), HC $20

Bo—Pitching and Wooing, by Maury Allen (Bo Belinsky), Dial (1973), HC, signed $45

Hardball, by George Bell with Bob Elliot, Key Porter (1990), HC.. $35

From Behind the Plate, by Johnny Bench with George Kalinsky, Rutledge (1972), HC $30

Johnny Bench—King of the Catchers, by Lou Sabin, Putnam (1977), HC $7.50

Catch You Later, by Johnny Bench with William Brashler, Harper & Row (1979), HC, $30, signed $75

Moe Berg—Athlete, Scholar, Spy, by Lewis Kaufman, et. al., Little, Brown (1974), HC $65

The Catcher Was a Spy, by Nicholas Dawidoff (Moe Berg), Pantheon (1994), HC $17

Yogi Berra—The Muscle Man, by Ben Epstein, Barnes (1951), HC $150

Yogi Berra, by Joe Trimble, Barnes (1952), HC...............................$40

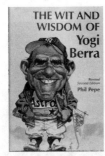

The Yogi Berra Story, by Gene Roswell, Messner (1958), HC $40

Yogi, Yogi Berra with Ed Fitzgerald, Doubleday (1961), HC $30-$45, signed $75

The Story of Yogi Berra, by Gene Schoor, Doubleday (1976), HC $40

Yogi, It Ain't Over, Yogi Berra with Tom Horton, McGraw Hill (1989), HC $12.50

When You Come to a Fork in the Road, Take It! Inspiration and Wisdom from One of Baseball's Greatest Heroes, by Yogi Berra with David Kaplan, Hyperion (2001), HC...............................$16

The Wit and Wisdom of Yogi Berra, by PHil Pepe, Hawthorn (1974) HC $17.50

Ewell Blackwell, by Lou Smith, Barnes (1951), HC $65

Vida, His Own Story, by Vida Blue and Bill Libby, Prentice Hall (1972), HC $12.50

Vida Blue—Coming Up Again, by Don Kowet, Putnam (1974), HC $12.50

Player-Manager, Lou Boudreau with Ed Fitzgerald, Little, Brown (1949), HC..$40

I'm Glad You Didn't Take It Personally, by Jim Bouton with Leonard Schecter, Morrow (1971), HC, signed $20

I Managed Good, But Boy Did They Play Bad, Jim Bouton with Neil Offen, Playboy (1973), HC, signed $20

Ball Four Plus Five: An Update (1970-80), by Jim Bouton, Stein & Day (1981), HC...$20.

Ken Boyer, by Jack Zanger, Nelson (1965), HC $60

You Can't Hit the Ball With the Bat on Your Shoulder, by Bobby Bragan and Jeff Guinn, Summit (1992), HC $25

The George Brett Story, by John Garrity, Coward McCann & Geoghegan (1981), HC $45

Stealing Is My Game, by Lou Brock with Franz Schulze, Prentice Hall (1976), HC ....$45-$65

The Jim Bunning Story, by Jim Bunning and Ralph Bernstein, Lippincott (1965), HC $40

Roy Campanella, by Dick Young, Grosset & Dunlap (1952), HC $30

It's Good to Be Alive, by Roy Campanella, Little, Brown (1959), HC $45

Roy Campanella—Man of Courage, by Gene Schoor, Putnam (1959), HC $60

Carew, by Rod Carew and Ira Berkow, Simon & Schuster (1979), HC ....$35, signed $60

A Dream Season, by Gary Carter and John Hough Jr. (recaps 1986 season), HBJ (1987), HC $10

The Gamer, by Gary Carter, Word (1993), HC, signed $40

Baby Bull: From Hardball to Hard Time and Back, by Orlando Cepeda with Herb Fagen Taylor, (1999).....................................$25

My Ups & Downs in Baseball, by Orlando Cepeda, Putnam (1968), HC ....$15-$50

Orlando Cepeda, by Bob Stevens and Richard Keller, Woodford (1987), HC, signed $25

Rocket Man, by Roger Clemens with Peter Gammons, S. Greene (1987), HC $30

Clemente, by Kal Wagenheim (Roberto Clemente), Praeger (1973), HC $45

The Life of Roberto Clemente, by Paul Robert Walker, HBJ (1988), HC $15

Ty Cobb—Idol of Baseball Fandom, by Sverre Braathen, Avondale (1928), HC, inscribed $800

The Tiger Wore Spikes, by John McCallum (Ty Cobb), Barnes (1956), HC ....$45.

My Life in Baseball—The True Record, by Ty Cobb with Al Stump, Doubleday (1961), HC ....$45-$125

Ty Cobb—The Greatest, by Robert Rubin, Putnam (1978), HC $75
Ty Cobb, by Charles Alexander, Oxford (1984), HC.........................$35
The Hank Aaron Story, by Milton Shapiro, Messner (1961), HC $15

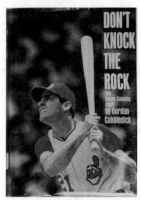

Don't Knock the Rock, by Gordon Cobbledick (Rocky Colavito), World (1966), HC..$150

"Commy," The Life Story of the Grand Old Roman of Baseball, by G.W. Axelson and Charles A. Comiskey, The Reilly & Lee Co. (1919), HC ....$150-$250

Seeing It Through, by Tony Conigliaro with Jack Zanger, MacMillan (1970), HC $15

Jocko, by Jocko Conlon and Robert Creamer, Lippincott (1967), HC $25

Inside Pitch, by Roger Craig and Vern Plagenhoef (pitching coach recaps 1984 Detroit Tigers season), Eerdmans (1984), HC $12.50

Slugging It Out in Japan, by Warren Cromartie and Robert Whiting, Kodansha Intl. (1991), HC...$20

When in Doubt, Fire the Manager, by Alvin Dark and John Underwood, Dutton (1980), HC $30

The Tommy Davis Story, by Patrick Russell, Doubleday (1969), HC $75

America's Dizzy Dean, by Curt Smith, Bethany Press (1978), HC ....$17.50-$25

Joe DiMaggio, Yankee Clipper, by Tom Meany, Barnes (1951), HC $65

Where Have You Gone Joe DiMaggio?, by Maury Allen, Dutton (1975), HC $25

The DiMaggio Albums, by Richard Whittingham (two volumes), Putnam (1982), HC..$25

Joe DiMaggio, by George DeGregorio, Scarborough (1983), HC $45

Joe DiMaggio: Baseball's Yankee Clipper, by Jack B. Moore, Praeger (1987), HC..$55

Joe DiMaggio: The Hero's Life, by Richard Ben Cramer, Simon & Schuster (2000), HC, 560 pages $28

Pride Against Prejudice, by Joseph Thomas Moore (Larry Doby), Praeger (1988), HC $12.50

One Last Round for the Shuffler, by Tom Clark (Shufflin Phil Douglas), Truck Books (1979), HC $35

The Don Drysdale Story, by Milton Shapiro, Messner (1964), HC $75

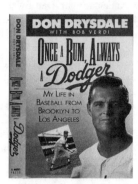

Once a Bum, Always a Dodger, by Don Drysdale with Bob Verdi, St. Martins (1990), HC $12.50

The Comeback, by Ryne Duren and Robert Drury, Lorenz (1978), HC $45

The Leo Durocher Story, by Gene Schoor, Messner (1955), HC $10

Nice Guys Finish Last, by Leo Durocher and Ed Linn, Simon & Schuster (1975), HC..$35

Nails, Lenny Dykstra with Marty Noble, Doubleday (1987), HC $25

Dock Ellis in the Country of Baseball, by Dock Ellis and Donald Hall, Coward McCann (1976), HC..$20-$25

Umpiring From the Inside, by Billy Evans, self-published (1947) $150

Strikeout Story, by Bob Feller, Barnes (1947), HC $40

Bob Feller, by Gene Schoor, Doubleday (1962), HC $45

Now Pitching, Bob Feller/A Baseball Memoir, by Bob Feller with Bill Gilbert, Birch Lane Press (1990) HC $25

No Big Deal, by Mark Fidrych with Tom Clark, Lippincott (1977), HC $20

Yankee Stranger, by Ed Figueroa and Dorothy Harshman, Exposition Press (1982), HC $20

Slick, by Whitey Ford and Phil Pepe, Morrow (1987), HC, signed ..$45

The George Foster Story, by Malka Drucker with George Foster, Holiday House (1979), HC $25

Double X: Jimmie Foxx Baseball's Forgotten Slugger, by Bob Gorman, Holy Name Society (1990), HC $15

Behind the Mask, by Bill Freehan, World (1970), HC $30

Frank Frisch—The Fordham Flash, by Frank Frisch and J. Roy Stockton, Doubleday (1962), HC $65

Garvey, by Steve Garvey with Skip Rozin, Times (1986), HC, $12.50, signed $30

Lou Gehrig—Pride of the Yankees, by Paul Gallico, Grosset & Dunlap (1942), HC,..$35

Lou Gehrig—Boy of the Sand Lots, by Guernsey Van Riper, Bobbs-Merrill (1949), HC $25

Iron Horse, by Ray Robinson (Lou Gehrig), Norton (1990), HC $17.50

Take Time for Paradise, by A. Bartlett Giamatti, Summit (1989), HC $15

From Ghetto to Glory, by Bob Gibson with Phil Pepe, Prentice Hall (1968), HC, signed $65

A Stranger to the Game, by Bob Gibson with Lonnie Wheeler, Viking (1994), HC, signed $50

Josh Gibson, by William Brashler, Harper & Row (1978), HC $125

Rookie, by Richard Woodley (Dwight Gooden), Doubleday (1985), HC $27.50

Dwight Gooden—Strikeout King, by Nathan Aaseng, Lerner (1988), HC $10

One Armed Wonder, by William C. Kashatus (Pete Gray), McFarland (1995), HC $14

The Story of My Life, by Hank Greenberg with Ira Berkow, Times Books (1989), HC ....$22.50-$30

Calvin: Baseball's Last Dinosaur, by Jon Kerr (Calvin Griffith), William C. Brown (1990) HC $40

Jolly Cholly's Story, by Charlie Grimm and Ed Prell, Regnery (1968), HC $25

Guidry, by Ron Guidry and Peter Golenbock, Prentice Hall (1980), HC $15

Tony!, by Tony Gwynn and Jim Geschke, Contempory (1986), HC. $25

Hawk, by Ken Harrelson and Al Hirshberg, Viking (1969), HC $25

Off Base, by Rickey Henderson with John Shea, Harper/Collins (1992), HC $10

If at First, by Keith Hernandez and Mike Bryan, McGraw Hill (1986), HC ....$15, signed, $35

Out of the Blue, by Orel Hershiser and Jerry Jenkins, Wolgemuth & Hyatt (1989), HC $15

White Rat, by Whitey Herzog with Kevin Horrigan, Harper & Row (1987), HC $10

The High Hard One, by Kirby Higbe and Martin Quigley, Viking (1967), HC $85

Gil Hodges: The Quiet Man, by Marino Amoruso, Erickson (1991), HC $25

My War With Baseball, by Rogers Hornsby with Bill Surface, McKay (1953), HC $85

The Willie Horton Story, by Hal Butler, Messner (1970), HC $25

The Jocks Itch, by Tom House, Contemporary (1989), HC $15

Frank Howard: The Gentle Giant, by Al Hirshberg, Putnam (1973), HC $40

Between the Lines, by Steve Howe with Jim Greenfield, Masters (1989), HC $12.50

Catfish, Million Dollar Pitcher, by Bill Libby (Jim Hunter), Coward McCann (1976), HC $12.50

Catfish Hunter, by Irwin Stambler, Putnam (1976), HC $20

Catfish, by Jim Catfish Hunter and Armen Keteyian, McGraw Hill (1988), HC..$10

Bo Knows Bo, by Bo Jackson with Dick Schaap, Doubleday (1990), HC $15

Reggie Jackson, The $3 Million Man, by Maury Allen, Harvey (1978), HC $15

The Reggie Jackson Story, by Bill Libby, Lothrop (1979), HC $20

Reggie, by Reggie Jackson with Mike Lupica, Villard (1984), HC $15

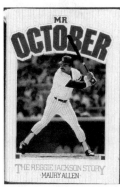

Mr. October, by Maury Allen (Reggie Jackson), Times (1981), HC $20

Say It Ain't So Joe—The Story of Shoeless Joe Jackson, by Donald Gropman, Little, Brown (1979), HC ....$50-$60

Shoeless Joe and Ragtime Baseball, by Harvey Frommer (Shoeless Joe Jackson), Taylor (1992), HC $15

Like Nobody Else, by Ferguson Jenkins and George Vass, Regnery (1973), signed..$60

The Tommy John Story, by Tommy and Sally John with Joe Muser, Revell (1978), HC, signed $40

Ban Johnson, by Gene Murdock, Greenwood (1982), HC $60

Walter Johnson, by Roger Treat, Messner (1948), HC $150

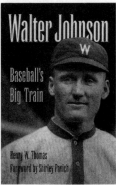

Walter Johnson—Baseball's Big Train, by Henry Thomas, Phenom (1995), HC $25

Temporary Insanity, by Jay Johnstone with Rick Talley, Contemporary (1985), HC, signed $20

Over the Edge, by Jay Johnstone with Rick Talley, Contemporary (1987), HC, signed $25

Cleon, by Cleon Jones with Ed Hershey, Coward McCann (1970), HC $25

The Al Kaline Story, by Al Hirshberg, Messner (1964), HC, signed $60

Al Kaline and the Detroit Tigers, by Hal Butler, Regnery (1973), HC $55

The Harmon Killebrew Story, by Hal Butler, Messner (1966), HC ..$15

Harmon Killebrew, Baseball's Superstar, Deseret (1971), HC $125

Ralph Kiner, The Heir Apparent, by Tom Meany, Barnes (1951), HC $45

Kiner's Korner, by Ralph Kiner and Joe Gergen, Arbor (1987), HC $25

Jim Konstanty, by Frank Yeutter, Barnes (1951), HC $17.50

Sandy Koufax—Strikeout King, Arnold Hano, Putnam (1964), HC ..$40

Koufax, by Sandy Koufax with Ed Linn, Viking (1966), HC, signed $100

Hardball, by Bowie Kuhn, Times (1987), HC $50

Judge Landis and 25 Years of Baseball, by J.G. Taylor Spink, Crowell (1947), HC $22.50

The Artful Dodger, by Tommy Lasorda with David Fisher, Arbor House (1985), HC...$20

The Wrong Stuff, by Bill Lee with Dick Lally, Viking (1984), HC $12.50

Breakout, by Ron LeFlore with Jim Hawkins, Harper & Row (1978), HC $15

Prophet of the Sandlots, by Mark Winegardner (scout Tony Luccadello), Atlantic Monthly (1990), HC $25

Fred Lynn, Young Star, by Bill Libby, Putnam (1977), HC, signed ...$40

Fred Lynn, The Hero from Boston, by Ed Dolan and Richard Lyttle, Icarus (1982), HC...$25

Connie Mack, by Fred Lieb, Putnam (1945), HC $35

My 66 Years in the Big Leagues, by Connie Mack, Winston (1950), HC $50

My Nine Innings, by Lee MacPhail, Meckler (1989), HC $25

The Sal Maglie Story, by Milton Shapiro, Messner (1966), HC ....$27.50-$45

The Mickey Mantle Story, by Mickey Mantle and Ben Epstein, Holt (1953) $150

Mickey Mantle of the Yankees, by Gene Schoor, Putnam (1958), HC $10

Mickey Mantle—Yankee Slugger, by Milton Shapiro, Messner (1962), HC $12.50

Mickey Mantle—Mr. Yankee, by Al Silverman, Putnam (1963), HC $50

The Quality of Courage, by Mickey Mantle, Doubleday (1964), HC $45

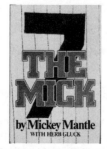

The Mick, by Mickey Mantle with Herb Gluck, Doubleday (1985), HC $25

A Pitcher's Story, by Juan Marichal with Charles Einstein, Doubleday (1967), HC $50

Roger Maris: A Man for All Seasons, by Maury Allen, Donald Fine & Co. (1986), HC ....$20-$30

Roger Maris: A Title to Fame, by Harvey Rosenfeld, Praire House (1991), HC $15

The Return of Billy the Kid, by Norman Lewis Smith (Billy Martin), Coward McCann (1977), HC $17.50

Billy Martin, by Gene Schoor, Doubleday (1980), HC $17.50

Billyball, Billy Martin with Phil Pepe, Doubleday (1987), HC ...$12.50

The Last Yankee, by David Falkner (Billy Martin), Simon & Schuster (1992), HC $15

Wild, High and Tight, by Peter Golenbock (Billy Martin), St. Martins (1994), HC $15

The Eddie Mathews Story, by Al Hirshberg, Messner (1961), HC, signed $75

Eddie Mathews and the National Pastime, by Eddie Mathews and Bob Buege, Douglas American (1994), HC, signed $45

Pitching in a Pinch, by Christy Mathewson, Putnam (1912), HC ..$350

Christy Mathewson, by Gene Schoor with Henry Gilfond, Messner (1953), HC $25

They Call Me Sarge, by Fred Mitchell with Gary Matthews, Bonus (1985), HC...$15

The Willie Mays Story, by Ken Smith, Greenberg (1954), HC $100

Born to Play Ball, Willie Mays and Charles Einstein, Putnam (1955), HC $45

Willie Mays Story, by Milton Shapiro, Messner (1960), HC $45

Mays, Mantle, Snider/A Celebration, by Donald Honig, MacMillan (1987) HC...$25

The Willie Mays Album, by Howard Liss, Hawthorn (1966), HC $75

My Life In and Out of Baseball, by Willie Mays and Charles Einstein, Dutton (1966), HC $15

Willie Mays—Baseball Superstar, by Sam and Beryl Epstein, Garrard (1975), HC $12.50

Willie's Time, by Charles Einstein (Willie Mays), Lippincott (1979), HC $30

Say Hey, Willie Mays with Lou Sahadi, Simon & Schuster (1988), HC, $10, signed $85

Oh, Baby, I Love It, by Tim McCarver with Ray Robinson, Villard (1987), HC $12.50

John McGraw, by Charles C. Alexander, Viking (1988), HC $35

Screwball, by Tug McGraw and Joe Durso, Houghton-Mifflin (1974), HC, signed $40

Nobody's Perfect, by Denny McLain with Dave Diles, Dial (1975), HC $20

Strikeout, by Denny McLain with Mike Nahrstedt, Sporting News (1988), HC, $15, signed $40

Joe Morgan: A Life in Baseball, by Joe Morgan with David Falkner, Norton (1933), HC, signed $60

Thurman Munson—Pressure Player, by Bill Libby, Putnam (1978), HC $30

Thurman Munson, by Thurman Munson with Martin Appel, Coward McCann (1978), HC $35

Ask Dale Murphy, by Dale Murphy with Curtis Patton, Algonquin (1987), HC $12.50

Stan Musial—The Man, by Tom Meany, Barnes (1951), HC $40

The Stan Musial Story, by Gene Schoor and Henry Gilfond, Messner (1955), HC $35

Stan Musial—The Man, by Irv Goodman, Nelson (1961), HC $30

Stan Musial, by Ray Robinson, Putnam (1963), HC $9

Stan Musial—The Man's Own Story, by Stan Musial and Bob Broeg, Doubleday (1964), HC $60

The Man, Stan Musial, Then and Now, Stan Musial and Bob Broeg, Bethany (1977), HC $45

Knuckler—The Phil Niekro Story, Wilfred Binette, Hallux Bros. (1970), HC, $25, signed $60

Knuckleballs, by Phil Niekro and Tom Bird, Freundlich (1986), HC $20

Sadahura Oh, by Sadahura Oh and David Falkner, Times (1984), HC $30

Pitchin' Man, by Satchel Paige and Hal Lebovitz, Cleveland News (1948), HC $35

Maybe I'll Pitch Forever, by Satchel Paige and David Lipman, Doubleday (1962), HC $75

Andy Pafko—The Solid Man, by John Hoffman, Barnes (1951), HC $65

Behind the Mask, by Dave Pallone and Alan Steinberg, Viking (1990), HC $12.50

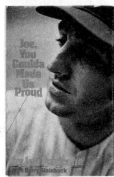

Joe, You Coulda Made Us Proud, by Joe Pepitone and Barry Stainback, Playboy (1975), HC $25

Me and the Spitter, by Gaylord Perry and Bob Sudyk, Sunday Review Press (1974), HC $50

The Truth Hurts, by Jimmy Piersall, Contemporary (1984), HC $12.50

Sweet Lou, by Lou Piniella and Maury Allen, Putnam (1986), HC $20

Snap Me Perfect, by Darrell Porter and William Deerfield, Nelson (1984), HC $10

Kirby Puckett—Fan Favorite, by Ann Bauleke (biography for younger readers), Lerner (1993), HC $15

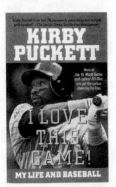

I Love This Game, by Kirby Puckett with Mike Bryan, Harper/Collins (1993), HC $12.50

Ted Double Duty Radcliffe, by Kyle McNary, McNary (1994), HC, signed $30

Phil Regan, by Phil Regan and James Hefley, Zondervan (1968), HC, signed $65

The Bobby Richardson Story, by Bobby Richardson, Revell (1965), HC, signed $50

Branch Rickey, by Arthur Mann, Houghton-Mifflin (1957), HC, inscribed $40

Branch Rickey, by Murray Polner, Atheneum (1982), HC $45

Phil Rizzuto, by Joe Trimble, Barnes (1951), HC $30

Phil Rizzuto: A Yankee Tradition, by Dan Hirshberg, Sagamore (1993), HC, signed $60

O Holy Cow! The Selected Verse of Phil Rizzuto, by Hart Seely and Tom Peyer, Ecco (1993) $10

The Brooks Robinson Story, by Jack Zanger, Messner (1967), HC $15

Putting It All Together, by Brooks Robinson and Fred Bauer, Hawthorn (1971), HC $30

Third Base Is My Home, by Brooks Robinson and Jack Tobin, Word (1974), HC..$30

Extra Innings, by Frank Robinson and Berry Stainback, McGraw-Hill (1988), HC...$17.50

My Life in Baseball, by Frank Robinson and Al Silverman, Doubleday (1975), HC..$12.50

My Own Story, by Jackie Robinson and Wendell Smith, Greenberg (1948), HC $100

The Jackie Robinson Story, by Arthur Mann, FJ Low (1950), HC ...$55

Wait Till Next Year, by Jackie Robinson and Carl Rowan, Random House (1960), HC $40

Jackie Robinson of the Brooklyn Dodgers, by Milton Shapiro, Messner (1965), HC $20

Jackie Robinson—Baseball's Gallant Fighter, by Sam and Beryl Epstein, Garrard (1974), HC $45

Jackie Robinson—A Life Remembered, by Maury Allen, Watts (1987), HC $25

I Never Had It Made, by Jackie Robinson and Alfred Duckett, Putnam (1972), HC $35

The Pete Rose Story, by Pete Rose, World (1970), HC $27.50

Pete Rose, They Call Him Charlie Hustle, by Bill Libby, Putnam (1972), HC $20

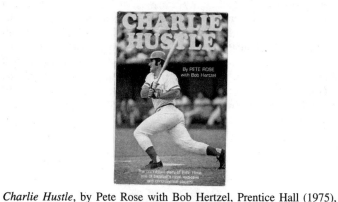

Charlie Hustle, by Pete Rose with Bob Hertzel, Prentice Hall (1975), HC $15

Pete Rose, Mr. .300, by Keith Brandt, Putnam (1977), HC $12.50

Pete Rose, My Life in Baseball, by Pete Rose, Doubleday (1979), HC $75

Pete Rose: My Story, by Pete Rose with Roger Kahn, MacMillan (1989), HC $7.50

Hustle: The Myth, Life and Lies of Pete Rose, by Michael Y. Sokolove, Simon & Schuster (1990), HC $17.50

Super Scout—Thirty Five Years of Major League Scouting, by Jim Russo and Bob Hammel, Bonus (1992), HC $15

Babe Ruth, by Tom Meany, Barnes (1947), HC $30

The Babe Ruth Story, by Babe Ruth and Bob Considine, Dutton (1948), HC $50

Babe Ruth—Baseball Boy, by Guernsey Van Riper, Bobbs-Merrill (1954), HC..$25

Babe Ruth, His Story in Baseball, by Lee Allen, Putnam (1966), HC $17.50

Babe Ruth's America, by Robert Smith, Crowell (1974), HC $40

Babe Ruth: His Life and Legend, by Karl Wagenheim, Praeger (1974), HC $45

The Life That Ruth Built, by Marshall Smelser (Babe Ruth), Quadrangle (1975), HC $75

Babe Ruth—Sultan of Swat, by Lois P. Nicholson, Goodwood (1994), HC $20

Nolan Ryan - Fireballer, by Bill Libby, Putnam (1975), HC $35

Throwing Heat, by Nolan Ryan and Harvey Frommer, Doubleday (1988), HC $15

Miracle Man: Nolan Ryan, by Nolan Ryan with Jerry Jenkins, Word (1992), HC $10

Second to None, by Ryne Sandberg, Bonus (1995), HC, signed........$50

Ron Santo: For Love of Ivy, by Ron Santo with Randy Minkoff, Bonus (1993), HC, signed $50

Sax!, by Steve Sax and Steve Delsohn, Contemporary (1986), HC, signed $20

Clowning Through Baseball, by Al Schact, Barnes (1941), HC $30

Tom Seaver of the Mets, by George Sullivan, Putnam (1971), HC $20

Inside Corner—Talks with Tom Seaver, by Joel Cohen, Atheneum (1974), HC, ...$30

Tom Seaver—Portrait of a Pitcher, by Malka Drucker with Tom Seaver, Holiday (1978), HC $20

Seaver, by Gene Schoor (Tom Seaver), Contemporary (1986), HC...$15

The Blooper Man, by Elson Smith (Rip Sewell), J. Pohl (1981), HC $25

The Ted Simmons Story, by Jim Brosnan, Putnam (1977), HC $30

Country Hardball, by Enos Slaughter and Kevin Reid, Tudor (1981), HC $45

Wizard, by Ozzie Smith with Rob Rains, Contemporary (1982), HC $25

The Duke Snider Story, by Irwin Winehouse, Messner (1964), HC $20

The Duke of Flatbush, by Duke Snider with Bill Gilbert, Zebra (1988), HC, $20, signed $50

A.G. Spalding and the Rise of Baseball, by Peter Levine, Oxford (1985), HC $30

Willie Stargell, by Bill Libby, Putnam (1973), HC..........................$10

Willie Stargell—An Autobiography, by Willie Stargell and Tom Bird, Harper & Row (1984), HC..$25

Rusty Staub of the Expos, by John Robertson, Prentice Hall (1971), HC $45

Casey Stengel—Baseball's Greatest Manager, by Gene Schoor, Messner (1953), HC $12.50

Casey Stengel, by Frank Graham Jr., John Day (1958), HC ......$15-$25

Casey at the Bat, by Casey Stengel and Harry T. Paxton, Random House (1962), HC $25

Casey, by Joseph Durso (Casey Stengel), Prentice Hall (1967), HC $25, signed $35

Casey Stengel, by Norman MacLean, Drake (1976), HC..................$40

Stengel: His Life and Times, by Robert W. Creamer, Simon & Schuster (1984), HC $30

Tomorrow, I'll Be Perfect, by Dave Stieb and Kevin Boland, Doubleday (1986), HC, signed $45

Darryl, by Darryl Strawberry and Art Rust Jr., Bantam (1992), HC $12.50

Triumph Born of Tragedy, by Andre Thornton and Al Janssen, Harvest House (1983), HC $25

El Tiante, by Luis Tiant and Joe Fitzgerald, Doubleday (1976), HC $25

Fernando!, by Mike Littwin (Fernando Valenzuela), Bantam (1981), HC $10

Veeck As In Wreck, by Bill Veeck with Ed Linn, Putnam (1962), HC, signed $200

The Hustlers Handbook, by Bill Veeck with Ed Linn, Putnam (1965), HC $65

The Kid from Cuba, James Terzian (Zoilo Versailles), Doubleday (1967), HC $30

The Ginger Kid, by Irving Stein (Buck Weaver), Brown and Benchmark (1992), HC $12.50

It's What You Learn After You Know It All That Counts, by Earl Weaver and Barry Stainback, Doubleday (1982), HC..................$20

Five O'Clock Comes Early, by Bob Welch and George Vecsey, Morrow (1982), HC..................$35

Billy, the Classic Hitter, by Billy Williams and Irv Haag, Rand McNally (1974), HC $50

Ted Williams, by Arthur Sampson, Barnes (1950), HC $45

My Turn at Bat, by Ted Williams with John Underwood, Simon & Schuster (1969) HC $45

Ted Williams: Seasons of the Kid, by Richard Cramer, Prentice Hall (1991), HC..................$45

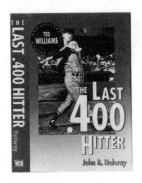

The Last .400 Hitter, by John B. Holway (Ted Williams), William C. Brown (1991), HC..................$20

Ted Williams—A Baseball Life, by Michael Seidel, Contemporary (1991), HC $20

It Pays to Steal, by Maury Wills and Steve Gardner, Prentice Hall (1963), HC $10

How to Steal a Pennant, by Maury Wills and Don Freeman, Putnam (1976), HC $12.50

On the Run, by Maury Wills and Mike Celizic, Carroll & Graf (1991), HC ....$15, signed, $30

Hack, by Robert Boone and Gerald Grunska (Hack Wilson), Highland Press (1978), HC $75

Dave Winfield—23 Million Dollar Man, by Gene Schoor, Stein & Day (1982), HC..................$30

Winfield—A Player's Life, by Dave Winfield with Tom Parker, Norton (1988), HC, $10, signed $35

Dave Winfield—3,000 and Counting, by the St. Paul Pioneer Press, Andrews & McMeel (1993), HC $15

Philip K. Wrigley, by Paul Angle, Rand McNally (1975), HC..........$65

Yaz, by Carl Yastrzemski with Al Hirshberg, Viking (1968), HC......$30

Batting, by Carl Yastrzemski with Al Hirshberg, Viking (1972), HC $25

Historical

The Autobiography of Baseball: The Inside Story from the Stars Who Played the Game, by Joseph Wallace and Ira Berkow, Abradale Press (2000), HC 224 pages $18

After the Miracle, by Maury Allen (1969 Mets, 20 years later), Watts (1989), HC..................$20

The Armchair Book of Baseball, by John Thorn, Scribners (1985), HC $15

Backstage at the Mets, by Lindsey Nelson and Al Hirshberg, Viking (1966), HC..................$30

Ballparks, by Robert Von Goeben and Red Howard, Metro Books (2000), HC 120 pages $15

The Baseball Anthology: 125 Years of Stories, Poems, Articles, Photographs, Drawings, Interviews, Cartoons and Other Memorabilia, by Joseph Wallace and Sparky Anderson, Abradale Press, (1998), HC 304 pages $25

Ballplayers Are Human Too, by Ralph Houk and Charles Dexter, Putnam (1962), HC..................$27.50

Baseball Between the Lines, by Donald Honig, Coward McCann (1976), HC $35

Baseball Is a Funny Game, by Joe Garagiola with Martin Quigley, Lippincott (1960), HC $30

Baseball's Golden Age: The Photographs of Charles M. Conlon, by Neal McCabe, Constance McCabe, Charles Martin Conlon, Abradale Press (1997), HC 198 pages $20

Baseball Rookies Who Made Good, by M.G. Bonner (Mantle, Williams, Ruth, etc.), Knopf (1954) $35

Baseball's 100, by Maury Allen (his picks as the best), Galahad (1982), HC $17.50

Baseball Through a Knothole, by Bill Borst (history of baseball in St. Louis), Krank (1980), HC $15

Baseball When the Grass Was Real, by Donald Honig, Coward McCann (1975), HC $35

Bats, by Davey Johnson and Peter Golenbock (New York Mets' 1985 season), Putnam (1986), HC $45

Beating the Bushes, by Frank Dolson (life in the minors), Icarus (1982), HC $30

The Best Seat in Baseball, But You Have to Stand, by Lee Gutkind (1974 season from an umpiring crews viewpoint), Dial (1975), HC, ...$30-$40

Beyond the Sixth Game, by Peter Gammons (Boston Red Sox from the sixth game of the 1975 World Series on), Houghton-Mifflin (1985), HC $25

Black Diamonds, by John Holway, Meckler (1989), HC $20

Bleachers—A Summer in Wrigley Field, by Lonnie Wheeler, Contemporary (1988), HC $30

The Boston Red Sox, by Fred Lieb, Putnam (1947), HC $45

The Boston Red Sox, by Tom Meany, Barnes (1956), HC $35

The Boys of Summer, by Roger Kahn, Harper & Row (1972), HC ...$50

The Boys Who Would Be Cubs, by Joseph Bosco (a year with the Class A Peoria Cubs), Morrow (1990), HC ....$12.50-$20

The Broadcasters, by Red Barber, Dial (1970), HC $50

The Bronx Zoo, by Sparky Lyle and Peter Golenbock, Crown (1979), HC, $10, signed $40

Bums, by Peter Golenbock (Brooklyn Dodgers baseball), Putnam (1984), HC $30

Bush League, by Robert Obojski (history of the minors), MacMillan (1975), HC $50

Can't Anybody Here Play This Game?, by Jimmy Breslin (New York Mets first year), Viking (1963), HC $40

Catch—A Major League Life, by Ernie Whitt and Greg Cable (Blue Jays 1988 season as seen by teams catcher), McGraw Hill - Ryerson, HC $27.50

Champagne and Baloney, by Tom Clark (recaps Oakland's prominence in the 1970s), Harper & Row (1976) $17.50

Charlie O & the Angry A's, by Bill Libby, Doubleday (1975) $20

The Chicago Cubs, by Warren Brown, Putnam (1946), HC ....$50-$75

The Chicago White Sox, by Warren Brown, Putnam (1952), HC ....$75-$90

The Chrysanthemum and the Bat, by Robert Whiting (baseball in Japan), Dodd, Mead (1977), HC $50

The Cincinnati Reds, by Lee Allen, Putnam (1948), HC $135

The Cincinnati Reds, by Ritter Collett, Jordan-Powers (1976), HC $125

Colorado Rockies—The Inaugural Season, by Rich Clarkson and Bob Baron, Fulcrum (1993), HC..............................$45

The Complete New York Yankees: The Total Encyclopedia of the Team, by Derek Gentile, Black Dog & Leventhal Pub., (1998), HC 600 pages $25

Cooperstown: Baseball's Hall of Fame, by Lowell Reidenbaugh, (1999), HC 400 pages $20

The Crooked Pitch, by Martin Quigley, Algonquin (1984), HC $35

The Cubs of 69, by Rick Talley (recaps the bittersweet 1969 season), Contemporary (1989), HC $20

The Curse of the Bambino, by Dan Shaughnessy, Dutton (1990), HC $25

Fair Ball, A Fan's Case for Baseball, by Bob Costas, Bantam Books (2000), HC 179 pages $25

Lightning in a Bottle, by Herbert F. Crehan with James W. Ryan (1967 Boston Red Sox), Branden (1992) $17.50

The Long Season, by Jim Brosnan (diary of the 1959 season), Harper & Row (1960), HC, $60, signed $85

Louisville Slugger, by Jan Arrow (history of bat making), Pantheon (1984), HC $30

Love Letters to the Mets, by Bill Adler, Simon & Schuster (1965) ...$50

Major League Memories Series, by Bruce Chadwick and David Spindel, team summaries and artifacts for the Los Angeles Dodgers (1993), $15; Boston Red Sox (1992), $12.50; Cincinnati Reds (1994) $8

The Man in the Crowd—Confessions of a Sports Addict, by Stanley Cohen, Random House (1981), HC $15

The Man in the Dugout, by Donald Honig, Follett (1977), HC $20

The Man Who Stole First Base, by Eric Nadel and Craig R. Wright (135 off-beat stories), Taylor (1989) $12.50

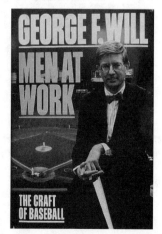

Men at Work, by George F. Will, MacMillan (1990), HC $10

The Men in Blue, by Larry Gerlach, Viking (1980), HC $35

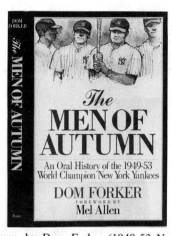

The Men of Autumn, by Dom Forker (1949-53 New York Yankees), Taylor (1989), HC $20

Men of the Reds Machine, by Ritter Collett (1970s Cincinnati Reds), Landfall (1976), HC $35

The Mets Will Win the Pennant, by William Cox, Putnam (1964), HC $40

The Milwaukee Braves, a Baseball Eulogy, by Bob Buege, Douglas (1988), HC $25

The Minors, by Neil J. Sullivan (historical overview of the minor leagues), St. Martins (1990), HC $17.50

Miracle at Coogans Bluff, by Thomas Kiernan (1951 Giants), Crowell (1975), HC..$35

Misfits!, J. Thomas Hetrick (1899 Cleveland Spiders), McFarland (1991) HC $25

My Baseball Diary, by James Farrell (novelists viewpoint on the game he followed all his life), Barnes (1957), HC .... $40-$50

My Baseball Scrapbook, by Bob Broeg (St. Louis Cardinal beat writer), River City (1983), HC $45

My Favorite Summer 1956, by Mickey Mantle and Phil Pepe, Doubleday (1991), HC $15

The Neighborhood of Baseball, by Barry Gifford (Chicago Cubs from the 1950s-80s), Dutton (1981), HC $20

The New Baseball Reader, by Charles Einstein (baseball anthologies), Viking (1991), HC $20

New York City Baseball, by Harvey Frommer (1947-57 baseball in New York), MacMillan (1980), HC $35

Nine Innings, by Daniel Okrent (1982 Brewer/Orioles game), Ticknor & Fields (1985), HC $15

1947: When All Hell Broke Loose in Baseball, by Red Barber, Doubleday (1982), HC $45

No Cheering in the Press Box, by Jerome Holtzman, Holt, Rinehart & Winston (1974), HC $30

No Joy in Mudville, by Ralph Andreano, Schenkman (1965), HC $25

October 1964, by David Halberstam (recaps pennant race and World Series), Villard (1994), HC $15

One Strike Away, by Dan Shaughnessy (1986 Red Sox season), Beaufort (1987), HC $25

Only the Ball Was White, by Robert Peterson (Negro Leagues), Prentice Hall, HC $100

The Only Ticket Off the Island, by Gare Joyce (a season in the Dominican Republic's Winter League), Lester & Orpen Dennys (1990), HC .$40

Our Game, by Charles C. Alexander (history of the game), Holt (1991), HC $17.50

Out of My League, by George Plimpton, Harper (1961), HC $25

Pen Men, by Bob Cairns (life in the bullpen), St. Martins (1992), HC $10

The Perfect Game, by Tom Seaver and Dick Schaap (1969 Mets), Dutton (1970), HC $12.50

The Philadelphia Phillies, by Fred Lieb and Stan Baumgartner, Putnam (1953), HC $225

The Philadelphia Phillies—The Team that Wouldn't Die, by Hal Bodley (1981), HC $45

Pine Tarred and Feathered, by Jim Kaplan (*Sports Illustrated* writer), Algonquin (1985), HC $17.50

Pinstripe Pandemonium, by Geoffrey Stokes (Yankees 1983 season), Harper & Row (1984), HC...$10

The Pirates—We Are Family, Lou Sahadi, Times (1980), HC............$25

Pitchers Do Get Lonely, by Ira Berkow, Atheneum (1988), HC $15

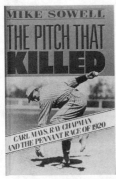

The Pitch That Killed, by Mike Sowell, MacMillan (1989), HC $20

The Pittsburgh Pirates, by Fred Lieb, Putnam (1948), HC ....$100-$135

Play Ball, by John Feinstein (baseballs troubled times), Villard (1993), HC $12.50

Playing Around, by Donald Hall, et. al. (1973 spring training with the Pittsburgh Pirates), Little, Brown (1974), HC $30

The Psychologist at Bat, by David F. Tracy (team psychologist for the St. Louis Browns), Sterling (1951), HC $50

Roger Maris at Bat, by Roger Maris and Jim Ogle, Duell (1961 season), Sloan and Pearce (1962), HC $60

The Rookies, by Ed Walton, Stein & Day (1982), HC $12.50

Safe at Home, by Sharon Hargrove (baseball wife tells her story), by Texas A&M (1989), HC $17.50

The St. Louis Cardinals, by Fred Lieb, Putnam (1944), HC $30

A Season in the Sun, by Roger Kahn, Harper & Row (1977), HC, signed $50

Season of Dreams, by Tom Kelly and Ted Robinson (Minnesota Twins 1991 season), Voyager Press (1992), HC $17.50

The Seattle Pilots Story, by Carson Van Lindt, Marabou (1993), HC $10

The Short Season, by David Falkner (spring training atmosphere), Times (1986), HC $45

Some Are Called Clowns, Bill Heward and Dimitri Gat (season with pitcher/manager of the 1973 Indianapolis Clowns), Crowell (1974), HC ....$50-$60

Streak: Joe DiMaggio and the Summer of 1941, by Michael Seidel, McGraw Hill (1988), HC ....$12.50-$20

The Suitors of Spring, by Pat Jordan, Dodd Mead (1973), HC $10

Superstars and Screwballs, by Richard Goldstein (baseball in Brooklyn), Dutton (1991), HC $15

Sweet Seasons, by Dom Forker (1955-64 New York Yankees), Taylor (1990), HC $20

Take Me Out to the Ballpark: An Illustrated Guide to Baseball Parks Past & Present, by Josh Leventhal, Black Dog & Leventhal Pub. (2000), HC 128 pages...$30

Ted Williams—The Golden Year 1957, by Edwin Pope, Prentice Hall (1970), HC, signed $275

The Twenty-Four Inch Home Run, by Michael Bryson (baseball oddities and anecdotes), Contemporary (1990), HC $15

The 26th Man, by Steve Fireovid and Mark Winegardner (story of a veteran minor leaguer), Macmillan (1991), HC $20

They Kept Me Loyal to the Yankees, by Victor Debs (tribute to former Yankees), Rutledge (1993), HC $25

Tomahawked, by Bill Zack (1992 Braves season), Simon & Schuster (1993), HC...$15

Total Baseball, by John Thorn and Pete Palmer, Warner (1989), HC $25

Two Spectacular Seasons, by William B. Mead (1930 and 1968 seasons recapped), Macmillan (1990), HC $12.50

Up From the Minor Leagues, by Donald Honig, Cowles (1970), HC $40

View From the Dugout, Ed Richter (1963 Philadelphia Phillies season), Chilton (1964), HC $27.50

Voices From the Great Black Baseball Leaguers, by John Holway, Dodd Mead (1975), HC $125

Voices of the Game, by Curt Smith (chronicles baseball broadcasting), Diamond (1987), HC $30

Wait Til Next Year, by Chris Jennison (New York City baseball from the 1940s and '50s), Norton (1974), signed by Duke Snider................$40

Want To Be a Baseball Champion?, by Ethan Allen (demonstrates baseball offensive strategies), General Mills (1946), HC $45

We Won Today, by Kathleen Parker (diary of a 1976 Mets fan), Doubleday (1977), HC ....$25-$35

When the Cheering Stops, by Lee Heiman, Dave Weiner and Bill Gutman (profiles 21 players from the 1950s and 1960s), MacMillan (1990), HC $15

The Whiz Kids, by Harry Paxton (1950 Phillies), McKay (1950), HC $110

Winning, by Earl Weaver and John Sammis (instructional), Morrow (1972), HC $20

Wild and Outside, by Stefan Fatsis (1994 season of the independent Northern League of Professional Baseball), Walker (1995), HC ...$25

The World Champion Pittsburgh Pirates, by Dick Groat and Bill Surface (1961 Pirates season), Coward McCann (1961), HC $65

Yankee Batboy, by Joe Carrieri and Zander Hollander, Barnes (1945), HC...$30

The Year of the Tiger, by Jerry Green, Coward McCann (1969), HC $40

The Year the Mets Lost Last Place, by Paul Zimmerman and Dick Schaap, World (1969), HC $20

The Year They Called Off the World Series, by Benton Stark (details the 1904 season), Avery (1991), HC $15

You Gotta Have Wa, by Robert Whiting (baseball in Japan), MacMillan (1989), HC ....$15-$20

BASEBALL COMIC BOOKS

A-1 Comics
Magazine Enterprises
1944-1955
89) Home Run, Stan Musial.............................$125

All-Pro Sports
1) Unauthorized bio—Bo Jackson, baseball (black and white).......$2.50

The All-Star Story of the Dodgers
Stadium Communications
April 1979
1F) Roy Campanella, Sandy Koufax, Jackie Robinson $2

All-Time Sports Comics
Hillman Periodicals
Oct.-Nov. 1949
5) Baseball...$75
7) Baseball...$75

The Amazing Willie Mays
Famous Funnies Publications
September 1954
1) Willie Mays...$400

The Amazon of the Ozarks
Prize/Headline Feature
June-July 1948
2) Baseball..$30

Babe Ruth Sports Comics
Harvey Publications
April 1949-February 1951
2) Baseball...$175
3) Joe DiMaggio.......................................$150
4) Bob Feller $125
8) Yogi Berra $115
9) Stan Musial $125

Baseball Classics
Personality
1) Willie Mays.......................................$2.75
1a) Willie Mays with trading cards $5
2) Lou Gehrig..$2.75
2a) Lou Gehrig with trading cards......................$5

Baseball Comics
Will Eisner Productions
Spring 1949
1) Rube Rooky $425

Baseball Comics
Personality
1) Frank Thomas $2.75
1a) Frank Thomas with cards $5

2) Rickey Henderson..................................$2.75
2a) Rickey Henderson with cards.........................$5
3) Nolan Ryan..$2.75
3a) Nolan Ryan with cards...............................$5
4) Cal Ripken Jr.....................................$2.75
4a) Cal Ripken Jr. with cards...........................$5

Baseball Greats
Dark Horse
1) Jimmy Piersall story...............................$2.95

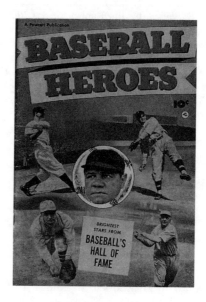

Baseball Heroes
Fawcett Publications
1952
Babe Ruth/Hall of Fame Biographies $450

Baseball Legends
Revolutionary
1) Babe Ruth $2.50
2) Ty Cobb...$2.50
3) Ted Williams $2.50
4) Mickey Mantle $2.50
5) Joe DiMaggio $2.50
6) Jackie Robinson $2.50
7) Sandy Koufax......................................$2.50
8) Willie Mays.......................................$2.50
9) Honus Wagner $2.50
10) Roberto Clemente $2.50
11) Yogi Berra $2.50
13) Hank Aaron $3
14) Carl Yastrzemski $3
15) Satchel Paige....................................$3
16) Johnny Bench $3

17) Shoeless Joe Jackson $3

18) Lou Gehrig $3

Baseball Sluggers
Personality Comics

1) Ken Griffey Jr..$2.75

1a) limited edition $5

2) Dave Justice $2.75

2a) limited edition $5

3) Frank Thomas $2.75

3a) limited edition $5

4) Don Mattingly $2.75

4a) limited edition $5

Baseball Superstars
Revolutionary

Hank Aaron; Jim Abbott; Alomar brothers; Steve Avery, Tom Glavine; Johnny Bench; Yogi Berra; George Brett; Jose Canseco; Roger Clemens; Joe DiMaggio; Dennis Eckersley; Carlton Fisk; Lou Gehrig; Ken Griffey Jr.; Rickey Henderson; Bo Jackson; Mickey Mantle; Billy Martin; Willie Mays; Mark McGwire; Kirby Puckett; Cal Ripken Jr.; Pete Rose; Nolan Ryan; Babe Ruth; Ryne Sandberg; Darryl Strawberry; Frank Thomas; Honus Wagner; Ted Williams; Dave Winfield; Carl Yastrzemski; Annual #1 Nolan Ryan. ....$3 ea.

Baseball Thrills
Ziff-Davis Publishing Co.
1951-1952

10) Bob Feller $200

2) Yogi Berra $150

3) Joe DiMaggio...$150

Baseball Thrills 3-D
3-D Zone
May 1990

1) Ty Cobb, Ted Williams..cover

Best Pitchers
Personality

1) Nolan Ryan...cover

1a) Nolan Ryan with cards ....cover

2) Dwight Gooden ....cover

2a) Dwight Gooden with cards.....................................cover

3) Roger Clemens ....cover

3a) Roger Clemens with cards ....cover

Bill Sterns Sports Book
Ziff-Davis Publishing Co.
1951-1952

1) Ewell Blackwell..$90

Blue Bolt
Funnies Inc./Novelty Press/Premium Group of Comics
1940-1949

8-1 Baseball cover $22

9-1 Baseball cover $22

10-1 Baseball cover $24

Blue Devil
DC Comics
1984-1986

26) Special baseball issue...$1.50

Brooks Robinson
Magnum
May 1992

1) Photo $1.75

Calling All Boys
Parents Magazine Institute
1946-1948

7) Baseball..$14

12) Baseball..$40

Comics Revue
St. John Publishing Co.
1947-48

3) Iron Vic baseball cover $27.50

Daredevil Comics
Lev Gleason Publications
July 1941-Sept. 1956

25) Baseball cover..$175

DC Superstars
National Periodical Publications/DC Comics
1976-1978

10) Superhero Baseball Special $4.25

Don Newcombe
Fawcett Publications
1950

1) Baseball Star $200

Famous Funnies
Eastern Color
1933-1955

22) Baseball cover..$300

58) Baseball cover..$140

Parents Institute
1947-1949
7) Baffling Mystery on the Diamond..$50

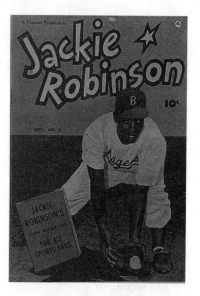

Jackie Robinson
Fawcett Publications
1950-1952
Famous Plays of Jackie Robinson..$450

2) Famous Plays of Jackie Robinson $300

3) Famous Plays of Jackie Robinson $250

4) Famous Plays of Jackie Robinson $250

5) Famous Plays of Jackie Robinson $250

6) Famous Plays of Jackie Robinson $250

King Comics
David McKay Publications
Starring Popeye
1936-1952
39) Baseball..$200

61) Phantom Baseball $125

156) Baseball..$35

Krazy Komics
Timely
1942-1948
24) Baseball..$40

Larry Doby, Baseball Hero
Fawcett Publications
1950
1) Baseball..$400

Lil' Abner
Harvey Publications
1947-1955
83) Baseball...$60

Mel Allen Sports Comics
Visual Editions
1949-1950
2) Lou Gehrig $70

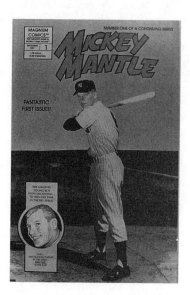

Mickey Mantle Comics
Magnum
1) Rise to Big Leagues..$3

Negro Heroes
Parents Magazine Institute
1947-1948
2) Jackie Robinson $375

Phil Rizzuto
Fawcett Publications
1951
The Sensational Story of the American Leagues MVP $350

Power Pack
1984-1991
13) Baseball issue...$2

The Pride of the Yankees
Magazine Enterprises
No # The Life of Lou Gehrig...$425

Ralph Kiner, Home Run King
Fawcett Publications
1950
No # Life Story of the Famous Pittsburgh Slugger $300

Real Heroes Comics
Parents Magazine Institute
1941-1946
6) Lou Gehrig $85
14) Pete Gray $30

Real Life Comics
Nedor/Better/Standard Publications
1941-1952
24) Babe Ruth $65
41) Jimmie Foxx..$35

Roy Campanella, Baseball Hero
Fawcett Publications
1950
No # Life Story of the Battling Dodgers Catcher............................$325

Sport Comics
Street & Smith Publications
1940-1941
1) Lou Gehrig..$275
3) Phil Rizzuto..$125

Sports Action
Marvel Comics
1950-1952
3) Hack Wilson..$100
7) Jim Konstanty $90
8) Ralph Kiner..$90

Sports Classics
Personality Comics
1) Babe Ruth $2.50
1a) with trading cards..................................$5
2) Mickey Mantle $2.50

2a) with trading cards..................................$5
3) Ty Cobb..$2.50
3a) with trading cards..................................$5
4) Ted Williams $2.50
4a) with trading cards..................................$5
5 Jackie Robinson $2.50
5a) with trading cards..................................$5

Sports Personalities
Personality Comics
1992
2) Nolan Ryan $2.50
2a) limited edition $5
3) Rickey Henderson $2.50
3a) limited edition $5
8) George Brett...$2.50
8a) limited edition $5
12) Ken Griffey Jr......................................$2.50
12a) with trading cards.................................$5
14) Pete Rose...$2.50
14a) with trading cards.................................$5

Sports Stars
Parents Magazine Institute
1946
2) Baseball Greats $125

Sport Thrills
Star Publications
1950-1951
11) Ted Williams, Ty Cobb $90
12) Joe DiMaggio, Phil Rizzuto..........................$65
14) baseball cover......................................$65
15) baseball cover......................................$65

Supersnipe Comics
Street & Smith's Publications
1942-1949
2-4 Baseball..$175
3-3 Baseball..$150
3-11 Baseball Pitcher $150
4-8 Baseball Star $115

Target Comics
Funnies Inc./Novelty Publishing/Star Publications
1940-1949
9-5 Baseball..$30

Thrilling True Story of the Baseball Giants
Thrilling True Story of the Baseball Yankees
Fawcett Publications
1952
Famous Giants of the Past...............................$375
Baseball Yankees $350

True Comics
True Comics/Parents Magazine Press
1941-1950

3) Baseball Hall of Fame $100

6) Baseball World Series $95

15) Bob Feller $45

37) Baseball...$25

44) El Senor Goofy, baseball $25

49) Baseball..$20

71) The Story of Joe DiMaggio $25

77) Lou Boudreau $25

78) Stan Musial $25

84) Includes baseball...$115

True Sport Picture Stories
Street & Smith Publications
1942-1949

1-5 Joe DiMaggio..$160

1-7 Mel Ott..$85

2-3 Carl Hubbell...$70

2-7 Stan Musial $75

2-10 Connie Mack...$70

3-2 The Philadelphia Athletics $60

3-3 Leo Durocher $60

3-12 Red Sox vs. Senators $60

4-1 Spring Training in full spring $55

4-2 How to Pitch 'Em Where They Can't Hit 'Em $55

Vic Verity Magazine
Vic Verity Publications
1945

5) Championship Baseball Game.............................$35

WOW Comics
Fawcett Publications
1940-1948

69) Tom Mix Baseball...$50

Yogi Berra
Fawcett Publications
1957

1) Yogi Berra $350

Young All-Stars
DC Comics
June 1987

7) Baseball Game ....cover

Chapter 5

Pins, Pennants, etc.

PRESS PINS AND MEDALLIONS

World Series Pins

1911 Philadelphia Athletics: Allen A. Kerr; brooch; blue ....$13,850-$18,000
1912 New York Giants: Whitehead & Hoag; brooch; blue...$6,500-$12,500
1912 Boston Red Sox: Unknown; threaded post; red...$3,500-$5,000
1913 New York Giants: Whitehead & Hoag; threaded post; blue ....$5,000-$10,000
1913 Philadelphia Athletics: J.E. Caldwell; brooch; blue/green...$6,000-$6,500
1914 Boston Braves: Bent & Bush; threaded post; blue..$5,000-$5,500
1914 Philadelphia Athletics: J.E. Caldwell; brooch; blue/white/green...............................$6,500-$11,000
1915 Philadelphia Phillies: J.E. Caldwell; brooch; red...$6,000-$11,000
1915 Boston Red Sox: Bent & Bush; threaded post; gold...$4,000-$5,500
1916 Brooklyn Dodgers: Dieges & Clust; threaded post; blue/white....................................$4,000-$4,400
1916 Boston Red Sox: Bent & Bush; threaded post; red/blue...$4,000-$5,000
1917 New York Giants: Unknown; brooch; gold ....$4,500-$7,000
1917 Chicago White Sox, with banner: Greenduck; threaded post; blue ....$4,000-$9,500
1918 Boston Red Sox: Bent & Bush; threaded post; gold...$3,000-$5,500
1919 Cincinnati Reds: Gustave Fox; threaded post; gold...$2,500-$4,750
1919 Chicago White Sox, with banner: Greenduck; threaded post; gold............................$5,000-$12,000
1920 Brooklyn Dodgers: Unknown; threaded post; red ....$2,500-$3,000
1920 Cleveland Indians, enamel: Unknown; threaded post; green/white................................$1,500-$3,000
1920 Cleveland Indians celluloid button: Unknown; safety brooch; black/white ....$2,500-$3,500
1921 New York Yankees/Giants: Whitehead & Hoag; brooch; blue/white.............................$2,000-$2,500
1922 New York Yankees/Giants: Whitehead & Hoag; brooch; blue/white.............................$3,000-$4,000
1923 New York Yankees: Dieges & Clust; threaded post; red/white/blue ....$2,300-$3,800
1924 New York Giants: Dieges & Clust; threaded post; blue...$845-$1,500
1924 Washington Senators: Dieges & Clust; threaded post; red/white/blue ....$1,000-$1,500
1925 Pittsburgh Pirates: Whitehead & Hoag; threaded post; black/white..............................$1,500-$2,500
1925 Washington Senators: Dieges & Clust; threaded post; blue...$1,375-$2,000
1926 St. Louis Cardinals: Unknown; threaded post; red ....$1,300-$2,400
1926 New York Yankees: Dieges & Clust; threaded post; red/white/blue ....$1,200-$1,500
1927 Pittsburgh Pirates: Whitehead & Hoag; threaded post; black/white..............................$1,100-$2,000
1927 New York Yankees: Dieges & Clust; threaded post; red/white/blue ....$2,000-$2,300
1928 St. Louis Cardinals: St. Louis Button; threaded post; red/white/blue ....$875-$1,200
1928 New York Yankees: Dieges & Clust; threaded post; red/white/blue ....$1,850-$2,400
1929 Chicago Cubs: Hipp & Coburn; threaded post; red/white/blue ....$1,500-$2,350
1929 Philadelphia Athletics: Unknown; threaded post; blue/white ....$375-$800
1930 St. Louis Cardinals: St. Louis Button; threaded post; red/white/blue ....$500-$1,000

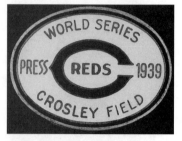

1930 Philadelphia Athletics: Unknown; threaded post; blue/white ....$3,000-$5,000
1931 St. Louis Cardinals: St. Louis Button; threaded post; red/white/blue ....$650-$900
1931 Philadelphia Athletics: Unknown; threaded post; blue/white ....$1,300-$1,500
1932 Chicago Cubs: Dieges & Clust; threaded post; black/white..$1,900-$2,200
1932 New York Yankees: Dieges & Clust; threaded post; gold......................................$1,000-$1,200
1933 New York Giants: Dieges & Clust; threaded post; red/green/blue..........................$235-$700
1933 Washington Senators: Dieges & Clust; threaded post; gold ....$700-$950
1934 St. Louis Cardinals: St. Louis button; threaded post; red/white ....$650-$800
1934 Detroit Tigers: Dieges & Clust; threaded post; black/white..$600-$750
1935 Chicago Cubs: S.D. Childs; brooch; red/white/blue ....$2,200-$3,000
1935 Detroit Tigers: Unknown; threaded post; black ....$600-$800
1936 New York Giants: Dieges & Clust; threaded post; black/white/orange ....$275-$400
1936 New York Yankees: Dieges & Clust; threaded post; red/white/blue ....$550-$800
1937 New York Giants: Dieges & Clust; threaded post; black/orange ....$225-$350
1937 New York Yankees: Dieges & Clust; threaded post; red/white/blue ....$450-$600
1938 Chicago Cubs: Lambert Bros.; brooch; red/white/blue ....$1,400-$2,250
1938 New York Yankees: Dieges & Clust; threaded post; red/white/blue ....$475-$750
1939 Cincinnati Reds: Bastian Bros.; threaded post, brooch; red/white/blue ....$275-$425
1939 New York Yankees: Dieges & Clust; threaded post; red/white/blue ....$400-$750
1940 Cincinnati Reds: Bastian Bros.; threaded post, brooch; red/white/blue ....$425-$475
1940 Detroit Tigers: Unknown; threaded post; gold..$475-$650
1941 Brooklyn Dodgers: Dieges & Clust; threaded post; red/white/blue ....$450-$725
1941 New York Yankees: Dieges & Clust; threaded post; red/white/blue ....$275-$475
1942 St. Louis Cardinals: St. Louis button; safety brooch; red/white/black ....$2,000-$2,400
1942 New York Yankees: Dieges & Clust; threaded post, brooch; silver ....$275-$400
1943 St. Louis: St. Louis button; safety brooch; red/black/white..$1,000-$2,000
1943 New York Yankees: Dieges & Clust; threaded post, brooch; silver ....$300-$500
1944 St. Louis Cardinals: St. Louis button; threaded post; copper ....$450-$575
1944 St. Louis Browns: St. Louis button; threaded post; copper ....$500-$575
1945 Chicago Cubs: Unknown; threaded post; red/white/blue..$400-$550
1945 Detroit Tigers: Unknown; threaded post; red/blue ....$425-$575
1946 St. Louis Cardinals: St. Louis button; threaded post; red/white/silver ....$350-$500
1946 Boston Red Sox: Balfour; threaded post; red/white ....$300-$575
1947 Brooklyn Dodgers: Dieges & Clust; threaded post, brooch; blue ....$400-$800
1947 New York Yankees: Dieges & Clust; threaded post; red/white/blue ....$500-$600
1948 Boston Braves: Balfour; threaded post; red/white/copper ....$400-$475
1948 Cleveland Indians: Balfour; threaded post; red/white/black ....$250-$400
1949 Brooklyn Dodgers: Dieges & Clust; threaded post, brooch; blue ....$350-$400
1949 New York Yankees: Dieges & Clust; threaded post, brooch red/white/blue ....$300-$400
1950 Philadelphia Phillies: Martin; needle post; red/silver ....$250-$350
1950 New York Yankees: Dieges and Clust; threaded post, brooch red/white/blue ....$250-$375
1951 New York Giants: Dieges & Clust; threaded post; black/white..$150-$175
1951 New York Yankees: Dieges & Clust; threaded post, brooch; red/white/blue..........................$125-$175
1952 Brooklyn Dodgers: Dieges & Clust; threaded post, brooch; red/blue ....$300-$400
1952 New York Yankees: Balfour; threaded post, brooch; red/white/blue ....$200-$300
1953 Brooklyn Dodgers: Dieges & Clust; threaded post, brooch; white/blue ....$275-$350
1953 New York Yankees: Balfour; threaded post and brooch; red/white/blue..........................$250-$325
1954 New York Giants: Dieges and Clust; threaded post; black/white ....$150-$200
1954 Cleveland Indians: Balfour; threaded post; red/white/blue/black..........................$250-$300
1955 Brooklyn Dodgers: Dieges & Clust; threaded post, brooch; silver/white/blue ....$400-$500
1955 New York Yankees: Balfour; threaded post, brooch; red/white/blue ....$125-$275
1956 Brooklyn Dodgers: Dieges & Clust; clasps; silver/white/blue ....$500-$750
1956 New York Yankees: Balfour; threaded post, brooch; red/white/blue ....$200-$300
1957 Milwaukee Braves: Balfour; threaded post; copper/red..$150-$200
1957 New York Yankees: Balfour; threaded post, brooch red/white/blue....................................$150-$200
1958 Milwaukee Braves: Balfour; threaded post; black/white ....$200-$275
1958 New York Yankees: Balfour; threaded post, brooch, white/blue..$175-$200
1959 Los Angeles Dodgers: Balfour; threaded post, charm, brooch; white/blue ....$125-$250
1959 Chicago White Sox: Balfour; threaded post, brooch; blue/green ....$175-$275
1960 Pittsburgh Pirates: Josten; threaded post; black/white ....$175-$250
1960 New York Yankees: Balfour; threaded post, brooch white/blue..$100-$150
1961 Cincinnati Reds: Balfour; threaded post, charm; red/white/blue ....$100-$175
1961 New York Yankees: Balfour; threaded post, brooch; red/white/blue ....$125-$225
1962 San Francisco Giants: Balfour; threaded post; white..$200-$275

1962 New York Yankees: Balfour; threaded post, brooch; red/white/blue ....$100-$150
1963 Los Angeles Dodgers: Balfour; threaded post; blue ....$125-$150
1963 New York Yankees: Balfour; needle post, brooch; red/white/blue..$100-$175
1964 St. Louis Cardinals: Josten; threaded post, brooch; red...$125-$200
1964 New York Yankees: Balfour; needle post; red/white/blue...$175-$200
1965 Los Angeles Dodgers: Balfour; needle post, charm; blue..$50-$150
1965 Minnesota Twins: Balfour; needle post; red/white/blue ....$50-$125
1966 Los Angeles Dodgers: Balfour; needle post, charm; blue..$50-$150
1966 Baltimore Orioles: Balfour; needle post, clasp, charm, brooch; black/white/orange ....$175-$200

1967 St. Louis Cardinals: Balfour; needle post, charms; red/white/black.....................................$75-$100
1967 Boston Red Sox: Balfour; needle post, charm; red/white/blue...$150-$200
1968 St. Louis Cardinals: Balfour; needle post, charms; red/white/black.....................................$75-$125
1968 Detroit Tigers: Balfour; needle post, charms; blue ....$125-$200
1969 New York Mets: Balfour; needle post, charm; blue/orange...$200-$300
1969 Baltimore Orioles: Balfour; needle post, charms, clasp, brooch; black/white/orange ....$150-$200
1970 Cincinnati Reds: G.B. Miller; needle post, charms; red/white/black ....$125-$150
1970 Baltimore Orioles: Jenkins; needle post, clasp, charm, brooch; black/white/orange ....$100-$150
1971 Pittsburgh Pirates: Balfour; needle post; black ....$75-$150
1971 Baltimore Orioles: Balfour; needle post, clasp, brooch; black/white/orange ....$100-$150
1972 Cincinnati Reds: Balfour; needle post, charm; red/white ....$100-$150
1972 Oakland A's: Balfour; needle post, charm; green/white...$125-$250
1973 New York Mets: Balfour; needle post, charm; orange/blue..$125-$150

1973 Oakland A's: Josten; needle post, charms; green/white ....$200-$275
1974 Los Angeles Dodgers: Balfour; needle post, charms; blue...$125-$150
1974 Oakland A's: Josten; needle post; green/white..$300-$375
1975 Cincinnati Reds: Balfour; needle post, charms; red..$100-$200
1975 Boston Red Sox: Balfour; needle post, charms; red/white ....$125-$200
1976 Cincinnati Reds: Balfour; needle post, charms; red..$125-$175
1976 New York Yankees: Balfour; needle post; red/white/blue..$125-$175
1977 Los Angeles Dodgers: Balfour; needle post, charms; red/white/blue...................................$125-$150
1977 New York Yankees: Balfour; needle post, charms; blue...$75-$125
1978 Los Angeles Dodgers: Balfour; needle post, charms; blue/white...$75-$100
1978 New York Yankees: Balfour; needle post, charms; red/white/blue ....$50-$125
1979 Pittsburgh Pirates: Balfour; needle post; gold...$50-$125
1979 Baltimore Orioles: Balfour; needle post, clasp, charm, brooch; white/black/orange ....$50-$100
1980 Philadelphia Phillies: Balfour; needle post; gold..$50-$75

1980 Kansas City Royals: Green Co.; needle post, charms; blue/white..$50-$175
1981 Los Angeles Dodgers: Balfour; needle post, charms; red/white/blue....................................$50-$100
1981 New York Yankees: Balfour; needle post; blue ....$75-$100
1982 St. Louis Cardinals: Balfour; needle post, charms; red ....$50-$75
1982 Milwaukee Brewers: Balfour; needle post, charms; blue ....$50-$100
1983 Philadelphia Phillies: Balfour; needle post, charms; red/white/green ....$40-$75
1983 Baltimore Orioles: Balfour; needle post, charm, brooch; orange/white/black ....$65-$100
1984 San Diego Padres: Balfour; needle post, charms; brown/white..$25-$75
1984 Detroit Tigers: Balfour; needle post, charms; blue ....$45-$75
1985 Kansas City Royals: Green Co.; needle post, charms; blue/white..$75-$100
1985 St. Louis Cardinals: Balfour; needle post, charms; red/black..$75-$100
1986 New York Mets: Balfour; needle post, charms; blue/orange...$100-$135
1986 Boston Red Sox: Balfour; needle post, charms; red/white/blue ....$75-$125
1987 St. Louis Cardinals: Balfour; needle post, charms; red/white/gold ....$100-$125
1987 Minnesota Twins: Josten; needle post, charms; gold...$75-$125
1988 Oakland A's..$60-$75
1988 Los Angeles Dodgers...$50-$75
1989 San Francisco Giants ....$75-$100
1989 Oakland A's..$75-$100
1990 Cincinnati Reds ....$125-$150
1990 Oakland A's..$75-$100
1991 Atlanta Braves..$60-$100
1991 Minnesota Twins..$60-$100
1992 Atlanta Braves..$100-$125
1992 Toronto Blue Jays..$125-$150

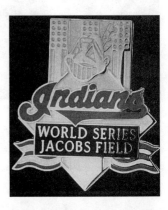

1993 Philadelphia Phillies ....$50-$100
1993 Toronto Blue Jays..$125-$150
1995 Atlanta Braves..$100-$150
1995 Cleveland Indians ....$100-$150

Phantom Press Pins

1938 Pittsburgh Pirates: Whitehead & Hoag; threaded post; red/white/black............................$500-$1,000
1944 Detroit Tigers: Unknown; threaded post; red/white/blue...$375-$500
1945 St. Louis Cardinals: St. Louis button; threaded post; red/white ....$475-$600
1946 Brooklyn Dodgers: Dieges & Clust; threaded post, brooch ....$125-$275
1948 Boston Red Sox: Balfour; threaded post; red/white/blue ....$1,200-$1,800
1948 New York Yankees: Dieges & Clust, threaded post; red/white/blue ....$1,600-$1,800
1949 St. Louis Cardinals: Unknown; threaded post; red/white/black ....$450-$725
1949 Boston Red Sox: Balfour; threaded post; red/white/blue ....$950-$1,400
1950 Brooklyn Dodgers: Balfour; threaded post; red/white/blue ....$1,600-$2,400
1951 Cleveland Indians: Balfour; threaded post; red/white/black.........................$1,200-$1,750
1951 Brooklyn Dodgers: Dieges & Clust; threaded post, brooch; red/white/blue ....$125-$400
1952 New York Giants: Dieges & Clust; threaded post, brooch; white/black ....$275-$350
1955 Chicago White Sox: Unknown; threaded post; red/white/blue.......................$800-$1,400
1955 Cleveland Indians: Balfour; threaded post; red/white/blue/black.............................$600-$800
1956 Milwaukee Braves: Balfour; threaded post; red/copper................................$100-$150
1959 San Francisco Giants: Balfour; threaded post; white/black...........................$550-$800
1959 Milwaukee Braves: Balfour; threaded post, charm; red/copper.......................$400-$500
1960 Chicago White Sox: Balfour; threaded post; red/white ....$1,200-$1,600
1960 Baltimore Orioles: Balfour; threaded post; red/green/black..........................$800-$1,250
1963 St. Louis Cardinals: Josten; threaded post; red ....$75-$150
1964 Philadelphia Phillies: Martin; needle post; red/blue ....$15-$30
1964 Chicago White Sox: Balfour; needle post; red/white/blue..........................$800-$1,100
1964 Baltimore Orioles: Balfour; needle post; orange/white/black..........................$625-$850
1964 Cincinnati Reds: Balfour; needle post, brooch; red/white/black ....$200-$250
1965 San Francisco Giants: Balfour; threaded post; white/black ....$125-$150
1966 Pittsburgh Pirates: Balfour; needle post; black...$375-$450
1966 San Francisco Giants: Balfour; threaded post; white/black...........................$950-$1,200
1967 Minnesota Twins: Balfour; needle post; red/white/blue ....$50-$60
1967 Chicago White Sox: Balfour; needle post; red/white/blue..............................$75-$100
1969 San Francisco Giants: Balfour; needle post; white/black ....$100-$150
1969 Atlanta Braves: Josten; needle post, charm; blue..$45-$75
1969 Minnesota Twins: Balfour; needle post; red/white/blue ....$75-$150
1970 California Angels: Balfour; needle post; red/white/blue...............................$450-$500
1970 Chicago Cubs: Balfour; needle post; blue/white...$450-$500
1971 San Francisco Giants: Balfour; needle post; black ....$125-$150
1971 Oakland A's (smaller pin): Unknown; needle post; green/white.......................$100-$150
1971 Oakland A's (larger pin): Balfour; needle post, charm; green/white ....$650-$750
1972 Chicago White Sox: Balfour; needle post; red/white/blue.............................$875-$1,000
1972 Pittsburgh Pirates: Balfour; needle post; no color..$600-$750
1974 Texas Rangers: Balfour; needle post; red/white/blue/gold ....$400-$550
1975 Oakland A's: Josten; needle post; green/white ....$300-$450
1976 Philadelphia Phillies: Balfour; needle post; no color......................................$35-$75
1977 Boston Red Sox: Balfour; needle post, charm; red/blue...................................$50-$75
1978 San Francisco Giants: Balfour; needle post; black/orange ....$30-$50
1978 Cincinnati Reds: Balfour; needle post, charm; red ....$75-$100
1978 Milwaukee Brewers..$50-$75
1979 Montreal Expos: Balfour; needle post; no color ....$50-$75
1979 California Angels: Balfour; needle post; red/white/blue..................................$200-$250
1979 Houston Astros: Balfour; needle post; white/blue ....$850-$900
1980 Houston Astros: Balfour; needle post, charm; blue/orange ....$150-$200
1981 Oakland A's: Balfour; needle post, charm; green..$55-$85
1981 Chicago Cubs: Balfour; needle post; red/white/blue ....$175-$200
1981 Philadelphia Phillies: Balfour; needle post; red/white ....$45-$75
1982 Los Angeles Dodgers: Balfour; needle post, charm; red/white/blue ....$125-$150
1983 Milwaukee Brewers: Balfour; needle post; white/black ....$200-$250
1983 Chicago White Sox: Balfour; needle post; red/blue..$40-$50
1983 Pittsburgh Pirates: Balfour; needle post; black ....$200-$275
1984 Chicago Cubs: Balfour; needle post, charm; red/black ....$125-$200
1985 Toronto Blue Jays: Balfour; needle post, charm; red/white/blue......................$200-$250
1986 California Angels: Gem Peddler; needle post, charm; no color ....$175-$200
1986 Houston Astros: Balfour; needle post, charm; red/blue....................................$75-$150
1987 Detroit Tigers: Balfour; needle post; blue/white/gold......................................$125-$175
1987 New York Yankees: Balfour; threaded post; blue/white/gold............................$175-$200
1987 New York Mets: Balfour; needle post; orange/black/white/gold ....$200-$225
1987 San Francisco Giants: Balfour; needle post; black/white/gold ....$75-$100
1987 Boston Red Sox..$150-$175
1988 Boston Red Sox..$75-$100
1990 Pittsburgh Pirates..$300-$350
1990 Boston Red Sox...$60-$75

All-Star Pins

1938 Cincinnati: Bastian Brothers; safety pin; red/white/blue ....$7,000-$8,000
1941 Detroit: Dodge; threaded post; blue ....$2,200-$2,500
1943 Philadelphia: Unknown; threaded post; silver...$1,200-$1,500
1946 Boston: Balfour; threaded post; red ....$575-$1,000
1947 Chicago: Unknown; threaded post; red/white/blue ....$1,100-$1,850
1948 St. Louis: St. Louis button; threaded post; brown/white...$650-$2,250
1949 Brooklyn: Balfour; threaded post, brooch; blue...$325-$400
1950 Chicago: Balfour; threaded post, brooch; red/white ....$150-$325
1951 Detroit: Unknown; threaded post, brooch; red/white/blue...$250-$375
1952 Philadelphia: Martin; needle post; red/white/blue ....$175-$400
1953 Cincinnati: Robbins; threaded post; red/white/black ....$225-$375
1954 Cleveland: Balfour; threaded post; red/white/black ....$250-$375
1955 Milwaukee: Balfour; brooch; gold ....$175-$350
1956 Washington: Balfour; threaded post, clasp; red/white/blue ....$225-$350
1957 St. Louis: Balfour; threaded post, brooch; black/red ....$300-$350
1958 Baltimore: Balfour; threaded post, charm; black/white/orange ....$400-$650
1959 Los Angeles: Balfour; threaded post, brooch; blue/white ....$100-$150
1959 Pittsburgh: Balfour; threaded post; red/white/black ....$225-$400
1960 Kansas City: Balfour; threaded post; red ....$200-$325
1960 New York Yankees: Balfour; threaded post; red/white/blue...$200-$400
1961 Boston: Balfour; needle post; red/white/blue...$400-$500
1961 San Francisco: Balfour; threaded post; white ....$475-$600
1962 Chicago: Balfour; needle post; red/white/blue...$250-$350
1962 Washington: Balfour; threaded post, clasp; white/blue ....$200-$250
1963 Cleveland: Balfour; threaded post; red/white/blue/black ....$75-$150
1964 New York (Shea Stadium): Balfour; needle post, charm; blue/orange ....$200-$250
1965 Minnesota: Balfour; needle post; red/white/blue ....$100-$175
1966 St. Louis: Balfour; needle post; red...$35-$80
1967 California: Balfour; needle post, charm; blue/white..$50-$150
1968 Houston: Balfour; needle post, charm; blue/white..$100-$125
1969 Washington: Balfour; needle post, clasp; blue ....$75-$150
1970 Cincinnati: Balfour; needle post, charm; red/white/black ....$75-$100
1971 Detroit: Balfour; needle post, charms; red/white/blue...$100-$175
1972 Atlanta: Balfour; needle post, charm; red/blue ....$75-$125
1973 Kansas City: Balfour; needle post, charm; blue ....$75-$150
1974 Pittsburgh: Balfour; needle post; gold...$175-$275
1975 Milwaukee: Unknown; brooch; gold ....$50-$100
1976 Philadelphia: Balfour; needle post; gold...$50-$75
1977 New York Yankees: Balfour; pin ....$100-$125
1977 New York: Balfour; charm; gold ....$30-$50
1978 San Diego: Balfour; needle post, charm, brooch; brown/blue ....$40-$80
1979 Seattle: Balfour; needle post, charm, brooch; blue/white..$30-$60
1980 Los Angeles: Balfour; needle post, charm; gold ....$30-$60
1981 Cleveland: Balfour; needle post, charm; red/white/blue...$25-$50
1982 Montreal: Balfour; needle post, straight pin; gold...$60-$75
1983 Chicago: Balfour; needle post, charms; red/blue ....$25-$50
1984 San Francisco: Balfour; needle post, charm; orange/black/white ....$20-$35
1985 Minnesota: Peter David; needle post, charms; red/white/blue..$20-$25
1986 Houston: Balfour; needle post, charms; red/white/blue/silver ....$65-$125
1987 Oakland: Josten; needle post; copper...$75-$90
1988 Cincinnati: Josten; needle post; red/white/blue/silver...$75-$100
1989 California ....$55-$75
1990 Chicago..$125-$150
1991 Toronto...$100-$125
1992 San Diego ....$20-$100
1993 Baltimore ....$100-$150
1994 Pittsburgh ....$125-$150
1995 Texas...$50-$100
1996 Philadelphia ....$50-$100
1997 Cleveland..$50-$100
1998 Denver...$50-$100
1999 Boston...$100-$150
2000 Atlanta...$75-$100

Hall of Fame Press Pins

1982: Balfour; charms and standard needle post: Hank Aaron, Happy Chandler, Travis Jackson, Frank Robinson...$400-$700

1983: Balfour; charms and standard needle post: Walter Alston, George Kell, Juan Marichal, Brooks Robinson...$400-$525

1984: Balfour; charms and standard needle post: Luis Aparicio, Don Drysdale, Harmon Killebrew, Rick Ferrell, Pee Wee Reese...$225-$375

1985: Balfour; charms and standard needle post: Lou Brock, Enos Slaughter, Arky Vaughan, Hoyt Wilhelm ....$250-$350

1986: Balfour; charms and standard needle post: Bobby Doerr, Ernie Lombardi, Willie McCovey ....$225-$350

1987: Balfour; charms and standard needle post: Ray Dandridge, Jim Hunter, Billy Williams ...$500-$650

1988: Balfour; charms and standard needle post: Willie Stargell...$500-$650

1989: Al Barlick, Johnny Bench, Red Schoendienst, Carl Yastrzemski ....$500-$650

1989: 50th Anniversary Medallion: Al Barlick, Johnny Bench, Red Schoendienst, Carl Yastrzemski ....$650-$700

1990: Joe Morgan, Jim Palmer..$450-$650

1990: (1936 inductees) Ty Cobb, Walter Johnson, Christy Mathewson, Babe Ruth, Honus Wagner $750

1991: Rod Carew, Fergie Jenkins, Gaylord Perry, Tony Lazzeri, Bill Veeck ....$375-$575

1991: (1937 inductees) Morgan Bulkeley, Ban Johnson, Nap Lajoie, Connie Mack, John McGraw, Tris Speaker, George Wright, Cy Young..$700

1992: Rollie Fingers, Bill McGowan, Hal Newhouser, Tom Seaver...$400

1992: (1938 inductees) Grover Cleveland Alexander, Alexander Cartwright, Henry Chadwick $375

1992: (1955 inductees) Frank Baker, Joe DiMaggio, Gabby Hartnett, Ted Lyons, Ray Schalk, Dazzy Vance $495

1993: Reggie Jackson $450

1993: (1939 inductees) Charles Comiskey, Buck Ewing, Cap Anson, Candy Cummings, Eddie Collins $400

1993: (1939 inductees) Charles Radbourne, George Sisler, Al Spalding, Lou Gehrig, Wee Willie Keeler $500

1994: Steve Carlton, Leo Durocher, Phil Rizzuto...$425-$450

1994: (1942 inductee) Rogers Hornsby..$375

1994: (1966 inductees) Casey Stengel, Ted Williams $375

1995: Richie Ashburn, Leon Day, William Hulbert, Mike Schmidt, Vic Willis $375

1995: (1944 inductee) Kenesaw Mountain Landis...$375

1995: (1969 inductees) Roy Campanella, Stan Coveleski, Waite Hoyt, Stan Musial...........................$375

1996: Jim Bunning, Earl Weaver, Ned Hanlon, B. Foster..$375

1996: (1974 inductees) Cool Papa Bell, Jim Bottomley, Jocko Conlan, Whitey Ford, Mickey Mantle, Sam Thompson $375

1997: Tommy Lasorda, Phil Niekro, Nellie Fox, Willie Wells $350

1997: (1962 inductees) Bob Feller, Bill McKechnie, Jackie Robinson, Edd Roush $350

1997: (1962 inductees) Yogi Berra, Josh Gibson, Lefty Gomez, Will Harridge, Sandy Koufax, Buck Leonard, Early Wynn, Ross Youngs $350

BASEBALL PENNANTS

The history of baseball pennants is perhaps the most difficult to track of all memorabilia. While a good deal is known about recent pennants, it's virtually impossible to determine how many were produced prior to 1970.

The first known baseball pennants appeared at ballparks around the turn of the century. From 1905-1910 the first pennants bearing team or city names were produced. The first commemorative pennant—celebrating the World Champion Boston Braves—appeared in 1914. By 1986, the market had grown considerably, as fans of the New York Mets had a selection of eight banners to choose from at Shea Stadium souvenir stands. Championship and single-season pennants through the years have evolved to include team rosters, facsimile signatures and team photos.

But the earliest pennants were not always season-specific. In the early years, fans might find the same pennants for sale at the ballpark for several years in a row. And these pennants were generally made with excess and scrap felt, so sizes and colors would differ at each stadium. Manufacturer labels can often be found sewn on the back of pennants produced before 1940, but for pennants issued between 1940 and 1970 it's nearly impossible to determine a specific producer.

Technology in the 1970s brought a change to the traditional felt pennants. Synthetics were added to the fabric, making pennants thinner, more rigid and less expensive to produce. Two companies—Trench Manufacturers of Buffalo and Wincraft of Winona, Minn.—established licensing agreements and have been the major players in the industry since 1970.

Event-specific and commemorative pennants seem to be the easiest to track, as well as being the most popular with collectors. They're often limited editions sold only at ballparks involved in the event. Pennants from the World Series, ballpark openings and retirement ceremonies fall into this category.

Attaching values to pennants is extremely difficult. Before the early 1990s, there were no checklists available, and previously unknown specimens are continually being discovered. The best places to find vintage pennants are in the traditional baseball cities, at card shows or through auctions.

In general, collectors prefer attractive pennants that can easily be displayed. Vibrant, colorful pennants, especially of the pre-1970 variety, are the most valuable and hardest to find. Many older pennants are faded, missing tassels or have pinholes around the tip—all direct results of being hung on bedroom walls.

Selected Pennants

1920s Cleveland Indians, red with white letters $135

1930s Boston Braves, batting scene, red..$125

1934-35 Detroit Tigers pennant winners, black-and-white on orange
....$375

1935 Detroit Tigers World Champs scroll pennant, orange on black
....$350

Early-1940s Boston Red Sox, large baseball over the stadium, gray and red..$100

Early-1940s Brooklyn Dodgers, batter and catcher, white on red....$285

Early-1940s Brooklyn Dodgers, Brooklyn Dodgers: Our Champs, white on purple..$395

Mid-1940s Boston Red Sox, batter hitting pitched ball, white on red
....$135

Late-1940s Brooklyn Dodgers, shows catcher and batter from backside, white on blue...$175

Late-1940s New York Yankees, player sliding into tag, white on blue
....$95

Late-1940s Philadelphia Phillies signature pennant with names and numbers, Fightin' Phillies, white and red $195

Late-1940s St. Louis Cardinals, two birds on a bat, red, yellow and white on red..$65

Late-1940s St. Louis Browns, player making a catch, orange on blue
....$175

1940s Boston Red Sox, runner sliding into base, white on red........$145

1940s Brooklyn Dodgers, player sliding into tag, blue on white $150

1940s Chicago Cubs, large C in Chicago, white on blue $110

1940s Chicago Cubs, player sliding into a tag, black on orange........$95

1940s Chicago White Sox, infield play in progress, white on dark blue
....$125

1940s Cincinnati Reds, Cincinnati in Gothic letters, white and red.....$150

1940s Cleveland Indians, Indian with full headdress, white on red ...$80

1940s Detroit Tigers, black tiger head on orange $85

1940s New York Giants, batter, catcher and umpire, white and blue
....$125

1948 Cleveland Indians American League Champs/World Series, multi-color on dark red $195

Early-1950s Brooklyn Dodgers, red, white and blue........................$295

Early-1950s Philadelphia A's, white on blue $85

1942 St. Louis Cardinals World Series pennant

Boston Red Sox pennant

1940s Brooklyn Dodgers pennant

1957 Milwaukee Braves pennant

1963 National League All-Stars pennant

Chicago White Sox pennant

Mid-1950s Chicago Cubs Wrigley Field $150

1965 World Series Los Angeles Dodgers vs. Minnesota Twins, multi-color on blue felt $85

1966 Baltimore Orioles team picture pennant $100

1966 Chicago White Sox team picture pennant, red and blue on white $110

1966 New York Mets team picture pennant $135

1966 World Series Los Angeles Dodgers vs. Baltimore Orioles, bird over Dodger Stadium $65

1966-67 California Angels, Anaheim Stadium $55

1967 Boston Red Sox vs. St. Louis Cardinals World Series at Fenway Park, black and red on white...$125

1967 St. Louis Cardinals National League Champions $40

1968 Chicago White Sox picture pennant...$85

1968 Detroit Tigers American League Champions, black and orange on white $85

1968 St. Louis Cardinals National League Champions/World Series, white and pink on red...$65

1969 Baltimore Orioles World Series picture pennant $110

1969 Boston Red Sox picture pennant..$55

1969 Cincinnati Reds picture pennant $95

1969 Houston Astros $20

1969 Kansas City Royals $40

1969 Montreal Expos $35

1969 Mickey Mantle Day at Yankee Stadium....................................$55

1969 New York Mets World Champions, orange on blue...................$95

1969 Seattle Pilots, MLB logo, Seattle in script, multi-colored on red $185

1969-71 Washington Senators, red and blue on white.........................$75

Early-1970s Chicago White Sox, batter on sock in red circle............$45

Early-1970s Cleveland Indians, Chief Wahoo with bat and ball $45

Early-1970s Minnesota Twins, TC in dot over in Minnesota, white on blue $35

1970s Baltimore Orioles $10

1970s Houston Astros $10

1970s Milwaukee Brewers $10

1970s St. Louis Cardinals $10

1970s San Diego Padres, crossed bats with Padre, white on brown...$55

1970s San Francisco Giants $10

1970 Baltimore Orioles team picture, orange and black on white $75

1970 Baltimore Orioles picture pennant $125

1970 Milwaukee Brewers, barrel man swinging a bat, gold on blue $55

1971 Pittsburgh Pirates color team photo pennant $95

1971 Pittsburgh Pirates National League Champs scroll, black and gold on white...$60

1972 All-Star Game in Atlanta, red and blue on white.......................$55

1973 Boston Red Sox Fenway Park, white and green on red $75

1973 Chicago White Sox American League Western Division Champions..$10

1973 New York Mets World Champs signature pennant $45

1973 New York Mets You Gotta Believe, Mets #1 Again, 1973 Champions, blue on white...$75

1973 New York Mets Eastern Division Champs scroll pennant, white and orange on blue $65

1973 Oakland A's American League Champs scroll pennant.............$45

1974 Cincinnati Reds picture pennant $95

1974 Hank Aaron Home Run King, dated April 8, 1974 ....$45

1974 Los Angeles Dodgers World Series signature pennant..............$50

1975 Boston Red Sox World Series signature pennant $55

1975 Boston Red Sox World Champions phantom $25

1975 Boston Red Sox American League Champions scroll pennant $50

1975 Cincinnati Reds picture pennant $65

1975 Cincinnati Reds World Champs signature pennant...................$65

1976 Cincinnati Reds World Champs trophy.................................$45

1977 New York Yankees picture pennant.....................................$55

1977 All-Star Game at Yankee Stadium......................................$30

1977 Los Angeles Dodgers National League Champs scroll pennant, blue on white $50

1978 Do it Pete! Do it Pete! for Rose's hitting streak, 7/25/78 at Shea Stadium $55

1979 Baltimore Orioles American League Champions signature pennant $45

1979 California Angels American League West Champions scroll pennant $65

1979 Philadelphia Phillies picture pennant, black and white $75

1979 Pittsburgh Pirates World Champions scroll pennant..................$45

1980 Kansas City World Series scroll pennant, blue and gold on white $45

1980 New York Yankees...$10

1980 New York Yankees American League Eastern Division Champs, blue and red on white $35

1980 Philadelphia Phillies World Champions scroll pennant, We're #1 ....$45

1981 All-Star Game in Cleveland, Chief Wahoo on a star $45

1981 New York Yankees American League Champions scroll pennant $45

1982 Milwaukee Brewers American League Eastern Division Champs, blue and gold on white..$40

1983 50th All-Star Game at Comiskey Park......................................$10

1983 Carl Yastrzemski retirement day pennant.................................$55

1983 Baltimore Orioles World Champions, scroll pennant, black and orange on white..$45

1983 Philadelphia Phillies National League Champs, maroon, blue and red on white..$40

1984 Chicago Cubs World Series...$20

1984 Detroit Tigers World Champions scroll pennant, blue and orange on black $55

1984 Kansas City Royals American League Western Division Champions, scroll..$35

1984 San Diego Padres National League Western Division Champions $10

1985 Kansas City Royals American League Western Division Champions, scroll..$35

1985 Los Angeles Dodgers National League Western Division Champions..$10

1986 Boston Red Sox American League Eastern Division Champions $10

1986 Boston Red Sox World Series $10

1986 New York Mets World Champs signature pennant $35

1986 New York Yankees color team picture $35

1987 Minnesota Twins World Series...$10

1988 All-Star Game in Cincinnati..$10

1989 Chicago Cubs N.L. East Champs...$10

1993 Florida Marlins Opening Day $20

1994 All-Star Game in Pittsburgh...$10

**1969 New York Yankees
Mickey Mantle Day pennant**

1969 Seattle Pilots pennant

**1970 Pittsburgh Pirates
N.L. Championship pennant**

1950 American Nut & Chocolate Pennants

Although there is nothing on these small (1 7/8 by 4) felt pennants to identify the issuer, surviving ads show that the American Nut & Chocolate Co. of Boston sold them as a set of 22 for 50 cents. The pennants of American League players are printed in blue on white, while National Leaguers are printed in red on white. The pennants feature crude line-art drawings of players on the left, along with a facsimile autograph. The pennants carry an American Card Catalog designation of F510. The complete set of 22 pennants is worth $350 in Near Mint condition.

Ewell Blackwell	$15
Harry Brecheen	$15
Phil Cavarretta	$15
Bobby Doerr	$17.50
Bob Elliott	$15
Boo Ferriss	$15
Joe Gordon	$15
Tommy Holmes	$15
Charles Keller	$15
Ken Keltner	$15
Whitey Kurowski	$15
Ralph Kiner	$20
Johnny Pesky	$15
Pee Wee Reese	$35
Phil Rizzuto	$30
Johnny Sain	$17.50
Enos Slaughter	$17.50
Warren Spahn	$30
Vern Stephens	$15
Earl Torgeson	$15
Dizzy Trout	$15
Ted Williams	$70

Current Pennants

When collecting current pennants, hobbyists can look to three manufacturers—Mitchell & Ness, Tag Express and WinCraft. Through extensive research, Mitchell & Ness has produced a line of replica pennants similar to those produced from 1907-1970. Each season, WinCraft produces a new pennant for every Major League team, but their specialty is a line of pennants featuring player caricatures. Recently WinCraft has begun to produce wool team pennants that feature current team logos. Tag Express, the company that purchased Trench, specializes in event- and ballpark-specific pennants.

Here is a list of some of the WinCraft caricature pennants with their latest secondary market values.

1991-1992 WinCraft

Player	Team	Quantity	Price
George Brett	Royals	Less than 5,000	$10
Jose Canseco	A's	Less than 5,000	$15
Roger Clemens	Red Sox	Less than 5,000	$7
Ken Griffey Sr. & Jr.	Mariners	More than 5,000	$10
Ken Griffey Jr.	Mariners	More than 5,000	$10
Tony Gwynn	Padres	Less than 5,000	$8
Don Mattingly	Yankees	More than 5,000	$7
Mark McGwire	A's	Less than 5,000	$6
Paul Molitor	Brewers	Less than 5,000	$5
Cal Ripken Jr.	Orioles	Est. 25,000	$8
Cal Ripken Jr. (MVP)	Orioles	More than 5,000	$10
Nolan Ryan	Rangers	Est. 8,922	$10
Nolan Ryan (Texas Heat)	Rangers	Est. 6,780	$10
Nolan Ryan (5,000 Ks)	Rangers	Est. 11,093	$8
World Champ '91	Twins	More than 5,000	$8
World Champ '92	Blue Jays	Less than 5,000	$6

1993 WinCraft
WinCraft began numbering its pennants in 1993.

No.	Player	Team	Quantity	Price
100	Kirby Puckett	Twins	More than 5,000	$6
103	Ken Griffey Jr.	Mariners	More than 5,000	$10
105	Mark McGwire	A's	Less than 5,000	$7
106	George Brett	Royals	Less than 5,000	$7
107	Ozzie Smith	Cardinals	Less than 5,000	$6
108	Braves Fever	Braves	More than 5,000	$5
112	Chiefs of Staff	Braves	Less than 5,000	$5
117	Barry Bonds	Giants	More than 5,000	$6
118	Nolan Ryan (Farewell)		More than 5,000	$8
120	George Brett (Thanks)	Royals	Est. 5,000	$8

1994-1998 WinCraft
Quantities not available.

No.	Player	Team	Price
121	Miracle Mets 25th Anniversary	Mets	$10
123	Frank Thomas (MVP)	White Sox	$10
128	Dave Winfield	Twins	$5
129	Mike Piazza	Dodgers	$7
134	Cleveland Tribe	Indians	$5
135	Barry Bonds	Giants	$6
138	David Cone	Royals	$5
139	Greg Maddux	Braves	$8
140	Randy Johnson	Mariners	$6
142	Nolan Ryan	Rangers	$8
147	Gary Sheffield	Marlins	$5
148	Roberto Clemente	Pirates	$10
150	Cal Ripken Jr.	Orioles	$10
151	Ken Griffey Jr.	Mariners	$10
156	Cal Ripken Jr.	Orioles	$10
158	Barry Bonds	Giants	$6
159	Mike Piazza	Dodgers	$7
160	Mo Vaughn	Red Sox	$5
161	Red Schoendienst—Stadium Exclusive	Cardinals	$6
162	Big Bats II	Rockies	$5
164	The Big Three	Rockies	$5
168	Cal Ripken Jr.	Orioles	$10
169	Cal Ripken Jr.	Orioles	$10
170	Mo Vaughn (MVP)	Red Sox	$6
171	Kirby Puckett	Twins	$6
172	Albert Belle	Indians	$6
173	Ken Griffey Jr.	Mariners	$10
174	David Cone	Yankees	$5
176	Paul Moliter	Twins	$5

No.	Player	Team	Price	No.	Player	Team	Price
177	Marty Cordova (ROY '95)	Twins	$5	209	Albert Belle	White Sox	$6
178	Hideo Nomo (ROY '95)	Dodgers	$7	210	Frank Thomas	White Sox	$10
179	Barry Larkin ('95 NL MVP)	Reds	$5	211	Mike Piazza	Dodgers	$8
180	Ryne Sandberg	Cubs	$6	215	Derek Jeter	Yankees	$7
184	Cal Ripken Jr.	Orioles	$10	216	Cal Ripken Jr. (Stadium Exclusive)	Orioles	$12
186	Chipper Jones	Braves	$8	218	Mo Vaughn	Red Sox	$6
189	Greg Maddux (4-time Cy Young)	Braves	$8	219	Roberto Clemente	Pirates	$10
192	Blake Street Bombers	Rockies	$5	220	Mark McGwire	A's	$7
195	Rey Ordonez	Mets	$5	225	Rockies Signature Pennant	Rockies	$6
198	White Sox Signature Pennant	White Sox	$8	226	Don Mattingly	Yankees	$6
199	Rockies Signature Pennant	Rockies	$6	231	Mark McGwire	Cardinals	$5
200	Reds Signature Pennant	Reds	$6	232	Roger Clemens (Cy Young)	Blue Jays	$7
203	All-Star Game Signature Pennant		$10	233	Ken Griffey Jr. (MVP)	Mariners	$10
204	Alex Rodriguez	Mariners	$7	235	Nomar Garciaparra	Red Sox	$7
205	Eddie Murray (3,000 hits)	Orioles	$7	236	Albert Belle	White Sox	$5
206	Paul Molitor (3,000 hits)	Twins	$7	237	Barry Bonds	Giants	$5
207	Ken Griffey Jr.	Mariners	$10	241	Cal Ripken Jr.	Orioles	$10
208	Cal Ripken Jr.	Orioles	$10	242	Frank Thomas	White Sox	$10

PROGRAMS

Collectors are always looking for remembrances of games they attended. Some of the least expensive and storage-friendly event-related collectibles are game programs. With rosters, feature stories and other information, programs are terrific for recalling the specifics of a special day at the ballpark.

Available from games as far back as the mid-1800s, programs have varied in size and cover subject but have remained one of the fixtures in the collections of baseball fans. Today's programs feature more historical information, including team statistics, along with the current player bios and, of course, tons of advertising.

In general, unscored programs carry a higher premium than editions in which the game has been scored.

Year	Price
Pre-1900	$500-$750

(only Braves, Cardinals, Dodgers, Giants, Indians, Orioles, Phillies, Pirates, Reds, Senators and Tigers have pre-1900s programs).

1900-1910	$200-$500
1910-1919	$75-$200

(certain Cubs, Indians, Reds, Senators and Tigers programs can be up to $250)

1920-1929	$35-$75

(certain Indians, Phillies, Pirates, Reds, Senators, Tigers and Yankees programs can be up to $100; 1920 Dodgers and Indians programs can be up to $135 each; Giants programs from 1921-24 are $80-$85)

1930-1939	$20-$35

(certain Indians, Phillies, Pirates, Tigers and Braves programs can be up to $40; certain Reds, Yankees and Dodgers programs have reached $50; Cubs programs from 1930-40 are $35-$50; A's programs from 1930-31 can be up to $75)

Below is a list of prices for Excellent to Near Mint programs from regular season games in each decade. Programs found in Near-Mint condition from the early 1900s command a premium due to their scarcity.

Between 1876 and 1900, there was only one professional baseball league, and the number of teams ranged from eight to 12 in any given year. During this time most teams underwent several city and nickname changes.

Exceptions to the price ranges below include teams that made the playoffs or teams that included a number of future Hall of Famers. For example, teams like the 1960s Baltimore Orioles, the 1920s New York Yankees and the 1970s Cincinnati Reds and Oakland A's carry a higher premium for regular season programs. Programs from regular season Yankee games in the 1920s have sold for as much as $125.

Year	Price
1940-1949	$15-$25

(certain Dodgers programs are up to $30; certain Yankees programs have reached $35)

1950-1959	$10-$25

(Baltimore programs from 1954-56 are $55-$75; 1953 Milwaukee Braves programs are $75; 1958 San Francisco Giants programs are $35; 1969 Seattle Pilots programs are $55)

1960-1969	$5-$25

(Houston Colt .45s programs can be up to $35; 1962 New York Mets programs are $60; 1961 Los Angeles Angels programs are $40; 1961 Minnesota Twins programs are $35; 1969 Montreal Expos programs are $30)

1970-1979	$5-$7.50

(1970 Milwaukee Brewer programs are $25; 1972 Texas Rangers programs are $20; 1977 Seattle Mariners programs are $15; 1977 Toronto Blue Jays programs are $12)

1990-1999 Florida Marlins, Colorado Rockies, Tampa Bay Devil Rays and Arizona Diamondbacks	$10-$15

World Series Programs

World Series programs have been produced since 1903 when Boston (A.L.) defeated Pittsburgh (N.L.) five games to three. Programs have been produced and saved as souvenirs each year since with the exception of 1904 (when John J. McGraw refused to allow his New York Giants to play an "inferior" team from the American League) and 1994 (MLB strike season).

In general, World Series programs, especially from championship teams, are in more demand than those from All-Star games and regular season games.

Since 1974, only one program has been produced for the World Series for both American and National League teams.

Like any other collectible, the better the condition, the more valuable the program. Programs that are unscored, not torn or faded and containing the original inserts, are more valuable.

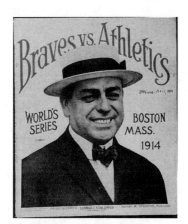

1914 World Series program

Year	Team	Price
1903	Pittsburgh	$15,000/$30,000
1903	Boston	$15,000/$30,000
1904	No series	
1905	Philadelphia	$7,000/$16,000
1905	New York Giants	$7,000/$10,000
1906	Chicago Cubs	$7,000/$10,000
1906	Chicago White Sox	$7,000/$7,500
1907	Detroit	$10,000/$14,000
1907	Chicago Cubs	$7,000/$10,000
1908	Detroit	$8,000/$12,000
1908	Chicago Cubs	$8,000/$12,500
1909	Detroit	$8,000/$10,000
1909	Pittsburgh	$6,000/$10,000

Year	Team	Price
1910	Chicago Cubs	$5,000/$7,500
1910	Philadelphia A's	$5,000/$10,000
1911	Philadelphia A's	$5,000/$6,000
1911	New York Giants	$3,000/$4,000
1912	New York Giants	$2,000/$4,000
1912	Boston Red Sox	$1,500/$3,000
1913	New York Giants	$2,000/$3,500
1913	Philadelphia A's	$2,000/$4,500
1914	Boston Braves	$3,000/$5,000
1914	Philadelphia	$2,000/$3,500
1915	Philadelphia A's	$2,500/$3,500
1915	Boston Red Sox	$2,000/$3,500
1916	Brooklyn	$2,000/$5,000
1916	Boston Red Sox	$2,000/$4,000
1917	New York Giants	$1,500/$3,500
1917	Chicago White Sox	$3,500/$5,000
1918	Boston Red Sox	$5,000/$10,000
1918	Chicago Cubs	$3,000/$5,000
1919	Cincinnati	$2,500/$4,000
1919	Chicago White Sox	$5,000/$9,000
1920	Brooklyn	$2,000/$5,000
1920	Cleveland	$3,000/$7,000
1921	New York Yankees	$1,500/$3,000
1921	New York Giants	$1,500/$3,000
1922	New York Yankees	$1,500/$2,500
1922	New York Giants	$1,500/$2,500
1923	New York Yankees	$1,500/$4,000
1923	New York Giants	$1,500/$3,500
1924	New York Giants	$1,500/$3,000
1924	Washington	$1,000/$2,000
1925	Pittsburgh	$3,000/$5,000
1925	Washington	$500/$1,000
1926	St. Louis Cardinals	$1,000/$2,000
1926	New York Yankees	$700/$1,500
1927	Pittsburgh	$2,000/$5,000
1927	New York Yankees	$2,000/$3,000
1928	St. Louis Cardinals	$1,000/$1,500
1928	New York Yankees	$1,500/$2,750
1929	Chicago Cubs	$500/$1,000
1929	Philadelphia A's	$1,000/$1,500
1930	St. Louis Cardinals	$400/$750
1930	Philadelphia A's	$500/$1,000
1931	St. Louis Cardinals	$350/$750
1931	Philadelphia A's	$450/$750
1932	Chicago Cubs	$700/$1,000
1932	New York Yankees	$750/$1,250
1933	New York Giants	$700/$1,000
1933	Washington	$550/$700
1934	St. Louis Cardinals	$350/$600
1934	Detroit	$450/$600
1935	Chicago Cubs	$350/$500
1935	Detroit	$500/$700
1936	New York Giants	$200/$400
1936	New York Yankees	$375/$400
1937	New York Giants	$275/$350
1937	New York Yankees	$250/$375
1938	Chicago Cubs	$250/$350
1938	New York Yankees	$200/$400
1939	Cincinnati Reds	$275/$350
1939	New York Yankees	$300/$350
1940	Cincinnati	$300/$350
1940	Detroit	$250/$325

1917 World Series program

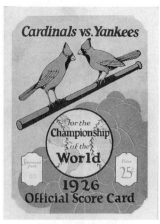

1926 World Series program

1927 World Series program

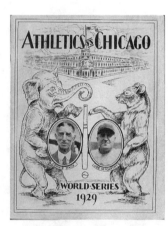

1929 World Series program

1931 World Series program

1933 World Series program

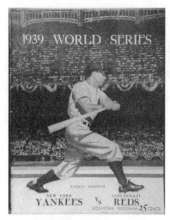

1939 World Series program

1942 World Series program

1956 World Series program

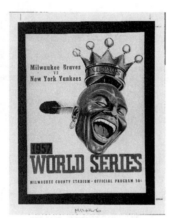

1957 World Series program

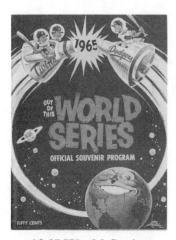

1965 World Series program

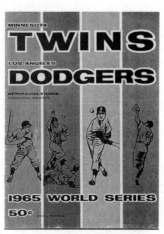

1965 World Series program

Year	Team	Price
1941	Brooklyn	$200/$400
1941	New York Yankees	$125/$250
1942	St. Louis Cardinals	$125/$250
1942	New York Yankees	$125/$250
1943	St. Louis Cardinals	$200/$250
1943	New York Yankees	$200/$250
1944	St. Louis Cardinals	$175/$250
1944	St. Louis Browns	$200/$350
1945	Chicago Cubs	$150/$200
1945	Detroit	$225/$350
1946	St. Louis Cardinals	$175/$200
1946	Boston Red Sox	$175/$225
1947	Brooklyn	$250/$300
1947	New York Yankees	$175/$250
1948	Boston Braves	$150/$175
1948	Cleveland	$100/$175
1949	Brooklyn	$200/$250
1949	New York Yankees	$175/$200
1950	Philadelphia Phillies	$125/$200
1950	New York Yankees	$150/$225
1951	New York Giants	$150/$225
1951	New York Yankees	$150/$225
1952	Brooklyn	$200/$275
1952	New York Yankees	$150/$200
1953	Brooklyn	$225/$325
1953	New York Yankees	$150/$200
1954	New York Giants	$200/$250
1954	Cleveland	$125/$200
1955	Brooklyn	$250/$300
1955	New York Yankees	$150/$225
1956	Brooklyn	$175/$300
1956	New York Yankees	$125/$200
1957	Milwaukee	$100/$175
1957	New York Yankees	$100/$175
1958	Milwaukee	$100/$175
1958	New York Yankees	$100/$175
1959	Los Angeles	$75/$125
1959	Chicago White Sox	$150/$200
1960	Pittsburgh	$100/$125
1960	New York Yankees	$75/$100
1961	Cincinnati	$100/$125
1961	New York Yankees	$100/$150
1962	San Francisco	$150/$225
1962	New York Yankees	$75/$100
1963	Los Angeles	$60/$75
1963	New York Yankees	$60/$75
1964	St. Louis	$100/$125
1964	New York Yankees	$60/$75
1965	Los Angeles	$30/$40
1965	Minnesota	$75/$100
1966	Los Angeles	$40/$50
1966	Baltimore	$85/$125
1967	St. Louis	$100/$125
1967	Boston	$100/$125
1968	St. Louis	$100/$125
1968	Detroit	$125/$225
1969	New York Mets	$125/$150
1969	Baltimore	$50/$75
1970	Cincinnati	$50/$75
1970	Baltimore	$25/$55
1971	Pittsburgh	$75/$100
1971	Baltimore	$40/$50

Year	Team	Price
1972	Cincinnati	$50/$75
1972	Oakland	$60/$75
1973	New York Mets	$20/$60
1973	Oakland	$60/$75
1974	Oakland/Los Angeles	$15/$35
1975	Cincinnati/Boston	$25/$50
1976	Cincinnati/New York Yankees	$15/$30
1977	New York Yankees/Los Angeles	$10/$25
1978	New York Yankees/Los Angeles	$10/$20
1979	Pittsburgh/Baltimore	$10/$15
1980	Philadelphia/Kansas City	$10/$15
1981	Los Angeles/New York Yankees	$12/$18
1982	St. Louis/Milwaukee	$15
1983	Philadelphia/Baltimore	$15
1984	Detroit/San Diego	$10
1985	Kansas City/St. Louis	$10
1986	New York Mets/Boston	$10
1987	Minnesota/St. Louis	$10
1988	Los Angeles/Oakland	$10
1989	Oakland/San Francisco	$10
1990	Cincinnati/Oakland	$10
1991	Minnesota/Atlanta	$10
1992	Atlanta/Toronto	$10
1993	Toronto/Philadelphia	$10
1995	Atlanta/Cleveland	$10
1996	New York Yankees/Atlanta	$10
1997	Florida/Cleveland	$10
1998	New York Yankees/San Diego	$10
1999	New York Yankees/Atlanta	$10
2000	New York Yankees/New York Mets	$10

1975 World Series program

1987 World Series program

1988 World Series program

Playoff Programs

The best-of-five League Championship series was initiated in 1969 and expanded to best-of-seven in 1985. With these additional playoff games came the usual parade of collectibles, including programs. These items, and their Division series counterparts, are the least popular of the post-season game programs. As with World Series programs, the programs from the winning team are generally more valuable.

American League

Championship programs
1969 Baltimore	$60-$65
1969 Minnesota	$60-$125
1970 Baltimore	$30-$50
1970 Minnesota	$100-$150
1971 Baltimore	$30-$50
1971 Oakland	$25-$50
1972 Detroit	$85-$115
1972 Oakland	$25-$50
1973 Baltimore	$30-$40
1973 Oakland	$20-$50
1974 Baltimore	$15-$40

1974 A.L. Playoff program

1976 A.L. Playoff program

1983 A.L. Playoff program

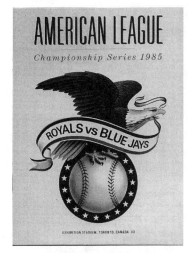

1985 A.L. Playoff program

1974 Oakland	$300-$350
1975 Boston	$40-$50
1975 Oakland	$40-$50
1976 New York	$10-$15
1976 Kansas City	$7-$15
1977 New York	$12-$15
1977 Kansas City	$10-$20
1978 New York	$7-$15
1978 Kansas City	$10-$20
1979 Baltimore	$60-$85
1979 California	$7-$15
1980 New York	$7-$10
1980 Kansas City	$7-$12
1981 New York at Oakland	$10-$20
1981 Oakland at New York	$10-$15
1981 K.C. at Oakland	$10-$20
1981 Oakland at K.C.	$40-$60
1981 Milwaukee at New York	$10-$15
1981 New York at Milwaukee	$40-$50
1982 Milwaukee	$60-$85
1982 California	$7-$10
1983 Baltimore	$7-$15
1983 Chicago	$10-$20
1984 Detroit	$7-$15
1984 Kansas City	$15-$20
1985 Toronto	$25-$35
1985 Kansas City	$25-$35

1986 Boston	$7-$15
1986 California	$20-$35
1987 Detroit	$6-$15
1987 Minnesota	$10-$20
1988 Boston	$6-$10
1988 Oakland	$75-$125
1989 Toronto	$20-$30
1989 Oakland	$20-$30
1990 Boston	$20-$30
1990 Oakland	$20-$30
1991 Toronto	$20-$30
1991 Minnesota	$20-$30
1992 Toronto	$20-$30
1992 Oakland	$20-$30
1993 Toronto	$10-$20
1993 Chicago	$10-$20
1995 Cleveland	$10-$20
1995 Seattle	$10-$20
1996 New York	$10-$15
1996 Baltimore	$8-$12
1997 Cleveland	$8-$12
1997 Baltimore	$8-$12
1998 New York	$10-$15
1998 Cleveland	$8-$12
1999 New York	$8-$12
2000 New York	$8-$12

National League Championship Programs

1969 New York	$100-$350
1969 Atlanta	$40-$65
1970 Pittsburgh	$300
1970 Cincinnati	$50-$75
1971 Pittsburgh	$30-$40
1971 San Francisco	$1,000
1972 Pittsburgh	$25-$40
1972 Cincinnati	$20-$30
1973 New York	$50-$75
1973 Cincinnati	$100-$175
1974 Pittsburgh	$200-$250
1974 Los Angeles	$150-$325

1975 Pittsburgh	$7-$15
1975 Cincinnati	$7-$15
1976 Philadelphia	$7-$15
1976 Cincinnati	$50-$75
1977 Philadelphia	$7-$15
1977 Los Angeles	$50-$75
1978 Philadelphia	$7-$12
1978 Los Angeles	$7-$15
1979 Pittsburgh	$7-$12
1979 Cincinnati	$12-$15
1980 Philadelphia	$10-$15
1980 Houston	$40-$50

1981 Houston at Los Angeles ....$10-$15
1981 Philadelphia at Montreal ....$15-$25
1981 Montreal at Philadelphia...$20-$25
1981 Los Angeles at Montreal ....$30-$40
1981 Montreal at Los Angeles ....$7-$30
1982 St. Louis ....$15-$25
1982 Atlanta ....$7-$10
1983 Philadelphia..$5-$15
1983 Los Angeles..$60-$85
1984 Chicago ....$15-$20
1984 San Diego...$20-$25
1985 St. Louis ....$25-$45
1985 Los Angeles.. $50-$60
1986 Houston ....$10-$20
1986 New York...$15-$30
1987 St. Louis ....$6-$10
1987 San Francisco ....$15-$30
1988 New York..$6-$10
1988 Los Angeles..$6-$10
1989 Chicago ....$10-$15
1989 San Francisco ....$10-$15
1990 Pittsburgh ....$15-$20
1990 Cincinnati ....$15-$20
1991 Pittsburgh ....$10-$20
1991 Atlanta ....$40-$50
1992 Pittsburgh ....$10-$20
1992 Atlanta ....$40-$50
1993 Philadelphia..$10-$20
1993 Atlanta ....$10-$20
1995 Atlanta ....$10-$20
1995 Cincinnati ....$10-$20
1996 Atlanta ....$10-$15
1996 St. Louis ....$10-$12
1997 Florida ....$10-$12
1997 Atlanta ....$10-$12

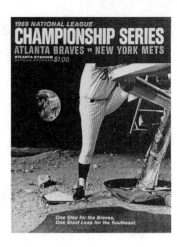

1969 N.L. Playoff program

1981 N.L. Playoff program

1998 San Diego..$10-$12
1998 Atlanta ....$10-$12
1999 Atlanta ....$10-$12
2000 New York Mets..$10-$12

Landmark Games

Programs and tickets from landmark games warrant a premium above the values of other regular-season programs and tickets from the same year. These include games in which a record was broken, a no-hitter was thrown or a milestone was reached.

The tickets from the games in which Cal Ripken Jr. tied and broke the consecutive games record weren't torn at the gate, so only full tickets are available. The same is true of Eddie Murray's 500th home run game. For other games, particularly those that took place decades ago, full tickets are scarce, so a value for the stubs is given. These tickets are denoted with an (S) after the value.

The following price list includes programs and tickets from some monumental games in baseball history.

ALL-TIME LEADERS

Date	Game/Player	Ticket	Program
7/1/41	Joe DiMaggio ties consecutive games w/hit record	$650 (S)	$400
7/2/41	Joe DiMaggio breaks consecutive games w/hit record	1,000 (S)	800
7/17/41	Joe DiMaggio's hitting streak ends	2,500	700
9/26/61	Roger Maris hits record-tying 61st home run	600 (S)	250
10/1/61	Roger Maris hits record 61st home run	1,000 (S)	1,000
4/1/74	Hank Aaron ties all-time home run record	600	100
4/8/74	Hank Aaron breaks all-time home run record	1,500	100
4/27/83	Nolan Ryan breaks all-time strikeout record	200	20
9/11/85	Pete Rose breaks all-time hit record	250	30
5/1/91	Rickey Henderson breaks all-time stolen base record	150	20
9/5/95	Cal Ripken Jr. ties all-time consecutive games played record	100	15
9/6/95	Cal Ripken Jr. breaks all-time consecutive games played record	200	20
9/6/95	Cal Ripken Jr. 2,131 consecutive games (commemorative)	100	30
6/14/96	Cal Ripken Jr. breaks world consecutive games played record	35	20

3,000th HIT GAMES

Date	Game/Player	Ticket	Program
9/30/72	Roberto Clemente	$1,000	$75
5/5/78	Pete Rose	200	20
9/12/79	Carl Yastrzemski	100	20
8/4/85	Rod Carew	100	15
9/9/92	Robin Yount	150	22
9/30/92	George Brett	200	22
9/16/93	Dave Winfield	55	20
6/30/95	Eddie Murray	50	15
9/16/96	Paul Molitor	30	12
8/6/99	Tony Gwynn	25	15
8/7/99	Wade Boggs	20	10
4/15/00	Cal Ripken Jr.	30	15

500th HOME RUN GAMES

Date	Game/Player	Ticket	Program
5/12/70	Ernie Banks	$200	$25
6/30/78	Willie McCovey	150	12
9/17/84	Reggie Jackson	175	25
4/18/87	Mike Schmidt	150	15
9/6/96	Eddie Murray	100	12
8/5/99	Mark McGwire	100	12
4/17/01	Barry Bonds	50	15

300th WIN GAMES

Date	Game/Player	Ticket	Program
5/6/82	Gaylord Perry	$100	$12
9/23/83	Steve Carlton	80	12
8/4/85	Tom Seaver	150	18
10/6/85	Phil Niekro	100	12
6/18/86	Don Sutton	100	12
7/30/90	Nolan Ryan	125	15
7/30/90	Nolan Ryan (commemorative)	n/a	20

NO-HIT GAMES

Date	Game/Player	Ticket	Program
5/15/73	Nolan Ryan-California	$800	$100
7/15/73	Nolan Ryan-California	700	75
9/28/74	Nolan Ryan-California	400	75
6/1/75	Nolan Ryan-California	400	75
5/30/77	Dennis Eckersley-Cleveland	125	30
6/16/78	Tom Seaver-Cincinnati	125	30
9/26/81	Nolan Ryan-Houston	800	100
6/2/90	Randy Johnson-Seattle	150	30
6/11/90	Nolan Ryan-Texas	125	40
5/1/91	Nolan Ryan-Texas	225	75
7/28/91	Dennis Martinez-Montreal	25	8
9/8/93	Darryl Kile-Houston	25	8
9/17/96	Hideo Nomo-Los Angeles	35	8
5/14/96	Dwight Gooden-New York Yankees	25	8
5/11/96	Al Leiter-Florida	25	8

PERFECT GAMES

Date	Game/Player	Ticket	Program
10/8/56	Don Larson-Yankees (World Series)	$500 (S)	$400
9/9/65	Sandy Koufax-Dodgers	400 (S)	100
5/8/68	Jim "Catfish" Hunter-Oakland	250	50
5/15/81	Len Barker-Cleveland	25	10
9/30/84	Mike Witt-California	25	10
9/16/88	Tom Browning-Cincinnati	25	10
7/28/91	Dennis Martinez-Montreal	25	8
7/28/94	Kenny Rogers-Texas	25	8

WORLD SERIES SPECIALS

Date	Game/Player	Ticket	Program
9/29/54	Willie Mays catch	$1,000	$350
10/21/75	Carlton Fisk's HR in 12th inning of Game 6	100	55
10/18/77	Reggie Jackson hits 3 consecutive HRs in Game 6	125	55
10/25/86	Buckner boots grounder in Game 6	75	20
10/15/88	Kirk Gibson's pinch-hit home run Game 1	50	20

SPECIAL REGULAR SEASON GAMES

Date	Game	Ticket	Program
4/18/23	First game at Yankee Stadium	$800 (S)	$800
7/4/41	Lou Gehrig Memorial Day	1,500	100
4/15/47	Jackie Robinson's first Dodgers games	1,000	500
4/27/47	Babe Ruth Day	1,000	200
10/1/51	Bobby Thomson's "Shot Heard Around the World"	800 (S)	750
4/30/52	Ted Williams Day	800	400
4/16/57	Roger Maris' first game	700	100
9/24/57	Last game at Ebbets Field	2,000	1,500
5/7/59	Exhibition game honoring Roy Campanella	450	100
9/29/59	Playoff between Los Angeles and Milwaukee Game 2	250	50
4/10/62	First game at Dodger Stadium	900	150
4/13/62	New York Mets first home game (Polo Grounds)	900	200
10/3/62	Playoff between Los Angeles and San Francisco Game 3	200	40
4/8/63	Pete Rose's first Major League game	500	200
9/29/63	Stan Musial's last game	450	400
4/8/69	San Diego Padres' first game (San Diego Stadium)	700	150
4/14/69	Montreal Expos' first home game	250	60
6/8/69	Mickey Mantle Day	1,000	100
6/30/70	First game at Riverfront Stadium	150	35
10/1/70	Last game at Shibe Park	300 (S)	80
4/6/77	Seattle Mariners' first game	75	20
4/7/77	Toronto Blue Jays' first game	100	50
10/2/78	Bucky Dent's three-run homer in playoff vs. Red Sox	200	50
8/1/79	Thurman Munson's last game	400 (S)	25
4/18/81	Tom Seaver's 3,000th strikeout	125	25
7/24/83	George Brett pine tar incident	250	20
4/29/86	Roger Clemens strikes out 20 batters	125	25
9/22/89	Nolan Ryan's 5,000th strikeout	100	18
9/14/90	Ken Griffey Sr. and Jr. hit back-to-back home runs	50	15
4/6/92	First game at Camden Yards	40	20
4/5/93	Colorado Rockies' first game	100	20
4/5/93	Florida Marlins' first game	85	30
4/5/93	Florida Marlins' first game commemorative ticket (2,500 made)	150	n/a
4/9/93	Colorado Rockies' first home game	85	25
9/22/93	Nolan Ryan's last game pitched	35	10
4/4/94	First game at Jacobs Field	75	20
9/18/96	Roger Clemens strikes out 20 batters	45	15
4/15/97	Jackie Robinson Day (Shea Stadium)	25	10

All-Star Game Programs

All-Star Game programs are generally scarcer than World Series programs since (with the exception of four years) there has been just one All-Star Game annually rather than a four-to-seven game World Series.

All-Star programs have been printed each year with the exception of 1945 when no game was played due to World War II. Programs from 1934, 1936 and 1942 are particularly scarce.

1935, Cleveland

1937, Washington

1941, Detroit

1946, Boston

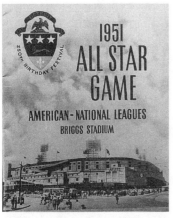

1951, Detroit

1952, Philadelphia

1955, Milwaukee

1960, Kansas City

1933 Chicago	$1,300-$2,500
1934 New York N.L.	$1,500-$3,000
1935 Cleveland	$450-$600
1936 Boston	$3,500-$5,500
1937 Washington	$500-$850
1938 Cincinnati	$700-$1,000
1939 New York A.L.	$800-$1,000
1940 St. Louis	$800-$900
1941 Detroit	$600-$850
1942 New York N.L.	$4,000-$4,500
1943 Philadelphia	$450-$700
1944 Pittsburgh	$1,000-$1,250
1945	no game
1946 Boston	$850-$1,100
1947 Chicago N.L.	$400-$550
1948 St. Louis	$300-$550
1949 Brooklyn	$900-$1,000
1950 Chicago A.L.	$250-$500
1951 Detroit	$150-$300

1952 Philadelphia	$150-$250
1953 Cincinnati	$175-$300
1954 Cleveland	$175-$250
1955 Milwaukee	$125-$175
1956 Washington	$150-$200
1957 St. Louis	$150-$250
1958 Baltimore	$200-$250
1959 Pittsburgh	$200-$250
1959 Los Angeles	$75-$100
1960 Kansas City	$125-$175
1960 New York A.L.	$75-$100
1961 San Francisco	$350-$500
1961 Boston	$300-$600
1962 Washington	$150-$250
1962 Chicago N.L.	$150-$200
1963 Cleveland	$75-$125
1964 New York N.L.	$200-$325
1965 Minnesota	$75-$125
1966 St. Louis	$150-$250

1961, Boston

1965, Minnesota

1967, Anaheim

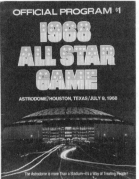

1968, Houston

1971, Detroit

1974, Pittsburgh

197, New York

1978, San Diego

1979, Seattle

1982, Montreal

1984, San Francisco

1985, Minnesota

1987, Oakland

1993, Baltimore

1998, Colorado

1967 California	$100-$200	1984 San Francisco	$5-$15
1968 Houston	$75-$150	1985 Minnesota	$5-$15
1969 Washington	$50-$85	1986 Houston	$5-$15
1970 Cincinnati	$75-$150	1987 Oakland	$10-$15
1971 Detroit	$100-$200	1988 Cincinnati	$10-$15
1972 Atlanta	$20-$40	1989 California	$10-$15
1973 Kansas City	$150-$200	1990 Chicago	$10-$15
1974 Pittsburgh	$20-$40	1991 Toronto	$10-$15
1975 Milwaukee	$40-$65	1992 San Diego	$10-$15
1976 Philadelphia	$15-$25	1993 Baltimore	$12-$15
1977 New York A.L.	$7-$20	1994 Pittsburgh	$10
1978 San Diego	$30-$50	1995 Texas	$10
1979 Seattle	$10-$25	1996 Philadelphia	$10
1980 Los Angeles	$20-$40	1997 Cleveland	$10
1981 Cleveland	$7-$20	1998 Colorado	$10
1982 Montreal	$25-$40	1999 Boston	$10
1983 Chicago A.L.	$10-$15	2000 Atlanta	$10

TICKET STUBS, SCHEDULES, BASEBALL TICKETS

Ticket stubs do not command high prices unless they are from World Series, All-Star or playoff games, or from a game in which a significant achievement or record occurred. Generally, the stubs are in either Poor or Fair condition, because they have been bent and are worn, or Very Good to Excellent because they have been preserved.

Full, unused tickets are worth more than stubs, and are generally for seats which went unsold for a playoff or World Series game, or one in which a baseball milestone occurred. Shortly after Nolan Ryan won his 300th game in 1990, unused tickets were being offered for $60; an unused ticket and program were priced at $75. Special commemorative certificates, printed by the respective teams, also add to the value and make for an attractive display.

Other tickets that would command premium prices would be those for games such as when Reggie Jackson hit three homers in the sixth game of the 1977 World Series, and the 1956 World Series game when Don Larsen pitched a perfect game against the Brooklyn Dodgers. One tick-et stub from that game sold for $532 in a 1992 auction. It was autographed, framed and matted and included a photo of the final pitch and a copy of the box score.

Other examples from auction results have shown prices realized from games from the 1922 and 1923 World Series (at the Polo Grounds and Yankee Stadium) were between $177-$296, while a 1920 Cleveland Indians full ticket from Game 4 sold for $967. A full ticket from Stan Musial's last game, Sept. 29, 1963, at St. Louis, sold for $242, while a full ticket from Catfish Hunter's perfect game on May 8, 1968, at Oakland, sold for $370. A 1978 All-Star Game full ticket from San Diego sold for $77. But in general, ticket stubs shouldn't cost more than $30.

The most valuable ticket stubs have seat numbers, which are generally printed in a different ink color in a separate press run. Those without, generally from the 1940s and 1950s, and sold in large blocks, are usually of little or no value because they are artist's proofs.

Year	Price
Pre-1900s*	$40-$60
1900-1910	$30-$40
1911-1920	$25-$30
1921-1930	$18-$25
1931-1940	$18-$20
1941-1950	$15-$18
1951-1960	$10-$15
1961-1970	$8-$10
1971-1980	$5-$8
1981-1990	$4-$6
1991-present	$3-$5

Pre-1900 tickets and stubs are available from only a very limited number of teams.

There can be a wide range in values even among tickets from the same team in the same era. For instance, tickets from the 1960-64 Chicago White Sox feature player photographs, and range in value from $5 for common players to $20 for Luis Aparicio.

A ticket from the 1957 World Series in Milwaukee

A ticket stub from 1942 All-Star Game at the Polo Grounds in New York

Note: The first ticket price is for a full ticket, the second is a stub. A means All-Star, P means playoff game, WS means World Series.

Boston Braves tickets: 1936 A ($400/$200); 1914 WS ($1,600/$800); 1948 WS ($200/$100-$145).

Brooklyn Dodgers tickets: 1949 A ($170/$85); 1916 WS ($1,200/$600-$750); 1920 WS ($800/$400); 1941-47-49 WS ($200-$250/$75-$200); 1952-53-56 WS ($125-$150/$75-$150); 1955 WS ($250/$95-$125).

Colorado Rockies tickets: 1998 A ($10).

Florida Marlins tickets: 1997 WS ($15).

Houston Colt .45s tickets: None.

Kansas City A's tickets: 1960 A ($70/$35).

Milwaukee Braves tickets: 1955 A ($150/$75-$150); 1957-58 WS ($150-$200/$40-$75).

New York Giants tickets: 1934 A ($400/$200); 1942 A ($200/$100); 1905 WS ($2,500/$1,200); 1911-12-13 WS ($1,600/$600-$800); 1917 WS (1,200/$600); 1921-22-23-24 WS ($800/$400); 1933-36-37 WS ($400/$125-$200); 1951 WS ($150/$75-$125).

Philadelphia A's tickets: 1943 A ($200/$100); 1905 WS ($2,500/$1,200); 1910-11-13-14 WS ($1,600/$800); 1915 WS ($1,200/$600); 1930-31 WS ($400/$175-$275).

St. Louis Browns tickets; 1948 A ($200/$100); 1944 WS ($200/$75-$125).

Seattle Pilots tickets: None.

Washington Senators tickets: 1937 A ($400/$200); 1956 A ($150/$75); 1962 A ($75/$35-$75); 1969 A ($75/$35); 1924-25 WS ($800/$400); 1933 WS ($400/$75-$200).

Atlanta Braves tickets: 1972 A ($55/$15); 1969 P ($30/$15); 1982 P ($15/$5); 1991-92 P ($10/$5); 1991-92 WS ($20/$10).

Cincinnati Reds tickets: 1938 A ($400/$200); 1953 A ($150/$75-$175); 1970 A ($40/$20-$65); 1988 A ($30/$15-$50); 1970-72-73-75-76-79 P ($35-$75/$20-$55); 1990 P ($18/$10); 1993-95 P ($100/$30-$60); 1919 WS ($2,000/$1,000); 1939 WS ($400/$200); 1940 WS ($200/$100-$125); 1961 WS ($70/$35-$75); 1970-75-76 WS ($40-$145/$15-$60); 1990 WS ($125/$45).

Houston Astros tickets: 1868 A ($70/$35-$100); 1986 A ($30/$15); 1981-86 P ($28/$15).

A ticket stub from 1993 All-Star Game
at Comiskey Park in Chicago

A ticket from the 1948 World Series at
Municipal Stadium in Cleveland

A ticket from the 1929
All-Star Game at Wrigley
Field in Chicago

A ticket from the Oct. 1, 1939 World Series
game at Yankee Stadium

A phantom World Series ticket from 1960

Los Angeles Dodgers tickets: 1959 A ($150/$100-$175); 1980 A ($30/$15-$25); 1974-77-78 P ($45/$20); 1981-83-85-88 P ($45/$25); 1959 WS ($150/$75); 1963-65-66 WS ($65-$125/$40-$50); 1974-77-78 WS ($75-$125/$35-$60); 1981-88 WS ($30-$75/$15-$40).

San Diego Padres tickets: 1978 A ($40/$20); 1992 A ($20/$10); 1984 P ($28/$15); 1984 WS ($75/$65).

San Francisco Giants tickets: 1961 A ($70/$35); 1984 A ($30/$15); 1971 P ($38/$15); 1987-89 P ($28/$15); 1962 WS ($300/$65-$125); 1989 WS ($30/$15).

Chicago Cubs tickets: 1947 A ($175-$200/$125); 1962 A ($150-$200/$35); 1990 A ($125/$60); 1984 P ($35/$15); 1989 P ($30/$15); 1906-07-08 WS ($2,000/$1,000); 1910 WS ($1,600/$800); 1918 WS ($1,200/$600); 1929 WS ($600/$250-$300); 1932-35-38 WS ($400/$150-200); 1945 WS ($200/$100).

Montreal Expos tickets: 1982 A ($175/$100); 1981 P ($28/$15).

New York Mets tickets: 1964 A ($70/$35); 1969 P ($65/$50); 1973 P ($125/$35); 1986-88 P ($28/$15); 1969 WS ($350/$95); 1973 WS ($225/$40-$75); 1986 WS ($250/$75-$100).

Philadelphia Phillies tickets: 1952 A ($150/$75); 1976 A ($40/$20); 1976-77-78 P ($38/$20-$35); 1980-83 P ($60/$25); 1993 P ($40/$20); 1915 WS ($1,200/$600); 1950 WS ($250/$100-$145); 1980-83 WS ($30/$15); 1993 WS ($100/$40).

Pittsburgh Pirates tickets: 1944 A ($200/$100); 1959 A ($150/$75); 1974 A ($100-$125/$30-$45); 1970-71-72-74-75-79 ($75/$20-$45), 1990-91-92 P ($18/$10); 1903 WS ($6,000/$3,000); 1909 WS ($2,000/$1,000); 1925 WS ($800/$400); 1927 WS ($600/$300); 1960 WS ($70/$40-$100); 1971-79 WS ($75-$100/$20-$45).

St. Louis Cardinals tickets: 1940 A ($200/$100); 1957 A ($85-$150/$45); 1966 A ($70/$35); 1982-85-87 P ($28/$15); 1926-28 WS ($600/$300-$375); 1930-31-34 WS ($400/$175-$200); 1942-43-44-46 WS ($200/$100); 1964-67-68 WS ($70/$45-$75); 1982-85-87 WS ($75-$100/$35-$45).

Baltimore Orioles tickets: 1958 A ($200/$100); 1993 A ($150/$40); 1969 P ($50-$75/$25-$50); 1970-71 P ($30-$65/$15-$45); 1973-74 P ($20-$50/$30-$40); 1979 P ($20/$7); 1983 P ($15/$5); 1966 WS ($100/$40); 1969-70 WS ($70/$35-$45); 1971 WS ($50/$20-$45); 1979 WS ($100/$40); 1983 WS ($50/$30).

Boston Red Sox tickets: 1946 A ($200/$100); 1961 A ($75/$35); 1975 P ($45/$20); 1986-88 P ($90/$15-$25); 1990 P ($20/$10); 1903 WS ($6,000/$3,000); 1915-16-18 WS ($1,200/$600); 1946 WS

($100/$70); 1967 WS ($70-$100/$40-$85); 1975 WS ($40/$20); 1986 WS ($30/$15).

Cleveland Indians tickets: 1935 A ($400/$200); 1954 A ($150/$75-$125); 1963 A ($70/$35); 1981 A ($30/$15); 1920 WS ($800/$200-$350); 1948 WS ($200/$75-$150); 1954 WS ($150/$55-$95).

Detroit Tigers tickets: 1941 A ($200/$100); 1951 A ($150/$75); 1971 A ($40/$20); 1972 P ($38/$18); 1984-87 P ($30-$50/$30); 1908-09 WS ($2,000/$1,000); 1934-35 WS ($400/$150-$200); 1940-45 WS ($200/$100-$125); 1968 WS ($70/$45); 1984 WS ($30-$50/$30).

Milwaukee Brewers tickets: 1975 A ($45/$20); 1982 P ($28/$15-$20); 1982 WS ($75-$100/$35).

New York Yankees tickets: 1939 A ($275-$400/$200); 1960 A ($70/$35); 1977 A ($40/$20); 1976-77-78 P ($38/$15-$20); 1980-81 P ($28/$15-$20); 1921-22-23 WS ($800/$400); 1926-27-28 WS ($600/$225-$300); 1932-36-37-38-39 WS ($400/$125-$200); 1941-42-43-47-49 WS ($200/$85-$150); 1950-51-52-53-55-56-57-58 WS ($125-$150/$75-$125); 1960-61-62-63-64 WS ($200/$35-$75); 1976-77-78 WS ($40/$25); 1981 WS ($30/$15).

Toronto Blue Jays tickets: 1991 A ($175-$65); 1985-89 P ($28-$35/$15); 1991-92 P ($20-$65/$10); 1993 P ($45/$20); 1992-93 WS ($100-$200/$15-$50).

California Angels tickets: 1967 A ($150/$85); 1989 A ($30-$60/$15-$45); 1979-82 P ($30/$15-$30); 1986 ($25/$10).

Chicago White Sox tickets: 1933 A ($400/$200-$250); 1950 A ($150/$75); 1983 A ($30-$75/$15); 1986 P ($15/$5); 1993 P ($60/$15); 1906 WS ($2,000/$1,000); 1917 WS ($1,200/$600); 1919 WS ($3,000/$1,500); 1959 WS ($150/$75-$95).

Kansas City Royals tickets: 1973 A ($40/$20); 1976-77-78 P ($38/$18); 1980-81-84-85 P ($28/$15); 1980-85 WS ($100-$125/$40-$45).

Minnesota Twins tickets: 1965 A ($70-$125/$35); 1985 A ($30/$15-$20); 1969 P ($65/$30); 1970-87 P ($35-$65/$15-$25); 1991 P ($20-$45/$10-$20); 1965 WS ($100-$150/$35-$50); 1987 WS ($75-$100/$35-$60); 1991 WS $100/$35-$50).

Oakland A's tickets: 1987 A ($30/$15); 1971-72-73-74-75 P ($38/$20-$30); 1988-89 P ($50-$65/$15-$20); 1990-92 P ($18/$10); 1972-73-74-75 WS ($75-$125/$40-$65); 1988-89 WS ($100-$125/$15-$45); 1990 WS ($20/$10).

Seattle Mariners tickets: 1979 A ($40/$20).

Texas Rangers tickets: 1995 A ($125/$50-$75).

Full Ticket Sheets

1965 Minnesota Twins: WS 1, 2, 6, 7..............................$265
1982 St. Louis Cardinals: WS 1, 2, 6, 7 ....$525
1982 Chicago White Sox (yellow): ALCS 1, 2; WS 3, 4, 5 ....$25
1982 Chicago White Sox (tan): ALCS 1, 2; WS 3, 4, 5 ....$25
1982 Chicago White Sox (green): ALCS 1, 2; WS 3, 4, 5 ....$25
1982 Chicago White Sox (orange): ALCS 1, 2; WS 3, 4, 5 ....$25

1982 Chicago White Sox (purple): ALCS 1, 2; WS 3, 4, 5..............$25
1984 Minnesota Twins: ALCS 1, 2; WS A, B, C, D....................$40
1987 St. Louis Cardinals: NLCS 1, 2, 6, 7; WS 3, 4, 5.................$595
1989 San Francisco Giants: WS 3, 4, 5 ....$295
1992 Minnesota Twins: ALCS 3, 4, 5; WS 3, 4, 5 ....$50

Miscellaneous Tickets/Stubs

- Arizona Diamondbacks inaugural season Opening Day ticket stub, 1998... $40
- American League pocket schedule $50
- Chicago Cubs first night game full ticket, Aug. 8, 1988..................$85
- Colorado Rockies inaugural season Opening Day ticket stub $50
- Hank Aaron hits #714, opening day ticket in Cincinnati, 1974 .....$145
- Hank Aaron hits #715, ticket in Atlanta, 1974 ....$300
- Barry Bonds hits #500, full ticket, April 17, 2001 ....$25
- Rod Carew 3,000th hit full ticket, $95, signed $150
- Steve Carlton 300th win ticket stub, signed $75
- Florida Marlins inaugural season Opening Day ticket stub $45
- Tony Gwynn's 3,000th hit Aug. 6, 1999, ticket stub..................... $15
- Reggie Jackson 500th home run full ticket, $175, signed...............$250
- Sandy Koufax's 1964 no-hitter ticket stub, June 4, 1964, with newspaper clippings $225
- Roger Maris' 60th home run ticket stub, Sept. 26, 1961.................$475
- Mark McGwire's 62nd home run full ticket $90
- Mark McGwire's 70th home run full ticket (original).....................$150
- Mark McGwire's 70th home run full ticket (souvenir reprint)...........$15
- Mark McGwire's 500th home run, Aug. 5, 1999........................$20
- Montreal Expos inaugural season Opening Day ticket $100
- Paul Molitor 3,000th hit ticket stub $50
- Eddie Murray's 500th home run ticket stub $60
- Eddie Murray's 3,000th hit ticket stub $55
- Phil Niekro's 300th win ticket stub $40
- Gaylord Perry's 300th win ticket.......................................$50
- Pittsburgh Pirates pocket mirror/schedule, has schedule on the celluloid front and a mirror on the back...................................$400

- Cal Ripken Jr. embossed ticket from Sept. 5, 1995...........................$90
- Cal Ripken Jr. embossed ticket from Sept. 6, 1995 ....$160
- Cal Ripken Jr. ticket from April 15, 2000 3,000th hit game $15
- Pete Rose 4,000 hit certificate, says "I Was There," signed.............$40
- Pete Rose's 4,192nd hit ticket, Sept. 11, 1985, signed....................$225
- Pete Rose's 4,192nd hit full ticket, framed, signed and matted with an autographed photo from the game, Sept. 11, 1985......................$325
- Nolan Ryan 6th no-hitter full ticket, framed and matted with an autographed photo from the game $225
- Nolan Ryan 7th no-hitter full ticket, May 13, 1991, unsigned, $65, signed $125
- Nolan Ryan 300th win full ticket, May 13, 1991.........................$75
- Nolan Ryan 300th win full ticket, May 13, 1991, autographed......$150
- Nolan Ryan first attempt at 300 wins, July 25, 1990, ticket vs. New York Yankees $35
- Nolan Ryan's last game full ticket, Sept. 22, 1993 ....$35
- Sammy Sosa's 62nd home run full ticket $60
- Sammy Sosa's 66th home run ticket....................................$65
- Mike Schmidt's 500th home run, full ticket, April 18, 1987, signed $165
- Tom Seaver's 300th win ticket stub....................................$100
- Don Sutton's 300th win ticket stub $45
- Tampa Bay Devil Rays inaugural season Opening Day ticket, 1998 ....$35
- Toronto Blue Jays inaugural season Opening Day ticket, 1977..... $100
- Dave Winfield's 3,000th hit ticket stub $55
- Robin Yount's 3,000th hit full ticket $60

An opening day ticket from the inaugural season (1993) for the Colorado Rockies

A ticket stub from the Oct. 1, 1969 game at Yankee Stadium in which Roger Maris hit his 61st home run

A ticket from the Sept. 27, 1998, game in which Mark McGwire hit his 69th and 70th home runs

A ticket from the April 17, 2001, game in which Barry Bonds hit his 500th home run

An opening day ticket from the inaugural season (1969) for the Montreal Expos

Baseball Schedules

Schedules come in all shapes and sizes and are distributed by a wide variety of sponsors

If you search through the scrapbooks, wallets and shoe boxes of memorabilia long enough, inevitably you'll find an annual schedule or two for a favorite team of yesteryear.

Schedules, or skeds for short, offer collectors an inexpensive alternative to the big-ticket items which anchor any fan's collection. The limits are endless.

Although the most common form is a pocket schedule, skeds come in all shapes, sizes and for all sports. Collegiate sports such as baseball, football and hockey often utilize sked-cards, which are usually a single piece of paper or tagboard stock with artwork on one side and a game schedule on the back. Professional sports teams generally use folded skeds, similar to sked-cards, but with multiple panels separated by folds. These types of schedules are commonly provided by the Major League teams' ticket offices. Other schedule varieties include matchbook covers, schedule cups, ticket brochures, decals, magnets, rulers, napkins, place mats, stickers, key chains, plastic coin purses and poster skeds.

The easiest way to begin or add to a schedule collection is to contact professional teams for ticket information. You'll usually get a response, especially if you send a self-addressed stamped envelope, which means the team isn't paying postage and already has a pre-addressed envelope to send back. When mailing to Canada, remember that any SASEs sent to the Montreal Expos or Toronto Blue Jays require Canadian postage.

Because schedules are primarily advertising pieces through which the sponsors can reach a wide, varying target audience, the sponsors themselves can be a source for schedules. Other possible sources can be found by determining who advertises in the team's yearbook and programs.

Radio and television sponsors, and stations which carry the broadcasts, also often produce skeds, as may those who advertise on the television and radio broadcasts.

Off-the-wall skeds can be found in a variety of locations, such as restaurants (which often offer matchbook schedules) liquor stores, sporting goods stores, museums, banks and credit unions, motels and hotels, and ticket offices. When traveling, remember to check gas stations, convenience stores, and kiosks which are located along interstate rest stops.

Another way to obtain schedules is by trading, searching for prospective partners in classified ads in hobby publications such as *Sports Collectors Digest* and sked newsletters.

If the conventional shoe box or scrapbook is not used for displaying schedules, many pocket schedules will fit into eight- or nine-pocket baseball card plastic sheets which are held together in an album. These sheets protect the skeds from getting dinged and folded. Oversized schedules may fit into a 5-by-7 inch, dollar bill-sized, or postcard-sized plastic sheets.

Condition is not a critical factor in determining a schedule's value, but it is important. It's more valuable if it isn't damaged, ripped or torn, or marked on. Schedules for defunct teams carry a slight premium value compared to other schedules of the same year, as do localized, scarcer schedules and those featuring team or player photos.

Schedules and their general values: 1901-1909 ($150); 1910-19 ($100); 1920-29 ($75); 1930-39 ($35); 1940-49 ($30); 1950-59 ($25); 1960-69 ($15); 1970-79 ($10); 1980-85 ($2); 1986-on ($1).

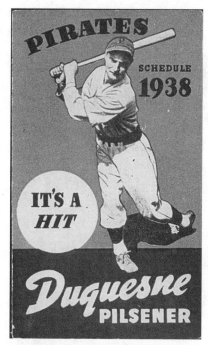

A 1971 Chicago White Sox schedule picturing Tommy John, Bill Melton and manager Chuck Tanner

A 1950 Pittsburgh Pirates schedule picturing Ralph Kiner

A 1938 Pittsburgh Pirates schedule sponsored by Duquesne Pilsener Beer picturing Hall of famer Paul Waner

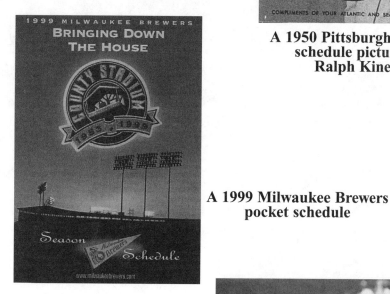

A 1999 Milwaukee Brewers pocket schedule

A 1999 Cleveland Indians pocket schedule

A 1985 New York Mets schedule picturing Dwight Gooden

Early 1980s Chicago White Sox schedules

AWARDS/RINGS/TROPHIES

Although each player, coach, front office worker and team dignitary receives one, less than 100 rings are made for each championship team. This makes them quite rare and more valuable compared to other memorabilia.

Jostens, of Minneapolis, Minn., has created many of the rings designed for championship teams. Each year the designs have become more expensive and complex; as more gold and diamonds are added to the design, the ring's value on the gold and precious gem market increases, too.

It generally takes four to six weeks to design a ring. The teams often request special design elements or graphics, words or logos. The sides (the shank) often feature a year, a message, symbol, team/league logo or game score. Most of the rings are made of gold and contain diamonds, but some contain other stones, either natural or synthetic, in the team's colors.

Most of the championship rings which are listed for sale in advertisements are marked "salesman's sample." These rings have a serial number inside the band and were not created for a player, but rather for a salesman to market and advertise the rings. Instead of real diamonds, they generally contain a diamond look-alike, called cubic zirconia.

Rings are also created for players entering their respective sport's Hall of Fame. Balfour, of Attleboro, Mass., has created the majority of these rings.

The best places to find rings are at memorabilia shows in larger cities, or for sale through auctions. Another alternative is to scan ads in pages of various hobby publications. Although they are generally on the high end of the monetary scale, rings offer a lasting memory from a championship season.

 **1988 L.A. Dodgers World Championship ring**

 **1990 Cincinnati Reds Championship ring**

 1993 Phillies N.L. Championship ring

Selected Rings/Pendants

George Brett Silver Gillette special award trophy for being the leading vote-getter for the 1981 All-Star Game, signed...................$3,250
Cito Gaston's San Diego Padres Baseball Writers Association MVP Award $895
Jostens National League Player of the Week presentation watch with box $295
100th anniversary of baseball commemorative watch, the face depicts a red, white and blue 100th anniversary baseball player logo, with baseball bats as hour hands, plus a black leather band and gold encasement $125
Babe Ruth wristwatch, working $595
Elroy Face Dapper Dan Award for outstanding contribution to baseball, sterling silver award $1,650
Mickey Mantle New York Yankees World Series Championship ring, salesman's sample $7,000
New York Yankees World Champs ladies watch, 14k with diamonds $895
Mickey Mantle/Roger Maris All-Star kids watch, with new band $145
New York Yankees 14k World Series ring, vs. the Pittsburgh Pirates $4,950
St. Louis Cardinals 14k World Series ring, white gold championship ring, vs. the New York Yankees $2,995
Sporting News/Rawlings Gold Glove Award, presented to California Angels shortstop Jim Fregosi, shows his model glove, flanked by two gold baseballs, on a base with his picture $3,995
Harmon Killebrew watch, Swiss-made, face features Killebrew photo with a facsimile autograph against a green baseball diamond background, includes a black imitation leather band $295
Nolan Ryan New York Mets 10k World Series ring, salesman's sample...$2,850
Baltimore Orioles World Series championship ring, Frank Robinson salesman's sample $1,795
Pittsburgh Pirates 10k World Series ring, vs. the Baltimore Orioles, salesman's sample $3,500
Oakland A's 10k World Series ring, Charles Finley salesman's sample, vs. the Los Angeles Dodgers $2,750
Rawlings Mitsui Japanese Central Gold Glove Award, just like an American version, presented to Clete Boyer $3,495
Cincinnati Reds 10k World Series ring, Joe Morgan salesman's sample white gold championship ring, vs. the Boston Red Sox $3,150
All-Star Game 10k yellow-gold ring, for the game in New York, belonged to a Yankee executive....................................$2,250
Los Angeles Dodgers 14k World Series ring, vs. the New York Yankees, salesman's sample $3,500
New York Yankees 10k World Series ring, Reggie Jackson salesman's sample $3,500
George Brett June 1979 Player of the Month Award $1,750
Philadelphia Phillies World Series ring, Pete Rose salesman's sample, vs. the Kansas City Royals...$2,100
Los Angeles Dodgers World Series trophy, presented to Danny Goodman...$3,850
Manny Mota presentation award/plaque, Los Angeles Dodgers 1981 World Champions and 145 Pinch Hits Major League Record $695
Bob Boone Eraser Mate 1982 Best Defensive Catcher Award, with a large lucite baseball diamond with an engraved colored plaque $995
All-Star Game ring, for the game in San Francisco, with original presentation box...$1,250
Kansas City Royals 10k World Series Champions pendant with diamonds $2,000
Kansas City Royals 10k World Series ring, George Brett salesman's sample...$3,695
Kansas City Royals World Series trophy, sample, autographed by Bret Saberhagen...$1,750
Boston Red Sox World Series ring, with presentation box, vs. the New York Mets $2,850
Minnesota Twins World Series ring, Frank Viola, vs. the St. Louis Cardinals $2,100
Los Angeles Dodgers World Championship 10k pendant, vs. the Oakland A's $1,500
San Francisco Giants National League Champions ring, 14k gold plated, Will Clark salesman's sample...................................$2,250
Oakland A's World Series ring, vs. the Cincinnati Reds, salesman's sample $3,500
Cincinnati Reds World Series ring, vs. the Oakland A's, salesman's sample $4,500
Atlanta Braves 10k World Series ring, yellow-gold salesman's sample, vs. the Minnesota Twins..$3,500
Roberto Alomar World Series MVP trophy, has his name engraved on the front, includes two press pins attached to the base of the award.......$6,000
All-Star Game ring, in Baltimore, made for a non-player $395
Philadelphia Phillies National League Champs 10k gold ring, Lenny Dykstra salesman's sample..$2,395
All-Star Game ring, in Texas, made for a front office executive $995

Chapter 6

FIGURES

BANKS

Figural banks for the most part have not yet become a mainstream collectible. That does not mean that they are not highly sought after or valuable. As collectors become more familiar with them, it is almost a certainty that they will become as desirable as other figural items. Some have mascot heads that compare favorably with the bobbing head series of the '60s. Others have team logos or player facsimile autographs. There are even a few that were made in the images of specific players. They are colorful and display beautifully. For these reasons, figural banks will almost assuredly pay "big dividends" in the future.

A number of companies emanating out of the Ohio area produced porcelain mascot banks relating to Major League teams. They were manufactured during the late '40s through the early '50s. Stanford Pottery was one of the leaders, issuing razor banks of the Cleveland Indians, Boston Braves, Pittsburgh Pirates, Brooklyn Dodgers, Detroit Tigers and various Minor League teams. They stand about 8 inches tall and glisten with color. The Gibbs-Connor Company made similar-looking banks of the Cleveland Indians using their familiar mascot "Chief Wahoo" as the model. Moyer made a generic baseball player reminiscent of the Stanford pottery line. Mint examples from these three companies can fetch very high prices.

There were also a series of glass banks in the shape of a baseball that were a give-away by Mobil Oil in the '30s and '40s. The company logo and a team logo were painted on separate panels of the ball. Known examples include the Cleveland Indians, Detroit Tigers, St. Louis Cardinals, Pittsburgh Pirates, Cincinnati Reds and the New York Yankees. Local banks used a plastic baseball with facsimile autographs of home-town team members to advertise their bank. There were probably issues for most of the Major League teams, with the Braves, Yankees and Dodgers being the more commonly found.

A Jackie Robinson brass bust bank was sold at souvenir stands in the late '40s and early '50s. There was also a tin litho Robinson bank that could be purchased through comic book offers. A Ted Williams bank is also known to exist. There is also a Ty Cobb look-alike cast iron bank from the early '20s.

Of all the figural baseball items, banks are probably the least known and the hardest to catalog. The banks mentioned above are only a handful of a growing list of these fabulous display pieces. With the advent of the Internet, never before seen banks are constantly "popping up" for sale. They will surely pique your interest.

Prices are based on Mint examples.

"Chief Yahoo" bank

New York Yankees bank

Porcelain Banks

Stanford Pottery (also known as "Gold Tooth" banks)

Boston Braves...$450
Boston Braves w/headdress (only one known example)..............$4,000
Brooklyn Dodgers $1,200
Cleveland Indians $300
Detroit Tigers (with mascot tiger head) $3,000
Detroit Tigers (human head) $2,000
Pittsburgh Pirates...$600
Minor League Teams...$300

Gibbs-Connor

Cleveland Indians (leaning on baseball) $475
Cleveland Indians (standing on base) $550

Moyer

Generic player $150

Glass Ball Banks

Cincinnati Reds $100
Cleveland Indians $75
Detroit Tigers..$75
Pittsburgh Pirates..$75
Pittsburgh Pirates (with Ralph Kiner facsimile autograph) $125
St. Louis Cardinals $200
New York Yankees (with Lou Gehrig & Bill Dickey facsimile
    autographs) $350

Plastic Ball Banks

Brooklyn Dodgers (all years).......................................$125-$200
Milwaukee Braves..$75-$100
New York Yankees...$125-$200
New York Giants ....$100-$150
L.A. Dodgers...$75-$100
All other teams..$50-$75

Miscellaneous

Ty Cobb (cast iron) ....$250-$400
Jackie Robinson - bust ....$750-$1,000
    (beware, a reproduction of this bank was issued in the '80s)
Jackie Robinson - tin litho...$150-$200
Generic tin litho baseball banks.....................................$25-$75
Plastic Bank with Major League team bats (wooden bats)..............$150
Plastic bank with Major League team bats (plastic bats)...........$50-$75

Banks portraying Braves, Pirates and Indians

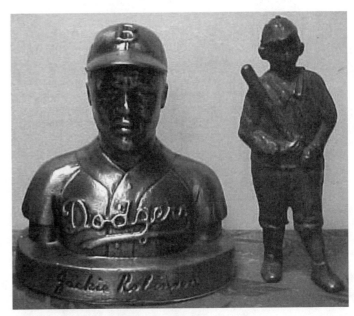

Jackie Robinson banks

BOBBING HEAD DOLLS

Bobbing head sports dolls have become a mainstream collectible over the past 10 years or so. Because of their figural mascot heads and rich colors, collectors have found that they display beautifully with their other sports and team memorabilia.

The Golden Age of the baseball bobbing head doll is generally considered to be from 1960 to 1971. This era produced six major series (these dolls are all made of papier-mâché). The series are classified by their base colors, size, or facial coloring. The Square Color Base series is generally considered the first baseball series, with its initial issue dating back to 1960-61. The White Base series would be next and would run from 1961 to 1963. Included in the White Base series are four actual player dolls (Mantle, Maris, Mays, and Clemente). Following closely would be the Mini series of 1961/62 (includes Mantle and Maris), the Green Base series from 1962 until 1965, Green Base Black players from 1963-65, and finally the Gold Base series of 1966-71. Subsequent bobbing heads were made of either a ceramic composition or plastic and are not highly thought of by advanced collectors.

The different series produce a large variation in pricing. Because of the figures' sensitive composition, condition is paramount in determining value. Gem Mint dolls with no chips or cracks and high gloss and color have been known to fetch prices significantly above book. Because of the high prices being generated, these dolls are not only a great collectible, but a good investment, too.

The White Base dolls are usually at the "top of the list" for collectors. The Roberto Clemente doll is considered the "Holy Grail" of the hobby with estimates of only 100-150 known examples. Black player dolls are even scarcer and command extremely high prices. The other series have risen in popularity over the last several years as collectors look to expand their collections.

The following price list is based on Mint and Near Mint (very minor flaws) conditions. Excellent condition is usually about one half the Mint price. Poorer grades are a fraction of the Mint value. Repaired and repainted dolls, although nice-looking, have little collectible value.

1960-61 SQUARE COLOR BASE

Team	Base color	Head Style	Mint/NrMt
Baltimore Orioles	Green	Mascot	$250/$200
Boston Red Sox	Green	Boy	$400/$325
Chicago Cubs	Blue	Boy	$350/$300
Cincinnati Reds	Red	Boy	$450/$400
Los Angeles Angels	Blue	Boy	$125/$100
Minnesota Twins	Blue	Boy	$100/$75
New York Mets	Blue	Boy	$250/$175
New York Yankees	Orange	Boy	$200/$175
Pittsburgh Pirates	Gold	Mascot	$225/$200
San Francisco Giants	Orange	Boy	$175/$150
Washington Senators	Blue	Boy	$1,200/$1,000

Note: Add 5 percent premium on all dolls if in the box.

1961-1963 WHITE BASE

Team	Head Style	Mint/NrMt
Anaheim Angels (label over base)	Boy	$225/$200
Baltimore Orioles	Mascot	$450/$400
Boston Red Sox	Boy	$275/$225
Chicago Cubs	Mascot	$500/$425
Chicago White Sox	Boy	$325/$275
Cincinnati Reds	Mascot	$500/$425
Cleveland Indians	Mascot	$650/$575
Detroit Tigers	Mascot	$425/$375
Houston Colt .45s (cowboy Hat)	Boy	$350/$300
Houston Colt .45s (with blue uniform)	Boy	$1,400/$1,000
Los Angeles Angels	Boy	$150/$125
Los Angeles Dodgers (embossed chest)	Boy	$150/$125
Los Angeles Dodgers (decal chest)	Boy	$200/$175

Detroit Tigers "Green" baseball mascot

Baltimore Orioles mascot

Chicago Cubs mascot

Cleveland Indians mascot

Kansas City mascot

New York Mets

Roberto Clemente

Mickey Mantle

Yankees black player

Roger Maris

Team	Head Style	Mint/NrMt
Kansas City Athletics	Boy	$300/$275
Milwaukee Braves	Mascot	$450/$400
Minnesota Twins	Boy	$300/$275
New York Mets	Boy	$350/$300
New York Yankees	Boy	$300/$275
Philadelphia Phillies	Boy	$225/$200
Pittsburgh Pirates	Mascot	$600/$500
St. Louis Cardinals	Mascot	$750/$600
San Francisco Giants (embossed chest)	Boy	$325/$300
San Francisco Giants (decal chest)	Boy	$350/$325
Washington Senators	Boy	$375/$325

Actual Player Dolls

Roberto Clemente...$2,200/$1,750
Mickey Mantle ....$750/$600
Roger Maris..$550/$450
Willie Mays (dark face) ....$550/$450
Willie Mays (light face) ....$500/$425

Note: The White Base boxes have a drawing of the doll on the box and are highly collectible. A box can add $50-$75. Mantle and Maris boxes are also picture boxes.

Bobbing head dolls made a resurgence as promotional giveaways at Major League ballparks in 2000 and 2001. Alexander Global Promotions manufactured dolls for up to 25 MLB teams. Minor league teams also produced bobbers, with the Columbus Clippers leading the way with 11 bobbing heads.

Houston and Minnesota led the majors in 2001 with four bobber giveaways each.

2000 Bobbers

Team	Figure	Quantity	Price
Baltimore Orioles	Majestic Cal Ripken	—	$40
Florida Marlins	Bobble Head Doll	—	$35
Minnesota Twins	Harmon Killebrew	—	$230
Minnesota Twins	Kent Hrbek	—	$175
Minnesota Twins	Tony Oliva	—	$75
Minnesota Twins	Kirby Puckett	—	$100
New York Mets	Tom Seaver	—	$90
Pittsburgh Pirates	Bill Mazeroski	—	$30-$50
Texas Rangers	Rafael Palmeiro	—	$45

2001 Bobbers

Team	Figure	Quantity	Price
Anaheim Angels	Tim Salmon	20,000	$40
Anaheim Angels	Garret Anderson	20,000	$40
Arizona Diamondbacks	Luis Gonzalez	15,000	$130
Arizona Diamondbacks	Mark Grace	15,000	$60
Arizona Diamondbacks	Tony Womack	15,000	$50
Arizona Diamondbacks	Matt Williams	15,000	$40
Baltimore Orioles	Brady Anderson	12,500	$60
Chicago Cubs	Sammy Sosa	10,000	$80
Chicago White Sox	Magglio Ordonez	10,000	$50
Chicago White Sox	Frank Thomas	10,000	$40
Cincinnati Reds	Barry Larkin	10,000	$60
Cincinnati Reds	Pete Harnisch	10,000	$25
Cincinnati Reds	Danny Graves	10,000	$20
Cleveland Indians	Omar Vizquel	—	$65
Cleveland Indians	Jim Thome	—	$50
Cleveland Indians	Dave Burba	—	$35
Cleveland Indians	Travis Fryman	—	$20
Cleveland Indians	Kenny Lofton	—	$25
Cleveland Indians	Bartolo Colon	—	$30
Cleveland Indians	Roberto Alomar	—	$25
Florida Marlins	Bobble Head Doll	—	$30
Houston Astros	Larry Dieker	10,000	$25
Houston Astros	Jeff Bagwell	10,000	$45
Houston Astros	Richard Hidalgo	10,000	$35
Houston Astros	Craig Biggio	10,000	$30
Los Angeles Dodgers	Tommy Lasorda	30,000	$60
Milwaukee Brewers	Geoff Jenkins	10,000	$40
Milwaukee Brewers	Bob Uecker	10,000	$25
Milwaukee Brewers	Robin Yount	10,000	$35
Minnesota Twins	Bert Blyleven	10,000	$100
Minnesota Twins	Rod Carew	10,000	$30
Minnesota Twins	Dave Winfield	10,000	$75
Minnesota Twins	Kirby Puckett	15,000	$100
New York Mets	Mookie Wilson	—	$65
New York Yankees	Andy Pettitte	15,000	$65
New York Yankees	Derek Jeter	15,000	$45
New York Yankees	Tino Martinez	15,000	$45
Oakland Athletics	Jason Giambi	15,000	$75
Philadelphia Phillies	Pat Burrell	—	$40
Pittsburgh Pirates	Roberto Clemente	—	$100

Tommy Lasorda

Team	figure	quantity	price
St. Louis Cardinals	Jim Edmonds	—	$20
San Diego Padres	Friar Bobble Head	—	$20
San Francisco Giants	Willie McCovey	—	$65
Seattle Mariners	Ichiro Suzuki	20,000	$150
Seattle Mariners	Kazuhiro Sasaki	20,000	$125
Tampa Bay Devil Rays	Raymond	7,500	$35
Texas Rangers	Nolan Ryan	25,000	$50
Texas Rangers	Ivan Rodriguez	25,000	$30
Toronto Blue Jays	Carlos Delgado	15,000	$35

GARTLAN

Gartlan U.S.A. was founded by Bob Gartlan in 1985. Most of the players in this line of fine porcelain figures were produced in both 8- and 5-inch (mini) versions. The large figures feature authentic autographs on the nameplate, while the smaller figures include facsimile signatures. Production runs vary from piece to piece. Most of the mini figures had production runs of 10,000, while the larger figures were more limited.

Pete Rose led off the Gartlan line in 1985 with an 8-inch signed pewter figure limited to 4,192 pieces—the number of hits that broke Ty Cobb's all-time record. Today, Gartlan figures are some of the most pop-ular in the hobby, with the 8-inch signed pieces attracting the most attention from collectors.

For a handful of players, Gartlan issued artist's proof figures that are more limited than either of the other series. The artist's proofs include the artist's signature along with that of the athlete.

Like other figure manufacturers, Gartlan started a collector's club for its loyal customers. A number of pieces were made available only to club members; these pieces are especially hard to find today.

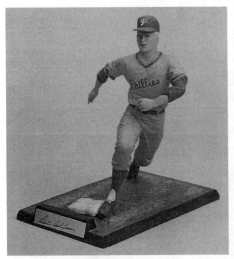

Johnny Bench

George Brett

Steve Carlton

	Quantity.	Issue Price	Mint
Hank Aaron			
Signed	1,982	$149.95	$150
Mini	10,000	39.95	40
Comm.	755	275	300
Club	—	79	125
Luis Aparicio			
Signed	1,984	120	100
Mini	10,000	39.95	40
Al Barlick			
Signed	1,989	124.95	125
"Cool Papa" Bell			
Signed	1,499	124.95	125
Johnny Bench			
Signed	1,989	150	175
Mini	10,000	39.95	75
AP	250	150	500
Yogi Berra			
Signed	2,150	225	250
Mini	10,000	39.95	75
AP	250	350	350

	Quantity	Issue Price	Mint
George Brett			
Signed	2,250	$199.95	$200
Mini	10,000	39.95	40
Club	—	79.95	125
Rod Carew			
Signed	1,991	124.95	125
Mini	10,000	39.95	40
Inc. Mini	125	99.95	200
Steve Carlton			
Signed	3,290	175	200
Mini	10,000	39.95	40
AP	300	350	425
Ray Dandridge			
Signed	1,987	124.95	125
Joe DiMaggio			
Signed	2,214	275	900
Signed Pin	325.00	695	1,800
AP	12	695	7,000

	Quantity	Issue Price	Mint
Carlton Fisk			
Signed	1,972	$149.95	$150
Mini	10,000	39.95	40
AP	300	350	350
Whitey Ford			
Signed	2,360	124.95	125
Mini	10,000	39.95	60
AP	250	350	350
Ken Griffey, Jr.			
Signed	1,989	199.95	200
Mini	10,000	39.95	40
Monte Irvin			
Signed	1,973	99.95	100
Mini	10,000	39.95	40
Ralph Kiner			
Signed	1,975	99.95	100
Mini	10,000	39.95	40

	Quantity	Issue Price	Mint
Buck Leonard			
Signed	1,972	$124.95	$125
Eddie Mathews			
Signed	1,978	149.95	150
Mini	10,000	39.95	40
Stan Musial			
Signed	1,969	199.95	200
Mini	10,000	39.95	40
AP	300	299.95	300
Pewter	500	850	850
Pete Rose			
Platinum	4,192	125	800
Mini	10,000	79.95	75

	Quantity	Issue Price	Mint
Mike Schmidt			
Signed	1,987	$150	$750
Mini	10,000	39.95	40
AP	20	275	1,500
Club	—	79	125
Tom Seaver			
Signed	1,992	125	125
Mini	10,000	39.95	40
Warren Spahn			
Signed	1,973	124.95	125
Darryl Strawberry			
Signed	2,500	99.95	100
Mini	10,000	39.95	60

	Quantity	Issue Price	Mint
Frank Thomas			
Signed	1,994	$199.95	$200
Mini	10,000	39.95	40
Ted Williams			
Signed	2,654	295	400
Mini	10,000	39.95	50
AP	250	650	825
Carl Yastrzemski			
Signed	1,989	150	250
Mini	10,000	79	80
AP	250	150	450

Ted Williams

Stan Musial

Carl Yastrzemski

HARTLAND STATUES

Hartland Statues are some of the pieces of sports memorabilia most recognized by the "Baby Boomer" generation today. Most collectors from the ages of 45 to 55 remember having them or wanting them as children. The superior workmanship and attention to detail have brought in new generations of collectors of these plastic masterpieces.

Hartland Plastics of Hartland, Wis., started producing a series of western, baseball and football statues in the mid- to late '50s. The baseball line was first introduced in 1958 with three home state players, Hank Aaron, Warren Spahn and Eddie Mathews of the then Milwaukee Braves. At the end of their run in 1962, an additional 15 players would be added to the series. Of the 18 player statues issued, all but one (Babe Ruth) were current players. Amazingly, all but three of these players would eventually be inducted into the Hall of Fame.

Hartland took great pride in depicting each player with incredible facial likenesses, physical attributes, and stances. Willie Mays was portrayed making his famous "basket catch," Mickey Mantle's forearms are bulging and Nellie Fox even has his trademark "chaw of tobacco" in his cheek. They all came in one of two styles of boxes and included neck tags, brochures and removable bats (for those shown batting). The stat-

ues have a realism that is unmatched by recent issues. In the early '90s, reissues and a new line were introduced with the Hartland name, but the consensus is that although they are well made, they don't match up to the "Original 18."

The usual factors are used in pricing Hartlands. Condition, completeness, and scarcity are the main determinates of obtaining value. Early runs of the Hartland baseball players used a plastic that in time had a tendency to yellow. A white statue will command a far greater price than one that is off-white or yellowed. The quantities of each player made range from an estimated high of 150,000 for Spahn, Mathews, Mantle, and Ruth to as low as 5,000 to 10,000 for Rocky Colavito and Dick Groat. Groat is by far the scarcest and most sought after of the series.

Boxes and neck tags can sometimes be worth as much as the actual statue. The same factors determine the value on the newer issues, although they are almost always found in their original boxes.

The following prices are based on Mint-condition statues. Excellent to near mint statues are usually 75 percent of the mint value.

1958-1962: THE "ORIGINAL 18"

(plus batboy & minor leaguer)

Player	Pose	Statue	Box	Tag
Hank Aaron	Batting	$275	$150	$150
Luis Aparicio	Fielding	$325	$150	$175
Ernie Banks	Batting	$325	$150	$175
Yogi Berra	Fielding (w/mask)	$150	$100	$125
Rocky Colavito	Batting	$1,000	$500	$500
Don Drysdale	Pitching (w/rubber)	$425	$200	$200
Nellie Fox	Fielding	$200	$100	$150
Dick Groat	Batting	$1,500	$500	$500
Harmon Killebrew	Batting	$750	$250	$250
Mickey Mantle	Batting	$300	$150	$150
Roger Maris	Batting	$450	$150	none*
Eddie Mathews	Fielding	$150	$100	$100
Willie Mays	Fielding	$250	$100	$100

Player	Pose	Statue	Box	Tag
Stan Musial	Batting	$250	$100	$100
Babe Ruth	Pointing	$200	$100	$100
Duke Snider	Batting	$450	$200	$200
Warren Spahn	Pitching	$150	$100	$100
Ted Williams	Batting	$275	$200	$200
Batboy (Little Leaguer)		$200		
Minor Leaguer	Batting	$150		

Notes: There is no known Roger Maris tag. Both Maris and Killebrew came with home plates that have a tendency to warp. Batters came with one of two sizes of bats. The batboy was originally issued as the Little Leaguer but was changed because of licensing rights. It came on a card under a plastic bubble. Most cards found have "Little League" cut off the top. Beware of reproduction tags.

In 1990 the above statues were reissued as 25th anniversary statues. They are heavier and not as well painted. All will be labeled "25th Anniversary." Their values range from $50-$75 with their boxes.

Original Hank
Aaron statue

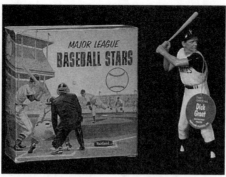

**Dick Groat Hartland statue with
original box and tag**

Batboy

1990s HARTLAND STATUES

(all prices include the box)

Player	Pose	Mint
Roberto Clemente	Batting	$125
Ty Cobb	Sliding	$750
Dizzy Dean	Pitching	$150
Bob Feller	Pitching	$1,500
Whitey Ford	Pitching	$100
Lou Gehrig	Batting	$200
Nolan Ryan	Pitching	$75
Honus Wagner	Batting	$125

Player	Pose	Mint
Carl Yastrzemski	Batting	$400
Cy Young	Pitching	$125
"Safe at Second" Sliding/Tagging		$125
"The Confrontation"	Arguing at Home	$2,000
Umpire		$75

Notes: There are two box styles for the Clemente and Ford statues. The green box (Dallas) is more desirable. A complete "The Confrontation" is very scarce. The Umpire was sent out separately without the "arguing manager." Dizzy Dean has a tendency to discolor even if it has never been removed from the box.

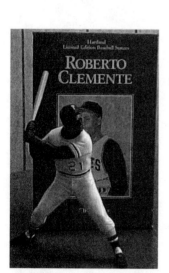

Roberto Clemente

**Nolan Ryan, Honus Wagner,
and Cy Young 1993
Hartlands**

1993 Whitey Ford

"Safe at Second"

1990 Babe Ruth

HALL OF FAME BUSTS

The Baseball Hall of Fame in Cooperstown, N.Y., opened its doors for the first time in 1936. The initial inductees included Ty Cobb, Babe Ruth, Honus Wagner, Christy Mathewson, and Walter Johnson. To honor these great players, busts were sculpted with their respective likenesses. On the pedestal was a plaque with each player's career highlights. The tradition continues today.

In 1963, the Hall of Fame commissioned a Long Island company (Sports Hall of Fame Inc.), to make miniature replicas of 20 of the existing Hall of Fame busts. They were to be sold at souvenir stands at Cooperstown and at Major League parks. They were made of plastic and stand about 6 inches tall. They came in a display window box with a listing of all the players in the series on the back. There were two separate series of 10, with the second series being slightly more rare than the first.

Collectors have found a new interest in them over the past several years. Because of their common size, they display beautifully with both Hartland statues and bobbing heads. Except for the Foxx and Greenberg statues, the set is relatively easy and inexpensive to complete. It is certainly one of the most underrated and undervalued series in the hobby today.

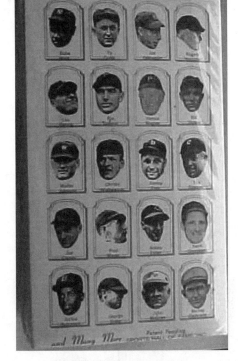

Hall of Fame series

Ty Cobb

Christy Mathewson

Player	Series	Mint in Box	Mint, No Box
Ty Cobb	1	$175	$100
Mickey Cochrane	2	$250	$150
Joe Cronin	2	$250	$150
Bill Dickey	1	$125	$75
Joe DiMaggio	1	$200	$125
Bob Feller	2	$250	$150
Jimmie Foxx	2	$450	$275
Lou Gehrig	1	$175	$100
Hank Greenberg	2	$400	$225
Rogers Hornsby	1	$175	$100
Walter Johnson	1	$175	$100
Christy Mathewson	1	$175	$100

Player	Series	Mint in Box	Mint, No Box
John McGraw	2	$300	$175
Jackie Robinson	2	$350	$200
Babe Ruth	1	$175	$100
George Sisler	2	$300	$175
Tris Speaker	2	$225	$150
Pie Traynor	1	$175	$100
Honus Wagner	1	$175	$100
Paul Waner	2	$225	$150

Note: All of the boxes are identical. A premium can be paid for boxes with the original cellophane unbroken. Statues that have yellowed or discolored are at least one-half the Mint price.

HEADLINERS

Some of the game's most popular players are featured in this series of 3" to 3-1/2" plastic statues by Corinthian Marketing. The figures have extra-long heads. Each figure was sold in a blister pack and includes a removable cap. Uniform details are painted on and there is a green base with the player's last name. Suggested retail price was about $4 each at retail stores, though inventory was quickly picked over by collectors and dealers who stocked up on the most popular players. Values shown are for unopened blister packs.

Fred McGriff

Mike Piazza

1997 Baseball

Complete Set (33)	$180
Common player	5
Roberto Alomar	5
Albert Belle	5
Wade Boggs	5
Barry Bonds	6
Ken Caminiti	5
Jose Caneco (A's)	5
Jose Canseco (Red Sox)	5
Lenny Dykstra	5
Andres Galarraga	5
Ken Griffey Jr.	12
Tony Gwynn	6
Orel Hershiser	5
Randy Johnson	6
Chipper Jones	12
David Justice	5
Eric Karros	5
Barry Larkin	5
Kenny Lofton (Indians)	5
Kenny Lofton (Braves)	5
Fred McGriff	5
Mark McGwire	8
Paul Molitor	5
Raul Mondesi	5
Hideo Nomo	6
Paul O'Neill	5
Mike Piazza	6
Cal Ripken Jr.	12
Ivan Rodriguez	5
Ryne Sandberg	5
Gary Sheffield	5
Frank Thomas	10
Mo Vaughn	5
Matt Williams	5

1998 Headliners Baseball

Complete Set (41)	$200
Common piece	6
Roberto Alomar	6
Wade Boggs	6
Barry Bonds	6
Jay Buhner	6
Ken Caminiti	6
Roger Clemens	10
Dennis Eckersley	6
Jim Edmonds	6
Juan Gonzalez	8
Ken Griffey Jr.	10
Tony Gwynn	6
Orel Hershiser (Giants)	6
Orel Hershiser (Indians)	6
Derek Jeter	8
Charles Johnson	6
Randy Johnson	6
Chipper Jones	8
David Justice	6
Eric Karros	6
Barry Larkin	6
Kenny Lofton (Braves)	6
Kenny Lofton (Indians)	6
Fred McGriff	6
Raul Mondesi	6
Hideo Nomo	6
Paul O'Neill	6
Rey Ordonez	6
Chan Ho Park	6
Mike Piazza	7
Cal Ripken Jr.	8
Alex Rodriguez	10
Ivan Rodriguez	6
Tim Salmon	6
Deion Sanders	6
Gary Sheffield	6

Sammy Sosa 10
Jim Thome 6
Frank Thomas 7
Bernie Williams 7
Matt Williams (Diamondbacks) 6
Matt Williams (Indians) 6

Jeff Bagwell

1998 MLB XL Home Run 2-Packs
McGwire/Griffey $30

1999 - 3" Figures
Brady Anderson $5
Jeff Bagwell 6
Jim Edmonds 5
Andres Galarraga 5
Mark Grace 4
Edgar Martinez 5
Blue Base..10
Mark McGwire 10
Tim Salmon 5
Red Base 10
Sammy Sosa 8
Larry Walker 4
Green Base 10

1999 MLB XL
Roger Clemens $15
Nomar Garciaparra 20
Nomar Garciaparra (CVS Excl.) 45
Juan Gonzalez 15
Green Base 20
Ken Griffey Jr. 20
Tony Gwynn 15
Red Base...20
Mark McGwire 30
Mark McGwire (CVS Excl.) 50
Chan Ho Park 12
Ivan Rodriguez 10
Sammy Sosa 25
Sammy Sosa (CVS Excl.) 50
David Wells 15
Blue Base..20
Matt Williams 10
Kerry Wood 15

1999 MLB XL 2-Packs
McGwire/Sosa $40

Mark McGwire

1998 Headliners Baseball XL
Complete Set (12) $200
Common piece 12

Set price doesn't include blue versions
Barry Bonds 20
Andres Galarraga 20
Ken Griffey Jr. (Blue)...25
Ken Griffey Jr. (White) 25
Derek Jeter..20
Chipper Jones 20
David Justice 20
Mark McGwire (Blue)...50
Mark McGwire (White) 85
Hideo Nomo 20
Mike Piazza 20
Cal Ripken Jr. 20
Alex Rodriguez..20
Frank Thomas..20

1998 MLB "Over the Fences" 3-Packs
McGwire/Griffey/Thomas $40

Sam's Exclusive 2-Packs
Bonds/McGwire 70
Griffey/Ripken...50

ROMITO

Romito Inc. released its first figurines in 1996 after obtaining a license from Major League Baseball. The first two figures were of Hall-of-Famer Roberto Clemente getting his 3,000th hit and of Clemente throwing from right field at Forbes Field.

Romito followed with Walter Johnson, nicknamed "The Big Train," standing on railroad tracks along with a figure of Jackie Robinson sliding into home plate.

The first four figures in the Hall of Fame series came out in 1998: Al Kaline, Bob Feller, Willie Stargell, and Rollie Fingers.

Brothers Rick and David Romito founded Romito Enterprises in 1990. At first, it specialized in selling Starting Lineup figures. It added other lines before issuing its own figurines.

Figure	Quantity	Price
Roberto Clemente at Forbes Field	1,000	$170
Roberto Clemente 3,000th hit	1,000	$90
Bob Feller autographed	400	$200
Bob Feller	100	$170
Rollie Fingers autographed	400	$200
Rollie Fingers	100	$170
Lou Gehrig	400	$170
Lou Gehrig HOF Edition	100	$170
Catfish Hunter	400	$170
Catfish Hunter HOF Edition	100	$170

Figure	Quantity	Price
Al Kaline autographed	400	$200
Al Kaline	100	$170
Bill Mazeroski autographed	500	$120
Thurman Munson	500	$170
Stan Musial autographed	100	$200
Stan Musial	400	$170
Babe Ruth	714	$120
Willie Stargell autographed	400	$200
Willie Stargell	100	$170

Roberto Clemente

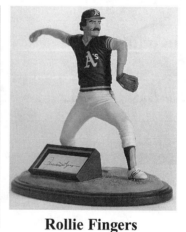

Bob Feller

Rollie Fingers

Lou Gehrig

Bill Mazeroski

Babe Ruth

Willie Stargell

STARTING LINEUP FIGURES

In 1986, Pat McInally, a Harvard graduate and 10-year veteran of the Cincinnati Bengals, was in the process of moving his family from Cincinnati to the West Coast. Preparations included selling his condominium, and the prospective buyer was a newly hired Kenner executive.

McInally was the author of a syndicated newspaper column called "Pat Answers For Kids." The Kenner executive was in the business of developing toys for those very readers. It was suggested that McInally come up with some ideas for Kenner.

A field trip to a toy store provided some inspiration. McInally and his wife journeyed across the Ohio River to wander the aisles of one of the major toy store chains. What they found in abundant quantity were "heroes" based upon fictional characters. The question that occurred to them both was, why not make toys of real world heroes such as sports stars?

Nothing further happened until McInally moved to California, but Kenner kept in touch. Finally, arrangements were made for him to return to Cincinnati and make a presentation of his idea to the company.

On his way to the meeting, he made a brief detour to a local store to pick up a pack of baseball cards to supplement his presentation. Grabbing one of Kenner's current action figures, McInally had the "total" package for his proposal. The reaction was overwhelming. Two hours of discussion ended with only one potential snag: How to get the licensing rights? McInally thought he could help with that, as well.

On the following Monday, a trip to New York to obtain licensing rights with the major sports leagues took place. McInally proved to be the key to success there as well. At NFL Properties, they met with John Flood. Flood had been a fullback at Harvard during McInally's tenure there. After a bit of reminiscing about college, the attendees sat down and negotiated an arrangement. The next stop was MLB Properties. Once again, McInally's college and professional background proved to be a key element in getting the ball rolling. The MLB Properties' legal counsel was Ed Durso, a former running back for the Bengals. Rick White, head of the division, was an alumnus of Chapman College in McInally's California neighborhood. The next morning, they visited the NBA's offices. The merit of the proposal and the prospect of a line featuring the full gamut of major league sports was impossible to reject. By the end of that week, commitments were in hand and Starting Lineup figurines soon became a reality.

Starting Lineups were owned and produced by Hasbro Toy Co. Hasbro obtained Tonka (which owned Kenner) in May 1990. The product development responsibility did not change, however. The Kenner logo appeared on the product through 1997 and was changed to the Hasbro logo in 1998. Prior to Tonka owning Kenner, Kenner had been a part of Kenner Parker Toys. And prior to that, it was a part of the General Mills group.

In January of 2001, Hasbro announced that it was discontinuing its entire line of figurines following the release of its 2001 baseball product lines.

1988 BASEBALL

	NM Price
Complete Set (124):	$3,200
5-player stand w/box	60
5-player stand w/o box	40
Blue Collector's Showcase	50
All-Star Baseball	40

Player	Mint
Ashby, Alan	$25
Baines, Harold	15
Bass, Kevin	12
Bedrosian, Steve	15
Bell, Buddy	25
Bell, George	15
Boddicker, Mike	40
Boggs, Wade	35
Bonds, Barry	95
Bonilla, Bobby	20
Bream, Sid	12
Brett, George	80
Brown, Chris	10
Brunansky, Tom	22
Burks, Ellis	40
Canseco, Jose	40
Carter, Gary	20
Carter, Joe	30
Clark, Jack	17
Clark, Will	25
Clemens, Roger	50
Coleman, Vince	10
Daniels, Kal	15
Davis, Alvin	10
Davis, Eric	10
Davis, Glenn	12
Davis, Jody	22
Dawson, Andre	20
Deer, Rob	16
Downing, Brian	12
Dunne, Mike	10
Dunston, Shawon	15
Durham, Leon	14
Dykstra, Lenny	10
Evans, Dwight	20
Fisk, Carlton	65
Franco, John	16
Franco, Julio	18
Gaetti, Gary	15
Gooden, Dwight	12
Griffey Sr., Ken	25
Guerrero, Pedro	10
Guillen, Ozzie	17
Gwynn, Tony	150
Hall, Mel	12
Hatcher, Billy	14
Hayes, Von	15
Henderson, Rickey	20
Hernandez, Keith	15
Hernandez, Willie	14
Herr, Tom	12
Higuera, Ted	15
Hough, Charlie	22
Hrbek, Kent	15
Incaviglia, Pete	18

Johnson, Howard 14
Joyner, Wally 12
Kennedy, Terry 20
Kruk, John 20
Langston, Mark 30
Lansford, Carney 20
Leonard, Jeffrey 15
Lynn, Fred 20
Maldonado, Candy 10
Marshall, Mike 14
Mattingly, Don 25
McGee, Willie 22
McGwire, Mark 160
McReynolds, Kevin 15
Molitor, Paul 65
Moore, Donnie 20
Morris, Jack 24
Murphy, Dale 14
Murray, Eddie 70
Nokes, Matt 12
O'Brien, Pete 12
Oberkfell, Ken 15
Parker, Dave 25
Parrish, Larry 12
Phelps, Ken 12
Presley, Jim 12
Puckett, Kirby 80
Quisenberry, Dan 25
Raines, Tim 20
Randolph, Willie 25
Rawley, Shane 12
Reardon, Jeff 40
Redus, Gary 12
Reuschel, Rick 12
Rice, Jim 24
Righetti, Dave 15

Sax, Steve 13
Schmidt, Mike 65
Scott, Mike 10
Seitzer, Kevin 14
Sierra, Ruben 25
Smith, Ozzie 70
Smith, Zane 15
Snyder, Cory 12
Strawberry, Darryl 10
Stubbs, Franklin 12
Surhoff, B.J. 25
Sutcliffe, Rick 17
Tabler, Pat 15
Tartabull, Danny 17
Trammell, Alan 20
Valenzuela, Fernando 10
Van Slyke, Andy 20
Viola, Frank 18
Virgil, Ozzie 12
Walker, Greg 12
Whitaker, Lou 24
White, Devon 30
Winfield, Dave 45
Witt, Mike 12

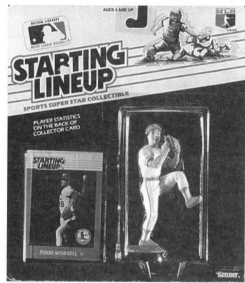

Worrell, Todd 18
Yount, Robin 75

CANADIAN

Complete Set (11): $500

Player	Mint
Bell, George	35
Brett, George	75
Boggs, Wade	50
Carter, Gary	35
Clemens, Roger	125
Dawson, Andre	35
Henderson, Rickey	50
Mattingly, Don	50
Raines, Tim	35
Strawberry, Darryl	35
Winfield, Dave	80

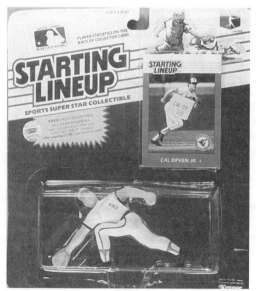

Ripken Jr., Cal 250
Rose, Pete 75
Ryan, Nolan 225
Saberhagen, Bret 20
Samuel, Juan 10
Sandberg, Ryne 70
Santiago, Benito 20

1989 BASEBALL

Player	NM Price / Mint
Complete Set (168):	$4,700

Player	Mint
Alomar, Roberto (R)	400
Anderson, Brady (R)	150
Baines, Harold	25
Barrett, Marty (R)	20
Bass, Kevin	15
Bedrosian, Steve	12
Bell, George	12
Berryhill, Damon (R)	20
Boggs, Wade	30
Bonds, Barry	100
Bonilla, Bobby	16
Bradley, Phil (R)	30
Braggs, Glenn (R)	20
Brantley, Mickey (R)	40
Brett, George	75
Brookens, Tom (R)	35
Brunansky, Tom	20
Buechele, Steve (R)	35
Burks, Ellis	25
Butler, Brett (R)	20
Calderon, Ivan (R)	25
Canseco, Jose	30
Carter, Gary	18
Carter, Joe	30
Clark, Will	22
Clemens, Roger	60
Coleman, Vince	10
Cone, David (R)	50
Daniels, Kal	12
Davis, Alvin	15
Davis, Chili (R)	130
Davis, Eric	10
Davis, Glenn	10
Davis, Mark (R)	30
Dawson, Andre	20
Deer, Rob	40
Diaz, Bo (R)	25
Doran, Billy (R)	35
Drabek, Doug (R)	30
Dunston, Shawon	25
Dykstra, Lenny	30
Eckersley, Dennis (R)	90
Elster, Kevin (R)	12
Fletcher, Scott (R)	110
Franco, John	12
Gaetti, Gary	12
Gant, Ron (R)	125
Gibson, Kirk (R)	15
Gladden, Dan (R)	25
Gooden, Dwight	10
Grace, Mark (R)	42
Greenwell, Mike (R)	10
Gubicza, Mark (R)	10
Guerrero, Pedro	10
Guillen, Ozzie	24
Gwynn, Tony	400
Hall, Albert (R)	30
Hall, Mel	40
Hatcher, Billy	15
Hayes, Von	12
Henderson, Rickey	20
Henneman, Mike (R)	20
Hernandez, Keith	12
Hershiser, Orel (R)	30
Higuera, Ted	30
Howell, Jack (R)	110
Hrbek, Kent	20
Incaviglia, Pete	40
Jackson, Bo (R)	25
Jackson, Danny (R)	30
Jacoby, Brook (R)	25
James, Chris (R)	12
James, Dion (R)	35
Jefferies, Gregg (R)	30
Jones, Doug (R)	20
Joyner, Wally	14
Kruk, John	30
Langston, Mark	30
Lansford, Carney	20
Larkin, Barry (R)	75
Laudner, Tim (R)	50
LaValliere, Mike (R)	30
Leiter, Al (R)	45
Lemon, Chet (R)	18
Lind, Jose (R)	40
Maddux, Greg (R)	300
Maldonado, Candy	12
Marshall, Mike	15
Mattingly, Don	27
McGee, Willie	25
McGwire, Mark	125
McReynolds, Kevin	18
Mitchell, Kevin (R)	20
Molitor, Paul	35
Morris, Jack	20
Murphy, Dale	25
Myers, Randy (R)	18
Nokes, Matt	15
Pagliarulo, Mike (R)	15
Parker, Dave	25
Pasqua, Dan (R)	25
Pena, Tony (R)	30
Pendleton, Terry (R)	25
Perez, Melido (R)	32
Perry, Gerald (R)	35
Plesac, Dan (R)	30
Puckett, Kirby	60
Quinones, Rey (R)	50
Raines, Tim	11
Ray, Johnny (R)	130
Reardon, Jeff	40
Reynolds, Harold (R)	50
Rice, Jim	20
Righetti, Dave	16
Ripken Jr., Cal	350
Russell, Jeff (R)	50
Saberhagen, Bret	16
Sabo, Chris (R)	20
Salazar, Luis (R)	25
Samuel, Juan	10
Sandberg, Ryne	45
Santiago, Benito	25
Schmidt, Mike	55
Schofield, Dick (R)	120
Scioscia, Mike (R)	130
Scott, Mike	10
Seitzer, Kevin	12

Sheets, Larry (R)	25
Shelby, John (R)	40
Sierra, Ruben	30
Slaught, Don (R)	15
Smith, Dave (R)	10
Smith, Lee (R)	70
Smith, Ozzie	50
Smith, Zane	50
Snyder, Cory	12
Stanicek, Pete (R)	30
Steinbach, Terry (R)	18
Stewart, Dave (R)	25
Stillwell, Kurt (R)	12
Strawberry, Darryl	10
Surhoff, B.J.	40
Sutcliffe, Rick	16
Sutter, Bruce (R)	75
Swindell, Greg (R)	20
Tabler, Pat	13
Tartabull, Danny	12
Thigpen, Bobby (R)	45
Thompson, Milt (R)	15
Thompson, Robby (R)	15
Trammell, Alan	18
Treadway, Jeff (R)	45
Uribe, Jose (R)	15
Valenzuela, Fernando	30
Van Slyke, Andy	20
Viola, Frank	10
Walk, Bob (R)	25
Walker, Greg	25
Weiss, Walt (R)	30
Welch, Bob (R)	20
Whitaker, Lou	25
White, Devon	140
Winfield, Dave	35
Witt, Mike	120
Worrell, Todd	14
Wynne, Marvell (R)	40
Young, Gerald (R)	20
Yount, Robin	80

Greenwell, Mike	35
Henderson, Rickey	45
Joyner, Wally	35
Mattingly, Don	50
McGwire, Mark	300
Raines, Tim	35
Ripken Jr., Cal	1,000
Sabo, Chris	35
Schmidt, Mike	100
Scott, Mike	35
Smith, Ozzie	100
Strawberry, Darryl	35
Trammell, Alan	35
Valenzuela, Fernando	35

1989 BASEBALL GREATS

Player	NM Price
Complete Set (10)	$450

Player	Mint
Banks/Williams	40
Bench/Rose	50
Drysdale/Jackson	60
Mantle/DiMaggio	90
Mathews/Aaron	50
Mays/McCovey	45
Musial/Gibson	30
Ruth/Gehrig	
(white/gray)	55
(white/white)	70
(gray/white)	45
Stargell/Clemente	55
Yastrzemski/Aaron	90

CANADIAN

Player	
Complete Set (20)	$1,500

Player	Mint
Bell, George	35
Boggs, Wade	50
Canseco, Jose	50
Carter, Gary	35
Clemens, Roger	200
Davis, Eric	35
Dawson, Andre	35
Gaetti, Gary	35
Gibson, Kirk	35
Gooden, Dwight	35

1990 BASEBALL

Player	NM Price
Complete Set (87)	$1,600

Player	Mint
Anderson, Allan (R)	12
Backman, Wally (R)	55

Player	
Ballard, Jeff (R)	12
Barfield, Jesse (R)	10
Bedrosian, Steve	10
Benzinger, Todd (R)	35
Berryhill, Damon (R)	20
Boggs, Wade	24
Bonds, Barry	75

Bonilla, Bobby	20
Bosio, Chris (R)	15
Burks, Ellis	15
Canseco, Jose	25
Clark, Will	
(Batting)	15
(Power)	15
Clemens, Roger	40
Coleman, Vince	10
Darling, Ron (R)	20
Davis, Eric	12
Dawson, Andre	18
Dibble, Rob (R)	25
Dykstra, Lenny	25
Eckersley, Dennis	50
Esasky, Nick (R)	30
Gaetti, Gary	12
Galarraga, Andres (R)	40
Gibson, Kirk	10
Gooden, Dwight	10
Grace, Mark	
(batting)	18
(power)	22
Greenwell, Mike	10
Griffey Jr., Ken	
(R, sliding)	125
Guerrero, Pedro	10
Hayes, Von	10
Henderson, Dave (R)	13
Henderson, Rickey	15
Herr, Tom	15
Hershiser, Orel	20
Hrbek, Kent	10
Jackson, Bo	10
Jefferies, Gregg	15
Johnson, Howard	10
Jordan, Rickey (R)	10
Kelly, Roberto (R)	15
Larkin, Barry	50

Nokes, Matt	15
O'Neill, Paul (R)	50
Oquendo, Jose (R)	25
Pettis, Gary (R)	50
Puckett, Kirby	40
Randolph, Willie	25
Reed, Jody (R)	15
Reuschel, Rick	10
Righetti, Dave	15
Ripken Jr., Cal	175
Ryan, Nolan	60
Sabo, Chris	12
Samuel, Juan	12
Sandberg, Ryne	35
Sax, Steve	10
Scott, Mike	10
Sheffield, Gary (R)	40
Smiley, John (R)	15
Smith, Ozzie	40
Stewart, Dave	15
Strawberry, Darryl	
(batting)	10
(fielding)	10
Sutcliffe, Rick	14
Tettleton, Mickey (R)	40
Trammell, Alan	14
Van Slyke, Andy	20
Viola, Frank	12
Walton, Jerome (R)	10
Whitaker, Lou	15
Williams, Mitch (R)	25
Winfield, Dave	45
Yount, Robin	70

Maddux, Greg	400
Magrane, Joe (R)	15
Mattingly, Don	
(bat in hand)	20
(power)	24
McGriff, Fred (R)	40
McGwire, Mark	90
McReynolds, Kevin	10
Mitchell, Kevin	12
Molitor, Paul	30
Murray, Eddie	150

EXTENDED

Complete Set (9) $200

Player	Mint
Abbott, Jim (R)	15
Alomar Jr., Sandy (R)	15
Canseco, Jose	20
Carter, Joe	25
Griffey Jr., Ken	
(R, jump)	115
Jackson, Bo	10
Ryan, Nolan	60
McDonald, Ben (R)	15
Walton, Jerome (R)	10

1991 BASEBALL

	NM Price
Complete Set (46)	$450
Mail-in Poster	10

Player	Mint
Abbott, Jim	10
Alomar Jr., Sandy	16
Armstrong, Jack (R)	12
Bonds, Barry	35
Bonilla, Bobby	14
Browning, Tom (R)	20
Canseco, Jose	15
Clark, Will	16
Davis, Eric	8
Dawson, Andre	10
DeShields, Delino (R)	10
Drabek, Doug	14
Dunston, Shawon	12
Dykstra, Lenny	14
Fielder, Cecil (R)	15
Franco, John	10
Gooden, Dwight	9
Grace, Mark	12
Griffey Jr., Ken (Batting)	40
Gruber, Kelly (R)	10
Guillen, Ozzie	12
Henderson, Rickey	12

Player	Mint
Maas, Kevin (R)	9
Magadan, Dave (R)	9
Martinez, Ramon (R)	20
Mattingly, Don	18
McDonald, Ben	10
McGwire, Mark	60
Mitchell, Kevin	10
Puckett, Kirby	25
Ryan, Nolan	40
Sabo, Chris	8
Sandberg, Ryne	30
Santiago, Benito	12
Sax, Steve	12
Stewart, Dave	13
Strawberry, Darryl (Mets)	10
Trammell, Alan	20
Viola, Frank	10
Williams, Matt (R)	36
Zeile, Todd (R)	14

EXTENDED

Complete Set (10)	$150

Player	Mint
Bell, George	10
Coleman, Vince	10
Davis, Glenn	10
Griffey Jr., Ken (running)	50
Griffey Sr., Ken	20
Jackson, Bo (White Sox)	15
Justice, Dave (R)	40
Raines, Tim	13
Ryan, Nolan	45
Strawberry, Darryl (Dodgers)	10

1991 HEADLINE BASEBALL

	NM Price
Complete Set (7)	$200

Player	Mint
Canseco, Jose	20
Clark, Will	20
Griffey Jr., Ken	60
Henderson, Rickey	25
Jackson, Bo	12
Mattingly, Don	42
Ryan, Nolan	60

Player	Mint
Jackson, Bo (Royals)	10
Jefferies, Gregg	13
Johnson, Howard	10
Kelly, Roberto	10
Larkin, Barry	20

1992 BASEBALL

	NM Price
Complete Set (37)	$500
Give-away Poster	10

Player	Mint
Alomar, Roberto	15
Bell, George	10

Player	Mint
Belle, Albert (R)	20
Biggio, Craig (R)	25
Bonds, Barry	25
Calderon, Ivan	8
Canseco, Jose	15
Clark, Will	15
Clemens, Roger	32
Dibble, Rob	8

Erickson, Scott (R) 10
Fielder, Cecil 10
Finley, Chuck (R) 10
Glavine, Tom (R) 35
Gonzalez, Juan (R) 35
Griffey Jr., Ken
  (bat in hand) 40
  (swing)...40
Gwynn, Tony 35
Henderson, Dave 7
Henderson, Rickey 10
Jackson, Bo
  (running) 9
  (bat in hand) 10
Johnson, Howard 10
Jose, Felix (R) 7
Justice, Dave..15
Maas, Kevin 8
Martinez, Ramon 8
McGriff, Fred 16
McRae, Brian (R) 9
Ripken Jr., Cal..75

Ryan, Nolan..35
Sabo, Chris 8
Sandberg, Ryne 18
Sierra, Ruben 14
Strawberry, Darryl 10
Thomas, Frank (R, fielding)...30
Williams, Matt 15

EXTENDED

Complete Set (9) $175

Player	Mint
Avery, Steve (R)	12
Bonilla, Bobby	10
Davis, Eric	8
Puckett, Kirby	18
Saberhagen, Bret	8
Seaver, Tom (R)	24
Tartabull, Danny	10
Thomas, Frank (R, batting)	40
Van Poppel, Todd (R)	10

1992 HEADLINE BASEBALL

	NM Price
Complete Set (7)	$140

Player	Mint
Brett, George	40
Fielder, Cecil	15
Griffey Jr., Ken	40
Henderson, Rickey	15
Jackson, Bo	10
Ryan, Nolan	50
Sandberg, Ryne	32

1993 BASEBALL

	NM Price
Complete Set (38)	$400

Player	Mint
Alomar, Roberto	10
Baerga, Carlos (R)	10
Bagwell, Jeff (R)	40
Bonds, Barry (Pirates)	15
Brown, Kevin (R)	20
Canseco, Jose	16
Clark, Will	8
Clemens, Roger	28
Cone, David	10
Fryman, Travis (R)	10
Glavine, Tom	25
Gonzalez, Juan	20
Griffey Jr., Ken	35
Grissom, Marquis (R)	10
Guzman, Juan (R)	8
Karros, Eric (R)	12
Kelly, Roberto	6

Kruk, John 10
Lankford, Ray (R) 12
Larkin, Barry 15
Mack, Shane (R)...6
McDowell, Jack (R) 9

McGriff, Fred 15
McGwire, Mark 60
Mussina, Mike (R) 30
Palmer, Dean (R) 10
Pendleton, Terry 6
Puckett, Kirby...15
Ripken Jr., Cal 40
Roberts, Bip (R) 9
Ryan, Nolan (regular).......................................40
Sandberg, Ryne 15
Sheffield, Gary 10
Smoltz, John (R)...30
Thomas, Frank 12
Van Slyke, Andy...10
Ventura, Robin (R) 15
Walker, Larry (R) 28

EXTENDED

Complete Set (7)	$400

Player	Mint
Bonds, Barry (Giants)	18
Fisk, Carlton	20
Jackson, Bo	10
Maddux, Greg	100
Neid, David (R)	10
Ryan, Nolan (Retire)	100
Santiago, Benito	10

1993 HEADLINE BASEBALL

	NM Price
Complete Set (8)	$175

Player	Mint
Abbott, Jim	14
Alomar, Roberto	15
Glavine, Tom	20
McGwire, Mark	70
Ripken Jr., Cal	50
Ryan, Nolan	50
Sanders, Deion	20
Thomas, Frank	20

1993 BASEBALL STADIUM STARS

	NM Price
Complete Set (6)	$175

Player	Mint
Clemens, Roger	32
Fielder, Cecil	20
Griffey Jr., Ken	40
Ryan, Nolan	60
Sandberg, Ryne	30
Thomas, Frank	32

1994 BASEBALL

	NM Price
Complete Set (57)	$450

Player	Mint
Appier, Kevin (R)	10
Avery, Steve	8
Baerga, Carlos	8
Bagwell, Jeff	17
Bell, Derek (R)	12
Bell, Jay (R)	14

Player	Mint
Belle, Albert	10
Boggs, Wade	8
Bonds, Barry	10
Burkett, John (R)	10
Carter, Joe	7
Clemens, Roger	20
Cone, David	12
Curtis, Chad (R)	10
Daulton, Darren (R)	12
DeShields, Delino	8
Fernandez, Alex (R)	7
Fielder, Cecil	8
Galarraga, Andres	8
Grace, Mark	8
Greene, Tommy (R)	8
Griffey Jr., Ken	30
Harper, Brian (R)	8
Harvey, Brian (R)	8
Hayes, Charlie (R)	8
Hoiles, Chris (R)	8
Hollins, Dave (R)	8
Jefferies, Gregg	7
Johnson, Randy (R)	40
Justice, Dave	10
Karros, Eric	8
Key, Jimmy (R)	15
Kile, Darryl (R)	12
Knoblauch, Chuck (R)	12
Langston, Mark	8
Mattingly, Don	10
Merced, Orlando (R)	8
Molitor, Paul	10
Mussina, Mike	10

Olerud, John (R)............15
Phillips, Tony (R) 10
Piazza, Mike (R)............70
Rijo, Jose (R)............8
Ripken Jr., Cal 42
Rodriguez, Ivan (R)............30
Salmon, Tim (R)............12
Sandberg, Ryne 15
Schilling, Curt (R)............20
Sheffield, Gary (regular)............7
Snow, J.T. (R)............12
Thomas, Frank............15
Thompson, Robby 7
Vaughn, Greg (R)............15
Vaughn, Mo (R)............18
Ventura, Robin............7
Williams, Matt............10
Winfield, Dave............10

EXTENDED

Complete Set (8) $175

Player	Mint
Carlton, Steve (R, HOF)	15
Clark, Will	12
Dykstra, Lenny	12
Gonzalez, Juan	20
Lofton, Kenny (R)	35
McGriff, Fred	15
Palmeiro, Rafael (R)	20
Sheffield, Gary (power)	8

1994 COOPERSTOWN

	NM Price
Complete Set (8)	$100

Player	Mint
Cobb, Ty	14
Gehrig, Lou	14
Jackson, Reggie	30
Mays, Willie	16
Robinson, Jackie	
(with #42)	14
(with #44)	350
Ruth, Babe	14
Wagner, Honus	30
Young, Cy	14

1994 BASEBALL STADIUM STARS

	NM Price
Complete Set (8)	$180

Player	Mint
Bonds, Barry	22
Clark, Will	18
Eckersley, Dennis	18
Glavine, Tom	25
Gonzalez, Juan	25
Jackson, Bo	50
Puckett, Kirby	20
Sanders, Deion	35

1995 BASEBALL

	NM Price
Complete Set (48)	$400

Player	Mint
Abbott, Jim	8
Alou, Moises (R)	15
Baerga, Carlos	8
Bagwell, Jeff	14
Belle, Albert	10
Berroa, Geronimo (R)	10
Bichette, Dante (R)	14
Bonds, Barry	12
Buhner, Jay (R)	14
Canseco, Jose (Rangers)	12
Carr, Chuck (R)	7
Carter, Joe	8
Cedeno, Andujar (R)	10
Clark, Will	8
Clemens, Roger	20
Conine, Jeff (R)	8
Cooper, Scott (R)	10
Daulton, Darren	10
Delgado, Carlos (R)	35
Fielder, Cecil	8
Floyd, Cliff (R)	12

Player	Mint
Franco, Julio	8
Gonzalez, Juan	10
Griffey Jr., Ken	30
Gwynn, Tony	20
Hamelin, Bob (R)	8
Hammonds, Jeffrey (R)	15
Johnson, Randy	16
Kent, Jeff (R)	25
King, Jeff (R)	10
Klesko, Ryan (R)	20
Knoblauch, Chuck	10
Kruk, John	10
Lankford, Ray	8
Larkin, Barry	12
Lopez, Javier (R)	25
Martin, Al (R)	10
McRae, Brian	8
Molitor, Paul	8
Mondesi, Raul (R)	25
Mussina, Mike	8
Neel, Troy (R)	10
Nilsson, Dave (R)	12
Olerud, John	8
O'Neill, Paul	10
Piazza, Mike (throwing)	30
Puckett, Kirby	12

Ripken Jr., Cal (regular) 35
Salmon, Tim 10
Sanders, Deion 12
Sanders, Reggie (R) 10
Sosa, Sammy (R) 75
Tettleton, Mickey 15
Thomas, Frank 12
Van Slyke, Andy 10
Vaughn, Mo 10
Wilkins, Rick (R) 10
Williams, Matt 10

EXTENDED

Complete Set (9) $300

Player	Mint
Canseco, Jose (Red Sox)	12
Greer, Rusty (R)	12
Lofton, Kenny	30
Pagnozzi, Tom (R)	10
Piazza, Mike (batting)	30
Ramirez, Manny (R)	70
Ripken Jr., Cal (Streak)	70
Rodriguez, Alex (R)	150
Schmidt, Mike (HOF)	15

1995 COOPERSTOWN

	NM Price
Complete Set (10)	$80

Player	Mint
Carew, Rod	12
Dean, Dizzy	10
Drysdale, Don	10
Feller, Bob	10
Ford, Whitey	10
Gibson, Bob	10
Killebrew, Harmon	18
Mathews, Eddie	25
Paige, Satchel	10
Ruth, Babe	15

1995 BASEBALL STADIUM STARS

	NM Price
Complete Set (9)	$200

Player	Mint
Daulton, Darren	20
Dykstra, Lenny	20
Griffey Jr., Ken	35
Johnson, Randy	65
Justice, Dave	20
Maddux, Greg	60
McGwire, Mark	62
Thomas, Frank	25
Vaughn, Mo	20

1996 BASEBALL

	NM Price
Complete Set (56)	$750

Player	Mint
Alomar, Roberto	10
Bagwell, Jeff (white bat)	15
(black bat)	10
Belle, Albert	10
Biggio, Craig	10
Bonds, Barry	12
Bones, Ricky (R)	8
Brogna, Rico (R)	12
Caminiti, Ken (R)	15
Castilla, Vinny (R)	12
Clark, Will	8
Cone, David	10
Cordero, Wil (R)	10
Cordova, Marty (R)	12
Dunston, Shawon	10
Dykstra, Lenny	8
Edmonds, Jim (R)	25
Eisenreich, Jim (R)	8
Gaetti, Gary	8
Gant, Ron	8
Griffey Jr., Ken (regular)	20
Grissom, Marquis	12
Guillen, Ozzie	8
Hunter, Brian (R)	10
Jeter, Derek (R)	80
Johnson, Charles (R)	12
Jones, Chipper (R)	150
Maddux, Greg	40
Manto, Jeff (R)	10
Martinez, Edgar (R)	30
McGriff, Fred	8
McGwire, Mark	35
Mondesi, Raul	8
Murray, Eddie	12
Nomo, Hideo (R, whitc)	18
(R, gray)	18
O'Neill, Paul	12
Piazza, Mike	18
Puckett, Kirby	20
Ripken Jr., Cal (diving)	32
(sliding)	32
(diving w/ sliding card)	32
(sliding w/ diving card)	32
Rodriquez, Ivan	10

Sanders, Deion 12
Smith, Ozzie 17
Sosa, Sammy 35
Steinbach, Terry 8
Thomas, Frank 12
Thome, Jim (R) 20
Thompson, Ryan (R) 8
Valentin, John (R) 10
Vaughn, Mo 8
Walker, Larry 15
White, Rondell (R) 10
Williams, Matt 8

EXTENDED

Complete Set (16)	$180

Player	Mint
Alou, Moises	12
Anderson, Garrett (R)	15
Baerga, Carlos	10
Bichette, Dante	12
Carter, Joe	10
Conine, Jeff	8
Curtis, Chad	10
Griffey Jr., Ken	50
Gonzalez, Juan	20
Justice, David	18
Karros, Eric	10
Larkin, Barry	15
Mattingly, Don	18
Morris, Hal	8
Neagle, Denny (R)	15
Palmeiro, Rafael	10

1996 BASEBALL STADIUM STARS

Complete Set (11)	NM Price $225

Player	Mint
Belle, Albert	20
Buhner, Jay	20
Canseco, Jose	20
Daulton, Darren	20
Grace, Mark	20
Knoblauch, Chuck	20
Lopez, Javy	35
Piazza, Mike	35
Ripken Jr., Cal	55
Ventura, Robin	20
Williams, Matt	20

1996 COOPERSTOWN

Complete Set (14)	NM Price $175

Player	Mint
Aaron, Hank	20
Alexander, Grover Cleveland	10
Ashburn, Richie (Clover)	20
Carew, Rod ('96 National)	20
Carlton, Steve ('96 Fanfest)	20

Clemente, Roberto	16
Foxx, Jimmy	15
Greenberg, Hank	10
Hornsby, Rogers	12
Killebrew, Harmon (*Tuff Stuff*)	25
Morgan, Joe	10
Ott, Mel	10
Roberts, Robin	15
Robinson, Jackie	18

1996 COOPERSTOWN 12" FIGURES

Complete Set (6)	NM Price $100

Player	Mint
Cobb, Ty	15
Gehrig, Lou	15
Ruth, Babe	
Red Sox (Kay-Bee)	15
Yankees	15
Wagner, Honus (Toys R Us)	15
Young, Cy	15

1997 BASEBALL

Complete Set (48)	NM Price $500

Player	Mint
Alomar, Roberto	10
Anderson, Brady	12
Bagwell, Jeff	10
Bell, Derek	8
Belle, Albert	12
Bichette, Dante	10
Bonds, Barry	12
Brosius, Scott (R)	12
Burks, Ellis	12
Clemens, Roger	15
Damon, Johnny (R)	15
Finley, Steve (R)	10
Glavine, Tom	15

Greer, Rusty...8
Griffey Jr., Ken..20
Hundley, Todd (R)...10
Isringhausen, Jason (R)..12
Jaha, John (R)...10
Johnson, Randy..15
Jones, Chipper..35
Jordan, Brian (R)...16
Joyner, Wally..8
Kendall, Jason (R)...24
Klesko, Ryan...15
Lopez, Javier...14
Martinez, Tino (R)..25
McRae, Brian...8
Mesa, Jose (R)...10
Molitor, Paul..10
Mondesi, Raul...10
Nomo, Hideo...12
Ordonez, Rey (R)...10
Park, Chan Ho (R)..15
Piazza, Mike..12
Ramirez, Manny...15
Ripken Jr., Cal...16
Rodriguez, Alex...23
Rodriguez, Henry (R)...15
Rodriguez, Ivan...12
Sandberg, Ryne...10
Sanders, Reggie..8
Smoltz, John..18
Snow, J.T...12
Thomas, Frank...12
Valdes, Ismael (R)..15
White, Devon...10
Williams, Bernie (R)...23
Williams, Matt...10

EXTENDED

Complete Set (14) $160

Player	Mint
Belle, Albert	10
Bottalico, Rickey (R)	7
Caminiti, Ken	10
Clark, Tony (R)	15
Clemens, Roger	18
Eckersley, Dennis	10
Jeter, Derek	25
Jones, Andruw (R)	35
McGwire, Mark	28
Mussina, Mike	10
Pettite, Andy (R)	20
Rodriguez, Alex	18
Sanders, Deion	10
Williams, Matt	10

1997 BASEBALL 12" FIGURES

Complete Set (4) $90

Player	Mint
Griffey Jr., Ken	35
Maddux, Greg	25
Piazza, Mike	25
Ripken Jr., Cal	25

1997 BASEBALL CLASSIC DOUBLES

	NM Price
Complete Set (11)	$225

Player	Mint
Aaron H./Robinson, J.	15
Griffey Jr./Griffey Sr.	30
Bonds Ba./Bonds Bo.	15
Maddux, G./Young, C.	50
Johnson, R./Ryan, N.	30
Thomas, F./Ruth, B.	25
Ripken Jr./Robinson, B.	25
Robinson, J./Doby L. (Fanfest)	25
Nomo, H./Drysdale, D.	15
McGwire, M./Maris, R.	65
Mantle, M./Maris, R.	30

1997 BASEBALL FREEZE FRAME

	NM Price
Complete Set (6)	$125

Player	Mint
Bichette, Dante	15
Gonzalez, Juan	15

Player	Mint
Griffey Jr., Ken	35
Jones, Chipper	35
Piazza, Mike	20
Thomas, Frank	20

1997 BASEBALL STADIUM STARS

	NM Price
Complete Set (7)	$140

Player	Mint
Aaron, Hank	20
Jenkins, Ferguson	20
Kaline, Al	20
Mantle, Mickey	35

1997 COOPERSTOWN

	NM Price
Complete Set (11)	$175

Player	Mint
Bench, Johnny	10
Fingers, Rollie	10
Gibson, Josh	10
Johnson, Walter	12
Kamenshek, Dottie	10
Mantle, Mickey	20
Robinson, Brooks	15
Robinson, Jackie (Dodgers)	75
Snider, Duke	10
Wilhelm, Hoyt	10
Yastzremski, Carl	10

Ruth, Babe	25
Schmidt, Mike	20
Yastrzemski, Carl	20

1998 BASEBALL

	NM Price
Complete Set (39)	$400

Player	Mint
Belle, Albert	8
Biggio, Craig	10
Bonds, Barry	10
Brown, Kevin	10
Canseco, Jose	12
Clark, Will	8
Erstad, Darin (R)	25
Galarraga, Andres	8

Player	Mint
Garciaparra, Nomar (R)	40
Glavine, Tom	15
Gonzalez, Juan	10
Grace, Mark	10
Grace, Mark (Cubs)	25
Griffey Jr., Ken	20
Grudzielanek, Mark (R)	12
Gwynn, Tony	12
Higginson, Bobby (R)	10
Hill, Glenallen (R)	8
Jeter, Derek	20
Jones, Chipper	25
Justice, Dave	10
Knoblauch, Chuck	12
Lankford, Ray	8
Larkin, Barry	10
Morandini, Mickey (R)	10

Player	Mint
Newfield, Marc (R)	8
Nomo, Hideo	10
Palmeiro, Rafael	10
Piazza, Mike	15
Ripken Jr., Cal	15
Rivera, Mariano (R)	30
Rodriguez, Alex	15
Sanders, Deion	12
Sheffield, Gary	10
Sosa, Sammy (Cubs)	100
Sprague, Ed (R)	10
Thomas, Frank	12
Thome, Jim	10
Vaughn, Mo	10
Walker, Larry	12
Williams, Bernie	10

EXTENDED

Complete Set (16)	$250

Player	Mint
Alomar, Sandy	8
Alou, Moises	12
Bell, Jay	10
Edmonds, Jim	12
Griffey Jr., Ken	18
Irabu, Hideki (R)	10
Maddux, Greg	20

McGriff, Fred 10
McGwire, Mark
  (extended) 75
  (home run) 35
Palmer, Dean 8
Rolen, Scott (R) 35
Sosa, Sammy
  (extended) 65
  (home run) 40
Walker, Larry 12
Womack, Tony (R) 15

1998 BASEBALL 12" FIGURES

	NM Price
Complete Set (4)	$75

Player	Mint
Jeter, Derek	30
Jones, Chipper	25
Nomo, Hideo	25
Rodriguez, Alex	30

1998 BASEBALL CLASSIC DOUBLES

	NM Price
Complete Set (11)	$225

Player	Mint
Griffey Jr./Rodriguez, A.	30
Ordonez, R./Jeter, D.	20
Belle, A./Thomas, F.	20
Rodriguez, I./Piazza, M.	24
Canseco, J./McGwire, M.	30
Ruth, B./Maris, R.	25
Ryan, N./Johnson, W.	25
Hunter, C./Jackson, R.	20
Berra, Y./Munson, T.	20
Bench, J./Morgan, J.	20
McGwire M. /Sosa S.	45

1998 BASEBALL FREEZE FRAME

	NM Price
Complete Set (6)	$120

Player	Mint
Bagwell, Jeff	20
Bonds, Barry	20

Jeter, Derek 25
Maddux, Greg 25
Ripken Jr., Cal 25
Rodriguez, Alex 25

1998 BASEBALL STADIUM STARS

	NM Price
Complete Set (7)	$140

Player	Mint
Belle, Albert	20
Griffey Jr., Ken	24
Piazza, Mike	25
Ripken, Cal	24
Rodriguez, Ivan	25
Smoltz, John	20
Williams, Bernie	20
Williams, Ted (Hills/Brad.)	27

1998 COOPERSTOWN

	NM Price
Complete Set (11)	$90

Player	Mint
Berra, Yogi	8
Brock, Lou	10
Campanella, Roy	8
Clemente, Roberto	12
Leonard, Buck	8
Niekro, Phil	8
Palmer, Jim	10
Robinson, Frank	8
Seaver, Tom	8
Spahn, Warren	10
Speaker, Tris	15

1999 BASEBALL

Player	NM Price
Complete Set (38)	$400

Player	Mint
Alfonzo, Edgardo (R)	25
Alvarez, Wilson (R)	10
Bagwell, Jeff	10
Cone, David	10
Cruz Jr., Jose (R)	15
Erstad, Darin	15
Castilla, Vinny	12
Clark, Tony	10
Clemens, Roger	14
Garciaparra, Nomar	
(regular)	18
(Fanfest)	20
Gonzalez, Juan	10
Griffey Jr., Ken	15
Guerrero, Vladimir (R)	90
Guillen, Jose (R)	10
Gwynn, Tony	12
Hernandez, Livan (R)	10
Jeter, Derek	15
Johnson, Randy	14
Jones, Chipper	15
Lee, Travis (R)	10
Lofton, Kenny	10
Martinez, Pedro (R)	60
Martinez, Tino	12

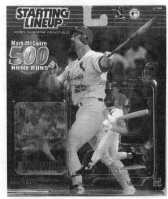

Player	Mint
McGwire, Mark	
(regular)	20
(Wal-Mart, red hat)	30
(Wal-Mart, blue hat)	65
Neagle, Denny	10
Park, Chan Ho	12
Piazza, Mike	15
Radke, Brad (R)	12
Ramirez, Manny	12
Renteria, Edgar (R)	12
Ripken, Cal	15
Rolen, Scott	15
Rodriguez, Alex	12
Rodriguez, Ivan	10
Sosa, Sammy	
(reguar)	20
(Wal-Mart)	20
Vizquel, Omar (R)	27
Walker, Larry	14
Wood, Kerry (R)	18

EXTENDED

Player	NM Price
Complete Set (10)	$120

Player	Mint
Brown, Kevin	10
Casey, Sean (R)	30
Drew, J.D. (R)	20
Garciaparra, Nomar	15
Grieve, Ben (R)	12
Maddux, Greg	12
Vaughn, Mo	10
Wells, David (R)	15
Williams, Bernie	10
Wright, Jaret (R)	10

1999 BASEBALL 12" FIGURES

Player	NM Price
Complete Set (6)	$125

Player	Mint
Clemens, Roger	25
Garciaparra, Nomar	25
Griffey Jr., Ken	25
Gwynn, Tony	25
McGwire, Mark	40
Sosa, Sammy	25

1999 BASEBALL CLASSIC DOUBLES

Player	NM Price
Complete Set (12)	$200

Player	Mint
Alomar, Sandy	20
Erstad, Darin	18
Garciaparra, Nomar	35
Griffey Jr., Ken	30
Jeter, Derek	30
Lopez, Javier	20
Maddux, Greg	25
McGwire, Mark	35
McGwire, M./Maris, R.	35
Mondesi, Raul	20
Rodriguez, Alex	30
Sosa, S./Maris, R.	35

1999 BASEBALL COOPERSTOWN

Player	NM Price
Complete Set (7)	$75

Player	Mint
Brett, George	16
Davis, Pepper	10
Gibson, Bob	10
Marichal, Juan	10

Ryan, Nolan...20
Weaver, Earl...12
Williams, Ted...16

1999 BASEBALL ONE-ON-ONE

	NM Price
Complete Set (5)	$90

Player	Mint
Alomar, S./Griffey, K.	30
Kendall, J./Ordonez, R.	20
Garciaparra/Edmonds, J.	22
Jones, C./Walker, L.	20
Ripken, C./Lofton, K.	20

1999 BASEBALL SPORT STAR

	NM Price
Complete Set (2)	$40

Player	Mint
McGwire, Mark	30
Sosa, Sammy	25

1999 BASEBALL STADIUM STARS

	NM Price
Complete Set (9)	$200

Player	Mint
Clemens, Roger	20
Garciaparra, Nomar	25
Jeter, Derek	25
Jones, Chipper	25
Lofton, Kenny	20
McGwire, Mark	
(regular)	35
(Wal-Mart)	25
Rodriguez, Alex	25
Sosa, Sammy (Wal-Mart)	25

2000 BASEBALL

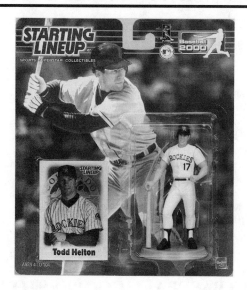

	NM Price
Complete Set (29)	$275

Player	Mint
Alomar, Roberto	12
Bonds, Barry	10
Boone, Bret (R)	8
Canseco, Jose	10
Clemens, Roger	10

Player	Mint
Drew, J.D.	10
Garciaparra, Nomar	10
Glaus, Troy (R)	20
Green, Shawn (R)	20
Griffey Jr., Ken	15
Guerrero, Vladimir	25
Helton, Todd (R)	35
Hernandez, Orlando (R)	18
Hoffman, Trevor (R)	10
Jeter, Derek	15
Johnson, Randy	8
Jones, Chipper (Fanfest)	25
Larkin, Barry	8
Maddux, Greg	10
Martinez, Pedro	20
McGwire, Mark	
(regular with shin guard)	25
(regular w/o shin guard)	20
(500 HR Wal-Mart Exclusive)	20
Millwood, Kevin (Fanfest)	15
Piazza, Mike	12
Reynolds, Shane (R)	10
Ripken Jr., Cal	10
Schilling, Curt	10
Sele, Aaron (R)	15
Sosa, Sammy	15
Stairs, Matt (R)	10
Ventura, Robin	10
Williams, Bernie	10

EXTENDED

Complete Set (9) $100

Player	Mint
Cedeno, Roger (R)	10
Griffey Jr., Ken	20
Gwynn, Tony	10
Hampton, Mike (R)	15
Jones, Chipper	15
Millwood, Kevin (R)	12
Ripken Jr., Cal	14
Rodriguez, Alex	12
Williamson, Scott (R)	12

2000 BASEBALL ALL-CENTURY

	NM Price
Complete Set (10)	$90

Player	Mint
Aaron, Hank	10
Bench, Johnny	10
Gehrig, Lou	10
Mantle, Mickey	15
Mathewson, Christy	30
Robinson, Jackie	10
Ruth, Babe	12
Schmidt, Mike	10
Wagner, Honus	25
Young, Cy	8

2000 BASEBALL CLASSIC DOUBLES

	NM Price
Complete Set (5)	$120

Player	Mint
Jeter, D./Piazza, M.	30
Clemens, R./Schilling, C.	18
Thome, J./Casey, S.	20
Martinez, P./Smoltz, J.	20
Ripken, C./Jones, C.	20

2000 BASEBALL ELITE

	NM Price
Complete Set (6)	$90

Player	Mint
Griffey Jr., Ken	20
Jeter, Derek	20
Maddux, Greg	15
McGwire, Mark	18
Piazza, Mike	18
Sosa, Sammy	18

2001 BASEBALL

	NM Price
Complete Set (21)	$325

Player	Mint
Ankiel, Rick (R)	20
Bonds, Barry	12
Burrell, Pat (R)	35
Furcal, Rafael (R)	30
Garciaparra, Nomar	15
Giambi, Jason (R)	20
Green, Shawn	10
Griffey Jr., Ken	15
Guerrero, Vladimir	15
Helton, Todd	15
Jeter, Derek	18
Johnson, Randy	10
Jones, Chipper	15
Martinez, Pedro	20
McGwire, Mark	20
Ordonez, Magglio (R)	20
Piazza, Mike	20
Reese, Pokey (R)	20
Ripken Jr., Cal	15
Rodriguez, Ivan	10
Sosa, Sammy	15

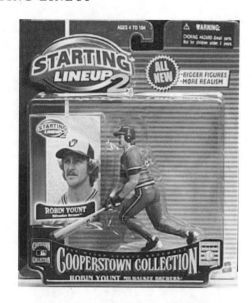

INSERT FIGURES

Player	Mint
Abreu, Bobby (R)	50
Giles, Brian (R)	65
Jones, Andruw	45
Wilson, Preston (R)	55

2001 BASEBALL COOPERSTOWN COLLECTION

	NM Price
Complete Set (7)	$90

Player	Mint
Jackson, Reggie	15
McCovey, Willie	12
Robinson, Brooks	10
Ryan, Nolan	20

Player	Mint
Seaver, Tom	15
Stargell, Willie	18
Yount, Robin	25

2001 BASEBALL WAL-MART EXCLUSIVES

	NM Price
Complete Set (7)	$80

Player	Mint
Dye, Jermaine	12
Galarraga, Andres	10
Griffey Jr., Ken	12
Jeter, Derek	22
Martinez, Pedro	20
McGwire, Mark	18
Sheffield, Gary	15

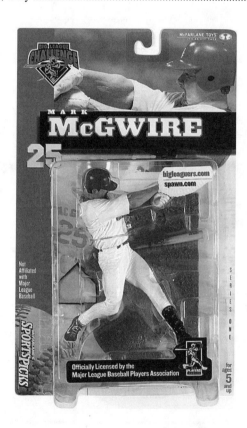

MCFARLANE 2000-01 BASEBALL SERIES I

	NM Price
Complete Set (6)	$100

Player	Mint
Bonds, Barry	20
Jones, Chipper	20
McGwire, Mark	25
Ramirez, Manny	20
Rodriguez, Alex	20
Sosa, Sammy	25

MISCELLANEOUS FIGURES

Bobbing heads, Hartland Statues, and Hall of Fame busts all were done in a series that makes them easy to catalog. There are quite a number of baseball figurines that do not fall into a specific category, but are highly collectible nonetheless.

Babe Ruth was and still is one of the most marketed athletes of all-time. There have been a number of statues, dolls, busts and other figurines made with his likeness. Shortly following his death in 1948, a mantle clock with his bust was produced. It has two baseballs on either side of it (one celebrates his 714 career homers, the other his 60 home run season). More recent Ruth memorabilia includes a '60s chalkware statue and an '80s doll by Effenbee. No matter what the vintage, "The Babe" sells.

Ruth is not the only baseball player to be immortalized with a figurine. Chalkware statues of Ty Cobb, Nap Lajoie and Shoeless Joe Jackson are some of the most sought-after pieces of memorabilia. Busts of Ted Williams and Roberto Clemente adorn many display cases. Jackie

Robinson's image appears on a candy container and a cane top. Mickey Mantle's likeness is featured on a '60s hand-held game. The list goes on and on from the early days of "America's National Pastime" right up to the present day.

But collecting figurines is not just confined to famous ballplayers or teams. There are a number of generic pieces that are also loved by collectors. Comical plaster baseball figures made by L.L. Rittgers compliment any display. There are also ashtrays, salt and pepper shakers, trophies, decanters and bookends that can spruce up your collection. Because of our fascination with the game, so many different and unique baseball items have been produced. Just when you think you've seen it all, something else is sure to pop up.

The following price guide is just a sampling of figurines available. Use your instincts when buying figures and make sure to have fun with the hobby.

Babe Ruth Clock	$2,500
Babe Ruth Chalkware Statue ('60s)	$150
Babe Ruth Effenbee Doll	$150
Rittgers Baseball Statues (umpire, batter & pitcher)	$300
Rittgers Baseball Statues (batter & catcher)	$600
Ty Cobb Chalkware Statue (circa 1910)	$3,000
Joe Jackson Chalkware Statue (circa 1910)	$3,000
Nap Lajoie Chalkware Statue (circa 1910)	$3,000
St. Louis Cardinals Mascot ashtray ('50s)	$250
Detroit Tigers Mascot ashtray ('40s)	$350
Pittsburgh Pirates Mascot ashtray ('40s)	$350
Jackie Robinson candy container	$300
Jackie Robinson cane top	$150
Blatz Beer display	$350
Brooks Robinson decanter	$250
Chicago Cubs decanter	$300
Baseball salt and pepper shakers	$50-$100 a pair

In addition to the major manufacturers, several other companies have issued a limited number of baseball figures over the years. These figures range from high-end statues—like the Art of Sport—to Hallmark ornaments, to low-end figures like Microstars. Some are still involved in the figure market, while others have come and gone. Here's the skinny on the remaining available baseball figures.

Babe Ruth clock

Cubs decanter

ART OF SPORT

British manufacturer Endurance Ltd. entered the figure market with its Art of Sport line of golf, cricket, and boxing figures issued in England. Their line of figures became available in the U.S. when the company issued its first baseball figure—Baltimore star Cal Ripken Jr. The Ripken piece, along with the follow-up Ken Griffey Jr. release, was well received in the hobby.

Cal Ripken Jr.

Player	Team	Edition	Mint Price
Cal Ripken Jr.			
(unsigned)	Orioles	4,515	$200
(signed)	Orioles	500	425
Ken Griffey Jr.			
(unsigned)	Mariners	1,500	225
(signed)	Mariners	500	450

HALLMARK ORNAMENTS

Greeting card giant Hallmark expanded its popular line of collectible ornaments with the addition of sports personalities in the 1990s. The "Baseball Heroes" series made its debut in 1994, with a Babe Ruth piece. Hallmark released three more ornaments in the series, with Jackie Robinson being the last before the line was retired.

A second baseball series, entitled "At the Ballpark," debuted in 1996 with Nolan Ryan and continued in 1997 with Hank Aaron.

At the Ballpark

Player	Team	Mint Price
Nolan Ryan ('96 w/MLB logo)	Rangers	$30
Nolan Ryan ('96 w/o MLB logo)	Rangers	30
Hank Aaron ('97)	Braves	15

Baseball Heroes

Player	Team	Mint Price
Babe Ruth ('94)	Yankees	$45
Lou Gehrig ('95)	Yankees	25
Satchel Paige ('96)	Kansas City	16
Jackie Robinson ('97)	Dodgers	13

MICROSTARS

MicroStars was a short-lived venture, lasting little more than two years before going out of business. The company hit the market with a 14-figure baseball set in 1995. The set of 2-inch figures included some of the biggest stars in the game, and the unique packaging allowed collectors to remove and later replace the figures without damaging the box. The baseball set was MicroStars' last, and today it draws little interest from collectors.

1995 Baseball

Complete Set (14):	$45
Jeff Bagwell	3
Albert Belle	4
Barry Bonds	4
Will Clark	3
Roger Clemens	3
Lenny Dykstra	3
Ken Griffey Jr.	6
Jimmy Key	3
Paul Molitor	3
Mike Piazza	5
Kirby Puckett	4
Cal Ripken Jr.	6
Deion Sanders	4
Frank Thomas	6

Prosport Creations

Figures from Prosport Creations look similar to figures from Sports Impressions. Unfortunately, most of the pieces don't look like the players they represent. Consequently, the line never caught on with collectors, and the company disappeared from the hobby in the early '90s.

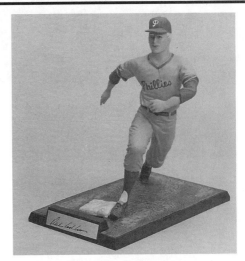

Richie Ashburn

	Height	Quantity	Mint
Richie Ashburn			
Auto	9"	1,990	$50
AP	9"	1,990	100
Mini	5"	3,000	40
Rod Carew			
Auto	9"	555	75
AP	9"	555	100
Bill Dickey			
Facsimile	9"	1,155	50
AP	9"	1,155	100
Mini	5"	3,000	40
Whitey Ford			
Auto	9"	2,072	75
AP	9"	2,072	100
Mini	5"	3,000	40
Steve Garvey			
Auto	9"	232	100
AP	9"	232	150
Bob Gibson			
Auto	9"	1,910	70
AP	9"	1,910	100
Mini	5"	3,000	40
Tony Gwynn			
Auto	9"	793	125
AP	9"	793	150
Ferguson Jenkins			
Auto	9"	490	75
Auto AP	9"	490	100
Harmon Killebrew			
Auto	9"	297	200
Auto. AP	9"	297	250

	Height	Quantity	Mint
Eddie Mathews			
Auto	9"	300	$125
Auto. AP	9"	300	150
Jim Palmer			
Auto	9"	1,499	80
Auto. AP	9"	1,499	150
Mini	5"	3,000	40
Brooks Robinson			
Auto	9"	800	125
Auto. AP	9"	800	150
Ozzie Smith			
Auto	9"	600	175
Auto. AP	9"	600	225
Willie Stargell			
Auto	9"	800	100
Auto. AP	9"	800	150

Salvino Figurines

Salvino Inc. was founded by brothers Rick and Wayne Salvino in 1988, with the goal of offering the most realistic-looking sports figures in the hobby. Since then, Salvino has become a leader in high-end porcelain sports figures and statues. Sandy Koufax and Don Drysdale were the first two figures released, and the success of these pieces allowed Salvino to expand its player selection into other sports.

Most Salvino figures come with the featured player's autograph on the base, an enhancement that helped the company rapidly gain a foothold in the market. Of all the Salvino figures, the Mickey Mantle pieces are the most popular with collectors.

		Quantity	Mint
Roy Campanella		2,500	$400
	SE	200	575
Roberto Clemente		1,750	125
Don Drysdale		2,500	185
	AP	300	225

Roy Campanella

Rickey Henderson

		Quantity	Mint
Rickey Henderson			
	HU	600	275
	AU	600	275
	SE	550	375
Reggie Jackson		1,500	275
Sandy Koufax		2,500	200
	AP	500	250
Mickey Mantle		2,000	125
	Field	682	800
	Bat	682	800
	HU, #6	368	1,300
	HU, #7	368	1,300
Roger Maris		2,000	125
Billy Martin		2,000	125

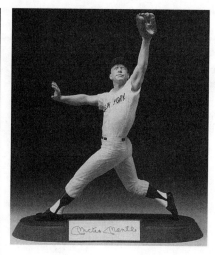

Mickey Mantle

		Quantity	Mint
Willie Mays			
	NY	750	400
	SF	750	400
	HU	368	600
Brooks Robinson		1,000	275
Duke Snider			
	HU	1,000	275
	AU	1,000	275

Sports Impressions

Sports Impressions was founded in 1987 by Joe Timmerman. Most of the early figures were produced in large quantities and without autographs. In 1991, Enesco, manufacturer of the popular Precious Moments figures and other porcelain collectibles, bought Sports Impressions and changed the company's philosophy. It began producing more limited runs that included the autographs of the featured players.

Enesco's Sports Impressions line falls in the middle of the sports figures market. The figures are nicer than most of the low-end sports figures, but when Salvino entered the market with a higher-priced product that more accurately depicted the players, Sports Impressions began losing its appeal. In 1996, Enesco issued its last sports figures and today there's little demand for Sports Impressions. Collectors tend to opt for the more popular Starting Lineup brand or the high-end Salvino figures.

		Height	Quantity	Mint
Hank Aaron		5"	—	$35
	500 HR	7"	5,755	75
	Auto	7"	975	125
Roberto Alomar				
	Auto	7"	975	125
Ernie Banks		5"	—	40
	500 HR	7"	5,512	100
Johnny Bench		6"	2,950	75
	Auto	9 1/2"	975	200
Wade Boggs		7"	2,500	75
Barry Bonds				
	Auto	8"	975	125
Ralph Branca				
	Auto	7"	1,951	100
Jose Canseco		10"	1,900	150
	Swing	5"	2,950	50
	Bat	5"	—	40
Rod Carew		7"	3,053	100

		Height	Quantity	Mint
Steve Carlton		9"	500	$120
Gary Carter		7"	5,009	50
Will Clark		10"	1,990	150
		7"	1,990	100
		5"	—	30
R. Clemens		5 1/2"	2,950	50
	Auto	7"	975	125
R. Clemente		7"	5,000	75
Ty Cobb		7"	5,000	80
Eric Davis		7"	1,990	60
		7"	2,950	40
Andre Dawson		7"	2,500	50
Lenny Dykstra		7"	1,990	75
		5"	2,950	35
Bob Feller		7"	2,500	75

Lou Gehrig

		Height	Quantity	Mint
Jimmie Foxx		7"	1,000	$175
Steve Garvey		7"	2,599	40
		4"	—	30
Lou Gehrig		7"	5,000	100
Kirk Gibson		7"	2,500	40
Tom Glavine				
	Auto	8"	975	150
Dwight Gooden		10"	1,990	125
		7"	5,016	60
		5"	2,950	35
Mike Greenwell		7"	2,500	40
		5"	2,950	30
Ken Griffey Jr.		7"	1,990	120
		5"	2,950	60
Tony Gwynn		7"	2,500	60
		5"	—	35
R. Henderson		8"	939	125
	AP	8"	94	200
K. Hernandez		7"	2,500	40
Orel Hershiser		7"	5,055	40
		5"	—	30
Bo Jackson		10"	2,950	100
		7"	2,950	75
		5"	—	25
Reggie Jackson				
	500 Oakland	7"	5,000	175
	Cal	7"	2,500	80
	N.Y.	7"	2,500	120
	N.Y.	9"	1,969	125
	Auto. Oakland	8"	975	150
	N.Y.	5"	—	40
Gregg Jefferies		7"	5,009	40
Howard Johnson		7"	5,020	60
		5"	—	30
Dave Justice				
	Auto	8"	975	150
Al Kaline		7"	2,500	50
Harmon Killebrew				
	500 HR	7"	5,573	200
Mark Langston		7"	1,990	50
Mickey Mantle		6"	2,950	200
	Auto	8"	975	250
		8"	7,500	150
		5"	—	40
		15"	1,956	150
	AP	15"	195	250
Eddie Mathews				
	500 HR	7"	5,512	100
Don Mattingly		10"	1,990	120
		7"	1,990	100
	Auto	8"	975	150
		6"	2,950	75
Fielding		5"	2,950	50
Batting		5"	—	40
		15"	1,990	100
	AP	15"	199	275
Willie Mays				
	500 HR	7"	5,660	70
	Catch	7"	5,000	70
		5"	—	40
Willie McCovey		7"	5,521	200
Mark McGwire		9 1/2"	1,990	150
		7"	2,500	75
		5"	—	35

		Height	Quantity	Mint
Kevin McReynolds		7"	5,022	$40
Kevin Mitchell		7"	1,990	70
		5"	—	30
Paul Molitor		7"	2,500	70
Joe Morgan		7"	1,990	120
		5"	—	30
Thurman Munson		10"	995	150
		7"	5,000	70
		5"	—	35
Mel Ott				
	500 HR	7"	1,008	175
Mike Piazza				
	Auto	7"	975	150
Kirby Puckett		7"	1,990	70
		5"	—	35
Cal Ripken Jr.		7"	1,990	100
		5"	—	40
Brooks Robinson		7"	2,848	70
		5"	—	35
Frank Robinson				
	500 HR	7"	5,586	75
Jackie Robinson		7"	5,042	75
		5"	—	30
Babe Ruth				
	500 HR	7"	5,000	125
	Club	4"	—	45
		9"	1,990	150
Nolan Ryan				
	Auto. '93	8"	975	250
	No Auto '93	8"	7,500	125
	Farewell Auto.	8"	975	200
	Farewell	8"	7,500	125
	AP	7"	500	200
	w/Plate NY	6 1/2"	3,000	100
	w/Plate Hou	5"	3,000	60
	w/Plate Cal	5"	3,000	60
	w/Plate Tex	5"	3,000	60
	Mini	5"	—	40
	Mini	5"	2,950	50
	Doll	15"	1,992	125
	AP	15"	199	300

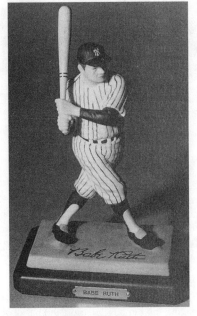

Babe Ruth

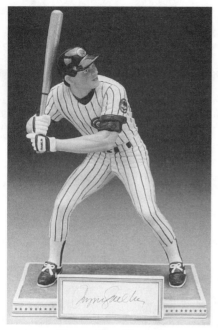

Ryne Sandberg

		Height	Quantity	Mint
Ryne Sandberg		6"	3,033	$50
	Auto	7"	975	175
Mike Schmidt				
	Auto	8"	975	200
Tom Seaver		9"	500	75
		7"	3,033	70
		5"	—	40
Duke Snider		7"	2,500	70
		5"	—	35
Darryl Strawberry		7"	5,018	50
		5"	2,950	30
Bobby Thomson		7"	1,951	100
Alan Trammell		7"	2,500	60
	Swing	7"	2,950	75
Andy Van Slyke		7"	2,500	50
Robin Ventura				
	Auto	8"	975	120
Frank Viola		7"	2,500	50
Honus Wagner		7"	5,000	70
Ted Williams				
	500 HR	7"	5,521	75
		10"	—	150
		5"	—	50
Dave Winfield		7"	2,500	70
Cy Young		7"	5,000	70

Aurora

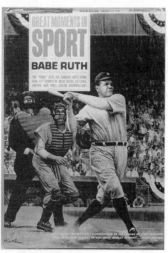

1965 Aurora

Great Moments in Sport

Plastic Model Kits

Aurora Plastics Corp. of West Hempstead, N.Y., was born in the late 1940s but came into production around 1952. It was founded by Abe Shikes, who started the company in an attempt to answer a demand for a better plastic hanger. Nabisco purchased the Aurora company in 1977 and quickly shut it down. Today some model molds from Aurora still exist and are being re-released under a different name on the box but with most of the original artwork. Aurora kits came unassembled as action figures that portray a famous event or accomplishment (such as Willie Mays making his famous catch off the bat of Vic Wertz in the 1954 World Series, Jimmy Brown getting his 10,000th career rushing

yard and Babe Ruth's 60th home run in 1927). These models were very basic with 15 to 30 parts. The most difficult task a modeler had to do was paint the figures prior to assembly.

Original packages contained booklets with text that was written by the editors of *Sport* magazine.

A small plaque was intended to be placed in front of each model.

Prices are for unassembled kits with original boxes in excellent-mint condition.

Jimmy Brown	$100-$150
Jack Dempsey/Louis Firpo	$60-$85
Willie Mays	$150-$200
Babe Ruth	$250-$300
Johnny Unitas	$100-$150
Jerry West	$35-$40

Southland Art Castings

Southland Plastics of Shreveport, La., produced its first figurines in 1998. Partners Joe Sterkx Jr. and Dr. Ray Maiwurm had originally hoped to produce Hartland-like statues and actually looked into acquiring the Hartland Plastics name. However, they couldn't reach an agreement with the owners of the defunct Hartland company name and the new company became Southland Plastics.

Cast bronze edition statues on walnut bases were limited to 100 each for Ryan, Griffey, Maddux and Gwynn. The "Shoeless" Joe Jackson was limited to 250 bronze.

Nolan Ryan (plastic) $80
Nolan Ryan (bronze) $750
Ken Griffey Jr. (plastic)..$80
Ken Griffey Jr. (bronze) $750
Greg Maddux (plastic) $70
Greg Maddux (bronze) $700
Tony Gwynn (plastic) $70
Tony Gwynn (bronze) $700
Shoeless Joe Jackson (plastic)..$90
Shoeless Joe Jackson (bronze) $800

1965 Big League Stars Statues

While the plastic statues in this set are virtually identical to the set issued in 1955 by Dairy Queen, the packaging of Big League Stars statues on a card with all the usual elements of a baseball card makes them more collectible. The DQ versions of the statues are white, while the Big League versions are bronze colored. The statues measure about 3 inches tall and were sold in a 4 x 5-inch cardboard and plastic blister pack for about 19 cents. Complete league sets were also sold in a large package. The singles package features the player's name in a large banner near the top with his team printed below and line drawings of ballplayers in action around the statue. Backs have a player portrait photo with facsimile autograph, position, team, previous year and career stats and a career summary. A perforated tab at bottom can be pulled out to make a stand for the display. Most packages are found with the hole at top punched out to allow for hanging on a hook. Values listed here are for complete statue/package combinations. Statues alone sell for $25-$50 for non-Hall of Famers; up to $800 for Mantle. Packages without the statue should be priced about one-third the values quoted here.

	NM	EX	VG
Complete Set (18):	$2500	$1250	$750
Common Player:	60	30	18
(1) John Antonelli	60	30	18
(2) Bob Avila	60	30	18
(3) Yogi Berra	185	92	55
(4) Roy Campanella	200	100	60
(5) Larry Doby	90	45	27
(6) Del Ennis	60	30	18
(7) Jim Gilliam	65	32	19
(8) Gil Hodges	125	62	37
(9) Harvey Kuenn	60	30	18
(10) Bob Lemon	75	37	22
(11) Mickey Mantle	800	400	240
(12) Eddie Mathews	125	62	37
(13) Minnie Minoso	65	32	19
(14) Stan Musial	250	125	75
(15) Pee Wee Reese	150	75	45
(16) Al Rosen	60	30	18
(17) Duke Snider	195	97	58
(18) Mickey Vernon	60	30	18

1968 Topps Plaks

Among the scarcest of Topps test issues of the late 1960s, "All Star" Baseball Plaks were plastic busts of two dozen stars of the era that came packaged like model airplane parts. The busts, which had to be snapped off a sprue, could be inserted into a base that carried the player's name. Packed with the plastic plaks was one of two checklist cards that featured six color photos per side. The 2 1/8" x 4" checklist cards, popular with superstar collectors, are considerably easier to find today than the actual plaks.

Complete set with the two checklist cards ($400 each) $4,500
1. Max Alvis..$40
2. Frank Howard...$60

3. Dean Chance $40
4. Catfish Hunter $90
5. Jim Fregosi $40
6. Al Kaline $120
7. Harmon Killebrew $100
8. Gary Peters $40
9. Jim Lonborg $40
10. Frank Robinson $120
11. Mickey Mantle.....................................$1,500
12. Carl Yastrzemski $125
13. Hank Aaron $250
14. Roberto Clemente $300
15. Richie Allen $60
16. Tommy Davis.......................................$40
17. Orlando Cepeda $80
18. Don Drysdale $120
19. Willie Mays...$250
20. Rusty Staub..$60
21. Tim McCarver......................................$60
22. Pete Rose $250
23. Ron Santo..$60
24. Jim Wynn $40

Chapter 7

PLATES

By Jerry Shaver

While limited-edition baseball plates are a relatively new hobby niche, the art of plate collecting has been around for more than a century. The first collectible plates—featuring Christmas themes and other popular subjects—were produced in Germany in the late 1800s. J. Roderick MacArthur brought the hobby to America in 1973 when he formed the Bradford Exchange. But plate collecting didn't cross over into the baseball world until the early 1980s.

In 1983, Hackett American began producing the first baseball-themed plates and several other manufacturers soon jumped on board. By the end of the decade, Gartlan USA and Sports Impressions had released numerous editions, and the Bradford Exchange entered the hobby in 1992.

If you're interested in collecting baseball plates, the usual caveats apply. Expect to pay a premium for Mint pieces in the original box, and an even bigger premium if the plate is extremely rare (check the edition size). Pay close attention to "autographed" editions. While several manufacturers—including Hackett and Sports Impressions—have produced autographed plates, many of the specimens on the market feature facsimile or "baked-in" signatures. The genuine autographs are usually signed in gold pen, and should be easily distinguishable by sight.

Since plates tend to take up a lot of room, you'll also want to give thought to display—especially if you don't have much shelf space. While most plates come with individual plastic or wooden stands, there are plenty of other options on the market, including plate frames (in all shapes and sizes), plate rails (featuring grooves that hold multiple plates securely), and shadow boxes.

BRADFORD EXCHANGE

J. Roderick MacArthur introduced collectible plates to the United States when he formed the Bradford Exchange to help collectors all over the world buy and trade collectible plates. Today, Bradford Exchange manufactures and distributes a wide variety of plates. Although most of its releases feature stars from the entertainment field, it has issued several sports plates with a number of themes.

Bradford Exchange

Ken Griffey Jr. Collection:

Most Valuable Player	$30
A.L. Home Run Leader	$30
M.L. RBI Leader	$30
All-Star Home Run Champ	$30
Welcome to the National League	$35

Mark McGwire Collection

Record Breaker 9-8-98	$35
Record 70 HRs	$35
50-50-50 Game	$40
70!	$35
Record Tying 61st HR	$40

**Mark McGwire
70th HR**

Full Speed to 40 ....$40
Historic 60th HR $40
The Triumph of 70 (4-plate set).........................$160

Cal Ripken Jr. Collection
3,000th Hit..$35
From Rookie to Legend (3-plate set)..................$120

Jackie Robinson Collection
Breaking Barriers $50
Player of the Year $50

Mickey Mantle

Mickey Mantle Collection
500th Home Run $50
1956 World Series $60
1961 Home Run Chase..$60
Bronx Bomber $50
The Oklahoma Kid $60
Triple Crown Season $45

Legends of Baseball
Babe Ruth: The Called Shot...............................$25
Lou Gehrig: The Luckiest Man...........................$35
Ty Cobb: The Georgia Peach..........................$35-$45
Cy Young: The Perfect Game ....$35-$45
Rogers Hornsby: The .424 Season....................$30-$40
Honus Wagner: The Flying Dutchman ....$30-$40
Jimmie Foxx: The Beast ....$30-$40
Walter Johnson: The Shutout..........................$30-$40
Tris Speaker: The Gray Eagle $30
Christy Mathewson: 1905 World Series ....$30-$40
Mel Ott: Master Melvin ....$30-$40
Lefty Grove: His Greatest Season ....$30-$40
Shoeless Joe Jackson ....$35-$50
Pie Traynor: Pittsburgh Champ.......................$30-$40
Mickey Cochrane: Black Mike $30
Grover Alexander ....$30-$40

Take Me Out to the Ball Game
Wrigley Field, the Friendly Confines.....................$60
Yankee Stadium, the House That Ruth Built $75

Polo Grounds

Fenway Park, Home of the Green Monster ....$25-$35
Briggs Stadium, Home of the Tigers.......................$25-$35
Comiskey Park, Home of the White Sox $60
Cleveland Stadium, Home of the Indians $60
Memorial Stadium, Home of the Orioles....................$75
County Stadium, Home of the Champs $35
Ebbetts Field, Home of the Dodgers.........................$60
Shibe Park...$50
Forbes Field...$60
Polo Grounds...$60

Lost Ballparks
Ebbetts Field..$100
Forbes Field..$75
Polo Grounds..$75
Shibe Field...$75

Joe DiMaggio

Great Moments in Baseball
Joe DiMaggio: The Streak $50
Stan Musial: 5-Homer Double-Header ....$45-$55

Bobby Thomson: The Shot Heard 'Round the World ....$25-$35
Bill Mazeroski: Winning Home Run $40
Don Larsen: Perfect World Series Game   ....$25-$33
Jackie Robinson: Saved Pennant $50
Satchel Paige: Greatest Games $40
Billy Martin: The Rescue Catch ....$25-$35
Dizzy Dean: World Series Shutout ....$25-$35
Carl Hubbell: The 1934 All-State $35
Ralph Kiner: The Home Run $50
Enos Slaughter: The Mad Dash .... $25-$35

Superstars of Baseball

Willie Mays $35
Carl Yastrzemski ....$70-$100
Frank Robinson ....$45-$65
Bob Gibson ....$45-$60
Harmon Killebrew $35
Don Drysdale ....$55-$80

Immortals of the Diamond

The Sultan of Swat, Babe Ruth...$50
The Pride of the Yankees, Lou Gehrig $50
The Georgia Peach, Ty Cobb $60
The Winningest Pitcher, Cy Young $60

Baseball's Diamond Moments

Ted Williams: Last Time at Bat...$40

Babe Ruth Centennial

The 60th Homer $30

Baseball Record Breakers

Yogi Berra $40
Lou Gehrig $40
Mike Schmidt $40
Cal Ripken Jr. $40

GARTLAN USA

Gartlan USA was based in Huntington Beach, Calif., and produced limited-edition ceramic and porcelain sports collectibles, including signed plates and ceramic plaques and cards. Plates range in size from 10 1/4" diameter to 8 1/2" to 3 1/4" mini plates. Artist's proofs are signed by the artist and player. Gartlan also offered a few plates directly through its club. Only collectors who were enrolled in the club received offers for the special plates, and Gartlan produced only enough product to cover the orders it received. These club-only plates can be very difficult to find on the secondary market.

Tom Seaver

Mike Schmidt

This list of players includes the number made and price. Artist's proofs are signed by the artist and player.

Luis Aparicio signed 10 1/4" plate, 1,984: $200
Luis Aparicio 10 1/4" proof plate, 250: $150
Luis Aparicio 8 1/2" plate, 10,000: ....$30-$40
Luis Aparicio 3 1/4" plate, open: ....$10-$20
Al Barlick 3 1/4" plate, open: $20
Al Barlick Club plate, club only: $110
Johnny Bench signed 10 1/4" plate, 1,989: $325
Johnny Bench 3 1/4" plate, open: $35
Johnny Bench proof plate, 100: $395
Yogi Berra Signed 10 1/4" plate, 2,150: $250
Yogi Berra proof plate, 250: $175
Yogi Berra 8 1/2" plate, 10,000: $40
Yogi Berra 3 1/4" plate, open: $20
George Brett signed 10 1/4" plate, 2,000: $475
George Brett proof plate, 24: $750
George Brett 3 1/4" plate, open: $20
George Brett tankard, open: $30
Rod Carew signed 10 1/4 " plate, 950: $175
Rod Carew 8 1/2" plate, 10,000: $40
Rod Carew 3 1/4" plate, open: $20
Carlton Fisk signed 10 1/4" plate, 950: $175
Carlton Fisk proof plate, 300: $175
Carlton Fisk 8 1/2" plate, 10,000: $40
Carlton Fisk 3 1/4" plate, open: $20
Carlton Fisk ceramic card, open: $18
Whitey Ford signed 10 1/4" plate, 2,360: $50
Whitey Ford proof plate, 250: $175
Whitey Ford 8 1/2" plate, 10,000: $25
Whitey Ford 3 1/4" plate, open: $15

Ken Griffey Jr. signed 10 1/4" plate, 1,989: $375
Ken Griffey Jr. 8 1/2" plate, 10,000: $40
Ken Griffey Jr. 3 1/4" plate, open: $20
Ken Griffey Jr. Club plate, club only: $75
Ken Griffey Jr. ceramic card, open: $12
Reggie Jackson 3 1/4 " plate, open: $20
Reggie Jackson artist's proof plate, 44: $450
Pete Rose signed 10 1/4" platinum plate, 4,192: $625
Pete Rose 3 1/4" platinum plate, open: $20
Pete Rose signed 10 1/4" Diamond plate, 950: $450
Pete Rose 3 1/4" Diamond plate, open: $20
Pete Rose Club plate, club only: $150
Pete Rose 10 1/4" Farewell plate, 50: $550
Pete Rose tankard, open: $30
Mike Schmidt signed 10 1/4" plate, 1,987: $800
Mike Schmidt proof plate, 56: $600
Mike Schmidt 3 1/4" plate, open: $25
Tom Seaver signed 10 1/4" plate, 1,992: $300
Tom Seaver 8 1/2" plate, 10,000: $40
Tom Seaver 3 1/4" plate, open: $20
Tom Seaver ceramic card, open: $18
Darryl Strawberry 10 1/4" plate, 1,979: $125
Darryl Strawberry 8 1/2" plate, 10,000: $40
Darryl Strawberry 3 1/4" plate, open: $20
Frank Thomas 10 1/4" plate, 1,994: $150
Frank Thomas 81/2" plate, 10,000: $35
Frank Thomas 3 1/4" plate, open: $25
Frank Thomas ceramic card, open: $12
Carl Yastrzemski 10 1/4" plate, 950: $100
Carl Yastrzemski 8 1/2" plate, 10,000: $225
Carl Yastrzemski 3 1/4" plate, open: $40
Carl Yastrzemski ceramic card, open: $20

HACKETT AMERICAN PLATES

Hackett American issued a handful of 8 1/2-inch full-color baseball plates during the mid-1980s. The plates, other than the Babe Ruth, Ty Cobb and Dwight Gooden issues, were all hand-signed by the player depicted. Hackett issued two different Reggie Jackson plates. The scarcity of these plates has made them some of the more desired and valuable sports plates in the hobby.

Hank Aaron signed	$150
Steve Carlton signed	$150
Gary Carter signed	$175
Roger Clemens signed	$300
Whitey Ford signed	$100
Steve Garvey signed	$50
Dwight Gooden, unsigned	$35
Reggie Jackson, Paluso	$300
Reggie Jackson, Alexander	$125
Wally Joyner signed	$295
Harmon Killebrew signed	$325
Sandy Koufax signed	$250
Eddie Mathews signed	$300
Willie Mays signed	$300
Pete Rose	$45
Babe Ruth unsigned	$100
Nolan Ryan signed	$800
Tom Seaver signed	$325
Tom Seaver 300	$250
Don Sutton signed	$325

Henry Aaron

Reggie Jackson

SPORTS IMPRESSIONS PLATES

Sports Impressions offered a wide variety of players on plates, as well as its line of figures. Most players have plates in three variations. Mini plates generally sell for $20. Regular-size (10 1/4") plates generally range from $75 to $150 and had production runs from 2,000 to 10,000. The Gold Edition is the most limited of all of the plates, with production runs of no more than 2,500. A Mickey Mantle gold plate sells for up to $200. The company also produced several player mugs.

Hank Aaron Gold Edition...$90
Wade Boggs 10 1/4" Red Sox plate, 2,000....................$50
Wade Boggs 10 1/4" Red Sox gold plate, 1,000 ....$125
Wade Boggs mini Red Sox plate.....................................$24
Jose Canseco 10 1/4" A's plate, 10,000 ....$50
Jose Canseco 10 1/4" A's gold plate, 2,500.................$150
Jose Canseco mini A's plate $24
Gary Carter 10 1/4" Mets plate, 2,000 ....$50
Gary Carter 10 1/4" Mets gold plate, 1,000...................$100
Gary Carter mini Mets plate..$15
Will Clark 10 1/4" Giants plate, 10,000 ....$65
Will Clark 10 1/4" Giants gold plate, 2,500 ....$50
Will Clark mini Giants plate $15
Roberto Clemente 10 1/4" Pirates plate,10,000 ....$75
Roberto Clemente mini Pirates plate...............................$20
Ty Cobb 10 1/4" Tigers plate, 10,000 ....$60
Ty Cobb mini Tigers plate..$20
Andre Dawson 10 1/4" Cubs plate, 10,000 ....$50
Andre Dawson 10 1/4" Cubs gold plate, 1,000 ....$125
Andre Dawson mini Cubs plate.......................................$20
Lenny Dykstra 10 1/4" Phillies plate, 10,000................$50
Lenny Dykstra 10 1/4" Phillies gold plate, 1,000 ....$125
Lenny Dykstra mini Phillies plate...................................$20
Bob Feller 10 1/4" Indians plate, 10,000.......................$50
Bob Feller 10 1/4" Indians gold plate, 2,500................$100
Bob Feller mini Indians plate..$15
Lou Gehrig 10 1/4" Yankees plate, 10,000 ....$100
Lou Gehrig mini Yankees plate $20
Kirk Gibson 10 1/4" Dodgers plate, 10,000 ....$30
Kirk Gibson 10 1/4" Dodgers gold plate, 2,500 ....$50
Kirk Gibson mini Dodgers plate $12

Team Griffey 10 1/4 " gold plate, Ken Sr. and Ken Jr., 1,991..........$125
Team Griffey mini plate, Ken Sr. and Ken Jr..................................$25
Tony Gwynn 7" Padres figurine, 2,500 ....$75-$125
Rickey Henderson 10 1/4" A's gold plate, 1,990 ....$125
Rickey Henderson mini A's plate...................................$24
Keith Hernandez 10 1/4" Mets plate, 2,000..................$50
Keith Hernandez 10 1/4 " Mets gold plate, 1,000 ....$100
Keith Hernandez mini Mets plate $20
Orel Hershiser 10 1/4" Dodgers plate, 10,000..............$35
Orel Hershiser 10 1/4" Dodgers gold plate, 2,500.........$150
Orel Hershiser mini Dodgers plate.................................$15
Gregg Jefferies 10 1/4" Mets gold plate, 3,500.............$125
Gregg Jefferies mini Mets plate $20
Al Kaline 10 1/4" Tigers plate, 10,000........................$60
Al Kaline 10 1/4" Tigers gold plate, 1,000...................$125
Al Kaline mini Tigers plate..$20
Mickey Mantle mini Yankees plate, Switch Hitter $20
Mickey Mantle 12 Yankees collectoval, The Life of a Legend, 1,968
....$195
Mickey Mantle 10 1/4" Yankees gold plate, Mickey 7, 1,500..........$100
Mickey Mantle 8 1/2" Yankees plate, The Golden Years, 5,000......$175
Mickey Mantle mini Yankees plate, The Golden Years $20
Mickey Mantle/Don Mattingly mini plate, Yankee Tradition $150
Don Mattingly 10 1/4" Yankees plate, Player of the Year, 5,000 ....$60
Don Mattingly 10 1/4" Yankees gold plate, Player of the Year, 2,500
....$125
Don Mattingly mini Yankees plate, Player of the Year....................$24
Don Mattingly 10 1/4" Yankees gold plate, Yankee Pride $150
Don Mattingly mini Yankees plate, Yankee Pride...........................$24
Don Mattingly 10 1/4" Yankees gold plate, #23, 1,991...................$175
Don Mattingly mini Yankees plate, #23.......................................$20
Willie Mays 8 1/2" Giants plate, The Golden Years, 5,000..............$125
Willie Mays mini Giants plate, The Golden Years...........................$20
Willie Mays 10 1/4" Giants gold plate, Famous Catch, 2,500 ....$150
Willie Mays mini Giants plate, Famous Catch $24

Dwight Gooden

Dwight Gooden 10 1/4 " Mets gold plate, 3,500.............$150
Dwight Gooden mini Mets plate.......................................$25

Mark McGwire

Mark McGwire 10 1/4" A's gold plate, 2,500...................$175
Mark McGwire mini A's plate...$20
Paul Molitor 10 1/4" Brewers plate, 10,000 ....$50

Paul Molitor 10 1/4" Brewers gold plate, 1,000 ....$125
Paul Molitor mini Brewers plate $20
Joe Morgan 10 1/4" Reds gold plate, 1,990.....................................$150
Joe Morgan mini Reds plate...$20
Thurman Munson 10 1/4" Yankees plate, 10,000...................... $50
Thurman Munson mini Yankees plate...$20
Stan Musial 10 1/4" Cardinals gold plate, 1,963 ....$150
Stan Musial mini Cardinals plate $20
Brooks Robinson 10 1/4" Orioles gold plate, 1,000......................$50
Brooks Robinson mini Orioles plate..$24
Jackie Robinson 10 1/4" Dodgers gold plate, 1,956.................$150
Jackie Robinson mini Dodgers plate..$24
Babe Ruth 10 1/4 " Yankees plate, 10,000..................................$175
Babe Ruth mini Yankees plate...$24
Nolan Ryan 10 1/4" Rangers gold plate, 5,000 Ks, 5,000................$175
Nolan Ryan mini Rangers plate, 5,000 Ks..$20
Nolan Ryan 10 1/4" Rangers gold plate, 300 Wins, 1,990.............$150
Nolan Ryan mini Rangers plate, 300 Wins.......................................$24
Tom Seaver 10 1/4" Mets gold plate, 3,311............................$175
Tom Seaver mini Mets plate...$24
Duke Snider 10 1/4" Dodgers gold plate, Boys of Summer,1,500...$125
Duke Snider 10 1/4" Dodgers plate, Boys of Summer, 5,000...........$50
Duke Snider mini Dodgers plate, Boys of Summer.........................$20
Duke Snider 8 1/2" Dodgers plate, 5,000, The Golden Years $125
Duke Snider mini Dodgers plate, The Golden Years $24

Darryl Strawberry

Darryl Strawberry 10 1/4" Mets gold plate, 3,500 ....$150
Alan Trammell 10 1/4 " Tigers plate, 10,000 ....$50
Alan Trammell 10 1/4" Tigers gold plate, 1,000 ....$125
Alan Trammell mini Tigers plate $50
Frank Viola 10 1/4" Twins gold plate, 2,500...........................$100-$125
Frank Viola mini Twins plate $20
Honus Wagner 10 1/4" Pirates plate, 10,000 ....$75
Honus Wagner mini Pirates plate $20

Ted Williams

Ted Williams 10 1/4" Red Sox gold plate, 1,960 ....$150
Ted Williams mini Red Sox plate $24
Carl Yastrzemski 10 1/4" Red Sox plate, 1,500...............................$50
Carl Yastrzemski 10 1/4" Red Sox gold plate, 1,500......................$100
Carl Yastrzemski mini Red Sox plate..$24
Cy Young 10 1/4 " Indians plate, 10,000 ....$75
Cy Young mini Indians plate $20

Theme Plates

Theme	Size	Quantity	Price
Boggs/Williams/Yastrzemski "Fenway Tradition"			
	12"	1,000	$200
Mantle/Mays/Snider "The Golden Years"			
	12"	1,000	200
Mantle/Mays/Snider "Greatest Centerfielders"			
	Gold Edition	3,500	150
	Mini Plate	—	20
Mantle/Mays/Snider	10G"	3,500	75
	Gold Edition	1,500	150
	Mini Plate	—	20
Robinson/Williams/Mantle/Yastrzemski "Living Triple Crown"			
	Gold Edition	1,000	150
	10G"	10,000	65
	Mini Plate	—	20
Ryan/Carlton/Seaver "Kings of Ks"			
	12"	1,990	195
Brooklyn Dodgers "Dem Bums"			
	10G"	1,000	50
	Mini Plate	—	20
Yankees "Living Triple Crown"			
	Mini Plate	—	20
	10G"	—	50
	Gold Edition	—	150
"Yankees Tradition"	Mini Plate	—	20
	10G"	10,000	65
Brooklyn Dodgers "Wait till next Year"			
	10G"	5,000	75
	Mini Plate	—	20
Yankee Stadium	10H"	5,000	75
	Mini Plate	—	20

Chapter 8

LIMITED EDITION

In an effort to attract collectors looking for a rare, high-end collectible, several companies have produced various precious-metal-based collectibles over the years. This group of collectibles is commonly referred to by the generic name of "limited-edition collectibles." While the print runs for these items don't always qualify as being "rare," they are generally produced in a publically announced quantity, hence the limited-edition designation.

While medallions make up the largest segment of the LEC category, precious metal trading cards have also been issued on numerous occasions in recent years.

As a rule, most LEC releases are produced and purchased as commemorative items which salute a specific event or individual accomplishment. Most collectors pick and choose which items they like based on their player or team preferences, but rarely purchase everything from a given company's print run. An active secondary market for these collectibles has never materialized, meaning most LEC releases maintain a value consistent with their original sale price.

BLEACHERS

Bleachers began releasing 23 Karat Gold Cards in 1993. The first cards were a tribute to a legend, Nolan Ryan, and the recognition of a future star, Ken Griffey Jr. In 1995, Bleachers joined dozens of other manufacturers in celebrating the record-breaking streak of Cal Ripken Jr. by issuing two cards. Other milestones honored by Bleachers include Eddie Murray's 500 home run and 3,000 hit plateau, and Griffey's chase of Roger Maris' record 61 home runs in a season. Most of these cards carry a sugested retail price of $30. The company is no longer in business.

Year	Player	Mintage	Price
1993	Griffey Jr., Ken #1 (Mega Star)	10,000	$30
1993	Ryan, Nolan #1 (27 Seasons)	10,000	30
1993	Ryan, Nolan #2 (Strikeout King)	5,714	90
1995	Griffey Jr., Ken #2 (silver/gold)	10,000	30
1995	Ripken Jr., Cal #1 (Iron Man)	75,000	30
1995	Ripken Jr., Cal/Gehrig, Lou (Iron Men)	20,000	30
1995	Thomas, Frank	10,000	30
1996	Ford, Whitey	25,000	30
1996	Mantle, Mickey #1 (Baseball's All-Time Great)	25,000	30
1996	Mantle, Mickey #2 (MVP)	10,000	30
1996	Mantle, Mickey #3 (Triple Crown)	10,000	30
1996	Mantle, Mickey #4 (#7)	10,000	30
1996	Mantle, Mickey #5 (Commerce Comet)	10,000	30
1996	Mantle, Mickey (Diamond Star)	10,000	30
1996	Murray, Eddie #1 (500 HRs)	10,000	30
1996	Murray, Eddie #2 (3,000 Hits & 500 HRs)	5,000	30
1996	Ripken Jr., Cal #2 (World Record)	10,000	30
1996	Ripken Jr., Cal (Diamond Star)	21,310	30
1996	Ripken Jr., Cal (Japanese)	10,000	30
1996	Rodriguez, Alex (black facsimile autograph)	5,000	30
1996	Rodriguez, Alex (pearl facsimile autograph)	5,000	30
1996	Ryan, Nolan (Diamond Star)	10,000	30
1996	Ryan, Nolan (laser cut Diamond Star)	10,000	30
1996	Thomas, Frank (Diamond Star)	10,000	30
1996	Williams, Ted	25,000	30
1996	Williams, Ted (Diamond Star)	10,000	30
1997	Clemente, Roberto (Diamond Star)	10,000	30
1997	Gehrig, Lou/Ruth, Babe (Avon)	50,000	30
1997	Griffey Jr., Ken #3 (triple image)	10,000	30
1997	Griffey Jr., Ken #4 (name in teal)	10,000	30
1997	Griffey Jr., Ken w/Chasing 62 HRs logo #1	4,997	40
1997	Griffey Jr., Ken w/Chasing 62 HRs logo #2	4,997	40
1997	Griffey Jr., Ken w/Chasing 62 HRs logo #3	4,997	40
1997	Jeter, Derek	10,000	30
1997	Ruth, Babe (Diamond Star)	10,000	30

CHICAGO PROCESSING
ENVIROMINT MEDALLIONS

Chicagoland first produced medallions in 1985 and continued through 1998. The company named its product Enviromint because the silver medallions are made from recycled silver taken from film scraps. Each coin issued commemorates a specific milestone or event, like George Brett's 3,000th hit, All-Star games, or division championship winners.

Starting in 1995, the coins were produced in bronze, silver, gold, and 24K versions, as well as proof sets. Mintage for these medallions ranged from 95 for some of the gold medallions to 25,000 for some of the first produced. The coins are individually numbered and are licensed by Major League Baseball.

Two of the most sought-after medallions are the 1990 Nolan Ryan 300th victory (limited to 1,500 coins and selling for $75), and the 1990 Ken Griffey Sr. and Jr. two piece set (3,300, $85).

Prices are for coins in mint condition. Listings below indicate the medallion, year, mintage and value.

World Series Champions
New York Mets, 1986, 25,000 . . . . $45
Minnesota Twins, 1987, 25,000 45
Los Angeles Dodgers, 1988, 25,000 35
Oakland Athletics, 1989, 6,550 35
Cincinnati Reds, 1990, 25,000 35
Toronto Blue Jays, 1992, 25,000 60
Atlanta Braves Silver, 1995, 10,000 40
Atlanta Braves 24K, 1995, 5,000 60
Atlanta Braves 3-pc. Proof Set, 1995, 1,995 140
Atlanta Braves Gold, 1995, 1,995 850
New York Yankees Silver, 1996, 10,000 40
New York Yankees 24K, 1996, 3,000 60
New York Yankees 3-pc. Proof Set, 1996, 1,000 140
New York Yankees Gold, 1996, 96 850
Florida Marlins 6-pc. Photo/Coin Set, 1997 500
Florida Marlins Silver, 1997, 25,000 35
Florida Marlins 24K, 1997, 7,500 50
Florida Marlins 3-pc. Proof Set, 1997, 1,000 125
Florida Marlins Gold, 1997, 197 850

American League Champions
Minnesota Twins, 1987, 5,000 . . . . $45
Oakland Athletics, 1988, 4,250 . . . . 32.50
Oakland Athletics, 1989, 6,550 . . . . 32.50
Oakland Atheltics, 1990, 10,000 30

1991 Minnesota Twins

Minnesota Twins, 1991, 10,000 30
Toronto Blue Jays, 1992, 10,000 55
Cleveland Indians Silver, 1995, 10,000 35
Cleveland Indians 24K, 1995, 3,000 40
Cleveland Indians 3-pc. Proof Set, 1995, 250 140
Cleveland Indians Gold, 1995, 95 850
New York Yankees Silver, 1996, 10,000 40
New York Yankees 24K, 1996, 3,000 60
NewYork Yankees 3-pc. Proof Set, 1996, 250 140

Cleveland Indians Silver, 1997, 10,000 35
Cleveland Indians 24K, 1997, 1,000 50
Cleveland Indians 10-pc. Proof Set, 1997, 500 125
Cleveland Indians 6-pc. WS Photo/Coin Set, 1997, 500 300

National League Champions
St. Louis Cardinals, 1987, 5,000 . . . . $45
Los Angeles Dodgers, 1988, 4,050 . . . . 30.50
San Francisco Giants, 1989, 8,100 . . . . 30.50

1993 Philadelphia Phillies

Philadelphia Phillies, 1993, 10,000 45
Cincinnati Reds, 1996, 10,000 30
Atlanta Braves, 1992, 10,000 45
Atlanta Braves Gold, 1994, 95 850
Atlanta Braves Silver, 1995, 10,000 40
Atlanta Braves 24K, 1995, 3,000 60
Atlanta Braves 3-pc. Proof Set, 1995, 95 140
Florida Marlins Silver, 1997, 10,000 35
Florida Marlins 24K, 1997, 3,000 45
Florida Marlins 10-pc. Proof Set, 1997, 500 125

American League East Division Winners
Detroit Tigers, 1987, 1,800 . . . . $35
Boston Red Sox, 1988, 500 45
Toronto Blue Jays, 1989, 2,300 70
Boston Red Sox, 1990, 450 50
Toronto Blue Jays, 1991, 5,000 70
Toronto Blue Jays, 1992, 5,000 55
Boston Red Sox Silver, 1995, 5,000 40
Boston Red Sox 24K, 1995, 1,995 60
Boston Red Sox Bronze, 1995, 500 20
Boston Red Sox 3-pc. Proof Set, 1995, 95 140
Baltimore Orioles Silver, 1997, 1,997 35
Baltimore Orioles 24K, 1997, 500 50
Baltimore Orioles 3-pc. Proof Set, 1997, 197 125

American League West Division Winners

Minnesota Twins, 1987, 3,000 . . . . $35
Oakland Athletics, 1988, 800 35
Oakland Athletics, 1989, 500 35
Oakland Athletics, 1990, 150 75
Minnesota Twins, 1991, 5,000 30
Seattle Mariners Silver, 1995, 5,000 40
Seattle Mariners 24K, 1995, 1,995 60
Seattle Mariners Bronze, 1995, 500 20
Seattle Mariners 3-pc. Proof Set, 1995, 95 140
Texas Rangers Silver, 1996, 1,996 35
Texas Rangers 24K, 1996, 500 55
Texas Rangers 3-pc. Proof Set, 1996, 196 130
Seattle Mariners Silver,1997, 1,997 35
Seattle Mariners 24K, 1997, 500 50
Seattle Mariners 3-pc. Proof Set, 1997, 197 125

National League East Division Winners

St. Louis Cardinals, 1987, 1,500 . . . . $35
New York Mets, 1988, 1,100 35
Chicago Cubs, 1989, 6,200 35
Chicago Cubs, 1989, 10,000 35
Pittsburgh Pirates, 1990, 1,300 35
Pittsburgh Pirates, 1991, 450 45
Atlanta Braves Silver, 1995, 5,000 40
Atlanta Braves 24K, 1995, 1,995 60
Atlanta Braves Bronze, 1995, 500 20
Atlanta Braves 3-pc. Proof Set, 1995, 95 125
Atlanta Braves Silver, 1997, 1,997 35
Atlanta Braves 24K, 1997, 500 50
Atlanta Braves 3-pc. Proof Set, 1997, 197 125

National League East Division Winners

San Francisco Giants, 1987, 1,000 . . . . $35
Los Angeles Dodgers, 1988, 800 35
San Francisco Giants, 1989, 600 35
Cincinnati Reds, 1990, 1,050 55
Atlanta Braves, 1991, 5,000 . . . . 32.50
Atlanta Braves, 1992, 5,000 . . . . 34.50
Los Angeles Dodgers Silver, 1995, 5,000 40
Los Angeles Dodgers 24K, 1995, 1,995 60
Los Angeles Dodgers Bronze, 1995, 500 20
Los Angeles Dodgers 3-pc. Proof Set, 1995, 95 125
San Francisco Giants Silver, 1997, 1,997 35
San Francisco Giants 24K, 500 50
San Francisco Giants 3-pc. Proof Set, 1997, 197 125

American League Central Division Winners

Cleveland Indians Silver, 1995, 5,000 . . . . $40
Cleveland Indians 24K, 1995, 1,995 60
Cleveland Indians 3-pc. Proof Set, 1995, 95 125
Cleveland Indians Silver, 1997, 1,997 35
Cleveland Indians 24K, 1997, 500 50
Cleveland Indians 3-pc. Proof Set, 1997, 197 125

National League Central Division Winners

Cincinnati Reds Silver, 1995, 5,000 . . . . $40
Cincinnati Reds 24K, 1995, 1,995 60
Cincinnati Reds Bronze, 1995, 500 20
Cincinnati Reds 3-pc. Proof Set, 1995, 95 125
Houston Astros Silver, 1997, 1,997 40
Houston Astros 24K, 1997, 500 60
Houston Astros 3-pc. Proof Set, 1997, 197 125

All-Star Game

Cincinnati, 1988, 2,000 . . . . $45
Anaheim,1989, 2,000 45
Toronto, 1991, 5,000 60
San Diego, 1992, 5,000 40
Baltimore, 1993, 5,000 35
Pittsburgh Silver, 1994, 5,000. 40
Pittsburgh 24K, 1994, 500 60
Texas Silver, 1995, 5,000 40
Texas 24K, 1995, 1,000 60
Texas Bronze, 1995, 5,000 20
Texas 3-pc. Proof Set, 1995, 95 125
Philadelphia Silver, 1996, 1,996 40
Philadelphia 24K, 1996, 500 60
Philadelphia 3-pc. Proof Set, 1996, 196 125
Philadelphia Ball/Coin, 1996, 500 50
Philadelphia Ball/Coin, 1996, 500 80
Cleveland Silver, 1997, 1,997 30
Cleveland 24K, 1997, 500 50
Cleveland 3-pc. Proof Set, 1997, 197 125
Cleveland Ball/Coin with Case, 1997, 1,997 125
Colorado Silver, 1998, 1,998 35
Colorado 24K, 1998, 500 50
Colorado 3-pc. Proof Set, 1998, 198 125

Player Coins

Roberto Alomar Silver, 1995, 1,500 . . . . $35
Roberto Alomar 24K, 1995, 125 60
Roberto Alomar Bronze, 1995, 500 20
Roberto Alomar Silver/All-Star, 1995, 1,995. 35
Roberto Alomar 24K/All-Star, 1995, 500 60
Roberto Alomar Bronze/All-Star, 1995, 1995 20
Roberto Alomar All-Star 3-pc. Proof Set, 1995, 95 125
Roberto Alomar All-Star Ball/Coin Set, 1996, 100 125
Roberto Alomar All-Star Photo/Coin Set,1997, 500. . . . 50
Roberto Alomar 3-pc. Photo/Coin Set, 1997, 197 150
Sandy Alomar WS Photo/Coin Set, 1997, 1,997 45
Moises Alou All-Star Photo/Coin Set 1997, 197 150
Moises Alou WS Photo/Coin Set 1997, 1,997 50
Brady Anderson All-Star Photo/Coin Set, 1997, 500 . . . 50
Brady Anderson 3-pc. Photo/Coin Set, 1997, 197 140
Paul Assenmacher WS Photo/Coin Set, 1997, 1,997 . . . 45
Carlos Baerga Silver/All-Star, 1995 1,995. 35
Carlos Baerga 24K/All-Star, 1995, 500 50
Carlos Baerga Bronze/All-Star 1995 1,995 20
Carlos Baerga All-Star 3-pc. Proof Set 1995, 95 130
Jeff Bagwell Silver, 1996, 1,996 30
Jeff Bagwell 24K Select, 1996, 500 50
Jeff Bagwell 3-pc. Proof Set, 1996, 196 125
Jeff Bagwell All-Star Ball/Coin Set, 1996, 100 125
Jeff Bagwell All-Star 3-pc. Photo Set, 1997, 197 150
Albert Belle Silver, 1995, 1,500 35
Albert Belle 24K, 1995, 125 60
Albert Belle Bronze, 1995, 500 20
Albert Belle Silver/All-Star, 1995, 1,995 35
Albert Belle 24K/All-Star, 1995, 500 60
Albert Belle Bronze/All-Star, 1995, 1,995 20
Albert Belle All-Star 3-pc. Proof Set, 1995, 95 130
Albert Belle All-Star Ball/Coin Set, 1996, 100 130
Albert Belle Framed Photo/Coin Set, 1996, 96 130
Albert Belle Silver, 1997, 1,997 35
Albert Belle 24K/All-Star, 1997, 500 50
Albert Belle 3-pc. Proof Set, 1997, 197 125
Albert Belle All-Star Photo/Coin Set, 1997, 500 50
Albert Belle 3-pc. All-Star Photo/Coin Set, 1997, 197 150
Johnny Bench Silver/Hall of Fame, 1989, 15,000 45
Dante Bichette Silver/All-Star, 1995 1,995 35
Dante Bichette 24K/All-Star, 1995, 500 60

Dante Bichette Bronze/All-Star, 1995, 1,995 20
Dante Bichette All-Star 3-pc. Proof Set, 1995, 95 130
Dante Bichette All-Star Ball/Coin Set, 1996, 100 125
Dante Bichette, Framed Photo/Coin Set1996, 96 125
Dante Bichette NL Photo/Coin Set 1997, 500 50
Craig Biggio All-Star Photo/Coin Set, 1997, 500 50
Craig Biggio 3-pc. Photo/Coin Set, 1997, 197 150
Jeff Blauser All-Star Photo/Coin Set1997, 500 50
Jeff Blauser All-Star Photo/Coin Set, 1997, 197 150
Wade Boggs Batting Title, 1993, 1,249 50
Wade Boggs 1993, 13,751 45
Wade Boggs, Silver/All-Star, 1995, 1,995 35
Wade Boggs, 24K/All-Star, 1995, 500 60
Wade Boggs, Bronze/All-Star, 1995, 1,995 20
Wade Boggs All-Star 3-pc. Proof Set, 1995, 95 130
Wade Boggs All-Star Ball/Coin Set, 1996, 100 130
Wade Boggs WS Reverse, 1996, 500 30
Wade Boggs, WS 3-pc. Proof Set, 1996, 96 125
Wade Boggs, WS Combo, 1996, 196 125
Wade Boggs, Framed Photo/Coin Set, 1996, 96 125
Barry Bonds Silver/NL MVP, 1993, 1,500 40
Barry Bonds 24K/NL MVP, 1993, 125 25
Barry Bonds Bronze/NL MVP, 1993, 500 20
Barry Bonds Silver/All-Star, 195, 1,995 40
Barry Bonds 24K/All-Star, 1995, 500 60
Barry Bonds Bronze/All-Star, 1995, 1,995 20
Barry Bonds All-Star 3-pc. Proof Set, 1995, 95 125
Barry Bonds All-Star Ball/Coin Set, 1996, 100 125
Barry Bonds All-Star Photo/Coin Set, 1997, 500 50
Barry Bonds All-Star 3-pc. Photo/Coin Set, 1997, 197 50
Bobby Bonilla WS Photo/Coin Set, 1997,1,997 50
George Brett Silver/3 Decades of Baseball, 1991, 2,033 45
George Brett Silver/3,000th Hit, 1992, 6,273 45
George Brett/RobinYount 2-pc. Set, 1992, 1,000 50
George Brett Silver 1992, 15,000 40
George Brett Silver/3,000 Hits, 1992, 15,000 40
Jay Buhner Silver, 1995, 1,995 35
Jay Buhner 24K ,1995, 500 60
Jay Buhner Bronze, 1995, 1,995 20
Jay Buhner 3-pc. Proof Set, 1995, 95 130
Jay Buhner All-Star Ball/Coin Set, 1996, 100 130
Ken Caminiti NL MVP 3-pc. Proof Set, 1996, 196 130
Ken Caminiti All-Star Photo/Coin Set, 1997, 500 50
Ken Caminiti All-Star 3-pc. Photo/Coin Set, 1997, 197 150
Jose Canseco Silver/40-40, Athletics, 1990, 6,000 45
Jose Canseco Silver/40-40, Rangers, 1992, 9,000 40
Jose Canseco Silver, 1995, 1,995 35
Jose Canseco 24K, 1995, 500 60
Jose Canseco Bronze, 1995, 1,995 20
Jose Canseco 3-pc. Proof Set, 1995, 95 125
Steve Carlton 4 Cy Youngs, 1990, 15,000 45
Joe Carter Silver, 1995, 1,500 35
Joe Carter 24K, 1995, 125 60
Joe Carter Bronze, 1995, 500 20
Joe Carter Silver, 1995, 1,995 35
Joe Carter 24K, 1995, 500 60
Joe Carter Bronze, 1995, 1,995 20
Joe Carter 3-pc. Proof Set, 1995, 95 130
Joe Carter All-Star Ball/Coin Set, 1996, 100 125
Vinny Castilla Silver/All-Star, 1995, 1,995 35
Vinny Castilla 24K/All-Star, 1995, 500 60
Vinny Castilla Bronze/All-Star, 1995, 1,995 20
Vinny Castilla All-Star 3-pc. Proof Set, 1995, 95 130
Will Clark 1990, 2,389 42
Will Clark Silver, 1995, 15,000 35
Will Clark Silver, 1995, 1,995 40
Will Clark 24K, 1995, 500 60
Will Clark Bronze, 1995, 1,995 20
Will Clark 3-pc. Proof Set, 1995, 95 130

Will Clark, All-Star Photo/Coin Set, 1997, 500 50
Roger Clemens Silver/'86-'87 Cy Young, 1990, 740 60
Roger Clemens Silver, 1995, 1,995 40
Roger Clemens 24K, 1995, 500 60
Roger Clemens Bronze, 1995, 1,995 20
Roger Clemens 3-pc. Proof Set, 1995, 95 135
R. Clemens Cy Young Photo/Coin Set, 1997, 500 50
Roger Clemens 24K/Cy Young, 1997, 1,000 35
Roberto Clemente Silver/1973 HOF, 1998, 15,000 55
R. Clemente Silver/All-Star Game, 1994, 5,000 40
Roberto Clemente 24K/All-Star Game, 1994, 1,000 75
Roberto Clemente Silver/Career, 1995, 5,000 40
Roberto Clemente 24K/Career 1995, 1,000 75
Roberto Clemente Silver/Card, 1995, 1,973 225
Roberto Clemente 24K/Card, 1995, 500 350
Roberto Clemente Silver Coin/Card Set, 1995, 500 275
Roberto Clemente 24K Coin/Card Set, 1995, 100 400
Ty Cobb 1988, 1,093 45
Ty Cobb Saver, 1995, 15,000 30
Jeff Conine WS Photo/Coin Set, 1997, 1,997 50
Craig Counsell WS Photo/Coin Set, 1997, 1,997 50
Darren Daulton Silver, 1995, 1,500 35
Darren Daulton 24K, 1995, 125 70
Darren Daulton Bronze, 1995, 500 20
Darren Daulton Silver/All-Star, 1995, 1,995 30
Darren Daulton 24K/All-Star, 1995, 500 60
Darren Daulton Bronze/All-Star, 1995, 1,995 20
Darren Daulton All-Star 3-pc. Proof Set, 1995, 95 130
Mark Davis 1989 Cy Young, 1989, 270 65
Andre Dawson 1987 MVP, 1990, 10,900 . . . . 32.50
Andre Dawson 1993, 4,100 45
Jason Dickson All-Star Photo/Coin Set, 1997, 500 50
Jason Dickson 3-pc. Photo/Coin Set, 1997, 197 150
Larry Doby Silver, 1997, 500 38
Larry Doby 24K, 1997, 500 55
Larry Doby 3-pc. Proof Set, 1997, 19 130
Lenny Dykstra 24K, 1995, 125 60
Lenny Dykstra Bronze, 1995, 500 20
Lenny Dykstra Silver/All-Star, 1995, 1,995 40
Lenny Dykstra 24K/All-Star, 1995, 500 60
Lenny Dykstra Bronze/All-Star, 1995, 1,995. 20
Lenny Dykstra All-Star 3-pc. Proof Set, 1995, 95 130
Dennis Eckersley 40 saves/3 years, 1992, 400 50
Dennis Eckersley 1992 Cy Young, 1992, 15,000 35
Dennis Eckersley Silver, 1995, 1,995 40
Dennis Eckersley 24K, 1995, 500 60
Dennis Eckersley Bronze, 1995, 1,995 20
Dennis Eckersley 3-pc. Proof Set, 1995, 95 130
Shawn Estes 3-pc. Photo/Coin Set, 1997, 197 150
Alex Fernandez, WS Photo/Coin, 1997, 1,997 50
Alex Fernandez, WS Photo/Coin Set, 1997, 1,997 50
Tony Fernandez WS Photo/Coin Set, 1997, 1,997 50
Cecil Fielder AL HR/RBI Leader, 1991, 15,000 30
Cecil Fielder Silver, 1996, 1,996 30
Cecil Fielder 24K, 1996, 500 50

Cecil Fielder

Cecil Fielder 3-pc. Proof Set, 1996, 196 125
Cecil Fielder WS Reverse Silver, 1996, 500 30
Cecil Fielder WS 3-pc. Proof Set, 1996, 96 130
Cecil Fielder WS Combo, 1996, 196 130
Cecil Fielder WS 24K, 1996, 196 50
Rollie Fingers Silver/Hall of Fame, 1995, 15,000 38
Carlton Fisk Most Hits by Catcher, 1990, 15,000 38
Andres Gallaraga Silver, 1995, 1,500 40
Andres Gallaraga Bronze, 1993, 500 20
Andres Gallaraga 24K, 1993, 125 60
Andres Gallaraga Silver, 1995, 1,995 40
Andres Gallaraga 24K, 1995, 500 60
Andres Gallaraga Bronze, 1995, 1,995 20
Andres Gallaraga 3-pc. Proof Set, 1995, 95 130
Andres Gallaraga Photo/Coin Set, 1996, 96 125
A. Gallaraga All-Star Photo/Coin Set, 1997, 197 150
Nomar Garciaparra 24K/ROY, 1997, 1,000 35
Nomar Garciaparra ROY Bronze Photo/Coin Set, 1997, 500 50
Steve Garvey 1,207 Consecutive Games, 1989, 15,000 . . . 35
Lou Gehrig 2,130 Consecutive Games, 1987, 1,352 45
Kirk Gibson 1988 MVP, 1988, 600 45
Kirk Gibson Silver, 1995, 1,995 40
Kirk Gibson 24K, 1995, 500 60
Kirk Gibson Bronze, 1995, 1,995 20
Kirk Gibson 3-pc. Proof Set, 1995, 95 130
Tom Glavine Silver/'91 Cy Young, 1991, 15,000 35
Tom Glavine Silver, 1995, 1,995 40
Tom Glavine 24K, 1995, 500 60
Tom Glavine Bronze, 1995, 1,995 20
Tom Glavine 3-pc. Proof Set, 1995, 95 130
Tom Glavine All-Star Ball/Coin Set, 1996, 100 20
Tom Glavine Silver/WS, 1996, 500 30
Tom Glavine 24K/WS, 1996, 196 50
Tom Glavine, WS 3-pc. Proof Set, 1996, 96 125
Tom Glavine, WS Combo Set, 1996, 196 125
Tom Glavine, All-Star 3-pc. Photo/Coin Set, 1997, 197 150
Juan Gonzalez, Bronze, 1995 20
Juan Gonzalez, Silver, 1995, 1,500 40
Juan Gonzalez 24K, 1995, 125 60
Juan Gonzalez Silver, 1995, 1,995 40
Juan Gonzalez 24K, 1995, 500 60
Juan Gonzalez Bronze, 1995, 1,995 20
Juan Gonzalez 3-pc. Proof Set, 1995, 95 130
Juan Gonzalez Silver/AL MVP, 1996, 1,996 40
Juan Gonzalez 24K/AL MVP, 1996, 500 60
Juan Gonzalez AL MVP 3-pc. Proof Set, 1996, 196 . . . 130
Juan Gonzalez AL Photo/Coin Set, 1997, 500 50
Dwight Gooden Silver, 1995, 15,000 35
Mark Grace Silver, 1995, 1,500 35
Mark Grace 24K, 1995, 125 60
Mark Grace Bronze, 1995, 500 20
Mark Grace Silver/All-Star, 1995, 1,995 40
Mark Grace 24K/All-Star, 1995, 500 60
Mark Grace Bronze/All-Star, 1995, 1,995 20
Mark Grace All-Star 3-pc. Proof Set, 1995, 95 130
Mark Grace Framed Photo/Coin Set, 1996, 96 130
Ken Griffey Jr. & Sr., 1990, 3,700 65
Ken Griffey Jr. & Sr., 1990, 3,300 85
Ken Griffey Jr. & Sr. Silver, 1995, 15,000 35
Ken Griffey Jr. Silver, 1995, 1,500 45
Ken Griffey Jr. 24K, 1995, 125 80
Ken Griffey Jr. Bronze, 1995, 500 25
Ken Griffey Jr. Silver/All-Star, 1995, 1,995 45
Ken Griffey Jr. 24K/All-Star, 1995, 500 65
Ken Griffey Jr. Bronze/All-Star, 1995, 1,995 25
Ken Griffey, Ken Jr. All-Star 3-pc. Proof Set, 1995, 95 140
Ken Griffey Ken Jr. All-Star Ball/Coin Set, 1996, 100 149
Ken Griffey Jr. Framed Photo/Coin Set, 1996, 96 140
Ken Griffey Jr. All-Star Photo/Coin Set, 1996, 500 65
Ken Griffey, Jr. MVP Photo/Coin Set, 1997, 500 65
Ken Griffey Jr. 24K/MVP, 1997, 1,000 45
Ken Griffey Jr. HR Leader Photo/Coin Set, 1997, 500 . . . 65
Ken Griffey Jr. 24K/HR Leader, 1997, 1,000 45
Ken Griffey Jr. 24K HR/MVP 2-pc. Set, 1997, 97 140
Ken Griffey Jr. Bronze HR/MVP 2-pc. Set, 1997, 197 . . . 95
Tony Gwynn Batting Title '87, '88, '89, 1990, 1,075 . . . 50
Tony Gwynn Silver/All-Star, 1995, 1,995 40
Tony Gwynn 24K/All-Star, 1995, 500 60
Tony Gwynn Bronze/All-Star, 1995, 1,995 20
Tony Gwynn All-Star 3-pc. Proof Set, 1995, 95 130
Tony Gwynn All-Star Ball/Coin Set, 1996, 100 125
Tony Gwynn Framed Photo/Coin Set, 1996, 96 125
Tony Gwynn Batting Title Photo/Coin Set, 1997, 500 . . . 50
Tony Gwynn 24K Batting Title, 1997, 1,000 35
Tony Gwynn/Frank Thomas 24K 2-pc. Set, 1997, 97 . . 130
Tony Gwynn /Frank Thomas Bronze 2-pc. Set, 1997, 197 . . . 80
Rickey Henderson, Stolen Bases, 1990, 7,109 45
Rickey Henderson 1993, 7,981 40
Rickey Henderson Silver, 1995, 1,995 40
Rickey Henderson 24K, 1995, 500 60
Rickey Henderson Bronze, 1995, 1,995 20
Rickey Henderson 3-pc. Proof Set, 1995, 95 130
Pat Hentgen Silver/AL Cy Young, 1996, 1,996 35
Pat Hentgen 24K/AL Cy Young, 1996, 500 50
Pat Hentgen AL Cy Young 3-pc. Proof Set, 1996, 196 . . . 125
Livan Hernandez WS Photo/Coin Set, 1997, 1,997 50
Livan Hernandez WS MVP Photo/Coin Set, 1997, 1,997 . . . 50
Livan Hernandez 2-pc. Card/Coin Set, 1997, 197 180
Orel Hershiser 1988 Cy Young, 1989, 600 45
Orel Hershiser Silver, 1997, 1,995 40
Orel Hershiser 24K, 1995, 500 60
Orel Hershiser Bronze, 1995, 1,995 20
Orel Hershiser 3-pc. Proof Set, 1995, 95 130
Orel Hershiser WS Photo/Coin Set, 1,997, 1,997 50
Todd Hollandsworth Silver/ROY 1996, 1,996 35
Todd Hollandsworth 24K/ROY, 1996, 500 50
Todd Hollandsworth ROY 3-pc. Proof Set, 1996, 196 . . 125
Bo Jackson Raiders/Royals, 1990, 4,400 45
Bo Jackson Raiders/White Sox, 1991, N/A 35
Reggie Jackson 1993 HOF Gold, 1993, 44 850
Reggie Jackson HOF 2-pc. Set, 1993, 100 125
Derek Jeter Silver/WS Reverse, 1996, 500 40
Derek Jeter WS Ball/Coin Set, 1996, 96 130
Derek Jeter 24K/WS, 1996, 196 60
Derek Jeter WS 3-pc. Proof Set, 1996, 96 125
Derek Jeter Framed Photo/Coin Set, 1996, 96 125
Derek Jeter Silver/ROY, 1996, 1,996 30
Derek Jeter 24K/ROY, 1996, 500 50
Derek Jeter ROY 3-pc. Proof Set, 1996, 196 125
Fergie Jenkins 1991 HOF, 1991, 15,000 35
Charles Johnson WS Photo/Coin Set, 1997, 1,997 50
Howard Johnson HR/RBI Champ, 680 35
Randy Johnson Silver, 1995, 1,500 40
Randy Johnson 24K, 1995, 125 60
Randy Johnson Bronze, 1995, 500 20
Randy Johnson Silver/All-Star, 1995, 1,995 40
Randy Johnson 24K/All-Star, 1995, 500 60
Randy Johnson Bronze/All-Star, 1995, 1,995 20
Randy Johnson All-Star 3-pc. Proof Set, 1995, 95 . . . 130
Randy Johnson Silver/Cy Young, 1995, 1,995 45
Randy Johnson 24K/Cy Young, 1995, 500 65
Randy Johnson Bronze/Cy Young, 1995, 1,995 50
R. Johnson Cy Young 3-pc. Proof Set, 1995, 95 135
Randy Johnson Framed Photo/Coin Set, 1996, 96 . . . 130

Randy Johnson 3-pc. Photo/Coin Set, 1997, 197 160
Chipper Jones Silver, 1995, 1,995 40
Chipper Jones 24K, 1995, 500 60
Chipper Jones Bronze, 1995, 1,995 20
Chipper Jones 3-pc. Proof Set, 1995, 95 130
Chipper Jones All-Star Ball/Coin Set, 1996, 100 125
Chipper Jones 24K/WS, 1996, 196 50
Chipper Jones WS 3-pc. Proof Set, 1996, 96 130
Chipper Jones WS Combo, 1996, 196. 125
Chipper Jones Framed Photo/Coin Set, 1996, 96 125
Chipper Jones All-Star 3-pc. Photo/Coin Set, 1997, 197 150
Bobby Jones All-Star Photo/Coin Set, 1997, 500 50
Bobby Jones All-Star Photo/Coin Set, 1997, 197 150
David Justice 1990 Rookie of Year, 1991, 15,000 38
David Justice Silver, 1995, 1,995 40
David Justice 24K, 1995, 500. 60
David Justice Bronze, 1995, 1,995 20
David Justice 3-pc. Proof Set, 1995, 95. 125
David Justice Silver/WS, 1996, 500 30
David Justice 24K/WS, 1996, 196 50
David Justice WS 3-pc. Proof Set, 1996, 96 125
David Justice WS Combo, 1996, 196. 125
David Justice Framed Photo/Coin Set 1996, 96 125
David Justice All-Star Photo/Coin Set, 1997, 500 50
David Justice 3-pc. Photo/Coin Set, 1997, 197 150
David Justice WS Photo/Coin Set, 1997, 1,997 50
Harmon Killebrew 1984 Hall of Fame, 1991, 15,000 45
Chuck Knoblauch 1993, 15,000 40
Chuck Knoblauch Silver, 1995, 1,995 40
Chuck Knoblauch 24K, 1995, 500 60
Chuck Knoblauch Bronze, 1995, 1,995. 20
Chuck Knoblauch 3-pc. Proof Set, 1995, 95 130
Chuck Knoblauch All-Star Ball/Coin Set, 1996, 100 130
Chuck Knoblauch 3-pc. Photo/Coin Set, 1997, 197. 150
Barry Larkin Bronze/All-Star, 1995, 1,995 20
Barry Larkin All-Star 3-pc. Proof Set, 1995, 95 130
Barry Larkin All-Star Photo/Coin Set, 1997, 500 60
Barry Larkin All-Star 3-pc. Photo/Coin Set, 1997, 197 150
Kenny Lofton Silver/All-Star, 1995, 1,995 40
Kenny Lofton 24K/All-Star, 1995, 500 60
Kenny Lofton Bronze/All-Star, 1995, 1,995 20
Kenny Lofton 3-pc. Proof Set 1995, 95. 130
Kenny Lofton All-Star Ball/Coin Set 1996, 100 130
Kenny Lofton Framed Photo/Coin Set 1996, 96 130
Kenny Lofton All-Star Photo/Coin Set 1997, 500 50
Kenny Lofton 3-pc. Photo/Coin Set 1997, 197 150
Greg Maddux Silver/Cy Young, 1992, 15,000 40
Greg Maddux Silver/Cy Young, 1993, 1,500 65
Greg Maddux Bronze/Cy Young, 1993, 500 40
Greg Maddux 24K/Cy Young, 1993, 125 100
Greg Maddux Silver/All-Star, 1995, 1,995 45
Greg Maddux, 24K/All-Star, 1995, 500 65
Greg Maddux, Bronze/All-Star, 1995, 1,995. 25
Greg Maddux All-Star 3-pc. Proof Set, 1995, 95 140
Greg Maddux Silver/4-Time Cy Young Winner, 1995, 1,995 45
Greg Maddux 24K/4 Time Cy Young Winner, 1995, 500 65
Greg Maddux Bronze/4 Time, 1995, Cy Young Winner, 1,995 25
Greg Maddux 4 Time Cy Young Winner 3-pc. Proof Set, 1995, 95 . 130
Greg Maddux All-Star Ball/Coin Set, 1996, 100 135
Greg Maddux WS Combo 1996, 196 135
Greg Maddux Framed Photo/Coin Set, 1996, 96 135
Greg Maddux All-Star 3-pc. Photo/Coin Set, 1997, 197. 150
Mickey Mantle Silver, 1997, 10,000 45
Mickey Mantle 24K, 1997, 1,956 75
Mickey Mantle Bronze, 1997, 25,000 25
Mickey Mantle 3-pc. Proof Set, 1997, 1,000 150
Mickey Mantle Gold, 1997, 100 850
Mickey Mantle Card/Coin 2-pc. Set, 1997, 1,956 65

Mickey Mantle

Pedro Martinez All-Star Photo/Coin Set, 1997, 500 50
Pedro Martinez All-Star 3-pc. Photo/Coin Set, 1997, 197 150
Pedro Martinez Cy Young 24K Bronze 1997, 1,000 35
Tino Martinez Silver, 1995, 1,995 40
Tino Martinez 24K, 1995, 500. 60
Tino Martinez Bronze, 1995, 1,995, ... 20
Tino Martinez 3-pc. Proof Set, 1995, 95 130
Tino Martinez All-Star Photo/Coin Set, 1997, 500 50
Tino Martinez 3-pc. Photo/Coin Set, 1997, 197 150
Edgar Martinez Silver/All-Star, 1995, 1,995 40
Edgar Martinez 24K/All-Star, 1995, 500. 60
Edgar Martinez Bronze/All-Star, 1995, 1,995 20
Edgar Martinez All-Star 3-pc. Proof Set, 1995, 95 130
Edgar Martinez All-Star Ball/Coin Set, 1996, 100 125
Edgar Martinez Framed Photo/Coin Set, 1996, 96 125
Edgar Martinez All-Star Photo/Coin Set, 1997, 500 50
Edgar Martinez 3-pc. Photo/Coin Set, 1997, 197. 150
Dennis Martinez Silver/All-Star, 1995, 1,995 40
Dennis Martinez 24K/All-Star 1995, 500 60
Dennis Martinez Bronze/All-Star, 1995, 1,995 20
D. Martinez, All-Star 3-pc. Proof Set, 1995, 95 130
Don Mattingly Most Grand Slams, 1988, 15,000 40
Don Mattingly Silver, 1995, 1,995 60
Don Mattingly 24K, 1995, 500 80
Don Mattingly Bronze, 1995, 1,995 20
Don Mattingly, 3-pc. Proof Set, 1995, 95 130
Jack McDowell Silver/1993 Cy Young, 1994, 1,500 40
Jack McDowell 24K/1993 Cy Young, 1994, 125 60
Jack McDowell Bronze/ 1993 Cy Young, 1994, 500 20
Jack McDowell/Frank/Thomas 2-pc. set, 1994, 100. 85
Jack McDowell Silver, 1995, 1,995 40
Jack McDowell 24K, 1995, 500 60
Jack McDowell Bronze, 1995, 1995 20
Jack McDowell 3-pc. Proof Set, 1,995, 95 130
Fred McGriff Silver/All-Star, 1995, 1,995. 40
Fred McGriff 24K/All-Star, 1995, 500 60
Fred McGriff Bronze/All-Star, 1995, 1,995. 20
Fred McGriff 3-pc. Proof Set, 1995, 95. 130
Fred McGriff All-Star Ball/Coin Set, 1996, 100 125
Fred McGriff WS Silver, 1996, 500 30
Fred McGriff WS 24K, 1996, 196 50
Fred McGriff WS 3-pc. Proof Set, 1996, 96 125
Fred McGriff WS Combo Set, 1996, 196 125
Fred McGriff NL Photo/Coin Set, 1997, 500 50
Mark McGwire 30 HR/4 season, 1991, 15,000 45
Mark McGwire Silver/All-Star, 1995, 1,995 45
Mark McGwire 24K/All-Star, 1995, 500. 65
Mark McGwire Bronze/All-Star, 1995, 1,995 25
Mark McGwire All-Star 3-pc. Proof Set, 1995, 95 135
Mark McGwire All-Star Ball/Coin Set, 1996, 100 125
Mark McGwire Framed Photo/Coin Set, 1996, 96 125
Mark McGwire 3-pc. All-Star Photo/Coin Set, 1997, 197 150

Mark McGwire HR Leader, 1997, 500 50
Mark McGwire 24K Bronze/HR Leader, 1997, 1,000 35
Jose Mesa WS Photo/Coin Set, 1997, 1,997 50
Kevin Mitchell 1989 MVP, 1990, 1,200 35
Kevin Mitchell 1992, 108 60
Kevin Mitchell 1993, 13,692 32
Paul Molitor 39-Game Hitting Streak, 1990, 11,001 35
Joe Morgan 1990 HOF, 1990, 15,000 45
Eddie Murray Silver/3,000 Hits, 1995, 3,000 45
Eddie Murray 24K/3,000 Hits, 1995, 1,995 65
Eddie Murray Gold/3,000 Hits, 1995, 100 850
Eddie Murray 3,000 Hits 3-pc. Proof Set, 1995, 95 130
Eddie Murray Silver/500th Home Run, 1996, 1,996 35
Eddie Murray 24K/500th Home Run, 1996, 1,000 55
Eddie Murray 500th Home Run 3-pc. Proof Set, 1996, 196 125
Eddie Murray Gold/500th Home Run, 1996, 33 850
Eddie Murray 500th HR/3,000th Hit 2-pc. Silver, 1996, 500 85
Eddie Murray 500th HR/3,000th Hit 2-pc. 24K, 1996, 100 140
Randy Myers Silver/All-Star, 1995, 1,995 40
Randy Myers 24K/All-Star, 1995, 500 60
Randy Myers Bronze/All-Star, 1995, 1,995 20
Randy Myers All-Star 3-pc. Proof Set, 1995, 95 130
Charles Nagy AL Photo/Coin Set, 1997, 500 50
Charles Nagy WS Photo/Coin Set, 1997, 1,997 50
C. Nagy 3-pc. All-Star Photo/Coin Set, 1997, 500 150
Robb Nen WS Photo/Coin Set 1997, 1,997 50
Hideo Nomo Silver/All-Star, 1995, 1,995 40
Hideo Nomo 24K/All-Star, 1995, 500 60
Hideo Nomo Bronze/All-Star, 1995, 1,995 20
Hideo Nomo All-Star 3-pc. Proof Set 1995, 95 130
Hideo Nomo Silver 1995, 1,995 40
Hideo Nomo 24K 1995, 500 60
Hideo Nomo Bronze, 1995, 1,995 20
Hideo Nomo Silver/Rookie, 1995, 1,995 40
Hideo Nomo 24K/Rookie, 1995, 500 60
Hideo Nomo, Bronze/Rookie, 1995, 1,995 20
Hideo Nomo, Rookie 3-pc. Proof Set, 1995, 95 130
Hideo Nomo, Framed Photo/Coin Set, 1995, 96 130
John Olerud Silver, 1993, 1,500 40
John Olerud 24K, 1993, 125 60
John Olerud Bronze, 1993, 500 20
John Olerud Silver, 1995, 1,995 40
John Olerud 24K, 1995, 500 60
John Olerud Bronze, 1995, 1,995 20
John Olerud 3-pc. Proof Set, 1995, 95 130
Gregg Olson '89 Rookie of the Year, 1990, 15,000 35
Paul O'Neil Silver/All-Star, 1995, 1,995 40
Paul O'Neil 24K/All-Star, 1995, 500 60
Paul O'Neil Bronze/All-Star, 1995, 1,995 20
Paul O'Neil All-Star 3-pc. Proof Set, 1995, 95 130
Terry Pendleton 1991 Batting Title, 1991, 900 45
Terry Pendleton, 1991 NL MVP, 1991, 15,000 40
Terry Pendleton Silver, 1995, 1,995 40
Terry Pendleton 24K, 1995, 500 60
Terry Pendleton Bronze, 1995, 1,995 20
Terry Pendleton 3-pc. Proof Set, 1995, 95 130
Andy Pettitte Silver WS Reverse, 1996, 500 35
Andy Pettitte WS Ball/Coin Set, 1996, 96 125
Andy Pettitte WS 24K, 1996, 196 55
Andy Pettitte WS 3-pc. Proof Set, 1996, 96 125
Mike Piazza Silver, 1993, 1,500 50
Mike Piazza 24K, 1993, 125 75
Mike Piazza Bronze, 1993, 500 25
Mike Piazza Silver/All-Star, 1995, 1,995 40
Mike Piazza 24K/All-Star, 1995, 500 60
Mike Piazza Bronze/All-Star, 1995, 1,995 20
Mike Piazza All-Star 3-pc. Proof Set, 1995, 95 130
Mike Piazza All-Star Ball/Coin Set, 1996, 100 125
Mike Piazza Framed Photo/Coin Set, 1996, 96 125

Mike Piazza 3-pc. Photo/Coin Set, 1997, 197 150
Kirby Puckett AL Batting Champ, 1990, 2,200 50
Kirby Puckett Silver/All-Star, 1995, 1,995 40
Kirby Puckett 24K/All-Star, 1995, 500 60
Kirby Puckett Bronze/All-Star, 1995, 1,995 20
Kirby Puckett All-Star 3-pc. Proof Set, 1995, 95 130
Kirby Puckett Silver/Retirement, 1996, 1,996 35
Kirby Puckett 24K/Retirement, 1996, 500 55
Kirby Puckett Retirement 3-pc. Proof Set, 1996, 196 130
Kirby Puckett Gold/Retirement 1996, 34 850
Kirby Puckett Framed Photo/Coin Set, 1996, 96 125
Manny Ramirez Silver/All-Star, 1995, 1,995 40
Manny Ramirez 24K/All-Star, 1995, 500 60
Manny Ramirez Bronze/All-Star, 1995, 1,995 20
Manny Ramirez All-Star 3-pc. Proof Set, 1995, 95 130
Manny Ramirez Framed Photo/Coin Set, 1996, 96 130
Manny Ramirez WS Photo/Coin Set, 1997, 1,997 50
Edgar Renteria, WS Photo/Coin Set, 1997, 1,997 50
Cal Ripken 1991 MVP, 1992, 15,000 40
Cal Ripken Silver, 1995, 1,500 50
Cal Ripken 24K, 1995, 125 80
Cal Ripken Bronze 1995, 500 30
Cal Ripken Silver/All-Star, 1995, 1,995 40
Cal Ripken 24K/All-Star, 1995, 500 60
Cal Ripken Bronze/All-Star, 1995, 1,995 20
Cal Ripken All-Star 3-pc. Proof Set, 1995, 95 130
Cal Ripken Silver/2,131 Coin, 1996, 10,000 40
Cal Ripken 24K/2,131 Coin, 1996, 2,131 75
Cal Ripken Jr. Gold/2,131 Coin, 1996, 95 850
Cal Ripken 2,131 Coin 3-pc. Proof Set, 1996, 500 135
Cal Ripken All-Star Ball/Card Set, 1996, 100 125
Cal Ripken All-Star Photo/Coin Set, 1997, 500 150
Brooks Robinson 1983 HOF, 1991, 15,000 35
Alex Rodriguez All-Star Ball/Coin Set, 1996, 100 125
Alex Rodriguez Silver, 1996, 1,996 40
Alex Rodriguez 24K, 1996, 500 60
Alex Rodriguez Bat. Champ. 3-pc. Proof Set, 1996, 196 125
Alex Rodriguez All-Star Photo/Coin Set, 1997, 500 50
Ivan Rodriguez, Silver/All-Star, 1995, 1,995 40
Ivan Rodriguez, 24K/All-Star, 1995, 500 60
Ivan Rodriguez, Bronze/All-Star, 1995, 1,995 20
Ivan Rodriguez All-Star 3-pc. Proof Set 1995, 95 130
Ivan Rodriguez All-Star Ball/Coin Set, 1996, 100 125
Ivan Rodriguez All-Star Photo/Coin Set, 1997, 500 50
Ivan Rodriguez 3-pc. Photo/Coin Set, 1997, 197 150
Scott Rolen ROY Photo/Coin Set, 1997, 500 50
Scott Rolen ROY 24K Bronze, 1997, 1,000 35
Pete Rose All Time Hit Leader, 1985, 25,000 65
Babe Ruth 1987, 15,000 50

Nolan Ryan

Nolan Ryan 5,000th Strikeout, 1989, 1,500 75
Nolan Ryan 300th Victory, 1990, 1,500 75
Nolan Ryan 7th No-Hitter, 1991, 1,500 65
Nolan Ryan Silver/Retirement, 1993, 15,000 45

Nolan Ryan Gold/Retirement, 1993, 100 850
Nolan Ryan Bronze/Retirement, 1993, 25,000 20
Nolan Ryan Retirement 2-pc. set, 1993, 500 145
Nolan Ryan Bat w/Silver Coin Set, 1993, 1,993 175
Nolan Ryan Bat w/24K Coin Set, 1993, 500 250
Nolan Ryan Silver/Jersey Retirement, 1996, 1,996 35
Nolan Ryan 24K/Jersey Retirement, 1996, 500 55
N. Ryan Jersey Retirement 3-pc. Proof Set, 1996, 196 135
Bret Saberhagen 1998 Cy Young, 1990, 300 65
Bret Saberhagen Silver, 1995, 1,995 40
Bret Saberhagen 24K, 1995, 500 60
Bret Saberhagen Bronze, 1995, 1,995 20
Bret Saberhagen 3-pc. Proof Set, 1995, 95 130
Chris Sabo '88 NL ROY, 1989, 1,315 45
Tim Salmon Silver, 1993, 1,500 45
Tim Salmon 24K, 1993, 125 65
Tim Salmon Bronze, 1993, 500 25
Tim Salmon Silver, 1995, 1,995 50
Tim Salmon 24K, 1995, 500 60
Tim Salmon Bronze, 1995, 1,995 20
Tim Salmon 3-pc. Proof Set, 1995, 95 130
Ryne Sandberg Errorless Streak, 1990, 15,000 38
Ryne Sandberg Framed Photo/Coin Set, 1996, 96 125
Ryne Sandberg Silver, 1996, 1,996 35
Ryne Sandberg 24K, 1996, 500 50
Ryne Sandberg 3-pc. Proof Set, 1996, 196 125
Ryne Sandberg Silver/HRs Record, 1997, 1,997 35
Ryne Sandberg 24K/HRs Record, 1997, 500 50
Ryne Sandberg HRs Record 3-pc. Proof Set, 1997, 197 125
Deion Sanders 1992, 15,000 32
Deion Sanders Silver, 1997 1,997 35
Deion Sanders 24K, 1997, 500 50
Deion Sanders 3-pc. Proof Set, 1997, 197 125
Tony Saunders, WS Photo/Coin Set, 1997, 1,997 50
Mike Schmidt Player of Decade, 1990, 10,000 45
Mike Schmidt Silver/Hall of Fame, 1995, 5,000 65
Mike Schmidt, 24K/Hall of Fame, 1995, 1,995 85
Mike Schmidt, Gold/Hall of Fame, 1995, 95 850
Mike Schmidt, Bronze/Hall of Fame, 1995, 5,000 25
Curt Schilling, All-Star Photo/Coin Set, 1997, 500 50
Curt Schilling All-Star 3-pc. Photo Set, 1997, 197 150
Tom Seaver 1992 HOF, 1992, 15,000 40
Gary Sheffield WS Photo/Coin Set, 1997, 1,997 50
Ozzie Smith Silver, 1995, 1,500 50
Ozzie Smith 24K, 1995, 125 70
Ozzie Smith Bronze, 1995, 500 25
Ozzie Smith Silver/All-Star, 1995, 1,995 40
Ozzie Smith 24K/All-Star, 1995, 500 60
Ozzie Smith Bronze/All-Star, 1995, 1,995 20
Ozzie Smith All-Star 3-pc. Proof Set, 1995, 95 130
Ozzie Smith All-Star Ball/Coin Set, 1996, 100 125
Ozzie Smith Framed Photo/Coin Set, 1996, 96 125
John Smoltz All-Star Ball/Coin Set, 1996, 100 125
John Smoltz Silver, 1996, 1,996 35
John Smoltz 24K, 1996, 500 55
John Smoltz 3-pc. Proof Set, 1996, 196 130
John Smoltz 24K/WS, 1996, 196 50
John Smoltz WS 3-pc. Proof Set, 1996, 96 125
John Smoltz Silver/NL Cy Young, 1996, 1,996 35
John Smoltz 24K/NL Cy Young, 1996, 500 50
John Smoltz NL Cy Young 3-pc. Proof Set, 1996, 196 125
John Smoltz NL Photo/Coin Set, 1997, 500 50
Sammy Sosa Bronze/All-Star, 1995, 1,995 20
Sammy Sosa 24K/All-Star, 1997, 500 50
Darryl Strawberry 1990, 1,200 45
Darryl Strawberry 1995, 13,800 32
Darryl Strawberry WS, 1996, 500 30
Darryl Strawberry WS 3-pc. Proof Set, 1996, 96 125

Frank Thomas Silver/AL MVP, 1993, 1,500 50
Frank Thomas 24K/AL MVP, 1993, 125 80
Frank Thomas Bronze/AL MVP, 1993, 500 28
Frank Thomas Silver/MVP, 1994, 1,500 50
Frank Thomas 24K/MVP, 1994, 125 80
Frank Thomas Bronze/MVP, 1994, 500 28
Frank Thomas Silver/All-Star, 1995, 1,995, ... 40
Frank Thomas 24K/All-Star, 1995, 500 60
Frank Thomas Bronze/All-Star, 1995, 1,995 20
Frank Thomas All-Star 3-pc. Proof Set, 1995, 95 120
Frank Thomas All-Star Ball/Coin Set, 1996, 100 125
Frank Thomas All-Star Photo/Coin Set, 1997, 197 140
Jim Thome WS Photo/Coin Set, 1997, 1,997 50
Mo Vaughn Silver/All-Star, 1995, 1,995 40
Mo Vaughn 24K/All-Star, 1995, 500 60
Mo Vaughn Bronze/All-Star, 1995, 1,995 20
Mo Vaughn All-Star 3-pc. Proof Set, 1995, 95 130
Mo Vaughn All-Star Ball/Coin Set, 1996, 100 125
Mo Vaughn AL Photo/Coin Set, 1997, 500 50
Frank Viola, '88 Cy Young, 1988, 15,000 32
Omar Vizquel WS Photo/Coin Set, 1997, 1,997 50
Larry Walker MVP Photo/Coin Set, 1997, 500 50
Larry Walker 24K Bronze MVP, 1997, 1,000 35
Jerome Walton '89 NL ROY, 1990, 900 55
John Wetteland Silver/WS MVP, 1996, 500 30
John Wetteland 24K/WS MVP, 1996, 196 50
John Wetteland WS MVP 3-pc. Proof Set, 1996, 96 125
Devon White WS Photo/Coin Set 1997, 1,997 45
Bernie Williams Silver/WS Reverse, 1996, 500 30
Bernie Williams 24K/WS, 1996, 196 50
Bernie Williams WS 3-pc. Proof Set, 1996, 96 125
Bernie Williams Photo/Coin Set, 1997, 500 40
Billy Williams 1987 HOF, 1991, 15,000 35
Matt Williams Silver, 1995, 1,500 40
Matt Williams 24K, 1995, 125 65
Matt Williams Bronze 1995, 500 22
Matt Williams Silver/All-Star 1996, 1,995 30
Matt Williams 24K/All-Star 1996, 500 50
Matt Williams Bronze/All-Star, 1996, 1,995 20
Matt Williams, All-Star 3-pc. Proof Set, 1996, 95 125
Matt Williams, AL Photo/Coin Set, 1997, 500 50
Matt Williams WS Photo/Coin Set, 1997, 1,997 50
Dave Winfield 1992, 389 60
Dave Winfield Twins, 1993, 14,611 40
Dave Winfield Silver, 1995, 1,995 40
Dave Winfield 24K, 1995, 500 60
Dave Winfield Bronze 1995, 1,995 20
Dave Winfield 3-pc. Proof Set, 1995, 95 130
Bobby Witt AL Photo/Coin Set 1997, 500 45
Mark Wohlers NL Photo/Coin Set 1997, 500 45
Jaret Wright WS Photo/Coin Set, 1997, 500 50

Robin Yount

Robin Yount 1989 MVP, 1990, 2,387 50
Robin Yount 3,000th Hit, 1992, 12,632 35

Team Commemorative Coins

Arizona Diamondbacks Silver, 1998, 5,000. . . . . $30
Arizona Diamondbacks 24K, 1998, 500 50
Arizona Diamondbacks Silver Inaugural, 1998, 1,998 40
Arizona Diamondbacks 24K Inaugural, 1998, 500 50
Arizona Diamondbacks Inaugural 1998 3-pc. Proof Set, 1998, 198
. . . . 125
New Arlington Stadium Silver, 1995, 5,000 40
New Arlington Stadium 24K, 1995, 500 60
New Arlington Stadium Gold, 1995, 100 850
Old Arlington Stadium Silver, 1995, 5000 40
Old Arlington Stadium 24K, 1995, 500. 60
Old/New Arlington Stadium 1995, 1,000 85
Old/New Arlington Stadium 2-pc. Silver Set , 1993, 1,000 75
Old/New Arlington Stadium 2-pc. 24K Set, 1995, 100 135
Atlanta Braves Silver Generic Coin, 1995, 1,000 30
Baltimore Orioles Silver Generic Coin, 1995, 1,000 30
Baltimore Orioles Silver/AL Wild Card, 1996, 1,996 30
Baltimore Orioles 24K/AL Wild Card, 1996, 500 50
Baltimore Orioles AL Wild Card, 1996, 196 125
Camden Yards/Orioles Silver, 1996, 1,000 30
Chicago Cubs Silver Generic Coin, 1991, 1,500 50
Chicago Cubs 24K/1984 Division Heir, 1990, 1,500 50
Chicago Cubs 24K/1989 Division Heir, 1990, 1,500 50
Chicago Cubs Silver/Wrigley Field, 1988, 39,012 30
First Night Game Chicago Cubs 24K/Wrigley Field, 1,500 60
Chicago Cubs/Wrigley 75th Anniversary 1990, 10,000 40
Chicago White Sox Silver Generic Coin, 1995, 1,000 45
Cleveland Indians Stadium Gold 1995, 61 850
Cleveland Indians/Eddie Murray 1995, 400 85
Cleveland Indians/Eddie Murray, 2-pc. Silver Set 1995, 100 135
Cleveland Indians 2-pc. 24K Set, 1,000 30
Cleveland Indians Silver Generic Coin, 1995, 1,000 30
Cleveland Indians Silver, 1995, 1,000 60
Cleveland Indians 24K, 1995, 196 85
Cleveland Indians Back-to-Back 2-pc. Set, 1996, 10,000 40
Colorado Rockies Franchise, 1991, 10,000 40
Colorado Rockies Inaugural, 1993, 5,000. 30
Colorado Rockies Silver/Record Attendance 1995, 5,000 40
Colorado Rockies Silver/1995 Wildcard, 1,995 60
Colorado Rockies 24K/1995 Wildcard, 1995, 500 20
Colorado Rockies Bronze/'95 Wildcard, 1995, 95 130
Colorado Rockies 3-pc. Proof Set, 680 75
Comiskey Park 75th Anniversary, 1985, 43,931 35
Old/New Comiskey Park, 1990, 195 185
Coors Field Silver 2-pc. Card/Coin Set, 1995 125
Coors Field 24K 2-pc. Card/Coin Set, 1995, 95 50
Coors Field Inaugural Silver, 1995, 1,999 75
Coors Field Inaugural Gold, 1995 850
Florida Marlins Franchise, 1991, 10,000. 40
Florida Marlins Inaugural, 1993, 10,000. 40
Florida Marlins Silver/Wild Card, 1,997 40
Florida Marlins 24K/Wild Card, 1997, 197 139

Florida Marlins Wild Card 3-pc. Proof Set, 1997, 500 400
Florida Marlins 10pc. Framed Set, 1997, 1,000 30
Houston Astros Silver Generic Coin, 1995, 5,000 40
Interleague Play Silver/Yankees-Mets, 1997,
Interleague Play 24K/Yankees-Mets, (Yankees side) 1,997 60
Interleague Play/Yankees-Mets 3-pc.Set, 1997, 500 125
(Yankees side) Interleague Play/Yankees-Mets 24K, 1997, (Mets side),
1,997 60
Interleague Play/Yankees-Mets 1997, 3-pc. Set (Mets side), 500 . . 125
Interleague Play Silver/Cubs-White Sox, 1997, 5,000 40
Interleague Play 24K/Cubs-White Sox, 1997, Cubs side), 1,997 60
Interleague Play Cubs-White Sox, 1997, 3-pc. Set (Cubs side), 500
. . . . 125
Interleague Play 24K Cubs-White Sox, 1997, (White Sox side), 1,997
. . . . 60
Interleague Play Cubs/White Sox, 1997, 3-pc. Set
(White Sox side), 500 125
Kansas City Royals 25th Anniversary, 1993, 5,000 40
Kansas City Royals Silver Generic Coin 1995, 1,000 30
Los Angeles Dodgers 100th Anniversary 1990, 5,000 65
Los Angeles Silver Generic Coin, 1995, 1,000 30
Los Angeles Dodgers Silver/Rookies, 1995, 1,995 40
Los Angeles Dodgers 24K/Rookies 1995, 500 60
Los Angeles Dodgers Bronze/Rookies, 1995, 1,995 20
Los Angeles Dodgers Rookies, 1995, 3-pc. Proof Set, 95 130
Los Angeles Dodgers Silver/Wild Card, 1996, 1,996 40
Los Angeles Dodgers 24K/Wild Card, 1996, 500 60
Los Angeles Dodgers Wild Card, 1996, 3-pc. Proof Set, 1,996 125
Montreal Expos 25th Anniversary, 1993, 5,000 45
Montreal Expos Silver Generic Coin, 1995, 1,000 30
Milwaukee Brewers Silver Generic Coin, 1995, 1,000 30
Milwaukee Brewers Silver/25th Anniversary, 1995, 5,000 30
Milwaukee Brewers 24K/25th Anniversary, 1995, 1,000 50
Minnesota Twins Silver Generic Coin, 1995, 1,000 30
New York Yankees Silver/Wildcard, 1995, 5,000 40
New York Yankees 24K/Wildcard, 1995, 1,995 60
New York Yankees Bronze/Wildcard 1995, 500 20
New York Yankees Wildcard, 1995, 3-pc. Proof Set, 95 130
New York Yankees Silver/Wildcard, 1997, 1,997 35
New York Yankees 24K/Wildcard 1997, 500 50
New York Yankees Wild Card, 1997, 3-pc. Proof Set, 1,997 125
Philadelphia Phillies Silver Generic Coin, 1995, 1,000 30
Rookies Mark McGwire/Jose Canseco, 1990, 15,000 65
Seattle Mariners Silver Generic Coin, 1995, 1,000 30
St. Louis Cardinals 100th Anniversary, 1992, 5,000 50
Tampa Bay Devil Rays Silver/Inaugural, 1998, 1,998 38
Tampa Bay Devil Rays 24K/Inaugural, 1998, 500 50
Tampa Bay Devil Rays Inaugural, 1998, 3-pc. Proof Set, 198 125
Texas Rangers Silver Generic Coin 1995, 1,000 30
Toronto Blue Jays Alomar/Carter/White, 1992, 15,000 45
Toronto Blue Jays Back-to-Back 2-pc. Set, 1993, 400 175
World Series 3-Pc. set, 1992, 500 290
World Series 3-Pc. set, 1993, 500 255

HIGHLAND MINT

LIMITED-EDITION TRADING CARDS

In 1992, Highland Mint issued reproductions of popular trading cards in bronze and silver. The cards are etched in remarkable detail to look exactly like the player's rookie card and recent-year issues. The cards retailed for $50 (bronze) and $235 (silver), but the prices didn't stay that low for long. Cards that sold out of the bronze and silver editions were reproduced in an extremely limited gold edition that retailed for $500 and also quickly grew in value.

The original license allowed for the reproduction only of Topps cards. In 1994, Pinnacle got into the mix, and in 1995, Highland Mint replicated an Upper Deck card of Michael Jordan playing baseball. This Jordan card was Highland Mint's last card release, as collector demand shifted to the company's less expensive line of coins.

In 1995, Highland Mint experimented with mini-cards, releasing a Cal Ripken Jr. and Lou Gehrig double mini-set to coincide with the consecutive game record held by Gehrig and about to be broken by Ripken. The set went over so well that four other pairings were introduced, including Greg Maddux and Cy Young, commemorating Maddux's fourth straight Cy Young Award.

MEDALLIONS

In 1994, Highland Mint built on the success of its limited edition cards with a line of sports medallions. The concept was the same, in that the company started with bronze and silver editions and didn't offer gold until later. The bronze mintage was 25,000 with a retail price of $9.99, while silver's numbers were 5,000 and $19.95. The gold line of the Gold Signature Series—featured silver coins with gold overlays of the featured players. Mintage was 1,500 of each, retailing for $49.95. All three of these products came encased in hard plastic capsules in velvet-lined jewelery boxes.

At the outset, the coins were red hot—medallion prices were rising within weeks of release. To further capitalize on the popularity, Highland Mint started offering collectors something different: jumbo medallions. The Magnum Series kicked off with Cal Ripken Jr. and Ken Griffey Jr., each depicted on bronze and silver medallions 2.5 inches in diameter—more than twice the size of the regular medallions. Each coin was packaged in a velvet box that opened like a book. Mintage was 3,500 bronze ($35 retail) and 750 silver ($150 retail). Like the cards, when bronze and silver sold out, gold versions were introduced (375 mintage, $250 apiece).

In 1997, Highland Mint showered the market with several new series, most in response to the success of these in other sports. Sets of two and three medallions encased in one box were issued. Bronze medallions with matching phone cards were introduced late in '97. The most popular of the new issues was the Elite Series. Griffey led the charge for these 44-millimeter medallions, issued in bronze (5,000 mintage), silver (2,500), and gold signature versions (1,000). Retail prices were $20, $40, and $80, respectively. As a bonus, 500 of the bronze medallions were replaced with gold-plated coins. Secondary market values have risen to the same level as the gold signature versions.

The player selection for all the series is stocked with baseball's big boys, the hottest rookies, and some of the biggest names from the past. The coins were individually numbered. Each of the medallions and sets comes with a numbered certificate of authenticity, matching the number on the coin(s).

PHOTO-MINTS

In 1999, The Highland Mint introduced a new line of collectibles entitled Photo Mints. These pieces usually consisted of a color photo of an individual player (sometimes autographed), a medallion describing some of his career accomplishments, and a piece of game-used memorabilia relating to the athlete. All three items were contained within a framed and matted setting.

Highland Mint Cards

Pinnacle

Bronze

Yr	Player	NM
'94	Bagwell, J. (2,500)	$75
'94	Maddux, G. (2,500)	80
'94	Mantle, M. (5,000)	180
'94	Ryan, N. (5,000)	175

Silver

Yr	Player	NM
'94	Bagwell, J. (750)	250
'94	Maddux, G. (750)	300
'94	Mantle, M. (1,000)	800
'94	Ryan, N. (1,000)	600

Gold

Yr	Player	NM
'94	Mantle, M. (500)	1,300
'94	Ryan, N. (500)	1,200

Topps

Bronze

Yr	Player	NM
'92	Alomar, R. (928)	80
'94	Banks, E. (920)	75
'94	Bench, J. (1,384)	80
'92	Bonds, B. (2,677)	100
'92	Brett, G. (3,560)	90
'92	Clark, W. (1,044)	80
'92	Clemens, R. (1,789)	90
'92	Gonzalez, J. (1,899)	90
'92	Griffey Jr., K. (5,000)	150
'94	Justice, D. (1,396)	75
'92	Mattingly, D. (1,550)	80
'94	Molitor, P. (639)	125
'93	Piazza, M. (2,500)	80
'92	Puckett, K. (1,723)	125
'92	Ripken, C. (4,065)	225
'92	Robinson, B. (2,043)	75

Barry Bonds

Yr	Player	NM
'92	Ryan, N. (5,000)	250
'94	Salmon, T. (768)	80
'92	Sandberg, R. (1,932)	80
'94	Sanders, D. (668)	55
'94	Schmidt, M. (1,641)	75
'92	Smith, O. (1,088)	100
'92	Thomas, F. (5,000)	125
'92	Winfield, D. (1,216)	75
'94	Yastrzemski, C. (1,072)	75
'92	Yount, R. (1.564)	80

Bronze Autograph

'92	Robinson, B. (350)	150

Silver

'92	Alomar, R. (214)	325
'94	Banks, E. (437)	350
'94	Bench, J. (500)	400
'92	Bonds, B. (596)	400
'92	Brett, G. (999)	325
'92	Clark, W. (150)	450
'92	Clemens, R. (432)	350
'92	Gonzalez, J. (365)	300
'92	Griffey Jr., K. (1,000)	600
'94	Justice, D. (265)	300

Yr	Player	NM
'92	Mattingly, D. (414)	350
'94	Molitor, P. (260)	350
'93	Piazza, M. (750)	450
'92	Puckett, K. (359)	500
'92	Ripken, C. (1,000)	800
'92	Robinson, B. (796)	350
'92	Ryan, N. (999)	1,200
'94	Salmon, T. (264)	300
'92	Sandberg, R. (430)	325
'94	Sanders, D. (187)	250
'94	Schmidt, M. (500)	350
'92	Smith, O. (211)	400
'92	Thomas, F. (1,000)	600
'92	Winfield, D. (266)	325
'94	Yastrzemski, C. (500)	300
'92	Yount, R. (349)	300

Silver Autograph

'92	Robinson, B. (150)	400

Gold

'92	Griffey Jr., K. (500)	1,300
'93	Piazza, M. (374)	1,000
'92	Thomas, F. (500)	1,200

Mini-Cards

Bronze

Yr	Player	NM
'96	Griffey/Thomas (5,000)	100
'96	Johnson/Ryan (2,500)	85
'96	Maddux/Young (2,500)	85
'96	Piazza/Campaneris (2,500)	75
'95	Ripken/Gehrig (2,500)	180

Silver

'96	Griffey/Thomas (1,000)	200
'96	Johnson/Ryan (500)	175
'96	Maddux/Young (500)	175
'96	Piazza/Campaneris (500)	175
'95	Ripken/Gehrig (500)	400

Gold

'96	Griffey/Thomas (500)	300
'95	Ripken/Gehrig (375)	700

Highland Mint Medallions

Bronze

Yr	Player Mintage	NM
'96	Bagwell, J. (25,000)	$15
'98	Garciaparra, N. (15,000)	20
'94	Griffey Jr., K. (25,000)	40
'98	Griffey Jr., K. .5lb (2,500)	60
'98	Griffey Jr., K. (15,000)	25
'97	Jeter, D. (25,000)	20
'96	Jones, C. (25,000)	20
'94	Maddux, G. (25,000)	18
'97	Mantle, M. (25,000)	30

Yr	Player Mintage	NM
'94	Mattingly, D. (25,000)	22
'98	McGwire, M. .5lb (2,500)	60
'98	McGwire, M. (25,000)	20
'99	McGwire, M. (3-pc. 2,500)	75
'99	McGwire, M. 500 HR (10,000)	20
'94	Piazza, M. (25,000)	18
'94	Ripken, C. (25,000)	20
'96	Ripken, C. (15,000)	20
'99	Ripken, C. .5lb. (1,500)	60
'96	Rodriguez, A. (25,000)	20
'94	Thomas, F. (25,000)	18

Will Clark

Silver

Yr	Player Mintage	NM
'96	Alomar, R. (5,000)	30
'94	Bagwell, J. (5,000)	30
'95	Belle, A. (5,000)	25
'94	Boggs, W. (5,000)	25
'99	Boggs, W. 3000 hit (5,000)	30
'94	Bonds, B. (5,000)	30
'95	Canseco, J. (5,000)	25
'95	Clark, W. (5,000)	20
'94	Clemens, R. (5,000)	40
'99	Drew, J.D. (1,999)	30
'96	Fielder, C. (5.000)	20
'98	Gonzalez, J. (5,000)	30
'94	Griffey Jr., K. (5,000)	55
'98	Griffey Jr., K. .5lb (1,500)	170
'95	Gwynn, T. (5,000)	25
'97	Irabu, H. (5.000)	25
'96	Jeter, D. (5,000)	45
'97	Jones, A. (5.000)	30
'95	Jones, C. (5.000)	45
'94	Maddux, G. (5,000)	40
'94	Mattingly, D. (5,000)	50
'97	McGwire, M. (5.000)	50
'98	McGwire, M. .5lb (1,500)	150
'98	McGwire, M. 70 HRs (7,500)	50
'99	McGwire, M. (3-pc. 1,500)	130
'99	McGwire, M. 500 HR (5,000)	40
'97	Mondesi, R. (5,000)	30
'96	Murray, E. (5,000)	35
'95	Nomo, H. (5,000)	30
'94	Piazza, M. (5,000)	40
'95	Puckett, K. (5,000)	35
'94	Ripken, C. (5,000)	75
'96	Rodriguez, A. (5,000)	40
'98	Ruth, B. (5,000)	40
'96	Sandberg, R. (5,000)	35

Yr	Player Mintage	NM
'95	Smith, O. (5,000)	30
'98	Sosa, S. (5,000)	40
'94	Thomas, F. (5,000)	35
'96	Vaughn, M. (5,000)	20

Gold

'99	McGwire, M. (3-pc. 500)	225

Ken Griffey Jr.

Gold Signature

'99	Boggs, W. 3,000 hit (1,000)	50
'95	Bonds, B. (1,500)	85
'95	Griffey Jr., K. (1,500)	125
'96	Jeter, D. (1,500)	85
'96	Jones, C. (1,500)	85
'95	Maddux, G. (1,500)	90
'98	McGwire, M. (1,273)	125
'98	McGwire, M. Err (227)	125
'98	McGwire, M. .5lb (500)	250
'99	McGwire, M. 500 HR (1,000)	70
'95	Nomo, H. (1,500)	50
'96	Piazza, M. (1,500)	100
'96	Puckett, K. (1,500)	70
'95	Ripken, C. (1,500)	125
'96	Rodriguez, A. (1,500)	80
'98	Sosa, S. (1,500)	75
'95	Thomas, F. (1,500)	85

Proof Set

'99	McGwire, M. (9-pc. 250)	550

Elite Series

	Bronze	
Yr	**Player**	**NM**
'97	Griffey Jr., K. (4,500)	40
'97	Jones, C. (4,500)	25

Yr	Player	NM
'98	Mantle, M. (4,500)	55
'97	Ripken, C. (4,500)	35
'97	Rodriguez, A. (4,500)	30
'97	Thomas, F. (4,500)	30

Frank Thomas

Silver

Yr	Player	NM
'97	Griffey Jr., K. (2,500)	60
'97	Jones, C. (2,500)	40
'98	Mantle, M. (2,500)	65
'97	Ripken, C. (2,500)	65
'97	Rodriguez, A. (2,500)	40
'97	Thomas, F. (2,500)	40

Gold Signature

Yr	Player	NM
'97	Griffey Jr., K. (1,000)	120
'97	Jones, C. (1,000)	80
'98	Mantle, M. (1,000)	130
'97	Ripken, C. (1,000)	120
'97	Rodriguez, A. (1,000)	80
'97	Thomas, F. (1,000)	75

Gold Plated Random Inserts

Yr	Player	NM
'97	Griffey Jr., K. (500)	200
'97	Jones, C. (500)	160
'97	Ripken, C. (500)	250
'97	Rodriguez, A. (500)	130
'97	Thomas, F. (500)	100

Proof Sets

Yr	Player	NM
'97	Griffey Jr., K. (350)	350
'97	Jones, C. (350)	170
'98	Mantle, M. (350)	200
'97	Ripken, C. (350)	250
'97	Rodriguez, A. (350)	175
'97	Thomas, F. (350)	150

Magnum

Bronze

Yr	Player	NM
'96	Griffey Jr., K. (5,000)	100
'96	Mantle, M. (3,500)	110
'96	Ripken, C. (3,000)	120

Yr	Player	NM
'97	Rodriguez, A. (3,000)	65
'96	Ruth, B. (3,500)	80
'96	Ryan, N. (3,500)	75
'97	Thomas, F. (3,000)	60

Silver

Yr	Player	NM
'96	Griffey Jr., K. (750)	200
'96	Ripken, C. (750)	200
'99	Ripken, C. .5lb. (500)	130
'97	Rodriguez, A. (750)	150
'96	Ruth, B. (750)	150
'96	Ryan, N. (750)	175
'97	Thomas, F. (750)	140

Gold

Yr	Player	NM
'96	Griffey Jr., K. (375)	350
'96	Ripken, C. (375)	350
'96	Ruth, B. (375)	200
'98	Ryan, N. (375)	300
'97	Mantle, M. (375)	400

Mickey Mantle

Magnum/Motion Set

Yr	Player	NM
'96	Ruth, B. (1,000)	130

MOTION MINTS

Bronze

Yr	Player	NM
'98	Mantle, M. 500 HR (2,500)	100

Nickel

Yr	Player	NM
'98	Mantle, M. #6 (2,500)	120
'99	McGwire, M. 62 HR (1,000)	75
'99	McGwire, M. 70 HR (1,500)	750

Gold

Yr	Player	NM
'99	McGwire, M. 62 HR (500)	150
'99	McGwire, M. 70 HR (500)	120

PHOTO-MINTS

Yr	Player	NM
'99	Griffey Jr., K. (w/piece of glove)	160
'99	McGwire, M. (w/piece of bat)	160
'99	Clemente, R. (w/piece of jersey)	160
'99	Griffey Jr., K. (2,500)	75
'99	Garciaparra, N. (2,500)	75
'99	Jeter, D. (2,500)	75
'99	McGwire, M. (2,500)	100
'99	Sosa, S. (2,500)	80
'99	Sosa/McGwire 2 Coins (2,500)	100
'99	Mantle, M. (2,500)	80
'99	Ryan, N. (2,500)	70
'99	Yankees WS (2,500)	80
	Musial auto	100
	Ruth, B.	200
	Ty Cobb	200
	Joe DiMaggio w/bat	200
	Derek Jeter w/bat	150
	Dave Winfield w/bat (525)	75
	Dave Winfield autographed (200)	160
01	Jimmie Foxx w/bat (250)	120

Rare Metal

Silver

Yr	Player	NM
'98	Griffey Jr., K. (2,500)	40
'98	Ripken, C. (2,500)	35

Signature Series

Yr	Player	NM
'99	Griffey Jr., K. (1,000)	60

Sculpt Monu-Mint

Bronze

Yr	Player	NM
'98	Mantle, M. (536)	400
'99	McGwire, M. (500)	350
'98	Ripken, C. (250)	350
'99	Ryan, N. (324)	300

Silver

Yr	Player	NM
'98	Mantle, M. (18)	550
'99	McGwire, M. (70)	500
'99	Ryan, N. (27)	600

Team 2000

Yr	Player	NM
'99	Griffey Jr., K. (2,000)	40
'99	Jeter, D. (2,000)	40
'99	Rodriguez, A. (2,000)	35

Medallion Sets

Litho-Mints

Yr	Player	NM
'98	Griffey, K. (2,500)	90
'98	Gwynn, T. (2,500)	90

Yr	Player	NM
'98	Jeter, D. (2,500)	70
'98	Jones, C. (2,500)	70
'98	Maddux, G. (2,500)	70
'98	McGwire, M. (2,500)	150
'98	Piazza, M. (2,500)	70
'98	Ripken, C. (2,500)	80
'98	Rodriguez, A. (2,500)	70
'98	Thomas, F. (2,500)	50

Silver Motion Mints

Yr	Player	NM
'98	Mantle, M. (2,500)	80
'99	McGwire, M. 70th HR (2,500)	50

Gold Motion Mints

Yr	Player	NM
'99	McGwire, M. 70th HR (500)	80

Tele-Mints

Yr	Player	NM
'97	Griffey, K. (1,743)	60
'97	Jeter, D. (748)	45
'97	Jones, C. (748)	40
'97	Maddux, G. (490)	45
'97	Piazza, M. (494)	40
'97	Ripken, C. (1,445)	50
'97	Rodriguez, A. (669)	45
'97	Thomas, F. (493)	35

Ring and coin set

Yr	Player	NM
'98	Clemens, R. (2,500)	60
'99	Garciaparra, N. (2,500)	65
'98	Griffey, K. (2,500)	70
'98	Jeter, D. (2,500)	70
'98	Jones, C. (2,500)	60
'98	McGwire, M. (2,500)	90
'98	Piazza, M. (2,500)	60
'98	Ripken, C. (2,500)	70
'98	Rodriguez, A. (2,500)	65
'98	Sosa, S. (500)	65

SETS

Bronze/Silver Set

Yr	Player	NM
'98	Griffey Jr., K. .5lb (250)	200
'98	McGwire, M. .5lb (250)	225

Bronze/Silver/Gold Set

Yr	Player	NM
'98	McGwire, M. (500)	130

Bronze

Yr	Player	NM
'99	Atlanta Braves Cy Young (2,500) (Glavine/Maddux/Smoltz)	40
'98	Chicago Connection (1,500) (Sosa/Wood)	35
'97	Pacific Power (2,500) (Rodriguez/Johnson/Griffey)	40
'97	Pinstripe Heroes (2,500) (Mattingly/Mantle/Jeter)	70
'97	Southern Pride (2,500) (C. Jones/A. Jones/Maddux)	40

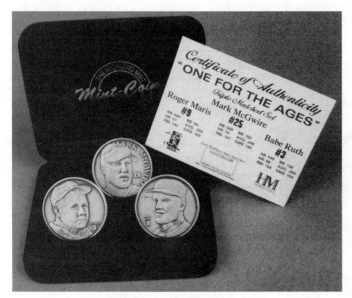

McGwire, Ruth, Maris

Silver

Yr	Player	NM
'99	Atlanta Braves Cy Young (250)	
	(Glavine/Maddux/Smoltz)	130
'99	Chicago Connection (500)	
	(Sosa/Wood)	70

Gold

Yr	Player	NM
'99	Chicago Connection (250)	
	(Sosa/Wood)	130

Bronze

'97	Belle/Thomas (2,500)	25
'97	Griffey/Thomas (2,500)	50
'97	Young Guns (2,500)	
	(Jeter/Jones/Rodriguez)	45

Silver

'97	Home Run Heroes (1,000)	
	(McGwire/Griffey)	100
'98	McGwire/Maris (2,500)	75
'98	One for the Ages Nickel	
	McGwire/Maris/Ruth (5,000)	100
'98	Sosa/Maris (2,500)	65

Gold

'98	McGwire/Maris (250)	175
'98	Sosa/Maris (250)	125

Gold Magnum

'99	Pure Power Cubed (100)	
	Ruth/Mantle/McGwire	300

TOPPS

1984 Topps Gallery of Immortals

The Gallery of Immortals bronze and silver replicas were the first metal miniature set from Topps and the start of an annual tradition (in 1985, the name was changed to Gallery of Champions). Each mini is an exact one-quarter scale replica of the featured player's 1984 Topps baseball card, both front and back, in minute detail. The three-dimensional metal cards were packaged in a velvet-lined case that bears the title of the set in gold-embossed let-

ters. A certificate of authenticity is included with each set. A Tom Seaver pewter metal mini-card was given as a premium to dealers who purchased sets. A Darryl Strawberry bronze was given as a premium to dealers who purchased cases of the 1984 Topps Traded sets. Issue price was about $100 for the cased bronze set, $500 for the silver edition of 1,000.

Complete Bronze Set (12):		**$100.00**	**$75.00**	(7b)	Joe Morgan(bronze)	5.00	3.75
Complete Silver Set (12):		**300.00**	**225.00**	(7s)	Joe Morgan(silver)	15.00	11.00
(1b)	George Brett(bronze)	12.50	9.50	(8b)	Jim Palmer(bronze)	5.00	3.75
(1s)	George Brett(silver)	40.00	30.00	(8s)	Jim Palmer(silver)	15.00	11.00
(2b)	Rod Carew(bronze)	7.50	5.75	(9b)	Pete Rose(bronze)	12.50	9.50
(2s)	Rod Carew(silver)	22.00	16.50	(9s)	Pete Rose(silver)	50.00	37.00
(3b)	Steve Carlton(bronze)	7.50	5.75	(10b)	Nolan Ryan(bronze)	40.00	30.00
(3s)	Steve Carlton(silver)	22.00	16.50	(10s)	Nolan Ryan(silver)	110.00	82.00
(4b)	Rollie Fingers(bronze)	5.00	3.75	(11b)	Mike Schmidt(bronze)	12.50	9.50
(4s)	Rollie Fingers(silver)	15.00	11.00	(11s)	Mike Schmidt(silver)	40.00	30.00
(5b)	Steve Garvey(bronze)	5.00	3.75	(12b)	Tom Seaver(bronze)	7.50	5.75
(5s)	Steve Garvey(silver)	15.00	11.00	(12s)	Tom Seaver(silver)	22.00	16.50
(6b)	Reggie Jackson(bronze)	9.00	6.75	(12p)	Tom Seaver(pewter)	22.00	16.50
(6s)	Reggie Jackson(silver)	25.00	18.50	(13)	Darryl Strawberry(bronze)	5.00	3.75

1985 Topps Gallery of Champions

This second annual metallic miniatures issue honors 12 award winners from the previous season (MVP, Cy Young, Rookie of Year, Fireman, etc.). Each mini is an exact reproduction at one-quarter scale of the player's 1985 Topps card, both front and back. The sets (editions of 1,000) were issued in a specially-designed velvet-like

case. A Dwight Gooden pewter replica was given as a premium to dealers who bought the sets. A Pete Rose bronze was issued as a premium to dealers purchasing cases of 1985 Topps Traded sets. Earlier listings of an aluminum version of the Gallery of Champions set were in error.

Complete Bronze Set (12):		**$135.00**	**$100.00**	(3p)	Dwight Gooden(pewter)	20.00	15.00
Complete Silver Set (12):		**325.00**	**245.00**	(4b)	Tony Gwynn(bronze)	40.00	30.00
(1b)	Tony Armas(bronze)	5.00	3.75	(4s)	Tony Gwynn(silver)	75.00	56.00
(1s)	Tony Armas(silver)	12.50	9.50	(5b)	Willie Hernandez(bronze)	5.00	3.75
(2b)	Alvin Davis(bronze)	5.00	3.75	(5s)	Willie Hernandez(silver)	12.50	9.50
(2s)	Alvin Davis(silver)	12.50	9.50	(6b)	Don Mattingly(bronze)	30.00	22.00
(3b)	Dwight Gooden(bronze)	10.00	7.50	(6s)	Don Mattingly(silver)	85.00	64.00
(3s)	Dwight Gooden(silver)	25.00	18.50	(7b)	Dale Murphy(bronze)	20.00	15.00

(7s)	Dale Murphy(silver)	50.00	37.00	(10s)	Mike Schmidt(silver)	55.00	41.00
(8b)	Dan Quisenberry(bronze)	5.00	3.75	(11b)	Rick Sutcliffe(bronze)	5.00	3.75
(8s)	Dan Quisenberry(silver)	12.50	9.50	(11s)	Rick Sutcliffe(silver)	12.50	9.50
(9b)	Ryne Sandberg(bronze)	20.00	15.00	(12b)	Bruce Sutter(bronze)	5.00	3.75
(9s)	Ryne Sandberg(silver)	50.00	37.00	(12s)	Bruce Sutter(silver)	12.50	9.50
(10b)	Mike Schmidt(bronze)	25.00	18.50	(13)	Pete Rose(bronze)	15.00	11.00

1986 Topps Gallery of Champions

For the third consecutive year Topps issued 12 metal "mini cards," adding an aluminum version to the bronze and silver. The metal replicas were minted 1/4-size (approximately 1 1/4" x 1 3/4") of the regular cards. The bronze and silver sets were issued in leather-like velvet-lined display cases, the aluminum in individual cello packs. A bronze 1952 Topps Mickey Mantle was given as a premium for dealers purchasing 1986 Traded sets, while a pewter Don Mattingly was issued as a premium to those ordering the sets.

Complete Aluminum Set:		**$45.00**	**$34.00**	(6p)	Don Mattingly(pewter)	60.00	45.00
Complete Bronze Set:		**135.00**	**100.00**	(7a)	Willie McGee(aluminum)	2.50	2.00
Complete Silver Set:		**300.00**	**225.00**	(7b)	Willie McGee(bronze)	7.50	5.75
(1a)	Wade Boggs(aluminum)	5.00	3.75	(7s)	Willie McGee(silver)	15.00	11.00
(1b)	Wade Boggs(bronze)	17.50	13.00	(8a)	Dale Murphy(aluminum)	5.00	3.75
(1s)	Wade Boggs(silver)	35.00	26.00	(8b)	Dale Murphy(bronze)	17.50	13.00
(2a)	Vince Coleman(aluminum)	2.50	2.00	(8s)	Dale Murphy(silver)	35.00	26.00
(2b)	Vince Coleman(bronze)	7.50	5.75	(9a)	Dan Quisenberry(aluminum)	2.50	2.00
(2s)	Vince Coleman(silver)	15.00	11.00	(9b)	Dan Quisenberry(bronze)	7.50	5.75
(3a)	Darrell Evans(aluminum)	2.50	2.00	(9s)	Dan Quisenberry(silver)	15.00	11.00
(3b)	Darrell Evans(bronze)	7.50	5.75	(10a)	Jeff Reardon(aluminum)	2.50	2.00
(3s)	Darrell Evans(silver)	15.00	11.00	(10b)	Jeff Reardon(bronze)	7.50	5.75
(4a)	Dwight Gooden(aluminum)	2.50	2.00	(10s)	Jeff Reardon(silver)	15.00	11.00
(4b)	Dwight Gooden(bronze)	7.50	5.75	(11a)	Pete Rose(aluminum)	12.50	9.50
(4s)	Dwight Gooden(silver)	15.00	11.00	(11b)	Pete Rose(bronze)	37.00	28.00
(5a)	Ozzie Guillen(aluminum)	2.50	2.00	(11s)	Pete Rose(silver)	100.00	75.00
(5b)	Ozzie Guillen(bronze)	7.50	5.75	(12a)	Bret Saberhagen(aluminum)	2.50	2.00
(5s)	Ozzie Guillen(silver)	15.00	11.00	(12b)	Bret Saberhagen(bronze)	7.50	5.75
(6a)	Don Mattingly(aluminum)	10.00	7.50	(12s)	Bret Saberhagen(silver)	15.00	11.00
(6b)	Don Mattingly(bronze)	35.00	26.00	(13)	Mickey Mantle(1952, bronze)	20.00	15.00
(6s)	Don Mattingly(silver)	75.00	56.00				

1987 Topps Gallery of Champions

Designed as a tribute to 1986's winners of baseball's most prestigious awards, the Gallery of Champions are metal "cards" that are one-quarter size replicas of the regular issue Topps cards. The bronze and silver sets were issued in leather-like velvet-lined display cases; the aluminum sets came cello-wrapped. Hobby dealers who purchased one bronze set or a 16-set case of aluminum "cards" received one free Jose Canseco pewter metal mini-card. The purchase of a silver set included five Canseco pewters. A 1953 Willie Mays bronze was given to dealers who bought cases of 1987 Topps Traded sets.

Complete Aluminum Set (12):		$20.00	$10.00
Complete Bronze Set (12):		125.00	94.00
Complete Silver Set (12):		250.00	185.00
(1a)	Jesse Barfield(aluminum)	2.00	1.50
(1b)	Jesse Barfield(bronze)	7.50	5.75
(1s)	Jesse Barfield(silver)	15.00	11.00
(2a)	Wade Boggs(aluminum)	4.00	3.00
(2b)	Wade Boggs(bronze)	15.00	11.00
(2s)	Wade Boggs(silver)	30.00	22.00
(3a)	Jose Canseco(aluminum)	4.00	3.00
(3b)	Jose Canseco(bronze)	15.00	11.00
(3s)	Jose Canseco(silver)	30.00	22.00
(3p)	Jose Canseco(pewter)	15.00	11.00
(4a)	Joe Carter(aluminum)	2.00	1.50
(4b)	Joe Carter(bronze)	8.75	6.50
(4s)	Joe Carter(silver)	17.50	13.00
(5a)	Roger Clemens(aluminum)	6.00	4.50
(5b)	Roger Clemens(bronze)	17.50	13.00
(5s)	Roger Clemens(silver)	37.00	28.00
(6a)	Tony Gwynn(aluminum)	6.00	4.50
(6b)	Tony Gwynn(bronze)	17.50	13.00
(6s)	Tony Gwynn(silver)	37.00	28.00
(7a)	Don Mattingly(aluminum)	7.50	5.75
(7b)	Don Mattingly(bronze)	25.00	18.50
(7s)	Don Mattingly(silver)	75.00	56.00
(8a)	Tim Raines(aluminum)	2.00	1.50
(8b)	Tim Raines(bronze)	7.50	5.75
(8s)	Tim Raines(silver)	15.00	11.00
(9a)	Dave Righetti(aluminum)	2.00	1.50
(9b)	Dave Righetti(bronze)	7.50	5.75
(9s)	Dave Righetti(silver)	15.00	11.00
(10a)	Mike Schmidt(aluminum)	6.00	4.50
(10b)	Mike Schmidt(bronze)	20.00	15.00
(10s)	Mike Schmidt(silver)	50.00	37.00
(11a)	Mike Scott(aluminum)	2.00	1.50
(11b)	Mike Scott(bronze)	7.50	5.75
(11s)	Mike Scott(silver)	15.00	11.00
(12a)	Todd Worrell(aluminum)	2.00	1.50
(12b)	Todd Worrell(bronze)	7.50	5.75
(12s)	Todd Worrell(silver)	15.00	11.00
(13)	Willie Mays(1953, bronze)	12.50	9.50

1988 Topps Gallery of Champions

These metal replicas are exact reproductions at one-quarter scale of Topps 1988 cards, both front and back. The set includes 12 three-dimensional raised metal cards packaged in a velvet-lined case that bears the title of the set in gold embossed letters. A deluxe limited edition of the set (1,000) was produced in sterling silver and an economy version in aluminum. A Mark McGwire pewter replica was given as a premium to dealers ordering the aluminum, bronze and silver sets. The special pewter card is distinguished from the regular issue by a diagonal name banner in the lower-right corner; regular replicas have a rectangular name banner parallel to the lower edge of the card). A 1955 Topps Duke Snider bronze was available to dealers purchasing cases of the 1988 Topps Traded sets.

Complete Aluminum Set (12):		$35.00	$26.00
Complete Bronze Set (12):		225.00	165.00
Complete Silver Set (12):		550.00	410.00
(1a)	Steve Bedrosian(aluminum)	2.00	1.50
(1b)	Steve Bedrosian(bronze)	10.00	7.50
(1s)	Steve Bedrosian(silver)	25.00	18.50
(2a)	George Bell(aluminum)	2.00	1.50
(2b)	George Bell(bronze)	10.00	7.50
(2s)	George Bell(silver)	25.00	18.50
(3a)	Wade Boggs(aluminum)	5.00	3.75

(3b)	Wade Boggs(bronze)	30.00	22.00	(8s)	Mark Langston(silver)	25.00	18.50
(3s)	Wade Boggs(silver)	65.00	49.00	(9a)	Mark McGwire(aluminum)	15.00	11.00
(4a)	Jack Clark(aluminum)	2.00	1.50	(9b)	Mark McGwire(bronze)	50.00	37.00
(4b)	Jack Clark(bronze)	10.00	7.50	(9s)	Mark McGwire(silver)	100.00	75.00
(4s)	Jack Clark(silver)	25.00	18.50	(9p)	Mark McGwire(pewter)	125.00	94.00
(5a)	Roger Clemens(aluminum)	7.50	5.75	(10a)	Dave Righetti(aluminum)	2.00	1.50
(5b)	Roger Clemens(bronze)	30.00	22.00	(10b)	Dave Righetti(bronze)	10.00	7.50
(5s)	Roger Clemens(silver)	75.00	56.00	(10s)	Dave Righetti(silver)	25.00	18.50
(6a)	Andre Dawson(aluminum)	4.00	3.00	(11a)	Nolan Ryan(aluminum)	15.00	11.00
(6b)	Andre Dawson(bronze)	15.00	11.00	(11b)	Nolan Ryan(bronze)	100.00	75.00
(6s)	Andre Dawson(silver)	40.00	30.00	(11s)	Nolan Ryan(silver)	250.00	187.00
(7a)	Tony Gwynn(aluminum)	7.50	5.75	(12a)	Benny Santiago(aluminum)	2.00	1.50
(7b)	Tony Gwynn(bronze)	35.00	26.00	(12b)	Benny Santiago(bronze)	10.00	7.50
(7s)	Tony Gwynn(silver)	75.00	56.00	(12s)	Benny Santiago(silver)	35.00	26.00
(8a)	Mark Langston(aluminum)	2.00	1.50	(13)	Duke Snider(bronze)	15.00	11.00
(8b)	Mark Langston(bronze)	10.00	7.50				

1989 Topps Gallery of Champions

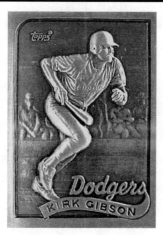

Topps continued its issue of 1/4-size metallic ingot reproductions of current-year baseball cards with aluminum, bronze and sterling silver sets in 1989. Again the players represented major award winners from the previous season. The metal mini-cards were sold only as complete sets. Dealers who ordered bronze and silver sets could receive as a bonus a pewter version of the Jose Canseco ingot. A bronze replica of Jackie Robinson's Topps debut card was offered to dealers who purchased Topps Traded sets for '89.

Complete Aluminum Set (12):		**$50.00**	**$37.00**	(6s)	Kirk Gibson(silver)	40.00	30.00
Complete Bronze Set (12):		150.00	110.00	(7a)	Tony Gwynn(aluminum)	10.00	7.50
Complete Silver Set (12):		425.00	325.00	(7b)	Tony Gwynn(bronze)	30.00	22.00
(1a)	Wade Boggs(aluminum)	9.00	6.75	(7s)	Tony Gwynn(silver)	75.00	56.00
(1b)	Wade Boggs(bronze)	30.00	22.00	(8a)	Orel Hershiser(aluminum)	8.00	6.00
(1s)	Wade Boggs(silver)	65.00	49.00	(8b)	Orel Hershiser(bronze)	25.00	18.50
(2a)	Jose Canseco(aluminum)	10.00	7.50	(8s)	Orel Hershiser(silver)	50.00	37.00
(2b)	Jose Canseco(bronze)	30.00	22.00	(9a)	Chris Sabo(aluminum)	3.00	10.00
(2s)	Jose Canseco(silver)	75.00	56.00	(9b)	Chris Sabo(bronze)	10.00	7.50
(2p)	Jose Canseco(pewter)	30.00	22.00	(9s)	Chris Sabo(silver)	25.00	18.50
(3a)	Will Clark(aluminum)	5.00	3.75	(10a)	Darryl Strawberry(aluminum)	6.00	4.50
(3b)	Will Clark(bronze)	15.00	11.00	(10b)	Darryl Strawberry(bronze)	20.00	15.00
(3s)	Will Clark(silver)	35.00	26.00	(10s)	Darryl Strawberry(silver)	50.00	37.00
(4a)	Dennis Eckersley(aluminum)	5.00	3.75	(11a)	Frank Viola	3.00	10.00
(4b)	Dennis Eckersley(bronze)	15.00	11.00	(11b)	Frank Viola(bronze)	10.00	7.50
(4s)	Dennis Eckersley(silver)	35.00	26.00	(11s)	Frank Viola(silver)	25.00	18.50
(5a)	John Franco(aluminum)	3.00	10.00	(12a)	Walt Weiss(aluminum)	3.00	10.00
(5b)	John Franco(bronze)	10.00	7.50	(12b)	Walt Weiss(bronze)	10.00	7.50
(5s)	John Franco(silver)	25.00	18.50	(12s)	Walt Weiss(silver)	25.00	18.50
(6a)	Kirk Gibson(aluminum)	5.00	3.75	(13)	Jackie Robinson(1952, bronze)	20.00	15.00
(6b)	Kirk Gibson(bronze)	15.00	11.00				

1990 Topps Gallery of Champions

The 1990 Topps 1/4-size metal baseball mini-cards were issued only as complete sets in a special display case. As with earlier editions, the 1 1/4" x 1 3/4" ingots do a creditable job of reproducing the players' 1990 Topps cards, right down to the tiny stats on the back. Players in the set represent the winners of major awards and statistical leaders from the previous season. A pewter Nolan Ryan 1/4-size card and 1954 Hank Aaron bronze mini-replica were issued as sales incentives for dealers purchasing the Gallery of Champions sets or 1990 Topps Traded sets.

Complete Aluminum Set (12):		**$40.00**	**$30.00**	(7a)	Kirby Puckett(aluminum)	6.00	4.50
Complete Bronze Set (12):		125.00	90.00	(7b)	Kirby Puckett(bronze)	20.00	15.00
Complete Silver Set (12):		375.00	275.00	(7s)	Kirby Puckett(silver)	60.00	45.00
(1a)	Mark Davis(aluminum)	3.00	2.25	(8a)	Jeff Russell(aluminum)	3.00	2.25
(1b)	Mark Davis(bronze)	6.00	4.50	(8b)	Jeff Russell(bronze)	6.00	4.50
(1s)	Mark Davis(silver)	15.00	11.00	(8s)	Jeff Russell(silver)	15.00	11.00
(2a)	Jose DeLeon(aluminum)	3.00	2.25	(9a)	Nolan Ryan(aluminum)	35.00	26.00
(2b)	Jose DeLeon(bronze)	6.00	4.50	(9b)	Nolan Ryan(bronze)	60.00	45.00
(2s)	Jose DeLeon(silver)	15.00	11.00	(9s)	Nolan Ryan(silver)	150.00	112.00
(3a)	Tony Gwynn(aluminum)	6.00	4.50	(9p)	Nolan Ryan(pewter)	125.00	94.00
(3b)	Tony Gwynn(bronze)	20.00	15.00	(10a)	Bret Saberhagen(aluminum)	3.00	2.25
(3s)	Tony Gwynn(silver)	60.00	45.00	(10b)	Bret Saberhagen(bronze)	10.00	7.50
(4a)	Fred McGriff(aluminum)	3.00	2.25	(10s)	Bret Saberhagen(silver)	25.00	18.50
(4b)	Fred McGriff(bronze)	7.50	5.75	(11a)	Jerome Walton(aluminum)	3.00	2.25
(4s)	Fred McGriff(silver)	25.00	18.50	(11b)	Jerome Walton(bronze)	6.00	4.50
(5a)	Kevin Mitchell(aluminum)	3.00	2.25	(11s)	Jerome Walton(silver)	15.00	11.00
(5b)	Kevin Mitchell(bronze)	6.00	4.50	(12a)	Robin Yount(aluminum)	5.00	3.75
(5s)	Kevin Mitchell(silver)	15.00	11.00	(12b)	Robin Yount(bronze)	15.00	11.00
(6a)	Gregg Olson(aluminum)	3.00	2.25	(12s)	Robin Yount(silver)	50.00	37.00
(6b)	Gregg Olson(bronze)	6.00	4.50	(13)	Hank Aaron(1954, bronze)	25.00	18.50
(6s)	Gregg Olson(silver)	15.00	11.00				

1991 Stadium Club Nolan Ryan Bronze

One of the premiums included with charter membership in the Topps Stadium Club was a bronze replica of the Nolan Ryan card from the Charter Member's card set. The replica measures 2 1/2" x 3 1/2" and reproduces both front and back of the Ryan card on a 10-ounce metal slab.

Nolan Ryan(bronze)	$10.00	$7.50

GULFSTREAM MINT SPORTSTRIKES

Gulfstream Mint issued metal baseball cards, called ingots, for two players, Mickey Mantle and Frank Thomas. Both players came in two editions—gold and silver—with mintages of 150 and 750, respectively. The cards are etched in great detail by Susan Wagner, sculptor of Hall of Fame plaques since 1984, and feature a facsimile autograph on both the card and the front of the display box. Each card is encased in a four-screw screw-down holder, which rests in a velvet-lined box. Cards are individually numbered, and registration was available through the company until Gulfstream ceased operation in 1997.

Year	Player	Gold Mintage	Gold Price	Silver Mintage	Silver Price	Set Price
1996	Mantle, Mickey	150	$725	750	$400	$1,125
1996	Thomas, Frank	150	700	750	375	1,000

HOBBY EDITIONS

Hobby Editions was formed by a former employee of Gulfstream Mint who retained the rights to distribute the Keeper Series porcelain replica cards. Each card in the 10-card set is a replica of the player's Topps rookie card, with production limited to 500 sets. Each card is protected in a screw-down holder and display box, and carries a retail price of $70. Mickey Mantle is included in this set, and a bonus card redeemable for one of 50 "Finders" series Mantle cards is inserted at a rate of one in 10 Keeper series cards.

In 1997, Hobby Editions released a new line called the Vintage Keeper Series consisting of porcelain cards replicating the 1914 Cracker Jack set, with a production run of 150 each. The first card issued was Shoeless Joe Jackson, with Tris Speaker, Honus Wagner and Ty Cobb following. In addition, there is a "Finders" series Honus Wagner T206 replica limited to 120 cards.

Keeper Series

Year	Player	Mintage	Price
1997	Griffey Jr., Ken ('89 Topps Traded)	500	$100
1997	Jeter, Derek ('93 Topps)	500	85
1997	Jones, Andruw ('97 Topps)	500	70
1997	Jones, Chipper ('91 Topps)	500	90
1997	Mantle, Mickey ('52 Topps)	500	125
1997	Puckett, Kirby ('85 Topps)	500	75
1997	Ripken Jr., Cal ('82 Topps Traded)	500	90
1997	Robinson, Jackie ('52 Topps)	500	75
1997	Thomas, Frank ('90 Topps)	500	90
1997	Williams, Ted ('54 Topps)	500	75

Vintage Keeper Series

Year	Player	Mintage	Price
1997	Alexander, Grover Cleveland	150	$75
1997	Cobb, Ty	150	90
1997	Jackson, Joe	150	75
1997	Johnson, Walter	150	75
1997	Lajoie, Napoleon	150	75
1997	Mathewson, Christy	150	75
1997	Speaker, Tris	150	75
1997	Wagner, Honus	150	125

Hobby Edition Medallions

Like Highland Mint, Hobby Editions also expanded from cards to medallions. The Chosen Few player medallions are also the work of Baseball Hall of Fame sculptor Susan Wagner. In addition to her work with the Hall, Wagner also sculpted the bronze statue of Roberto Clemente that was unveiled at the 1994 All-Star Game in Pittsburgh.

The player selection in the Chosen Few series includes sluggers Ken Griffey Jr. and Frank Thomas and newcomers Alex Rodriguez and Derek Jeter. Each release entailed 1,000 bronze, 500 silver, and 250 gold, with 50 proof sets including one of each medallion. Issue prices were $19, $35, $55 and $130, respectively.

Year	Player	Gold Mintage	Gold Price	Silver Mintage	Silver Price	Bronze Mintage	Bronze Price
1997	Griffey Jr., Ken	250	$90	500	$50	1,000	$30
1997	Jeter, Derek	250	65	500	40	1,000	25
1997	Jones, Chipper	250	80	500	45	1,000	25
1997	Maddux, Greg	250	55	500	40	1,000	20
1997	Piazza, Mike	250	65	500	40	1,000	20
1997	Ripken Jr., Cal	250	80	500	45	1,000	25
1997	Rodriguez, Alex	250	55	500	40	1,000	20
1997	Thomas, Frank	250	65	500	40	1,000	20

Chosen Few Medallion Proof Sets

Year	Player	Mintage	Price	Year	Player	Mintage	Price
1997	Griffey Jr., Ken	50	$140	1997	Piazza, Mike	50	$130
1997	Jeter, Derek	50	130	1997	Ripken Jr., Cal	50	135
1997	Jones, Chipper	50	135	1997	Rodriguez, Alex	50	130
1997	Maddux, Greg	50	130	1997	Thomas, Frank	50	130

PREMIER INSTANT REPLAY

Premier Instant Replay cards feature motion prints in a 6- by 7-inch frame. Each print in the 30-card set showcases a career highlight from players like Ken Griffey Jr., Cal Ripken Jr., and Nomar Garciaparra, and they retail for $7 a piece.

Year	Player	Mintage	Price
1997	Alomar, Roberto	5,000	$10
1997	Bagwell, Jeff	5,000	12
1997	Belle, Albert	5,000	12
1997	Bonds, Barry	5,000	12
1997	Clark, Tony	5,000	12
1997	Erstad, Darin	5,000	10
1997	Garciaparra, Nomar	5,000	15
1997	Gonzalez, Juan	5,000	12
1997	Griffey Jr., Ken	5,000	22
1997	Guerrero, Vladimir	5,000	12
1997	Gwynn, Tony	5,000	12
1997	Hollandsworth, Todd	5,000	8
1997	Jeter, Derek	5,000	20
1997	Jones, Andruw	5,000	15
1997	Jones, Andruw (WS home run)	5,000	15
1997	Jones, Chipper	5,000	$20
1997	Jordan, Brian	5,000	8
1997	Maddux, Greg	5,000	15
1997	McGwire, Mark	5,000	15
1997	Piazza, Mike	5,000	15
1997	Ramirez, Manny	5,000	11
1997	Ripken Jr., Cal	5,000	20
1997	Rodriguez, Alex	5,000	20
1997	Rolen, Scott	5,000	12
1997	Sandberg, Ryne	5,000	10
1997	Sheffield, Gary	5,000	12
1997	Sosa, Sammy	5,000	10
1997	Thomas, Frank	5,000	22
1997	Vaughn, Mo	5,000	12
1997	Young, Dimitri	5,000	8

PRO MINT

Pro Mint tried to repeat the success of Highland Mint with its own line of gold-etched cards, featuring a lower price point and larger print run. The cards weren't as thick as Highland Mint's, and Pro Mint used its own card design instead of forming a relationship with an existing manufacturer. Most cards can be found for around the original issue price of $29.95.

Year	Player	Promo Mintage	Promo Price	Card Mintage	Card Price
1993	Ryan, Nolan (Gold Sig.)	1,000	$150	50,000	$50
1993	#1 Ryan, Nolan	250	200	50,000	40
1993	#2 Bonds, Bobby	1,000	100	50,000	30
1993	#3 Ryan, Nolan (Anniversary)	1,000	100	50,000	30
1993	#4 Puckett, Kirby	1,000	100	50,000	30
1993	#5 Brett, George	1,000	110	50,000	40
1994	#6 Thomas, Frank	1,000	110	50,000	40
1994	#7 Griffey Jr., Ken	1,000	125	50,000	50
1994	#8 Piazza, Mike	1,000	100	50,000	30
1994	#9 Clemens, Roger	1,000	100	50,000	35
1994	#10 Bagwell, Jeff	1,000	100	50,000	30
1994	Ruth, Babe (Diamond)	100	500	25,000	150
1995	#11 Mattingly, Don	1,000	100	50,000	30
1995	#12 Smith, Ozzie	1,000	100	50,000	30
1995	#13 Gwynn, Tony	1,000	110	50,000	35
1995	#14 Belle, Albert	1,000	100	50,000	30
1995	#15 Maddux, Greg	1,000	115	50,000	40
1995	#16 Ripken Jr., Cal	1,000	115	50,000	45
1995	#17 Sanders, Deion	1,000	100	50,000	30
1995	#18 Fielder, Cecil	1,000	100	50,000	30
1995	#19 Nomo, Hideo	1,000	110	50,000	40
1995	#20 Bichette, Dante	1,000	100	50,000	30
1995	#21 Vaughn, Mo	1,000	100	50,000	30
1995	#22 Canseco, Jose	1,000	100	50,000	30
1996	#23 Sandberg, Ryne	1,000	100	50,000	30
1996	#24 McGwire, Mark	1,000	125	50,000	50
1996	#25 Griffey Jr., Ken	1,000	125	50,000	50
1996	#26 Murray, Eddie	1,000	100	50,000	30

UPPER DECK

Upper Deck issued two single gold baseball cards through its Upper Deck Authenticated division. These cards were produced by Authentic Images for Upper Deck, and the design was unlike Upper Deck's regular card releases. A poor marketing effort prevented these cards from becoming popular in the hobby. Currently Upper Deck has no plans for additional cards.

Year	Player	Mintage	Price
1996	Griffey Jr., Ken "The Natural"	1,996	$150
1996	Nomo, Hideo "Rookie of the Year"	1,996	150

World Series program, 1917

All-Star Game program, 1955

Tiger Stadium, final game program, 1999

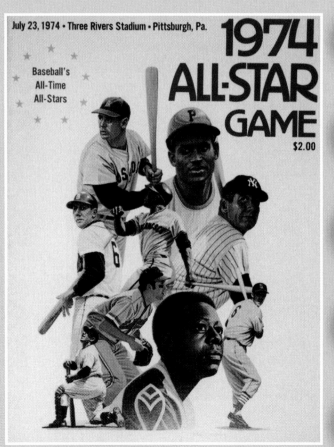

All-Star Game program, 1974

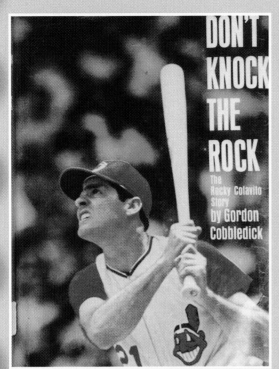

Don't Knock The Rock, The Rocky Colavito Story

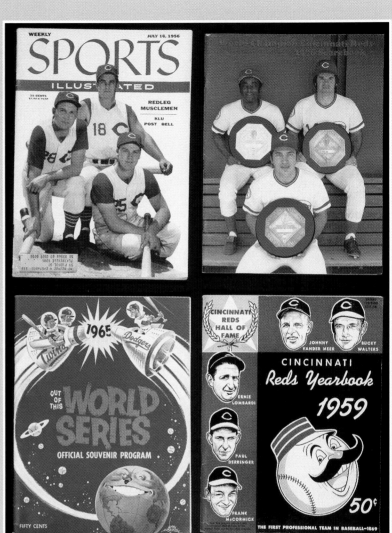

Cincinnati Reds on the covers: *Sports Illustrated*, program,
1965 World Series program, 1959 yearbook

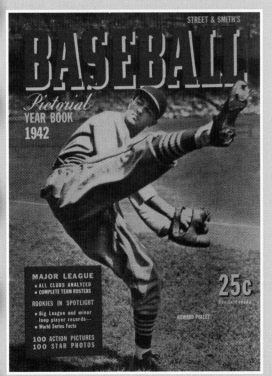

Street & Smith's Baseball Yearbook, 1942

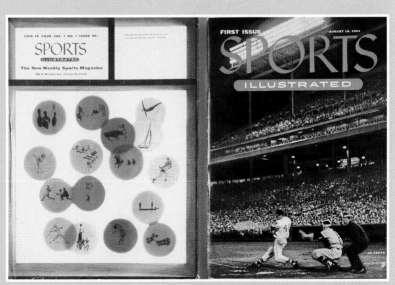

First issue of *Sports Illustrated*

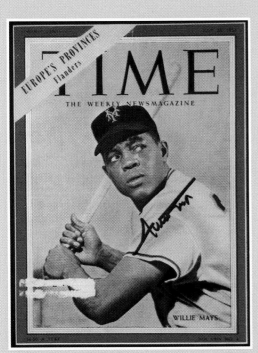

Time magazine Willie Mays cover, July 26, 1954

Sport magazine baseball covers

Playboy magazine, first issue, signed by Joe DiMaggio

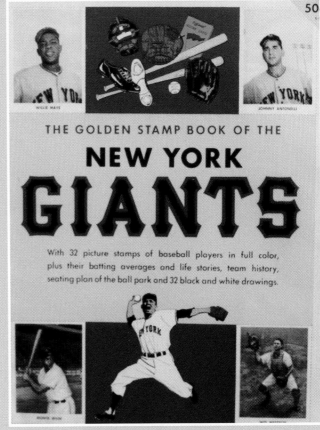

The Golden Stamp Book of the New York Giants

Roger Maris, Auravision Records, 1964

The Greatest Moments in Sports record

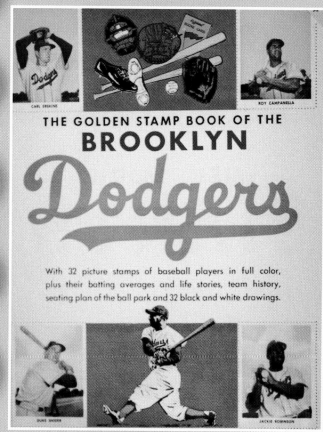

The Golden Stamp Book of the Brooklyn Dodgers

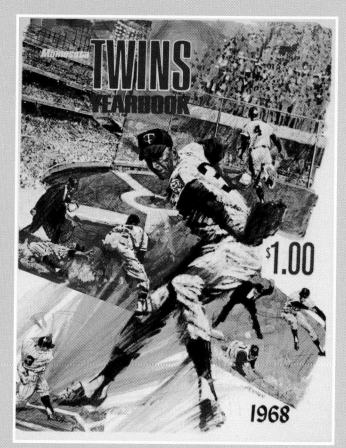

Minnesota Twins yearbook, 1968

1989 WHITE SOX TICKET ORDER FORM

GAME DATE	NUMBER OF TICKETS	AMOUNT
	BOX $8.50*	
	MEZZ./TERR. $6.50*	
	RESERVED $5.50*	
	SVC/HANDLING	$2.00

*All Monday night games are half price.

LOCATION PREFERENCE: ☐ Upper Deck ☐ Lower Deck
☐ Home Plate ☐ First Base ☐ Third Base

CREDIT CARD: ☐ American Express ☐ VISA ☐ MasterCard
Card Number _____ Exp. Date _____

NAME:
ADDRESS:
CITY: STATE: ZIP:
HOME PHONE: WORK PHONE:
Mail to: Chicago White Sox Ticket Office, 324 W. 35th Street, Chicago, IL 60616

SEASON TICKET PLANS

COMPLETE GAME PLAN (82 GAMES)
The Ted Lyons plan offers a choice seat for all 81 regular-season White Sox home games plus the exhibition contest against the crosstown rival Cubs. Golden box seats are $861, loge box seats are $779, upper or lower deck box seats are $697, and reserved mezzanine or terrace seats are $533.

HALL OF FAME PLANS (28 GAMES)
A choice seat for one of three different 28-game plans, each offering the opportunity to see every American League opponent. The Luke Appling Plan A and Ray Schalk Plan B offer weeknight contests. The Ed Walsh Plan C offers all Saturdays and Sundays plus Memorial Day. Golden box seats are $292, loge box seats are $265, upper or lower deck box seats are $238, and reserved mezzanine or terrace seats are $182.

DOUBLE PLAY COMBINATION PLANS (15 GAMES)
A seat for one of two separate 15-game plans, both affording the chance to see each American League team. The Luis Aparicio Plan D offers assorted weeknights. The Nellie Fox Plan E offers all Sundays plus Memorial Day. Upper or lower deck box seats are $127.50 and reserved mezzanine or terrace seats are $97.50.

All the above plans include tickets for the May 18 White Sox-Cubs exhibition game at Comiskey Park. For additional season ticket information, call the White Sox sales department (312/924-1000).

When It's Miller Lite, Less Filling Tastes Great

Miller Brewing Co., Milw., WI

1989 WHITE SOX SCHEDULE

		APRIL				
SUNDAY	MONDAY	TUESDAY	WEDNESDAY	THURSDAY	FRIDAY	SATURDAY
			CAL	CAL	CAL	OAK	OAK
OAK	SEA	SEA	SEA		OAK	OAK
OAK	CAL	CAL	CAL	SEA	SEA	SEA
SEA			BOS	BOS	BOS	NY	NY
NY						

		MAY				
	MIL	MIL	BOS	BOS	NY	NY
NY	MIL	MIL	MIL		BAL	BAL
BAL	DET	DET	DET	CUBS	TOR	TOR
TOR	BAL	BAL	BAL		TOR	TOR
TOR	DET	DET	DET			

		JUNE				
				MIN	MIN	MIN
MIN	TEX	TEX	TEX	TEX	MIN	MIN
MIN	CLE	CLE	CLE		BOS	BOS
BOS	BOS	NY	NY	NY	MIL	MIL
MIL		TEX	TEX	KC	KC

		JULY				
						KC
KC	CLE	CLE	CLE		KC	KC
KC			ALL-STAR GAME (CAL)	MIL	MIL	MIL
MIL	NY	NY	NY		BOS	BOS
BOS	SEA	SEA	SEA	CAL	CAL
OAK						

		AUG				
	OAK	OAK	OAK	DET	DET
DET		OAK	OAK	OAK	SEA	SEA
SEA	KC	KC	KC	TEX	TEX	TEX
TEX		MIN	MIN	MIN	CLE	CLE
CLE		TOR	TOR	TOR		

		SEPT				
					BAL	BAL
BAL	TOR	TOR	TOR		DET	DET
DET	BAL	BAL	BAL		CAL	CAL
CAL	KC	KC	KC		TEX	TEX
TEX	MIN	MIN	MIN		CLE	CLE

		OCTOBER				
CLE						

☐ HOME   ☐ ROAD   WMAQ ALL NEWS 67

TICKET INFORMATION

MAIL
Specify game dates, number of tickets, and price. Include a $2 handling fee with each order. Send check or money order, payable to the Chicago White Sox, to: Chicago White Sox Ticket Office, 324 W. 35th Street, Chicago, IL 60616.

CREDIT CARD
Order Sox tickets with American Express, MasterCard, or Visa. Credit card purchases are available until three hours prior to game time. Tickets will be mailed or held at the special Ticketmaster "will call" window if time does not permit mailing. A convenience charge per ticket is assessed. Call Ticketmaster (312/559-1212).

COMISKEY PARK
The Comiskey Park box office is open during the season from 10 a.m.-6 p.m. and weekends from 10 a.m.-4 p.m. On game days, the box office opens at 9 a.m. and remains open until 9 p.m. during night games.

OUTLETS
All Ticketmaster ticket centers, including all Rose Records and Carson, Pirie, Scott and Company stores, offer White Sox tickets.

White Sox baseball is televised by WFLD-TV and SportsVision. The club's flagship radio station is WMAQ-AM (670). WTAQ-AM (1300), Radio Fiesta, offers Spanish-language description of all home games and selected road contests.

Chicago White Sox schedule, 1989

Hank Greenberg autographed Perez-Steele postcard

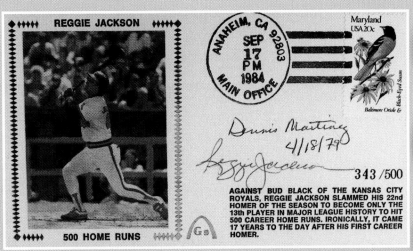

REGGIE JACKSON — 500 HOME RUNS

ANAHEIM, CA 92803 SEP 17 PM 1984 MAIN OFFICE

Maryland USA 20c — Baltimore Oriole & Black-Eyed Susan

Dennis Martinez 4/18/79

343/500

AGAINST BUD BLACK OF THE KANSAS CITY ROYALS, REGGIE JACKSON SLAMMED HIS 22nd HOMER OF THE SEASON TO BECOME ONLY THE 13th PLAYER IN MAJOR LEAGUE HISTORY TO HIT 500 CAREER HOME RUNS. IRONICALLY, IT CAME 17 YEARS TO THE DAY AFTER HIS FIRST CAREER HOMER.

Reggie Jackson commemorative postcard, 1984

MICKEY CHARLES MANTLE
NEW YORK A.L. 1951-1968
HIT 536 HOME RUNS. WON LEAGUE HOMER TITLE
AND SLUGGING CROWN FOUR TIMES. MADE
2415 HITS. BATTED .300 OR OVER IN EACH
OF TEN YEARS WITH TOP OF .365 IN 1957.
TOPPED A.L. IN WALKS FIVE YEARS AND
IN RUNS SCORED SIX SEASONS. VOTED
MOST VALUABLE PLAYER 1956-57-62. NAMED
ON 20 A.L. ALL-STAR TEAMS. SET WORLD
SERIES RECORDS FOR HOMERS, 18; RUNS, 42;
RUNS BATTED IN, 40; TOTAL BASES, 123;
AND BASES ON BALLS, 43.

NATIONAL BASEBALL HALL OF FAME & MUSEUM
Cooperstown, New York

STANLEY FRANK MUSIAL
"THE MAN"
ST. LOUIS CARDINALS 1941-1963
HOLDS MANY NATIONAL LEAGUE RECORDS,
AMONG THEM: GAMES PLAYED 3026; AT
BAT 10972 TIMES; 3630 HITS; MOST RUNS
SCORED 1949; MOST RUNS BATTED IN 1951;
TOTAL BASES 6134. LED N.L. IN TOTAL
BASES 6 YEARS. SLUGGING PERCENTAGE
6 YEARS. MOST VALUABLE PLAYER 1943-
1946-1948. NAMED ON 12 ALL STAR TEAMS.
LIFETIME BATTING AVERAGE .331.

NATIONAL BASEBALL HALL OF FAME & MUSEUM
Cooperstown, New York

Mickey Mantle autographed Hall of Fame card

Stan Musial autographed Hall of Fame card

World Series ticket stub, 1919

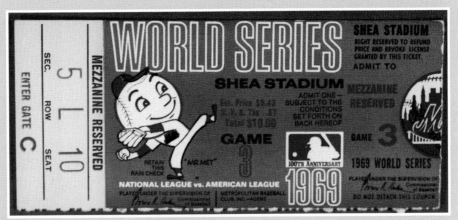

World Series
ticket stub, 1969

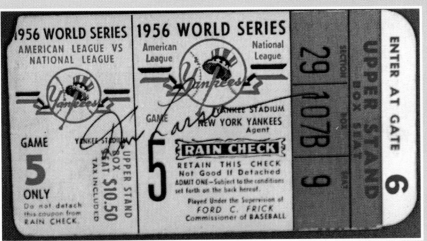

World Series
ticket stub, 1956,
autographed by
Don Larsen

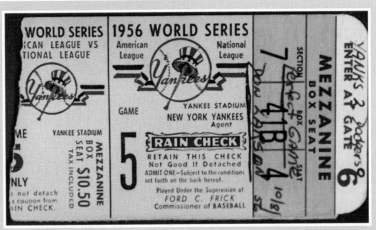

World Series
ticket stub,
1956

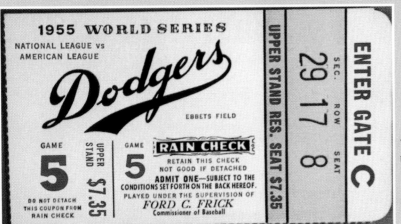

World Series
ticket stub,
1955

World Series press pin, 1962

World Series pin, 1966

World Series phantom pin, 1951

All-Star Game press pins, 1950, 1951

Babe Ruth Mrs. Sherlock's Bread pin

National League Champions
ring, 1993

World Series press
pins from 1911 on

Triple Crown trophy, Mickey Mantle, 1956

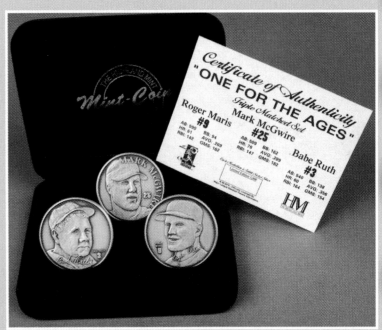

Highland Mint Mint-Coin set of Babe Ruth, Roger Maris, Mark McGwire

Cy Young Award, 1977, Steve Carlton

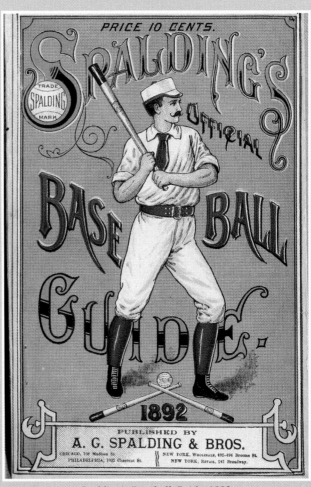

Spalding's Baseball Guide, 1892

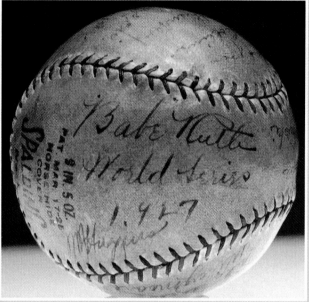

Baseball autographed by Babe Ruth in 1927

Ty Cobb autographed baseball

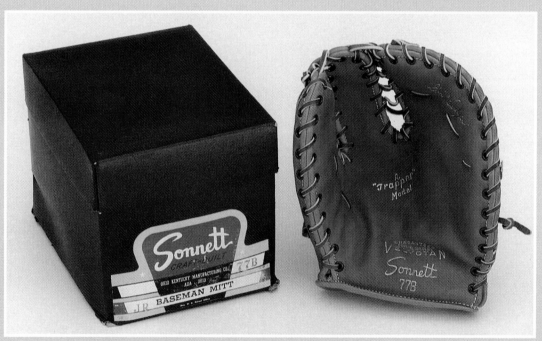

Sonnett Gil Hodges model first baseman's mitt

Babe Ruth model bat

Dave Winfield autographed glove

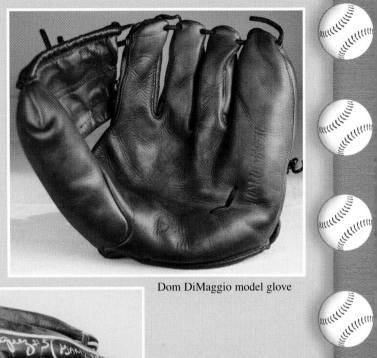

Dom DiMaggio model glove

Alex Rodriguez autographed Rawlings glove

Mickey Mantle
model glove

Jeff Kent model glove

Ted Williams autographed jersey

Hank Aaron autographed Milwaukee Braves jersey

Pedro Guerrero Montreal Expos jersey

Mark McGwire Oakland A's road jersey, 1993

Milwaukee Braves pennant

Joe DiMaggio and Stan Musial Wheaties boxes

Sandy Koufax autographed cap

Ted Williams:
Ted's Root Beer

Charles Klein matchbook

Moxie soda, featuring Ted Williams

"The Dugout,"
Norman Rockwell

Milwaukee Braves
Bobbing Head doll

Mickey Mantle,
Willie Mays,
Duke Snider
artwork

Roberto Clemente Bobbing Head doll

New York Mets
Bobbing Head doll

Complete Hartland baseball statue set

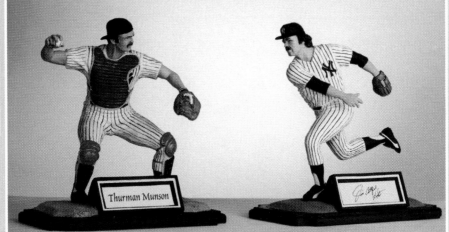

Thurman
Munson,
Catfish Hunter
Romito figures

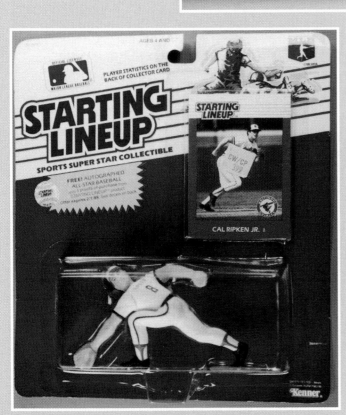

Cal Ripken Jr. Starting Lineup

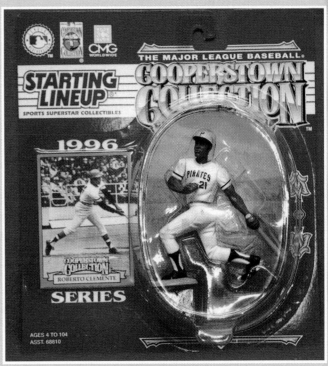

Roberto Clemente Cooperstown Collection Starting Lineup

Base Ball game, J.H. Singer Co.

Say Hey! Willie Mays Baseball, Centennial Games, 1954

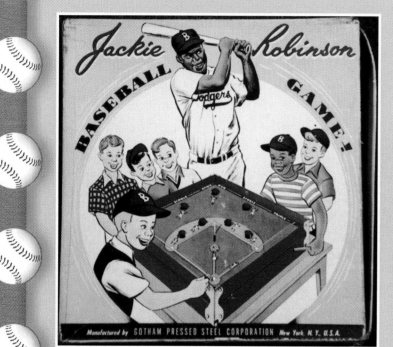

Jackie Robinson Baseball Game, Gotham Pressed Steel Corp., 1948

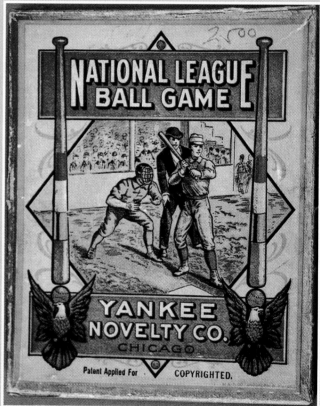

National League Ball Game, Yankee Novelty Co., 1890

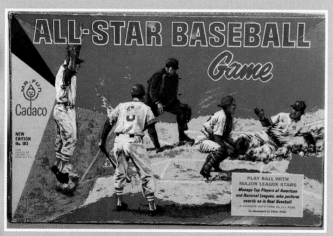

All-Star Baseball Game by Cadaco-Ellis, 1959-60

Chapter 9

STADIUM MEMORABILIA

By Paul N. Ferrante

Ballparks are magical places. Every baseball fan remembers that first trip to his home team's diamond—the sights, the smells, the ambience. Collectors love to rhapsodize about the green cathedrals of their youth. Which is why, in our era of high-tech era, old ballparks and their fixtures (most notably the seats) have taken off like no other segment of the hobby.

It used to be that when a park was torn down its fixtures were either given away, sold for a few dollars apiece, recycled by minor league clubs, fairgrounds or anyplace else where large numbers of people gathered, or simply sent to the scrap heap. Even such now-hallowed venues as Ebbets Field or the Polo Grounds attracted minimal interest when they were demolished. (In Forbes Field and Shibe Park, some people simply ripped out their seats at the last game and left with them.) Most seats from the first half of the 20th century were either destroyed or relocated to other facilities where they would hold on for another few years before being replaced themselves due to obsolescence.

Yankee Stadium's renovation in the early '70s altered the pattern somewhat. Seats and other fixtures were sold directly to the public and through advertising promotions, most notably by Winston cigarettes. Comiskey Park in 1991 held a formal, organized sale in which thousands of seats were purchased. Arlington Stadium, Cleveland Stadium, Memorial Stadium and others would follow. With each sale, prices bumped up a little more, and the rarer pieces from pre-'70s demolitions soared. Today, fixtures from even "modem" parks such as Three Rivers Stadium are commanding considerable cash. A plastic seat from that '70s doughnut may cost you $450, whereas in 1974 a Yankee Stadium original wooden box seat from 1923 could be had for $10.

Stadium seats, especially, have a secondary attraction to collectors. Besides being striking examples of period architecture (note the figural seats of 1900-1930s), they are functional items. What better place to watch a ballgame in your own rec room than an actual box seat?

To study "Stadia," we'll start by taking a look at the most sought-after items—the seats—by breaking them into time period groups. We'll go back as far as the turn of the century, when some seats sported mud scrapes on the legs (horses outside the park), and work our way to the present.

It is important to note that in any time-period mentioned, only a few companies supplied seats, most notably Heywood-Wakefield and American Seating Co. As a result, many parks from the same time period featured similar seats, except for the more rare figural aisle models available in some parks.

A collector ideally wants a seat displaying its original paint color (although it may have been recoated many times over its life in the park) as well as its wood. (If the seat was exposed to the elements, chances are a slat or two was replaced during its lifespan). He also wants the seat to be generally free of rust or splinters. Of course, if the seat was relocated to a racetrack, say, for 20 years, it was most likely painted over and provenance becomes tricky. That is why, unless a collector purchases a seat directly from a soon-to-be-demolished stadium, he must be wary and do his homework. Restoration, of course, lowers the value of a seat somewhat, but at times it cannot be avoided. (Let us note that both collectors and dealers disagree over whether a restored seat, even with all its original parts, holds the same value as an unrestored one. This ultimately depends on the collector. Does he regard his seat like a '57 Chevy that should be returned to mint condition, or a piece of antique furniture that should have its original patina?)

The prices quoted here are estimates gleaned from discussions with dealers and collectors, as well as auction results. We will suppose that we are pricing a single seat that has its original paint and parts and is in Excellent condition. (Wear is OK - an unrestored seat is supposed to show wear, runs or drips from numerous coatings, or even an old piece of gum on the seat bottom!)

We will differentiate between figurals and non-figurals only. We will not differentiate between floor mount and riser mount seats (although floor mounts are somewhat more desirable for ease of mounting) or between the many styles (Comiskey had more than 12 when it was demolished after 80 years) that may have been present. Remember that because this is a relatively new collecting area, and that large quantities of these items may suddenly become available with the closing of a park (example, Fenway), prices can fluctuate. Some parks to date have only seen them leak out a few at a time in minor renovations, hence their inflated prices.

SEATS

Original 16 Teams' Parks

These are the classic parks, some of which predate the turn of the last century. A few parks such as Shibe (later known as Connie Mack) and Sportsman's housed two clubs, and three are left: Yankee Stadium, Fenway and Wrigley, although they have undergone renovations of varying scope. Only Fenway still features wooden seats - thousands of them.

Though the New York triumvirate far outdistances the others for collectors, there are classic seats sprinkled throughout this list. The most rare, by far, are Baker Bowl, League Park and Braves Field, whose demolitions met with indifference, but whose seats are among the most attractive, especially the figurals.

Shibe Park figural (ribbon-end)

Listed According to Opening Date

Ballparks	First Used	Team(s)	Wood Figural	Wood Non-Figural	Plastic
Sportsman's Park	1875	Cardinals (NL)	N/A	$450	N/A
		Browns (AL)			
Baker Bowl	1887	Phillies (NL)	$5,000	$3,500	N/A
Shibe Park	1909	Athletics (AL)	$800	$600	N/A
		Phillies (NL)			
Forbes Field	1909	Pirates (NL)	$1,200	$800	N/A
Comiskey Park	1910	White Sox (AL)	$700	$500	$300
League Park	1910	Indians (AL)	$5,000	$3,500	N/A
Griffith Stadium	1911	Senators (AL)	N/A	$400	N/A
Polo Grounds	1911	Giants (NL)	$3,000	$800	N/A
Crosley Field	1912	Reds (NL)	$1,800	$850	N/A
Tiger Stadium	1912	Tigers (AL)	$1,800	$650	N/A
Fenway Park	1912	Red Sox (AL)	N/A	$1,000	$600
Ebbets Field	1913	Dodgers (NL)	N/A	$2,000	N/A
Wrigley Field	1914	Cubs (NL)	N/A	$850	$425
Braves Field	1915	Braves (NL)	$2,700	$1,800	N/A
Yankee Stadium	1923	Yankees (AL)	N/A	$1,300	N/A
Cleveland Stadium	1932	Indians (AL)	N/A	$450	$300

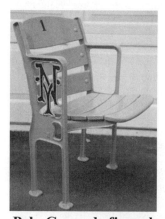

Polo Grounds figural

Crosley Field figural

Tiger Stadium figural

Ebbets Field

Yankee Stadium

Expansion/Relocation Era Parks

This group is a hodgepodge of the old (County Stadium, which was recently torn down), the new (Fulton County, which was a quasi-doughnut) and the temporary (Seals Stadium). Most notable here is Dodger Stadium, the standard bearer for westward expansion, which replaced some wooden seats within the past few years. Five of these parks held formal sales for the public.

Arlington Stadium

Alphabetically Listed

Ballparks	First Used	Team(s)	Wood Figural	Wood Non-Figural	Plastic
Arlington Stadium	1972	Rangers (AL)	N/A	N/A	$250
County Stadium	1953	Braves (NL) Brewers (AL-NL)	N/A	$200	$150
Dodger Stadium	1962	Dodgers (NL)	N/A	$675	N/A
Fulton County Stadium	1966	Braves (NL)	N/A	$550	$275
Memorial Stadium	1954	Orioles (AL)	N/A	$250	N/A
Metropolitan Stadium	1961	Twins (AL)	N/A	$400	$225
Municipal Stadium	1955	Athletics (AL)	N/A	$700	N/A
Seals Stadium	1958	Giants (NL)	N/A	$500	N/A

Milwaukee County Stadium

Memorial Stadium

Bowls/Domes Era

This group is exclusively plastic. Three of the parks still exist but have been renovated. Three Rivers held an extensive auction before its demolition. The Kingdome also sold seats before it was fittingly imploded.

Three Rivers Stadium (double)

Alphabetically Listed

Ballparks	First Used	Team(s)	Wood Figural	Wood Non-Figural	Plastic
Busch Stadium	1966	Cardinals (NL)	N/A	N/A	$300
Kingdome	1977	Manners (AL)	N/A	N/A	$250
Royals Stadium	1973	Royals (AL)	N/A	N/A	$275
Three Rivers Stadium	1970	Pirates (NL)	N/A	N/A	$400
Veterans Stadium	1971	Phillies (NL)	N/A	N/A	$225

Veterans Stadium

SIGNS

There are three types of signs. First are the older, wooden type, which were hand painted. Then there are those fashioned from metal alloys and from plastic. The most desirable are the wooden ones, obviously, but there are other factors that influence value. Condition is one. Another is whether the sign can be attributed to a specific team through words or a logo. Signs have been hot items at recent ballpark demolition auctions and make for terrific display items. Prices can vary from $50-$200 for a simple plastic section marker to $1,000 or more for hand-painted examples pre-1970 or the enameled beauties that came from Yankee Stadium's renovation in the 1970s.

Cleveland Stadium wooden sign, 1950s

Memorial Stadium metal sign

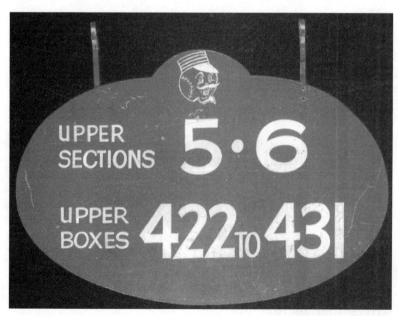

Crosley Field metal sign

TURNSTILES

These fixtures are among the most alluring for collectors. Imagine the millions of people who passed through them, the anticipation of the game as the machine clicked and whiffed! These devices fall into two basic categories. First is the older, rotary style found in the older parks. They are big, bulky and beautiful. Next is the style still used today in many parks: the side-winding model. You can expect to pay upwards of $6,500 for a Forbes Field or Shibe turnstile, providing it is not repainted and is complete, meaning that the brass cap that houses the counting mechanism is intact (many were removed for scrap). A "side winder" will run from $2,000-$4,000, depending on the park and the vintage. No matter what style, these are awesome stadium relics.

Polo Grounds rotating turnstile

Shibe Park rotating turnstile, 1909

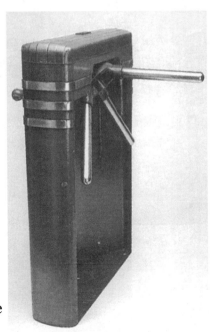

Wrigley Field sidewinding turnstile

USHER/VENDOR/POLICE ITEMS

It is somewhat ironic that those old-time ballpark employees with the most menial jobs sported some of the most desirable collectibles. Usher's hats and uniforms (primarily the jackets, especially those bearing a team logo) are highly desirable. The older the park, the better. A 1940s hat from Tiger Stadium will easily surpass $1,000. A full uniform from Ebbets Field would be considered priceless. And what of those who served us hotdogs or ice-cold drinks? Their coolers or shirts can range from a couple hundred dollars on up. A "Yankee Stadium Police" badge will set you back at least $500, with a hat pushing $1,000.

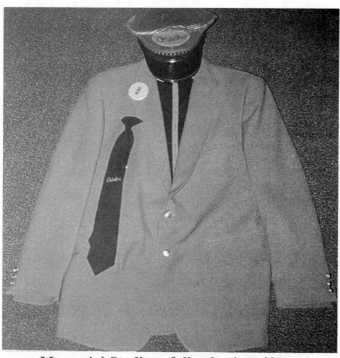

Memorial Stadium full usher's uniform

Yankee Stadium police badge

OTHER FIXTURES

If one attends a ballpark demolition auction today he will be amazed at what people will purchase, sometimes for great sums of money. Flagpoles, bullpen phones, wall padding, ticket boxes and player lockers make interesting conversation pieces. Even restroom fixtures have popped up in collectors' homes! Probably the two most popular items from this area are banners/flags that adorned the stadium roofs, and scoreboard numerals from the older parks. Flags, many of them made of canvas and sporting the names of MLB cities, range from $250 to $1,000, depending on the park. Banners used for World Series or All-Star games can run a few thousand dollars. Scoreboard numerals or letters can range from $250 to $1,000 as well. With the truly oddball items, it comes down to what a collector will pay—whether it be a garbage can, piece of synthetic turf, brick or cornerstone.

Comiskey Park brick

Wrigley Field stadium flag

Forbes Field scoreboard numeral No. 9.

Yankee Stadium ticket box

MINIATURE STADIUMS

Bridgeport Collectibles

Bridgeport Marketing of Cedarhurst, N.Y., produces miniature stadiums of cold-cast porcelain. They are hand-painted and available in a variety of sizes.

Candlestick Park - San Francisco $50
Pro Player Stadium - Miami $50
Three Rivers Stadium - Pittsburgh $55

Sport Collectors Guild Stadium Replicas

Sport Collectors Guild of Phoenix, Ariz., has produced stadium replicas from ground stone mixed with pine tar resin and secret ingredients since 1995. The patented process allows for original designs with extreme detail. Three series of stadia are produced, including Silver Series (miniature, measuring approximately 3 x 3 x 2, not numbered), Gold Series (approximately 5 x 5 x 2, individually numbered to 4,750) and Platinum Series (approximately 11 x 10 x 3, individually numbered to 4,750). Visit the company's Web site at www.replicastadiums.com.

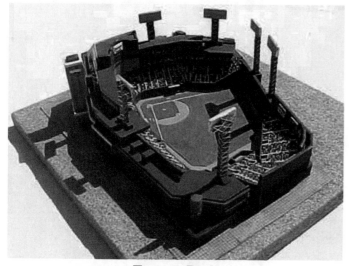

Fenway Park

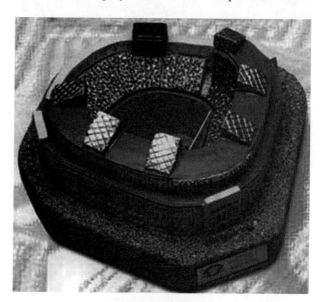

Yankee Stadium

Coors Field

County Stadium

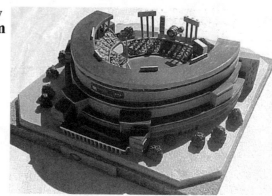

Gold Series

Atlanta's Fulton County $50
The Ballpark at Arlington $50
Bank One, Arizona $50
Busch Stadium $50
Camden Yards w/warehouse $60

Candlestick Park $50
Cleveland Stadium $50
Comiskey Park $50
Coors Field $50
County Stadium, Milwaukee $50
Crosley Field $50
Dodger Stadium $50

Dodger Stadium

Wrigley Field

Ebbets Field	$50
Fenway Park	$50
Forbes Field	$50
Griffith Stadium	$40
Jacobs Field	$50
Kingdome	$50
League Park	$50
Metrodome	$50
Oakland Alameda	$50
Old Memorial Stadium	$50
Polo Grounds	$50
Riverfront Stadium	$50
Shea Stadium	$50
Skydome	$50
Three Rivers Stadium	$50
Tiger Stadium	$50
Turner Field	$50

Veterans Stadium	$50
Wrigley Field	$50
Yankee Stadium	$50
Yankee Stadium (old)	$50

Silver Series (Mini stadiums)

Camden Yards	$15
Cleveland Stadium	$15
County Stadium	$15
Old Comiskey Park	$15
Old Yankee Stadium	$15
Polo Grounds	$15
Shea Stadium	$15
Shibe Park	$15
Wrigley Field	$15
Yankee Stadium	$15

Chapter 10

BASEBALL CEREAL BOXES

By Tom Hultman

Baseball cereal box collectors can thank quarterback Doug Flutie for the explosion in commemorative packages featuring collectors' favorite players from the diamond.

When Flutie Flakes were released by PLB Sports in the fall of 1998, it opened the door for other player cereal boxes to hit the market, including Cal Ripken's Classic O's in May of 1999 and Sammy's (Sosa) Frosted Flakes shortly thereafter from Famous Fixins.

Other player cereals that hit the store shelves were A-Rod's (Alex Rodriguez) 40/40 Crunch, Barry Bonds MVP Crunch, (Derek) Jeter's Frosted Flakes, Houston's Triple Play (Jeff Bagwell, Craig Biggio and Ken Caminiti) and Amazing Mets Frosted Flakes.

Of course, that's just the background on the player cereals. To get the history of athletes appearing on cereal boxes, one would have to go back to 1935 when General Mills showcased Olympians on boxes of Wheaties.

Today, Wheaties has become famous for honoring championship teams or a monumental feat on the front of its boxes. Over the past three years, Wheaties has honored the New York Yankees, Mark McGwire, Nolan Ryan and the Arizona Diamondbacks on the front of its boxes.

It truly is a wonderful time to be a cereal box collector.

"If you wanted to start collecting boxes today and you went to six different grocery stores, you could put 40 boxes on your shelf," cereal box collector Ron Schwinnen said. "It's good for starters. Forty boxes times

$3 apiece is $120. There are people who pay thousands of dollars to get started in other hobbies. It's a tremendous thing what Wheaties is doing."

There is one question that remains a constant within this collecting genre—Should collectors keep the boxes full of cereal, empty or flat? Schwinnen, who owns more than 400 boxes, said it doesn't matter. He said a majority of collectors prefer to have the boxes empty.

"There's always been an argument about this," he said. "One dealer says keep the boxes full with the cereal in it. Well, if you've got a warehouse where you can maintain a 72-degree temperature, do that. About 95 percent of all collectors take the cereal out and donate it to charity kitchens. Then the boxes are easier to store and easier to ship. I don't know of a collector who wanted to add a box to his collection that would refuse to buy it or trade for it based on the fact that it didn't have cereal in it."

Collectors say the easiest way to remove the cereal from the box is to melt the glue on the top and bottom flaps by using a hair dryer on the hottest setting. Blowing the hot air back and forth on the flaps will melt the glue. Then, gently pry the box open with a butter knife. Collectors who want to keep the package looking full may fill the box with styrofoam peanuts. To reseal the box, reheat the glue with a hair dryer and, when the glue has melted, seal the flaps.

In addition, other hobbyists prefer to collect cereal boxes straight from the presses. These packages, which are not folded, glued or filled with cereal, are called flats.

The following list prices mint, unopened cereal boxes. Original flats are worth 10-20 percent more than the listed price. The year reflects the date when the box was issued. The brand is the type of cereal. Regional issues are indicated by R. We also note which boxes were Canadian issues.

Cheerios
1998 Marlins '97 WS Champs $8

General Mills Grand Slam Baseball
1998 McGwire/Thomas/Piazza. $7

Kellogg's Corn Flakes
1970 Willie Mays $75
1983 San Diego Chicken 50
1983 Mike Reilly (umpire) 50
1983 Fernando Valenzuela 40

1991 Hank Aaron 40
1991 Ernie Banks 25
1991 Yogi Berra 25
1991 Lou Brock 25
1991 Steve Carlton 25
1991 Bob Gibson 25
1991 Aaron/Berra/Mays/Spahn 30
1992 Mike Schmidt 30

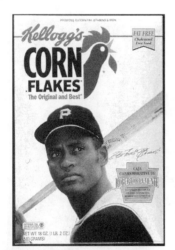

1993 Roberto Clemente (Spanish) 35

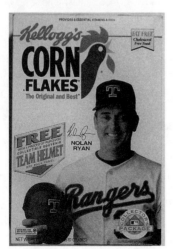

1993 Nolan Ryan 20
1993 Nolan Ryan farewell 30

1994 Roberto Clemente batting 30
1994 Roberto Clemente bat (Spanish). 40

Kellogg's Corn Pops
1993 Tom Seaver $20

Kellogg's Frosted Flakes
1991 Atlanta Braves NL Champs $30
1991 Braves WS (phantom) 75
1991 Twins WS Champs. 35
1992 Blue Jays Champs (*Canada). 35
1992 Braves NL Champs 35
1992 St. Louis Cardinals. 35

1993 Ken Griffey Jr. (20/25). 20
1993 Florida Marlins Inaugural. 18

1993 Colorado Rockies Inaugural. 18
1995 Carlos Baerga (Spanish). 15
1995 Colorado Rockies (Spanish). 15

Frosted Mini-Wheats
1995 Reggie Jackson (20). $25

Kellogg's Froot Loops
1983 Reggie Jackson/ Robin Yount/ Fernando Valenzuela $20

Post Alpha-Bits Canadian
1994 Joe Carter $20

Post 40% Bran Flakes
1960s Baseball cards on back ....$50-$100

Post Grape Nuts
1960s Baseball cards on back ....$50-$100

Post Grape Nut Flakes
1959 Warren Spahn $45

Post Honeycomb
1993 Barry Bonds, Ken Griffey, Jr.......................$15
1994 Mattingly/ Gonzalez/ Bonds/ Thomas/ Olerud/ Bonilla 20

Post Sugar Crisp
1955 Ted Williams.....................................$50
1960s Baseball cards on back............................50
1994 Mattingly/Gonzalez, Bonds, Thomas, Olerud, Bonilla 15

Post Raisin Bran
1960s Baseball Cards on back ....$50-$100

Post Sugar Crisp Canadian
1994 Joe Carter $20
1995 Devon White 15
1997 Moises Alou.......................................15

Post Toasties
1960s Baseball cards on back ....$50-$100

Ralston Cookie Crisp
1981 Jim Palmer $12
1984 Dale Murphy 10

Ralston Donkey Kong
1983 Jim Palmer.......................................$12

General Mills Wheaties

1935

Fancy Frame with Script Signature

Jack Armstrong $20
Wally Berger 20

Tommy Bridges 20
Mickey Cochrane 175
James "Rip" Collins 20
Dizzy Dean 55
Paul Dean 22
William Delaney 20

Jimmie Foxx 50
Frank Frisch 37

Lou Gehrig..225
Goose Goslin 30
Lefty Grove 45
Carl Hubbell 35
Travis Jackson 30
"Chuck" Klein 30
Gus Mancuso 20
"Pepper" Martin 20
Joe Medwick 35
Melvin Ott 50
Harold Schumacher 20
Al Simmons 30
"Jo Jo" White 20

1936

Fancy Frame with Printed Name and Data

Earl Averill..$30
Mickey Cochrane 40
"Jimmie" Foxx 45
Lou Gehrig 225

Hank Greenberg 40
"Gabby" Hartnett 30
Carl Hubbell 35
"Pepper" Martin 17
Van L. Mungo 20
"Buck" Newsom 20
"Arky" Vaughan 30
Jimmy Wilson 20

1936

How to Play Winning Baseball

Lefty Gomez. $35
Billy Herman 30
Luke Appling 35
Jimmie Foxx 45
Joe Medwick 35
Charlie Gehringer 35
Mel Ott 45
Odell Hale 20
Bill Dickey 50
"Lefty" Grove 50
Carl Hubbell 40
Earl Averill 35

1936

Thin Orange Border/Figures In Border

Curt Davis $20
Lou Gehrig 250
Charlie Gehringer 40
Lefty Grove 40
Rollie Hemsley 20
Billy Herman 30
Joe Medwick 30
Mel Ott. 45
Schoolboy Rowe 20
Arky Vaughan 30
Joe Vosmik 20
Lon Warneke 20

1937

Color Series

Zeke Bonura $20
Tom Bridges 20
Harland Clift 20
KiKi Cuyler 30
Joe DiMaggio. 225
Robert Feller 75
Lefty Grove 50
Billy Herman 30
Carl Hubbell 35
Buck Jordan 20
"Pepper" Martin 20
Wally Moses 20
Van L. Mungo 20
Cecil Travis 20
Arky Vaughan 30

1937

How to Star In Baseball

Bill Dickey. $50
Red Ruffing 30
Zeke Bonura. 20

Charlie Gehringer 35
"Arky" Vaughan 20
Carl Hubbell 35
John Lewis 20
Heinie Manush 30
Lefty Grove 40
Billy Herman 30
Joe DiMaggio. 225
Joe Medwick 30

1937

Small Panels with Orange Background Series

Zeke Bonura $40
Tom Bridges 40
Dolph Camilli 40
Frank Demaree 40
Joe DiMaggio 250
Billy Herman 70
Carl Hubbell 75
Ernie Lombardi 55
"Pepper" Martin 40
Jo Jo Moore 40
Van L. Mungo 40
Mel Ott. 75
Raymond Radcliff 40
Cecil Travis 40
Harold Trosky 40
ArkyVaughan 55

1937

Speckled Orange, White and Blue Series

Luke Appling $30
Earl Averill. 30
Joe DiMaggio 175
Robert Feller 75
Charles Gehringer 40
Lefty Grove 45
Carl Hubbell 45
Joe Medwick 35

1937

29 Series

"Zeke" Bonura $20
Cecil Travis 20
Frank Demaree 20
Jo Jo Moore 20
Ernie Lombardi 30
John "Pepper" Martin. 25
Harold Trosky 20
Raymond Radcliff 20
Joe DiMaggio 225
Tom Bridges 20
Van L. Mungo 20
"Arky" Vaughan 30
Arnold Statz 150
Fred Muller 150
Gene Lillard 150

1938

Biggest Thrills In Baseball

Bob Feller $75
Cecil Travis 20

Joe Medwick 35
Gerald Walker. 20
Carl Hubbell 35
Bob Johnson. 20
Beau Bell 20
Ernie Lombardi 30
Lefty Grove 40
Lou Fette 20
Joe DiMaggio 250
Pinky Whitney 20
Dizzy Dean 55
Charlie Gehringer 40
Paul Waner 30
Dolph Camilli 20

1938

Dress Clothes or Civilian Series

Lou Fette $20
Jimmie Foxx 40
Charlie Gehringer 35
Lefty Grove 35
Hank Greenberg 35
Ernie Lombardi 30
Joe Medwick 35
Lon Warneke 20

1938

Small Panels with Orange, Blue and White Background

Zeke Bonura $40
Joe DiMaggio. 250
Charley Gehringer 80
Hank Greenberg 80
Lefty Grove 60
Carl Hubbell 60
John "Buddy" Lewis 40
Heinie Manush 60
Joe Medwick 60
Arky Vaughan 60

1939

100 Years of Baseball

Design of First Diamond. $20
Gets News of Nomination on Field. 20
Crowd Boos First Baseball Glove. 20
Curve Ball Just an Illusion. 20
Fencer's Mask Is Pattern 20
Baseball Gets "All Dressed Up" 20
Modern Bludgeon Enters Game 20
"Casey at the Bat" 20

1939

Personal Pointers Series

Ernie Lombardi $30
Johnny Allen 20
Lefty Gomez 35
Bill Lee 20
Jimmie Foxx. 45
Joe Medwick 35
Hank Greenberg 35
Mel Ott. 50
Arky Vaughan. 30

1940

Champs of the U.S.A.

Bob Feller
Lynn Patrick
Charles "Red" Ruffing $50
Leo Durocher
Lynn Patrick
Charles "Red" Ruffing 45

Joe DiMaggio
John Duge
Hank Greenberg 150
Joe DiMaggio
Mel Ott
Ellsworth Vines 150
Bernie Bierman
Bill Dickey
Jimmie Foxx 40
Morris Arnovich
Capt. R.L. Baker
Earl "Dutch" Clark 20
"Matty" Bell
Ab Jenkins
Joe Medwick 20
Ralph Guldahl
John Mize
Davey O'Brien 20
Ralph Guldahl
Gabby Hartnett
Davey O'Brien 20
Bob Feller
John Mize
Rudy York 45
Joe Cronin
Hank Greenberg
Byron Nelson 20
Ernie Lombardi
Jack Manders
George Myers 20
Bob Bartlett
Capt. R.C. Hanson
Terrell Jacobs 20
Lowell "Red" Dawson
Billy Herman
Adele Inge 20
Dolph Camilli
Antoinette Concello
Wallace Wade 20
Luke Appling
Stanley Hack

Hugh McManus 20
Felix Adler
Hal Trosky
Mabel Vinson 20

1941

Champs of the U.S.A.

Felix Adler
Jimmie Foxx
Capt. R.G. Hanson $45
Bernie Bierman
Bob Feller
Jessie McLeod 45
Lowell "Red" Dawson
Hank Greenberg
J.W. Stoker 35
Antoinette Concello
Joe DiMaggio
Byron Nelson. 125
Capt. R.L. Baker
Frank "Buck" McCormick
Harold "Pee Wee" Reese 45
Harry Danning
Barney McCosky
Bucky Walters 20
William Robbins
Gene Sarazan
Gerald "Gee" Walker 20
Joe "Flash" Gordon
Stan Hack
George Myers 20

1951

Bob Feller (Baseball) $100
John Lujack (Football) 60
George Mikan (Basketball). 100

Stan Musial (Baseball) 150
Sam Snead (Golfer) 40
Ted Williams (Baseball) 150

1952

Larry "Yogi" Berra $40
Roy Campanella 40
Bob Feller 30
George Kell 12
Ralph Kiner 20
Bob Lemon. 20
Stan Musial 50
Phil Rizzuto 25

Elwin "Preacher" Roe 10
Ted Williams 75

Wheaties

1964 Tom Tresh $50
1985 Pete Rose (8 oz.) 45
1985 Pete Rose (12/18 oz.). 40
1987 Minnesota Twins WS Champs R 15
1989 Johnny Bench HOF R 40
1990 Jim Palmer HOF R. 40
1990 Cincinnati Reds R 25
1991 Rod Carew R 125
1991 Twins WS Champ (.75 oz) R 100
1991 Twins WS Champs R 30
1993 Lou Gehrig 10
1993 Willie Mays 10
1993 Babe Ruth 10
1995 Cal Ripken no O's logo R 25
1995 Cal Ripken w/O's logo. 10
1995 Braves WS Champs R 18
1995 Indians AL Champs R 18
1996 Ken Griffey Jr. (HF). 5
1996 Ken Griffey Jr. (HF 14.75 oz.) 8
1996 Griffey Jr. gold emb. (HF) 10
1996 Ken Griffey Jr. (HF). 15
1996 Kirby Puckett R 20
1996 Braves NL Champs R 12
1996 Cards Champs (phantom). 75
1996 Negro Leagues (75th Anniversary). 10
1996 Yankees AL Champs R. 12
1997 Jackie Robinson (Al) 7
1997 Mariners '97 WD champs 20
1997 Cone/Maddux/Nomo 6
1997 Bonds/Griffey/Gwynn 8
1997 Piazza/Ripken/Sandberg. 8
1997 Bonds/Griffey/C. Jones 8
1997 Griffey/Ripken/Thomas 8
1998 R. Clemens (Canada) (MFW) 10
1998 McGwire/Griffey/T. Martinez 15
1998 A. Rod/Maddux/Garciaparra (HF) 8
1998 Arizona Diamondbacks 10
1998 Mark McGwire/70HR 6
1998 Yankees WS Champs 15

1998 Nolan Ryan Leg. 5
1998 Nolan Ryan Leg. (CWR) 5
1998 Nolan Ryan Leg. (HW) 5
1999 Joe Torre/Yankees WS 10

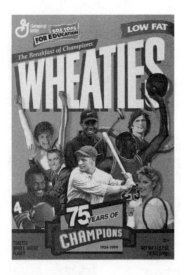

Wheaties 75 Years of Champions
1999 L. Gehrig/W. Payton/C. Evert/etc. $10

Additional Cereal Boxes

Famous Fixins
1999 Cal's Classic O's $10
1999 Slammin' Sammy's Frosted Flakes 10

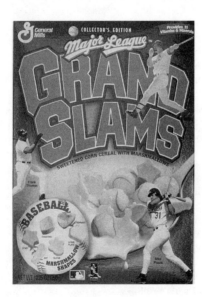

General Mills Corp.
1998 Major League Grand Slams (McGwire, F. Thomas, Piazza)
. . . . $10

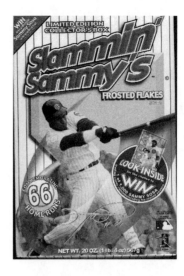

Famous Fixins 1999
Slammin' Sammy's (Sosa) Frosted Flakes. $10

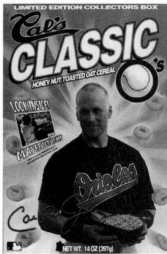

Cal's (Ripken) Classic O's 10
A-Rod's (Alex Rodriguez) 40/40 Crunch 10
Barry Bonds MVP Crunch 10
(Derek) Jeter's Frosted Flakes. 10
Houston's Triple Play (Jeff Bagwell, Craig Biggio and Ken Caminiti)
. . . . 10
Amazing Mets Frosted Flakes. 10

Global Sports & Promotions 1999
Albert Belle's Slugger Cereal $10
Roberto Clemente. 10

GENERAL MILLS CORP.
1960 POST CEREAL BOX BACKS

These cards were issued on the backs of Grape Nuts cereal and measure an oversized 7" x 8"? The nine cards in the set include five baseball players, two football players (Johnny Unitas and Frank Gifford) and two basketball players (Bob Pettit and Bob Cousy). The full-color photos were placed on a color background and bordered by a wood frame design. The cards covered the entire back of the cereal box and were blank-backed. Card fronts also include the player's name and team and a facsimile autograph. A panel on the side of the box contains player biographical information. A scarce set, the cards are very difficult to obtain in Mint condition. A Mint condition set of all nine is worth $4,500.

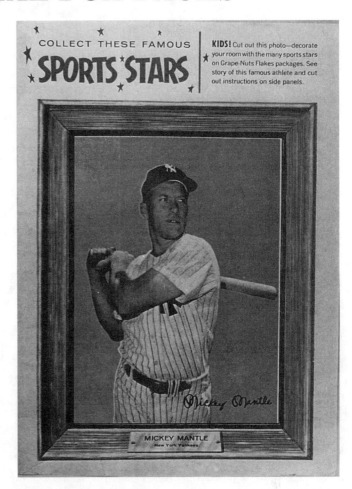

Bob Cousy	$450
Don Drysdale	400
Frank Gifford	350
Al Kaline	450
Harmon Killebrew	300
Eddie Mathews	300
Mickey Mantle	1,500
Bob Pettit	400
Johnny Unitas	400

BOTTLES & CANS

BEER CANS

Cold drinks and baseball go together. So it's no surprise that a large number of beer and soft drink cans have been produced over the years commemorating baseball teams and players.

The earliest-known examples date to 1906, when six different bottles known as the "Champions of 1906" were released. Featuring Christy Mathewson, John McGraw, Joe McGinnity, Billy Gilbert, Leon "Red" Ames and Mike Donlin from the 1905 World Champion New York Giants, the set is virtually one of a kind. It's tough to price the entire set, but individually at auction the bottles have attracted bids totaling $18,000.

In the 1950s, the Moxie Co. released root beer bottles featuring Ted Williams. These bottles are generally considered the first sports bottles to be widely available to the collecting public.

Over the last 50 years, more than 250 beer cans with sports-related themes have been issued. Generally, the cans feature team/player photos, drawings, schedules or statistics in the design. The most appealing cans usually salute pro sports teams and their stars, but lower levels of competition have also been represented.

More than 50 commemorative baseball-related beer cans have been produced featuring major league players, minor league teams and six major league teams (Pirates, Twins, Cubs, White Sox, Reds and Orioles). Many have team/player photos, drawings, schedules or stats incorporated into the design and were sold for a limited time in a limited area. Beer can trade shows are the best places to find older cans no longer sold in stores. Most collectors prefer cans that have been opened from the bottom.

Anheuser-Busch, St. Louis, Mo., issued a Red Schoendienst commemorative bank can in 1977, honoring the dedication of Schoendienst Field, Feb. 20, 1977, in Germantown, Ill.

C. Schmidt & Sons Inc., Philadelphia, Pa., issued four Caseys Lager Beer cans in 1980 featuring Duke Snider, Richie Ashburn, Whitey Ford and Monte Irvin.

National Brewing Co., Baltimore, Md., issued a National Bohemian Beer can with a 1970 Baltimore Orioles schedule and a can in 1992 commemorating Baltimore's Memorial Stadium from 1954-91. Adolph Coors Co., Golden, Colo., issued a can in 1992 commemorating the Baltimore Orioles' 1991 season.

G. Heileman Brewing Co., La Crosse, Wis., has done several cans. Old Style 16-ounce brands in 1990 featured the Chicago White Sox' Comiskey Park, Ron Santo, Billy Williams, Ferguson Jenkins and the 1990 Divisional Championship. A 1991 Old Style Light can featured Billy Williams, while 1992 Special Export 16-ounce green cans and 1992 Special Export Light 16-ounce blue cans honor the 1961-91 Minnesota Twins.

Hudepohl Brewing Co., Cincinnati, Ohio, issued cans in 1976 and 1977 commemorating the 1975 and 1976 World Champion Cincinnati Reds. There are two varieties in 1976 — with either a cream or grey box score background.

Pittsburgh Brewing Co., Pittsburgh, Pa., issued Iron City Beer & Draft cans, focusing on the Pittsburgh Pirates. The 1973 cans featured Three Rivers Stadium. Ten 1974 cans featured the Pirates' team record from 1887-1973; participation in the World Series; 1974 home schedule; 1974 TV schedule; 1974 roster of pitchers, catchers; 1974 roster of infielders, outfielders; 1960 World Series; 1971 World Series; World Championships from 1950-73; and a letter from the brewery's president. Two 1980 cans featured the 1979 World Champions and a salute to the 1979 champs. A 1988 can featured Hardball 88, while a 1990 can honored the Pittsburgh Tradition. Two 1991 cans were issued featuring the Eastern Division Championship and ticket stubs.

Places to search for beer cans include flea markets, antique shops and malls, along the roadside, at hunting camps and cabins, in old farms and at the town dump. There are also clubs to join, such as the Beer Can Collectors of America (in Fenton, Mo.) and the American Breweriana Association (in Pueblo, Colo.).

Bottle price

1906 Christy Mathewson	$6,500
1906 John McGraw	3,500
1906 Joe McGinnity	3,500
1906 Billy Gilbert	1,500
1906 Leon "Red" Ames	1,500
1906 Mike Donlin	1,500
1950s Ted Williams Moxy Co. (unopened)	200
1950s Ted Williams Root Beer 6-pack w/carton (opened)	300
1976 Pepsi Cincinnati Reds 1975 World Champions (unopened)	12
1976 Hudepohl Brewing Co. Cincinnati Reds World Champions	15
1977 Hudepohl Brewing Co. Cincinnati Reds World Champions	15
1980 C. Schmidt & Sons Casey's Lager Beer Duke Snider	15
1980 C. Schmidt & Sons Casey's Lager Beer Richie Ashburn	15
1980 C. Schmidt & Sons Casey's Lager Beer Whitey Ford	15
1980 C. Schmidt & Sons Casey's Lager Beer Monte Irvin	15

COCA-COLA PRODUCTS

Commemorative Coca-Cola Bottles

Over the years, numerous baseball events have been commemorated on Coke. Various events have been covered including championships, All-Star games, new stadium openings, anniversaries of team foundings, new logos, old logos, inaugural seasons, attendance records, etc. Generally, bottles are issued regionally for professional, college and other amateur sporting events. Commemorative bottles have been produced in 6 1/2, 8, 10, 12, 16 and 32 oz. sizes.

The first 8 oz. sports commemorative was issued in 1991. According to Coca Cola, there are three basic guidelines when considering issuing a commemorative Coke bottle. First, it must commemorate a special event which has a potentially high level of interest. Next, issuance of the bottle would be expected to generate interest in the prod-uct in the geographic area of the event. Finally, it should be sought after by collectors as a keepsake to remember the event, team, or person. Subjects for commemorative bottles are limited to three general areas: 1. major national events or local events with a relatively large following, 2. Coca-Cola Collectors Club-related events, and 3. internal Coca-Cola Bottling Co. events such as anniversaries and retirements.

In order to be "collectible," bottles should be full, since the contents can be seen. This differs from collectible cans that may be opened (usually from the bottom) and emptied without losing value.

There are two versions of the Jackie Robinson bottle. The first was issued in Los Angeles and includes shades of blue, gold, red and white with a glossy finish. The second was issued in southern Michigan and includes blue and white only with a flat finish.

8 oz. Coca-Cola Bottles

Event	Year	Price
St. Louis Cardinals 100 Anniversary	1992	$8
Baltimore Orioles, MLB All-Star Game at Camden Yards	1993	6
Best of the Bay - Oakland A's (set of 6)	1993	4
Best of the Bay - S.F. Giants (set of 6)	1993	4
Colorado Rockies Inaugural Season	1993	6
Florida Marlins Inaugural Season	1993	6
San Diego Padres 25th Year	1993	10
Ballpark at Arlington	1994	4
Cincinnati Reds 5 World Championships	1994	5
Cincinnati Reds First Season Central Division	1994	3
Colorado Rockies MLB Attendance Record (D. Baylor sign.)	1994	3
Colorado Rockies MLB Attendance Record (McMorris sign.)	1994	3
Florida Marlins Second Season	1994	3
Johnny Mize - The Big Cat - Hall of Fame 1981	1994	50
Milwaukee Brewers 25th Anniversary	1994	3
Ty Cobb -The Georgia Peach	1994	125
All-Star Fan Fest (Baseball)	1994	3
Astrodome 30th Anniversary	1995	5
Cal Ripken Jr. Record-Breaking Year	1995	3
Cincinnati Reds Logo (1869) (1st of 5)	1995	3
Cincinnati Reds Logo (1907) (2nd of 5)	1995	3
Cincinnati Reds Logo (1911) (3rd of 5)	1995	3
Cincinnati Reds Logo (1939) (4th of 5)	1995	3
Cincinnati Reds Logo (1995) (5th of 5)	1995	3
Norwich Navigators Baseball	1995	3
Ty Cobb - Baseball's Best (1,008 bottles made)	1995	100
Atlanta Braves World Champs	1996	3
Cincinnati Reds Big Red Machine 20th Anniversary	1996	3
Jackie Robinson - 50th Anniversary (California version)	1997	3
Jackie Robinson - 50th Anniversary (Michigan version)	1997	3
John Smoltz - Cy Young Award Winner	1997	3
Reds (Cincinnati) Rally 25th Anniversary	1997	3
St. Louis Cardinals - Central Division Champs	1997	3
Texas Rangers - Western Division Champs	1997	3
Turner Field - Home of the Braves - Inaugural Season	1997	3
Zephyrs Field - Inaugural Season	1997	3
Florida Marlins - World Series Champs	1998	3
Roger Dean Stadium - Inaugural Season	1998	3
Yankee Stadium 75th Anniversary	1998	3

10 oz. Coca-Cola Bottles

Event	Year	Price
Baseball Winter Meetings - Hollywood, Fla.	1981	$125
Dizzy Dean Graduate League World Series	1982	15
St. Louis Cardinals - World Champions (Error)	1982	15
Birmingham Barons 1983 Southern League Baseball Champs	1983	5
Orioles - 1983 World Champions	1984	6
Johnston Coca-Cola Youth Baseball Classic	1985	10
Kansas City Royals - World Champions "Show Me Series"	1985	15
Ty Cobb - The Georgia Peach	1985	250
Johnston Coca-Cola Youth Baseball Classic	1985	10
Tyrus Raymond Cobb - Royston Lodge 52 Remembers Ty	1986	1,200
Johnston Coca-Cola Youth Baseball Classic	1988	10
Ty Cobb - First in the Hall of Fame	1989	175

1977-78 ROYAL CROWN COLA SODA CANS

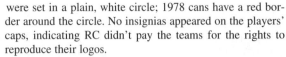

They don't fit into plastic sheets, they rust and they may leak, and all they do is collect dust. But if you have the room to display or store them, Royal Crown cans featuring baseball players pose a fairly inexpensive challenge to collectors.

The cans, issued in 1977-78, feature more than a dozen Hall of Famers. The cans, produced prior to the introduction of today's one-piece aluminum pop cans, are constructed in three parts — a top, center and bottom — which are crimped and soldered together. Rust may appear at the seams if the cans are in storage for a while; if the can still has soda inside it, you can expect it to spring a leak, due to the acidity of the cola. Cans are more valuable when they appear to be full, so they should be opened from the bottom.

There were 70 cans produced in 1977; in 1978, 100 cans were made. Many of the players appeared in both sets, some with the same black-and-white pictures, some with different ones. The photos

were set in a plain, white circle; 1978 cans have a red border around the circle. No insignias appeared on the players' caps, indicating RC didn't pay the teams for the rights to reproduce their logos.

Both years used the same basic blue color scheme, with red and white trim. Cans from 1977 had player biographical data in a square, while those produced in 1978 had a career-highlights summary inside a baseball. At the bottom of the ball was the can number, designated as No. x of 100.

The biggest problem with buying RC cans is not the cost, but rather finding the cans. Many dealers do not take them to shows because they are too bulky and take up valuable table space. Nor are the cans generally advertised for sale in hobby papers because it usually costs more to mail them than they are worth. The first price listed below is for a can; the second value is for the can flats, the 5x8 3/8" square tin strips used to make the cans.

1977 Royal Crown Soda Cans

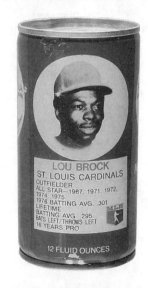

Sal Bando .... $3/$6	Fred Lynn .... $2-$3.50/$6
Mark Belanger .... $1-$3.50/$6	Bill Madlock .... $1/$6
Johnny Bench.................................. $10/$30	Jon Matlack .... $1-$4/$8
Vida Blue .... $3-$5/$6	Gary Matthews.............................. $1-$3/$6
Bobby Bonds .... $2-$3/$6	Bake McBride .... $1/$6
Bob Boone .... $1-$3/$6	Hal McRae .... $2-$3/$6
Larry Bowa .... $1/$6	Andy Messersmith .... $1-$3/$6
Steve Braun .... $3/$6	Rick Monday .... $1/$6
George Brett .... $10/$25	John Montefusco .... $1-$3/$6
Lou Brock .... $10-$15/$20	Joe Morgan .... $10/$20
Bert Campaneris .... $2/$6	Thurman Munson .... $5-$10/$10
Bill Campbell .... $1-$3/$6	Al Oliver .... $2-$3.50/$6
Jose Cardenal .... $1/$6	Amos Otis .... $1/$6
Rod Carew .... $5-$10/$25	Jim Palmer .... $5-$10/$25
Dave Cash .... $1-$3/$6	Dave Parker .... $2-$3/$6
Cesar Cedeno .... $1-$3/$6	Fred Patek .... $1/$6
Ron Cey .... $2/$6	Gaylord Perry .... $10/$20
Chris Chambliss .... $2-$4/$6	Marty Perez .... $1/$6
Dave Concepcion .... $2/$7	Tony Perez .... $2-$4/$8
Mark Fidrych .... $2/$6	J.R. Richard.................................... $1/$6
Rollie Fingers .... $8-$10/$15	Pete Rose .... $10/$35
George Foster .... $2-$3/$6	Joe Rudi .... $2-$3/$6
Wayne Garland .... $3/$6	Mike Schmidt.................................. $10/$35
Ralph Garr .... $1-$3/$6	Tom Seaver .... $10-$12/$35
Steve Garvey .... $3.50-$5/$7	Bill Singer .... $1/$6
Bobby Grich .... $1-$3/$6	Rusty Staub .... $1-$4/$6
Ken Griffey .... $2-$3.50/$6	Don Sutton .... $2/$7
Don Gullett .... $1-$3/$6	Gene Tenace .... $2/$6
Mike Hargrove .... $3/$6	Luis Tiant .... $2/$7
Catfish Hunter .... $5/$15	Ellis Valentine .... $1-$3/$6
Randy Jones .... $1-$3/$6	Claudell Washington .... $1-$3/$6
Dave Kingman .... $4/$8	Butch Wynegar .... $1/$6
Dave LaRoche .... $1/$6	Carl Yastrzemski .... $10-$15/$30
Ron LeFlore .... $2/$6	Robin Yount .... $10-$15/$20
Greg Luzinski .... $2-$3/$6	Richie Zisk .... $1.50-$2/$6

1978 Royal Crown Soda Cans

1. Don Sutton ....$2-$3.50/$6
2. Bill Singer ....$1/$5
3. Pete Rose ....$10-$15/$30
4. Gene Tenace ....$1-$3/$5
5. Dave Kingman ....$2-$3.50/$5
6. Dave Cash ....$1-$3/$5
7. Joe Morgan ....$10/$15
8. Mark Belanger ....$1-$3.50/$5
9. Steve Braun ....$1/$5
10. Butch Wynegar ....$3/$5
11. Ken Griffey ....$2-$3.50/$5
12. Ron LeFlore ....$1-$3/$5
13. George Foster ....$2-$3/$5
14. Tony Perez ....$4/$7
15. Thurman Munson ....$5-$10/$10
16. Bill Campbell ....$1-$3/$5
17. Andy Messersmith ....$1-$3/$5
18. Mike Schmidt ....$10-$15/$30
19. Ron Cey ....$3/$5
20. Chris Chambliss ....$3/$5
21. Ralph Garr ....$1-$3/$5
22. Dave LaRoche ....$1-$3/$5
23. George Brett ....$10/$20
24. Bob Boone ....$3/$5
25. Jeff Burroughs ....$1-$3/$5
26. Bake McBride ....$3/$5
27. Gary Matthews ....$3/$5
28. Don Gullett ....$1/$5
29. Rick Monday ....$1-$3/$5
30. Al Oliver ....$3.50/$5
31. Ellis Valentine ....$3/$5
32. Mike Hargrove ....$3/$5
33. Hal McRae ....$2/$5
34. Rollie Fingers ....$7-$10/$12
35. Dave Parker ....$3/$5

36. Tom Seaver ....$10/$30
37. Wayne Garland ....$3/$5
38. Jon Matlack ....$3/$5
39. Richie Zisk ....$3/$5
40. Joe Rudi ....$3/$5
41. Sal Bando ....$3-$5/$5
42. Greg Luzinski * ....$2/$5
43. Vida Blue * ....$3/$5
44. Bobby Bonds ....$2-$3/$6
45. Jim Palmer ....$7/$20
46. Claudell Washington ....$1-$3/$5
47. Dave Concepcion ....$2/$6
48. Rod Carew ....$10/$20
49. J.R. Richard ....$3/$5
50. Rich Gossage ....$2/$6
51. Cesar Cedeno ....$2/$5
52. Bert Campaneris ....$2/$5
53. Marty Perez ....$1/$5
54. Bill Madlock ....$2/$5
55. Amos Otis ....$2/$5
56. Robin Yount ....$10/$15
57. Bobby Grich ....$1-$3/$5
58. Catfish Hunter ....$5-$10/$12
59. Butch Hobson ....$3/$5
60. Larry Bowa ....$2/$5
61. Randy Jones * ....$1-$3/$5
62. Richie Hebner ....$1/$5
63. Fred Patek ....$1/$5
64. John Denny ....$1/$5
65. Johnny Bench ....$10/$25
66. Doyle Alexander ....$3/$5
67. Dusty Baker ....$2/$5
68. Bert Blyleven ....$3/$5
69. Lyman Bostock ....$1/$5
70. Bill Buckner ....$1-$3/$5

71. Steve Carlton ....$10-$12/$25
72. John Candelaria ....$1/$5
73. Andre Dawson ....$4/$6
74. Al Cowens ....$1/$5
75. Eddie Murray ....$7/$30
76. Dan Driessen ....$3/$5
77. Jim Rice ....$3.50/$6
78. Garry Maddox ....$3/$5
79. Larry Hisle ....$3/$5
80. Al Hrabosky ....$3/$5
81. Reggie Jackson ....$10/$25
82. Tommy John ....$3/$5
83. Willie McCovey ....$10/$15
84. Sparky Lyle ....$3/$5
85. Tug McGraw ....$3/$5
86. Paul Splittorff ....$3/$5
87. Bobby Murcer ....$4/$8
88. Graig Nettles ....$4/$6
89. Phil Niekro ....$4/$7
90. Lou Piniella ....$3.50/$6
91. Rick Reuschel ....$3/$5
92. Frank Tanana ....$3/$5
93. Nolan Ryan ....$40/$75
94. Garry Templeton ....$3/$5
95. Reggie Smith....................................$3/$5
96. Bruce Sutter ....$1-$3/$5
97. Jason Thompson ....$3/$5
98. Mike Torrez....................................$3/$5
99. Rick Wise ....$1/$5
100. Bump Wills ....$3/$5

• Indicates the player photo is different from that used on the 1977 can.

BOTTLE CAPS

1967-68 Coca-Cola Baseball

These bottle caps were issued in 1967-68. Some of the players had changed teams from one year to the next, so some were dropped and others were added in 1968. The caps issued in 1967 are identified by an a; those issued in 1968 have a b. The caps were issued on bottles of Coke, Tab, Sprite, Fresca and some flavors of Fanta.

Although Coke caps are more common, there is no difference in price for the same player on different sodas. This was a national promotion, but only the All-Stars were issued across the country. Each major league team at the time was produced, except the St. Louis Cardinals. They were distributed in the local area of that team only, which makes completing a set of all 19 teams very difficult. The All-Stars are the most readily available, so a cap of the same player is generally more valuable from the regional set than the All-Star set. The numbering is on the inside of the cap. The system for the regional sets begins with an alphabetical designation sometimes corresponding to the team name (T for Tigers) and a number from 1-18. However, for the two cities which have two teams (New York and Los Angeles), the numbers go to 35. The All-Stars are numbered in one of two ways. The Major League All-Stars are numbered from 1-35 with no alphabetical designation; this set was produced for those areas which did not have a major league city near by. The other set is divided between National (N19-N35) and American (A19-A35) League All-Stars. This set is a continuation of the regional sets. There were also eight game caps which could be sent in to Coca-Cola along with complete team sets for prizes, among which were the 1967 Dexter Press oversized cards. The bottle caps are condition-sensitive because most were bent with a bottle opener and discarded.

Major League All-Stars

1. Richie Allen $2.50
2. Pete Rose............................ $25
3. Brooks Robinson $15
4. Marcelino Lopez $1
5. Rusty Staub $2
6. Ron Santo $2.50
7. Jim Nash...............................$1
8. Jim Fregosi.........................$1.50
9. Paul Casanova $1
10. Willie Mays $35
11. Willie Stargell $7
12. Tony Oliva $2.50
13. Joe Pepitone $1.50
14. Juan Marichal $6
15. Jim Bunning $2.50
16. Claude Osteen $1
17. Carl Yastrzemski $20
18. Harmon Killebrew $8.50
19. Henry Aaron $35
20. Joe Torre $2.50
21. Ernie Banks $15
22. Al Kaline $15
23. Frank Robinson $14
24. Max Alvis..............................$1
25. Elston Howard $2.50
26. Gaylord Perry $5
27. Bill Mazeroski $2.50
28. Ron Swoboda $1
29. Vada Pinson.......................$1.50
30. Joe Morgan $7
31. Cleon Jones $1
32. Willie Horton $1
33. Leon Wagner $1
34. George Scott..........................$1
35. Ed Charles $1

National League All-Stars

N19. Henry Aaron $35
N20. Jim Bunning.....................$2.50
N21. Joe Torre $2.50
N22. Claude Osteen $1
N23. Ron Santo $2.50
N24. Joe Morgan $7
N25. Richie Allen......................$2.50
N26. Ron Swoboda $1
N27. Ernie Banks $15
N28. Bill Mazeroski $2.50
N29. Willie Stargell.....................$7

N30. Pete Rose $25
N31. Gaylord Perry $5
N32. Rusty Staub $2
N33. Vada Pinson $1.50
N34. Juan Marichal $6
N35. Cleon Jones $1

American League All-Stars

A19. Al Kaline $15
A20. Frank Howard $2.50
A21. Brooks Robinson $15
A22. George Scott.......................$1
A23. Willie Horton $1
A24. Jim Fregosi $1.50
A25. Ed Charles $1
A26. Harmon Killebrew................ $8.50
A27. Tony Oliva $2.50
A28. Joe Pepitone $1.50
A29. Elston Howard $2.50
A30. Jim Nash...........................$1
A31. Marcelino Lopez $1
A32. Frank Robinson $14
A33. Leon Wagner $1
A34. Max Alvis..........................$1
A35. Paul Casanova $1

Atlanta Braves

B1a. Gary Geiger $1.50
B1b. Cecil Upshaw.....................$1.50
B2a. Ty Cline $1.50
B2b. Tito Francona....................$1.50
B3. Henry Aaron $45
B4a. Gene Oliver......................$1.50
B4b. Pat Jarvis $1.50
B5. Tony Cloninger $1.50
B6a. Denis Menke $1.50
B6b. Phil Niekro......................$7.50
B7a. Denny LeMaster $1.50
B7b. Felix Milan $1.50
B8. Woody Woodward $1.50
B9. Joe Torre $3
B10. Ken Johnson $1.50
B11a. Bob Bruce $1.50
B11b. Marty Martinez...................$1.50
B12. Felipe Alou $1.50
B13. Clete Boyer $1.50
B14a. Wade Blasingame $1.50
B14b. Sonny Jackson $1.50
B15a. Don Schwall $1.50

B15b. Deron Johnson $1.50
B16a. Dick Kelley.....................$1.50
B16b. Claude Raymond $1.50
B17. Rico Carty.........................$2
B18. Mack Jones $1.50

Baltimore Orioles

O1. Dave McNally $1.50
O2a. Luis Aparicio $5
O2b. Jim Hardin $1.50
O3. Paul Blair $1.50
O4. Frank Robinson.................... $18
O5a. Jim Palmer $14
O5b. Bruce Howard $1.50
O6a. Russ Snyder $1.50
O6b. John O'Donoghue $1.50
O7a. Stu Miller $1.50
O7b. Dave May $1.50
O8. Dave Johnson $1.50
O9. Andy Etchebarren $1.50
O10. Brooks Robinson................. $20
O11. John Powell........................$3
O12a. Sam Bowens $1.50
O12b. Pete Richert $1.50
O13. Curt Blefary $1.50
O14a. Ed Fisher........................$1.50
O14b. Mark Belanger $1.50
O15. Wally Bunker $1.50
O16a. Moe Drabowsky $1.50
O16b. Don Buford $1.50
O17. Larry Haney $1.50
O18. Tom Phoebus $1.50

Boston Red Sox

R1. Lee Stange $1.50
R2a. Carl Yastrzemski $25
R2b. Gary Waslewski $1.50
R3a. Don Demeter.......................$1.50
R3b. Gary Bell $1.50
R4a. Jose Santiago $1.50
R4b. John Wyatt $1.50
R5. Darrell Brandon $1.50
R6. Joe Foy $1.50
R7a. Don McMahon $1.50
R7b. Ray Culp $1.50
R8. Dalton Jones $1.50
R9a. Mike Ryan $1.50
R9b. Gene Oliver $1.50
R10a. Bob Tillman $1.50

R10b. Jose Santiago $1.50
R11. Rico Petrocelli $1.50
R12. George Scott $1.50
R13a. George Smith $1.50
R13b. Mike Andrews $1.50
R14a. Dennis Bennett $1.50
R14b. Dick Ellsworth $1.50
R15a. Hank Fischer $1.50
R15b. Norm Sieburn $1.50
R16. Jim Lonborg $1.50
R17a. Jose Tartabull $1.50
R17b. Jerry Adair $1.50
R18a. George Thomas...............$1.50
R18b. Elston Howard $3.50

California Angels

L19. Len Gabrielson $1.50
L20. Jackie Hernandez $1.50
L21. Paul Schaal $1.50
L22. Lou Burdette $1.50
L23. Jimmie Hall $1.50
L24. Fred Newman $1.50
L25. Don Mincher $1.50
L26. Bob Rodgers $1.50
L27. Jack Sanford $1.50
L28. Bobby Knoop....................$1.50
L29. Jose Cardenal $1.50
L30. Jim Fregosi $1.50
L31. George Brunet $1.50
L32. Marcelino Lopez $1.50
L33. Minnie Rojas....................$1.50
L34. Jay Johnstone $1.50
L35. Ed Kirkpatrick $1.50

Chicago Cubs

C1. Ferguson Jenkins $12
C2. Ernie Banks $20
C3. Glenn Beckert....................$1.50
C4. Bob Hendley $1.50
C5. John Boccabella.................$1.50
C6. Ron Campbell $1.50
C7. Ray Culp $1.50
C8. Adolfo Phillips $1.50
C9. Don Bryant $1.50
C10. Randy Hundley $1.50
C11. Ron Santo $3
C12. Lee Thomas $1.50
C13. Billy Williams $8.50
C14. Ken Holtzman....................$1.50
C15. Cal Koonce $1.50
C16. Curt Simmons....................$1.50
C17. George Altman $1.50
C18. Byron Browne $1.50

Chicago White Sox

L1. Gary Peters $1.50
L2. Jerry Adair $1.50
L3. Al Weiss $1.50
L4. Pete Ward $1.50
L5. Hoyt Wilhelm $6
L6. Don Buford $1.50
L7. John Buzhardt.....................$1.50
L8. Wayne Causey.....................$1.50
L9. Gerald McNertney $1.50
L10. Ron Hansen $1.50
L11. Tom McCraw $1.50
L12. Jim O'Toole $1.50
L13. Bill Skowron $1.50
L14. Joel Horlen $1.50

L15. Tommy John $4
L16. Bob Locker $1.50
L17. Ken Berry $1.50
L18. Tommie Agee $1.50

Cincinnati Reds

F1. Floyd Robinson $1.50
F2. Leo Cardenas $1.50
F3. Gordy Coleman $1.50
F4. Tommy Harper $1.50
F5. Tommy Helms $1.50
F6. Deron Johnson $1.50
F7. Jim Maloney $1.50
F8. Tony Perez $10
F9. Don Pavletich $1.50
F10. John Edwards $1.50
F11. Vada Pinson $1.50
F12. Chico Ruiz $1.50
F13. Pete Rose $25
F14. Billy McCool $1.50
F15. Joe Nuxhall $1.50
F16. Milt Pappas $1.50
F17. Art Shamsky $1.50
F18. Dick Simpson $1.50

Cleveland Indians

I1. Luis Tiant $5
I2. Max Alvis $1.50
I3. Larry Brown $1.50
I4a. Rocky Colavito $4
I4b. Tommy Harper $1.50
I5a. John O'Donoghue $1.50
I5b. Vern Fuller $1.50
I6a. Pedro Gonzalez $1.50
I6b. Jose Cardenal $1.50
I7a. Gary Bell $1.50
I7b. Dave Nelson $1.50
I8. Sonny Siebert $1.50
I9. Joe Azcue $1.50
I10. Lee Maye $1.50
I11. Chico Salmon $1.50
I12. Leon Wagner $1.50
I13a. Fred Whitfield $1.50
I13b. Eddie Fischer $1.50
I14. Jack Kralick $1.50
I14b. Stan Williams $1.50
I15. Sam McDowell $2.00
I16a. Dick Radatz $1.50
I16b. Steve Hargan $1.50
I17. Vic Davallio $1.50
I18a. Chuck Hinton $1.50
I18b. Duke Sims $1.50

Detroit Tigers

T1a. Larry Sherry.....................$1.50
T1b. Ray Oliver........................$1.50
T2. Norm Cash $5
T3a. Jerry Lumpe $1.50
T3b. Mike Marshall $5
T4a. Dave Wickersham $1.50
T4b. Mickey Stanley $1.50
T5. Joe Sparma $1.50
T6. Dick McAuliffe $1.50
T7a. Fred Gladding $1.50
T7b. Gates Brown $1.50
T8. Jim Northrup $1.50
T9. Bill Freehan $1.50
T10. Earl Wilson $1.50
T11. Dick Tracewski $1.50
T12. Don Wert $1.50

T13a. Jake Wood $1.50
T13b. Dennis Ribant $1.50
T14. Mickey Lolich $5
T15a. Johnny Podres $1.50
T15b. Denny McLain $6.50
T16a. Bill Monbouquette $1.50
T16b. Ed Mathews $12
T17. Al Kaline $20
T18. Willie Horton $2

Houston Astros

H1. Dave Guisti $1.50
H2. Bob Aspromonte...................$1.50
H3. Ron Davis $1.50
H4a. Claude Raymond $1.50
H4b. Julio Gotay $1.50
H5a. Barry Latman $1.50
H5b. Fred Gladding $1.50
H6a. Chuck Harrison...................$1.50
H6b. Lee Thomas $1.50
H7a. Bill Heath $1.50
H7b. Wade Blasingame $1.50
H8a. Sonny Jackson $1.50
H8b. Denis Menke......................$1.50
H9. John Bateman $1.50
H10. Ron Brand $1.50
H11a. Aaron Pointer $1.50
H11b. Doug Rader $1.50
H12. Joe Morgan $9
H13. Rusty Staub $3
H14. Mike Cuellar......................$1.50
H15. Larry Dierker $1.50
H16a. Dick Farrell......................$1.50
H16b. Denny LeMaster $1.50
H17a. Jim Landis $1.50
H17b. Jim Wynn $1.50
H18a. Ed Mathews $12
H18b. Don Wilson $1.50

Kansas City Athletics

K1. Jim Nash $1.50
K2. Bert Campaneris...................$1.50
K3. Ed Charles $1.50
K4. Wes Stock $1.50
K5. John Odom $1.50
K6. Ozzie Chavarria...................$1.50
K7. Jack Aker $1.50
K8. Dick Green $1.50
K9. Phil Roof $1.50
K10. Rene Lachemann $1.50
K11. Mike Hershberger.................$1.50
K12. Joe Nossek $1.50
K13. Roger Repoz $1.50
K14. Chuck Dobson $1.50
K15. Jim Hunter $12
K16. Lew Krausse $1.50
K17. Danny Cater $1.50
K18. Jim Gosger $1.50

Los Angeles Dodgers

L1. Phil Regan..........................$1.50
L2. Bob Bailey $1.50
L3. Ron Fairly $1.50
L4a. Joe Moeller $1.50
L4b. Jim Brewer $1.50
L5. Don Sutton $8.50
L6a. Ron Hunt $1.50
L6b. Tom Haller $1.50
L7a. Jim Brewer $1.50
L7b. Rocky Colavito $4

L8a. Lou Johnson....................................$1.50
L8b. Jim Grant $1.50
L9a. John Roseboro..............................$1.50
L9b. Jim Campanis................................$1.50
L10. Jeff Torborg..................................$1.50
L11a. John Kennedy..............................$1.50
L11b. Zoilo Versalles.............................$1.50
L12. Jim Lefebvre $1.50
L13. Wes Parker $1.50
L14a. Bob Miller....................................$1.50
L14b. Bill Singer $1.50
L15. Claude Osteen...............................$1.50
L16a. Ron Perranoski............................$1.50
L16b. Len Gabrielson............................$1.50
L17. Willie Davis $1.50
L18. Al Ferrara.....................................$1.50

Minnesota Twins

M1a. Ron Kline......................................$1.50
M1b. Rich Reese $1.50
M2. Bob Allison....................................$1.50
M3a. Earl Battey....................................$1.50
M3b. Ron Perranoski.............................$1.50
M4a. Jim Merritt $1.50
M4b. John Roseboro $1.50
M5. Jim Perry.......................................$1.50
M6. Harmon Killebrew $10
M7. Dave Boswell..................................$1.50
M8. Rich Rollins $1.50
M9. Jerry Zimmerman $1.50
M10. Al Worthington $1.50
M11. Cesar Tovar $1.50
M12a. Sandy Valdespino.........................$1.50
M12b. Jim Merritt $1.50
M13a. Zoilo Versalles $1.50
M13b. Bob Miller....................................$1.50
M14. Dean Chance..................................$1.50
M15a. Jim Grant $1.50
M15b. Ted Uhlaender..............................$1.50
M16. Jim Kaat $4
M17. Tony Oliva $3
M18a. Andy Kosco..................................$1.50
M18b. Rod Carew $50

New York Mets

V19. Chuck Hiller..................................$1.50
V20. Johnny Lewis.................................$1.50
V21. Ed Kranepool $1.50
V22. Al Luplow......................................$1.50
V23. Don Cardwell................................$1.50
V24. Cleon Jones $1.50
V25a. Bob Shaw $1.50
N7. Tom Seaver......................................$50
V26. John Stephenson.............................$1.50
V27. Ron Swoboda.................................$1.50
V28. Ken Boyer $1.50

V29. Ed Bressoud $1.50
V30. Tommy Davis $1.50
V31. Roy McMillan $1.50
V32. Jack Fisher.....................................$1.50
V33. Tug McGraw $1.50
V34. Jerry Grote.....................................$1.50
V35. Jack Hamilton................................$1.50

New York Yankees

V1. Mel Stottlemyre...............................$3.50
V2. Ruben Amaro $1.50
V3. Jake Gibbs $1.50
V4. Dooley Womack...............................$1.50
V5. Fred Talbot $1.50
V6. Horace Clark $1.50
V7. Jim Bouton $3.50
V8. Mickey Mantle $75
V9. Elston Howard.................................$3.50
V10. Hal Reniff $1.50
V11. Charley Smith................................$1.50
V12. Bobby Murcer.................................$3.50
V13. Joe Pepitone $1.50
V14. Al Downing $1.50
V15. Steve Hamilton $1.50
V16. Fritz Peterson $1.50
V17. Tom Tresh $1.50
V18. Roy White $1.50

Philadelphia Phillies

P1. Richie Allen $3
P2. Bob Wine $1.50
P3. Johnny Briggs $1.50
P4. John Callison $1.50
P5. Doug Clemons $1.50
P6. Dick Groat.......................................$1.50
P7. Dick Ellsworth $1.50
P8. Phil Linz..$1.50
P9. Clay Dalrymple $1.50
P10. Bob Uecker.....................................$8.50
P11. Cookie Rojas $1.50
P12. Tony Taylor $1.50
P13. Bill White.......................................$1.50
P14. Larry Jackson.................................$1.50
P15. Chris Short $1.50
P16. Jim Bunning....................................$3
P17. Tony Gonzalez $1.50
P18. Don Lock $1.50

Pittsburgh Pirates

E1. Al McBean $1.50
E2. Gene Alley $1.50
E3. Donn Clendenon $1.50
E4. Bob Veale $1.50
E5. Pete Mikkelsen $1.50
E6. Bill Mazeroski $3
E7. Steve Blass......................................$1.50

E8. Manny Mota $1.50
E9. Jim Pagliaroni $1.50
E10. Jesse Gonder $1.50
E11. Jose Pagan......................................$1.50
E12. Willie Stargell $9
E13. Maury Wills $4
E14. Roy Face $1.50
E15. Woodie Fryman...............................$1.50
E16. Vernon Law $1.50
E17. Matty Alou $1.50
E18. Roberto Clemente $50

San Francisco Giants

G1. Bob Bolin $1.50
G2. Ollie Brown $1.50
G3. Jim Davenport..................................$1.50
G4a. Tito Fuentes $1.50
G4b. Bob Barton $1.50
G5a. Norm Sieburn $1.50
G5b. Jack Hiatt $1.50
G6. Jim Hart..$1.50
G7. Juan Marichal $7.50
G8. Hal Lanier.......................................$1.50
G9a. Tom Haller $1.50
G9b. Ron Hunt $1.50
G10a. Bob Barton $1.50
G10b. Ron Herbal $1.50
G11. Willie McCovey $10
G12. Mike McCormick $1.50
G13. Frank Linzy $1.50
G14. Ray Sadecki $1.50
G15. Gaylord Perry $6
G16. Lindy McDaniel $1.50
G17. Willie Mays....................................$45
G18. Jesus Alou.....................................$1.50

Washington Senators

S1. Bob Humphreys $1.50
S2. Bernie Allen $1.50
S3. Ed Brinkman $1.50
S4. Pete Richert......................................$1.50
S5. Camilio Pascual $2.00
S6. Frank Howard $3
S7. Casey Cox $1.50
S8. Jim King..$1.50
S9. Paul Casanova $1.50
S10. Dick Lines......................................$1.50
S11. Dick Nen $1.50
S12. Ken McMullen.................................$1.50
S13. Bob Saverine $1.50
S14. Jim Hannan $1.50
S15. Darold Knowles $1.50
S16. Phil Ortega.....................................$1.50
S17. Ken Harrelson $1.50
S18. Fred Valentine $1.50

7-ELEVEN CUPS

These unnumbered white plastic cups feature color-line portraits of baseball, basketball and football players. In most cases, a facsimile signature appears below the portrait and above the player's name and team. In 1972-73, 7-Eleven convenience stores gave away, with the purchase of a soda or 14-ounce Slurpee crushed-ice drink, cups that feature portraits of Major League baseball players.

The 5 5/16-inch tall plastic cups are 3 1/4 in diameter at the top and 2 1/8 inches at the bottom. The player's full-color sketched picture is on one side of the cup above his name and the team name; on the opposite side, in between his team's logo and the 7-Eleven logo, is a brief biography.

The 1972 60-cup set includes 18 Hall of Famers. Twenty-one of the players were carried over to the 1973 set; all but seven (Dick Allen, Lou Brock, Cesar Cedeno, Ralph Garr, Willie Mays, Vada Pinson and Tom Seaver) were the same portraits. The 1973 cups differed little from the 1972 cups; the major change in format was that in 1972 the player's name and team name are flush left above his biography, while in 1973 they were centered.

The 80-cup 1973 series includes 20 old-time Hall of Famers, whose cups were the same format and styles as the current players' cups, except the portraits were done in gold rather than in color.

7-Eleven later produced full-color cups using reproduced photos. These, and the earlier cups, have not survived in quantity or quality, in part because too much dishwashing took its toll on them.

The backs include some basic biographical information and a handful of career highlights. A 7-Eleven logo is at the top, while a team helmet is at the bottom.

The cups are very susceptible to cracking, so don't put too much pressure on them, and keep them out of direct sunlight so they don't fade.

1972 7-Eleven Baseball Cups

Hank Aaron .... $25-$30	Reggie Jackson $40	Jim Perry $6
Tommie Agee $6	Ferguson Jenkins $15	Lou Piniella .... $7-$10
Rich Allen .... $7-$8	Alex Johnson $7	Vada Pinson $10
Sal Bando $6	Deron Johnson $8	Dave Roberts $6
Johnny Bench $25	Al Kaline $15	Brooks Robinson .... $25-$30
Steve Blass $6	Harmon Killebrew .... $15-$20	Frank Robinson .... $15-$20
Vida Blue .... $7-$8	Mickey Lolich .... $7-$12	Pete Rose $25
Lou Brock $20	Jim Lonborg $7	George Scott $6
Norm Cash $6	Juan Marichal .... $15-$25	Tom Seaver $25
Cesar Cedeno $6	Willie Mays $35	Sonny Siebert $8
Orlando Cepeda $10	Willie McCovey .... $15-$25	Reggie Smith $8
Roberto Clemente .... $35-$50	Denny McLain $7	Willie Stargell .... $12-$25
Nate Colbert $7	Dave McNally .... $6-$7	Bill Stoneman $7
Willie Davis $7	Bill Melton $7	Mel Stottlemyre .... $7-$9
Ray Fosse .... $6-$7	Andy Messersmith $6	Joe Torre $8
Ralph Garr $6	Bobby Murcer .... $7-$12	Maury Wills $7
Bob Gibson $20	Tony Oliva .... $7-$10	Don Wilson $6
Bud Harrelson .... $7-$8	Amos Otis $6	Rick Wise .... $7-$8
Frank Howard $9	Jim Palmer .... $15-$20	Wilbur Wood $7
Ron Hunt .... $6-$7	Joe Pepitone .... $7-$8	Carl Yastrzemski $25

1973 7-Eleven Baseball Cups

Hank Aaron $15	Ty Cobb * .... $15-$35	Toby Harrah $6
Dick Allen .... $7-$8	Nate Colbert .... $4-$6	Richie Hebner $4
Dusty Baker .... $4-$6	Willie Davis $4	Ken Henderson .... $4-$8
Johnny Bench $15	Bill Dickey * $10	Carl Hubbell * .... $6-$35
Yogi Berra .... $10-$12	Bob Feller * .... $10-$35	Jim Catfish Hunter .... $7-$13
Larry Biittner $6	Carlton Fisk .... $6-$8	Reggie Jackson .... $15-$20
Steve Blass .... $4-$6	Bill Freehan .... $4-$7	Walter Johnson * .... $10-$15
Lou Boudreau * $6	Ralph Garr .... $4-$6	Don Kessinger .... $4-$8
Lou Brock $5	Lou Gehrig * $15, $65	Leron Lee .... $4-$6
Roy Campanella * .... $10-$15-$35	Charlie Gehringer * .... $8-$10-$35	Mickey Lolich .... $4-$8
Bert Campaneris .... $4-$6	Bob Gibson $10	Sparky Lyle $4
Rod Carew $9	Hank Greenberg * .... $10-$15-$35	Greg Luzinski $5
Steve Carlton $9	Bobby Grich .... $4-$8	Mike Marshall .... $4-$6
Cesar Cedeno $4	Lefty Grove * .... $6-$35	Mickey Mantle * .... $20-$25-$95

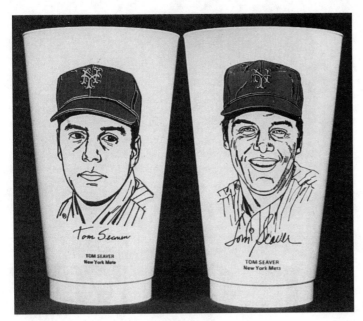

Al Oliver ....$4-$6
Claude Osteen ....$4-$6
Jim Palmer $6
Gaylord Perry ....$5-$12
Lou Piniella $4
Vada Pinson $4
Brooks Robinson $15
Ellie Rodriguez ....$4-$6
Joe Rudi ....$4-$6
Red Ruffing * ....$6-$12
Babe Ruth * ....$15-$25-$55
Nolan Ryan ....$35-$45
Manny Sanguillen ....$4-$6
Ron Santo $9
Richie Scheinblum $4
Tom Seaver $25
Ted Simmons $6
Reggie Smith $4
Chris Speier ....$4-$6
Don Sutton ....$5-$12
Luis Tiant $4
Pie Traynor * ....$8-$12-$35
Honus Wagner * ....$10-$20-$35
Billy Williams ....$6-$10
Wilbur Wood ....$4-$7
Carl Yastrzemski ....$15-$20
• Old-time Hall of Famer

Carlos May..$4-$6
Lee May ....$4-$6
John Mayberry ....$4-$6
Willie Mays * $20
John McGraw * ....$6-$10-$35
Joe Medwick * ....$6-$35

Joe Morgan...$5-$12
Thurman Munson.................................$9-$25
Bobby Murcer ....$8-$12
Stan Musial * ....$12-$15-$35
Gary Nolan..$4-$6
Tony Oliva..$8-$9

Chapter 12

BASEBALL GAMES

Generally, player- or team-related games are in greater demand than generic games, while board games are more valuable than card games. Game values are also determined in part by age (older is more valuable); company (Milton Bradley and Parker Bros. are two of the top); graphics/illustrations (those with higher quality of lithography and highly-detailed, colorful illustrations, especially on the box, are more valuable); box and board style (wooden boxes are more valuable than heavy cardboard; metal games are more valuable than cardboard ones); theme; the region in which the item is being sold; rarity; implements (game parts): and completeness (missing game cards or integral parts may drop a value by 50 percent). The American Game Collectors Association has archives of game instructions and can supply copies by contacting AGCA, 49 Brooks Ave., Lewiston, Maine 04240.

The game recognized as the first professional baseball game, The New Parlor Game of Baseball, was produced in 1869. Published by M.B. Sumner, the game included team rosters and lineup cards.

The first data-enhanced game based on player statistics appeared in 1950, when APBA Game Co. of Lancaster, Pa., created a dice and card game. The company produces new player game cards annually. The first game to be endorsed by a player—the Rube Walker & Harry Davis Baseball Game—was produced in 1905 by Champion Athletics. Since that time, several athletes have loaned their names to games—Hank Aaron, Bob Feller, Lou Gehrig, Walter Johnson, Mickey Mantle, Christy Mathewson, Willie Mays, Babe Ruth and Carl Yastrzemski, to name a few.

Generally, player- or team-related games are in greater demand than generic games. Condition is also a big factor in determining game values. Look for games that are in Very Good or Excellent condition—those that are not faded, water-stained, covered with soot or mildew, and have all the parts and instructions.

The best places to find games are at game conventions, collectibles shows, antique shops, flea markets, and through auction houses and hobby publications, such as Krause Publications' Toy Shop and Warman's Today's Collector publications. When buying sight-unseen through the mail, however, get a detailed description about condition and inquire if the seller has a return policy if the material is not satisfactory.

Many games are repairable, but that's best left to an archivist or other professional who can clean your game using special materials such as acid-free glue and paper. Rubber cement thinner can be used to remove price stickers or tape on the outside box covers on games that are taped shut. Mildew can be cleaned with a bathroom mildew remover and a damp sponge, but test a small area first.

Games should be kept out of extremely cold or hot temperatures and places with wide temperature fluctuations. Direct sunlight, spotlights and other bright lights should be avoided, too, to prevent fading. Damp areas can cause mildew buildup, so a dehumidifier is recommended. Also, although stacking is not suggested, if you are going to stack your games, do so by cross-stacking them, alternating them vertically and horizontally, so that the weight of the games on top do not crush those underneath.

Note: Because so few exist in that condition, games from 1844-1945 are virtually impossible to find in mint condition. Prices fluctuate, too, oftentimes based on auction fever, which tends to drive prices up. Remember, value is what someone is willing to pay, not necessarily the selling price.

SELECTED BASEBALL BOARD GAMES

ABC Baseball Game, 1910s . . . . $430-$715
Action Baseball, Pressman, 1965 . . . . $35-$75
Alexander's Baseball Game, 1930s . . . . $245-$400
All Pro Baseball, Ideal, 1950 . . . . $45-$110
All-Star Baseball Game, Whitman, 1935 . . . . $100-$165
All-Star Baseball, Cadaco-Ellis, 1959-60 . . . . $40-$90
All-Star Baseball Game, Cadaco-Ellis, 1962 . . . . $40-$50
All-Star Baseball, Cadaco, 1989 . . . . $12-$30
All-Star Electric Baseball & Football, Harett-Gilmar, 1955 . . . $35-$90
All-Time Greats Baseball Game, Midwest Research, 1971 . . . . $15-$35

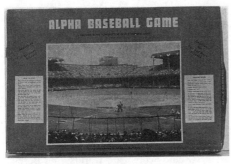

Alpha Baseball Game, Redlich Mfg. Co., 1930s .... $110-$275
APBA Baseball Master Game, APBA, 1975 .... $35-$90
ASG Baseball, 3M, 1989...................................$12-$30
ASG Major League, Baseball, Gerney Games, 1973 .... $55-$135
Atkins Real Baseball, Atkins & Co., 1915 .... $450-$750
Autograph Baseball Game, F. J. Raff, 1948 .... $110-$275
Auto-Play Baseball Game, Auto-Play Games Co., 1911.... $425-$700
Aydelott's Parlor Baseball, Aydelott's Base Ball Card Co., 1910
....$195-$325
Babe Ruth Baseball Game, 1933 .... $640-$1,075
Babe Ruth National Game of Baseball, Keiter-Fry Mfg. Co., 1929
....$550-$910

Babe Ruth's Baseball Game, Milton Bradley, 1936 .... $200-$500
Babe Ruth's Official Baseball Game, Toy Town Corp., 1940s
....$430-$715
Ballplayer's Baseball Game, Jon Weber, 1955 .... $30-$75
Bambino, Johnson Store Equipment Co., 1933........... $295-$490
Bambino Baseball Game, Mansfield-Zesiger Mfg. Co., 1946
....$145-$250
Base-Ball Game of 1886, McLoughlin Bros., 1886 ...... $750-$1,300
Baseball, George Parker, 1885.....................$700-$1,000
Baseball, George B. Doan & Co., 1920 .... $70-$100
Baseball, J. Ottman Litho Co., 1915.................$140-$200
Baseball Game, All-Fair, 1930 ....$100-$125
Baseball, All-Fair, 1946..........................$30-$60
Baseball, Milton Bradley, 1940s ....$35-$50
Baseball, Samuel Lowe Co., 1942 ....$15-$25
Baseball, Football & Checkers, Parker Bros., 1957 .... $35-$90
Baseball & Checkers, Milton Bradley, 1910s........... $75-$150
Baseball Card All-Star Game, Captoys, 1987............$6-$15
Baseball Card Game, Ed-U-Cards, 1950s..............$20-$50
Baseball Challenge, Tri-Valley Games, 1980 .... $15-$35
Baseball Dominoes, Evans, 1910....................$250-$400
Baseball Game, Brinkman Engineering, 1925 .... $95-$135
Baseball Game, Corey Games, 1943 ....$70-$100
Baseball Game, Parker Bros., 1949 ....$10-$25
Baseball Game, Parker Bros.,1950..................$10-$22
The Baseball Game, Horatio, 1988 ....$12-$30
Baseball Game & G-Man Target Game, Marks Bros., 1940
....$100-$165
Baseball's Greatest Moments, Ashburn, Ind., 1979 ....$5-$12
Baseballitis Card Game, Baseballitis Card Co., 1909 ..... $125-$205
Baseball Knapp Electro Game Set, Knapp, 1929 .... $125-$175
Baseball Mania The Board Game, Baseball Mania, 1993..... $14-$30

Baseball Strategy, Avalon Hill, 1973 .... $10-$20
Baseball Wizard Game, Morehouse Mfg., 1916......... $265-$450
Base Hit, Games Inc.,1944 ....$55-$90
Bases Full Hand Skill Game, 1930 ....$45-$70
Batter-Rou Baseball Game, Memphis Plastic, 1950s...... $100-$250
Batter-Up Card Game, Ed-U-Cards, 1949 .... $25-$60
Batter Up, M. Hopper, 1946..........................$75-160
Bee Gee Baseball Dart Target, Bee Gee, 1935 .... $70-$115
Bible Baseball, Standard Publishing Co., 1950 .... $10-$25
Big League Baseball Card Game, Whitman Publishing, 1933 .. $35-$60
Big League Baseball Game, J. Chein & Co., 1930s .... $42-$60
Big League Baseball Game, A.E. Gustafson, 1938........ $85-$125
Big League Baseball, Saalfield, 1959.................$55-$135
Big League Baseball Game, 3M Corp., 1966 .... $55-$135
Big League Baseball, 3M Corp., 1971 ....$14-$30
Big Six: Christy Mathewson Indoor Baseball Game, Piroxloid Products
Corp., 1922...$775-$1,300
Big 6 Sports Games, Gardner & Co., 1950s..........$175-$450
Bob Feller's Big League Baseball, Saalfield Artcraft, 1950 .. $75-$250
Bobby Shantz's Baseball Game, Realistic Games, 1954..... $80-$225
Boston Baseball Game, Boston Game Co., 1906 .... $495-$825
Boston Red Sox Game, Ed-U-Cards, 1964.............. $55-$135
Broadcast Baseball, J. Pressman & Co., 1938-40 .... $70-$100
Carl Hubbell Mechanical Baseball, Gotham, 1950....... $100-$300
Carl Yastrzemski's Action Baseball, Pressman, 1962 ...... $90-$195
Casey on the Mound, Kamm Games Inc., 1947 .... $190-$275

Challenge the Yankees, Hasbro, 1960s $325-635
The Champion Game of Base Ball, Schultz, 1889 ..... $4,100-$6,800
The Champion Base Ball Game, New York Game Co., 1913
....$140-$200

The Champion Game of Base Ball, Proctor Amusement Co., 1890s
....$60-$100
Championship Baseball, Championship Games Inc., 1966.... $10-$30
Championship Baseball, Milton Bradley, 1984............ $18-$40
Championship Base Ball Parlor Game, Grebnelle Novelty Co. 1914
....$1,050-$1,750
Charlie Brown's All-Star Baseball Game, Parker Bros., 1965.. $35-$90
Chicago Game Series Base Ball, George Doan Co., 1890s
....$1,175-$1,950

Classic Major League Baseball Classic green, 1987 . . . . $115-$250
Classic Major League Baseball, Classic, yellow update, 1987
. . . . $18-$40
Classic Major League Baseball, Classic red, 1988 . . . . $7.50-$15
Classic Major League Baseball, Classic blue, 1988 . . . . $10-$20
Classic Major League Baseball, Classic, 1989 . . . . $18-$40
Classic Major League Baseball, Classic travel orange, 1989 . . $10-$20
Classic Major League Baseball, Classic, 1989. . . . . $7.50-$15
Classic Major League Baseball, Classic, 1990. . . . . $7.50-$15
Classic Major League Baseball, Classic, 1990 . . . . $6-$13
Classic Major League Baseball, Classic 1990 . . . . $7.50-$15
Classic Major League Baseball, Classic, 1991 . . . . $6-$14
College Base Ball Game, Parker Bros., 1898 . . . . $350-$900
Computer Baseball, Epoch Playtime, 1966 . . . . $25-$65
Danny McFayden's Stove League Baseball Game, National Games
Co., 1927 . . . . $295-$490
Dennis The Menace Baseball Game, 1960 . . . . $20-$70
The Diamond Game of Base Ball, McLoughlin Bros., 1894
. . . . $1,275-$2,150
DiceBall, Ray-Fair Co., 1938. . . . . $90-$145
DiceBall, Intellijedx, 1993. . . . . $12-$25
The Dicex Baseball Game, Chester S. Howland, 1925 . . . . $195-$325
Double Game Board, Parker Bros., 1926 . . . . $165-$275
Double Header Baseball, Redlich Mfg. Co., 1935 . . . . $145-$250
Durgin's New BaseBall Game, Durgin & Palmer, 1885 . . . . $425-$700
Earl Gillespie Baseball Game, Wei-gill Inc., 1961 . . . . $25-$65
Ebbets Field Pro Baseball Game, Montminy Games, LLC, 1998
. . . . $10-$12
Egerton R. Williams Baseball Game, The Hatch Co., 1886
. . . . $2,500-$5,000
Electric Baseball, Einson-Freeman Publishing Corp., 1935 . . . $35-$60
Electric Baseball, Jim Prentice, 1940s . . . . $55-$80
Electric Baseball, Jim Prentice, 1950s . . . . $30-$65
Electric Magnetic Baseball, 1900. . . . . $175-$295
Ethan Allen's All-Star Baseball, Cadaco Ltd., 1941 . . . . $60-$150

Ethan Allen's All-Star Baseball Game, Cadaco-Ellis, 1942 . . $60-$150
Ethan Allen's All-Star Baseball Game, Cadaco-Ellis, 1946 . . . $28-$60
Ethan Allen's All-Star Baseball Game, Cadaco-Ellis, 1955 . . . $22-$50
Extra Innings, J. Kavanaugh, 1975. . . . . $15-$35
Fan-I-Tis, C.W. Marsh, 1913 . . . . $110-$180
Follow The Stars Watts Indoor Baseball League, H. Allan Watts, 1922
. . . . $225-$375
Fortune Telling & Baseball Game, 1889 . . . . $85-$140

Game of Base Ball, J.H. Singer, 1888 . . . . $325-$550
Game of Baseball, Milton Bradley, 1910 . . . . $100-$150

Game of Baseball, Milton Bradley, 1925 . . . . $42-$60
Game of Baseball, Canada Games Co., 1925 . . . . $210-$300
Game of Batter Up, Fenner Game Co., 1908 . . . . $100-$165
George Brett's 9th-Inning Baseball Game, Brett Ball, 1981 . . . $16-$40
Get The Balls Baseball Game, 1930 . . . . $20-$30
Gil Hodges Pennant Fever, Research Games, 1970 . . . . $65-$150
Golden Trivia Game, Western Pub., 1984. . . . . $6-$15
Gonfalon Scientific Baseball, General Specialties Corp., 1930
. . . . $110-$180
Goose Goslin's Scientific Baseball Game Wheeler Toy Co., 1935
. . . . $250-$400
Graham McNamee Radio Scoreboard World Series Baseball Game,
Radio Sports Inc., 1937 . . . . $250-$400
Grand Slam, Sming Game Co.,1979 . . . . $14-$30
Graphic BaseBall, North Western, 1930s . . . . $165-$275
The Great American Baseball Game, William Dapping, 1906
. . . . $145-$250
The Great American Game, Frantz Toys, 1925. . . . . $110-$180
The Great American Game of Baseball, Pittsburgh Brewing Co., 1907
. . . . $145-$250
The Great American Game of Baseball, Hustler Toy Co., 1923
. . . . $105-$175
Great American Game of Pocket Baseball, Neddy Pocket Game Co.,
1910. . . . . $140-$200
Great Mails Baseball Card Game, Walter Mails Baseball Game Co.,
1919 . . . . $2,475-$4,100
Great Pennant Races, Great Pennant Races 1980 . . . . $14-$28
Grebnelle Championship Base Ball Parlor Game, Grebnelle Novelty
Co., 1914 . . . . $150-$250
Hank Aaron Baseball Game, Ideal, 1973 . . . . $50-$125
Hank Aaron's Eye Ball Game, 1960s . . . . $85-$215
Hank Bauer's "Be A Manager," Bamo Enterprises, 1953 . . . . $75-$175
Hatfield's Parlor Base-Ball Game, Hatfield Co., 1914 . . . . . $140-$200
Hening's In-Door Game of Professional Baseball, Inventor's Co., 1889
. . . . $525-$875
Home Baseball Game, McLaughlin Bros., 1900 . . . . $900-$1,700
Home Baseball Game, McLaughlin Bros., 1910 . . . . $775-$1,100
Home Baseball Game, Rosebud Art. Co., 1936 . . . . $100-$150
Home Diamond The Great Baseball Game, Phillips Co., 1913
. . . . $175-$295
Home Plate, 1996, signed by Barry and Bobby Bonds $110
Home Run King, Selrite Products Inc., 1930s . . . . $275-$450
Home Run With Bases Loaded, T.V. Morrison, 1935 . . . . . . $205-$350
Home Team Baseball Game, Ben Dickenson, 1917 . . . . $140-$200
Home Team Baseball Game, Ben Dickenson/Selchow & Righter, 1918
. . . . $140-$200
Home Team Baseball Game, Selchow & Righter, 1957 . . . . . . $35-$90
Home Team Baseball Game, Selchow & Righter, 1964 . . . . . . $14-$30
Houston Astros Baseball Challenge Game Croque Ltd., 1980
. . . . $15-$35
In-Door Baseball, E. Bommer Foundation, 1926 . . . . $100-$180
Inside Base Ball Game, Popular Games Co., 1913 . . . . $300-$500
Jackie Robinson Baseball Game, Gotham Pressed Steel Corp., 1948
. . . . $425-$725
Jacmar Big League Electric Baseball, Jacmar, 1952. . . . . . . $100-$250
JDK Baseball, JDK Baseball, 1982 . . . . $10-$25
Jim Thome's Pro Baseball Game, Montminy Games LLC, 1998
. . . . $10-$12
Joe "Ducky" Medwick's Big Leaguer Baseball Game, Johnson-Breier
Co., 1939. . . . . $125-$200
Jose Canseco's Perfect Baseball Game, Perfect Game Co., 1991
. . . . $8-$20
Junior Baseball Game, Benjamin-Seller Mfg. Co., 1913. . . . $100-$165
Kellogg's Baseball Game, Kellogg's, 1936 . . . . $21-$30
KSP Baseball, Koch Sports Products, 1983 . . . . $15-$35
Las Vegas Baseball, Samar Enterprises, 1987. . . . . $8-$20
Lawson's Patent Base Ball Playing Cards, T.H. Lawson & Co., 1884
. . . . $350-$700

League Parlor BaseBall, Bliss, 1880s . . . . $1,050-$1,750
League Parlor BaseBall, R. Bliss Mfg., 1889s . . . . $600-$1,000
Leslie's Base Ball Game, Perfection Novelty & Advertising Co., 1909
. . . . $145-$250
Lew Fonseca The Carrom BaseBall Game, Carrom Co., 1930s
. . . . $525-$875
LF Baseball, Len Feder, 1980 . . . . $12-$30
Line Drive, Lord & Freber Inc., 1953 . . . . $60-$125
Little League Baseball Game, Standard Toycraft Inc., 1950s . . $25-$70
LongBall, Ashburn Industries, 1975 . . . . $30-$75
Look All-Star Baseball Game, Progressive Research, 1960 . . . $35-$90
Lou Gehrig's Official Play Ball, Christy Walsh, 1930s . . . . . $525-$875
Lucky 7th BaseBall Game, All-American Games Co., 1937. . . $55-$90
"Mac" Baseball Game, McDowell Mfg. Co., 1930s . . . . $145-$250
Main Street BaseBall, Main Street Toy Co., 1989 . . . . $20-$55
Major League Ball, National Game Makers, 1921 . . . . $325-$550

Major League Indoor Base Ball, Philadelphia Game Mfg. Co., 1913
. . . . $650-$1,000
The Major League BaseBall Game, 1910 . . . . $85-$145
Major Legue BaseBall, Negamco, 1959 . . . . $12-$25
Major League BaseBall Magnetic Dart Game, Pressman, 1958
. . . . $55-$135
Major League Indoor BaseBall Game, Philadelphia Game Mfg. Co.,
1912 . . . . $4,200-$6,000
Manage Your Own Team, Warren, 1950s . . . . $55-$135
Mather's Parlor Base Ball Game, Mathers, 1908 . . . . $350-$500
Mickey Mantle's Baseball Action Game, Kohner Bros., 1960s
. . . . $50-$175

Mickey Mantle's Big League Baseball, Gardner & Co., 1962
. . . . $125-$325
Mickey Mouse Baseball, Post Cereal, 1936 . . . . $55-$90

Monopoly: Boston Red Sox Collectors Edition, Parker Bros., 1999
. . . . $20-$25
Monopoly: New York Yankees Collectors Edition, Parker Bros., 1999
. . . . $20-$25
Montreal Expos Super Baseball, Super Sports Games, 1979
. . . . $7.50-$15
MVP Baseball The Sports Card Game, Ideal, 1989 . . . . $8-$20
National American Base Ball Game, Parker Bros., 1910 . . . $110-$180
The National Base Ball Game, National Baseball Playing, 1913
. . . . $700-$1,200
The National Game of Base Ball, McLoughlin, 1901 . . . . . . $500-$875
The National Game, National Game Co., 1889 . . . . $875-$1,450

National League Ball Game, Yankee Novelty Co., 1890 . . . . $350-$575
NBC Baseball Game of the Week, Hasbro, 1969 . . . . $25-65
New Baseball Game, Clark & Martin, 1885 . . . . $165-$275
The New Parlor Game Baseball, M.B. Summer, 1869 . $7,000-$10,000
New York Recorder Newspaper Supplement Baseball Game, 1896
. . . . $430-$715
Official Baseball Game, Milton Bradley, 1965 . . . . $175-450
Official Baseball Game, Milton Bradley, 1953 . . . . $100-$250
Official Baseball Game, Milton Bradley, 1970 . . . . $55-$125
Official Denny McLain Magnetik Game, Gotham, 1968 . . . $115-$295
Official Dizzy and Daffy Dean Nok-Out Baseball Game, Nok-Out
Manufacturing Co., 1930 . . . . $350-$575
Our National Ball Game, McGill & DeLany, 1887 . . . . $425-$650
Our No. 7 Baseball Game Puzzle, Satisfactory Co.,1910 . . . $110-$180
Ozark Ike's Complete 3 Game Set, Builtrite, 1956 . . . . $55-$135
Parlor Baseball, E.B. Pierce, 1878 . . . . $1,750-$2,900
Parlor Base Ball, American Parlor Base Ball Co., 1903 . . . . $165-$250
Parlor BaseBall Game Chicago vs. Boston, 1880s . . . . . $2,100-$3,000
Parker Bros. Baseball Game, Parker Bros., 1950 . . . . $45-$110
Pat Moran's Own Baseball Game, Smith, Kline & French, 1919
. . . . $325-$550
Pee-Wee (Pee Wee Reese Marble Game), Pee Wee Enterprises, 1956
. . . . $175-$450
Peg Base Ball, Parker Bros., 1908 . . . . $105-$175
Pennant Chasers Baseball Game, Craig Hopkins, 1946 . . . . . $25-$70
Pennant Drive, Accu-Stat Game Co., 1980 . . . . $8-$20
Pennant Puzzle, L.W. Harding, 1909 . . . . $250-$400
Pennant Winner Wolverine Supply & Manufacturing Co., 1939
. . . . $175-$295
The Philadelphia Inquirer Baseball Game Philadelphia Inquirer, 1896
. . . . $145-$250
Photo-Electric Baseball, Cadaco-Ellis, 1951 . . . . $55-$135
Pinch Hitter, J&S Corp., 1938 . . . . $110-$180
Play Ball, National Game Co., 1920 . . . . $145-$250
Pocket Baseball, Toy Creations, 1940 . . . . $15-$25
Pocket Edition Major League Baseball Game, Anderson, 1943
. . . . $85-$140
Polar Ball Baseball, Bowline Game Co., 1940 . . . . $90-$145
Poosh-em-up Slugger, Bagatelle, North Western Products, 1946
. . . . $30-$105
Popular Indoor Baseball Game, Egerton R. Williams, 1896
. . . . $500-$850

Pro Baseball, 1940s . . . . $70-$115

Pro Baseball Card Game, Just Games, 1980s $6-$60 . . . .

Pursue the Pennant, Pursue the Pennant, 1984 . . . . $25-$60

Psychic Base Ball Game, Psychic Baseball Corp., 1927 . . . . . $60-$150

Psychic Base Ball Game, Parker Bros., 1935 . . . . $175-$295

Radio Baseball, Toy Creations, 1939 . . . . $50-$125

Real Action Baseball Games, Real-Action Games, 1966 . . . . . $20-$50

Real BaseBall Card Game, National Baseball, 1900 . . . . . . $110-$275

Realistic Baseball Realistic Game & Toy Co., 1925 . . . . . . $205-$350

Red Barber's Big League Baseball Game, G&R Anthony Inc., 1950s

. . . . $350-$900

Replay Series Baseball, Bond Sports Ent., 1983 . . . . $6-$15

Robin Roberts Sports Club Baseball Game, Dexter Wayne, 1960

. . . . $100-$250

Roger Maris' Action Baseball, Pressman Toy Co., 1962 . . . . $50-$175

Roll-O Junior Baseball Game, Roll-O Mfg., 1922 . . . . $325-$550

Roulette Base Ball Game, W. Bartholomae, 1929 . . . . $115-$195

Rube Bressler's Baseball Game, Ray B. Bressler, 1936 . . . . $130-$215

Rube Waddell & Harry Davis Baseball Game, Inventors and Investors

Corp., 1905 . . . . $875-$1,450

St. Louis Cardinals Baseball Card Game, Ed-U-Cards, 1964 . . $35-$85

Sandlot Slugger, 1960s . . . . $35-$90

Say Hey! Willie Mays Baseball Game, Toy Development Co., 1954

. . . . $200-$525

Scott's Baseball Card Game, Scott's BaseBall Cards, 1989 . . . $12-$30

Skor-It Bagatelle, Northwestern Products, 1930s . . . . $145-$250

Slide Kelly! Baseball Game, B.E. Ruth Co. 1936 . . . . $70-$115

Slugger Baseball Game, Marks Bros., 1930 . . . . $110-$180

Snappet Catch Game with Harmon Killebrew, Killebrew Inc., 1960

. . . . $55-$135

Spin Cycle Baseball, Pressman, 1965 . . . . $25-$65

Sporting News BaseBall, Mundo Games, 1986 . . . . $8-$20

Sport-O-Rama Pin-Bo, 1950s . . . . $35-$90

A Sports Illustrated Game Baseball, Time Inc., 1975 . . . . $25-$65

Sports Illustrated Baseball, Sports Illustrated 1972 . . . . $25-$65

Sports Illustrated Pennant Race Avalon Hill-Sports Illustrated, 1982

. . . . $7.50-$15

Star Baseball Game, W.P. Ulrich, 1941 . . . . $70-$115

Statis Pro Baseball, Avalon Hill, 1979 . . . . $17-$40

Strategy Manager Baseball, McGuffin-Ramsey, 1967 . . . . $20-$50

Strat-O-Matic Baseball, Strat-O-Matic, 1961 . . . . $100-$250

Strat-O-Matic Baseball, Strat-O-Matic, 1969 . . . . $10-$25

Strike-Like, Saxon Toy Corp., 1940's . . . . $55-$90

Strike-Out, All-Fair Inc., 1920s . . . . $175-$295

Strike 3 by Carl Hubbell, Tone Products Corp., 1946 . . . . . $275-$725

Superstar Baseball, Sports Illustrated, 1966 . . . . $30-$75

Superstar Baseball, Sports Illustrated-Time Inc., 1974 . . . . . $12-$25

Swat Baseball, Milton Bradley, 1948 . . . . $20-$50

Tiddle Flip Baseball, Modern Craft Ind., 1949 . . . . $20-$50

Time Travel Baseball, Time Travel, 1979 . . . . $8-$18

Tom Seaver Game Action Baseball, Pressman Toy Co., 1969

. . . . $50-$175

Toto The New Game BaseBall, Toto Sales Co., 1925 . . . . $55-$90

Triple Play, National Games Inc., 1930s . . . . $12-$20

Tru-Action Electric Baseball Game, Tudor, 1955 . . . . $25-$80

Ty Cobb's Own Game of Baseball, National Novelty Co., 1924

. . . . $350-$650

U-Bat-It, Schultz III Star Co., 1920s . . . . $70-$115

Ultimate Sports Trivia, Ram Games, 1992 . . . . $17-$35

Uncle Sam's Base Ball, J.C. Bell, 1890 . . . . $525-$875

Wachter's Parlor Base Ball, Wachter, 1888 . . . . $145-$250

Walter Johnson Base Ball Game, Walter Johnson Baseball Game,

1920s . . . . $125-$250

Walter Johnson Base Ball Game, Walter Johnson Baseball Game,

1930s . . . . $195-$325

Waner's Baseball Game, Waner's BaseBall Inc., 1939 . . . . . $350-$575

Whirly Bird Play Catch, Game Innovation Industries, 1958 . . . $20-$50

Whiz BaseBall, Electric Game Co., 1945 . . . . $42-$60

Wil-Croft Baseball, Wil-Croft, 1971 . . . . $10-$25

William's Popular Indoor Baseball, Hatch Co., 1889 . . . . . $700-$1,175

Willie Mays Push Button Baseball, Eldon Champion, 1965

. . . . $175-$450

Willie Mays "Say Hey" Baseball, Centennial Games, 1958

. . . . $190-$450

Win A Card Trading Game, Milton Bradley, 1965 . . . . $350-$900

Winko Baseball, Milton Bradley, 1945 . . . . $45-$70

Wiry Dan's Electric Baseball Game, Harrett-Gilmore, 1950 . . . $15-$65

World's Championship Baseball, Champion Amusement Co., 1910

. . . . $175-$295

World's Championship Baseball Game, Beacon Hudson Co., 1930s

. . . . $100-$150

World's Greatest Baseball Game, J. Woodlock, 1977 . . . . $30-$80

World Series Baseball Game, Radio Sports, 1940s . . . . $205-$350

World Series Big League Baseball Game, E.S. Lowe, 1945

. . . . $115-$150

World Series Parlor Baseball, Clifton E. Hooper, 1916 . . . . . $150-$250

Yaz Action Baseball, unknown, 1962 . . . . $15-$20

"You're Out" Baseball Game, Corey Games, 1941 . . . . $85-$140

Zimmer BaseBall Game, McLoughlin Bros., 1885 . . . . . $1,300-$2,150

BASEBALL CARD GAMES

Card games are another offshoot of collector interest involving all things baseball. The earliest games were produced in the mid-1880s, but aside from sporadic production since then, the majority of baseball card games were created in the 1990s. A sizable portion of the collectible card game market is comprised of playing card sets created regionally for local teams, and sets celebrating milestones such as World Series victories and inaugural season team lineups. Most of these recent playing card sets don't command a huge premium, and are easily obtained for $5-$10.

Game	Manufacturer	Year	Price
Ask Me Game of Baseball Facts	Quaker Oats	1930s	$300
Atlanta Braves Playing Cards	USPC	1992	6
Atlanta Braves Playing Cards (Silver)	USPC	1992	8
Atlanta Braves Playing Cards	USPC	1994	6
Atlanta Braves World Series Playing Cards	USPC	1992	6
Baltimore Orioles Playing Cards	USPC	1994	5
Baseball Card All-Star Game	Captoys	1987	10
Base Ball Card Game	Allegheny	1904	30,000
Baseball Card Game	Ed-U-Cards	1950s	35
Baseballitis Card Game	Baseballitis Card Co.	1909	205
Batter Up Card Game	Ed-U-Cards	1949	25
Big League Baseball Card Game	Whitman Pub.	1933	35
Boston Red Sox Game	Ed-U-Cards	1964	55
Boston Red Sox Playing Cards	USPC	1992	4
Chicago Cubs Playing Cards	USPC	1992	5
Cincinnati Reds Playing Cards	USPC	1993	4
Colorado Rockies Playing Cards	USPC	1993	4
Detroit Tigers Playing Cards	USPC	1992	4
E285 Rittenhouse Candy	Unknown	1933	7,000
Egerton R. Williams Baseball Game	The Hatch Co.	1888	8,000
Florida Marlins Playing Cards	USPC	1993	5
Game of Batter Up	Fenner Game Co.	1908	250
Joe "Duckey" Medwick Big Leaguer Baseball Game	Johnson-Breier Co.	1939	125
Lawson's Patent Base Ball Playing Cards	T.H. Lawson & Co.	1884	350
MLB All-Stars Playing Cards	USPC	1990	7
MLB All-Stars Playing Cards (Silver)	USPC	1990	8
MLB All-Stars Playing Cards	USPC	1991	6
MLB All-Stars Playing Cards (Silver)	USPC	1991	8
MLB All-Stars Playing Cards	USPC	1992	6
MLB Aces Playing Cards	USPC	1993	6
MLB Aces Playing Cards	USPC	1994	6
MLB Aces Playing Cards	USPC	1995	6
MLB Rookies Playing Cards	USPC	1993	5
MLB Rookies Playing Cards	USPC	1994	5
Minnesota Twins Playing Cards	USPC	1992	4
Minnesota Twins Playing Cards (Silver)		1992	4
National American Base Ball Game	Parker Bros.	1910	500
Official Baseball Game	Milton Bradley	1965	295
Philadelphia Phillies Playing Cards	USPC	1994	4
Pro Baseball Card Game	Just Games	1980s	10
Psychic Base Ball Game	Psychic	1927	150
San Francisco Giants Playing Cards	USPC	1994	5
Scott's Baseball Card Game	Scott's	1989	20
Star Baseball Game	W.P. Ulrich	1941	115
T.J. Jordan Card Game	Unknown	1900s	500
Topps Blue Backs	Topps	1951	2,500
Topps Red Backs	Topps	1951	1,500
Topps Dice Game	Topps	1961	5,000
Topps Game Cards	Topps	1968	1,000
Toronto Blue Jays Playing Cards	USPC	1994	4
Toronto Blue Jays Playing Cards	USPC	1994	4
W502 Baseball Game	Unknown	1927	700
W560 Playing Cards	Unknown	1929	1,500
WG1 Baseball Card Game	Unknown	1888	20,000
WG2 Fan Craze AL Game	Unknown	1904	5,000
WG3 Fan Craze NL Game	Unknown	1906	5,000
WG5 The National Game	Unknown	1913	3,500
WG4 Polo Grounds Game	Unknown	1910	3,000
WG-6 Tom Barker Game	Tom Barker	1913	3,000
WG7 Walter Mails Game	Unknown	1923	4,000
WG8 National Game	S and S Games	1936	900

Donruss

Top of the Order 1996

Complete Set (360) $200
Dual Starter Box (5) 90
Dual Starter Deck (160) 16
Starter Deck (80) 8
Booster Box (36) 75
Booster Pack (12) . . . . .2..50
Unlisted Commons 20

Atlanta Braves
Chipper Jones (C) $7
Tom Glavine (U) 1.50
Ryan Klesko (U) 1
Greg McMichael (U) 1
Marquis Grissom (R) 2
David Justice (R) 2
Greg Maddux (R) 15
Fred McGriff (R) 4
John Smoltz (R) 4
Mark Wohlers (R) 2

Baltimore Orioles
Harold Baines (U) $1
Bret Barberie (U) 1
Bobby Bonilla (U) 1
Ben McDonald (U) 1
Mike Mussina (U) 2
Curtis Goodwin (R) 2
Rafael Palmerio (R) 2
Cal Ripken Jr. (R) 15

Boston Red Sox
Jose Canseco (U) $2
Mike Greenwell (U) 1
Troy O'Leary (U) 1
Lee Tinsley (U) 1
Tim Naehring (R) 2
John Valentin (R) 2
Mo Vaughn (R) 5

California Angels
Chuck Finley (U) $1
Tony Phillips (U) 1
J.T. Snow (U) 1
Chili Davis (R) 2
Gary DiSarcina (R) 2
Jim Edmonds (R) 2
Troy Percival (R) 2
Tim Salmon (R) 2
Lee Smith (R) 2

Chicago Cubs
Jim Bollinger (U) $1
Jaime Navarro (U) 1
Rey Sanchez (U) 1
Steve Trachsel (U) 1
Shawon Dunston (R) 2
Mark Grace (R) 2
Brian McRae (R) 2
Randy Myers (R) 2
Sammy Sosa (R) 3

Chicago White Sox
Mike Devereaux (U) $1
Lance Johnson (U) 1
Tim Raines (U) 1
Robin Ventura (U) 1
Ozzie Guillen (R) 2
Frank Thomas (R) 15

Cincinnati Reds
Jeff Branson (U) $1
Mariano Duncan (U) 1
Jose Rijo (U) 1
Pete Schourek (U) 1
Bret Boone (R) 2
Jeff Brantley (R) 2
Ron Gant (R) 2
Barry Larkin (R) 3
Reggie Sanders (R) 3

Cleveland Indians
Jose Mesa (U) $1
Sandy Alomar, Jr. (R) 2
Carlos Baerga (R) 4
Albert Belle (R) 10
Kenny Lofton (R) 6
Eddie Murray (R) 3
Eric Plunk (R) 2
Manny Ramirez (R) 8
Jim Theme (R) 3

Colorado Rockies
Vinny Castilla (U) $1
Joe Girardi (U) 1
Bruce Ruffin (U) 1
Bret Saberhagen (U) 1
Dante Bichette (R) 3
Andres Galarraga (R) 2
Steve Reed (R) 2
Larry Walker (R) 3

Detroit Tigers
Cecil Fielder (U) $2
John Flaherty (U) 1
Travis Fryman (U) 1
Alan Trammell (U) 1
Mike Henneman (R) 2
Lou Whitaker (R) 2

Florida Marlins
Terry Pendleton (U) $1
Jeff Conine (R) 2
Chris Hammond (R) 2
Gary Sheffield (R) 3

Houston Astros
Jeff Bagwell (U) $3
Craig Biggio (U) 1
Tony Eusebio (U) 1
Brian Hunter (U) 1
Dave Magadan (U) 1
Derek Bell (R) 2
Todd Jones (R) 2

Kansas City Royals
Kevin Appier (R) $2
Vince Coleman (R) 2
Tom Goodwin (R) 2
Wally Joyner (R) 2

Los Angeles Dodgers
Tom Candiotti (U) $1
Jose Offerman (U) 1
Ismael Valdes (U) 1
Eric Karros (R) 2
Raul Mondesi (R) 4
Hideo Nomo (R) 7
Mike Piazza (R) 8
Todd Worrell (R) 2

Milwaukee Brewers
Joe Oliver (U) $1
Kevin Seitzer (U) 1
B.J. Surhoff (U) 1

Minnesota Twins
Alex Cole (U) $1
Chuck Knoblauch (R) 2
Kirby Puckett (R) 6

Montreal Expos
Sean Berry (U) $1
Wil Cordero (U) 1
Carlos Perez (U) 1
Mel Rojas (U) 1
David Segui (U) 1
Tony Tarasco (U) 1
Moises Alou (R) 2
Pedro Martinez (R) 2
Tim Scott (R) 2

New York Mets
Joe Orsulak (U) $1
Ryan Thompson (U) 1

New York Yankees
David Cone (U) $1
Paul O'Neill (U) 1
Wade Boggs (R) 3
Don Mattingly (R) 8
John Wetteland (R) 2

Oakland Athletics
Mike Bordick (U) $1
Rickey Henderson (U) 1
Steve Ontiveros (U) 1
Mark McGwire (R) 4
Todd Stottlemyre (R) 2

Philadelphia Phillies
Ricky Bottalico (U) $1
Lenny Dykstra (U) 1
Jim Eisenreich (U) 1
Tyler Green (U) 1
Charlie Hayes (U) 1

Mickey Morandini (U) 1
Heathcliff Slocumb (U) 1
Curt Schilling (R) 2

Pittsburgh Pirates
Dave Clark (U) $1
Nelson Liriano (U) 1
Al Martin (U) 1
Orlando Merced (U) 1
Dan Miceli, (U) 1
Dan Plesac (R) 2

San Diego Padres
Andy Ashby (U) $1
Brad Ausmus (U) 1
Ken Caminiti (U) 1
Steve Finley (R) 2
Tony Gwynn (R) 7
Bip Roberts (R) 2

San Francisco Giants
Rod Beck (U) $1
Mike Benjamin (U) 1
Steve Scarsone (U) 1
Barry Bonds (R) 8
Deion Sanders (R) 3
Matt Williams (R) 5

Seattle Mariners
Alex Rodriguez (C) $7
Andy Benes (U) 1
Jay Buhner (U) 1
Joey Cora (U) 1
Tino Martinez (U) 1
Bobby Ayala (R) 2
Ken Griffey, Jr. (R) 15
Randy Johnson (R) 4
Edgar Martinez (R) 3
Billy Risley (R) 2

St. Louis Cardinals
Ray Lankford (U) $1
John Mabry (U) 1
Ozzie Smith (U) 2
Bernard Gilkey (R) 2
Tom Henke (R) 2
Brian Jordan (R) 2

Texas Rangers
Juan Gonzalez (C) $2
Jeff Frye (U) 1
Otis Nixon (U) 1
Will Clark (R) 2
Mark McLemore (R) 2
Dean Palmer (R) 2
Ivan Rodriguez (R) 2

Toronto Blue Jays
Paul Molitor (C) $1
Devon White (U) 1
Roberto Alomar (R) 6
Joe Carter (R) 3

MISCELLANEOUS BASEBALL GAMES

Baseball has inspired innumerable games and gaming paraphernalia including darts, pinball, and, as technology has improved, video games. The more obscure items are frequently prized by niche collectors. As is the case with board games, player likenesses, team and league logos, and official licensing, have a direct bearing on a game's value.

The following list provides examples of baseball gaming collectibles that have been featured in several recent auctions. The list is by no means exhaustive, but should give some indication of the wide range of baseball-related games and gaming collectibles available on the secondary market.

Casino Chips

Bally's Grand Atlantic City 60th Anniversary Baseball Hall of Fame $75	Bally's Park Place Atlantic City Willie Mays set of four 60
	Four Queens Hotel Limited Edition "Perfect Game" 50
Babe Ruth 18	Don Larsen 14
Ty Cobb 18	Enos Slaughter 10
Christy Mathewson 18	Hank Bauer 10
Walter Johnson 18	Andy Carey 10
Honus Wagner 18	Gil McDougald 10

Dart Games

Game	Manufacturer	Price
1935 Bee Gee Baseball Dart Game	Bee Gee	$70
1950s Clown Shoot/Dart Baseball	Bar Zim Toys	50
1998 Electronic Baseball Dart Game	QVC	65
1958 Major League Baseball Magnetic Darts	Pressman	150
1960s Rocky Colavito's Own Baseball 2 in 1	Dart Game	400
1950s Safe T Dart Magnetic Dart Game	Unknown	50

Punch Boards/Scratch Offs

Game	Manufacturer	Price
Baseball Tavern Gambling Game	Unknown	$50
Baseball One Cent Punch Board	Unknown	20
1950s Diamond Dust (Mantle, Kaline, Berra, Martin, Snider, Ashburn)		425
Garcia Grande Very Mild Cigars	Garcia Grande	45
1915 National Base Ball Game	National	300
1938 Play Ball! Punch Board (Gehrig, Ruth, Cobb, Wagner, Johnson, DiMaggio)		800
1920s Two Baseball Games Play Ball Punch Board (Cy Young and Jimmy Foxx)		400

Pinball/Arcade Games

Game	Manufacturer	Price
1920s Baffle Ball Baseball	Unknown	$1,200
1933 Bambino Pinball Machine	Bally	8,000
1940s Baseball Coin-Op Machine	Unknown	800
1950s Baseball Dexterity Game	Elmar Products	50
1950s Baseball Pinball/Gumball Machine	Unknown	800
1920s Electric Baseball World Champion Game	Unknown	600
Jim Prentice Electric Baseball	Holyoak Electric Toys	200
1930s Lou Gehrig's Official Playball	Christy Walsh	1,000
Mr. Pinball Game	Marx Toys	20
1920s Play Ball Penny Arcade Game	Exhibit Supply	1,200
1940s Play Ball Penny Arcade Game	Unknown	200
1940s Play Ball Pinball Game	Unknown	100
1920s Poosh-M-Up Jr.	Northwestern Products	100
1932 Poosh-M-Up 4 in 1 Game	Northwestern	75
1946 Poosh-M-Up Slugger Bagatelle	Northwestern	200
1950 Poosh-M-Up Table Pinball	Northwestern	150
Poosh-M-Up Streamliner 5 Games in 1	Northwestern	60
1930s Skor-It Bagatelle	Northwestern	300
1934 World Series Pinball Game	Unknown	2,070

Outdoor Games

Game	Manufacturer	Price
1880/90s Champion Bean Bag Game	Champion	$1,835
Jimmy Piersall's Little Pro Bat A Round	Unknown	600
1960 Mickey Mantle's Backyard Baseball	Unknown	300
Mickey Mantle's Batmaster Game	Unknown	250
Mike Schmidt Pitch en' Field Game	Unknown	150
Whirly Bird Game with Warren Spahn	Unknown	75

Video/Electronic Games

Game	Manufacturer	Price
Atari Real Sports Baseball	Atari (2600)	$10
Atari Baseball	Atari (7800)	8
Aaron vs. Ruth	Mindscape	35
All-Star Baseball '97 Featuring Frank Thomas	Acclaim	40
All-Star Baseball '98	Acclaim	50
All-Star Sports	Encore Software	35
Backyard Baseball GT	Interactive Software	32
Baseball Mogul GT	Value/Wizard Works	33
Baseball's Greatest Hits	Voyager	30
Cal Ripken Jr. Fantasy Baseball	Fantasy Sports	25
Coleco Head-to-Head Baseball	Coleco	30
Colecovision Baseball	Coleco	15
Dinomight Baseball	Microform Manf.	40
Eurekas Sports	Nodtronics PTY LTD	15
Fantasy League Baseball	IBM Multimedia	45
Frank Thomas Big Hurt Baseball	Acclaim	15
Front Page Baseball '98	Sierra On-Line	35
Game Gear World Series Baseball '97	Sega	25
Hardball 3 Featuring Al Michaels	Accolade	20
Hardball 5 Enhanced	Electronic Arts	25
High Heat Baseball	3DO Company	40
Intellivision Baseball	Mattel	15
Intellivision World Championship Baseball	Mattel	25
King of Baseball (Japanese)	Nintendo	60
Mattel Handheld Baseball	Mattel	20
Mego Pulsonic Baseball	Mego	20
Mego Pulsonic Baseball II	Mego	15
MS Baseball 3D	Microsoft	50
Nintendo 8 Bit Baseball	Nintendo	20
Odyssey 2 Baseball	Magnivox	10
Pro League Baseball '97	Micro League	25
Reggie Jackson Baseball	Sega	20
Roger Clemens MVP Baseball	Sega	15
Sega Championship Baseball	Sega	20
Sega Sports Talk Baseball	Sega	15
SI Microleague Baseball 6.0	Micro League	40
Talking Baseball Handheld Game	VTech	20
Tony La Russa Baseball 4	Maxis	50
Topps Cybercards	Topps	
Alex Rodriguez		25
Barry Bonds		25
Bernie Williams		25
Cal Ripken Jr.		25
Chipper Jones		25
Derek Jeter		25
Frank Thomas		25
Juan Gonzalez		25
Mark McGwire		25
Mike Piazza		25
Mo Vaughn		25
Total Baseball '93	Z Master Prod.	17
Triple Play '98	EA Sports	45
Ultimate Baseball Series	Electronic Arts	33
Virtual Boy Professional Baseball (Japanese)	Kemco	15
Virtual Boy League Baseball (American)	Kemco	25
VR Baseball '96	Interplay	50
VR Baseball '97	Interplay	40
World Series Baseball '98	Sega	50

Chapter 13

MOVIES, MUSIC

MOVIE MEMORABILIA

By Jerry Shaver

In the years before television, baseball was America's national pastime and the movies were the country's most popular form of entertainment, so it's no wonder that Hollywood has often turned to the sport for material. For collectors, baseball movies combine the best of both worlds, and auctions for baseball movie memorabilia can become quite heated as sports fans and film buffs compete for rare and valuable items.

If you're interested in collecting baseball movie memorabilia, take some time to familiarize yourself with the hobby's terminology. A press book, for example, is a book given out to the media that contains information about a movie and its stars. A press kit, on the other hand, usually contains a press book plus 6–8 stills (usually black-and-white photos) and other trinkets. So press kits are definitely the more prized of the two.

Movie posters also come in all shapes and sizes. The prices listed here—unless otherwise noted—are for original posters that hung in theaters either before (advance posters) or during (release posters) a movie's initial run. Back before television, movies were often re-run in theaters, so be aware that posters from re-releases are generally not as valuable as their first-run counterparts (which should feature copyright dates corresponding with the film's original release). Condition also is a key factor, since movie posters are designed to hang in theaters and often suffer varying degrees of damage.

The type of movie poster can also affect its value. A one sheet (27x41-inches) is the industry standard, and generally the most prized by collectors. Half sheets (28x22-inches) are usually printed on heavier stock and command about 35 percent of a one sheet's value. Three sheets (41x81-inches) are far less common, and these giants can go for almost twice as much as a one-sheet. Lobby cards (14x11-inches) are generally

produced in sets of eight, and the first card in the series is almost always the most expensive.

Other prices in this section are for costumes, props, autographed publicity stills, and other movie memorabilia. Many of these items—like the Oscar statue from *Pride of the Yankees*—are one-of-a-kind pieces that come up for sale periodically. Prices given are based on auction results, but can be considered highly speculative.

Notes on price listings:

Video and Laserdiscs: Prices given for new copies only. In cases where the video is out-of-print, or no longer widely available, no price is listed.

Posters: Prices given for Excellent/Near Mint examples of original posters that hung in movie theaters. Posters are used for advertising purposes, and nearly all examples will show some type of wear from use. Unless otherwise noted, prices are for posters from a film's original run—corresponding with the date given in the header—and not a re-release. Posters bearing later dates are from re-releases, or are replicas, and are worth considerably less.

Photos: Autographed photo prices are given for publicity photos from the film. For example, a Ty Cobb 8x10 signed by Tommy Lee Jones indicates a photo of Jones in character as Ty Cobb, not a Jones-signed picture of Ty Cobb, the baseball player.

Jerseys/Uniforms: Prices given are for actual prop uniforms worn by the actors in the movie. The term "replica" is used to avoid confusion in cases where actors portrayed real ballplayers. The Lou Gehrig jersey from *Pride of the Yankees* isn't an actual Lou Gehrig jersey, but a replica made by the Western Costume Company. Manufacturer names have been given, where possible.

Unless otherwise noted, all dimensions given are in inches.

61*—Barry Pepper, Thomas Jane; HBO; 2001
Commemorative Baseball $40
Commemorative Cap (given out at Yankee Stadium) $60

Angels in the Outfield (original)—Ty Cobb, Joe DiMaggio; MGM; 1951
Video . . . . $12-$13
Laserdisc $25
One-Sheet Movie Poster . . . . $150-$300
Insert Poster $75

Angels in the Outfield (remake)—Danny Glover; Disney; 1994
Video . . . . $12-$13
One-Sheet Movie Poster . . . . $10-$20

The Babe—John Goodman; Universal; 1992
Video . . . . $8-$10
Laserdisc $30
One-Sheet Movie Poster . . . . $15-$20
Baseball—signed by Goodman $80
Bat—signed by Goodman $200
Replica Babe Ruth Uniform—worn by Goodman $3,000

The Babe Ruth Story—William Bendix; Allied Artists; 1948
One-Sheet Movie Poster—27x41 . . . . $600-$800
Six-Sheet Movie Poster—82x41 . . . . $1,500
Half-Sheet Movie Poster and Press Book $900
Insert Poster $800
Lobby Card $300

The Bad News Bears—Walter Mathau, Tatum O'Neal; Paramount; 1976
Video $15
One-Sheet Movie Poster . . . . $40-$50

Bang the Drum Slowly—Robert DeNiro; Paramount; 1973
Video $15
Half-Sheet Movie Poster $30
One-Sheet Movie Poster . . . . $50-$100
Press Book . . . . $10-$15
Lobby Card (set of 8) . . . . $50-$60
Baseball—signed by DeNiro $120
Bat—signed by DeNiro $300
Replica Yankees Jersey—McAuliffe, worn by DeNiro $1,500

Big Leaguer—Edward G. Robinson; MGM; 1953
Lobby Card—14x17 . . . . $300

Bingo Long Traveling All-Stars—Richard Pryor; Universal; 1976
One-Sheet Movie Poster . . . . $50-$75
Half-Sheet Movie Poster . . . . $30-$60
Video . . . . $10-$15
Lobby Cards (set of 8) $60
Bingo Long Uniform—worn by Pryor $1,500

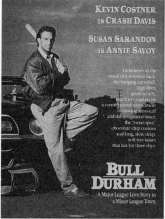

Bull Durham—Kevin Costner, Susan Sarandon, Tim Robbins; Orion; 1988
Video $15
DVD . . . . $25-$30
One-Sheet Movie Poster—Costner and Sarandon . . . . $150-$225
One-Sheet Movie Poster—Costner alone $300
Mini-Poster $90
Promotional Baseball Cards (4) $25
Press Kit $75
Mini Lobby Cards $5
Lobby Standee $40
Baseball—signed by Costner $100
Baseball—signed by Robbins $200
Bat—signed by Costner, Sarandon, Robbins $400

The Busher—Charles Ray; Paramount; 1919
One-Sheet Movie Poster $3,000

Casey at the Bat—Wallace Beery; Paramount; 1927
Lobby Cards—11x14, set of four $1,200

Cobb—Tommy Lee Jones; Warner Bros.; 1994
Video $15
Laserdisc $35
One-Sheet Movie Poster $20

Ty Cobb 8x10—signed by Jones $50
Baseball—signed by Jones $90
Bat—signed by Jones $200

Damn Yankees—Ray Walston, Jean Stapleton; Warner Bros.; 1958
Video . . . . $12-$17
One-Sheet Movie Poster $300
Lobby Card . . . . $10-$15
Lobby Card (set of 8) $90
8x10 Photo Still $6

Eight Men Out—John Cusak, Charlie Sheen; Orion; 1988
Video . . . . $10-$15
DVD . . . . $15-$20
One-Sheet Movie Poster . . . . $40-$60
Ring—presented to cast members, "Miller St. Louis Browns" . . $1,200
Replica White Sox Jersey—Western Costume Co., worn by extra
. . . . $1,000

Fear Strikes Out—Anthony Perkins; Paramount; 1957
Video $15
One-Sheet Movie Poster $300

Field of Dreams—Kevin Costner, Ray Liotta; Universal; 1989
Video $15
DVD . . . . $30-$35
One-Sheet Movie Poster $100
One-Sheet Movie Poster—signed by Costner $150
Joe Jackson 8x10—signed by Liotta $50
Ray Kinsella 8x10—signed by Costner $50
Press Kit $30
Baseball—signed by Costner $100
Baseball—signed by Liotta $100
Baseball—signed by Costner, Liotta $150
Bat—signed by Costner, Liotta $300

For Love of the Game—Kevin Costner, Kelly Preston; Universal; 1999
Video $15
DVD $25
One-Sheet Movie Poster $25
Press Kit $30

Headin' Home—Babe Ruth; Yankee Pictures; 1920
Theater Give-Away Card—11 3/16x3 5/16 . . . . $5,000
Lobby Card—set of eight* $20,700
*Only one set known to exist.
Sold in 1995 as a complete set, but has since been broken up.

It Happens Every Spring—Ray Milland; 20th Century Fox; 1949
Video $17
One-Sheet Movie Poster . . . . $150-$400
Lobby Card $50
Press Kit $20

The Jackie Robinson Story—Jackie Robinson, Ruby Dee; MGM; 1950
Video $15
DVD . . . . $20-$25
One-Sheet Movie Poster—27x41 . . . . $500-$2,000
Half-Sheet Poster—22x28 . . . . $1,000
Insert Poster—14x36 . . . . $1,000
Lobby Card—Robinson in Montreal Royals Uniform $500
Lobby Card—Robinson and Minor Watson $200
Lobby Cards—set of eight $1,000
Baseball—signed by Robinson, 17 other cast members $1,200

The Kid From Cleveland—George Brent; Republic; 1949
One-Sheet Movie Poster—27x41 . . . . $800
Three-Sheet Movie Poster—78x41 . . . . $1,000

A League of Their Own—Tom Hanks, Geena Davis, Madonna; Columbia; 1992
Video . . . . $10-$12
VHS Gift Set $25
DVD $20
One-Sheet Movie Poster $50
Baseball—signed by Hanks $100
Baseball—signed by Davis $100
Baseball—signed by Madonna $400
Bat—signed by Hanks, Madonna, Davis, Rosie O'Donnell $1,000
Replica Rockford Peaches Manager's Uniform—worn by Hanks . $5,000
Replica Rockford Peaches Uniform—worn by Madonna $7,500

Major League—Tom Berenger, Wesley Snipes; Paramount; 1989
Video $10
DVD $15
One-Sheet Movie Poster . . . . $25-$30
Baseball—signed by Snipes $200
Pedro Cerano Jersey—worn by Dennis Haysbert $1,000

Major League 2—Tom Berenger, Charlie Sheen; Warner Bros.; 1994
Video $10
DVD $15
One-Sheet Movie Poster $15
Press Kit $15
Replica Cleveland Indians Uniform—worn by David Keith $700
Willie Mays Hayes Uniform—worn by Omar Epps $1,200

Manhattan Merry-Go-Round—Joe DiMaggio; Republic; 1938
Video $20
One-Sheet Movie Poster $400
Lobby Card—signed by DiMaggio $400

Mr. Baseball—Tom Selleck; Universal; 1992
Video $15
DVD $15
One-Sheet Movie Poster . . . . $15-$35
Press Kit—10 stills $20
Replica Japanese Uniform—Descente, worn by Selleck $1,000

The Natural—Robert Redford, Glenn Close; Tristar; 1984
Video $15
DVD . . . . $20-$25
One-Sheet Movie Poster . . . . $40-$100
Press Kit $45
Roy Hobbes 8x10—signed by Redford $100
Baseball—signed by Redford $120
Bat—signed by Redford $300
Prop Tickets—Knights vs. Cubs, Knights vs. Phillies, etc. . . . . . $5 ea.
Prop Scorecards—Knights vs. Braves, Knights vs. Reds, etc.
. . . . $10-$25 ea.
Prop Life Magazine—Roy Hobbes on cover $500
Cardboard Extras—31x42, 75 photo cutouts used as stadium crowds
. . . . $800
New York Knights Jersey—worn by extra $900
Roy Hobbes Jersey—worn by Redford $2,000

The Naughty Nineties—Bud Abbott, Lou Costello; Universal; 1945
Video $15
"Who's On First?" Video $13
"Who's On First?" Lobby Card $200

The Pride of St. Louis—Dan Daily, Joanne Dru; 20th Century Fox; 1952
Video $17
One-Sheet Movie Poster—29x38 . . . . $400
Lobby Card $50

Pride of the Yankees—Gary Cooper, Babe Ruth; RKO; 1941

One-Sheet Movie Poster—27x41, Cooper Only (1941 original run)
. . . . $3,500
One-Sheet Movie Poster—27x41, Cooper and Ruth (1949 reissue)
. . . . $2,000
Half-Sheet Movie Poster—22x28 . . . . $900
Insert Poster—13x30, Cooper and Teresa Wright $800
Lobby Card—11x14 (1941 original run). $600
Lobby Card—11x14 (1949 reissue) $400
Movie Pressbook—22x17, color. $800
Publicity Stills—set of eight $500
Publicity Still—7x9, Ruth with Cooper, signed by Ruth. $5,000
Cast Photo—9Hx7H, signed by Cooper, Ruth, Samuel Goldwyn
. . . . $5,500
Yankee Press Statements—signed by Joe DiMaggio, Bill Dickey, others $1,500
Letter—signed by Ruth on Samuel Goldwyn stationery $2,500
Check Stub—$2,750 to Ruth from Goldwyn Inc. $800
Baseball—signed by Cooper, Ruth, Dickey, Walter Brennen, others
. . . . $4,000
Replica Lou Gehrig Jersey—Western Costume Co., worn by Cooper
. . . . $20,000
Replica Lou Gehrig Uniform—WCC, worn by Cooper $30,000
Replica Miller Huggins Uniform—WCC, worn by Ernie Adams
. . . . $1,500
Academy of Motion Picture Arts & Sciences Certificate of Nomination
. . . . $1,500
Academy Award "Oscar" Statue—to Daniel Mandell for Film Editing
. . . . $25,000

Rawhide—Lou Gehrig; 20th Century Fox; 1938

One-Sheet Movie Poster—27x41 . . . . $3,000
Lobby Card. $150
Movie Press Book—11x17H cover $500
Publicity Stills—8x10, set of eight $250
Publicity 8x10—signed by Gehrig $2,000
Publicity 9x7H photo—signed by Gehrig. $2,500
Publicity 13Hx10Hphoto—signed by Gehrig, Jacob Ruppert . . . $3,000

Roogie's Bump—Roy Campanella, Carl Erskine; Republic; 1954

One-Sheet Movie Poster—27x41 . . . . $700-$900
Advertising Poster—48x24 . . . . $900

Safe At Home—Mickey Mantle, Roger Maris; Columbia; 1962

One-Sheet Movie Poster—27x41 . . . . $700
Half-Sheet Movie Poster—22x28 . . . . $500
Half-Sheet Movie Poster—signed by Maris $800
Movie Poster—14x36. . . . . $500
Movie Poster—60x40 . . . . $1,500
Lobby Cards—11x14, set of eight. $800
Lobby Card—signed by Maris $300
Lobby Card—signed by Mantle, Maris. $700
Movie Press Book. $200

Soul of the Game*—Blair Underwood; HBO; 1996

Video $15
DVD . . . . $15-$20
Replica K. C. Monarchs Jersey—worn by Underwood $800
*Also known as Baseball in Black and White.

The Stratton Story—James Stewart, June Allyson; MGM; 1949

Video $15
One-Sheet Movie Poster . . . . $350-$400
Half-Sheet Movie Poster. $300
Lobby Card $25

Take Me Out to the Ballgame—Frank Sinatra, Gene Kelley; MGM; 1949

Video $17
Laserdisc $30
One-Sheet Movie Poster—27x41 . . . . $600
Half-Sheet Movie Poster. $400

The Winning Team—Ronald Reagan; Warner Bros.; 1952

Video $15
Laserdisc $30
Insert Poster $300
Lobby Card $40
Baseball—signed by Reagan. $300

VIDEOS

Baseball videos range from stirring documentaries like Ken Burns' *Baseball*, to any of the numerous "blooper" tapes issued by Major League Baseball. Regardless of your tastes, you can bet that someone has produced a baseball video—or series of videos—to suit almost every fan of the game. The list below is by no means complete, but it should give you a good indication of the range of titles available on the market. Unless otherwise noted, prices given are for Mint/Near-Mint copies of VHS tapes.

A Great Beginning (1993 Florida Marlins) $20
A Tale of Two Cities (New York/San Francisco Giants) 20
All-Star Game (single tapes from each year, starting in 1940s) . . 20 ea.
All-Time A's (Oakland A's 25th Anniversary) 20
An Amazin' Era (New York Mets 25th Anniversary) 20
Angels '62 (Los Angeles Angels) 25
An Hour of a Legend (Ted Williams) 35
Back to Back Bucs (Pittsburgh Pirates) 20
Back 2 Back (Toronto Blue Jays) 20
The Baltimore Orioles in Action (1962 Baltimore Orioles) 25
Baseball: A Film by Ken Burns (9 tapes). 150
Baseball: A Film by Ken Burns (DVD) 180
Baseball in Boston 25
Baseball in the '70s 20
Baseball in the '80s 20
Baseball Like it Oughta Be (1996 St. Louis Cardinals) 20
Baseball's Greatest Games (continuing series) . . . . 20 each
Baseball's Greatest Moments 15
Baseball's Greatest Pennant Series 15
Baseball's Main Street 20
Baseball News 1951 20
Baseball News 1955-56 20
Baseball News 1959 20
Baseball's Greatest World Series Moments 20
Battlin' Bucs (Pittsburgh Pirates). 20
The Best of Baseball 10
The Boys of Zimmer (1988 Chicago Cubs) 20
The Braves Family (Boston Braves) 25
Bravesland USA (Milwaukee Braves) 25
The Brooklyn Dodgers: The Original America's Team (5 tapes) . . . 100
The Cardinal Tradition 25
Centennial (Philadelphia Phillies 100th Anniversary) 20
Century of Success (St. Louis Cardinals) 20
Champions by the Bay (1989 San Francisco Giants/Oakland A's) . . . 20
Chicago and the Cubs 20
Chicago White Sox: A Visual History 20
Cleveland Rocks: The Story of the 1995 Cleveland Indians 20
Cooperstown: Baseball's Mail St. 20
Dodgers On-Line (1995 Los Angeles Dodgers). 20
Dodger Stadium (Los Angeles Dodgers 25th Anniversary) 20
Dusty Baker You Can Teach Hitting (3 tapes) 100
   Vol. 1: A Systematic Approach to Hitting 30
   Vol. 2: Ten Common Hitting Mistakes. 30
   Vol. 3: Twenty Hitting Drills. 30
Expressway to the Big Leagues (New York Mets) 25
Ferguson Jenkins: King of the Hill 25
The 50 Greatest Home Runs in Baseball History 15
The Fighting Braves of '59 (Milwaukee Braves) 25
The First Century of Baseball, American League 25
The First Century of Baseball, National League 25
The First 10 Years (Seattle Mariners) 20
The 500 Home Run Club 30
Forever Fenway (Boston Red Sox) 20
Funny Side Up 10
The Game Nobody Saw. 25
Generations of Heroes 20
The Glory of Their Times 45
The Greatest League Championship Series 15

Hall of Fame Weekend 1997 20
Hail to the Braves (1957 Milwaukee Braves) 25
The History of Baseball Card Collecting 20
Hitting the Ted Williams Way Part 1 20
Home of the Braves (Milwaukee Braves) 25
Jackie Robinson: Breaking Barriers 20
The Kansas City A's in Action. 25
Lefty: The Life and Times of Steve Carlton 20
Major League Baseball: All Century Team 20
  DVD. 25
MLB '98: Baseball's Record Breakers 15
MLB '99: A Season of Heroes. 15
MLB Unbelievable: Bloopers and Great Plays 20
Mr. Kansas City: The Life of Buck O'Neil (DVD) 30
The National Pastime (5 tapes) 50
Nolan Ryan's 7th No-Hitter 20
The Official History of Baseball 25
Pinstripe Destiny (1996 New York Yankees). 20
Pinstripe Power: The Story of the '61 Yankees 20
Play Ball the Major League Way (3 tapes) 50
   Vol. 1: Pitching and Catching 15
   Vol. 2: Hitting and Baserunning 15
   Vol. 3: Infield and Outfield Play 15
Play Ball with the Red Sox 25
Pride of New England (Boston Red Sox) 25
Pride of the Upper Midwest (Minnesota Twins) 25
Prime 9 Hosted by Ozzie Smith. 15
Race for the Record (McGwire/Sosa) 15
The Reds. 20
The Red Sox at Home 25
Roberto Clemente 20
Rotisserie League Baseball. 20
Sammy Sosa: Making History. 15
Silver Odyssey (Houston Astros 25th Anniversary) 20
The Story of the Washington Nationals (Washington Senators). 35
Super Duper Baseball Bloopers 10
Super Duper Baseball Bloopers 2 15
Super Sluggers 20
10 Greatest Moments in Yankee History 20
This Week in Baseball: 20 Years of Unforgettable Plays and Bloopers
 15
Tigertown USA (Detroit Tigers) 25
T is for Team (1996 Texas Rangers) 20
Wahoo, What a Finish (1995 Cleveland Indians). 20
We Had 'Em All the Way (1960 Pittsburgh Pirates) 25
Whatever it Takes, Dude (1993 Philadelphia Phillies) 20
When It Was a Game Vol. 1. 15
  DVD. 20
When It Was a Game Vol. 2. 12
  DVD. 20
When It Was a Game Vol. 3. 15
  DVD. 20
Winning with the Yankees 25
Wire to Wire (1990 Cincinnati Reds). 20
World Series Highlights (one tape for each year from 1943-present)
 . . . . 20 ea.
Year of Change (New York Mets) 25

MUSIC AND RECORDINGS

More than 500 records in the form of baseball recordings have been made. The first actual baseball record–*Casey at the Bat*–was released in 1907 as performed by T. Wolfe Hopper, a prominent actor of that era. This piece is one of the most prolific pieces of baseball literature, as is *Take Me Out to the Ballgame*, whose lyrics are sung the third most frequently in the United States (behind *Happy Birthday* and the *National Anthem*). The song has been done by more than 30 different artists since it was first released in 1910. Historical broadcasts and significant events such as Carlton Fisk's dramatic home run in the 1975 World Series have also been captured on record. The best place to find records are at garage sales, flea markets and used record stores and thrift shops.

Some of the players who have been featured on records include Joe DiMaggio (*Little Johnny Strikeout*, without dust jacket $45, $175 with); Jackie Robinson and Pee Wee Reese (*Slugger at the Bat*, two records, 1949, $200); Babe Ruth (*Babe Ruth, Babe Ruth, We Love You*); Mickey Mantle (*I Love Mickey*, sung by Theresa Brewer, $85); Willie Mays (*Say Hey, Willie Mays*, $100); Mays, Mantle and Duke Snider (*Willie, Mickey and the Duke*); Tony Oliva (*My Favorite Music*); and Waite Hoyt (*The Best of Waite Hoyt In The Rain*, $50).

Baseball Players

Move Over Babe, Here Comes Henry Aaron, 45 rpm, $15, 33 1/3 rpm
. . . . $35

Hank Aaron, A Night To Remember, 45 rpm $15

The Ballad of Roberto Clemente, 45 rpm $20

Tony Conigliaro, Limited Man, 45 rpm $20

That Holler Guy by Joe Garagiola, 45 rpm with original sleeve
. . . . $40-$100

Ralph Kiner Talks to the Amazin Mets–Gil Hodges, Tom Seaver,
Tommie Agee, etc., 33 1/3 rpm $75

Sandy Koufax Talks With Vin Scully, Union 76 record in original sleeve,
1966 . . . . $50

My Favorite Hits, Mickey Mantle album 1969 . . . . $150-$175

Mickey Mantle, A Day To Remember, 45 rpm $40

A Day To Remember, Mickey Mantle, 33 1/3 rpm $75

Ode to Billy Martin, 45 rpm $25

Denny McLain's Greatest Hits, 1963, 33 1/3 rpm $45

Stan the Man Musial's Hit Record, by Phillips 66, includes booklet
with Musial demonstrating hitting techniques . . . . $25-$60

He's a Hero to Us All, Nolan Ryan, by Jerry Jeff Walker, 1990 . . . . $12

Babe Ruth: The Legend Comes to Life, 33 1/3 rpm $35

Babe Ruth's Home Run Story, 1920, 78 rpm, with Ruth's actual voice
. . . . $350-$1,200

Ted Williams, 78 rpm photo record (1946), includes original envelope
. . . . $225

Carl Yastrzemski, album $25

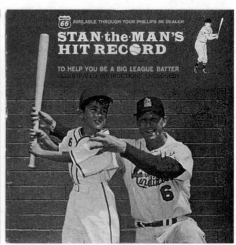

Baseball Teams/Other

The Impossible Dream: 1967 Red Sox . . . . $20-$35
Super Sox 75, Boston's 1975 season $20
Yes We Can, highlights of the California Angels first 19 years, from
  1961-79. . . . . $50
The Sound of the Dodgers, Vin Scully, Jimmy Durante and Stubby
  Kaye, with Willie Davis and Maury Wills on the cover $35
Go Get 'Em Braves, 33 1/3 rpm 1961 Braves $40
Meet the Mets, 33 1/3 rpm, with dust jacket $70
The Amazing Mets, 1969 season recap . . . . $20-$30
Get Metsmerized, 1986 Mets recap $20
Return to Glory, Yankees 1977 season $35
Ain't No Stoppin Us Now, 45 rpm, 1980 Phillies season recap $55
The Phantastic Phillies, 1980 recap $30
The Impossible Pirates, 1960 recap, Bill Mazeroski home run cover, 33
  1/3 rpm . . . . $45-$250
The Impossible Pirates, 1960 season, 331/3 rpm. $250
St. Louis Cardinals World Champions 1964, narrated by Harry Caray,
  Jack Buck $45
The Giants Win The Pennant, 1962 Giants recap $50

Baseball - The First 100 Years, 33 1/3 rpm. . . . . $20-$45
Baseball in the Great Yankee Tradition, 45rpm $65
Casey at the Bat, 45 rpm, $45, 33 1/3 rpm $35
The Greatest Moments in Sports, 33 1/3 rpm, with Ruth/Gehrig cover
  . . . . $45-$65
Yankee Stadium's 50 Years $45
Yankee Stadium, The Sounds of Half a Century, narrated by Mel Allen
  . . . . $20
Baseball Tips from the Stars, by Willie Mays, #1 How to Bat, 1962
  . . . . $25
Baseball Tips from the Stars, by Spahn, Drysdale, Podres and Jay, #2
  How to Pitch, 1962 . . . . $25
Baseball Tips from the Stars, by Willie Mays, #3 How to Field, 1962
  . . . . $25
Talkin' Baseball records for the Mets, Astros, Phillies, Indians, Orioles,
  Red Sox, Pirates, Reds, Tigers, Cubs, Dodgers, Braves, Rangers and
  Giants . . . . $25 each
Sears/Ted Williams Batting Tips, with 45 rpm on how to be a better
  hitter $135

1971 Mattel Instant Replay Records

These 2 3/8" diameter plastic records were produced in conjunction with a hand-held, battery operated record player. Paper inserts featured illustrations of players in baseball, football and basketball, as well as various racing vehicles and airplanes. The audio recounts career highlights of the depicted player. Additional records were sold in sets of four. The complete set of 11 records sells for $200. Individual prices, in Near Mint, are: Hank Aaron ($25), Ernie Banks ($20), Al Kaline ($20), Sandy Koufax ($30), Roger Maris ($40), Willie Mays ($25, plays one side only, was included with record player purchase), Willie McCovey ($20), Tony Oliva ($10), Frank Robinson ($20), Tom Seaver ($25), and Willie Stargell ($20).

1962 Auravision Records

Similar in design and format to the 16-record set which was issued in 1964, this test issue can be differentiated by the stats on the back. On the 1962 record, Mantle is shown in a right-handed batting pose, as compared to a follow-through on the 1964 record. Where Jim Gentile and Rocky Colavito are shown in the uniform of Kansas City A's on the 1964 records, they are shown as a Tiger (Colavito) and the Oriole (Gentile) on the earlier version. The set is checklisted here alphabetically.

		NM	EX	VG
Complete set (6):		500	250	150
Common player:		45	22	150
(1)	Rocky Colavito	95	47	28
(2)	Whitey Ford	75	37	22
(3)	Jim Gentile	45	22	13.50
(4)	Mickey Mantle	125	62	37
(5)	Roger Maris	80	40	24
(6)	Willie Mays	100	50	30

1964 Auravision Records

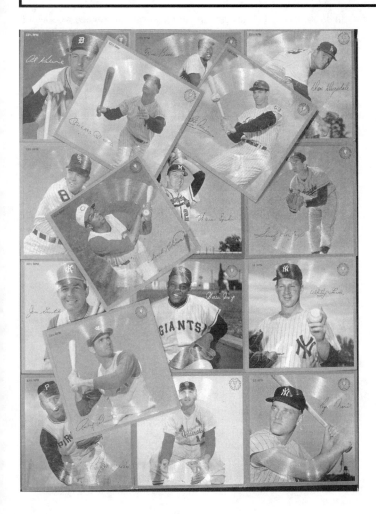

Never a candidate for the Billboard "Hot 100," this series of baseball picture records has been popular with collectors due to the high-quality photos on front and back. On the grooved front side of the 6 3/4" by 6 3/4" plastic-laminated cardboard record, is a color player photo with facsimile autograph, Sports Record trophy logo and 33 1/3 RPM notation. A color border surrounds the photo and is carried over to the unrecorded back side. There is another photo on the back, along with a career summary and complete major and minor league stats and instructions for playing the record. In the bottom border is a copyright notice by Sports Champions Inc., and a notice that the Auravision Record is a product of Columbia Records. A hole at center of the record could be punched out for playing and the records featured a five-minute interview with the player by sportscaster Marty Glickman. Large quantities of the records made their way into the hobby as remainders. For early-1960s baseball items, they remain reasonably priced today. The unnumbered records are checklisted here alphabetically. The Mays record is unaccountably much scarcer than the others.

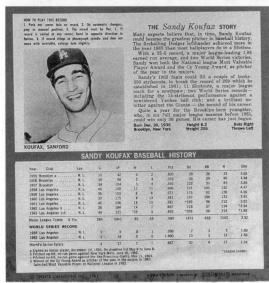

		NM	EX	VG
Complete set (16):		400	200	120
Common player:		10	5	3
(1)	Bob Allison	10	5	3
(2)	Ernie Banks	35	17.50	10.50
(3)	Ken Boyer	18	9	5.50
(4)	Rocky Colavito	25	12.50	7.50
(5)	Don Drysdale	35	17.50	10.50
(6)	Whitey Ford	35	17.50	10.50
(7)	Jim Gentile	10	5	3
(8)	Al Kaline	35	17.50	10.50
(9)	Sandy Koufax	50	25	15
(10)	Mickey Mantle	95	47	28
(11)	Roger Maris	45	22	13.50
(12)	Willie Mays	110	55	33
(13)	Bill Mazeroski	25	12.50	7.50
(14)	Frank Robinson	35	17.50	10.50
(15)	Warren Spahn	35	17.50	10.50
(16)	Pete Ward	10	5	3

1966 Los Angeles Dodgers 76 Union Oil 45 RPM Records

In 1966, Union Oil gas stations in California distributed a series of eight 45 rpm recordings featuring two Dodgers players per record. Dodgers broadcaster Vin Scully did the narration.

Complete set (8): $175
Common player: 15

1. Walter O'Malley/Claude Osteen 15
2. Buzzie Bavasi/Jim Gilliam 15
3. Walt Alston/Phil Regan 15
4. Sandy Koufax/John Kennedy 35
5. Don Drysdale/Jeff Torborg 30
6. Don Sutton/Maury Wills 25
7. Willie Davis/Al Ferrara 20
8. Wes Parker/Nate Oliver 20

SHEET MUSIC

Babe Ruth! Babe Ruth! We Know What He Can Do, by J. W. Spencer $650

Oh! You Babe Ruth. $1,150

Bucky Boy, by Al Stern, dedicated to Bucky Walters $40

Safe at Home, ... $60

I Can't Get To First Base With You, Fred Fisher and Mrs. Lou Gehrig, dedicated to Lou Gehrig $100

I Can't Miss That Ball Game, 1910 . . . . $50

I Love Mickey, by Teresa Brewer, Ruth Roberts and Bill Katz . . . . $75-$100

It's a Grand Old Game, by Harry S. Faunce $40

Joltin' Joe DiMaggio, by Allan Courtney and Ben Homer. $60

Leave Us Go Root for the Dodgers, Rodgers, by Dan Parker and Bud Green $50

Let's Get the Umpire's Goat, by Nora Bayes and Jack Norworth . . . $100

Loyal Giants Rooters, by Dr. Charles Mandelbaum, dedicated to John J. McGraw and the New York Giants. $75

Meet the Mets, official songsheet of the team $95

Take Me Out To The Ball Game, by Jack Norworth and Albert Von Tilzer $600

The Hustler's Pennant March, by Edward S. Dotter and Harry Abramsom $90

The Milwaukee Braves Song, 1953 . . . . $45

Go Get 'Em Braves, by Joe Staudacher and Bill Ehlert. $40

The National Game sheet music, by John Phillip Sousa, 1925. . . . $145

Tigers on Parade sheet music, 1934, roaring Tiger on the front, dedicated to Mickey Cochrane and his Tigers . . . . $85-$95

Ty Cobb King of Clubs sheet music, Cobb pose on the front . . . $1,500

Come Play Ball With Me Deary, 1909 sheet music, features women playing baseball, wearing Chicago and Yankee uniforms $175

Where The Shy Little Violets Grow, 1928 sheet music, features photo of Hall-of-Fame pitcher Waite Hoyt at the piano $30

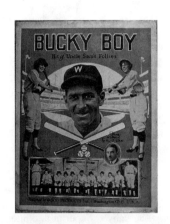

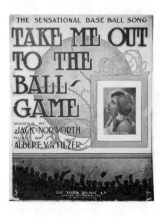

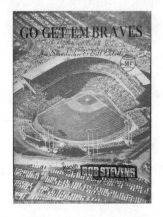
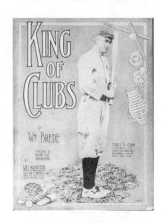

Chapter 14

AUCTIONS

By T.S. O'Connell

In the fascinating compilation of 100 items that follows, we have selected a wide assortment of some of the most spectacular pieces that have changed hands over the last several years. Though many of the items are extraordinarily expensive, it was hardly a principal criterion, since the list would wind up being horribly repetitive.

Instead, we tried to come up with a group that is representative of the whole range of memorabilia collecting, and at the same time is as visually appealing as possible. The prices range from a low of $522 for a Mickey Mantle/Roger Maris Safe at Home movie poster, to the king of

the Barry Halper Collection sale, Lou Gehrig's final glove, which sold for a whopping $387,500.

Despite the concerted effort to find items other than from Halper's Collection, it still wound up representing about 40 percent of the total, which is hardly out of line for anyone familiar with his holdings. And though we insisted that price was only one factor considered along the way, it's fun to point out that this entire "collection" could be had for a mere $3,680,905.

Tax not included.

(The photos in this section are provided courtesy of the following auction houses: Grey Flannel, Hunt's, Leland's, Lew Lipset, MastroNet Inc., Sotheby's, Superior and Sports Cards Plus.)

1935 R327 Diamond Stars original artwork of Ossie Bluege
The remarkable art deco-inspired artwork of National Chicle's 1935 R327 Diamond Stars set is highly coveted by collectors of original art because of the colorful watercolor backgrounds adorning a popular vintage set. Only a small group of the original artwork from the Diamond Stars set is known to have survived. $5,829

1991 Perez-Steele Tony Lazzeri original art
The original watercolor piece by noted sports artist Dick Perez was used in the company's famed Hall-of-Fame Postcard Series. $1,484

1954 Amazing Willie Mays comic original art
This is a fascinating piece depicting one of the greatest players of the 1950s and 1960s, featuring 26 interior pages and the cover. . . . $3,215

1912 Major League Indoor Baseball Game
Probably the most sought-after pre-World War I tabletop baseball game, it features an ornate wooden box with cameo photos of the greatest players of the period. $17,026

Charles Martin Conlon Ty Cobb photo
Original print from the premier photographer of baseball from the turn of the century to the end of World War II. This is perhaps the most highly recognized of the tens of thousands of Conlon photos. . $22,225

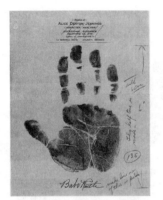

Babe Ruth signed hand print
Under the heading of unusual material, it's hard to beat an original ink hand print of the greatest player in baseball history impressed on stationery, complete with Ruth's signature. $14,950

1948 complete run of *The Sporting News*
A complete week-by-week account from the most-respected magazine at the time, in an era when baseball ruled the American sporting scene. The collection includes articles from the most famous sportswriters of the day and the incredible artwork that was a staple of the magazine.
. . . . $766

Babe Ruth's last will and testament
This was obtained from Claire Ruth and resided for years in the famed Barry Halper Collection. It is dated 1938 and includes a stamp from the New York Surrogate Court in 1954. . . . . $31,971

Circa 1927 Lou Gehrig derby
This collectible comes with a photo showing the Hall of Famer wearing the derby. The derby is signed on the inside by Gehrig. This also came from the Barry Halper Collection. $5,756

1921-22 Ty Cobb single-signed ball
Signed in his familiar green ink, the ball is an Official American League ball with the distinctive signature of the game's greatest pre-World War I player. $8,050

Lou Gehrig wax figure
It's hard to beat a life-size figure of one of the game's most beloved players in the memorable pose of his farewell speech at Yankee Stadium. The wax figure had originally been created for a baseball museum, along with several other legendary stars. $5,811

1998 All-Star Game Mark McGwire jersey
Incredible jersey from McGwire's finest season. The All-Star Game jerseys were donated to the Baseball Assistance Team and ultimately auctioned, with the proceeds to BAT. $27,782

1953 *Playboy Magazine* **No. 1**
Perhaps not technically a baseball item, it certainly qualifies as one with a Joe DiMaggio signature included. Originally owned by Barry Halper, the famed collector once asked his friend, DiMaggio, if he would sign the issue with the Marilyn Monroe centerfold. DiMaggio agreed, but only with the stipulation that Halper never show it to anyone while DiMaggio was alive. And he did not. $40,250

1948 "The Dugout" Norman Rockwell art
This is one of several Rockwell originals of the artwork that graced the cover of the *Saturday Evening Post*. This original had resided at the Hall of Fame in Cooperstown until offered at auction. $345,000

1907 Joe Jackson Victor Mills team photo
Rare photo of the 1907 Victor Mills baseball team with what is regarded as one of the earliest images of Joe Jackson, then 18 years old.
. . . . $11,480

1923-24 Tomas Gutierrez Cuban League baseball photo album
Remarkable photo album offers a glimpse of many of the great Cuban players of the period, along with a number of the greatest Negro League players of all time, including John Henry Lloyd and Oscar Charleston. $1,808

1921 Yankees/Giants World Series pennant
Pennant from Babe Ruth's first World Series as a member of the Yankees, one of the rarest pennants known within the hobby. . . $5,418

1968-70 Willie Mays game-used, signed bat
Uncracked, 35-inch, 36-ounce bat with light game use from one of the all-time greats as he neared the end of his career. $4,261

1931 Babe Ruth single-signed ball
Among the most treasured single-signed balls in the hobby and also the most expensive, even though Ruth was easily the most prolific signer of his day. This one includes a light inscription that also features the date. $36,170

Hartland Baseball Statue complete set
Popular statues from the late 1950s and early 1960s remain a hobby mainstay 40 years later. This high-grade set includes all 18 statues, plus the Batboy and Minor Leaguer, and the boxes. $10,572

Mickey Mantle and Roger Maris *Safe at Home* **movie poster**
One-sheet movie poster of the 1962 film that actually featured the two Yankees greats in the production.
. . . . $522

1951 Ted Williams Moxie Root Beer six-pack
Soda pop that is 50 years old doesn't usually attract this kind of attention, but Ted's affiliation with the famed drink helps out here. Teddy Ballgame is pictured on each full bottle, along with on the carton itself. $894

One dozen unopened Warren Giles baseballs
Case of unopened baseballs from the National League president who reigned from 1951-69. . . . . $3,491

World Series press pin collection
Among the most elegant of baseball collectibles, this grouping includes 47 assorted pins from the 1930s to modern day. $3,608

1969 Topps Decal factory roll of 10,000
Complete factory roll of 10,000 decals from the quirky 1969 Topps issue, with more than 800 of each decal of a dozen different players, including Willie Mays, Pete Rose and Carl Yastrzemski. $30,203

1951 Yogi Berra AL MVP Award
This was the first of three Most Valuable Player Awards won by the Hall of Fame catcher. $6,722

1960s Roberto Clemente Bobbin' Head
Easily the rarest of the 1960s nodders and one of the most actively pursued, this specimen includes the even tougher original box. $3,780

Rare Dick Groat Hartland statue
The most seldom-seen statue in the classic Hartland series, the Groat statue was produced in much smaller numbers than any of the other 18.
. . . . $1,312

Gil Hodges' 1954 Brooklyn jersey
Dodgers home flannel of the immensely popular first base-man who has unfortunately been denied admission to the Hall of Fame. Collector inter-est in virtually of his memora-bilia is yet another indication of the Veterans Committee slight. $8,419

1977 Steve Carlton Cy Young Award
This was the second Cy Young for the first pitcher to ever nail down four.
. . . . $32,754

Ultimate Spalding Guide collection
This is a run of 56 Spalding Guides from 1894 to 1941, a beautiful group that was originally sold at the epic Copeland sale in 1991.
. . . . $6,325

1955 Brooklyn Dodgers Schaefer Beer sign
This is one of the most spectacular advertising display pieces in the hobby, of one of the most beloved teams in history upon the occasion of their first championship. The three-dimensional sign appears periodically in the major auctions, always bringing top dollar in the upper grades. $2,954

1955 Brooklyn Dodger Sandy Koufax jersey
This is a signed jersey from the rookie campaign of the Hall of Famer. It contains an inscription, "My first uniform, 1955" and is dated and signed by Koufax. $24,019

1986 World Series "Mookie Ball"
The ball that dribbled between Bill Buckner's legs and turned the tide of the 1986 World Series remains one of the most talked-about specimens in the hobby. It was once owned by noted actor and collector Charlie Sheen, who sold it in 2000, along with many of the other prized pieces from his collection.
He had made national news when he ponied up $93,500 for the ball when it first sold in 1992. . . . . $63,945

1950s Ted Williams Moxie advertising display
One of the great 1950s advertising display pieces from perhaps the greatest player of the era, the counter display sign is signed by Williams. $2,195

1941 Ted Williams game-worn uniform
Thought to be the finest Teddy Ballgame uniform known, it comes from his epic season in 1941 when he was the last batter to top the .400 mark for an entire season. Though he shared (maybe relinquished) the national spotlight with his archrival Joe DiMaggio and his 56-game hitting streak, it is worth noting that Williams hit for a higher batting average for the entire season than DiMaggio did during his streak. This specimen was owned at one time by Charlie Sheen. $120,097

1956 Jackie Robinson last game-used glove
An amazing piece from one of the most important players in the history of the game, this glove came from Robinson's widow, Rachel, and included a letter of authenticity from her. $15,296

1903 World Series program
This is the original scorecard of the very first World Series between the Boston Pilgrims and the Pittsburgh Pirates. Only a handful of these are known to exist; this is regarded as one of the top artifacts in the hobby.
.... $43,671

1920 Chicago White Sox team-signed ball
One of only two known baseballs signed by the 1920 club that include the signature of Joe Jackson. The signatures of the Black Sox appear on an Official American League ball (Ban Johnson). $21,836

Complete run of All-Star Game programs
This is a high-grade run of programs from the inaugural game in 1933 to 1984 .... $8,149

1961 Roger Maris home flannel jersey
One of only a couple Maris jerseys known from his historic 1961 season, the pinstriped flannel is from Maris' record-breaking season when he topped the Babe's home run record. $26,847

1964 Jim Bunning perfect game program
An excellent specimen of the game program from Father's Day, 1964, when the Phillies' ace Bunning tossed a perfecto at the Mets. $510

1933 American League All-Star team ball
A ball from the American League squad that played in the very first All-Star Game in 1933 at Comiskey Park in Chicago. The ball contains signatures of the greatest AL stars of the day, including Ruth, Gehrig, Jimmie Foxx, Al Simmons, Joe Cronin, Bill Dickey and Lefty Grove. $18,490

1903 Boston Red Sox Cabinet photograph
Vintage studio shot of four stars of the first World Series, including Hall of Famer Jimmy Collins and the season's home run champ, Buck Freeman. $575

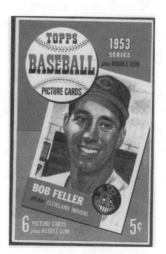

1953 Topps cardboard advertising display
Printed on heavy cardboard, the display piece features a giant version of Bob Feller's 1953 Topps card. Easily one of the most attractive of the early Topps baseball cards advertising displays. $3,617

1950s Stan Musial glove box
Rawlings cardboard box that housed a store-model Musial glove. The top of the box is made up of six "trading cards" of Musial that comprise the complete 1955 Rawlings set that is valued at nearly $1,000 by itself. $1,233

Ty Cobb game-worn glove
The only known glove once used by Cobb, it was originally given by Cobb to the noted actor Joe E. Brown, and came from the Joe E. Brown Collection. It later belonged to Charlie Sheen, who purchased it at auction in 1993. . . . . $62,301

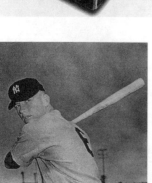

1951 Mickey Mantle Bowman card photo
Posed photograph of the Yankee great from his first season is the inspiration for the artist who designed Mantle's 1951 Bowman rookie card.
. . . . $3,220

1928 Fro-Joy Ice Cream store display
Huge advertising piece of the fabled Babe, and probably one of the most actively pursued advertising display pieces in the hobby.
. . . . $21,846

Finest known set of B18 Blankets
A complete set of the B18 Blankets that were attached to tobacco product packs in 1914. The 181-card set was assembled over a 20-year span by one of the most famous collectors/dealers in the country, Bill Mastro, and is regarded as the best such set ever accumulated.
. . . . $14,571

Lou Gehrig single-signed ball
Incredibly high-grade Reach ball signed by one of the greatest players in the history of the game.
. . . . $37,950

1979 Ken Boyer game-worn jersey
The 1964 National League MVP for the Cardinals returned to the club in the late-1970s as manager. $677

1954 Roogie's Bump movie poster
Colorful three-sheet movie poster of 1954 feature film that tells the story of "Roogie, the Miracle Kid, with the Super Zoom Ball!" Poster features portraits of four actual members of the Dodgers: Roy Campanella, Billy Loes, Russ Meyer and Carl Erskine. $731

1951 Mickey Mantle rookie road flannel
One of the great uniforms from the beloved Mantle, and includes the coveted 1951 American League 50-Year Anniversary patch on the sleeve. The jersey originated in the Halper Collection. $73,386

1939 Lou Gehrig's last glove
The actual glove used by Gehrig in his final game on April 30, 1939. The glove had to be included in this listing for a number of reasons, including the fact that it was the most expensive item sold at the historic Barry Halper Collection Auction at Sotheby's in September of 1999. The Gehrig glove, one of the final items to be sold, was hammered down for nearly $400,000 in the closing moments of the weeklong sale. $387,500

500-HR Club signed Andy Jurinko paintings
Incredible grouping of 15 individual paintings from sports artist Andy Jurinko, each measuring almost three-foot square. From the Halper Collection, each painting is signed by the player, with autograph cuts included for Ruth, Foxx and Ott. $37,375

Gaylord Perry signed Vaseline jar
Barry Halper set the standard for thinking of unusual, but significant, items for ballplayers to sign, and he outdid himself by getting Hall of Famer Perry to sign a bottle of this particular foreign substance. $862

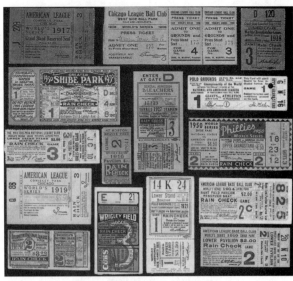

1903-98 World Series ticket collection
This is a 256-ticket run of stubs and tickets from the Fall Classic, compiled over a 40-year span by Barry Halper. $140,000

1911 *Breaking Into the Big League* poster
Incredibly artistic and colorful movie poster was issued to advertise the film that starred Christy Mathewson and John McGraw, both pictured on the poster. $33,350

Pair of Polo Grounds seats
A pair of attached seats from the famous park that passed into history in the 1960s after a brief stay by the then-fledgling New York Mets.
. . . . $14,950

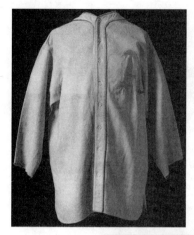

1928 Ty Cobb Philadelphia A's signed jersey

This is the jersey that captured the imagination of collectors and dealers at the Halper auction, selling for $332,500 and later being one of the marquee items in the 2000 Upper Deck Sweepstakes. $332,500

1942 Oscar from *Pride of the Yankees*

The only Oscar ever presented to honor a baseball movie, the Oscar was awarded for film editing of the 1942 film that starred Gary Cooper.
.... $57,500

1953 Topps Mickey Mantle original art

One of the most famous baseball card paintings has been auctioned a couple of times in the last dozen years. The artwork initially entered the hobby in the historic sale of the Topps archives in 1989, selling for an extraordinary $121,000. Bought by the Marriott Corp., it was later donated to the Children's Miracle Network, which auctioned the 3 1/2-by-4 1/2-inch painting in 2000. .... $150,000

Alexander Cartwright Hall of Fame plaque

The actual plaque from the family of the man regarded as the "Father of Baseball." Given the historical significance of the item, its $14,950 sale price at the 1999 Halper sale was one of the few lots thought to have been something of a bargain at the historic event. $14,950

1917-21 Babe Ruth H & B Pro Model bat

Earliest known bat bearing Ruth's facsimile signature, the white ash bat measures nearly 36 inches and weighs a whopping 45 ounces, and shows considerable game use. $36,098

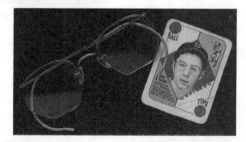

Dom DiMaggio's eyeglasses

The actual glasses worn by the youngest of the three DiMaggio brothers. The glasses came with a note from the former ballplayer attesting to the fact that he had worn them during his playing days. $1,840

Jackie Robinson's golf shoes

Size 14D golf shoes from the all-time great who loved golf until he was slowed by the diabetes that would eventually end his life in 1972. The shoes come with a letter of authenticity from Rachel Robinson.
.... $1,390

Yankee Stadium turnstile

Quite a few collectors have stadium seats, but the number with actual turnstiles is a bit smaller. This turnstile was removed from the Stadium during the renovation in the 1970s that sent the Yankees briefly to Shea Stadium to board with the Mets. $10,350

Joe DiMaggio's 1951 World Series ring
This is the ring from The Yankee Clipper's final World Series in 1951, and "Joe DiMaggio" is engraved on the inside of the band. $37,350

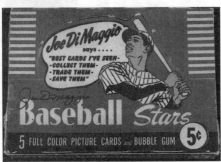

1953 Bowman Color display box
A display box from one of the most spectacular vintage sets of all time – the 1953 Bowman Color set. The box features a drawing of DiMaggio on the top and also bears his signature. $3,737

1956 Mickey Mantle Triple Crown Award
This is the actual trophy awarded to Mantle for his amazing 1956 season, considered by many to be his finest. The trophy came with a signed note from Mantle. $211,500

1986 Darryl Strawberry World Series glove
Black Gold Glove Series mitt worn by the Mets star in the play-offs and World Series in 1986 when the Mets upended the Red Sox. The glove is signed by Strawberry in silver. $2,875

1992 Roberto Alomar World Series Trophy
The trophy awarded to the players comes with 26 flags surrounding a crown at the center, with Blue Jays and Braves emblems below on a circular black base. The trophy comes with a signed note from Alomar. $37,375

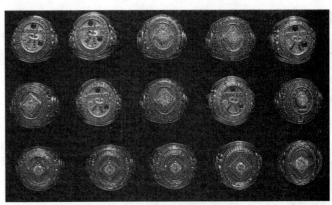

1947-64 Del Webb Yankees World Series rings
Staggering collection of World Series and American League Championship rings once owned by one of the team's owners, Del Webb. The collection includes 10 World Series rings and five AL championship rings. $310,500

1973 Pete Rose Silver Slugger bat
This is the stunning silver bat awarded to the league's batting champion. It is engraved with Rose's facsimile signature and batting mark for that season. $40,250

Billy Martin's boots
These boots came to Barry Halper by way of former A's coach Charlie Metro, who was given the boots by Martin. The custom-made dark brown boots belonged to the scrappy former player and manager, who was also a close friend of Halper's and a periodic visitor to Halper's home. Martin even appeared with Halper in a video shot in Halper's basement that chronicled many of the treasures within. . . . $2,875

Circa 1910 Mordecai Brown cigar box
The Hall of Fame pitcher endorsed this particular brand of cigars which was marketed by a local tobacco company based in his hometown of Terre Haute, Ind. The lid of the wooden box opens to reveal a full-color label showing Brown pitching. $2,875

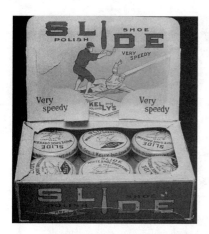

Circa 1920s Kelly's Shoe Polish and display
One of the great 19th century stars, the product and display box are inspired by the popular song Slide Kelly Slide. The box holds 12 containers of shoe polish. $1,380

Ty Cobb "Safe" bronze statue
Superb likeness of the Hall of Famer in an elegant bronze statue atop a wooden base. The statue is not dated but is thought to be from the 1920s. $18,400

Babe Ruth's Underwear and box
From the icon who endorsed more products during his career than any other player comes "Babe Ruth All American Athletic Underwear."
. . . . $1,840

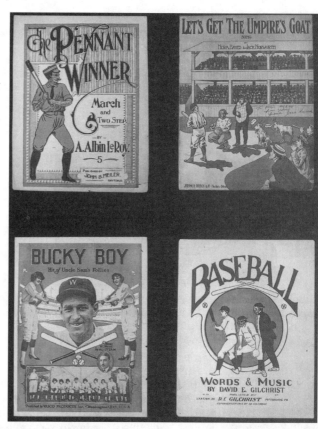

Baseball sheet music collection
This incredible assortment of sheet music, touching upon the National Pastime, came from the Halper Collection and spanned more than a century. It also bears the distinction of being the final lot out of more than 2,400 in the historic, weeklong auction in 1999. . . . . $48,875

Connie Mack bronze bust
This is a life-size bust of the Hall of Fame manager in his traditional suit and tie outfit. . $2,012

Al Barlick's signed NL umpire's suit
This is the last umpire's suit worn by the Hall of Fame umpire. Barlick signed the suit and noted the year of his HOF induction (1989) on the inside. $6,325

Ty Cobb's robe
This was given to Cobb's biographer, Al Stump, and is elaborately embroidered with Cobb's monogram in silver letters above two crossed bats on the front pocket. $5,750

Ryne Duren's glasses
There may not be a more famous pair of glasses from any postwar player. The hard-throwing reliever was noted for his thick eyewear, and would take advantage of the impression by whizzing a couple of warm-up pitches over the catcher's head. The glasses come with a letter from Duren noting that the glasses were the actual ones he wore during day games. . . . $2,587

1960 Mickey Mantle game-worn glove
Billy Crystal, who would go on to delight millions of baseball fans by directing the movie 61* just two years later, charmed the auction attendees at Sotheby's in 1999 at the Halper Auction by being the winning bidder on this item. $239,000

1903 American League composite photograph
Elaborate composite photography was a mainstay for baseball clubs at the turn of the century, and this remarkable Imperial Cabinet photograph illustrates the allure of the format. It features photos from virtually every player in the league. $35,650

1920 large Babe Ruth signed photograph
This is an amazing photo of Ruth, regarded as perhaps the finest signed Ruth photo in existence. Almost three feet high and two feet wide, it comes in an ornate frame and is signed and dated (1921) by Ruth. $35,650

1927 New York Yankees team photo
A large, detailed photograph of a team widely regarded as perhaps the greatest of all time, it comes with the facsimile signatures of many of the players. $18,400

1966 Luis Aparacio's World Series ring
This is the Hall of Famer's World Series ring from the 1966 affair when the Orioles unceremoniously dumped the Dodgers in Sandy Koufax's final appearance as a player. $18,400

Hank Aaron signed photo collection
The all-time home run king is the focus of this staggering photo lot from Barry Halper, which included nearly four-dozen signed photos, documents, and baseball cards bearing Hank's signature, including the photo shown with Aaron and legendary Negro Leaguer Satchel Paige. $10,925

Panoramic photo of the 1926 Yankees
These kinds of interesting elongated photos were very popular in the pre-World War II major leagues, with a camera mounted on a tripod that would slowly revolve, occasionally allowing a prankster player to appear at both ends of the photo. This particular photo from the Halper Collection is 41 inches wide and about 7 inches high. $27,600

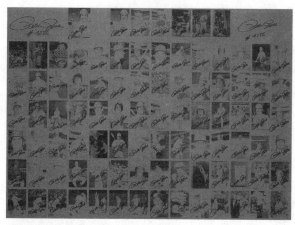

1985 Pete Rose multi-signed proof sheet
Barry Halper showed he was years ahead of his time when he got Pete Rose to sign every "card" from this 1985 black-ink proof uncut sheet from a card set that was made exclusively for Rose. $3,162

Rare baseball pin collection (no photo)
This assortment of 17 pin rarities spanned nearly four decades from the 1910s to the 1940s, mostly featuring individual players and often linked to specific products. $4,312

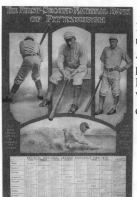

1913 Honus Wagner advertising schedule
A full-color, cardboard advertising display piece that was issued by the First National Bank of Pittsburgh, this originated from Wagner's personal collection and is the only known example of the schedule.
. . . . $16,100

1961 Exhibit card machine
Few pieces illustrate the scope of the hobby better than the various card vending machines that collectors saved from the scrap heap. These machines were often found in penny arcades and amusement parks around the country, dispensing The Exhibit Supply Co. cards created by the company for its own machines. $10,350

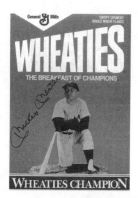

Mickey Mantle promotional Wheaties box
An enterprising collector created this one-of-a-kind piece by submitting a Mantle photo to General Mills in a 1980 promotion designed to allow fans to have their own photos appear as "Wheaties Champions" on a cereal box. This item was subsequently signed by Mantle.
. . . . $2,587

1986 Bill Buckner World Series glove
Blame the leather. This is the actual glove worn by the ill-fated Buckner in Game Six when history would be so cruel to an otherwise highly respected and talented ballplayer. Though he would later chafe a bit under the strain of disputes about the ball in question, he was a good sport with the leather, signing it and identifying it as the culprit from Game Six. $19,851

1940s baseball pinball machine
Freestanding, coin-operated "Keeney's Deluxe Texas Leaguer" arcade machine is designed to pitch marbles to the batter by means of a ramp extending from above the centerfield fence. This specimen is in working order. $17,250

1953 Cleveland Indians team-signed photo
This large black-and-white photograph features most of the ballplayers who would be part of the record-setting club that swept to 111 regular-season wins the following year. The players signed the photo in black ink. $3,737

Chapter 15

MISCELLANEOUS

ARTWORK/LITHOGRAPHS

Baseball Prints

A large number of artists have captured baseball's dramatic moments and all-time stars. Here is a sampling of baseball artwork:

Hank Aaron and Sadaharu Oh - lithograph, by Michael Elpins, signed by all $155
Roberto Alomar - 18x24 lithograph, by Angelo Marino, signed by both $90
Johnny Bench, the Catcher - 38x19, serigraph, limited edition, by Leroy Neiman, signed by both. $2,500
Roger Clemens - lithograph, by Michael Garner, signed by both. . $130
Roberto Clemente - 18x24 lithograph, by Angelo Marino $75

Old Comiskey Park - 15x34 oil on canvas original by Terrence Fogarty $6,000
Joe DiMaggio - 24x18, open edition, autographed, by Angelo Marino $700
Joe DiMaggio - 16x20, oil, by Frank Stapleton $500
Joe DiMaggio - 18x24 lithograph, by Angelo Marino, signed by both $595

500 Home Run Club by Doo S. Oh, signed by 11 . . . . $1,300

500 Home Run Club, poster by Ron Lewis, signed by 11 . . . . . $1,350
500 Home Run Club Lightning Bolt poster by Ron Lewis, signed by 11 . . . . $1,200
Whitey Ford - 18x24 lithograph, by Angelo Marino, signed by both. . $10
Ken Griffey Jr. - 16x20 lithograph, by J. Charles, signed by both . . $75
Tony Gwynn - 18x24 lithograph, by Angelo Marino, signed by both. . . $95
Sandy Koufax 28x22, limited edition, autographed, by Leroy Beachy $350

"Lefty and Robin" (Steve Carlton and Robin Roberts) 36x24 lithograph by Cliff Spohn, signed by all $320
Mickey Mantle, Hall of Fame Performance - 20x16, by James Amore $20

Mickey Mantle, "Life of a Legend" by James Fiorentino $225
Mickey Mantle - 10x16, limited edition, by James Amore. $225
Mickey Mantle, the Last World Series - 12x16, limited edition, by James Amore $200

Mickey Mantle - 24x21, pencil, autographed, by Glen Banse . . . $3,600

Mickey Mantle - 3D, 12x14 of his 1952 Topps card, autographed, by Jeff Frankel $3,000

Mickey Mantle - 24x18, open edition, autographed, by Angelo Marino $700

Mickey Mantle – 37 1/2x24, limited edition, autographed, by Burt Silverman $800

Willie Mays - 16x20 Lithograph, by Ron Lewis, signed by both . . $125

1969 Mets - 28x22, limited edition, by Joseph Catalano $200

"Stan the Man" - by Lewis Watkins 22x36, signed by both $650

Cal Ripken Jr. - 18x24 lithograph, by Angelo Marino $75

Pete Rose - 26x22, limited edition, autographed by Lewis Watkins, A Tradition of Excellence (Brooks Robinson and Cal Ripken Jr.) - 30x41, limited edition, autographed by both, by Tony Capperellio $700

Young Babe Ruth 27x34 1/2 litho by Gregory Perillo $175

Nolan Ryan - 24x18, open edition, autographed, by Angelo Marino $600

Ryan Express - 20x17, open edition, by Kenneth Gatewood $35

Mike Schmidt - 28x22, limited edition, autographed, by Frank Stapleton $375

Warren Spahn and Johnny Sain - 17x22 lithograph, by Ron Lewis, signed by all. $80

Frank Thomas - 25x36 lithograph, by Frank Stapleton $275

We Wanna Play (Ken Griffey Jr. and Frank Thomas) 21x16, open edition, by Kenneth Gatewood $35

Ted Williams - 18x24 lithograph, by Angelo Marino. $75

Ted Williams, the End of an Era - 22x26, limited edition, autographed, by Lewis Watkins. $950

Ted Williams, 1941 - 30x22, limited edition, autographed, by Lewis Watkins $950

Yankee Greats - Lou Gehrig, Mickey Mantle, 300-Win Club poster by Carlo Benaniti $270

3,000 Strikeout Club poster by Ron Lewis signed $330

Babe Ruth and Joe DiMaggio, 28x22, limited edition by Joseph Catalano $200

Carl Yastrzemski, Triple Crown - 22x28, limited edition, autographed, by Walt Peterson $200

Posters

Costacos Brothers

Founded in 1985 by brothers Tock and John Costacos, Seattle-based Costacos Sports grew rapidly to become the largest producer of creative licensed sports posters.

In 1994, Costacos entered into an agreement in which the company became the exclusive distributor for Nike posters. In 1996, Costacos was purchased by Indianapolis-based Day Dream, Inc., the world's largest poster and wall calendar company.

In 1997, Day Dream was purchased by Sidney, N.Y.-based AT-A-GLANCE Group, the world's largest manufacturer of time management products including desk calendars, student planners, three-ring binders, pocket portfolios and notebooks.

From the beginning, Costacos made an impact on the sports world with its innovative "fantasy" sports posters. Throughout the 1980s, superstar athletes would pose for some classic posters. Roger Clemens was "The Rocket," standing on the mound holding a smoking rocket-ball.

Costacos produces more than 200 new posters each year and has never kept a complete list of all the posters it has created since the mid-1980s.

In general, most poster prices in near mint condition do not fluctuate much and maintain their original suggested retail price on the current collectibles market.

Early Costacos Brothers Posters

Roger Clemens (The Rocket) $6

Eric Davis (44 Magnum) $5

Andre Dawson (The Hawk) $5

McGwire/Canseco (Bash Brothers). $8

Dave Winfield (Class). $5

Cory Snyder (Gunsmoke) $4

Frank Viola (Sweet Music) $4

Barry Bonds (License to Thrill) $5

Rickey Henderson (Lethal Weapon) $6

Andy Van Slyke (Pirates Treasure) $4

Ken Griffey Jr. (Kid Dynamite). $10

Sports Illustrated posters

During the late 1960s and early 1970s, *Sports Illustrated* produced several posters featuring hockey, basketball, football and baseball players. The posters, made available through ads in the magazine beginning in 1969, originally sold for $1.50 each. Today, some have reached $200, including Mickey Mantle, Roberto Clemente and Willie Mays. The year listed behind a player's name is the year the poster was released. The year of release of some posters is not known, so those posters are indicated by 1968-70.

Player	Value
Hank Aaron, 1968	$35-$45
Tommie Agee, 1968-70	$8-$15
Richie Allen, 1968	$10-$15
Gene Alley, 1968	$8-$15
Felipe Alou, 1968	$8-$15
Max Alvis, 1968	$8-$15
Mike Andrews, 1969	$8-$12
Bob Aspromonte, 1968-70	$10-$15
Ernie Banks, 1968	$20-$30
Glenn Beckert, 1968-70	$8-$20
Gary Bell, 1968 (Indians)	$10-$15
Gary Bell, 1968 (Pilots)	$10-$20
Bobby Bonds, 1970	$10-$18
Clete Boyer, 1968	$8-$12
Lou Brock, 1968	$18-$25
Johnny Callison, 1968	$10-$15
Bert Campaneris, 1968	$10-$15
Leo Cardenas, 1968	$10-$15
Rod Carew, 1970	$25-$45
Paul Casanova, 1968	$10-$15

Orlando Cepeda, 1968	$20-$30
Roberto Clemente, 1968	$125-$200
Tony Conigliaro, 1968	$12-$20
Mike Cuellar, 1970	$8-$15
Tommy Davis, 1968	$10-$20
Willie Davis, 1968	$10-$15
Don Drysdale, 1968	$18-$30
Mike Epstein, 1970	$8-$15
Al Ferrara, 1968	$8-$12
Curt Flood, 1968	$10-$15
Bill Freehan, 1968	$10-$15
Jim Fregosi, 1968	$8-$15
Bob Gibson, 1968	$18-$25
Bud Harrelson, 1968	$8-$15
Ken Holtzman, 1970	$8-$15
Joe Horlen, 1968	$8-$15
Tony Horton, 1968	$8-$12
Frank Howard, 1968	$12-$20
Reggie Jackson, 1969	$90-$120
Ferguson Jenkins, 1968-70	$25-$50
Tommy John, 1968	$10-$18
Cleon Jones, 1970	$8-$15
Al Kaline, 1968	$18-$25
Harmon Killebrew, 1968	$25-$35
Jerry Koosman, 1968	$10-$18
Let's Go Mets, 1969	$25-$45
Mickey Lolich, 1970	$10-$18

Jim Lonborg, 1968	$8-$15
Jim Maloney, 1968	$8-$15
Mickey Mantle, 1968	$150-$225
Juan Marichal, 1968	$20-$35

Willie Mays, 1968	$125-$200
Bill Mazeroski, 1968	$12-$18
Tim McCarver, 1968	$10-$15
Mike McCormick, 1968	$8-$15
Willie McCovey, 1968	$75-$150
Sam McDowell, 1970	$8-$15
Denny McLain, 1968	$12-$18
Don Mincher, 1968 (Angels)	$8-$15
Don Mincher, 1968 (Pilots)	$8-$20
Rick Monday, 1968	$10-$15
Bobby Murcer, 1968-70	$10-$18
Phil Niekro, 1970	$12-$20
John Odom, 1968-70	$10-$15
Tony Oliva, 1968	$12-$18
Wes Parker, 1970	$8-$12
Tony Perez, 1970	$12-$20
Rico Petrocelli, 1968	$8-$15
Boog Powell, 1968-70	$10-$18
Rick Reichart, 1968	$8-$15

Brooks Robinson, 1968	$50-$100

Frank Robinson, 1968	$30-$50
Pete Rose, 1968	$25-$50
Ron Santo, 1968	$10-$15
Tom Seaver, 1968	$50-$85
Chris Short, 1968	$8-$15
Bill Singer, 1970	$8-$15
Reggie Smith, 1968	$8-$15
Rusty Staub, 1968	$10-$18
Mel Stottlemyre, 1968	$10-$15
Ron Swoboda, 1968	$8-$15
Cesar Tovar, 1968	$10-$15
Roy White, 1968-70	$8-$12
Walt Williams, 1970	$8-$12
Earl Wilson, 1968	$8-$15
Jimmy Wynn, 1968	$8-$15
Carl Yastrzemski, 1968	$25-$40

PEREZ-STEELE POSTCARDS

Baseball Hall of Fame Art Postcards

In its first postcard set issued in 1980, Perez-Steele Galleries of Fort Washington, Pa., produced the first of four limited-edition sets. The first set is devoted to members of the Hall of Fame and is updated every two years to add the new inductees. The 10,000 numbered sets of postcards produced each time are generally collected autographed; the prices below are for autographed postcards. I means it's impossible that the player could have signed the postcard. Generally, unsigned postcards range from $5-$35, with the following exceptions: Jackie Robinson, Roberto Clemente, Sandy Koufax and Willie Mays are $40 each; Satchel Paige is $45; Earl Averill, Joe DiMaggio and Ted Williams are $50 each; Stan Musial is $55; Lou Gehrig is $60; Ty Cobb is $75; Babe Ruth is $100; and Mickey Mantle is $150. The first value is for an unsigned card; the second is for an autographed one.

First Series (Brown, 1980)
1. Ty Cobb . . . .$75 un, I
2. Walter Johnson . . . .$30 un, I
3. Christy Mathewson . . . .$10 un, I
4. Babe Ruth . . . .$100 un, I
5. Honus Wagner. . . . .$10 un, I
6. Morgan Bulkeley. . . . .$5 un, I
7. Ban Johnson . . . .$5 un, I
8. Nap Lajoie . . . .$5 un, I
9. Connie Mack. . . . .$5 un, I
10. John McGraw . . . .$5 un, I
11. Tris Speaker . . . .$10 un, I
12.George Wright . . . .$5 un, I
13. Cy Young. . . . .$10 un, I
14. Grover Alexander . . . .$5 un, I
15. Alexander Cartwright . . . .$5 un, I
16. Henry Chadwick . . . .$5 un, I
17. Cap Anson. . . . .$5 un, I
18. Eddie Collins . . . .$5 un, I
19. Candy Cummings . . . .$5 un, I
20. Charles Comiskey . . . .$5 un, I
21. Buck Ewing . . . .$5 un, I
22. Lou Gehrig . . . .$60 un, I
23. Willie Keeler . . . .$5 un, I
24. Hoss Radbourne . . . .$5 un, I
25. George Sisler. . . . .$10 un, I
26. A.G. Spalding . . . .$5 un, I
27. Rogers Hornsby. . . . .$10 un, I
28. Kenesaw Landis . . . .$5un, I
29. Roger Bresnahan . . . .$5 un, I
30. Dan Brouthers . . . .$5 un, I

Second Series (Green, 1980)
31. Fred Clarke . . . .$5 un, I
32. Jimmy Collins. . . . .$5 un, I
33. Ed Delahanty. . . . .$5 un, I
34. Hugh Duffy. . . . .$5 un, I
35. Hughie Jennings . . . .$5 un, I
36. King Kelly. . . . .$5 un, I
37. Jim O'Rourke . . . .$5 un, I
38. Wilbert Robinson. . . . .$5 un, I
39. Jesse Burkett . . . .$5 un, I
40. Frank Chance . . . .$5 un, I
41. Jack Chesbro . . . .$5 un, I
42. Johnny Evers. . . . .$5 un, I
43. Clark Griffith. . . . .$10 un, I
44. Thomas McCarthy . . . .$5 un, I
45. Joe McGinnity. . . . .$5 un, I
46. Eddie Plank . . . .$5 un, I
47. Joe Tinker . . . .$5 un, I
48. Rube Waddell . . . .$5 un, I
49. Ed Walsh . . . .$5 un, I
50. Mickey Cochrane . . . .$10 un, I

51. Frankie Frisch . . . .$15 un, I
52. Lefty Grove. . . . .$20 un, I
53. Carl Hubbell . . . . $25 un, $60-$80

54. Herb Pennock . . . .$10 un, I
55. Pie Traynor . . . .$5 un, I
56. Mordecai Brown . . . .$5 un, I
57. Charlie Gehringer . . . . $20 un, $60
58. Kid Nichols. . . . .$5 un, I
59. Jimmie Foxx . . . .$15 un, I
60. Mel Ott . . . .$10 un, I

Third Series (Blue, 1980)
61. Harry Heilmann. . . . .$5 un, I
62. Paul Waner . . . .$5 un, I
63. Edward Barrow . . . .$5 un, I
64. Chief Bender. . . . .$5 un, I
65. Tom Connolly . . . .$5 un, I
66. Dizzy Dean . . . .$35 un, I
67. Bill Klem . . . .$5 un, I
68. Al Simmons. . . . .$10 un, I
69. Bobby Wallace . . . .$5 un, I
70. Harry Wright. . . . .$5 un, I
71. Bill Dickey. . . . . $20 un, $75-$80
72. Rabbit Maranville . . . .$5 un, I
73. Bill Terry . . . . $20 un, $65-$80
74. Frank Baker. . . . .$5 un, I

75. Joe DiMaggio. . . . . . $50 un, $250-$300
76. Gabby Hartnett . . . .$5 un, I

77. Ted Lyons . . . . $10 un, $200-$250
78. Ray Schalk . . . .$5 un, I

79. Dazzy Vance . . . .$5 un, I
80. Joe Cronin. . . . .$15 un, $750

81. Hank Greenberg . . . .$20 un, $300
82. Sam Crawford . . . .$5 un, I
83. Joe McCarthy . . . .$10 un, I
84. Zack Wheat. . . . .$10 un, I
85. Max Carey . . . .$ 5un, I
86. Billy Hamilton . . . .$5 un, I
87. Bob Feller . . . . $15 un, $25-$35
88. Bill McKechnie . . . .$5 un, I
89. Jackie Robinson . . . .$40 un, I
90. Edd Roush . . . . $10 un, $65-$80

Fourth Series (1981, Red)
91. John Clarkson . . . .$5 un, I
92. Elmer Flick . . . .$5 un, I
93. Sam Rice. . . . .$5 un, I
94. Eppa Rixey . . . .$5 un, I
95. Luke Appling . . . .$10 un, $40
96. Red Faber . . . .$5 un, I

97. Burleigh Grimes . . . . $10 un, $200
98. Miller Huggins . . . .$10 un, I
99. Tim Keefe . . . .$5 un, I
100. Heinie Manush . . . .$5 un, I
101. John Ward . . . .$5 un, I
102. Pud Galvin . . . .$5 un, I
103. Casey Stengel . . . .$25 un, I

104. Ted Williams . . . . . . $50 un, $225-$325
105. Branch Rickey. . . . .$5 un, I
106. Red Ruffing. . . . .$10 un, $400

107. Lloyd Waner. . . . . $10 un, $3,500
108. Kiki Cuyler . . . . $5 un, I
109. Goose Goslin. . . . . $10 un, I
110. Joe Medwick . . . . $10 un, I
111. Roy Campanella . . . . $20 un, $175
112. Stan Coveleski . . . . $10 un, $400
113. Waite Hoyt . . . . $10 un, $450-$550

114. Stan Musial. . . . . $55 un, $80
115. Lou Boudreau . . . . $10 un, $20
116. Earle Combs . . . . $10 un, I
117. Ford Frick . . . . $5 un, I
118. Jesse Haines . . . . $10 un, I
119. David Bancroft . . . . $5 un, I
120. Jake Beckley . . . . $5 un, I

Fifth Series (1981, Yellow)
121. Chick Hafey . . . . $10 un, I
122. Harry Hooper . . . . $5 un, I
123. Joe Kelley . . . . $5 un, I
124. Rube Marquard . . . . $5 un, I
125. Satchel Paige . . . . $45 un, $3,500
126. George Weiss. . . . . $5 un, I
127. Yogi Berra. . . . . $15 un, $25
128. Josh Gibson. . . . . $5 un, I
129. Lefty Gomez . . . . $20 un, $55-$65
130. William Harridge. . . . . $5 un, I
131. Sandy Koufax . . . . $40 un, $70
132. Buck Leonard . . . . $15 un, $30
133. Early Wynn . . . . $10 un, $20
134. Ross Youngs . . . . $5 un, I
135. Roberto Clemente . . . . $40 un, I
136. Billy Evans . . . . $5 un, I
137. Monte Irvin. . . . . $10 un, $20
138. George Kelly. . . . . $10 un, $300

139. Warren Spahn. . . . . . . $10 un, $20-$30
140. Mickey Welch . . . . $5 un, I
141. Cool Papa Bell . . . . . . $20 un, $65-$80
142. Jim Bottomley. . . . . $5 un, I
143. Jocko Conlan . . . . $10 un, $45-$60
144. Whitey Ford . . . . $15 un, $25
145. Mickey Mantle . . . . $150 un, $300-$350
146. Sam Thompson . . . . $5 un, I
147. Earl Averill . . . . $50 un, $550
148. Bucky Harris . . . . $10 un, I

149. Billy Herman . . . . $10 un, $25
150. Judy Johnson. . . . . $20 un, $80

Sixth Series (1981, Orange)
151. Ralph Kiner . . . . $10 un, $15-$25
152. Oscar Charleston . . . . $5 un, I

153. Roger Connor . . . . $5 un, I
154. Cal Hubbard . . . . $5 un, I
155. Bob Lemon . . . . $10 un, $20
156. Freddie Lindstrom . . . . $5 un, I
157. Robin Roberts . . . . $10 un, $20

158. Ernie Banks . . . . $15 un, $30-$35
159. Martin DiHigo. . . . . $5 un, I
160. John Lloyd . . . . $5 un, I
161. Al Lopez . . . . $15 un, $75
162. Amos Rusie . . . . $5 un, I
163. Joe Sewell . . . . $10 un, $45-$60
164. Addie Joss . . . . $5 un, I
165. Larry MacPhail . . . . $5 un, I
166. Eddie Mathews . . . . $10 un, $20
167. Warren Giles . . . . $20 un, I

168. Willie Mays. . . . . $40 un, $60
169. Hack Wilson . . . . $10 un, I
170. Al Kaline . . . . $15 un, $20
171. Chuck Klein . . . . $10 un, I
172. Duke Snider . . . . $10 un, $25
173. Tom Yawkey . . . . $5 un, I
174. Rube Foster . . . . $5 un, I
175. Bob Gibson . . . . $10 un, $20
176. Johnny Mize . . . . $15 un, $25
A. Abner Doubleday . . . . $5 un, I
B. Stephen C. Clark . . . . $5 un, I
C. Paul S. Kerr . . . . $5 un, I
D. Edward W. Stack . . . . $5 un, $15

Seventh Series (1983, Brown)

177. Hank Aaron. . . . . $15 un, $25
178. Happy Chandler . . . . . . $15 un, $35
179. Travis Jackson. . . . . $10 un, $75

180. Frank Robinson. . . . . $10 un, $25
181. Walter Alston . . . . $20 un, $800

182. George Kell. . . . . $10 un, $12
183. Juan Marichal . . . . $10 un, $20
184. Brooks Robinson. . . . . . . $10 un, $20

Eighth Series (1985, Green)
185. Luis Aparicio . . . . $10 un, $20
186. Don Drysdale . . . . $10 un, $30

187. Rick Ferrell. . . . . $10 un, $30
188. Harmon Killebrew. . . . . . $15 un, $25
189. Pee Wee Reese . . . . $15 un, $30
190. Lou Brock. . . . . $10 un, $20

191. Enos Slaughter . . . . $10 un, $20
192. Arky Vaughan . . . . $5 un, I

193. Hoyt Wilhelm . . . . $10 un, $15

Ninth Series (1987, Blue)
194. Bobby Doerr . . . . $10 un, $15
195. Ernie Lombardi . . . . $5 un, I
196. Willie McCovey . . . . $5 un, $20
197. Ray Dandridge . . . . $5 un, $20
198. Catfish Hunter. . . . . $10 un, $20
199. Billy Williams . . . . $5 un, $10-$15

Tenth Series (1989, Red)
200. Willie Stargell . . . . $5 un, $15
201. Al Barlick . . . . $5 un, $15
202. Johnny Bench . . . . $5 un, $20-$25

203. Red Schoendienst. . . . . . $5 un, $15-$20
204 .Carl Yastrzemski . . . . $5 un, $30

Eleventh Series (1991)
205. Joe Morgan . . . . $5 un, $15
206. Jim Palmer . . . . $5 un, $15-$20
207. Rod Carew . . . . $5 un, $25
208. Ferguson Jenkins . . . . . . $5 un, $10-$15
209. Tony Lazzeri . . . . $5 un, I
210. Gaylord Perry . . . . $5 un, $15
211. Bill Veeck . . . . $5 un, I

Twelfth Series
212. Steve Carlton . . . . $5 un, $30
213. Leo Durocher . . . . $5 un, I
214. Rollie Fingers . . . . $5 un, $15
215. Reggie Jackson . . . . $5 un, $25
216. Bill McGowan. . . . . $5 un, I

217. Hal Newhouser . . . . $5, $15-$20
218. Phil Rizzuto . . . . $15 un, $35
219. Tom Seaver $15, $35

Thirteenth Series
220. Richie Ashburn . . . . $5 un, $30
221. Jim Bunning . . . . $5 un, $15
222. Leon Day . . . . $5 un, I
223. Bill Foster . . . . $5 un, I
224. Ned Hanlon . . . . $5 un, I
225. William Hulbert . . . . $5 un, I
226. Mike Schmidt. . . . . . $10 un, $25-$30
227. Earl Weaver. . . . . $5 un, $15
228. Vic Willis . . . . $5 un, I

Fourteenth Series
229. Nellie Fox . . . . $5 un, I
230. Tom Lasorda . . . . $5 un, $15-$20
231. Phil Niekro . . . . $5 un, $15-$20
232. Willie Wells . . . . $5 un, I
233. George Davis . . . . $5 un, I

234. Larry Doby . . . . $5 un, $20
235. Lee MacPhail . . . . $5 un, $15
236. Joe Rogan . . . . $5 un, I
237. Don Sutton . . . . $5 un, $20

238. George Brett . . . . $5 un, $25-$30
239. Orlando Cepeda . . . . $5 un, $20
240. Nestor Chylak . . . . $5 un, I
241. Nolan Ryan . . . . . . $10 un, $35-$40
242. Frank Selee . . . . $5 un, I
243. Joe Williams . . . . $5 un, I
244. Robin Yount . . . . $5 un, $20

Perez-Steele Great Moments

In 1985, Perez-Steele Galleries offered 5,000 numbered sets of Great Moments postcards, with periodical updates. These cards are generally purchased for the autograph, or to be autographed; the prices listed are for signed postcards. I means it's impossible that the player could have signed the card. Generally, unsigned cards sell for about $5-$15 each, except for higher priced cards for players such as Babe Ruth, Lou Gehrig, Ted Williams, Mickey Mantle, Stan Musial and Charlie Gehringer.

First Series (1985)
1. Babe Ruth . . . . $20 un, I
2. Al Kaline. $25
3. Jackie Robinson. I
4. Lou Gehrig . . . . $30 un, I
5. Whitey Ford . . . . $20-$30
6. Christy Mathewson I
7. Roy Campanella . . . . $12 un, $200
8. Walter Johnson. I
9. Hank Aaron . . . . $30-$35
10. Cy Young I
11. Stan Musial $75
12. Ty Cobb . . . . $20 un, I

Second Series (1987)
13. Ted Williams. . . . . $100-$135
14. Warren Spahn $20
15. The Waner Brothers I

16. Sandy Koufax. . . . . $35-$60
17. Robin Roberts. . . . . $12-$15
18. Dizzy Dean I
19. Mickey Mantle . . . . $150-$250
20. Satchel Paige I
21. Ernie Banks . . . . $25-$35

22. Willie McCovey. $25
23. Johnny Mize $20
24. Honus Wagner I

Third Series (1988)
25. Willie Keeler I
26. Pee Wee Reese. $35
27. Monte Irvin . . . . $12-$15
28. Eddie Mathews. . . . . $10-$20
29. Enos Slaughter. $20
30. Rube Marquard I

31. Charlie Gehringer. . . . . $30-$40

32. Roberto Clemente I
33. Duke Snider. $25
34. Ray Dandridge. $20
35. Carl Hubbell. . . . . $35-$50
36. Bobby Doerr. . . . . $10-$15

Fourth Series (1988)
37. Bill Dickey. . . . . $55-$60
38. Willie Stargell. . . . . $10-$15
39. Brooks Robinson . . . . $10-$15
40. Tinker-Evers-Chance I
41. Billy Herman. $20
42. Grover Alexander. I
43. Luis Aparicio . . . . $10-$20
44. Lefty Gomez . . . . $40-$50
45. Eddie Collins I

46. Judy Johnson I
47. Harry Heilmann I
48. Harmon Killebrew $25

Fifth Series (1990)
49. Johnny Bench $30
50. Max Carey. I
51. Cool Papa Bell. $80
52. Rube Waddell. I
53. Yogi Berra . . . . $15-$25
54. Herb Pennock I
55. Red Schoendienst . . . . $10-$20
56. Juan Marichal . . . . $10-$20
57. Frankie Frisch I
58. Buck Leonard . . . . $15-$25

59. George Kell . . . . $10-$15
60. Chuck Klein. I

Sixth Series (1990)

61. King Kelly. I
62. Jim Hunter . . . . $10-$15
63. Lou Boudreau. . . . . $10-$20
64. Al Lopez. . . . . $60-$70
65. Willie Mays. $30
66. Lou Brock $20
67. Bob Lemon. . . . . $10-$20
68. Joe Sewell . . . . Improbable, $50
69. Billy Williams . . . . $10-$15
70. Rick Ferrell . . . . $15-$20
71. Arky Vaughan I
72. Carl Yastrzemski. . . . . $15-$30

Seventh Series (1991)

73. Tom Seaver $35
74. Rollie Fingers $20
75. Ralph Kiner $20
76. Frank Baker I
77. Rod Carew. $25
78. Goose Goslin I
79. Gaylord Perry $15
80. Hack Wilson I
81. Hal Newhouser $15
82. Early Wynn $20
83. Bob Feller $20
84. Branch Rickey I

Eighth Series (1992)

85. Jim Palmer $25
86. Al Barlick $15
87. Willie, Mickey & Duke $150
88. Hank Greenberg. I
89. Joe Morgan $20
90. Chief Bender I
91. Reese, Robinson. I
92. Jim Bottomley I
93. Ferguson Jenkins $15
94. Frank Robinson $25
95. Hoyt Wilhelm $15
96. Cap Anson I

Perez-Steele Celebration

This 45-card set was issued in 1989 to commemorate the 50th anniversary of the Baseball Hall of Fame and the Galleries' 10th anniversary. There were 10,000 sets made. The set will not be updated; a complete set has 44 Hall of Famers and one checklist. Cards are 3 1/2-by-5 1/4 inches in size. The prices below are for signed cards. I means it is impossible that the player could have signed the card. Unsigned cards are generally about $8-$10 each, but are generally more for players such as Mickey Mantle, Stan Musial and Ted Williams.

1. Hank Aaron . . . . $22-$25
2. Luis Aparicio. $20
3. Ernie Banks . . . . $20-$35
4. Cool Papa Bell . . . . $35-$50
5. Johnny Bench. . . . . $15-$30
6. Yogi Berra . . . . $15-$20
7. Lou Boudreau. . . . . $10-$15
8. Roy Campanella $200

9. Happy Chandler. $25
10. Jocko Conlan . . . . $150-$500
11. Ray Dandridge . . . . $15-$20
12. Bill Dickey. . . . . $45-$50
13. Bobby Doerr. . . . . $10-$15
14. Rick Ferrell . . . . $15-$20
15. Charlie Gehringer . . . . $25-$40

16. Lefty Gomez I
17. Billy Herman . . . . $10-$15

18. Catfish Hunter . . . . $10-$15
19. Monte Irvin . . . . $10-$15
20. Judy Johnson I
21. Al Kaline. $20
22. George Kell . . . . $10-$15
23. Harmon Killebrew . . . . $10-$20
24. Ralph Kiner . . . . $10-$20
25. Bob Lemon. . . . . $10-$20
26. Buck Leonard. . . . . $15-$25
27. Al Lopez. . . . . $45-$70
28. Mickey Mantle . . . . $125-$250
29. Juan Marichal. . . . . $10-$15
30. Eddie Mathews . . . . $10-$15

31. Willie McCovey . . . . $10-$20
32. Johnny Mize. . . . . $15-$20
33. Stan Musial . . . . $30-$50

34. Pee Wee Reese . . . . $15-$35
35. Brooks Robinson . . . . $10-$15
36. Joe Sewell . . . . $25-$40
37. Enos Slaughter . . . . $10-$20
38. Duke Snider . . . . $10-$25
39. Warren Spahn . . . . $10-$20
40. Willie Stargell . . . . $10-$15
41. Bill Terry I
42. Billy Williams . . . . $10-$15
43. Ted Williams. . . . . $80-$175
44. Carl Yastrzemski. . . . . $15-$25

Perez-Steele Master Works

This 50-card set was produced in two 25-card series beginning in 1990 and features 10 players on five different postcard styles. The players are Charlie Gehringer, Mickey Mantle, Willie Mays, Duke Snider, Warren Spahn, Yogi Berra, Johnny Mize, Willie Stargell, Ted Williams and Carl Yastrzemski. Four designs are modeled after the 1888 Goodwin Champions baseball card set, the 1908 Rose cards, the Ramly 1909 set and the 1911 gold-bordered T205 set. The last design was created by the artist, Dick Perez. There were 10,000 sets produced. Prices are for individual cards.

Charlie Gehringer
1. Ramly..........................($6 unsigned, $50 signed)
2. Goodwin.......................($6 unsigned, $50 signed)
3. Rose...........................($6 unsigned, $50 signed)
4. Gold Border...................($6 unsigned, $50 signed)
5. Perez-Steele..................($6 unsigned, $50 signed)

Mickey Mantle
6. Ramly.........................($20 unsigned, $150 signed)
7. Goodwin......................($20 unsigned, $150 signed)
8. Rose..........................($20 unsigned, $150 signed)
9. Gold Border..................($20 unsigned, $150 signed)
10. Perez-Steele................($20 unsigned, $150 signed)

Willie Mays
11. Ramly.........................($7 unsigned, $35 signed)
12. Goodwin......................($7 unsigned, $35 signed)
13. Rose..........................($7 unsigned, $35 signed)
14. Gold Border..................($7 unsigned, $35 signed)
15. Perez-Steele.................($7 unsigned, $35 signed)

Duke Snider
16. Ramly.........................($6 unsigned, $20 signed)
17. Goodwin......................($6 unsigned, $20 signed)
18. Rose..........................($6 unsigned, $20 signed)
19. Gold Border..................($6 unsigned, $20 signed)
20. Perez-Steele.................($6 unsigned, $20 signed)

Warren Spahn
21. Ramly.........................($6 unsigned, $20 signed)
22. Goodwin......................($6 unsigned, $20 signed)
23. Rose..........................($6 unsigned, $20 signed)
24. Gold Border..................($6 unsigned, $20 signed)
25. Perez-Steele.................($6 unsigned, $20 signed)

Yogi Berra
26. Ramly.........................($7 unsigned, $25 signed)
27. Goodwin......................($7 unsigned, $25 signed)
28. Rose..........................($7 unsigned, $25 signed)
29. Gold Border..................($7 unsigned, $25 signed)
30. Perez-Steele.................($7 unsigned, $25 signed)

Johnny Mize
31. Ramly.........................($6 unsigned, $35 signed)
32. Goodwin......................($6 unsigned, $35 signed)
33. Rose..........................($6 unsigned, $35 signed)
34. Gold Border..................($6 unsigned, $35 signed)
35. Perez-Steele.................($6 unsigned, $35 signed)

Willie Stargell
36. Ramly.........................($6 unsigned, $20 signed)
37. Goodwin......................($6 unsigned, $20 signed)
38. Rose..........................($6 unsigned, $20 signed)
39. Gold Border..................($6 unsigned, $20 signed)
40. Perez-Steele.................($6 unsigned, $20 signed)

Ted Williams
41. Ramly........................($20 unsigned, $125 signed)
42. Goodwin......................($20 unsigned, $125 signed)
43. Rose.........................($20 unsigned, $125 signed)
44. Gold Border.................($20 unsigned, $125 signed)
45. Perez-Steele................($20 unsigned, $125 signed)

Carl Yastrzemski
46. Ramly........................($10 unsigned, $30 signed)
47. Goodwin......................($10 unsigned, $30 signed)
48. Rose.........................($10 unsigned, $30 signed)
49. Gold Border.................($10 unsigned, $30 signed)
50. Perez-Steele................($10 unsigned, $30 signed)

STAMPS

There have been several general issue sports-related postage stamps issued by the United States. They are listed using Fine-Very Fine grading conditions.

1) 1939 3-cent Baseball Centennial, violet - a sheet for $110; block of 4 for $11; unused stamp, $2.30; used stamp, 20 cents.

2) 1969 6-cent Professional Baseball Centenary, multicolored - a sheet for $50; block of 4 for $4.95; an unused stamp, $1.10; a used stamp, 15 cents.

3) 1982 20-cent Jackie Robinson, multicolored - a sheet for $95; block, $9.50; unused, $1.95; used, 15 cents.

4) 1983 20-cent Babe Ruth, blue - sheet, $100; block, $10.50; unused, $2.75; used, 15 cents.

5) 1984 20-cent Roberto Clemente, multicolored - sheet, $130; block, $12.75; unused, $3; used, 15 cents.

6) 1988 25-cent Lou Gehrig, multicolored - sheet, $38.50; block, $4; unused, 85 cents; used, 15 cents.

Two post offices in the Caribbean, Grenada and St. Vincent, have issued multi-player sheets of stamps. (Values for these stamps are from Scotts Standard Postage Stamp Catalogue, Volume 1A). In 1988, Grenada, licensed by Major League Baseball, issued nine sheets portraying 79 past and present baseball stars. Sheets of nine stamps (each stamp is 30 cents in East Caribbean currency) can be purchased from stamp dealers for $2 each; the whole set can be purchased for $17.50-$20. Three players from each team were depicted, except the Yankees. Individual stamps generally sell for 20 cents each.

The groups of nine are: A) Johnny Bench, Dave Stieb, Reggie Jackson, Harold Baines, Wade Boggs, Pete O'Brien, Stan Musial, Wally Joyner and Grover Cleveland Alexander.

B) Jose Cruz, American League logo, Al Kaline, Chuck Klein, Don Mattingly, Mike Witt, Mark Langston, Hubie Brooks and Harmon Killebrew.

C) Jackie Robinson, Dwight Gooden, Brooks Robinson, Nolan Ryan, Mike Schmidt, Gary Gaetti, Nellie Fox, Tony Gwynn and Dizzy Dean.

D) Luis Aparicio, Paul Molitor, Lou Gehrig, Jeffrey Leonard, Eric Davis, Pete Incaviglia, Steve Rogers, Ozzie Smith and Randy Jones.

E) Gary Carter, Hank Aaron, Gaylord Perry, Ty Cobb, Andre Dawson, Charlie Hough, Kirby Puckett, Robin Yount and Don Drysdale.

F) Mickey Mantle, Roger Clemens, Rod Carew, Ryne Sandberg, Mike Scott, Tim Raines, Willie Mays, Bret Saberhagen and Honus Wagner.

G) George Brett, Joe Carter, Frank Robinson, Mel Ott, Benito Santiago, Teddy Higuera, Lloyd Moseby, Bobby Bonilla and Warren Spahn.

H) Ernie Banks, National League logo, Julio Franco, Jack Morris, Fernando Valenzuela, Lefty Grove, Ted Williams, Darryl Strawberry and Dale Murphy.

I) Roberto Clemente, Cal Ripken Jr., Bob Feller, George Bell, Mark McGwire, Alvin Davis, Pete Rose, Dan Quisenberry and Babe Ruth.

On Dec. 7, 1988, St. Vincent issued a $2 stamp honoring Hall of Famer Babe Ruth. This stamp is worth $1.50. On May 3, 1989, St. Vincent issued another sheet of two $2 stamps - one features team logos for the 1988 World Series participants - the Oakland A's and Los Angeles Dodgers; the other shows the Dodgers celebrating. Individual stamps are worth $1.50; the sheet is worth $3.

On July 23, 1989, St. Vincent issued a set of 12 $2 stamps featuring Hall of Famers Bob Feller, Ernie Banks, Al Kaline, Stan Musial, Ty Cobb, Jackie Robinson, Ted Williams, Willie Mays, Lou Gehrig, Red Schoendienst, Carl Yastrzemski and Johnny Bench. Individual stamps are worth $1.50 each; the complete set is worth $18. Major League Baseball and the Major League Baseball Players Association gave approval for the stamps. A $5 1989 All-Star Game stamp, listing the starting lineups for the game in California, was also issued; it's worth $3.75.

Three other sheets of nine 60-cent stamps were also issued at the same time. Two sheets feature rookies, mainly from 1989. The first sheet shows Tom McCarthy, Jerome Walton, Dante Bichette, Gaylord Perry, Ramon Martinez, Carl Yastrzemski, John Smoltz, Ken Hill and Randy Johnson. The second has Bob Milacki, Babe Ruth, Jim Abbott, Gary Sheffield, Gregg Jefferies, Kevin Brown, Cris Carpenter, Johnny Bench and Ken Griffey Jr. The third sheet has nine award winners - Chris Sabo, Walt Weiss and Willie Mays (Rookie of the Year winners); Kirk Gibson, Ted Williams and Jose Canseco (MVP winners); and Gaylord Perry, Orel Hershiser and Frank Viola (Cy Young Award winners). In each case, sheets of nine are worth $4; individual stamps are worth 45 cents.

In September 1989, St. Vincent issued two sheets of nine 60-cent stamps featuring members of the World Champion Los Angeles Dodgers. The sheets are worth $4 each; individual stamps are worth 45 cents. One sheet has Jay Howell, Alejandro Pena; Mike Davis, Kirk Gibson; Fernando Valenzuela, John Shelby; Jeff Hamilton, Franklin Stubbs; Dodger Stadium; Ray Searage, John Tudor; Mike Sharperson, Mickey Hatcher; coaches Amalfitano, Cresse, Ferguson, Hines, Mota, Perranoski and Russell; and John Wetteland, Ramon Martinez. The second sheet has Tim Belcher, Tim Crews; Orel Hershiser, Mike Morgan; Mike Scioscia, Rick Dempsey; Dave Anderson, Alfredo Griffin; team emblem; Kal Daniels, Mike Marshall; Eddie Murray, Willie Randolph; Tommy Lasorda, Jose Gonzalez; and Lenny Harris, Chris Gwynn and Billy Beane.

On Nov. 30, 1989, St. Vincent issued nine more sheets of nine 30-cent stamps. The sheets are $2 each; individual stamps are 22 cents each. The sheets feature 1) Early Wynn, Cecil Cooper, Joe DiMaggio, Kevin Mitchell, Tom Browning, Bobby Witt, Tim Wallach, Bob Gibson and Steve Garvey; 2) Rick Sutcliffe, Bart Giamatti, Cory Snyder, Rollie Fingers, Willie Hernandez, Sandy Koufax, Carl Yastrzemski, Ron Darling and Gerald Perry; 3) Mike Marshall, Tom Seaver, Bob Milacki, Dave Smith, Robin Roberts, Kent Hrbek, Bill Veeck, Carmelo Martinez and Rogers Hornsby; 4) Barry Bonds, Jim Palmer, Lou Boudreau, Ernie Whitt, Jose Canseco, Ken Griffey Jr., Johnny VanderMeer, Kevin Seitzer and Dave Drabecky; 5) Glenn Davis, Nolan Ryan, Hank Greenberg, Richie Allen, Dave Righetti, Jim Abbott, Harold Reynolds, Dennis Martinez and Rod Carew; 6) Joe Morgan, Tony Fernandez, Ozzie Guillen, Mike Greenwell, Bobby Valentine, Doug DeCinces, Mickey Cochrane, Willie McGee and Von Hayes; 7) Frank White, Brook Jacoby, Boog Powell, Will Clark, Ray Kroc, Fred McGriff, Willie Stargell, John Smoltz and B.J. Surhoff; 8) Keith Hernandez, Eddie Mathews, Tom Paciorek, Alan Trammell, Greg Maddux, Ruben Sierra, Tony Oliva, Chris Bosio and Orel Hershiser; 9) Casey Stengel, Jim Rice, Reggie Jackson, Jerome Walton, Bob Knepper, Andres Galarraga, Christy Mathewson, Willie Wilson and Ralph Kiner. Two misspellings occurred; Fingers is spelled Finger, while Cochrane is Cochpane.

Nolan Ryan is featured on a sheet of nine $2 stamps issued Nov. 30, 1989. Individual stamps are worth $1.50; the sheet is worth $13.50. Ryan's achievements recognized on the stamps include: a) 383 league-leading strikeouts in 1973, b) no-hitter on May 15, 1973, c) no-hitter on July 15, 1973, d) no-hitter on Sept. 28, 1974, e) no-hitter on June 1, 1975, f) no-hitter on Sept. 26, 1981, g) won 100+ games in both leagues, h) struck out 200+ batters in 13 seasons, and i) 5,000 career strikeouts. Boston Red Sox outfielder Mike Greenwell was also featured on a 30-cent stamp; individual stamps are worth 22 cents.

On Aug. 5, 1992, St. Vincent issued a boxed set of 64 x 89mm $4 stamps featuring 12 Hall of Famers; a complete set is worth $36. The stamps were printed on thin cards; to affix the stamps, one had to remove the backing, which contained the players' statistics. The players in the set are Ty Cobb, Dizzy Dean, Bob Feller, Whitey Ford, Lou Gehrig, Rogers Hornsby, Mel Ott, Satchel Paige, Babe Ruth, Casey Stengel, Honus Wagner and Cy Young. Two $5 stamps, honoring players from New York - the Mets' Howard Johnson and the Yankees' Don Mattingly - were issued Nov. 9, 1992. These stamps are worth $3.75 each. On Dec. 21, 1992, three $2 stamps were issued honoring Hall of Famers Roberto Clemente, Hank Aaron and Tom Seaver. These stamps are worth $1.50 each. A $2 stamp for Hall of Famer Reggie Jackson was issued Oct. 4, 1993. The stamp is also worth $1.50.

UPPER DECK COMMEMORATIVE SHEETS

It started at the National Convention in Chicago in 1989. Upper Deck, then in its infancy and looking for ways to promote its products, handed out 8 1/2- by 11-inch sheets of cardboard that featured photos of some of the company's 1989 baseball cards. Each of the sturdy souvenir sheets was individually numbered.

Most of the subsequent sheets that were printed were theme-oriented and numbered. Print runs averaged about 40,000 per sheet. Sheet backs are mostly blank.

Some of the sheets featured artwork, while others featured photographs of Upper Deck card products. Many were produced to honor events that Upper Deck sponsored, such as the Heroes of Baseball old-timer games.

The sheets were created for promotional purposes by Upper Deck.

1991 Heroes of Baseball

Sheet	Value
Heroes of Baseball	$22
Heroes of Baseball	$35
Baltimore Orioles	$45
Boston Red Sox	$30
Cleveland Indians	$30

Atlanta Braves	$20
Oakland A's	$30
New York Mets	$25
Cincinnati Reds	$30
Milwaukee Brewers	$30
Toronto All-Star Game	$15
California Angels	$18
Pittsburgh Pirates	$20
St. Louis Cardinals	$20
Houston Astros	$28
New York Yankees	$30
Philadelphia Phillies	$14
Texas Rangers	$24
San Diego Padres	$17
San Francisco Giants	$12
Chicago Cubs	$40
Detroit Tigers	$15
Montreal Expos	$20

1992 Heroes of Baseball

Sheet	Value
Orioles Park at Camden Yards Opening Day	$40
Toronto Blue Jays	$14
Atlanta Braves	$10
Chicago White Sox	$10
Boston Red Sox	$10
San Francisco Giants	$10
Milwaukee Brewers	$10
Houston Astros	$18

New York Mets	$10
St. Louis Cardinals	$12
Texas Rangers	$10

California Angels	$10
Cincinnati Reds	$10
Los Angeles Dodgers	$12
San Diego "FanFest"	$35
New York Yankees	$14
All-Star (San Diego)	$12
Kansas City Royals	$10
Pittsburgh Pirates	$10
Seattle Mariners	$18
Montreal Expos	$12
Cleveland Indians	$12
Philadelphia Phillies	$12
Baltimore Orioles	$12
Rollie Fingers Hall of Fame	$10
Oakland A's	$18
Chicago Cubs	$14
Minnesota Twins	$12
Detroit Tigers	$10

1993 Heroes of Baseball

Sheet	Value
Heroes of Baseball Autograph Summer '93	$8
Toronto Blue Jays	$12
Atlanta Braves	$10
St. Louis Cardinals	$10
Kansas City Royals	$10
Ewing Kauffman Tribute (K.C. Royals)	$14
Boston Red Sox	$12
San Francisco Giants	$12
Cincinnati Reds	$10
Milwaukee Brewers	$12
New York Mets	$12
Philadelphia Phillies	$10
Colorado Rockies	$14
San Diego Padres	$10

Chicago White Sox	$12
Minnesota Twins	$12
Negro League Tribute	$12
Baltimore (All-Star)	$10
Fanfest Autograph	$5
Houston Astros	$10
New York Yankees	$12
World Children's Baseball Fair	$12
California Angels	$12
Oakland A's	$14
Seattle Mariners	$10
Detroit Tigers	$14
Montreal Expos	$10
Florida Marlins	$14
Cleveland Indians	$12
Texas Rangers	$10

1994 Baseball

Sheet	Value
Colorado Rockies	$12
FanFest Autograph Sheet	$5

New York Mets	$12
Pirates All-Star	$10
St. Louis Cardinals	$12

LOUISVILLE SLUGGER NOVELTIES

Over the years, the Hillerich and Bradsby Company, makers of Louisville Slugger bats, produced numerous novelty items and promotional materials including miniature bats, banks, pens and pencils. Some items were issued as team novelties while others were produced with individual star player items.

• Famous Slugger plastic bat rack and miniature player bats; circa late 1950s, offered by Famous Slugger Yearbooks . . . . $75-$100
• Louisville Slugger plastic bats bank, includes Mantle, Clemente and Rose, with original box $85
• Joe DiMaggio Bakelite plastic pencil bat, 1940s Louisville Slugger, facsimile autograph on the barrel $80

• Roger Maris/Eddie Mathews Louisville Slugger pen and pencil bat set, 1960s $60
• Duke Snider/Ted Williams combination pen

MATCHBOOKS

One of the most popular categories of matchcover collecting is sports matchcovers. The category is very broad, encompassing individuals, teams, stadiums, schedules and special events.

Collecting matchcovers has been an organized hobby since the 1939 New York World's Fair. Today, there are more than 25 clubs. Among the gamut of subjects, ranging from beer, to politics to transportation, sports covers remain the most popular, with an estimated thousands of people having sports covers in their collections. The easiest types to find are those from motels, banks and restaurants, with more than 50 percent coming from restaurants. Sports VIPs—players such as Jack Dempsey, Joe DiMaggio, Mickey Mantle and Lefty O'Doul who have lent their likenesses and names for advertising purposes—remain quite popular among those who collect restaurant/lounge covers.

In the late 1870s, nearly 100 small companies joined to form the Diamond Match Co., in Barberton, Ohio. The company's first baseball set, which appeared in 1934, is the largest. The set, called the silver border (because of the silver line framing the player's photo), or U-1 (Sports Collectors Bible designation set), has 200 different players featured, each with four different background colors - red, green, blue and orange. Thus, there are 800 covers to challenge collectors.

Hall of Famers in the set include Jim Bottomley, Kiki Cuyler, Dizzy Dean, Leo Durocher, Rick Ferrell, Frankie Frisch, Charlie Gehringer, Chick Hafey, Jesse Haines, Gabby Hartnett, Billy Herman, Waite Hoyt, Carl Hubbell, Chuck Klein, Bill Klem, Ernie Lombardi, Al Lopez, Ted Lyons, Rabbit Maranville, Bill McKechnie, Joe Medwick, Met Ott, Casey Stengel, Dazzy Vance, Lloyd Waner, Paul Waner and Hack Wilson. Prices for the non-Hall of Famers range from $6-$25, while HOFers are about $75-$90 each in Mint condition, with all matches in the book.

A second set, U-2, was produced in 1935. It is the most difficult to assemble. Each of the 24 covers has a black border entirely around the picture on the front and history on the back. There are eight each of three colors — red, green and blue.

A third set, U-3, was produced in 1935 and 1936 with red, green and blue. Two smaller sets were also produced through 1938. Those designated as U-4 and U-5 consist of a combined 23 players, each having three different colors (red, green and blue), making the total set 69 matchcovers. The set is available in two styles — with either brown or black ink. The final set, U-6, has 14 covers in all.

1961 Minnesota Twins, F&M Savings Bank

(1) Bob Allison $7.50
(2) Earl Battey 6
(3) Reno Bertoia 6
(4) Billy Gardner 6
(5) Lenny Green 6
(6) Harmon Killebrew 20
(7) Cookie Lavagetto 6
(8) Jim Lemon 6.50
(9) Camilo Pascual 7
(10) Pedro Ramos 7

1962 Minnesota Twins, F&M Savings Bank

(1) Bob Allison $7.50
(2) Earl Battey 6
(3) Lenny Green 6
(4) Jim Kaat 9
(5) Harmon Killebrew 25
(6) Jack Kralick 6
(7) Jim Lemon 6
(8) Camilo Pascual 7
(9) Pedro Ramos 7
(10) Zoilo Versalles 7

PLAYER-RELATED SOUVENIRS

•Hank Aaron 715 Home Runs Magnavox bat in original box $375
•Hank Aaron 715 Home Run King T-shirt. $65
•Hank Aaron theme spiral notebook, color photo of Aaron on the front
. . . . $20
•Frank "Home Run" Baker cigar box $300
•Johnny Bench's red baseball school nylon jacket, signed "Catch Ya
Later," Johnny Bench $175
•Johnny Bench/Pete Rose Lincoln-Mercury dealership 8x11 1/2 letter-
head $20
•Johnny Bench/Pete Rose Lincoln-Mercury dealership bumper decals,
unused $40
•Johnny Bench/Willis Reed Keds gym shoe box, with size 12 shoes
included, has large cards of Bench and Reed on the top $175
•Johnny Bench Strohs Beer keychain, shaped like a ticket, dated Aug.
11, 1984, commemorates the retirement of Bench's uniform . . . $40
•Ty Cobb writing tablet, 6 x 9 lined notepad with Cobb on the cover
surrounded by baseball-related newspaper clippings. $175
•Rocky Colavito 2-in-1 baseball dart game $40
•Del Crandall porcelain glove ashtray $110

• Dizzy Dean "Ole Diz" charcoal briquets bag $6
• Dizzy Dean Winner's Bread pin, brass bat and ball with a facsimile
autograph down the bat $45
•Joe DiMaggio Fisherman's Wharf Restaurant menu, with facsimile
autograph. $50
•Joe DiMaggio Fisherman's Wharf Restaurant pennant, red, 1940s. . $200
•Joe DiMaggio paper placemat, from his San Francisco restaurant
. . . . $30-$40
•Lou Gehrig wooden bat pencil, with mechanical lead, features image
of Gehrig batting $50
•Gil Hodges Rheingold Beer serving tray $50
•Harmon Killebrew 500 Home Runs insulated plastic mug, miniature
baseballs depict his milestone home runs, shows the then six mem-
bers of the 500 Home Run Club. $25
•Don Larsen Oct. 6, 1956, World Series commemorative plate, has
Yankee Stadium box score, signed by Larsen and Yogi Berra . . $400
•Mickey Mantle clock with portrait of Mantle in batting pose. . . . $90
•Mickey Mantle's Restaurant in New York, menu and napkins $30
•Waiter's vest from Mickey Mantle's New York restaurant $150
•Mickey Mantle's Isometric Minute a Day Home Gym, exercise sys-
tem, shows Mantle's face on the box $95
•Mickey Mantle pencil set $25
•Mickey Mantle/Willie Mays 1968 Transogram Zippee bat and ball set
with cardboard picture container $150
•Roger Maris' Batting Secrets flipbook, 1961, by David Blumenthal
. . . . $25

•Roger Maris' Zipee plastic practice baseball in original package . . $20
•Eddie Mathews plastic wiffle ball. . . . . $15-$20
•Say Hey! Buy USA Willie Mays bumper sticker $45
•Willie Mays/Ronald Reagan postcard from the White House. $55
•Joe Medwick 1930s wooden pencil bat, facsimile autograph on the
barrel $35
•Joe Morgan Kahn's Wieners commemorative coin, still in the bubble
pack $4
•Stan "The Man" Musial harmonica, signed $50
•Stan Musial replica Beechnut Gum metal poster, autographed . . . $20
•Pedro Ramos cigar box $75
•Babe Ruth knife keychain $75
•Bambino Tobacco rolling papers, original pack of papers made for
Bambino Tobacco, wrapper pictures Babe Ruth swinging a bat $300
•Babe Ruth belt buckle $265
•Babe Ruth 1933 Feen-A-Mint lifesize mask $600
•Babe Ruth musical bat, 1930s, wooden harmonica $150
•50 Babe Ruth League booster pin, red, white and blue with a silhou-
ette of Ruth $24
•Babe Ruth model pocket knife. $40
•Slide picturing Babe Ruth and William Bendix during filming of the
Babe Ruth Story, a promo item for the world premier $25
•Nolan Ryan "He's a Hero to Us All" CD. $75
•Bag of Purina dogfood picturing Nolan Ryan $25
•Menu from Nolan Ryan's Restaurant. $40
•Early-1980s Nolan Ryan Gillette premium blue windbreaker, with fac-
simile autograph. $125
•Mike Schmidt retirement glass mug by Courier-Post newspaper . . $12
•Al Simmons cigar box $400
•Willie Stargell stars, two, given to Pittsburgh Pirates players during
the 1979 season $85
•Tony Taylor Night keychain, from Aug. 9, 1975, has two photos and
facsimile autograph $45
•Joe Tinker cigar band $125
•Joe Tinker cigar box $400

•Life-size Bob Uecker face mask, by Miller Lite $6
•Likeness of Ted Williams on package of Champ prophylactics . . $100
•Ted Williams Sears box of Target Load Shotgun shells, 12-gauge,
25 in box $150
•Ted Williams model Sears lunch box. $50
•Ted Williams model Sears Movie camera $110
•Ted Williams Sears fishing reels — set of three — spinning, fly and
spin cast. $130
•Spool of Ted Williams Sears monofilament fishing line. $20
•Ted Williams Jimmy Fund tag. $45
•Ted Williams Sears shotgun and rifle cleaning kits $55
•Ted Williams 1959 Jimmy Fund membership card and hang tab . $150

TEAM SOUVENIRS

- Baltimore Orioles round metal pocket schedule $75
- Baltimore Orioles popcorn holder/megaphone $40
- Baltimore Orioles matchbook, 1966 and 1970 World Champions . $25
- Baltimore Orioles glasses, set of six, includes Ripken, Davis, Murray, Boddicker, Dempsey and Lynn $150
- Boston Braves World Series leather wallet, features Indian head and tomahawk on the front with the date, made to hold playing cards, etc $185
- Baseball team visors, banana-shaped, visors have team name, date and baseball logo, Boston Red Sox, New York Giants, Chicago Cubs and New York Yankees . . . . $45 each
- Boston Red Sox crystal dish, etched with date $195
- Brooklyn Dodgers team letterhead, 8 1/2x11, pictures an engraving of Ebbets Field, includes return address envelope $100
- Chicago White Sox charm bracelet, gold, with small bat and ball, White Sox and 51 are attached $75
- Chicago Cubs bullpen white glass coffee cup, features facsimile autographs of the teams relievers $55
- Chicago Cubs tobacco tin . . . . $70-$90
- Chicago White Sox Lite Beer beer tapper handle, 3 x 6, heavy plastic $10
- Chicago White Sox 12 metal ruler $12
- Pocket hanky with letter H on it, attached to a 1960 Chicago White Sox schedule, 3 1/2x7 . . . . $10
- Cincinnati Reds ice scraper, mounted on original cardboard display $30
- Cincinnati Reds Marathon Oil bumper sticker, Team of the '70s . . $10
- Cincinnati Reds ashtray with Cincinnati Inquirer headline honoring the 1961 N. L. champions $35
- Cincinnati Reds World Champs drinking glass, 5 1/2 tall, with facsimile autographs $20
- Cincinnati Reds Icee plastic drinking glass, 5 1/2 tall, with Icee Bear on one side, playoff and World Series stats on the other $5
- Cleveland Indians Chief Wahoo rubber doll, by Rempel Co. of Akron, Ohio, without feather $45
- Cleveland Indians 10″ plate, center features Cleveland Stadium . . $250
- Cleveland Indians cloth iron-on patch $25
- Cleveland Indians Coca-Cola plastic place mat, features Bell, Manning and Grubb $10
- Detroit Tigers or New York Yankees bat pencils . . . . $12 each
- Los Angeles Dodgers keychain on original card $45
- Milwaukee Braves souvenir fan, red and black Braves mascot, black wooden handle $20
- Milwaukee Braves plastic ring $30
- Milwaukee Braves beaded belt $65
- Milwaukee Braves drinking glasses, lot of seven, each has a team logo and opponents (Mets, Cubs, Giants, Dodgers, Reds, Cards and Phillies) $100
- Play Ball With the Braves! placemat, red, white and blue design features Milwaukee County Stadium and schedule, 10x14 . . . . $20
- Milwaukee Braves ashtray with Milwaukee Sentinel headline honoring the 1957 World Champs $35
- Milwaukee Brewers Harvey's Wallbangers ceramic coffee cup . . . $35
- Minnesota Twins Metropolitan Stadium bricks, original stadium bricks, available with red, blue, orange or gray paint edge $35
- Minnesota Twins charm bracelet, gold, with gold bat and ball . . . $25
- Minnesota Twins pen/pencil set, in original placard $40
- Minnesota Twins American League Champions souvenir patch, red, white and blue, with Twins logo in the center, 4 1/2x6 1/2, from the World Series $50
- Minnesota Twins all-time team ruler, red on white, features Killebrew, Carew, Oliva, Allison and Kaat $25
- House of Pancakes placemat featuring New York Mets players . . . $75
- New York Mets World Champions glass mug $45
- New York Mets cigarette lighter, silver-toned, features 1973 World Series logo $150
- New York Yankees beach towel, signed by Joe DiMaggio $200
- New York Yankees fountain pen and retractable pencil, each shaped like a baseball bat, with Yankee logo $200
- New York Yankees or Boston Red Sox straw hats, with felt band including team name and baseball player, sold at stadiums . . . . $50 each
- New York Yankees Yankee Stadium Special Police badge, #160, 1950s-1960s, silver metal, worn by police $295
- 1963 New York Yankees/New York Mets plastic bat pen $25
- Oakland A's inflatable seat cushion, 1972-74 World Champions . . $45

- Philadelphia A's tin parking plate $60
- Philadelphia Athletics fishing hat, blue and white $65
- Philadelphia Phillies set of six sandwich bags, feature Schmidt, Luzinski, Bowa, Lonborg, McGraw and Cash $95
- Philadelphia Phillies World Champs metal ashtray $45
- Philadelphia Phillies World Champs ceramic plate $50
- Philadelphia Phillies World Champions ceramic baseball bank . . . $55
- Pittsburgh Pirates souvenir fan from 1909 team picturing team members $475
- Pittsburgh Pirates ice scraper, in original package $15
- Pittsburgh Pirates souvenir scrapbook, empty, front cover has a gold Pirate mascot head and the words 1960 World Champions $40
- Pittsburgh Pirates plastic baseball bank, with facsimile autographs $195
- Pittsburgh Pirates World Champions glass mug $35
- World Series pen/pencil set, in original box, barrels read 1944 World Series St. Louis Cardinals vs. St. Louis Browns $135
- St. Louis Cardinals schedule on a vinyl car litter bag $45
- San Francisco Giants Christmas card, photo of Candlestick Park on the cover $35
- Washington Senators beach baseball $135
- Washington Senators popcorn holder/megaphone $45
- Washington Senators ceramic baseball glove dish with bat in pocket $65
- Mid-1960s megaphone, has all the American and National League team logos, by F. R. Woods of Cooperstown, N.Y. $75
- Uniform patches, 3″ diameter each, for Senators, Royals, Brewers, Red Sox, Yankees, Indians, Twins, Mets, Astros and Reds, each $20

GLOSSARY OF HOBBY TERMS

Airbrushing: The touching up of a photo by an artist, sometimes done to avoid licensing fees.

ALS: A letter that has been signed.

Ask Price: The price a dealer, investor or collector offers to sell his items for.

Autograph guest: A current or former player or other celebrity who attends a sports convention to sign autographs for fans. A fee, which can range from a few dollars to more than $75 for an athlete such as Muhammad Ali, is usually charged for the autograph.

Autopen: A mechanical device that is programmed to duplicate a precise signature. Autopens are often used by celebrities who receive numerous requests for their autographs.

Base brand: Basic set of sports cards produced by a card maker, usually the lowest priced.

Bid price: The price an investor, dealer, etc., offers to buy items.

Blank back: A card with no printing on the back, usually because of a printing error.

Blanket: An early 20th-century collectible consisting of a square piece of felt or other fabric that came wrapped around a package of cigarettes. Baseball players were one of the several subjects found on blankets. Most popular are the 5 1/2x5 B18 blankets from 1914, so-called because they were sometimes sewn together to form a blanket.

Bobbing Heads: A series of fragile hand-painted ceramic sports dolls that first came over from Japan in 1960. Sports, Accessories & Memorabilia (S.A.M.) reintroduced new dolls in the 1990s.

Book price: The retail selling price that appears in a price guide.

Buy price: The price that a dealer is willing to pay for cards or memorabilia. A dealer's buy price is usually quite a bit lower than that item's catalog or retail price.

Cachet: A specifically designed and produced envelope to commemorate a specific historical or sporting event that is usually postmarked on the anniversary or actual day of the event.

Centering: Refers to the positioning of a photo on a card. If all other things are the same, the better the centering, the more valuable the card.

Certificate of Authenticity: A piece of paper, usually of minimal value, that guarantees that the signature or piece of memorabilia is authentic and legitimate.

Checklist: A list of every item in a particular set. A checklist can appear on a card, in a book or elsewhere.

Coin: A metal or plastic coin-sized disc that depicts a player. It can also refer to an actual coin that depicts a player. It can also refer to an actual coin or a coin-sized silver piece that commemorates an actual event.

Condition: One of the major factors in determining the value of memorabilia, this term applies to the wear and tear on an item.

Convention: Also known as a trading card show. A gathering of anywhere from one to 600 or more card dealers at a single location (convention center, hotel, school auditorium or gymnasium) for the purpose of buying, selling or trading memorabilia. A convention is open to the public, and oftentimes a fee is required to attend the show. Many conventions feature a player or several players to sign autographs.

Counterfeit: A card or collectible made to look like a real item. Counterfeits have no collectible value.

Cut: A signature that has been literally "cut" away from a check, card, letter or notebook on which it was originally signed.

Dealer: A person who buys, sells and trades sports cards and other memorabilia for profit. A dealer may be full-time, part-time, own a shop, operate a mail-order business from his home, deal at baseball card shows on weekends or do any combination of the above.

Distributor: Persons or organizations that buy cards and memorabilia directly from the manufacturers or from other dealers and resells them on a large scale. Sometimes distributors receive exclusive products, and thus are the only source of distribution for the product.

eBay: The huge Internet trading source in which thousands of items are offered for auction daily.

Facsimile autograph: A reproduced autograph. Facsimile autographs are often found on bats, gloves and other equipment.

F.D.C.: An envelope or cachet that is designed to be postmarked to celebrate a specific event on the day or anniversary of the event. F.D.C. stands for "first-day cover."

Felt: A baseball item consisting of a felt pennant, usually with a photograph or likeness of the player attached. Felts were made in 1916 and again from 1936-37.

Find: A "find" normally happens because of a chance encounter or casual comment that results in the purchase of an item of exceptional quality or rarity, usually at a favorable and economical price. What makes a "find" possible is that people look at souvenirs in a special way and tend to keep scorecards, autographs and other odd pieces of memorabilia to accumulate over the years that eventually turn up as a treasure for someone else. The belief that most "finds" have already been found is not true. There are still "finds" out there waiting to be discovered.

Flannel: A jersey made of a cotton or wool material. Most flannels were discontinued and replaced by knit jerseys in the early 1970s.

Flat: A term used at autograph shows to describe a picture, poster, magazine, postcard or card. Usually "flats" have a different pricing structure than equipment, uniforms or balls.

Fixtures: Any non-seat items that came out of a stadium, such as turnstiles, aisle signs, restroom signs, etc.

Fleer: The Pennsylvania-based maker of baseball, basketball and football cards.

Foil Pack: A tamperproof card packaging widely used since 1989.

Game: A uniform, cap, helmet or piece of equipment manufactured and designed for use in a college or professional game or sporting event. A "game" bat was ordered by the player to be used but is not "game-used" until it actually makes its way into an actual game.

Game-used or game-worn: A uniform, hat or piece of equipment actually used or worn in a professional or college sporting event.

Grade: The state of preservation of a piece of memorabilia. An item's value is based in large part on its grade (condition).

GPC: The initials GPC stand for "government postcard." These pre-stamped postcards were especially popular for obtaining autographs by mail from outside stadiums. That way, a fan could hand a player a self-addressed stamped postcard that the player could sign and return at a more convenient time.

Grading service: A company that charges a fee to grade cards or memorabilia. Most grading services work like this: After a card is graded, it is placed in a tamper-proof plastic holder. A network of member-dealers then agrees to buy that card sight-unseen at that grade. Grading services are a recent innovation, patterned after similar services in the coin-collecting hobby.

Hall of Famer (HOFer): a member of a sports hall of fame. Hall of Famer items often command a premium over non-Hall of Famer items.

Hall of Fame plaque: A postcard that is sold at the Baseball Hall of Fame gift shop in Cooperstown, N.Y. The postcard is a photo of each individual's plaque honored as a member of the Hall of Fame.

Hartland: A statue produced by a Wisconsin plastics company in the late 1950s and early 1960s. Eighteen major league baseball players were models for Hartlands. The company also produced football player statues and a long line of Western and historical figures, horses and farm animals. Hartland baseball figures were reissued in the late 1980s and early 1990s.

Headliners: A series of sports figurines produced by Corinthian Marketing, beginning in 1997.

Hobby: A folksy term used by veteran collectors that refers to the sports collectibles business/industry.

Hologram: The silvery, laser-etched trademark printed as an anti-counterfeiting device on Upper Deck cards and Upper Deck Authenticated memorabilia.

Kellogg's: The Battle Creek, Mich., cereal company that packaged three-dimensional baseball and football cards in its cereal from 1970-83. The company has also produced cereal boxes picturing famous athletes.

Knits: The modern, polyester-based fabrics used in modern sports uniforms.

Letter of authenticity (LOA): A letter stating that a certain piece of memorabilia, such as a uniform, is authentic.

Limited edition: A term often used by makers of cards and memorabilia to indicate scarcity. A limited edition means just that—production of the item in question will be limited to a certain number. However, that number may be large or small.

Lithograph: An art print made by a specific process that results in a print of outstanding clarity. Most lithographs are limited editions—though, as always, some lithographs are more limited than others.

Mail-bid auction: A form of auction where all bids are sent in through the mail. The person who sends in the highest bid gets the merchandise.

Manufacturer's tag: A tag sewn or attached into a jersey identifying it as from a particular company, such as Rawlings or Russell.

Matted out: A term used in the framing process to describe the covering of something not wanted in the finished product. For example, if a 3x5 card is personalized to "William" and the owner of the autograph is named "Bob," the owner would probably want to have the name "William" matted out.

Memorabilia: Usually referred to as items other than cards that mark or commemorate a player and his career, a team or an event.

Minimum Bid: The lowest acceptable offer that an auction company or individual will take for a particular item to begin the auction.

Mylar: Type of plastic from which many card holders, plastic sheets and other protection devices are made.

National: A sports memorabilia show held annually in different parts of the United States that draws hundreds of dealers and thousands of collectors.

Obverse: The front of the card displaying the picture. Opposite of reverse.

Oddball: A catchall category of sports collectibles other than cards, autographs and game-worn uniforms. Examples include beer and soda cans, cereal boxes, ticket stubs, publications and sports movie posters.

O-Pee-Chee: A longtime Canadian licensee of Topps that produced bilingual (French/English) baseball and hockey cards.

Paint pen: Gold or silver markers with opaque ink that can be difficult to use because of inconsistent ink flow.

Parkhurst: A Canadian manufacturer of hockey cards in the 1950s and 1960s. In recent years, the name was licensed to major manufacturers of hockey cards.

Perez-Steele: Line of popular Baseball Hall of Fame art postcards that is ideal for autographs, produced by artist Dick Perez and his late business partner, Franklin Steele.

Phantom: A ticket or press pin produced in anticipation of a team making the playoffs, but not used when the team failed to make it.

Phone auction: An auction where bids for memorabilia are taken over the phone. The highest bidder gets the merchandise.

Post: A cereal company that made baseball and football cards from 1960-63 and put them on the backs of its cereal boxes. Today the most valuable Post cards are uncut panels found on boxes. The company has also pictured athletes on its cereal boxes.

PPD: Postage paid.

Premium: An extra. Something inserted in a package of some other product. "Premium" can also refer to the extra money a star's item commands.

Price guide: A periodical or book that contains checklists of cards, sets and other memorabilia and their values in varying conditions.

Price on request (P.O.R.): A dealer will advertise an item P.O.R. if he believes the price will fluctuate from the time he places his ad until the time the ad is seen by the public.

Private signing: An autograph signing event where a dealer employs a celebrity to sign a number of items or "pieces" that have been mailed in or ordered by collectors. A private signing is not a public event.

Provenance: The history of ownership of a particular item. It allows the buyer to secure additional insight as to the origin of the item.

Puzzle piece, poster piece: The back of a card containing a partial design that, when pieced together with corresponding pieces, forms a large picture or poster.

Rare: Difficult to obtain and limited in number.

ROY: Rookie of the Year.

Salesman's Sample: An example of a commemorative championship ring or a jersey produced by companies for players and team officials to preview. Not as collectible, but often mistaken for the real thing.

SASE: A term used in hobby advertisements and elsewhere to indicate "self-addressed, stamped envelope."

SCD: The weekly magazine known as *Sports Collectors Digest* that is published in Iola, Wis.

Sell price: The price at which a dealer will sell cards. Generally much higher than his buy price.

Sepia: A dark reddish-brown coloration used in some photos instead of traditional black and white.

Series: A group of items that is part of a set and was issued at one time.

Set: A complete run of items.

Sharpie: A permanent marker made by Sanford in a variety of colors and pen points for use on paper, cloth or leather. It is not advisable to use for autographs on baseballs because the ink has a tendency to bleed.

Single-signed: An item (often a ball) with only one signature on it.

Slabbing: Process of independent, professional grading on a scale of 1-10 or 1-100 and placing cards in hard plastic casings.

Stamp: An adhesive-backed paper that depicts a player. When the stamp, which can be an individual or a sheet of many stamps, is moistened, it can be attached to another surface or corresponding stamp album.

Stamped: An autograph applied to a photo, card or other item with a rubber stamp, not hand signed.

Starting Lineup: A line of plastic figures with accompanying cards produced by Kenner/Hasbro since 1988. Also, the trademark for a computer-based baseball game with cards produced by Parker Brothers.

Stub: A portion of a ticket left over from attending a game. Not as valuable as an untorn ticket, but usually still collectible.

Sweet spot or manager's spot: The section of a baseball reserved for the team manager on baseballs. It is usually the most desirable spot for an autograph on single-signed baseballs.

Tobacco cards: Baseball cards packaged with tobacco products in the late 1800s and early 1900s.

Topps: The oldest existing sports card manufacturer. Based in New York, the company has produced baseball cards continuously since 1951 and has also produced basketball, football and hockey cards.

Upper Deck: The Carlsbad, Calif., manufacturer of baseball, basketball, football and hockey cards.

Upper Deck Authenticated (UDA): The sister company of The Upper Deck Co., which produces authentic autographed memorabilia items under contracts with star athletes including Michael Jordan.

Uncut sheet: A full press sheet of cards that was never cut and collated into individual cards.

UV: A glossy coating applied to sports cards.

3 x 5 (lined or unlined): A 3-inch by 5-inch card that may have a lined side and a blank side. Autograph collectors prefer that signatures be on the unlined side of the card.

Variation: A card printed in more than one manner, usually to correct an error or printing mistake.

Want list: A collector's or dealer's list of items he is wishing to buy. Often, a collector will send a dealer a "want list," and the dealer will try to locate the items on the list.

Wax: Type of card packaging (for example, wax pack) widely used until the late 1980s. Wax-sealed wrappers could be easily removed and the contents tampered with.

Wheaties: The breakfast cereal by General Mills that often pictures sports personalities and championship teams on the fronts of boxes.

ADDRESSES

AMERICAN LEAGUE TEAM ADDRESSES

Anaheim Angels
Edison Field
2000 Gene Autry Way
Anaheim, CA 92806
Phone: (714) 940-2000
angels.mlb.com

Baltimore Orioles
Oriole Park at Camden Yards
333 West Camden Street
Baltimore, MD 21201
Phone: (410) 685-9800
orioles.mlb.com

Boston Red Sox
Fenway Park
4 Yawkey Way
Boston, MA 02215
Phone: (617) 267-9440
redsox.mlb.com

Cleveland Indians
Jacobs Field
2401 Ontario Street
Cleveland, OH 44115
Phone: (216) 420-4200
indians.mlb.com

Chicago White Sox
Comiskey Park
333 West 35th Street
Chicago, IL 60616
Phone: (312) 674-1000
whitesox.mlb.com

Detroit Tigers
Comerica Park
2100 Woodward Avenue
Detroit, MI 48201
Phone: (313) 471-2000
tigers.mlb.com

Kansas City Royals
Kauffman Stadium
1 Royal Way
Kansas City, MO 64141-6969
Phone: (816) 921-8000
royals.mlb.com

Minnesota Twins
Metrodome
34 Kirby Puckett Place
Minneapolis, MN 55415
Phone: (612) 375-1366
twins.mlb.com

New York Yankees
Yankee Stadium
161st Street and River Avenue
Bronx, NY 10451
Phone: (718) 293-4300
yankees.mlb.com

Oakland Athletics
Network Associates Coliseum
7677 Oakport, Suite 200
Oakland, CA 94621
Phone: (510) 638-4900
athletics.mlb.com

Seattle Mariners
Safeco Field
P.O. Box 4100
Seattle, WA 98104
Phone: (206) 346-4000
mariners.mlb.com

Tampa Bay Devil Rays
Tropicana Field
One Tropicana Drive
St. Petersburg, FL 33705
Phone: (727) 825-3137
devilrays.mlb.com

Texas Rangers
The Ballpark in Arlington
1000 Ballpark Way
Arlington, TX 76011
Phone: (817) 273-5222
rangers.mlb.com

Toronto Blue Jays
Skydome
1 Blue Jays Way, Suite 3200
Toronto, Ontario, Canada M5V1J1
Phone: (416) 341-1000
bluejays.mlb.com

NATIONAL LEAGUE TEAM ADDRESSES

Arizona Diamondbacks
Bank One Ballpark
401 East Jefferson Street
Phoenix, AZ 85001
Phone: (602) 462-6500
diamondbacks.mlb.com

Atlanta Braves
Turner Field
755 Hank Aaron Drive
Atlanta, GA 30315
Phone: (404) 552-7630
braves.mlb.com

Chicago Cubs
Wrigley Field
1060 West Addison
Chicago, IL 60613-4397
Phone: (773) 404-2827
cubs.mlb.com

Cincinnati Reds
Cinergy Field
100 Cinergy Field
Cincinnati, OH 45202

Phone: (513) 421-4510
reds.mlb.com

Colorado Rockies
Coors Field
2001 Blake Street
Denver, CO 80205-2000
Phone: (303) 292-0200
rockies.mlb.com

Florida Marlins
Pro Player Stadium
2269 Dan Marino Boulevard
Miami, FL 33056
Phone: (305) 626-7400
marlins.mlb.com

Houston Astros
Enron Field
501 Crawford Street
Houston, TX 77002
Phone: (713) 259-8000
astros.mlb.com

Los Angeles Dodgers
Dodger Stadium
1000 Elysian Park Avenue
Los Angeles, CA 90012-1199
Phone: (213) 224-1500
dodgers.mlb.com

Milwaukee Brewers
Miller Park
One Brewers Way
Milwaukee, WI 53214
Phone: (414) 902-4400
brewers.mlb.com

Montreal Expos
Olympic Stadium
4549 Avenue Pierre de Coubertin
Montreal, Quebec, Canada H1V3N7
Phone: (514) 253-3434
expos.mlb.com

New York Mets
Shea Stadium
123-01 Roosevelt Avenue

Flushing, NY 11368-1699
Phone: (718) 507-6387
mets.mlb.com

Philadelphia Phillies
Veterans Stadium
3501 South Broad Street
Philadelphia, PA 19148
Phone: (215) 463-6000
phillies.mlb.com

Pittsburgh Pirates
PNC Park
115 Federal Street
Pittsburgh, PA 15212
Phone: (412) 323-5000
pirates.mlb.com

San Diego Padres
Qualcomm Stadium
8880 Rio San Diego Drive, Suite 400
San Diego, CA 92112-2000
Phone: (619) 881-6500
padres.mlb.com

San Francisco Giants
Pacific Bell Park
24 Willie Mays Plaza
San Francisco, CA 94107
Phone: (415) 972-2000
giants.mlb.com

St. Louis Cardinals
Busch Stadium
250 Stadium Plaza
St. Louis, MO 63102
Phone: (314) 421-3060
cardinals.mlb.com

HALLS OF FAME, MUSEUMS

Alabama Sports Hall of Fame and Museum
2150 Civic Center Blvd
Birmingham, AL 35203
(205) 323-6665
Web site: www.tech-comm.com/ashof

The American Sportscasters Association Hall of Fame
5 Beekman St., Suite 814
New York, NY 10038
(212) 227-8080
Web site: www.americansportscasters.com

The Babe Ruth Museum
216 Emory St.
Baltimore, MD 21230
(410) 727-1539
Web site: www.baberuthmuseum.com

Bob Feller Hometown Exhibit
310 Mill St. P. O. Box 95
Van Meter, IA 50261
(515) 996-2806,
Web site: www.bobfellermuseum.org

Ivan Allen Jr., Braves Museum and Hall of Fame
755 Hank Aaron Dr.
Atlanta, GA 30315
(404) 614-2310

Kansas Sports Hall of Fame
213 N. Broadway, P. O. Box 35
Abilene, KS, 67410
(785) 262-7403
Web site: www.kshof.org

Louisiana Sports Hall of Fame
6007 Financial Plaza, Suite 401
Shreveport, LA 71129
Web site: www.lasportshof.com

Louisville Slugger Museum
800 West Main St.
Louisville, KY 40202
(502) 588-7228
Web site: www.slugger.com/museum

MCI National Sports Gallery
601 F. St.
N.W., Washington, DC 20001
(202) 661-5133
Web site: www.mcicenter.com

Michigan Sports Hall of Fame
32985 Hamilton Court, Suite 218
Farmington Hills, MI 48334
(248) 848-0252

National Baseball Hall of Fame and Museum
P.O. Box 590
Cooperstown, NY 13326
(607) 547-7200
Web site: www.baseballhalloffame.org

Negro League Baseball Museum
1601 E. 18th St., Suite 260
Kansas City, MO 64108
(816) 221-1920

Oklahoma Sports Museum
315 W. Oklahoma Ave.
Guthrie, OK 73044
(405) 260-1342
Web site: www.oksports.qpg.com

Pennsylvania Sports Hall of Fame
P.O. Box 2034
Cleona, PA 17042
(717) 274-3644
Web site: www.pasportshalloffame.com

St. Louis Cardinals Hall of Fame Museum
111 Stadium Plaza
St. Louis, MO 63102
(314) 231-6340
Web site: www.stlcardinals.com

Ted Williams Museum and Hitters Hall of Fame
2455 N. Citrus Hills Blvd.
Hernando, FL 34442-5349
(352) 527-4163
Web site: http: twmuseum.com

Ty Cobb Museum
461 Cook St.
Royston, GA 30662
(706) 245-1825
Web site: www.tycobbmuseum.org

SPORTS RELATED WEB ADDRESSES

Auction Companies

All American Collectibles
www.aacauction.com

Amazon
www.amazon.com

American Memorabilia
www.Ami21.com

AcuBid.com
www.acubid.com

Andalé
www.andale.com

Auction Anything.com
www.auctionanything.com

AuctionBytes.com
www.auctionbytes.com

The Auction Channel
www.theauctionchannel.com

Auction Helper.com
www.auctionhelper.com

AuctionInvoice.com
www.auctioninvoice.com

Auction Watch
www.auctionwatch.com

Auction Works
www.auctionworks.com

Baseball Planet
www.baseballplanet.com

Beckett.com
www.beckett.com

Bidhop.com
www.bidhop.com

Boxlot.com
www.boxlot.com

Card Hobby
www.cardhobby.com

Clean Sweep Auctions
www.csauctions.com

Coach's Corner Sports Auctions
www.ccsauction.com

Collectit.net
www.collectit.net

Collectors Universe
www.collectors.com

Compares.com
www.compares.com

eBay
www.ebay.com

eWanted
www.ewanted.com

Gavel Net
www.gavelnet.com

GoTo Auctions
auctions.goto.com

Grey Flannel Collectibles
www.greyflannel.com

Hunt Auctions Inc.
www.huntauctions.com

InterNet's Baseball Card Store
www.baseball-cards.com

Leland's
www.lelands.com

Greg Manning Auctions Inc.
www.gregmanning.amazon.com

Mastro Fine Sports Auctions
www.mastronet.com

MintXpress
www.mintxpress.com

M.S. Auctions
www.msauctions.com

PSA Auctions
www.psaauctions.com

Ron Oser Enterprises
www.ronoserent.com

Rotman Auctions
www.rotmanauction.com
www.wwcd.com/rotman

R&R Enterprises
www.rrauction.com

Sotheby's
www.sothebys.amazon.com

Sports Auction.com
www.sportsauction.com

Sports Collective Network
www.sportscollective.net

Sports Investments International
www.air23.com

Superior Galleries
www.superiorgalleries.com

Superior Sports Auctions
www.collectors.com

Teletrade Sports Auctions
www.teletrade.com

Todays Sports
www.todayssports.com

Triple Threat Cards
www.ttcards.com

Yahoo Auctions
www.auctions.yahoo.com

Autograph Collectors

Autographs.com
www.autographs.com

The Autograph Zone
www.autographzone.com

Baseball Autographs
www.expage.com/page/autographsby-mail

BD's Autograph Shack
www.members.aol.com/cb4sports/index.html

Celebrity Address Emporium
www.springrose.com/celebrity/b.html

JD's Baseball Autographs
www.geocities.com/Colosseum/Base/2-611/index.html

Mac Maroon's Sports Autographs
www.geocities.com/Colosseum/Bench/2126/

Mark's Signing Bonus
www.angelfire.com/mb/markssigning-bonus/

NBO Baseball
www.nbobaseball.com

Net's Best Autograph Collecting Links
www.rightguide.com/topics/hobby/autograph.htm

Signatures of Success
www.signaturesofsuccess.com

Signings Hotline
www.signingshotline.com

The Star Archive
www.stararchive.com

Stu's Super Autograph Page
www.stu-man.com

Card Graders, Authentication Services

Action Figure Authority
toygrader.com

Advanced Grading Specialists
www.advancedgrading.com

ASA Accugrade
www.asa-accugrade.com

Authentic Autographs Unlimited
www.aaunlimited.com

Beckett Grading Services
www.beckett.com

Certified Sports Authentication Inc.
www.csacards.com
www.certifiedsports.com

CTA Grading Experts, Inc.
www.ctagradingexperts.com

Certified Express
www.certifiedexpress.com

Forensic Autograph Authenticators
www.authenticators.net

Grey Flannel
www.greyflannel.com

Online Authentics
www.onlineauthentics.com

Professional Grading Service
www.prograding.com

Pro Sports Grading Inc.
www.prograding.net

PSA
www.collectors.com/psa
www.psacard.com

PSA/DNA Authentication Services
www.collectors.com/psadna

SCD Authentic
www.SCDAuthentic.com

Sportscard Guaranty Corp.
www.SGCcard.com

Ultimate Sportscard Authority
www.usasportscards.com

Card Manufacturers

Collector's Edge
www.edgefootball.com
Donruss
www.donruss.com
Fleer
www.fleerskybox.com

Just Minors
www.justminors.com
Pacific Trading Cards
www.pacifictradingcards.com
Playoff
www.playoffinc.com

Press Pass/Racing Champions
www.racingchampions.com
Roox Sports
www.roox.com
SA-GE
www.SA-GE.com

Score
www.scoreonline.com
Starting Lineup Authenticated
www.sluauthenticated.com
Team Best
www.teambest.com

Topps
www.topps.com
Upper Deck
www.upperdeck.com
Warning Track Cards
www.warningtrackcards.com

Collectors

Card Links
www.cardlinks.com

The Card Mall
www.cardmall.com

Collect.com
www.collect.com

Collectibles.com
www.collectibles.com

Collecting Channel
www.collectingchannel.com

Collectors Universe
www.collectors.com

Collector Link
www.collector-link.com

Graded Sports Cards.net
www.gradedsportscards.net

Krause Publications
www.krause.com

Oddball Mall
www.oddball-mall.com

Old Links Golf Collectibles
www.oldlinks.com

Pack Ripper
www.packripper.com

Philadelphia A's Historical
www.philadelphiaathletics.org

PriceIs.com
www.priceis.com

Seth Swirsky
www.sethsroom.com

Sports Investments Network
www.sinetwork.com

Network Top 50 sites
www.top50network.com

T206 Museum
www.t206museum.com

Top Prospect Alert
www.topprospectalert.com

Trading Card Central
www.tradingcardcentral.com

Trading Card Source
www.tradingcardsource.com

World-Wide Collectors Digest
www.wwcd.com

Worth Guide
www.worthguide.com

Dealers

Adelson Sports
www.adelsonsports.com

A. J. Sports Cards
www.ajcards.com

A & K Sports Collectibles
www.wwcd.com/a_k

All American Collectibles
www.allamericancollectible.com

All Star Cards
www.allstar-cards.com

Rich Altman Hollywood Collectibles
www.hollywoodcollectibles.com

American Card Management
www.americancardmgmt.homestead.com

American Memorabilia
www.ami21.com

America's Memories
www.americasmemories.com

Anaconda Sports
www.anacondasports.com

Antiquities of the Prize Ring
www.antekprizering.com

Thomas Appleby
www.applebyarchives.com

AU Sports
www.ausports.com

Authentics Handsigned Collectibles
www.hometown.aol.com/handsigned

Autographs For Sale.com
www.autographsforsale.com

B2 Sports Art
www.b2sportsart.com

Jeremy Bachman
www.spectatorsportcards.com

Ballpark Legends
www.ballparklegends.net

Bammerland.com
www.bammerland.com

The Baseball Card Kid
www.bbckid.com

Baseball Cards Unlimited
www.baseballcardsunlimited.com

Baseball Fanatic Superstore
www.members.aol.com/baseball

Baseball Tapes.com
www.baseballtapes.com

BB Cards 4 U.com
www.bbcards4u.com

B & J Collectibles
www.b-j.com

Big Al "The Collector's Pal"
www.sportsillustratedmags.com

Blue Chip Sports
www.bc-sports.com

Bob's Archives
www.bobsarchives.com

The Bobbinator
www.bobbinator.com

Boca Cards and Investments
www.bocacards.com

Broadway Rick's Strike Zone
www.strikezone.net

Byron's Hockeyland
www.byronshockeyland.com

California Sports Investments
www.californiasportsinv.com

Capital Cards
www.capitalcards.com

Card Collectors' Co.
www.wwcd.com/cardhaven

Cards 'n Stars
www.americasmemories.com

Steve Ciniglio
www.sportsautograph.com

Clarks Trading Stores
www.ctagradingexperts.com

Classic Collectibles
classiccollect.com

Kevin Cloutier's Hartland Figurines and Sports Memorabilia
www.hartlands.com

Joe Colabella
www.joecolabella.com

Collect Baseball.com
www.collectbaseball.com

The Collectible Closet
www.ccplayball.com

Collectibles.com
www.collectibles.com

Consolidated Sports
www.consolidatedsports.com

Creative Sports Enterprises Inc.
www.creativesportsonline.com

Danrick Enterprises
www.baseballtapes.com

Dan's Dugout
www.dansdugout.com

Dave's Vintage Baseball Cards
www.gfg.com/baseball

Dedicated Fan
www.dedicatedfan.com

Ed Dolan Jr.'s Baseball Fanatic Super Store
www.eddolan.com

Dot and Lou's Collectibles
www.dotandloucollectibles.com

The Edge-Man
www.edgeman.com

Empire State Sports Memorabilia and Collectibles
www.empirestatesports@beckett.com

The Endzone
members.aol.com/endzone494

Epic Sports and Collectibles
www.epicsportsonline.com

Everlasting Images
www.everlastingimages.com

Ewaxpax.com
www.ewaxpax.com

Doak Ewing Rare Sports Films
www.raresportsfilms.com

Fat Stacks
www.fatstacks.com

Field of Dreams
www.field-of-dreams.com

Terrence Fogarty Studio
www.terrencefogarty.com

Larry Fritsch Cards
www.fritschcards.com

Frozen Pond
www.frozenpond.com

Georgetown Card Exchange
www.gcxonline.com

Good As Gold Investments
www.goodasgold-inv.com

Grad, Ink. Autographs
www.autographs.gradink.com

Graf Baseball Card Co.
www.grafcard.com

Grandstand Sports and Memorabilia
www.grandstandsports.com

Great Traditions
www.greattraditions.com

Grosnor Sportscards Inc.
www.grosnor.com

Halsports
www.halsports.com

Bill Hendersons Cards
www.azww.com/hendo

High End Sports Cards
www.UDAautos.com

Ira Hirshhorn and Co.
www.irahirshhornandcompany.com

Hobby Store 4U
www.hobbystore4u.com

Neil Hoppenworth Cards
www.hoppenworthcards.com

Hot Rookies.com
www.hotrookies.com

Howard's Sports Collectibles
www.howardsauction.com

Robert Hurst
www.adamnfineartist.com

InterNet's Baseball Card Store
www.baseball-cards.com

Jake's Toy Chest
www.jakestoys.com

Norman James
www.normanjames.com

J. Paul Sports Promotions Inc.
www.jpaulsports.com

Jeff's Baseball Corner
www.members.aol.com/jbcorner

J & J Distributing
www.forcomm.net/jjdistributing

J & J Sports Section
www.jjsports1.com

Johnson & Johnson Sportcards
www.johnsonsportscards.com

Dennis A. Jose "Mr. Mint Tix"
www.chicagotix.com

JM Sports
www.footballhelmets.com

J. T. Sports
www.gameusedbats.com

Kaiser Cards
www.kaisercards.com

Bob "The Card" Kauffman
www.voicenet.com/~vintbase

Kings
www.dking-gallery.com

Kruk Cards Inc.
www.krukcards.com

Lake Country Minor League Prospects
www.members.xoom.com/lake_country

Carl and Maryanne Laron
www.laronsports.com

LCG Signatures
www.lcgsignatures.com

Left Field Collectibles
www.leftfieldcollectibles.com

Legends Sports
www.legendsports.com

Leisure Time Industries
www.LTIsports.com

Lew Lipset
www.oldjudge.com

Lost in Sports
www.lostinsports.com

Andy Madec Sportscards Inc.
www.andymadecsportscards.com

Greg Manning Sports
www.gregmanning.com

McAvoy Sportcards
www.mcavoysportcards.com

MeiGray Group
www.meigray.com

Mencik's Sportscards
www.mencik.com

Mile High Card Co.
www.milehighcardco.com

Minfords Minors
www.minfordsminors.com

Minnesota Connection
www.mnconn.com

Monicore Inc.
www.wheatiestrophy.com

MOS Sports Inc.
www.mos-sports.com

MVP Autographs
www.mvpautographs.com

Adam Nemeth
www.adamnemeth.com

Leroy Neiman
www.leroyneiman.com

No Bull Sports
www.nobullsports.com

Steve Novella
www.megalink.net/~damone/home.html

Official Stuff
www.officialstuff.com

Ondeck Sports
www.ondecksports.com

Oriole's Trading Post
www.geocities.com/Colosseum/5115

Osports
www.osports.com

Bob Pace's Boxing Memorabilia
www.bobpaceboxing.com

Paladins
www.paladins.com

Pastime Portfolio Collection Inc.
www.pastime-portfolio.com

Past Time Sports
www.coachhelp.com/ptsports.htm

PC Sports Inc.
www.pcsportsinc.com

Perfect Image
www.wwcd.com/pimage

Phil's Collectibles
www.sportsillustrateds.com

Port Sports
www.portsports.net

Quality Autographs and Memorabilia of Virginia Inc.
www.qualityautographs.com

Rainbow Card Co.
www.rainbowcardco.com

Real Deal Memorabilia
www.realdealmemorabilia.com

Real Legends.com
www.reallegends.com

Recollectics
www.presspins.com

James J. Reeves
www.jamesjreeves.com

Retro-Sports
www.retro-sports.com

Rick's Coin Shop
www.rickscoinshop.com

Riverwood Gallery
www.riverwoodgallery.com

Romito Enterprises
www.romito.com

Alan Rosen
www.mrmint.com

R&R Collectibles
www.joedimaggioestate.com

707 Sportscards
www.707sportscards.com

SLS Sports
www.slssports.com

Spectator Sportcards
www.spectatorsportcards.com

James Spence Vintage Autographs
www.jspence.com

Sportan Direct
www.sportandirect.com

Sport Card Heaven Inc.
www.sportcardheaven.com

Sport Collectibles and Supplies
www.sportcollectibles.com

SportsCards Plus
www.sportscardsplus.com

Sports Center Collectibles
www.sccol.com

Sports Collectibles Inc.
www.spcollect.com

Sportsend
www.sportsend.com

The Sports Gallery
www.sports-gallery.com

Sports Investments International
www.air23.com

Sportsman's Park
www.members.spree.com/sip/sportspark/home.htm

Sports Pages International
www.headlineclassics.com

SportsPro Marketing Inc.
www.sportspromarketing.com

Sportstop
www.sportstop.net

Stan the Man Inc.
www.stan-the-man.com

Stan "The Man" Sportscards
www.stanthemansportscards.com

Star Box
www.starbox.com

Steiner Sports Memorabilia
www.steinersports.com

Jim Stinson Sports
www.stinsonsports.com

Strictly Mint
www.smcci.com

Superstar Greetings
www.superstargreetings.net

Supercards
www.supercards.net

Ed Taylor's Baseball Dreams
www.petemaravich.com

T.C. Card Co.
www.tccardco.com

Team Wear Athletic
www.teamwearathletic.com

Texas Sportcard Co.
www.txsportcard.com

Trademark Sportscards
www.trademarksportscards.com

Trendco Inc.
www.trendco.com

TNT Collectibles
www.nb.net/~tntcoll

Trading Card Source
www.tradingcardsource.com

T-Rex Collectibles
www.trexcard.com

Triple Threat Cards
www.ttcards.com

Truly Unique Collectibles
www.uniquecollectibles.com

Trumpets East
www.calltrumpets.com

V & J Cards
www.psafootball.com

Vintage Baseball Cards
vintagebbcards.tripod.com

Visionary Art Inc./James Fiorentino
www.jamesfiorentino.com

VP Sport
www.vpsport.com

Wall of Fame
www.walloffame.com

Wallos.com
www.wallos.com

Gary Walter Baseball Cards
www.garywalterbaseballcards.com

Scott Welkowsky
www.scottwelkowsky.com

Mike Wheat Cards
www.mikewheatcards.com/index.htm

Les Wolff
members.aol.com/lwolff1823

When It Was A Game
www.wiwag.com

Wright Plaque
www.wrightplaque.com

Yankee Doodle Sports Products
www.yddsp.com

Kit Young Cards
www.kityoung.com

Zindler's Baseball Card Co.
www.zindlers.com

Halls of Fame, Sports Museums

Alabama Sports Hall of Fame
www.tech-comm.com/ashof

American Sportscasters Association Hall of Fame
www.americansportscasters.com

Ty Cobb Museum
www.tycobbmuseum.org

Bob Feller Museum
www.bobfellermuseum.org

Kansas Sports Hall of Fame
www.kshof.org

Louisiana Sports Hall of Fame
www.lasportshof.com

Louisville Slugger Museum
www.slugger.com/museum

MCI National Sports Gallery
www.mcicenter.com

National Baseball Hall of Fame
www.baseballhalloffame.org

Oklahoma Sports Museum
www.oksports.qpg.com

Pennsylvania Sports Hall of Fame
www.pasportshalloffame.com

Cal Ripken Museum
www.ripkenmuseum.com

Babe Ruth Museum
www.baberuthmuseum.com

St. Louis Cardinals Hall of Fame
www.stlcardinals.com

Ted Williams Museum and Hitters Hall of Fame
www.twmuseum.com

Hobby Supplies, Software

Absolute Best Acrylics
www.acrylics.com

All Sports Labels
www.allsportslabels.com

APBA Card Collector 6.0
www.APBAgames.com

A Pro Image Sports Supply
www.aproimagess.com

Atfab
www.atfabcompany.com

BCW Supplies
www.bcwsupplies.com

Lin Terry
www.linterry.com

LK2 Card Collecting Software
www.lk2.com

Memories on Display
www.memoriesondisplay.qpg.com

Pennzoni Display Co.
www.displayco.com

Pick-N-Click Software
www.cardsoftware.com

Rembrandt/Ultra Pro
www.ultra-pro.com

Showcase Your Collectibles
www.showcaseshowplace.com

Sportan Direct
www.sportandirect.com

Sports Fulfillment
www.sportsfulfillment.com

Memorabilia Manufacturers

APBA
www.apbastadium.com
www.apbagames.com

Classic Collectible Products
www.ccpweb.com

Cooperstown Bat Co.
www.cooperstownbat.com

Crown Pro
www.crownpro.com

Enviromint
www.enviromint.com

Equity Marketing/Headliners
www.headliners.com

Famous Fixins
www.famousfixins.com
www.celebrityfixins.com

Fotoball USA
www.fotoball.com

Bill Goff/Good Sports Art
www.goodsportsart.com

Hasbro
www.hasbrocollectors.com

Harris Management Group
www.reggiejackson.com

Limited Treasures
www.limitedtreasures.com

Mattel
www.mattelhoops.com

Nikco Sports
www.nikcosports.com

Photo File
www.photofile.com

PLB Sports
www.plbsports.com
www.vpsport.com

Revolving Rainbow
www.bobbinbobbers.com

Romito Inc.
www.romito.com

Salvino's Bammers
www.salvinos.com

SAMAC
www.bobbing.com

Sierra Sun Editions
www.sierrasuneditions.com

Silk Road Gifts
www.silkroadgifts.com

Southland Art Castings
www.southlandartcastings.com

Southland Plastics
www.southlandplastics.com

Sport Collectors Guild
www.replicastadiums.com

White Rose Collectibles
www.whterose.com

Upper Deck Authenticated
www.udauthenticated.com

USAopoly
www.usaopoly.com

Players, Coaches

Dusty Baker
www.dustybaker.com

Derek Bell
www.hit14.com

Johnny Bench
www.johnnybench.com

Yogi Berra/LTD Enterprises
www.yogi-berra.com

Tom Candiotti
www.tomcandiotti.com

Steve Carlton
www.carlton32.com

Roger Clemens
www.rocketroger.com

Roberto Clemente
www.robertoclemente21.com

Ty Cobb
www.cmgww.com/baseball/cobb/cobb.html

Rollie Fingers
www.fingers34.com

Whitey Ford – Whitey's
www.whitey-ford.com

Dwight Gooden
www.dwightgooden.com

"Shoeless" Joe Jackson
www.cmgww.com/baseball/jackson/jackson.html

Reggie Jackson
www.reggiejackson.com

Geoff Jenkins
www.geoffjenkins.com

Mike Liebethal
www.lieberthal.com

Roger Maris
www.rogermaris.com

Don Mattingly
www.don-mattingly.com

Willie McGee
www.williemcgee.com

Stan Musial
www.stan-the-man.com

C. J. Nitkowski
www.cjbaseball.com

Paul O'Neill
www.pauloneill21.com

Chan Ho Park
www.chanhopark61.com

Cal Ripken Jr.
www.2131.com

Rick Reed
www.vvm.com/~dthacker/reed.html

Robin Roberts
www.robinrobertswhizkid.com

Alex Rodriguez
www.arod.com

Pete Rose
www.peterose.com

Babe Ruth
www.baberuth.com

WEB ADDRESSES

Nolan Ryan
www.nolanryan34.com

Ozzie Smith
www.ozziesmith.com

Darryl Strawberry
www.dstrawberry.com

Jim Thome
www.teamthome.com

Omar Vizquel
www.omarvizquel.com/ov.html

Honus Wagner
www.cmgww.com/baseball/honus/honus.html

Ted Williams
www.tedwilliams.com

Steve Woodard
www.stevewoodard.com

Carl Yastrzemski
www.yaz8.com

Multiple Player

Athletes Direct.com
www.athletesdirect.com

MLB Players Choice
www.bigleaguers.com

Rivals.com
www.rivals.com

Professional Leagues

Major League Baseball
www.majorleaguebaseball.com

Sports Collectors Magazines

Krause Publications
www.fantasysportsmag.com
www.sportscollectorsdigest.com
www.tuffstuffonline.com

Beckett
www.beckett.com

Show Promoters/Shows

A Gloria Rothstein Show Inc.
www.grshows.com

Atlantique City
www.atlantiquecity.com

The Autograph Zone
www.autographzone.com

B & L Sports Memorabilia
www.b-n-lsports.com

Central New York Promotions
www.cnypromotions.com

Collectors' Showcase of America
www.csashows.com

Gibraltar Trade Center Inc.
www.gibraltartrade.com

International Collectibles Exposition
www.collectibleshow.com

J. Paul Sports Promotions Inc.
www.jpaulsports.com

Krause Publications
www.krause.com/shows

National Sports Collectors Convention
www.thenational.net

Signings Hotline
www.signingshotline.com

Sport Card and Memorabilia Expo
www.sportcardexpo.com

SportsFest
www.sportsfestshow.com

St. Louis Sports Collectors Inc.
www.stlsportscollectors.com

Sports Collectibles of Houston
www.ghg.net/spocoho

Star Shows.com
www.starshows.com

Toronto Sportscard/Memorabilia Expo
www.sportcardexpo.com

Tri-Star Productions Inc.
www.tristarproductions.com

World Wide Show.com
www.worldwideshow.com

Sports Memorabilia Insurance

Cornell and Finkelmeier Inc.
www.cf-insurance.com

Internet Consulting

Jireh
www.jireh.com

Right Click Solutions Inc
www.sportscardswww.com

Just for Fun

The Baseball Archive
www.baseball1.com

Baseball Heckle Depot
www.heckledepot.com

Negro Leagues
www.blackbaseball.com

Total Baseball
www.totalsports.com/baseball

Wiffle Ball
www.wiffleball.com